Neural Networks

Neural Networks:

Deterministic Methods of Analysis

Steve Ellacott
and
Deb Bose

School of Computing and Mathematical
Sciences
University of Brighton

INTERNATIONAL THOMSON COMPUTER PRESS

I(T)P An International Thomson Publishing Company

London • Bonn • Boston • Johannesburg • Madrid • Melbourne • Mexico City • New York • Paris
Singapore • Tokyo • Toronto • Albany, NY • Belmont, CA • Cincinnati, OH • Detroit, MI

Neural Networks:
Deterministic Methods of Analysis

I(T)P A division of International Thomson Publishing Inc.
The ITP logo is a trademark under licence.

For more information, contact:

International Thomson Computer Press
Berkshire House
168–173 High Holborn
London WC1V 7AA
UK

International Thomson Computer Press
20 Park Plaza
Suite 1001
Boston, MA 02116
USA

Imprints of International Thomson Publishing

International Thomson Publishing GmbH
Königswinterer Straße 418
53227 Bonn
Germany

International Thomson Publishing Asia
60 Albert Street #15–01
Albert Complex
Singapore 189969

Thomas Nelson Australia
102 Dodds Street
South Melbourne, 3205
Victoria
Australia

International Thomson Publishing Japan
Hirakawacho Kyowa Building, 3F
2–2–1 Hirakawacho
Chiyoda-ku, 102 Tokyo
Japan

Nelson Canada
1120 Birchmount Road
Scarborough, Ontario
Canada M1K 5G4

International Thomson Editores
Campos Eliseos 385, Piso 7
Col. Polenco
11560 Mexico D. F. Mexico

International Thomson Publishing South Africa
PO Box 2459
Halfway House
1685 South Africa

International Thomson Publishing France
Tours Maine-Montparnasse
33 avenue du Maine
75755 Paris Cedex 15
France

British Library Cataloguing-in-Publication Data
A catalogue record for this book is available from the British Library

Library of Congress Cataloging-in-Publication Data
A catalog record for this book is available from the Library of Congress

First Printed 1996
Typeset by WestKey Ltd., Cornwall
Printed in the UK by Cambridge University Press

ISBN 1–85032–244–9

Commissioning Editor Liz Israel Oppedijk

Contents

1 Mathematical fundamentals

There is nothing new under the sun. Is there anything of which one can say 'Look, this is something new?' It was here already, long ago; it was here before our time.
King Solomon (Ecclesiastes 1, vv 9,10. New International Version)

1.1 What this book is not

In this book, you will not find an introduction to, or survey of, the field of neural networks. Such are readily available, for example by Simpson (1990), Aleksander and Morton (1990), Wasserman (1989), Carling (1992), or a host of others. You will certainly meet some of the common neural net models and architectures, but these are there to illustrate the underlying mathematical ideas. It is not claimed that the examples used are necessarily the best methods to use in any particular application. The book aims rather to explore the mathematical roots of deterministic connectionist computation, and to show that these concepts are founded in well established theory. Many aspects of the subject have parallels and equivalents in classical branches of mathematics such as optimisation, approximation theory, or control theory. The educated researcher or user of neural networks needs to be aware of these links, or development will simply recapitulate known territory. The reader should find here the key mathematical tools in accessible form. Moreover, the book aspires to be more than just an encyclopaedia: it is the authors' view that only by uniting the diverse ideas into a coherent theory can the analysis and synthesis of neural computing systems become a mature and comprehensible field.

Whether this aspiration has been achieved, the reader must judge. The reader may be surprised by the focus on deterministic theory. The authors in no way deny the importance of the stochastic theories of learning which have received considerable attention in recent years (Amari, 1989; Anthony, 1994; Bishop, 1995). However this development has often been at the expense of the dynamic and numerical aspects: this book aims to fill that gap. In many cases the imposition of statistical variation hides the simple underlying algebraic properties of the network models. Another topic you will not find is discrete mathematics: complexity theory, automata theory and so on. Again this is a subject of some importance, but we have chosen here to focus on continuous models and to address the question of the computational power of networks via approximation theory.

The material found here should be accessible to those readers with a level of mathematical attainment found in numerate degree courses, such as engineering or computer science. Regrettably, in order to keep the volume down to a reasonable size, it is not possible to provide an introduction to the mathematics at a level comprehensible to those with very little background, although it is acknowledged that the need for such support exists. To assist those readers in this situation, advice on further reading is provided within the chapters.

In this chapter, we remind the reader of some basic ideas and notation, and discuss the analytical tools required. We also introduce some of the basic concepts of neural computation, such as linear transformations, and linear and non-linear separability. Chapters 2 and 3 contain an extensive introduction to the field of linear algebra, on which the rest of the book depends. Equipped with these fundamental tools, an exposition is given of three key theories: Chapter 4 discusses optimisation, Chapter 5, dynamical systems and Chapter 6, approximation theory.

1.2 Sets

Any computing system, whether connectionist or conventional, is concerned with the manipulation of data. A rigorous approach to the analysis of such systems needs to start from a precise specification of the nature of this data, and the forms of manipulation that are to be performed on it. In the language of mathematics, a collection of objects to be operated on is called a *set*. The objects in the set are called the *elements*, and are delimited by curly brackets. For example

$S = \{a, b\}$ or $P = \{$ neural net researchers$\}$

The set S has two elements, whereas P has a finite but unknown number. The order of elements in a set is unimportant. In symbolic approaches to artificial intelligence, we often consider sets such as strings of characters. However, in neural computation, data is more often encoded in some numerical form. The set of all whole numbers (positive, negative or zero) is called the set of *integers* and is denoted by $\mathbb{Z}$ (from the German Zahl), i.e.

$$\mathbb{Z} = \{ 0, \pm 1, \pm 2, \ldots \}.$$

Note that this set has infinitely many elements. The set of numbers that we can think of as representing (positive, negative or zero) distances along a line is called the set of *real numbers*, $\mathbb{R}$. 1.2, $\sqrt{2}$ and π are all examples of real numbers. We indicate that an element belongs to a set by the symbol $\in$, e.g. $\pi \in \mathbb{R}$. Most of the sets that we refer to in this book are constructed from one of these two basic number sets. We shall often need to refer to the magnitude of an integer or real number x, ignoring its sign. This is called the *modulus* of x, denoted $|x|$. For example, $|2.7| = 2.7$, but $|-3.1| = 3.1$. Note that $|x + y| \leq |x| + |y|$: this result, known as the *triangle inequality*, we shall use frequently.

Another set of numbers that we will need from time to time is the *complex numbers*. These are numbers of the form $z = x + iy$, where $i^2 = -1$. We call x the *real part* of z, written $\mathrm{Re}(z)$, and y the *imaginary part* of z, $\mathrm{Im}(z)$.

Now consider the set $T = \{2, 1\}$. All the elements of this set are also in $\mathbb{Z}$: we say that T is a *subset* of $\mathbb{Z}$, written $T \subset \mathbb{Z}$. Since in this case $T \neq \mathbb{Z}$, we say that T is a *proper subset*. If $U = \{1, 7\}$, we can construct the *union* of T and U, written $T \cup U$ by taking those elements in either set (or both), thus

$$T \cup U = \{7, 1, 2\}.$$

The *intersection* of T and U, $T \cap U$, is the set of elements which are in both T and U, so

$$T \cap U = \{ 1 \}.$$

A set with no elements is called the *empty set* denoted $\{\}$ or $\varnothing$. (Do not confuse this with $\{0\}$ which contains the integer 0.) Two sets T and U, such that $T \cap U = \varnothing$, are said to be *disjoint*.

A third set operation that is often useful is the difference $T - U$. This is the set of elements in T that are not in U, or more formally, $T - U = \{x \in T \mid x \notin U\}$. For the sets above, $T - U = \{2\}$.

Two sets T and U are said to be *in one-to-one correspondence* if each element of T can be associated with exactly one element of U. For example let $T=\{\text{tea, coffee, beer}\}$ and let $u=\{\text{Jim, Susan, Jane}\}$. Then a correspondence is Jim $\leftrightarrow$ tea, Susan $\leftrightarrow$ beer, Jane $\leftrightarrow$ coffee. Roughly speaking, two sets can be put in one-to-one correspondence if they have the same number of elements. Note, however, that it is possible for an infinite set to be put in one-to-one correspondence with a proper subset of itself. For instance, let E be the set of even integers. The association $n \leftrightarrow 2n$ is a one-to-one correspondence between $\mathbb{Z}$ and E. A set that can be put into one-to-one correspondence with a subset (not necessarily a proper subset) of $\mathbb{Z}$ is said to be *countable*. Thus E is countable, as is any set with a finite number of elements. Roughly speaking, a set is countable if we can write the elements out in a list: if the element $x_i \leftrightarrow i$ we can write the list $x_1, x_2, \ldots$ and conversely such a list defines a one-to-one correspondence.

The number $r \in \mathbb{R}$ is said to be *rational* if it can be written as p/q, where $p, q \in \mathbb{Z}$ (with, of course, $q \neq 0$). The set of rational numbers is denoted by $\mathbb{Q}$. Somewhat surprisingly, it is countable. To see this note that the following algorithm will list all the rational numbers greater than zero and less than or equal to one.

For $q=1$ to ∞, step 1
  For $p=1, 2, \ldots q$, step 1
    Check if p/q is already on the list, and if not, add it to the list.

Note that it is necessary to check each time to see if we have already listed p/q, since for example 1/2 is the same as 2/4.

It can be shown that the real numbers $\mathbb{R}$ are not countable, but we will not give a proof here.

1.3 Functions and relations

A formal model of a computing system must not only describe what data is to be manipulated, but also what manipulations are permitted. Traditional computing machines make use of a small number of processing units (often only one). These processing units are capable of quite complex operations (although ultimately these operations are expressible in terms of a few very simple logical ones). Mammalian brains employ a different strategy. They rely on having a very large number of processing units called *neurons*, each performing an apparently simple task. The neurons are connected together by *synapses*, and it is through the interaction of these units that computation takes place. As in most biological systems, study of neurons has shown them to be rather more sophisticated than is at first apparent, and in fact their behaviour is far from well understood. Nevertheless, it is this basic idea of an interconnected network of simple units which inspires the connectionist paradigm for computation, and is at the heart of the multitude of artificial neural network architectures now available. In artificial systems, the term *processing unit* is often substituted for neuron, and *connection* for synapse: we shall use both terminologies as appropriate.

Now let us consider a very simple model of such a neuron, due to McCulloch and Pitts (see Fig. 1.1). The input synapses are considered to be carrying signals which are represented by real numbers. The unit processes these inputs and then passes its result onto the output connection. How can we describe this mathematically? The input to the unit consists of several copies of the real numbers: four in the neuron shown in Fig. 1.1. The set of objects consisting of ordered pairs of elements of two sets T and U is known as the *Cartesian product* of the sets, written $T \times U$. The elements are written (t, u) where $t \in T$ and $u \in U$. (Note that in this definition the order of the sets is important.) For example

$$\mathbb{Z} \times \mathbb{Z} = \{ (p, q), \text{where } p \text{ and } q \text{ are integers} \}.$$

When the sets T and U are the same, we use a superscript notation for short. We write $\mathbb{Z} \times \mathbb{Z} = \mathbb{Z}^2$. Clearly this concept is not limited to two sets. The input data for the unit in Fig. 1.1 consists of four real numbers, (x_1, x_2, x_3, x_4) say, and we can think of this as an element of $\mathbb{R}^4$. Let $\mathbf{x}$ denote the element (x_1, x_2, x_3, x_4):

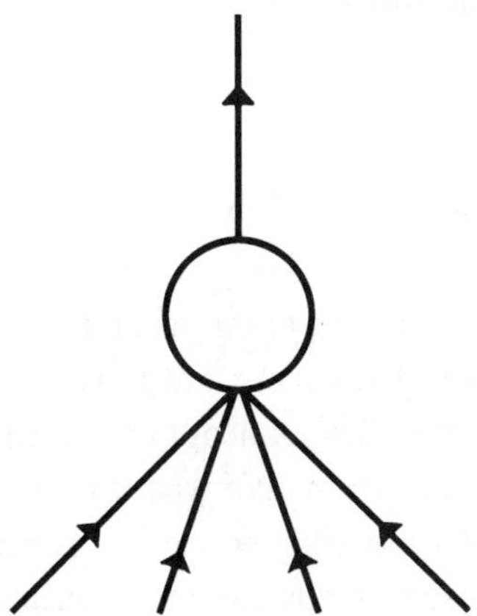

Fig. 1.1

elements of $\mathbb{R}^n$ where n is an integer > 1 are called *vectors*, and are printed in bold type.

Our simple processing unit is required to take $\mathbf{x}$ and perform some operation on it, producing an output which is an element of $\mathbb{R}$. In the language of mathematics, the output is a *function* of the input. More precisely, a function takes an element of an input set called the *domain*, and produces an element of an output set called the *codomain*. Thus our processing unit is a function f mapping the domain $\mathbb{R}^4$ to the codomain $\mathbb{R}$, which we write in mathematical shorthand as $f: \mathbb{R}^4 \rightarrow \mathbb{R}$. We insist that f should produce an answer $f(t)$ for every element t of the domain, and moreover that this should be a unique, well defined element of the codomain: thus we do not allow it to have more than one possible output corresponding to a given input.

Of course, it remains to specify the precise recipe for producing the output from the input. When describing a neuron, it is usual to split the function f into two simpler functions. The first, g say, is a simple summation. Thus, $g: \mathbb{R}^4 \rightarrow \mathbb{R}$, and

$$y = g(\mathbf{x}) = x_1 + x_2 + x_3 + x_4 = \sum_{i=1}^{4} x_i.$$

in mathematical notation: the Σ symbol means add up all the x_i from $i=1$ to $i = 4$. The output is then a function of y, say $\sigma: \mathbb{R} \rightarrow \mathbb{R}$. This function σ is called the *activation function* of the unit. Popular choices for σ are

(a) $\sigma(y) = y$ (the identity function),

(b) $\sigma(y) = \begin{cases} 1 \text{ if } y > 0 \\ 0 \text{ if } y \leq 0 \end{cases}$ (the threshold function)

or

(c) $\sigma(y) = \dfrac{1}{1+e^{-y}}$ (the logistic function).

Note that example (b) is different from (a) and (c) in that it has a jump at 0 where the value changes suddenly from 0 to 1. Mathematically, we say that the function is *discontinuous* at 0. The concept of continuity is an important one, so we will give a formal definition. We wish to say that a function $f: S \rightarrow \mathbb{R}$, where S is a subset of $\mathbb{R}$ (or possibly $\mathbb{R}$ itself) is continuous at a point x, if we can always, by choosing y sufficiently close to x, ensure that $f(y)$ is as close as we like to $f(x)$. In other words, given any 'accuracy' $\varepsilon > 0$, we wish to be able to make $|f(x)-f(y)| < \varepsilon$. The following definition captures this idea. At first sight, it may seem a little convoluted, but close examination should make it clear.

Definition 1.1

Let $S \subset \mathbb{R}$, and $f\colon S \to \mathbb{R}$. The function f is said to be *continuous* at $x \in S$, if, given any $\varepsilon > 0$, there exists a positive real number δ such that for every $y \in S$ with $|x-y| < \delta$, $|f(y)-f(x)| < \varepsilon$.

If f is continuous at every point x of S, f is said to be *continuous* on S.

□

Obviously, this definition is too clumsy for everyday use. To determine in practice whether a function is continuous, we make use of the following theorem which enables us to build up complicated continuous functions from simple ones. We can add, multiply or divide continuous functions, or substitute one continuous function into another. This last process is known as *composition* and is denoted by the symbol $\circ$. (See (d) in the theorem below.)

Theorem 1.2

Let f, g be continuous at x, and l continuous at $f(x)$. Then

(a) $(f+tg)(x)=f(x)+tg(x)$ $(t \in R)$
(b) $(fg)(x)=f(x)\times g(x)$
(c) $(f/g)(x)=f(x)/g(x)$ (unless $g(x)=0$)
(d) $l \circ f(x)=1[f(x)]$

are all continuous.

Proof

We give the proof of (a) in the case $t=1$ for illustration. The other parts of the theorem are proved in a similar way. [See, e.g. Spivak (1967, Chapter 6) or any other textbook of elementary analysis.]

Given $\varepsilon > 0$ choose δ such that for $|x-y| < \delta$, $|f(x)-f(y)| < \varepsilon/2$ and $|g(x)-g(y)| < \varepsilon/2$. Then

$$\begin{aligned} |(f+g)(x)-(f+g)(y)| &= |f(x)+g(x)-f(y)-g(y)| \\ &= |f(x)-f(y)+g(x)-g(y)| \\ &< |f(x)-f(y)| + |g(x)-g(y)| \\ &< \varepsilon/2+\varepsilon/2=\varepsilon. \end{aligned}$$

□

It is very easy to show from Definition 1.1 that $f(x)=x$ is continuous on $\mathbb{R}$: just choose $\varepsilon=\delta$. Then, by repeated application of Theorem 1.2, we can show that, for instance, any polynomial function is continuous. It can also be shown that the elementary functions sin, cos and exp are continuous on $\mathbb{R}$, and that the logarithmic function *ln* is continuous on the positive real numbers.

A very common problem when working with functions concerns finding an *inverse*, i.e. given a transformation f, find a transformation f^{-1} such that

$$f^{-1} \circ f(\mathbf{x}) = x$$

for any x. We will start with some general observations about this problem.

A function is said to be *1–1* (read 'one-to-one') or *injective* if distinct points have distinct images, i.e. if $f(x_1)=f(x_2)$ implies $x_1=x_2$. Also f is said to be *onto* or *surjective* if for *each* y there is an x with $f(x)=y$. If f is 1–1 and onto then the inverse exists and moreover it is also true that

$$f \circ f^{-1}(y) = y \text{ for any } y \text{ [just put } y = f(x)].$$

We normally require this condition that f is 1–1 onto in the definition of an inverse. However, to solve the equation

$$f^{-1} \circ f(x) = x$$

for any x actually only requires the condition that f is 1–1. If f is 1–1 but not onto, we call f^{-1} a *left inverse*. In this case $f \circ f^{-1}(y)=y$ does *not* necessarily hold, since there may not be a y such that $y=f(x)$. For example, let $\mathbb{R}^+=\{x \in \mathbb{R} \mid x >0\}$, i.e. the set of positive real numbers. The exponential function exp: $\mathbb{R} \rightarrow \mathbb{R}^+$ is denoted by $\exp(x)=e^x$. This mapping is 1–1 and onto, and the inverse function is called *ln*. If $y=e^x$, then $x= ln\ y$. However if we had defined the codomain of exp to be the whole of $\mathbb{R}$, the mapping would be 1–1 but not onto, and we could only think of *ln* as a left inverse. Similarly if f is onto but not 1–1 we can define a right inverse.

A more general concept than function is a *relation*. This is simply a way of associating elements of sets together: a function is, of course, a particular way of doing this. There are two (equivalent) ways to think about a relation. The more formal way is as a subset of the cartesian product of the sets involved. For simplicity, we will restrict discussion to so-called binary relations involving only two sets. Then, given two sets T and U, a *binary relation* R on T and U is a subset of $T \times U$, i.e. a set of elements of the form (t, u) where $t \in T$ and $u \in U$. In the case in which T and U are the same set, we simply refer to a relation on T.

We write $t\ R\ u$ ('t is related by R to u') if $(t, u) \in R$. This rather mysterious definition becomes much clearer if, less formally, we think of $t\ R\ u$ as being a statement that is either true or false. This idea is exactly equivalent to the previous one: the statement 't is related to u' is true if and only if $(t, u) \in R$. As a concrete example, let $T = U = \mathbb{Z}$, and consider the 'equals' relation $x = y$. This defines the subset of elements of $\mathbb{Z} \times \mathbb{Z}$ consisting of pairs of the form (x, x).

A less trivial example is the 'less than or equal to' relation on $\mathbb{R}$. The element (x, y) belongs to this relation if and only if $x \leq y$. This relation has the following obvious properties.

$x \leq x$.
If $x \leq y$ and $y \leq x$ then $x = y$.
If $x \leq$ and $y \leq z$ then $x \leq z$.

These properties turn out to be surprisingly general. Given a set X we say that a relation R on X is an *order relation* if for all $x, y, z \in X$,

$x\ R\ x$ (we say R is *reflexive*).
If $x\ R\ y$ and $y\ R\ x$ then $x = y$ (R is *antisymmetric*).
If $x\ R\ y$ and $y\ R\ z$ then $x\ R\ z$ (R is *transitive*).

As another example of an order relation, let U be any non-empty set, and let S be its *power set*, the set of all subsets of U. Set inclusion is an order relation on S, i.e. for $A, B \in S$, A is related to B if $A \subset B$.

Another important type of relation is the equivalence relation. A relation R is an *equivalence relation* if it is reflexive and transitive, and also *symmetric*, i.e. if $x\ R\ y$ implies $y\ R\ x$. The 'equals' relation is a (trivial) example of an equivalence relation. Equivalence relations have an important property described in the following theorem.

Theorem 1.3

Let R be an equivalence relation on a set X. Then the following property holds for each y and $z \in X$:

Let $Y = \{\text{all } x \text{ such that } x\ R\ y\}$ and $Z = \{\text{all } x \text{ such that } x\ R\ z\}$. Then if $y\ R\ z$, $Y = Z$, and on the other hand if $y\ R\ z$ is false, $Y \cap Z = \varnothing$.

Proof

Let $x \in Z$, i.e. $x\ R\ z$.

If $z\ R\ y$, then $x\ R\ y$ (R is transitive), hence $x \in Y$. But x was an arbitrary element of Z so $Z \subset Y$. Similarly, $Y \subset Z$, whence $Y = Z$.

On the other hand suppose $Y \cap Z \neq \emptyset$. Let $u \in Y \cap Z$. Then $u\ R\ y$ and $u\ R\ z$. But since R is symmetric, it follows that $y\ R\ u$, and hence, by the transitivity property, $y\ R\ z$.

□

This theorem means that an equivalence relation on a set X divides the set up into mutually disjoint subsets of elements that are related to each other. The theorem also has a trivial converse, in that given any partition of X into disjoint subsets, we can define an equivalence relation R by $x\,R\,y$ if and only if x and y are in the same subset. An equivalence relation can be thought of as identifying some common property by means of which the elements of a set can be classified. A neural net used as a pattern classifier can thus be thought of as concrete realisation of an equivalence relation.

1.4 Graphs

One neuron cannot do very much on its own. To build useful computing systems, we must consider networks of neurons linked by synapses. A neural network is therefore a concrete example of the mathematical structure known as a graph. A *graph* consists of a set of *vertices* or *nodes*, joined by lines called *arcs* or *edges*. The study of such abstract structures is known as *graph theory*. Since neural networks are, in an obvious sense, graphs, it might be expected that graph theory would play an important role in their analysis. However, in practice, it has been found that the special properties of neural networks have enabled much more powerful theoretical tools to be employed, and relatively few papers depending heavily on graph theory have appeared in the literature. Although the reader should be aware of the concept, we will not make any use of graph theoretic methods in this book.

1.5 Limits, sequences and series

The concepts of function, relation and graph that we have discussed up to now are adequate to describe the static behaviour of systems, but not those properties that change with time: the so-called *dynamical systems*. We can discuss both learning systems that adapt in a continuous fashion as their environment changes (a *continuous time* model), and those that respond to stimuli occurring at discrete intervals (a *discrete time* model). We shall meet features that are common to both types of system, and also some differences. A key concept in analysing any dynamical system is that of limit: i.e. of a value approached by the system over time. Many extensions and generalisations of this concept will be encountered in this book, so it is convenient at this point to remind the reader of the idea of limit as found in elementary calculus. However, space does not permit a detailed exposition. Readers completely unfamiliar with the ideas described here and in the next few sections would be well advised to consult one of the many excellent introductory texts in this field, such as Spivak (1967), before proceeding further.

Consider the following sequences of numbers:

(a) 1, 2, 3, 4, 5, 6, . . . ,
(b) −1, +1, −1, +1, −1, . . . ,
(c) 1, 1.5, 1.75, 1.875, 1.9375, ...

Note that the third of these sequences gets closer and closer to 2. Mathematically, we say that the limit of the sequence is 2. However, in order to discuss this notion rigorously, we need to make the ideas here more precise. Firstly, it is obviously not very sensible to specify a sequence just as a list of numbers. Most people would guess that the next term in sequence (a) is 7, but of course logically it could equally well be −366! Thus the only satisfactory way to define a sequence is to give a formula to generate the terms. For instance the sequences above are generated by these formulae for the nth term u_n:

(a) $u_n = n$,
(b) $u_n = (-1)^n$,
(c) $u_n = 2 - 2^{(1-n)}$.

Observe that a sequence can actually be considered as a function: the expression for the term is a function of n. Here we will be concerned with sequences of real numbers, so we can give the following formal definition.

Definition 1.4

A real sequence is a function $u_n: \mathbb{N} \to \mathbb{R}$, where $\mathbb{N}$ denotes the natural numbers $\{1, 2, 3, \ldots\}$.

□

Now we need to distinguish between sequence (c), which appears to approach 2, and the other sequences which do not approach a value. To do this we need the idea of a limit. This is quite a subtle idea to define precisely. In essence, we wish to say that by going far enough along the sequence, we can get as close to 2 as we like. First then, we must specify how close we like. To do this specify some number ε which we can think of as giving the required accuracy. For instance we might chose $\varepsilon=0.1$ or .01 or 1E−6. Clearly, how far we need to go along the sequence depends on this number. Thus, after a suitable period of fasting and meditation, we arrive at the following definition.

Definition 1.5

We say that u is the *limit* of the sequence (u_n) as n tends to infinity if, given any $\varepsilon > 0$, there exists N such that for $n>N$, $|u-u_n| < \varepsilon$.

We also say in this case that (u_n) *tends* or *converges* to u, and write

$$\lim_{n\to\infty} u_n = u \text{ or } u_n \to u.$$

□

For example, for (c) above, $u_n = 2 - 2^{(1-n)}$.

Given any $\varepsilon > 0$, we wish to find a corresponding N such that

$$|2 - [2 - 2^{(1-n)}]| < \varepsilon.$$

In this case this means that we want

$$2^{(1-n)} < \varepsilon \text{ or } 2^{(n-1)} > 1/\varepsilon.$$

This will be satisfied if

$$(n-1)\, ln\, 2 > ln\, (1/\varepsilon),$$

so we chose N to be any integer $>1 - (ln\, \varepsilon / ln\, 2)$.

As an exercise, you might like to use the definition to show that the following sequences $\to 0$ as $n\to\infty$.

(a) $u_n=(1/n)$

(b) $u_n=x^n$ if $|x| <1$.

Obviously, Definition 1.5 is a bit clumsy for everyday use. We need more manageable tools for practical evaluation of limits. The most usual way to evaluate simple limits is by means of the following theorem.

Theorem 1.6

Suppose $u_n\to u$, $v_n\to v$ and t is a real number. Then

(a) $(u_n+tv_n)\to u+tv$,

(b) $(u_n \times v_n) \rightarrow uv$ and
(c) $(u_n/v_n) \rightarrow u/v$ (provided v is not zero, and ignoring any n for which v_n is zero).
(d) Let $S \subset \mathbb{R}$, $u \in S$, and f: $S \rightarrow \mathbb{R}$ be continuous at u. Then the sequence $f(u_n) \rightarrow f(u)$.

Proof

We give the proof that $(u_n + v_n) \rightarrow (u + v)$ for illustration.

Suppose we are given some $\varepsilon > 0$. Since $u_n \rightarrow u$ and $v_n \rightarrow v$, we know that given $\varepsilon > 0$ we can find N such that for $n > N$,

$$|u_n - u| < \varepsilon/2 \text{ and } |v_n - v| < \varepsilon/2.$$

(Choose $\varepsilon/2$ instead of ε in Definition 1.5, and use the larger of the two N's.)

Hence, if $n > N$, we have

$$|(u_n - v_n) - (u - v)| < |(u_n - u) + (v_n - v)| < |u_n - u| + |y_n - v|$$

$$< \varepsilon/2 + \varepsilon/2 = \varepsilon,$$

which completes the proof.

The other parts of the theorem are proved in a similar manner.

□

Armed with this theorem it is easy to evaluate many limits. Consider for instance the common case of a rational function of n, for example

$$\frac{3n^3 + 4n^2 + 2}{4n^3 + 8n}.$$

To evaluate the limit of this we divide the top and bottom by the highest power of n, in this case n^3. This gives

$$\frac{3 + (4/n) + (2/n^3)}{4 + (8/n^2)}.$$

Since the limit of $(4/n)$ is 0, etc., we see by applying the theorem that the limit of the whole expression is

$$\frac{3 + 0 + 0}{4 + 0}.$$

$$\text{i.e. } \frac{3}{4}.$$

We will now describe an important property of the real numbers which will prove very useful later. Consider the sequence

3, 3.1, 3.14, 3.141, 3.14159, . . .

i.e. the digits in the decimal expansion for π. Each of these is a rational number (see Section 1.2): for instance 3.141 is 3141/1000. However π is not a rational number. Thus we have a sequence of rational numbers that seems to be converging, but there is no rational limit for it to arrive at. A fundamental property of the real numbers (note this is an axiom, not a theorem) is that this cannot happen for sequences of reals. We first need a preliminary definition. A sequence (u_n) is said to be *monotone increasing* if $u_n+1>u_n$ for all n. Similarly we may define monotone decreasing sequences, and strictly monotone sequences if the inequality is strict. Also, any set $S\subset\mathbb{R}$ is said to be *bounded above* if there is a number $B\in\mathbb{R}$ such that $x<B$ for each x in S. We now state the axiom.

Axiom 1.7

If a sequence (u_n) of real numbers is monotone increasing and bounded above, then it converges to a real number u.

□

Note that this axiom only guarantees the existence of a limit: it does not tell us what it is.

Some of the most interesting and important sequences occurring in neural computation are defined recursively, i.e. the state at the next time step is defined in terms of the state at the current time, and possibly some of the previous ones. Any learning system must have both a *memory*, and the *ability to adapt to new inputs*. Therefore the theory of recursive expressions and functions is natural in this context. Expressions defining such sequences are known variously according to context as *recurrence relations*, *difference equations*, *iterations* or *recursions*. Mathematically, these are essentially the same.

A good example of a system with ‘learning’ and ‘memory’ is known in control theory as a *digital filter*. This involves a given ‘input’ sequence (v_n), say, and produces a corresponding ‘output’ sequence, say (u_n). A simple example of such a filter is

$$u_{n+1}=(u_n+v_n)/2. \tag{1.1}$$

Consider the case, for instance, in which the system is initially quiescent (u_0

$=0$) and the input sequence takes the constant value 1 ($v_n=1$). Thus

$$u_{n+1} = (u_n + 1)/2, \; u_0 = 0. \tag{1.2}$$

Thus, $u_1 = (0 + 1) / 2 = ½$, $u_2 = ¾$, etc.

We use this example to illustrate the ideas discussed in this section. The function $f(u)=(u+1)/2$ is obviously continuous. The iteration (1.2) can be written

$$u_{n+1} = f(u_n). \tag{1.3}$$

Note that *if* u_n tends to a limit u, then by Theorem 1.6(d) we have

$$u = f(u). \tag{1.4}$$

In general, a number u satisfying (1.4) is called a *fixed point* of the iteration (1.3). For our particular example, we see that a fixed point must satisfy

$$u = (u + 1)/2.$$

Solving this equation gives $u=1$ as the only fixed point. Thus, the only *possible* candidate for a limit of the sequence defined by (1.2) is $u=1$: however, it is important to realise that this does *not* prove that the sequence converges to this value. For example, the recurrence

$$x_{n+1} = 2x_n$$

has a fixed point $x=0$, but the reader may easily verify by experiment that with any non-zero choice of x_0, the sequence does not converge. How, then, can we show that the sequence u_n defined in (1.2) does converge to 1?

We first observe that u_n+1 is the average of u_n and 1. Thus, provided $0 \leq u_n \leq 1$, we have $0 \leq u_n+1 \leq 1$. Hence, the sequence u_n is bounded above by 1. (Compare the remark before Axiom 1.7.) Moreover, if $u_n \leq 1$, then $u_n+1 \leq u_n$. The sequence u_n is monotone increasing. Thus, by Axiom 1.7 we know that the sequence converges to *some* limit. In view of the remarks above, this limit must be a fixed point of (1.2), i.e. 1. We now have a completely rigorous proof that the sequence $u_n \to 1$.

The techniques discussed so far are all right to show that the sequence converges when we can make a guess at the limit. However, suppose we do not know the limit. Can we still decide if the sequence is convergent? In one important case the answer is 'yes'. We introduce the idea of a *Cauchy sequence*: we will find in later chapters that this is the key to discussing convergence in much more complicated situations.

Definition 1.8

A real sequence (u_n) is said to be *Cauchy* if, given $\varepsilon > 0$ there exists N such that for m and $n > M$, $|u_m - u_n| < \varepsilon$.

□

In other words, a sequence is Cauchy if the terms become arbitrarily close together the farther we go along the sequence.

Theorem 1.9

If a real sequence (u_n) is Cauchy, then it is convergent.

Proof

To prove this we first observe that a Cauchy sequence must be bounded above and below: if not then by fixing m in Definition 1.8, and letting n vary, we can obviously make $|u_m - u_n|$ arbitrarily large.

Now call n a *peak point* of the sequence (u_n) if $u_m < u_n$ for all $m > n$. We identify two cases. Firstly, the sequence may have infinitely many peak points, n_1, n_2, ... If so $u_{n1} > u_{n2} > u_{n3} > \dots$ is a monotone decreasing subsequence of (u_n) which must have a limit. On the other hand if the sequence has only finitely many peak points, then there exists n_1 greater than all the peak points. Thus there is some $n_2 > n_1$ such that $u_{n2} \geq u_{n1}$. Since n_2 is not a peak point, there is some $n_3 > n_2$ such that $u_{n3} \geq u_{n2}$ and so on. Thus we have a monotone increasing subsequence, which again must converge. In either case, let the limit of this subsequence be u. Given $\varepsilon > 0$, choose M such that for m, $n > M$, $|u_m - u_n| < \varepsilon/2$. In particular $|u_m - u_{nj}| < \varepsilon/2$ for j sufficiently large. Letting $j \to \infty$ we have [using Theorem 1.6(d)], $|u_m - u| \leq \varepsilon/2 < \varepsilon$. This proves that the whole sequence (u_n) converges.

□

Observe that the proof also shows that any sequence contains a monotone subsequence, and therefore that any bounded sequence contains a convergent subsequence.

A natural extension of the idea of a system that has memory is one that retains all of its previous values. For simplicity, we will first consider an example here that is not derived from a neural model.

Consider the well known series for the base e of the natural logarithms. What do we mean by the statement

$$e = 2 + \frac{1}{2!} + \frac{1}{3!} + \frac{1}{4!} + \ldots ?$$

(Here 4! means $4\times3\times2\times1$, etc.) Intuitively, we think that if we add up more and more terms we will get closer and closer to e. More precisely, the sequence of numbers we get by successively adding on more terms should converge to e. We call the sum S_n of the first n terms the *partial sum* of the series, and we expect that the sequence (S_n) will converge to e. To avoid all the '+'s and dots we employ this symbol Σ meaning 'add up over the given range of integers'.

Thus

$$\sum_{n-1}^{3} n^2 = (1^2 + 2^2 + 3^2) = 1 + 4 + 9 = 14.$$

The series for e can be written

$$e = \sum_{n=0}^{\infty} \frac{1}{n!}.$$

Now consider the general *infinite series*

$$\sum_{k=1}^{\infty} u_k . \tag{1.5}$$

Definition 1.10

(a) The *partial sum* S_n of the series (1.5) is defined as

$$S_n = \sum_{k=1}^{n} u_k .$$

(b) The series (1.5) is said to *converge* or *sum* to S if $S_n \to S$ as $n \to \infty$. If it does not converge, it is said to *diverge*.

□

For example, for the series for e above we have

$S_1 = 2$
$S_2 = 2 + 1/(2!) = 2.5$
$S_3 = 2.5 + 1(/3!) = 2.666. . . .$
$S_4 = 2.666\ldots + 1/(4!) = 2.70833\ldots$ etc.

We can see that the partial sums appear to be converging to e=2.718281828 .... (We omit a proof, since this requires Taylor's Theorem which is discussed later in this chapter: see Section 1.8.)

Now let us consider a model of a neuron with memory built in. More specifically, consider a neuron like Fig. 1.1 but with only a single input. Now, however, assume that constant signals of strength a arrive at equal time steps, and that the output at the nth time step is the current input plus r times the output at time step $n-1$ (this model is much simpler than any realistic neuron, but does capture features found in more sophisticated models). Thus

at time step 0, the output is a,
at time step 1, the output is $a+ar$,
at time step 2, the output is $a+r(a+ar)=a+ar+ar^2$,

and so on. At time step n we find that the output is

$$S_n = a + ar + ar^2 + ... + ar^n = \sum_{k=0}^{n} ar^k. \tag{1.6}$$

Series of this type (i.e. in which each term is in constant ratio to the previous one) occur in almost every branch of mathematics and are said to be *geometric series*. The number r is called the *common ratio*.

There is a useful trick to obtain a simple formula for S_n. We multiply (1.6) by r to obtain

$$rS_n = ar + ar^2 + ... + ar^{n+1}. \tag{1.7}$$

Subtracting (1.7) from (1.6), we observe that all but the first term on the right of (1.6), and the last on the right of (1.7), cancel out, leaving

$$(1 - r)S_n = a - ar^{n+1}.$$

If $r=1$ the series is just $a+a+a+a$ . . . and the partial sum S_n is just $(n+1)a$. Discarding this trivial case we see that $1-r$ is not zero, so we may divide by it to obtain

$$S_n = \frac{a(1 - r^{n+1})}{1 - r}. \tag{1.8}$$

This formula gives the output after n time steps or, of course, the partial sum of any other geometric series such as the accumulation of capital at compound interest. To see what happens ultimately we need only let $n \to \infty$ in (1.8). If $r > 1$, then the output increases without bound. However if $|r| < 1$, we obtain as the sum of the infinite geometric series

$$S = \frac{a}{(1-r)}. \tag{1.9}$$

For example if $a=1$ and $r=0.5$, the ultimate output of the neuron is $1/(1-0.5) = 2$.

For the geometric series we can obtain a simple formula for the partial sum S_n and hence find the limit as $n \to \infty$. Unfortunately for most other series of practical interest this is not the case. The only way to estimate the sum is to add up enough of the terms (although sometimes transformations can be applied to make the series converge quicker). Before embarking on this tedious task, it is a good idea to ensure that the series does actually converge! One obvious test to apply is to see if the individual terms tend to zero.

Proposition 1.11
If the series (1.5) converges, then $u_n \to 0$ as $n \to \infty$.

Proof
Let the sum of the series be S. We have $u_n - S_{n-1}$. Hence

$$\lim_{n\to\infty} u_n = \lim_{n\to\infty} S_n - \lim_{n\to\infty} S_{n-1} = 0 - 0 = 0.$$

□

Unfortunately, the converse of this theorem is false, i.e. *it is possible for the terms of a series to tend to zero, but the series still diverge*. Since this fact causes endless confusion and dismay to those unfamiliar with series, it is worth giving a detailed example.

Consider the so called *harmonic series*

$$\sum_{n=1}^{\infty} \frac{1}{n}.$$

Writing out the terms and bracketing them we get

$$1 + (1/2 + 1/3) + (1/4 + 1/5 + 1/6 + 1/7) + (1/8 + 1/9 + 1/10 + \ldots + 1/15) + \ldots$$

which is greater than

$$1 + (1/4 + 1/4) + (1/8 + 1/8 + 1/8 + 1/8) + (1/16 + 1/16 + 1/16 + \ldots + 1/16) + \ldots$$

which in turn is equal to

$$1 + 1/2 + 1/2 + 1/2 + \ldots .$$

Clearly the partial sums can be made as large as we like, and the series is divergent.

Because of examples such as this one which 'appear' to converge but may not actually do so, great care is required when dealing with infinite series. There are a range of tests available to determine whether or not a series actually converges. However, we discuss only two here. These will be required later. Before stating the test, we need to introduce a new concept. The series

$$\sum_{k=1}^{\infty} u_k$$

is said to be *absolutely convergent* if the series

$$\sum_{k=1}^{\infty} |u_k|$$

is convergent.

Lemma 1.12

If a series is absolutely convergent, then it is convergent.

Proof

Let $a_n = u_n$ if $u_n > 0$, and 0 otherwise. Similarly let $b_n = u_n$ if $u_n < 0$ and 0 otherwise. Let

$$T_k = \sum_{n=1}^{k} |u_n| .$$

By the hypothesis of the lemma, T_k converges as $k \to \infty$. Say the limit is T. Obviously

$$A_k = \sum_{n=1}^{k} a_n$$

forms a monotone increasing sequence bounded above by T, and similarly the partial sums B_k of the b_n are bounded below by $-T$. Hence both these sequences of partial sums converge. But if S_k denotes the partial sum of the original sequence, then

$$S_k = A_k + B_k$$

whence we see that the limit of the left-hand side exists, since both limits on the right exist.

□

A series which is convergent but not absolutely convergent is said to be *conditionally convergent*. It can be shown that for an absolutely convergent series, we will get the same answer if we re-order the terms. If the series is only conditionally convergent, it is possible to re-order the terms to get any sum at all! Similarly, absolutely convergent series that depend on a variable (e.g. power series) can be differentiated termwise, limits exchanged with sums and so on. See Spivak (1967, Chapter 4).

We now come to a fundamental test for absolute convergence: most other such tests are based on this one.

Theorem 1.13 (The Comparison Test)

Suppose $|u_n| < a_n$ for each n, and

$$A = \sum_{n=1}^{\infty} a_n \text{ converges.}$$

Then

$$S = \sum_{n=1}^{\infty} u_n \text{ converges absolutely.}$$

Moreover $S < A$.

Proof

We need merely note that the partial sums of the $|u_n|$'s are monotone increasing and bounded above by the sum of the a_n's.

□

Theorem 1.14 (The Alternating Series Test)

Suppose $u_n \to 0$, $|u_{n+1}| < |u_n|$, and $u_{n+1} \times u_n < 0$ (i.e. the terms alternate in sign) for each n. Then

$$S = \sum_{n=1}^{\infty} u_n \quad \text{converges (not necessarily absolutely of course).}$$

Moreover S lies between any two successive partial sums of the series.

Proof

Let us suppose for definiteness that u_1 is positive, u_2 is negative and so on. $S_1 = u_1$. Now $S_3 = u_1 + (u_2 + u_3)$. The term in brackets is negative since u_2 is negative and $|u_3| < |u_2|$. Hence $S_3 < S_1$ and proceeding in this way we have $S_1 > S_3 > S_5 > \ldots$. Similarly $S_2 < S_4 < S_6 < \ldots$. Moreover, since $S_{n+1} = S_n + u_{n+1}$, and the even numbered terms are negative, it follows that if n is odd, $S_{n+1} < S_n$, i.e. $S_2 < S_1$, $S_4 < S_3$ and so on. Hence the even numbered partial sums form a monotone increasing sequence bounded above by S_1, and thus converge: say to S_e. Similarly the odd numbered partial sums converge: say to S_o. But since $u_n \to 0$, the difference between even and odd partial sums tends to zero so we must have $S_e = S_o = S$, say. Thus the whole series converges. The final part of the theorem is the observation that S is less than all the odd sums and greater than the even sums.

□

This test shows that the series

$$\sum_{n=1}^{\infty} \frac{(-1)^n}{n}$$

does converge conditionally, even though the harmonic series does not. It is difficult to give realistic neural examples on the tests at this stage: however, the results will be used later.

1.6 Differentiable functions and extreme values

'What are these infinitesimals: the ghosts of departed quantities?'
(Bishop Berkely)

The concept of a sequence is ideal for discussing discrete time models. However, when working in continuous time, it is necessary to make use of the techniques of the calculus.

The calculus is perhaps the greatest contribution to knowledge of modern western mathematics: only the discovery of the principles of automatic computation rivalling its importance. Much of physics and engineering would simply be impossible without calculus. There are two approaches to the precise definition of the derivative. The classical approach is to use the idea of limit, reducing the infinitesimal to a mere notational convenience. An alternative approach (called non-standard analysis) uses the concept of infinitesimal in a much more profound way. This latter approach has certain attractions, but is much more difficult to set up, so we will adhere to the standard approach.

Definition 1.15
Let f: $\mathbb{R} \to \mathbb{R}$. We say that

$$\lim_{x\to\infty} f(x) = A$$

if given any $\varepsilon > 0$, there exists δ such for $0 < |x - y| < \delta \mid f(x) - A| < \varepsilon$.

□

Clearly this definition of limit is closely related to that for sequences. Similar results on combinations of limits and techniques for evaluation also hold. We will therefore take these as read, and give only a simple example.

$$\lim_{x\to\infty} \frac{x^2 + 2x + 3}{3x^2 + 4} = \lim_{x\to\infty} \frac{1 + (2/x) + [3/(x^2)]}{3 + [4/(x^2)]}$$

$$= 1/3.$$

It is now not too difficult to give a precise definition of the derivative, although surprisingly it took some 200 years from the time of Newton and Leibnitz for mathematicians to arrive at this exact definition. Figure 1.2 illustrates the concept.

Intuitively, the idea of the derivative is (like all the best ideas!) quite simple. We wish to evaluate the slope of a curve at a point x. To estimate the slope, we consider a point $x + \delta x$. Note that δx is not a product, it is simply a notation for a small real number. The slope of the chord joining the function values at these points is

$$\frac{f(x+\delta x)-f(x)}{(x+\delta x)-x}=\frac{f(x+\delta x)-f(x)}{\delta x}.$$

Provided the curve is sufficiently smooth, our intuition suggests that the smaller we make δx, the better the slope of the chord will approximate the slope of the curve. Thus

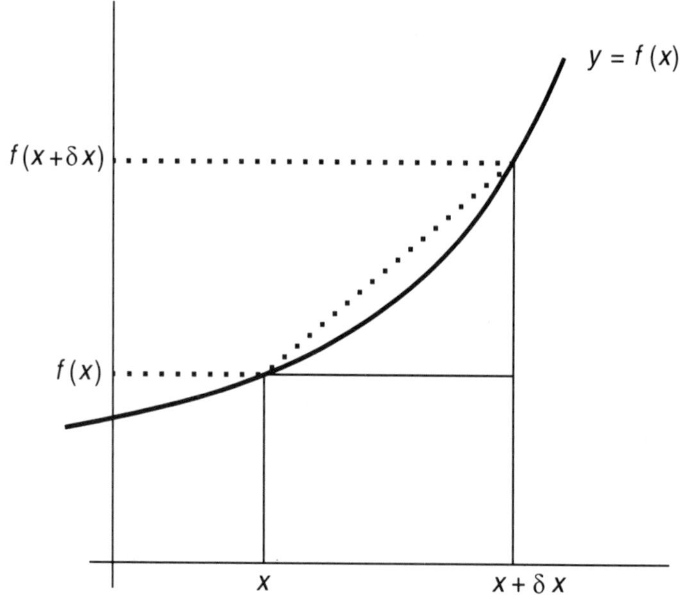

Fig. 1.2

Definition 1.16

(a) Let $x \in \mathbb{R}$ and f be a real function. We say that f is *differentiable* at x, and that $f'(x)$ is its *derivative* at x, if

$$f'(x)=\lim_{x\to 0}\frac{f(x+\delta x)-f(x)}{\delta x}$$

exists.

(b) If $X \subset \mathbb{R}$, and f is differentiable at each $x \in X$ we say that f is *differentiable* on X.

□

For example, let $f(x)=x^2$. Then

$$f(x+\delta x)=(x+\delta x)^2=x^2+2x\,\delta x+\delta x^2.$$

Hence

$$\begin{aligned}\frac{f(x+\delta x)-f(x)}{\delta x}&=\frac{\delta x^2+2x\,\delta x}{\delta x}\\&=2x+\delta x\\&\to 2x \text{ as } x\to 0.\end{aligned}$$

Remarks 1.17

(a) Sometimes, if $y=f(x)$, the notation $\mathrm{d}y/\mathrm{d}x$ or $\mathrm{d}f/\mathrm{d}x$ is used instead. This is to remind us that the derivative is the limit of the difference of y divided by the difference of x. The objects '$\mathrm{d}x$' and '$\mathrm{d}y$' are sometimes called *infinitesimals*. However in standard analysis they have no real meaning: they are simply a notational convenience.
(b) Clearly we can also define higher derivatives $f'', f''', \ldots : f''$ is the derivative of f'. We will use the notation $f^{[n]}$ to denote the nth derivative of f.
(c) If a function is differentiable at x, it must be continuous there. (Think of what would happen to the chord at a discontinuity!)
(d) The derivatives of standard functions are tabulated and covered in elementary calculus courses, and we will take them for granted. (See, for example, Abramowitz and Stegun (1964).)

□

Since the elementary rules of differentiation are likely to be familiar to the reader, we list them here without proof. Again the reader totally unfamiliar with the calculus is referred to Spivak (1967, Part III) or a similar textbook.

Theorem 1.18 (Properties of the derivative)
Let $X \subset \mathbb{R}$, f, g: $X \to \mathbb{R}$, h: $\mathbb{R} \to \mathbb{R}$ and $\lambda \in \mathbb{R}$. Then

(a) $(f+\lambda g)'=f'+\lambda g'$.
(b) If $y=f(x)$, and f has locally an inverse $g(y)$ so that $x=g(y)$, then

$$\frac{dy}{dx} = 1/\frac{dx}{dy},$$

provided the right-hand side is finite.

(c) If $y=f(x)$ and $z=h(y)$, then

$$\frac{dz}{dx} = \frac{dz}{dy}\frac{dy}{dx} = h'(y)f'(x) = h'[f(x)]f'(x).$$

(d) If $u=f(x)$, $v=g(x)$ and $y=uv$, then

$$\frac{dy}{dx} = u\frac{dv}{dx} + v\frac{du}{dx}.$$

(e) $$\frac{d(u/v)}{dx} = \frac{v\dfrac{du}{dx} - u\dfrac{dv}{dx}}{v^2}.$$

□

A very important application of the derivative is in finding the extreme (i.e. maximum and minimum) values of a function. We shall use this idea repeatedly in this book to find the minimum error of a neural system.

The first question to consider when examining a function to determine its extrema is whether it is continuous (see Definition 1.1). If a function is not continuous, finding extrema can be very problematical, and we will not go into this here. Figure 1.3 shows a function whose extrema we may wish to determine. Normally, we wish to work on a so-called *closed interval*, i.e. a set $[a, b] \subset \mathbb{R}$ defined to be $\{x \in \mathbb{R} \mid a \leq x \leq b\}$. On occasions we may also work on an *open interval* (a, b), which is $\{x \in \mathbb{R} \mid a < x < b\}$. We first state the following basic property.

Theorem 1.19 (The Intermediate Value Theorem)

Let $f: [a, b] \to \mathbb{R}$ be continuous. Then there are real numbers $\lambda, \mu \in [a, b]$ such that $f(x) \geq f(\lambda)$ and $f(x) \leq f(\mu)$ for all $x \in [a, b]$ (i.e. the extreme values of f are achieved). Moreover if $y \in \mathbb{R}$ satisfies $f(\lambda) < y < f(\mu)$, then there exists $\nu \in [a, b]$ such that $f(\nu) = y$ (i.e. every value intermediate between the two extrema is also achieved).

□

The numbers λ, μ, ν are illustrated in Fig. 1.3. Note that it is essential that the interval $[a, b]$ be closed. We will not give a proof of the Intermediate Value

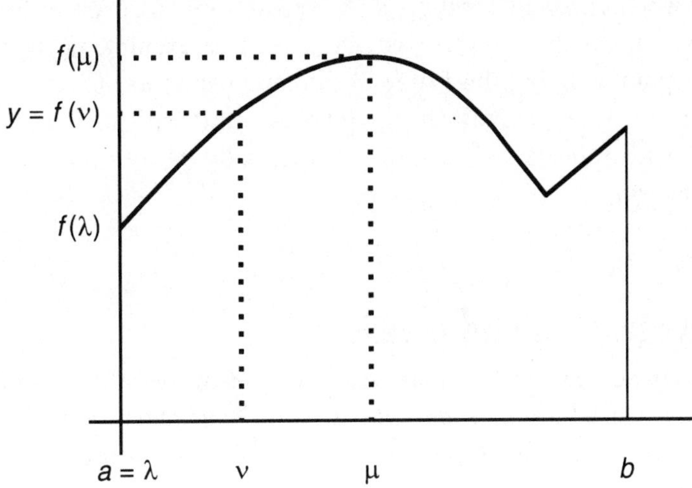

Fig. 1.3

Theorem. At this stage, the result may appear to the reader to be obvious and not worth proving. However, it is possible to find continuous functions which have astonishingly complicated behaviour, at which point the Intermediate Value Theorem might seem far less obvious! Nevertheless, it is true for an arbitrary continuous real function, and a proof may be found in Spivak (1967).

By examining Fig. 1.3, it is now easy to identify possible candidates for the extrema.

Theorem 1.20

Let f, λ and μ be as in Theorem 1.19. Then at least one of the following properties must hold for λ (and similarly μ).

(i) λ is an end point, i.e. $\lambda=a$ or $\lambda=b$.
(ii) f is not differentiable at λ, or
(iii) $f'(\lambda)=0$.

□

If we are working on an open interval (a, b) or the whole of $\mathbb{R}$, there is no guarantee that either extrema is achieved. On the other hand, if we know that it is achieved, finding it is rather easier since then case (i) cannot occur. In the simplest case of a function differentiable throughout $\mathbb{R}$, we need only examine points at which the derivative vanishes: such points are called *stationary points*.

Note that whereas, except for the 'special' cases (i) and (ii), extrema are always stationary points, the converse is not true. For example $f(x)=x^3$ has a stationary point at 0, but this is not an extremum, even locally. Another case to beware of is where a stationary point η is an extreme point of $f(x)$ when compared with values close to η, but not globally. Such a point is called a *local extremum*.

1.7 Integration and measure

Readers may be familiar with the construction of the definite integral due to Riemann, in which the area under a curve is approximated by upper and lower sums. Unfortunately, the Riemann integral is insufficient for our purposes: we will need a more general construction due to Lebesgue. Although the Lebesgue integral does not require any analytical machinery other that the results on limits and sequences that we have already seen, some of the proofs are quite difficult. Readers not interested in coming to grips with every detail might wish to skip over some of these technical proofs, but should aim to understand the basic idea of the construction of the integral, and the meaning of the theorems.

We consider functions defined on a subset X of $\mathbb{R}^n$. The reader to whom this construction is totally new may prefer to think of the case where $n=1$ and X is an interval: the illustrations are given for this case. However there is no added difficulty in handling the general multidimensional case, and we will require it later. There are two basic approaches to the Lebesgue integral: one is to define the measure of a set in an abstract way, and construct the integral from this. A good description of this approach is given in Komolgorov and Fomin (1961) or Hewitt and Stromberg (1965). However we shall adopt the more concrete route of first defining the integral. This is the approach taken by Weir (1973), and readers requiring a more comprehensive and less terse discussion than we can give here are recommended to consult this book. Bartle (1966) adopts something of a hybrid of the two methods. Our discussion here focuses on the main ideas and results: one or two technical difficulties are skated over!

An *interval* on $\mathbb{R}^n$ is the Cartesian product of n real intervals. (Thus an interval is a rectangle in $\mathbb{R}^2$, or a cuboid in $\mathbb{R}^3$.) We start by defining the integral for a very simple class of functions.

Definition 1.21

Let X be a subset of $\mathbb{R}^n$, and let $\varphi: X \to \mathbb{R}$ satisfy the following conditions.

(a) $\varphi(x)=0$ except for a finite number of disjoint intervals $I_1, I_2, \ldots, I_N$ for some positive integer N.
(b) $\varphi(x)$ is constant and positive on each interval, i.e. there exist N numbers $\varphi_1, \varphi_2, \ldots, \varphi_N$ (not necessarily different) such that $\varphi(x)=\varphi_i$ for $x \in I_i$.

The φ is said to be a *step function*.

□

In other words a step function is piecewise constant and takes only a finite number of non negative values. The set of values on which a function is non-zero is called the *support* of the function. Step functions must have bounded support. Rather illogically, a function whose support is bounded is said to have *finite support*, although the support is not necessarily a finite set!

Definition 1.22

Suppose an interval I is given by $(a_1, b_1)\times(a_2, b_2)\times\ldots\times(a_n, b_n)$. The *Lebesgue measure* $\mu(I)$ of I is defined to be $(b_1-a_1)\times(b_2-a_2)\times\ldots\times(b_n-a_n)$. More generally if $I_1, I_2, I_3, \ldots$ are disjoint intervals, we may define $\mu(I_1 \cup I_2 \cup I_3 \cup \ldots)$ as $\mu(I_1)+\mu(I_2)+\mu(I_3)+\ldots$. This is valid even if there are countably infinitely many I_k, provided of course that the sum converges.

□

Thus the measure of a real interval is simply its length, the measure of a rectangle is its area, and the measure of a cuboid is its volume.

Definition 1.23

If φ is a step function, we define its *Lebesgue integral* by

$$\int_{\mathbb{R}n} \varphi(\boldsymbol{x})\,\mathrm{d}\boldsymbol{x} = \sum_{i=1}^{N} \varphi_i\,\mu(I_i).$$

□

Thus in the case of the real line and assuming the φ_i's are all positive, the integral is simply the area under the function φ. Our aim now is to generalise the integral to much more general functions, and, at the same time, extend the concept of measure to more general sets.

Definition 1.24

A set $X \subset \mathbb{R}$ is said to have *Lebesgue measure zero*, if, given any $\varepsilon > 0$, there exists a countable (see Section 1.2) set of intervals $J_1, J_2, \ldots$ (not necessarily disjoint) such that

(a) $X \subset \bigcup_{i=1}^{\infty} J_i$ (the J_i are said to *cover* X), and

(b) $\sum_{i=1}^{\infty} \mu(J_i) \leq \varepsilon$

A property that is true except on a set of measure zero is said to be *essentially* true or true *almost everywhere* (a.e.)

□

Any countable subset C of $\mathbb{R}$, (for instance $\mathbb{Q}$) has measure zero. For each $c_i \in C$, define $t_i = 2^{-i}$, and $J_i = (c_i - \frac{1}{4}\varepsilon t_i,\ c_i + \frac{1}{4}\varepsilon t_i)$. Then

$$\sum_{i=1}^{\infty} \mu(J_i) = \tfrac{1}{2} \sum_{i=1}^{\infty} \varepsilon t_i = \tfrac{\varepsilon}{2} \sum_{i=1}^{\infty} 2^{-i} = \varepsilon/2 \text{ by (1.9).}$$

A simple extension of this argument shows that a countable union of sets of measure zero has measure zero. The next results form the core of the construction of the Lebesgue integral. We give the proofs here, but most readers will not find it necessary to come to grips with these details!

Lemma 1.25

Let (φ_m) be a monotone increasing sequence of non-negative step functions, and K a positive real number, such that

$$\int_{\mathbb{R}^n} \varphi_m(\mathbf{x})\, d\mathbf{x} < K \text{ for every } m.$$

Then for almost every $\mathbf{x} \in \mathbb{R}^n$, $[\varphi_m(\mathbf{x})]$ converges.

Proof

Since for each $\mathbf{x}$ the sequence $[\varphi_m(\mathbf{x})]$ is monotone increasing, there are only two possibilities: either it converges or tends to $+\infty$.

Denote by X the set of $\mathbf{x}$ for which $\varphi_m(\mathbf{x}) \to +\infty$. We need to show that X has measure zero. Given any $\varepsilon > 0$, define

$$S_m{}^{\varepsilon} = \{x \in \mathbb{R}^n \mid \varphi_m(x) \geq K/\varepsilon\}.$$

$S_m{}^{\varepsilon}$ consists of a finite number of disjoint intervals: it is a subset of the support of $\varphi_m(\mathbf{x})$. We have

$$\int_{\mathbb{R}^n} \varphi_m\,(\mathbf{x})\,d\mathbf{x} > \mu\,(S_m{}^{\varepsilon})\,(K/\varepsilon),$$

whence $\mu(S_m{}^{\varepsilon}) < \varepsilon$. Moreover $S_m^{\varepsilon} \subset S^{\varepsilon}{}_{m+1}$ since $\varphi_m(\mathbf{x})$ is monotone increasing for each $\mathbf{x}$. Also, observe that if $\mathbf{x} \in X$, $\varphi_m(\mathbf{x}) \geq K/\varepsilon$ for some m, so $X \subset S^{\varepsilon} = \cup\, S_m{}^{\varepsilon}$ where the union is taken over all m. But we may decompose S^{ε} as a countable union of disjoint intervals as follows: Set $J_1 = S_1{}^{\varepsilon}$, $J_2 = S_2 - J_1$ and in general $J_k = S_k - J_{k-1}$. Observe that $S_m{}^{\varepsilon} = J_1 \cup J_2 \ldots \cup J_m$ so the sum of the measures of $\mu(J_1 \cup J_2 \ldots \cup J_m) = \sigma_m{}^{\varepsilon} < \varepsilon$. Hence $\mu(S^{\varepsilon}) = \mu(J_1 \cup J_2 \ldots) \leq \varepsilon$. Since we can perform this construction for any $\varepsilon > 0$, X has zero measure.

□

This lemma suggests that we define the (non-negative) integrable functions as those which can be expressed a.e. as the limit of step functions, and the integrals as the limits of the integrals of the step functions. However, the problem is that a function f might be the limit a.e. of two distinct sequences of step functions *which might therefore give different values for the integral.* We need to show that this cannot occur. We also need to show that if two functions are equal except on a set of measure zero, then they have the same integral. The following theorem achieves both these objectives.

Theorem 1.26

Suppose (φ_m) and (ψ_m) are increasing sequences of step functions such that $\varphi_m(\mathbf{x}) \to f(\mathbf{x})$ a.e. and $\psi_m(\mathbf{x}) \to g(\mathbf{x})$ a.e. and that $f(\mathbf{x}) = g(\mathbf{x})$ a.e. Suppose moreover that

$$\lim_{m \to \infty} \int_{\mathbb{R}^n} \varphi_m\,(\mathbf{x})\,d\mathbf{x} = I.$$

Then

$$\lim_{m\to\infty}\int_{\mathbb{R}^n} \psi_m(\mathbf{x})\,\mathrm{d}\mathbf{x} = I.$$

Proof

Given any $\varepsilon > 0$, we start by fixing some subscript k_0. Suppose $M=\max\ \psi_{k_0}(\mathbf{x})$, T the support of ψ_{k_0} and $L=\mu(T)$. Recall also that $\psi_{k_0}(\mathbf{x})\leq f(\mathbf{x})$ for almost all x.

Let $S_k=\{\mathbf{x}\ |\varphi_k(\mathbf{x}) < \psi_{k_0}(\mathbf{x})-\varepsilon/L\}$. Since φ_k and ψ_{k_0} are step functions, S_k consists of a finite union of intervals. Thus $\mu(S_k)$ is defined. Now the φ_k are monotone increasing, so the S_k form a monotone decreasing sequence of sets, i.e. $S_{k+1}\subset S_k$. The sequence $\mu(S_k)$ is monotone decreasing and bounded below by 0, so it converges. Let the limit be μ_∞. We have

$$\mu_\infty = \mu(S_1) - \sum_{k=1}^{\infty}[\mu(S_k) - \mu(S_{k+1})].$$

Each term of the sum represents the measure of the intervals deleted in passing from S_k to S_{k+1}. Let S_D denote the union of all these deleted intervals. Thus the sum is $\mu(S_D)$. Let $S_N=S_1-S_D$. For $\mathbf{x}\in S_N$, $\varphi_k(\mathbf{x})\leq f(\mathbf{x})-\varepsilon/L$ for all k. Hence $\mu(S_N)=0$, since $\varphi_k(\mathbf{x})\to f(\mathbf{x})$ almost everywhere. Thus

$$\mu_\infty = \mu(S_1) - \mu(S_D) = \mu(S_D) + \mu(S_N) - \mu(S_D) = 0.$$

Then

$$\begin{aligned}\int_{\mathbb{R}^n} \psi_{k_0}(\mathbf{x})\,\mathrm{d}\mathbf{x} &= \int_{T-S_k} \psi_{k_0}(\mathbf{x})\,\mathrm{d}\mathbf{x} + \int_{S_k} \psi_{k_0}(\mathbf{x})\,\mathrm{d}\mathbf{x}\\ &\leq \int_{T-S_k} (\varphi_k(\mathbf{x}) + \varepsilon/L)\,\mathrm{d}\mathbf{x} + \int_{S_k} \psi_{k_0}(\mathbf{x})\,\mathrm{d}\mathbf{x}\\ &\leq I + \varepsilon + \int_{S_k} \psi_{k_0}(\mathbf{x})\,\mathrm{d}\mathbf{x}.\end{aligned}$$

Now let $k\to\infty$. Since $\mu(S_k)\to\mu_\infty=0$, the integral term goes to zero and we conclude

$$\int_{\mathbb{R}^n} \psi_{k_0}(\boldsymbol{x})\,\mathrm{d}\boldsymbol{x} \leq I + \varepsilon.$$

Now the integral increases monotonically with k_0, so we may allow $k_0\to\infty$ establishing that

$$\lim_{k_0\to\infty}\int_{\mathbb{R}^n}\psi_{k_0}(\mathbf{x})\,\mathrm{d}\mathbf{x}\le I+\varepsilon.$$

But $\varepsilon>0$ was arbitrary, so we must have

$$\lim_{k_0\to\infty}\int_{\mathbb{R}^\Delta}\psi_{k_0}(\mathbf{x})\,\mathrm{d}\mathbf{x}\le I.$$

A similar argument reversing the roles of φ_k and ψ_k shows that

$$\int_{\mathbb{R}^n}\psi_{k_0}(\mathbf{x})\,\mathrm{d}\mathbf{x}\ge I.$$

completing the proof.

□

We are now in a position to define the Lebesgue integrable functions.

Definitions 1.27

(a) With the notation of Theorem 1.26, we say that f is *positive Lebesgue integrable*, and define

$$\int_{\mathbb{R}^n} f(\mathbf{x})\,\mathrm{d}\mathbf{x}=I.$$

(b) If S is a subset of $\mathbb{R}^n$, let

$$f_s(\mathbf{x})=\begin{cases} f(\mathbf{x}) \text{ if } \mathbf{x}\in S\\ 0 \text{ otherwise}\end{cases}$$

If f_S is Lebesgue integrable, then we define

$$\int_S f(\mathbf{x})\,\mathrm{d}x=\int_{\mathbb{R}^n} f_s(\mathbf{x})\,\mathrm{d}\mathbf{x}.$$

In the particular case that $n=1$ and S is just an interval $[a, b]$ we write alternatively

$$\int_a^b f(x)\,\mathrm{d}x \text{ for } \int_S f(x)\,\mathrm{d}x.$$

(c) Clearly f can only satisfy the conditions of Theorem 1.26 if it is non-negative. However, this restriction is easily removed. For a function f that may take both positive and negative values, define S^+ to be the set on which $f(\mathbf{x})\ge$

0, and S^- to be the set on which $f(\mathbf{x})<0$. Then we define

$$\int f(\mathbf{x})\,d\mathbf{x} = \int_{S^+} f(\mathbf{x})\,d\mathbf{x} - \int_{S^-} [-f(\mathbf{x})]\,d\mathbf{x}$$

provided both integrals on the right-hand side exist.

□

The construction detailed above may seem unpleasantly complex to those unfamiliar with mathematical analysis. Even readers familiar with the Riemann integral may find the details confusing. However, the Lebesgue integral is an essential tool in describing the behaviour of non-linear systems, and in the rigorous definition of function spaces. The remarks following will hopefully elucidate the construction and bring out some simple properties.

Remarks 1.28

(a) It is fairly easy to see that any continuous function on an interval is integrable. For simplicity, consider the case of a non-negative continuous function on the closed interval $[0,1]$ of the real line. Split this into two subintervals $[0,0.5]$ and $(0.5,1]$. In view of the Intermediate Value Theorem (Theorem 1.19) we may define

$$v_1 = \min_{x\in[0,.5]} f(x)$$

and

$$v_2 = \min_{x\in[.5,1]} f(x).$$

Now construct a step function $\varphi_1(x)$ to take the value v_1 on $[0, 0.5]$ and v_2 on $(0.5, 1]$. Similarly we construct φ_2 by dividing $[0, 1]$ into four intervals, φ_3 by dividing into eight intervals and so on. The sequence (φ_k) so produced is obviously monotone increasing and in view of the continuity of f will converge to it almost everywhere.

(b) The integrals of Definition 1.27 satisfy the following linearity property: if f and g are Lebesgue integrable on a set S and $\lambda \in \mathbb{R}$, then

$$\int_S [f(\mathbf{x}) + \lambda g(\mathbf{x})]\,d\mathbf{x} = \int_S f(\mathbf{x})\,d\mathbf{x} + \lambda \int_S g(\mathbf{x})\,d\mathbf{x}.$$

To see this, first consider the case $S=\mathbb{R}^n$, $\lambda > 0$ and non-negative functions with $(\varphi_k)\rightarrow f$ a.e. and $(\psi_k)\rightarrow g$ a.e. Observe that $(\varphi_k + \lambda\psi_k)$ defines a monotone sequence of step functions converging a.e. to $f+\lambda g$. Removal of the various restrictions is straightforward and is left as an exercise for the reader.

Similarly, one can show that the product function $f(x)g(x)$ is integrable. In this case there is not such a simple representation for the integral of the product, but see Theorem 1.30.

(c) A useful and important consequence of Definition 1.27(c) is that if the integrals on its right-hand side exist, then $|f|$ is also integrable, and moreover

$$\left|\int_S f(\mathbf{x})\,d\mathbf{x}\right| \leq \int_S |f(\mathbf{x})|\,d\mathbf{x}.$$

(d) Readers familiar with the Riemann integral might wish to note that any Riemann integrable function is also Lebesgue integrable, and gives the same value. To see this, observe that lower Riemann sums define a sequence of monotone increasing step functions satisfying the required conditions. On the other hand it is possible for a function to be Lebesgue integrable, but not Riemann integrable: for example consider f: $[0, 1]\rightarrow[0, 1]$ defined by

$$f(x)=\begin{cases}0 \text{ if } x \text{ is rational}\\ 1 \text{ otherwise.}\end{cases}$$

The lower Riemann sums for this function always give 0, while the upper sums give 1. Thus the function is not Riemann integrable. On the other hand the function differs from the function $g(x)=1$ only on the set $\mathbb{Q}$ of rational numbers. Since $\mathbb{Q}$ has measure zero (see the remark following Definition 1.24), f is Lebesgue integrable and has integral 1.

(e) It is important to note that there is no significance attached to name **x** of the variable appearing as the argument of f and in the '$d\mathbf{x}$' part. It is merely there to indicate that integration is with respect to the argument. The integral is a real number and it would be perfectly valid to refer to the variable by any other name instead of **x**, e.g. **y** or **t**. A variable used in this way is called a *dummy variable*.

(f) The integral is *set additive*: i.e. if S_1 and S_2 are disjoint sets, and f is integrable on each, then the integral on $S_1 \cup S_2$ exists and

$$\int_{S_1\cup S_2} f(\mathbf{x})\,d\mathbf{x} = \int_{S_1} f(\mathbf{x})\,d\mathbf{x} + \int_{S_2} f(\mathbf{x})\,d\mathbf{x}$$

To see this, note that we can form a sequence of step functions on $S_1 \cup S_2$ by combining the sequences on S_1 and S_2.

□

Closely related to the Lebesgue integral is the concept of *measure*. We have already met the measure of intervals, and sets of measure zero. We can now give a definition of measure for much more general sets.

Definition 1.29

(a) Let g: $\mathbb{R}^n \rightarrow \mathbb{R}$ satisfy $g(\mathbf{x}) > 0$ for all $\mathbf{x}$, and let $S \subset \mathbb{R}^n$. Then

$$\mu_g(S) = \int_S g(\mathbf{x})\, d\mathbf{x}$$

is called a *Lebesgue–Stieltjes measure* of S, provided the integral exists, and the corresponding g is called a *density function*. (A more general definition of Lebesgue–Stieltjes measure will be introduced in Chapter 6.)

(b) The particular case $g(\mathbf{x})=1$ for all $\mathbf{x}$ is called the *Lebesgue measure*. In this case we will omit the subscript and refer simply to $\mu(S)$.

(c) Any choice of g for which $\mu_g(\mathbb{R}^n)=1$ is said to be a *probability measure*.

□

Of course the Lebesgue measure reduces to the definition given previously for intervals and sets of measure zero. The reader may wonder whether there are any bounded subsets of $\mathbb{R}^n$ for which the measure does *not* exist. In fact, the existence of such sets is known but their construction is difficult and will not be considered here. Clearly all countable unions of intervals are measurable.

Note that if two measurable sets S_1 and S_2 are such that $S_1 \cap S_2$ is also measurable, then by Remark 1.28(f),

$$\mu(S_1 \cup S_2) = \mu(S_1) + \mu(S_2) - \mu(S_1 \cap S_2),$$

which is obviously an essential property when discussing probability! The reader may well be familiar with the well known *Gaussian* or *normal* probability measure on the real line defined by

$$g\mathbf{x} = \exp(-x^2/\sqrt{2\pi})$$

(See Example 6.53 for evaluation of the integral required to prove that this is a probability measure.) The quantity $\mu_g(S)$ is simply the probability of a random variable x taking a value in S: for example, if $S=\{x \mid x \leq y\}$ and g is the normal density function, then $\mu_g(S)$ is the probability of a normally distributed variable x taking a value less than or equal to y.

We can now leave the loftier regions of analysis and return to more prosaic

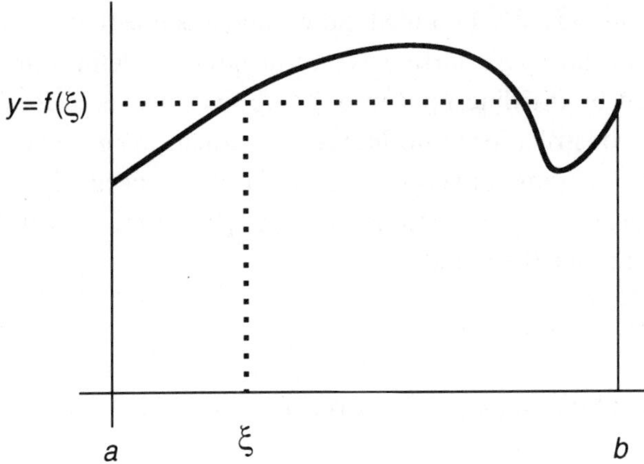

Fig. 1.4

matters. The next part of our discussion of integration will be concerned only with intervals of the real line. The link between the relatively esoteric topic of measure theory and the traditional concerns of applied calculus is provided by a result known as the Integral Mean Value Theorem. A special case of this result is easily illustrated (see Fig. 1.4). If f is a continuous function on an interval $J=[a, b]$, then it is not difficult to see that there exists a number ξ between a and b for which the area under f is the same as the area under the constant line of height $f(\xi)$. In terms of integrals, we have

$$\int_a^b f(x)\,\mathrm{d}x = (b-a)f(\xi).$$

Since $\mu(J)=(b-a)$, we may re-write the right-hand side of this equation as $f(\xi)\mu(J)$. This simple special case is in fact all that is needed for most applications, but we may as well give a proof for a more general measure.

Theorem 1.30 (The Integral Mean Value Theorem)
Let $J=[a, b]$ and let μ_g be a Lebesgue–Stieltjes measure corresponding to the continuous density function g, and such that $\mu_g(S)$ exists. Moreover, let $f\colon I\to\mathbb{R}$ be continuous. Then there exists $\xi\in J$ such that

$$\int_a^b f(x)g(x)\,\mathrm{d}x = f(\xi)\mu_g(S).$$

Proof

Since f is continuous, it is bounded. So we may assume that f is non-negative: if not add a constant. Of course, g is non-negative by definition.

We proceed by dividing up J into 2^k subdivisions, as in Remark 1.28(a). However we construct separate increasing sequences (φ_k) and (ψ_k) of non-negative step functions converging a.e. to f and g respectively. Clearly $(\varphi_k\psi_k)$ defines a sequence of step functions converging a.e. to fg, and If T is the value of the integral in the theorem,

$$T = \lim_{k\to\infty} \int_S \varphi_k(x)\psi_k(x)\,\mathrm{d}x.$$

But for each k, the integrand is defined to be constant on each of the 2^k subdivisions of J. Thus

$$\int_I \varphi_k(x)\psi_k(x)\,\mathrm{d}x = \frac{(b-a)}{2^k}\sum_{i=1}^{m} \varphi_k(x_i)\psi_k(x_i) = T_k, \text{ say,}$$

where x_i is any point in the ith subinterval. Now provided φ_k is constructed as in Remark 1.28(a) so that $\varphi_k(x_i)$ is the minimum of $f(x)$ in the ith subinterval, we have

$$m_1 \sum_{i=1}^{\infty} \psi(x_i) \le \sum_{i=1}^{\infty} \varphi_k(x_i)\,\psi_k(x_i) \le m_2 \sum_{i=1}^{\infty} \psi(x_i),$$

where m_1 and m_2 are respectively the minimum and maximum values of f in the interval $[a, b]$, which exist from the Intermediate Value Theorem (Theorem 1.19). This is because the values $\psi(x_i)$ are all positive. Now divide these inequalities by $(b-a)/2^k$ and let $k\to\infty$. We obtain

$$m_1 \int_a^b g(x)\,\mathrm{d}x \le \int_a^b f(x)g(x)\,\mathrm{d}x \le m_2 \int_a^b g(x)\,\mathrm{d}x$$

which by definition is

$$m_1\mu_g(I) \le \int_a^b f(x)g(x)\,\mathrm{d}x \le m_2\mu_g(I).$$

Thus

$$\frac{1}{\mu_g(I)} \int_a^b f(x)g(x)\,\mathrm{d}x$$

is a value intermediate between m_1 and m_2, the minimum and maximum values of f on $[a, b]$. Hence, again by Theorem 1.19, there must be a point ξ at which $f(\xi)$ is equal to it.

□

This result frees us from the necessity to work with step functions and enables us to deal directly with limits of integrals. In particular, we may address our next target, which is the Fundamental Theorem of Calculus. This is the result which links together the differential and integral calculus.

Definition 1.31

Let f be a continuous real valued function on $[a, b]$. Then any function $F(x)$ satisfying $F'(x)=f(x)$ is called an *indefinite integral* of f.

□

The reason for this definition should be apparent from the next result.

Theorem 1.32 (First version of the Fundamental Theorem)

Let f be a continuous real valued function on $[a, b]$. Then $F(x)$ defined by

$$F(x) = \int_a^x f(t)\,dt$$

is an indefinite integral of f.

Proof

We are required to show that F is differentiable and that its derivative is f. Thus we consider

$$\begin{aligned}\frac{F(x+\delta x) - F(x)}{\delta x} &= \frac{1}{\delta x}\left(\int_a^{x+\delta x} f(t)\,dt - \int_a^x f(t)\,dt\right) \\ &= \frac{1}{\delta x}\int_x^{x+\delta x} f(t)\,dt \text{ by Remark 1.28}(f). \\ &= \frac{1}{\delta x}\,\delta x\, f(\xi) \text{ (where } x < \xi < x+\delta x\text{) from Theorem 1.30} \\ &\qquad \text{with } g(x) = 1 \\ &= f(\xi).\end{aligned}$$

Since f is continuous, this tends to $f(x)$ as $\delta x \to 0$, as required.

□

Note that what we have done here is to show that the definite integral can be used to construct an indefinite integral. This is sometimes useful, but often we want it the other way round.

Corollary 1.33 (Fundamental Theorem of Calculus)

Let f be a continuous real valued function on $[a, b]$, and let G be any indefinite integral of f. Then

$$\int_a^b f(t)\,\mathrm{d}t = G(b) - G(a).$$

Proof

We know that F as defined in Theorem 1.32 is an indefinite integral. But 'clearly' only constants can have derivative vanishing identically in a non-empty interval. (Actually, this depends on a result known as the Mean Value Theorem. Examination of Fig. 1.2 suggests that if f is differentiable in $[a, b]$, there exists $\xi \in (a, b)$ with $f'(\xi) = [f(a) - f(b)]/(a - b)$, i.e. the curve must have the same slope at some intermediate point as the chord. For a formal proof of this statement, see Spivak (1969, p. 169). If $f'(\xi) = 0$, it follows that $f(a) = f(b)$, and since this equally applies to any points in the closed interval, f must be constant.)

Hence $G(x) = F(x) + c$ for some real constant c. However from the definition of $F(x)$, $F(a) = 0$. Hence $c = G(a)$, i.e. $G(x) - G(a) = F(x)$. We need now only put $x = b$ in Theorem 1.31.

□

The expression $G(b) - G(a)$ is evaluated so often that we have a special notation for it. We write

$$G(b) - G(a) = [G(x)]_a^b.$$

For example

$$\int_0^1 x^2\,\mathrm{d}x = \left[\frac{x^3}{3}\right]_0^1 = 1/3.$$

It is not the purpose of this book to give a course in elementary integration: it is assumed that most readers willing to tackle the material herein will already be familiar with basic calculus. See Spivak, (1967) for a development of the theory, or Abramowitz and Stegun (1964) for integrals of elementary functions. However, we will require the two basic rules for practical integration: Substitution and Integration by Parts. Thus, for completeness we give a proof of these here.

Theorem 1.34 (The Substitution Rule)

(a) Let $F(x)$ be an indefinite integral of $f(x)$, and suppose that x is a function of t. Then $F[x(t)]$ is an indefinite integral of

$$f(x)\frac{\mathrm{d}x}{\mathrm{d}t}.$$

(b) $\int_c^d f[x(t)]\frac{\mathrm{d}x}{\mathrm{d}t}\mathrm{d}t = \int_a^b f(x)\,\mathrm{d}x$

where $a=x(c)$ and $b=x(d)$.

Proof

(a) is simply Theorem 1.18(c) rewritten, since

$$\frac{\mathrm{d}F}{\mathrm{d}t} = \frac{\mathrm{d}F}{\mathrm{d}x}\frac{\mathrm{d}x}{\mathrm{d}t}.$$

(b) follows from (a) and Corollary 1.33.

□

Theorem 1.35 (Integration by Parts)

$$[uv]_a^b = \int_a^b u\frac{\mathrm{d}v}{\mathrm{d}x}\,\mathrm{d}x + \int_a^b v\frac{\mathrm{d}u}{\mathrm{d}x}\,\mathrm{d}x$$

Proof

Again, this is just a rewrite of one of the rules for differentiation, in this case Theorem 1.18(d).

□

When studying learning rules and dynamical systems in general, a key technique is the approximation of the functions involved by polynomials in one or more variables. The basic tool for doing this is known as Taylor's theorem: we consider the one variable case in this section. There are various proofs of Taylor's theorem. The one given here is not the shortest, but it is fairly 'natural' and also yields at an intermediate stage another form of the theorem which is sometimes useful. We make use of the Integral Mean Value Theorem (Theorem 1.30) and instead of differentiation we use repeated Integration by Parts (Theorem 1.35). We assume that f has n continuous derivatives and start from the Fundamental Theorem of Calculus (Corollary 1.33).

$$f(x) - f(a) = \int_a^x f'(t)\,\mathrm{d}t.$$

We introduce into the integrand a dummy multiplier $(x-t)^0$. (This is of course equal to 1: the special form is only to get the correct indefinite integral). Integration by parts (with respect to t, of course) yields

$$f(x) = f(a) + [-(x-t)f'(t)]_a^x + \int_a^x (x-t)f''(t)\,\mathrm{d}t$$

$$= f(a) + (x-a)f'(a) + \int_a^x (x-t)f''(t)\,\mathrm{d}t.$$

Integrating by parts again gives

$$f(x) = f(a) + (x-a)f'(a) + \left[\frac{-(x-t)^2 f''(a)}{2}\right]_a^x + \int_a^x \frac{(x-t)^2 f''(t)}{2}\,\mathrm{d}t$$

$$= f(a) + (x-a)f'(a) + \frac{(x-a)^2 f''(a)}{2} + \int_a^x \frac{(x-t)^2 f''(t)}{2}\,\mathrm{d}t.$$

Repeating again gives for the right-hand side

$$f(a) + (x-a)f'(a) + \frac{(x-a)^2 f''(a)}{2} + \left[\frac{-(x-t)^3 f''(a)}{3\times 2}\right]_a^x + \int_a^x \frac{(x-t)^3 f^{[4]}(t)}{3\times 2}\,\mathrm{d}t.$$

$$= f(a) + (x-a)f'(a) + \frac{(x-a)^2 f''(a)}{2} + \frac{(x-a)^3 f''(a)}{3\times 2} + \int_a^x \frac{(x-t)^3 f^{[4]}(t)}{3\times 2}\,\mathrm{d}t$$

Clearly we can continue this process for as long as f has continuous derivatives. We obtain Theorem 1.36 (using the factorial notation $k! = k\times(k-1)\times(k-2)\times\ldots\times 2\times 2\times 1$).

Theorem 1.36 (Taylor's theorem with integral remainder)

Let J be an open interval, and $f: J \to \mathbb{R}$. Suppose further that f has n continuous derivatives, and that $a \in J$. Then for each x in J,

$$f(x) = f(a) + \frac{(x-a)f'(a)}{1!} + \frac{(x-a)^2 f''(a)}{2!} + \frac{(x-a)^3 f''(a)}{3!} + \ldots +$$

$$\frac{(x-a)^{(n-1)} f^{[n-1]}(a)}{(n-1)!} + R_n,$$

$$\text{where } R_n = \int_a^x \frac{(x-t)^{n-1} f^{[n]}(t)}{(n-1)\,!} \mathrm{d}t.$$

□

The integral form of the *remainder term* R_n as given in Theorem 1.36 is the basis of a theorem due to Peano which can be used to obtain the error term for Simpson's rule and similar numerical integration formulae, but we will not pursue this here. Various other forms for R_n are known, but the following is the most commonly used, and will suffice for all the applications we consider.

Theorem 1.37

R_n in Theorem 1.36 can be written

$$R_n = \frac{(x-a)^n f^{[n]}(\xi)}{n!} \text{ where } \xi \in (a, x).$$

(Note that if $x<a$, we interpret the interval (a, x) as (x, a). From now on we shall assume this.)

Proof

We assume $x>a$. The other case requires only a change of sign throughout. We have

$$R_n = \int_a^x \frac{(x-t)^{n-1} f^{[n]}(t)}{(n-1)!} \mathrm{d}t.$$

Since $(x-t) > 0$ for $t \in [a, x]$, we may apply Theorem 1.30 (the Integral Mean Value Theorem) to obtain

$$R_n = f^{[n]}(\xi) \int_a^x \frac{(x-t)^{n-1}}{(n-1)!} \mathrm{d}t \text{ for some } \xi \in (a, x)$$

$$= f^{[n]}(\xi)\left[\frac{-(x-t)^n}{n(n-1)!}\right]_a^x$$

$$= f^{[n]}(\xi)\frac{(x-a)^n}{n!}.$$

□

This form is easy to remember since the remainder is of almost the same form as the other terms. It is essential to note that the formula is finite and exact: there are no truncated infinite series here. The price we pay for this is the indeterminate form of the remainder. However, in most cases this turns out not to be a serious drawback.

We complete this section on integration with some rather more technical theorems about the Lebesgue integral. These are required for establishing analytical properties of sets of integrable functions which will be required in later chapters. Recall that two integrable functions are said to be equal almost everywhere (a.e.) if they are equal except on a set of measure zero. We consider integrals on $\mathbb{R}^n$ again.

Theorem 1.38 (The Beppo Levi Monotone Convergence Theorem)
Let A be a measurable subset of $\mathbb{R}^n$ and (f_i) a sequence of integrable functions on A with the property that $f_{i+1}(\mathbf{x}) \geq f_i(\mathbf{x})$ for almost all $\mathbf{x} \in A$. Suppose moreover that there exists a real number M such that

$$\int_A f_i(\mathbf{x})\, d\mathbf{x} \leq M$$

for all i. Then there is a function f such that $f_i(\mathbf{x}) \to f(\mathbf{x})$ for almost all $\mathbf{x}$, f is integrable and

$$\int_A f_i(\mathbf{x})\, d\mathbf{x} \to \int_A f(\mathbf{x})\, d\mathbf{x} \text{ as } i \to \infty.$$

Proof

We may assume without loss of generality that the f_i are non-negative: subtract f_1 from each function if not. If the f_i's are step functions, the theorem is simply the definition of the Lebesgue integral (compare Lemma 1.25 and Theorem 1.26). For general f_i, each f_i is itself a.e. the limit of a sequence of step functions, say $\psi_{i,m}$. The main step in the proof is to construct a sequence of step functions ψ_k that converges monotonically to f. We would like to choose ψ_k to be $\varphi_{i,m}$

for a suitable choice of m, but this will not necessarily make the sequence monotone. However if we set $\psi_k(\mathbf{x})=\max(\varphi_{i,m}(\mathbf{x}), 1\le i, m\le k)$ we obtain a monotone sequence. We have $\psi_k(\mathbf{x})=\varphi_{j,m}(\mathbf{x})$ for some $j\le k$ and $m\le k$, and hence $\psi_k(\mathbf{x})\le f_m(\mathbf{x})\le f_k(\mathbf{x})$. The integral of $\psi_k(\mathbf{x})$ is therefore bounded above by M and by Lemma 1.25, there is a function f such that $\psi_k(\mathbf{x})\to f(\mathbf{x})$ a.e.

Now $\varphi_{i,k}\le\psi_k$ for $i\le k$. Fix i and let $k\to\infty$. Since $\varphi_{i,k}(\mathbf{x})\to f_i(\mathbf{x})$ a.e., $f_i(\mathbf{x})\le f(\mathbf{x})$ a.e. Hence for any j, $\psi_j(\mathbf{x})\le f_j(\mathbf{x})\le f(\mathbf{x})$ a.e., and since $\psi_j(\mathbf{x})\to f(\mathbf{x})$ a.e., $f_j(\mathbf{x})\to f(\mathbf{x})$ a.e. Moreover we have also

$$\int_A \psi_j(\mathbf{x})\,\mathrm{d}\mathbf{x}\le\int_A f_j(\mathbf{x})\,\mathrm{d}\mathbf{x}\le\int_A f(\mathbf{x})\,\mathrm{d}\mathbf{x}$$

and the integral on the left tends to the integral on the right (by definition) as $k\to\infty$.

□

Clearly the theorem also holds for decreasing sequence of functions whose integrals are bounded below. The second theorem is similar, but has the major advantage of not requiring monotone convergence.

Theorem 1.39 (The Lebesgue Dominated Convergence Theorem)
Let A be a measurable subset of $\mathbb{R}^n$ and (f_i) a sequence of integrable functions on A with the property that $|f_i(\mathbf{x})|\le g(\mathbf{x})$ for almost all $\mathbf{x}\in A$ and for some integrable function g. Suppose moreover that there is a function f such that $f_i(\mathbf{x})\to f(\mathbf{x})$ for almost all $\mathbf{x}$. Then

$$\int_A f_i(\mathbf{x})\,\mathrm{d}\mathbf{x}\to\int_A f(\mathbf{x})\,\mathrm{d}\mathbf{x} \text{ as } i\to\infty.$$

Proof
If g_1 and g_2 are integrable, then $\min\{g_1, g_2\}=\frac{1}{2}(g_1+g_2)-\frac{1}{2}|g_1-g_2|$ is integrable as is $\max\{g_1,g_2\}=\frac{1}{2}(g_1+g_2)+\frac{1}{2}|g_1-g_2|$.

Hence $l_{ik}=\min\{f_i, f_{i+1}, \ldots, f_{i+k}\}$ is integrable, as is $u_{ik}=\max\{f_i, f_{i+1}, \ldots, f_{i+k}\}$. Letting $k\to\infty$, we obtain monotone sequences with integrals bounded by the integral of g, which therefore converge by Theorem 1.38 a.e. to integrable functions, say l_i and u_i respectively. Note that a.e. l_i is a monotone increasing sequence and u_i a monotone decreasing sequence with i. Now for any $\varepsilon>0$ and for almost any $\mathbf{x}$, there exists M such that for $m>M$, $|f_i(\mathbf{x})-f(\mathbf{x})|<\varepsilon$ and hence $|l_i(\mathbf{x})-f(\mathbf{x})|<\varepsilon$. So $l_i\to f$ a.e. Similarly $u_i\to f$ a.e. From Theorem 1.38, the integrals of l_i and u_i both converge to the integral of f.

Also $l_i \leq f_i \leq u_i$ from the construction of l_i and u_i, which shows that the integral of f_i converges to the integral of f.

□

1.8 Metric spaces

Questions concerning the convergence of a learning algorithm for a neural net, or finding the stable states of a system such as a Hopfield net, are central in the study of neural computation. In order to make these questions precise, we need to have a clear understanding of what convergence and stability mean.

We have already looked at these ideas for real numbers: you will have noticed that the modulus of a number (i.e. the size, or the distance between two numbers) played a fundamental role. To analyse the stability of neural nets we need to generalise this idea of modulus so that we can talk about convergence, or measure the distance between objects more general than numbers (e.g. input and output patterns). When discussing stability of dynamical systems in Chapter 5, we will need to talk about the distance between solutions of such systems.

In this section we will introduce the *metric space* which is in a sense rather weak in that it applies to more or less any abstract set in which the concept of distance makes any sense at all. In subsequent chapters we shall meet stronger ideas of distance which depend upon the structure of the set (for example a vector space). These ideas of distance are special cases of the one we introduce here, and constitute a rather less abstract idea of distance. So why bother with metric spaces then? The first reason is that some of the topological properties of sets, such as openness or closedness do not really depend on the algebraic structure of the sets, and are best discussed independently. Secondly, we can in this context prove a very important theorem about the existence of fixed points, and convergence of sequences of points. Again this does not depend on any algebraic structure of our spaces, only the topological structure.

To aid us in arriving at a definition of distance, let us abstract from the real numbers $\mathbb{R}$ the vital properties of the modulus. Let d: $\mathbb{R}\times\mathbb{R}\rightarrow\mathbb{R}$ be defined by $d(x, y)=|x-y|$. We call d a *distance function*, or *metric*, and observe that it satisfies the following properties.

Firstly $d(x, y) \geq 0$, and $d(x, y)=0$ if and only if $x=y$. In words, the distance between two real numbers is non-negative, and is zero if and only if they are the same number.

Secondly, the distance from x to y should be the same as the distance from y to x: $d(x, y)=d(y, x)$.

The third property is slightly less obvious. When using the modulus to talk about convergence, for example, we make frequent use of the inequality $|a+b| \leq |a|+|b|$ for all $a, b \in \mathbb{R}$. If we set $a=x-y$, $b=y-z$ for $x, y, z \in \mathbb{R}$, we get $|x-y|+|y-z| \geq |x-z|$. This gives us a third property of the distance function: the distance from x to z cannot be greater than the distance from x to y plus the distance from y to z. Thus $d(x, y)+d(y, z) \geq d(x, z)$. This property is called the *triangle inequality*: we shall see why shortly.

We formalise these three properties into the definition of a metric.

Definition 1.40

A *metric d* on a non-empty set A is a map $d\colon A \times A \to \mathbb{R}$ that satisfies the three properties

(a) $d(x, y) \geq 0$, and$d(x, y)=0$ if and only if $x=y$.
(b) $d(x, y)=d(y, x)$
(c) $d(x, y)+d(y, z) \geq d(x, z)$

The pair (A, d) is called a *metric space*.

□

There are many different kinds of metric spaces. In fact, most of the ones we shall meet in this book are so called *normed vector spaces* (see Chapter 3). However we give here some simple examples.

Examples 1.41

(a) Let A by any non-empty set, and define

$$d(x, y) = \begin{cases} 0 \text{ if } x=y \\ 1 \text{ if } x \neq y. \end{cases}$$

Then d satisfies Definition 1.40 (a), (b) and (c) and (A, d) is a metric space. This choice of d is called the *Discrete metric*. It measures only if x and y are distinct or not, and is of limited usefulness. However it does show that a metric can be put on any set A.

(b) More usefully, let $A=\mathbb{R}^2$. Our normal definition of distance in two dimensions is

$$d(\mathbf{x}, \mathbf{y}) = \sqrt{(x_1^2 - y_1^2) + (x_2^2 - y_2^2)},$$

where $\mathbf{x}=(x_1, x_2)$ and $\mathbf{y}=(y_1, y_2)$. Again d satisfies Definition 1.40 (a), (b) and (c). The third property expresses the fact that the sum of the lengths of any two sides of a triangle is not less than the length of the third side, hence the name 'triangle inequality'. In Chapter 3, we will generalise this idea of distance to n-dimensional spaces and later use it to measure the error in networks such as multilayer perceptrons.
(c) Let $A=C\,[0, 1]$, the set of all continuous real-valued functions on the real interval [0, 1].

$$d\,(f, g) = \max_{x \in [0,1]} |f\,(x) - g\,(x)|$$

is a metric on this set of functions. This example is very important. For example, suppose g is an approximation to f. Then $d(f, g)$ measures the maximum error of the approximation.

□

Having introduced the idea of a metric, we now work towards a statement and proof of the Contraction Mapping Theorem. Many of the learning algorithms used in neural sets employ an iteration scheme involving the weight vector. A central question is whether the weight vectors generated by this scheme converge. The Contraction Mapping Theorem can often help us to answer this question. First of all, let us make precise what we mean by convergence. (Compare Definition 1.5.)

Definition 1.42

We say that $u \in A$ is the *limit* of the sequence (u_n) of points in a metric space as n tends to infinity if, given any $\varepsilon > 0$, there exists N such that for $n>N$, $d(u, u_n)$ $<\varepsilon$. We also say in this case that (u_n) *tends* or *converges* to u, and write

$$\lim_{n \to \infty} u_n = u \text{ or } u_n \to u.$$

□

Before we can prove our theorem, we need to consider the idea of *completeness*. The key to this is the Cauchy sequence. (Compare Definition 1.8.)

Definition 1.43

A (u_n) in a metric space (A, d) is said to be *Cauchy* if, given $\varepsilon > 0$ there exists M such that for m and $n>M$, $d(u_m, u_n) <\varepsilon$.

□

It follows directly from the triangle inequality that every convergent sequence is Cauchy. However in general the converse is not true.

Definition 1.44

If every Cauchy sequence in a metric space (A, d) converges (to an element of A, of course), (A, d) is said to be *complete*.

□

This definition looks (and is) rather technical, but unfortunately is unavoidable. Complete metric spaces are nearly always required in applications. The advantage of such spaces is that convergence of a sequence can be established without a knowledge of what the limit actually is. An intuitive notion of completeness is that the space has no 'holes' to which a sequence might try to converge. For example, consider the sequence of rational numbers 1, 1.4, 1.41, 1.414, . . . which are heading towards $\sqrt{2}$. This sequence fails to converge in the rational numbers $\mathbb{Q}$, since $\sqrt{2}$ is not a rational number. On the other hand it does converge in the complete metric space $\mathbb{R}$ (Theorem 1.9). One of the reasons for introducing the Lesbesgue integral is that it leads to complete metric spaces of functions, whereas the Riemann integral does not. It is often rather difficult to prove that a space is compete. Proofs for many important spaces will be given in Chapter 3. We note here only that $\mathbb{R}^2$ is complete with the metric of Example 1.41(b). To see why this is, this note that if sequence is Cauchy, it is also Cauchy in each of its co-ordinates. Thus the individual co-ordinates converge, which implies convergence of the sequence. (If this is not convincing, a more formal proof may be found in Chapter 3.)

Closely related to (but not the same as!) completeness is the idea of a *closed* set.

Definition 1.45

Let (A, d) be a metric space, and let $S \subset A$.

(a) S is said to be *closed* if for every sequence $(u_n) \subset S$ such that $u_n \to u \in A$, it is true that $u \in S$. In words, S contains all its limit points.
(b) The *open neighbourhood* $N(a, \varepsilon)$ of a point $a \in A$ is the set of $b \in A$ such that $d(a, b) < \varepsilon$ for some $\varepsilon > 0$. (So $N(a, \varepsilon)$ is a small 'disc' around a.)
(c) S is said to be *open* if for every $a \in S$, there exists $\varepsilon > 0$ such that $N(a, \varepsilon) \subset S$. In other words, S is open if it contains a neighbourhood of each of its points.

(d) A *boundary point* of a subset S is a point $a \in A$ such that every $N(a, \varepsilon)$ contains a point of S and a point *not* in S.

□

For example, in $\mathbb{R}$,

the closed interval $[a, b] = \{x \in \mathbb{R} \mid a \leq x \leq b\}$ is closed;
the open interval $(a, b) = \{x \in \mathbb{R} \mid a < x < b\}$
the interval $(a, b] = \{x \in \mathbb{R} \mid a < x \leq b\}$ is neither open nor closed;

In any metric space (A, d), A itself is both closed and open, as is the empty set $\varnothing$. For the case of $\mathbb{R}$, $\mathbb{R}$ and $\varnothing$ are in fact the only sets that are both open and closed. In any metric space a set S is open if and only if its set theoretic complement in A (i.e. the set of $a \in A$ with $a \notin S$) is closed. (As an exercise, you might like to try and prove this. It is not hard once you really understand all the definitions!)

Boundary points of S may or may not be in S. Each of the three intervals above have the boundary points a and b. A set is closed if and only if it contains all its boundary points: this is an immediate consequence of the definition of limit. The *closure* of S is the union of S and its boundary points. Obviously it is the smallest closed set containing S. In $\mathbb{R}$, every point is a boundary point of $\mathbb{Q}$, and thus the closure of $\mathbb{Q}$ is $\mathbb{R}$ itself.

In an incomplete space, it may not be immediately obvious if a set is closed. For example it is very difficult to see if a set in $\mathbb{Q}$ is closed since we cannot easily identify the limit points of subsets. By contrast in complete spaces, any sequence that seems to be converging really does have a limit, so it is much easier to check that S is closed. Roughly speaking in a complete metric space, a set will be closed if it is defined by '≤' conditions or '=' only, and will be open if it is defined by strict inequalities. For example, the unit closed disc

$$D = \{\mathbf{x} \in \mathbb{R}^2 \mid d(\mathbf{x}, \mathbf{0}) \leq 1\} \text{ is closed},$$

as is the unit circle

$$C = \{\mathbf{x} \in \mathbb{R}^2 \mid d(\mathbf{x}, \mathbf{0}) = 1\}.$$

(Here $\mathbf{0} = (0, 0)$ is the origin in $\mathbb{R}^2$.) On the other hand the open disc $N(\mathbf{0}, 1)$ is open because of the '<' in Definition 1.45(b). The set of all open subsets of a metric space is called the *topology* of the space. (Actually, it is possible to define a topology without reference to a metric, but we will not need to do so in this book.) The reader may come across references to the 'topological properties' of a space. This is not a precisely defined concept: it is a general term for the properties of openness, closedness, completeness and similar issues.

Now if (A, d) is a metric space and $S \subset A$, then (S, d) is a metric space: obviously d will do just as well as a metric on S. But unfortunately completeness may not be inherited. For example consider the open interval with the usual modulus metric of $\mathbb{R}$. The sequence $(1/n) \subset (0, 1)$ is Cauchy: it converges to 0. But $0 \notin (0, 1)$. However, if S is a closed set, completeness will be inherited.

Theorem 1.46

Let (A, d) be a complete metric space, and let $S \subset A$ be closed. Then (S, d) is a complete metric space.

Proof

The example of the preceding paragraph illustrates the idea. A Cauchy sequence in S is *a fortiori* a Cauchy sequence in A and thus has a limit a, say, in A. But if S is closed it contains, by definition, all its limit points, so $a \in S$, which establishes the result.

□

Up to now we have only introduced very general properties of limits. We need some tools to help us to establish convergence of particular sequences. In particular we need to know about mappings between metric spaces. One useful property is continuity (compare Definition 1.1).

Definition 1.47

Let (A, d_A) and (B, d_B) be metric spaces. Suppose $f: A \to B$. The function f is said to be *continuous* at $x \in A$, if, given any $\varepsilon > 0$, there exists a positive real number δ such that for every $y \in A$ with $d_A(x, y) < \delta$, $d_B[f(y), f(x)] < \varepsilon$.

If f is continuous at every point x of A, f is said to be *continuous on A*.

□

The analogue of Theorem 1.2 holds in this context: we will not bother with a formal statement and proof. However we should particularly note the following (compare Theorem 1.6(d)).

Theorem 1.48

Let (A, d_A) and (B, d_B) be metric spaces. Suppose $f: A \to B$ is continuous. Suppose further that the sequence $(u_n) \subset A$ converges, say $u_n \to u$. (By definition, $u \in A$.) Then the sequence $f(u_n) \to f(u)$ (in the metric of B).

Proof

The proof is a straightforward extension of that of Theorem 1.6(d).

□

We now introduce the idea of a contraction map. This is a deceptively simple and surprisingly powerful condition that enables one to show that an iteration scheme based on that map will give rise to a Cauchy sequence. In Chapter 5, we will employ this apparently trivial idea to prove some very general theorems about the properties of systems of differential equations.

Definition 1.49

Let (A, d) be a metric space. Suppose f: $A \to A$. Then f is said to be a *Lipschitz* if

$$d[f(x), f(y)] \leq \alpha\, d(x, y) \tag{1.10}$$

for some positive real number α. If, in addition, (1.10) holds with $\alpha < 1$, then f is said to be a *contraction with parameter* α, or is described as *contractive*.

□

Note that any Lipschitz function is continuous: simply set $\delta = \varepsilon/\alpha$ in Definition 1.47. Now for the *piece de la resistance*. A very common problem in mathematics is to solve an equation of the form

$$x = f(x). \tag{1.11}$$

Definition 1.50

An x satisfying (1.11) is called a *fixed point* of f.

□

On other occasions we wish to know about the convergence of an *iteration*, which is a sequence generated by a mapping, for example of the form

$$x_{n+1} = f(x_n). \tag{1.12}$$

If we can show that f is contractive, we can solve both these problems at a stroke.

Theorem 1.51 (The Contraction Mapping Theorem)

Let (A, d) be a complete metric space and f: $A \to A$ be a contraction with parameter α. Then

(a) f has precisely one fixed point x and

(b) from any $x_0 \in A$, the iteration (1.12) will generate a sequence (x_n) with $x_n \to x$.

(c) Moreover

$$d(x_n, x) \leq \frac{\alpha^n}{1-\alpha} d(x_1, x_0).$$

Proof

We show that the sequence (x_n) is Cauchy. In fact

$$\begin{aligned} d(x_n, x_m) &= d[f(x_{n-1}), f(x_{m-1})] \\ &\leq \alpha d(x_{n-1}, x_{m-1}) \\ &= \alpha d[f(x_{n-2}), f(x_{m-2})] \\ &\leq \alpha^2 d(x_{n-2}, x_{m-2}), \text{ ect.} \end{aligned}$$

Assuming without loss of generality $m>n$, we arrive eventually at

$$d(x_n, x_m) \leq \alpha^n d(x_0, x_{m-n}) \tag{1.12}$$

$$\leq \alpha^n \{d(x_0, x_1) + d(x_1, x_2) + \ldots + d(x_{m-n-1}, x_{m-n})\} \tag{1.13}$$

by repeated application of the triangle inequality. But

$$d(x_{k-1}, x_k) \leq \alpha^{k-1} d(x_0, x_1)$$

using (1.12) with $n=k-1$ and $m=k$. Hence (1.13) together with (1.9) yields

$$\begin{aligned} d(x_n, x_m) &\leq \alpha^n d(x_0, x_1)\{1+\alpha+\alpha^2+\ldots\alpha^{m-n-1}\} \\ &\leq \alpha^n d(x_0, x_1)\{1+\alpha+\alpha^2+\ldots\} \text{ (continuing the sum to infinity)} \\ &\leq d(x_0, x_1)[\alpha^n/(1-\alpha)]. \end{aligned}$$

We can make the right-hand side as small as we like by choosing n sufficiently large, so the sequence (x_n) is indeed Cauchy. Thus $x_n \to x$ for some $x \in A$. Moreover $d(x_n, y)$ is a continuous function of y (the triangle inequality shows this), so by Theorem 1.48,

$$d(x_n, x) \leq d(x_0, x_1)[\alpha^n/(1-\alpha)].$$

It remains to show that x is a fixed point of f. Again using Theorem 1.46, we conclude that the sequence $f(x_n)$ also converges, and indeed $f(x_n) \to f(x)$. But $f(x_n) = x_{n+1}$, so we also have $f(x_n) \to x$. Thus $f(x) = x$, i.e. x is a fixed point of f.

□

The bound of part (c) is really quite remarkable. It enables us to compute a rigorous estimate of where the fixed point is, given only a knowledge of the contraction parameter and the distance between the first two estimates.

(Very Important) Remark 1.52

We have stated the Contraction Mapping Theorem for the case of a mapping f of the whole metric space (A, d) into itself. In many applications to non-linear systems, the mapping f might well be a contraction only locally. This is where Theorem 1.46 comes in. If $S \subset A$ is closed, and $f(S) \subset S$ (i.e. each element of S is mapped to an element of S), and f is contractive on S, then f has a unique fixed point in S. It can be found by iteration from any $x_0 \in S$, and the bound of Theorem 1.51(c) applies.

□

We will make considerable use of this theorem in the ensuing chapters. The simple example which follows gives a taster of these applications.

Example 1.53

Let A be $\mathbb{R}^2$ with the usual metric. Defined f: $\mathbb{R}^2 \to \mathbb{R}^2$ by $\mathbf{u} = f(\mathbf{x})$ where

$$u_1 = ax_1 + bx_2 + c$$
$$u_2 = px_1 + qx_2 + r,$$

$a, b, c, p, q, r \in \mathbb{R}$. (The delta rule used in neural networks is a mapping of this type.) Then if $\mathbf{y} \in \mathbb{R}^2$, and $\mathbf{v} = f(\mathbf{y})$ we have

$$\begin{aligned} d^2[f(\mathbf{x}), f(\mathbf{y})] &= d^2(\mathbf{u}, \mathbf{v}) \\ &= \{a(x_1 - y_1) + b(x_2 - y_2)\}^2 + \{p(x_1 - y_1) + q(x_2 - y_2)\}^2. \end{aligned}$$

But

$$\begin{aligned} &(a^2 + b^2)\{(x_1 - y_1)^2 + (x_2 - y_2)^2\} \\ &\quad = a^2(x_1 - y_1)^2 + b^2(x_2 - y_2)^2 + b^2(x_1 - y_1)^2 + a^2(x_2 - y_2)^2 \\ &\quad = a^2(x_1 - y_1)^2 + b^2(x_2 - y_2)^2 + 2ab(x_1 - y_1)(x_2 - y_2) \\ &\qquad - 2ab(x_1 - y_1)(x_2 - y_2) + b^2(x_1 - y_1)^2 + a^2(x_2 - y_2)^2 \\ &\quad = \{a(x_1 - y_1) + b(x_2 - y_2)\}^2 + \{b(x_1 - y_1) - a(x_2 - y_2)\}^2 \\ &\quad \geq \{a(x_1 - y_1) + b(x_2 - y_2)\}^2. \end{aligned}$$

Hence

$$d^2[f(\mathbf{x}), f(\mathbf{y})) \leq (a^2 + b^2 + p^2 + q^2)\{(x_1 - y_1)^2 + (x_2 - y_2)^2\}$$

so

$$d[f(\mathbf{x}), f(\mathbf{y})] \leq (a^2 + b^2 + p^2 + q^2)d(\mathbf{x}, \mathbf{y}).$$

Thus f is Lipschitz, and is contractive if $\alpha = (a^2 + b^2 + p^2 + q^2) < 1$. If this is the case, then the iteration $\mathbf{x}_{k+1} = f(\mathbf{x}_k)$ (starting from any $\mathbf{x}_0$) will converge to a fixed point of f, i.e. a solution of the equations

$$\begin{aligned} x_1 &= ax_1 + bx_2 + c \\ x_2 &= px_1 + qx_2 + r, \end{aligned}$$

or

$$\begin{aligned} c &= (a - 1)x_1 + bx_2 \\ r &= px_1 + (q - 1)x_2. \end{aligned}$$

You might like to verify this by putting in actual numbers for a, b, c, p, q, r and performing the iteration.

□

Fortunately, in our later applications, we will be able to develop more sophisticated tools for proving contraction, rather than the 'brute force' approach of this example.

1.9 The order notation

One item of notation that we shall make use of is the so-called *order notation*. At first sight this notation looks a little vague, but in fact it can be made perfectly precise. Consider two sequence real (x_n) and (y_n) as $n \to \infty$. We say that $x_n = O(y_n)$ (read 'big order y_n') if

$$\lim_{n \to \infty} \frac{x_n}{y_n} = K$$

where K is a non-zero real number. If this expression holds, but with $K = 0$, we say that $x_n = o(y_n)$ (read 'small order y_n'). The point of this is that normally y_n is a simpler sequence than x_n. For example we might say that the sequence $(3n^3 + 4n)/n^2)$ is $O(n)$ or $o(n^2)$ as $n \to \infty$.

A similar notation is used for limits of functions at zero. For example we may write $\sin x = O(x)$ as $x \to 0$.

1.10 Concluding remarks

In this chapter, we have reviewed the fundamental ideas of sets, limits and the calculus. However, with the exception of the integral and the idea of a metric space, we have largely restricted ourselves to the study of functions of a single variable. Obviously this is insufficient to describe neural computing systems which by definition involve many processing units working in parallel together. Thus, in the next chapter we will investigate the properties of functions of several variables.

2 Linear algebra

2.1 Linear systems

In Chapter 1 we met some of the fundamental mathematical ideas required in order to model neural systems. In describing the input to the McCulloch–Pitts neuron (see Section 1.3), we encountered $\mathbb{R}^n$, the set of n-dimensional vectors. Indeed the construction of the integral was also described for this set. Since neural systems are essentially parallel in nature, it is clear that any mathematical formalism used to describe them must be defined in terms of the properties of this set, and the structures that can be imposed on it.

Throughout much of this chapter, we shall use illustrations based on the simplest types of neural networks, *perceptrons* and *linear associative memories*. As we shall see shortly, there are severe restrictions on what can be achieved with these simple models. However, the language and mathematical machinery that we shall develop in our descriptions of the relatively simple straightforward linear models is also essential in discussing non-linear and recursive ones. Moreover, it is possible to gain some understanding of aspects of the generic behaviour of neural systems by a detailed analysis of linear ones, whereas the corresponding analysis of non-linear systems may be much more difficult. (However, it should be emphasised at this point that there are some types of dynamical behaviour which are specific to non-linear systems.) Our development of linear algebra will be motivated by the simple perceptron, but of course the subject is much older than this! There are many good introductory books on matrix theory, which may be used for further reading. For example, Gerber (1990) approaches the subject from the viewpoint of linear equations. Finkbeiner

(1966) takes a more formal approach, but is still clearly explained. If these books are not available, the mathematics section of any general academic library will provide a host of alternatives!

2.2 Column vectors, matrices and perceptrons

Figure 2.1 shows a simple single layer perceptron. It is made up of McCulloch–Pitts type neurons as shown in Fig. 1.1 and described in Section 1.3. Neurons are shown as small circles, and the synapses connecting them as lines. The lower layer neurons are the *input units* and the upper layer are the *output units*. Since we are dealing with an abstract mathematical system here, rather than a biological model, we will in fact avoid the physiological implications of the term *neuron* and refer merely to *units*. Similarly, we will describe the synaptic connections as merely *connections*, or *edges*. Let us suppose that we have n input units and m output units (in Fig. 2.1, $n=4$ and $m=3$). The input units simply distribute their input values along their output edges. Associated with each such edge is a *synaptic weight*: the weight attached to the edge joining input unit j to output unit i will be called w_{ij}. Weights w_{11} and w_{43} are shown on Fig. 2.1. Thus, suppose the input to input unit j is denoted by x_j. Then the total input to the ith output unit is given by

$$\sum_{j=1}^{n} w_{ij}x_j.$$

According to the use to which the perceptron is to be put, the output unit may simply output this value or it may apply a thresholding operation to it. For the moment, we assume that the value is simply output as y_i. Thus

$$y_i = \sum_{j=1}^{n} w_{ij}x_j. \tag{2.1}$$

The input to the system consists of the n input values $x_1, x_2, \ldots, x_n$. Thus the input can be though of as an element of $\mathbb{R}^n$. With the usual notation for $\mathbb{R}^n$, we might expect to write this element as $(x_1, x_2, \ldots, x_n)$. This is known as a *row vector*, since it is written as a row. However we wish to use the theory of matrices and it is conventional to represent the vector as a *column vector*, i.e.

$$x = \begin{pmatrix} x_1 \\ x_2 \\ \cdot \\ \cdot \\ \cdot \\ x_n \end{pmatrix}.$$

Here $x_1, x_2, \ldots, x_n$ are called the *entries* or *elements* of the vector. Similarly we may represent the output values $y_1, y_2, \ldots, y_m$ as a column vector in $\mathbb{R}^m$,

$$y = \begin{pmatrix} y_1 \\ y_2 \\ \cdot \\ \cdot \\ \cdot \\ y_m \end{pmatrix}$$

The weights w_{ij} form an $m \times n$ array of numbers, which we call a *matrix*. More formally,

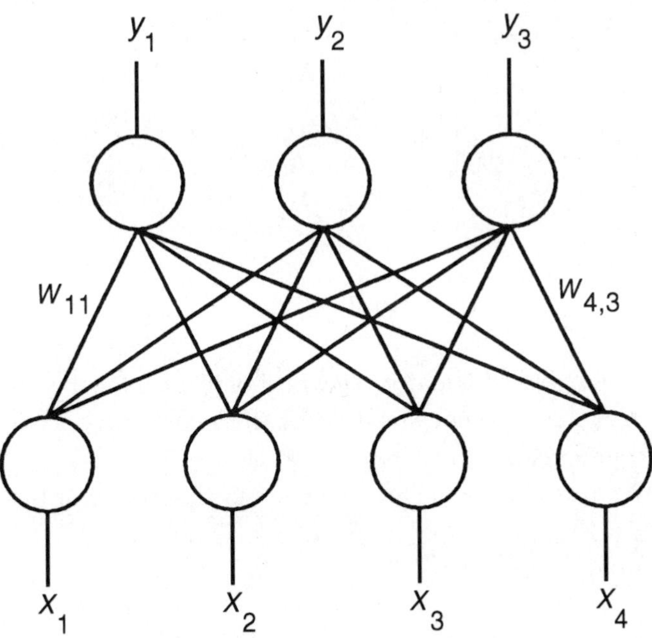

Fig 2.1

Definition 2.1

An $m \times n$ (read 'm by n') *real matrix* W is a rectangular array of real numbers with m rows and n columns. The number in the ith row and jth column is called the *ijth element* (or *entry*) and is denoted by either $(W)_{ij}$ or w_{ij} as convenient.

□

For example, in the case of Fig. 2.1, we can represent the weights by the 3×4 matrix

$$W = \begin{pmatrix} w_{11} & w_{12} & w_{13} & w_{14} \\ w_{21} & w_{22} & w_{23} & w_{24} \\ w_{31} & w_{32} & w_{33} & w_{34} \end{pmatrix}.$$

It is of course important to remember which subscript refers to the row and which to the column: the rule is always **row number first**.

Now (2.1), applied for $i=1, 2, \ldots, m$, defines a transformation t: $\mathbb{R}^n \to \mathbb{R}^m$ which we denote by $\mathbf{y}=t(\mathbf{x})$. This transformation is completely determined by the weight matrix W, and we call $\mathbf{y}$ the *matrix product* of W with $\mathbf{x}$. We write

$$y = t(\mathbf{x}) = W\mathbf{x}.$$

To avoid too many numbers, we illustrate this with a numerical example smaller than Fig. 2.1. Specifically, take $m=2$ and $n=3$. With

$$W = \begin{pmatrix} 3 & 1 & 2 \\ 4 & 0 & -5 \end{pmatrix} \text{ and } \mathbf{x} = \begin{pmatrix} 1 \\ 1 \\ 2 \end{pmatrix}$$

we have

$$\begin{pmatrix} 3 & 1 & 2 \\ 4 & 0 & -5 \end{pmatrix} \begin{pmatrix} 1 \\ 1 \\ 2 \end{pmatrix} = \begin{pmatrix} 3\times1 + 1\times1 + 2\times2 \\ 4\times1 + 0\times1 - 5\times2 \end{pmatrix}$$

Readers unfamiliar with matrix algebra should compare this example carefully with (2.1), as an understanding of the matrix product is crucial in modelling neural systems.

Formally, we can define the product of a matrix and vector by

$$(W\mathbf{x})_i = \sum_k w_{ik} x_k.$$

To get the ith element of the product, we multiply the entries in the ith row of W by the corresponding entries in x, and then add up these quantities. An important special matrix is the *identity* (or *unit*) matrix I. This matrix always has $m=n$, i.e. the same number of rows as columns. With $m=n=3$ it is

$$I=\begin{pmatrix}1&0&0\\0&1&0\\0&0&1\end{pmatrix}.$$

More generally, the identity matrix I has $(I)_{jj}=1$ for $j=1, \ldots, m$ and all other elements are 0. This matrix has the property that for any vector $\mathbf{x}$, $I\mathbf{x}=\mathbf{x}$. Any matrix W with $m=n$ is said to be *square*. The entries w_{jj} for $j=1, \ldots, m$ constitute the *main* or *leading diagonal*. Thus I is a square matrix with main diagonal elements 1 and all other elements 0.

Of course, the language of vectors and matrices was not created to model neural computing systems! Originally, it was invented to describe the geometry of two- and three-dimensional space, and other quantities such as velocities and forces which have both magnitude and direction. This link with geometry can help us to visualise the behaviour of neural systems, at least in simple cases, so at this point we will digress a little and explore the geometry of $\mathbb{R}^2$ and $\mathbb{R}^3$. We assume that the reader is familiar with the description of points in two- or three-dimensional space as cartesian co-ordinates (x, y) and (x, y, z) respectively. Since we shall later need to work in more than three dimensions, we will in fact use co-ordinates (x_1, x_2) in two dimensions, and (x_1, x_2, x_3) in three dimensions. It is tempting to identify the column vector

$$\begin{pmatrix}x_1\\x_2\end{pmatrix}$$

with the point (x_1, x_2), but in fact it is better to think of the column vector as representing the **line segment** from the origin $O=(0, 0)$ to the point. This line segment has, of course, both a length and direction, and it is called the *position vector* of the point (see Fig. 2.2a). We add two column vectors by adding their corresponding elements, i.e. if

$$\mathbf{x}=\begin{pmatrix}x_1\\x_2\end{pmatrix} \text{and } \mathbf{y}=\begin{pmatrix}y_1\\y_2\end{pmatrix} \text{then } \mathbf{x}+\mathbf{y}=\begin{pmatrix}x_1+y_1\\x_2+y_2\end{pmatrix}.$$

Geometrically, this corresponds to the *parallelogram law of addition* (Fig. 2.2b). Readers familiar with mechanics will recognise this as the basic law for adding forces, velocities, etc. If we think of the column vectors as just representing a line segment of a given length and direction, not necessarily starting from the origin, then this law can be replaced by the *triangle law of addition* (Fig. 2.2c).

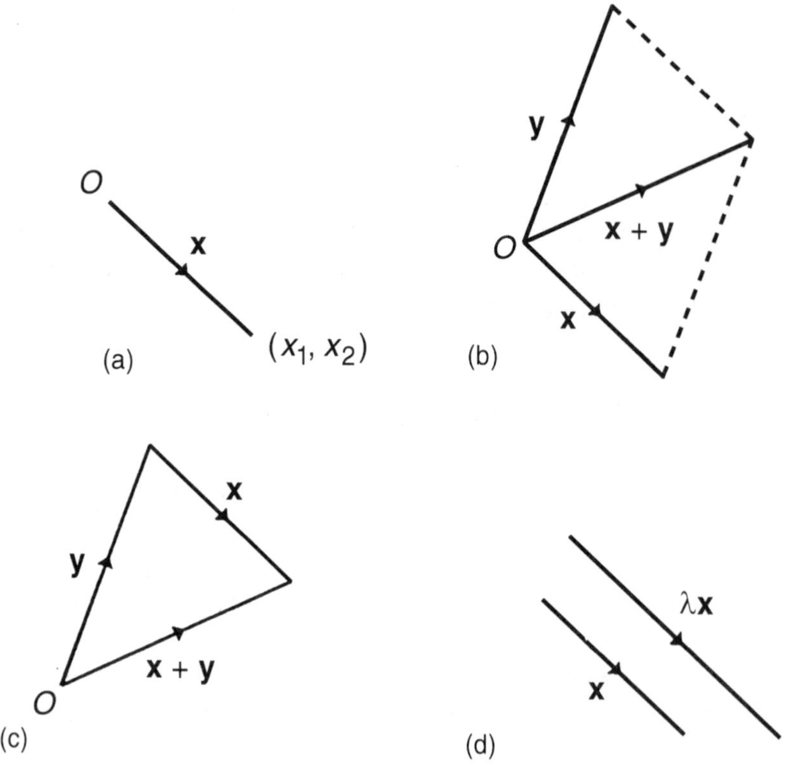

Fig. 2.2

Finally, we note that we can also multiply vectors by a real number λ (usually called a *scalar* in this context, to distinguish it from vector quantities.)

$$\lambda\mathbf{x} = \begin{pmatrix} \lambda x_1 \\ \lambda x_2 \end{pmatrix}.$$

This corresponds to multiplying the length of **x** by the factor λ without changing its direction if λ is positive (Fig. 2.2d), or reversing the direction if λ is negative.

Now let us see how this geometric representation of vectors can help us to understand the behaviour and limitations of the perceptron used as a pattern classifier. Consider the four vectors

$$\begin{pmatrix} 0 \\ 0 \end{pmatrix}, \begin{pmatrix} 0 \\ 1 \end{pmatrix}, \begin{pmatrix} 1 \\ 0 \end{pmatrix}, \begin{pmatrix} 1 \\ 1 \end{pmatrix} \text{in } \mathbb{R}^2.$$

Obviously these are the position vectors of four points distributed at the corners of a square (Fig. 2.3). Now suppose that we wish to separate these into two classes, according to whether the logical OR of the x_1 and x_2 values is 1 or 0, i.e. x_1 OR $x_2=1$ if either x_1, x_2 or both is 1. Thus we wish to divide the vectors into two classes, namely

$$\left\{\begin{pmatrix}0\\0\end{pmatrix}\right\} \text{ and } \left\{\begin{pmatrix}0\\1\end{pmatrix},\begin{pmatrix}1\\0\end{pmatrix},\begin{pmatrix}1\\1\end{pmatrix}\right\}$$

We will use a perceptron similar to Fig. 2.1, but with only two input units and a single output y. The weight matrix W is thus 1×2 and for each pattern vector $\mathbf{x}$ we have

$$y = w_1x_1 + w_2x_2, \tag{2.2}$$

where we have deleted the row subscript on the w's as there is only one row: in fact we can regard W as a row vector in this case. Clearly the output y will in general be neither 0 nor 1: this is why thresholding is required. We decide to interpret the output as '1' if $y > 0.5$, and '0' if $y < 0.5$. (At this point the reader may wonder whether this construct is not rather artificial. However, there is evidence to suggest that biological neurons may well incorporate some form of thresholding, and in electronic networks similar results can be achieved by circuits such as the Schmidt trigger.) **The effect of the perceptron is thus to separate the plane $\mathbb{R}^2$ into two sets**, according to $y>0.5$ or $y<0.5$. The boundary between these two sets is defined by the condition

$$w_1x_1 + w_2x_2 = 0.5. \tag{2.3}$$

This is of course the equation of a straight line in the (x_1, x_2) plane. Our aim is to choose w_1 and w_2 so that all elements of the first class of input vectors lie on one side, and all elements of the second class lie on the other. Obviously there are many possible choices for w_1 and w_2: one is to choose the line through the points (0, 0.5) and (0.5, 0) as in Fig. 2.3. This gives $w_1=w_2=1$.

Now consider a different classification problem: suppose we wish to separate the input vectors according to the 'exclusive or' XOR. x_1XOR$x_2=1$ if $x_1 \neq x_2$. The required classes are therefore

$$\left\{\begin{pmatrix}0\\0\end{pmatrix},\begin{pmatrix}1\\1\end{pmatrix}\right\} \text{ and } \left\{\begin{pmatrix}0\\1\end{pmatrix},\begin{pmatrix}1\\0\end{pmatrix}\right\}.$$

An inspection of the position of these points on Fig. 2.3 will reveal there is no straight line which will divide the plane in such a way that all the elements

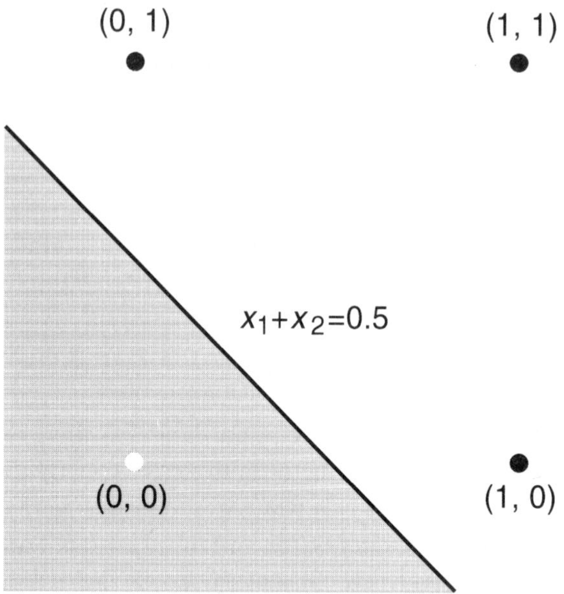

Fig. 2.3

of one class lie on one side of the line and all the elements of the other class lie on the other side. It was the observation by Minsky and Pappert (1969) that many simple classification problems were not linearly separable that delayed the development of neural systems for many years, until it was discovered that these problems could be overcome by the use of non-linear systems.

Classes of points which can be separated by a simple thresholded perceptron are said to be *linearly separable*. Of course, these ideas can easily be extended to higher dimensions. If the input vectors are in $\mathbb{R}^3$, the separating surfaces are planes. In $\mathbb{R}^n$, they are 'n-dimensional planes' called *hyperplanes*.

Returning to two dimensions, it is worth noting at this point that there is an alternative geometric representation that we could use: one, indeed, which may seem more natural in a machine learning context. In equation (2.1), the values x_1 and x_2 are specified in the input vectors. The 'variables' that we are trying to find are the weights w_1 and w_2. These we may think of as forming a 1×2 matrix, or row vector, (w_1, w_2). It would seem sensible, then, to display the possible choices of weights on a plane, which we might call the **w**-*plane*.

Any learning algorithm for choosing the weights will 'live' in this plane, which is called the *dual space* of the original **x**-plane shown in Fig. 2.3. Figure 2.4 shows the representation of our separation problem in the w-plane. Classifying according to the OR relation, we see that for each input vector **x** we have a condition to satisfy. Specifically, we require w_1 and w_2 to satisfy the conditions $0<0.5$ for the first class and

$$\begin{aligned} w_2 &> 0.5 \\ w_1 \quad &> 0.5 \\ w_1 + w_2 &> 0.5 \end{aligned}$$

for the second class. For this problem, the first condition is vacuous since it is satisfied for any choice of w_1 and w_2. Each of the other three conditions excludes a half plane, shown shaded in Fig. 2.4. The unshaded region, known as the *feasible region*, is therefore the set of acceptable weights. Our previous choice, $w_1 = w_2 = 1$, is illustrated. For the XOR problem, the fourth condition is replaced by

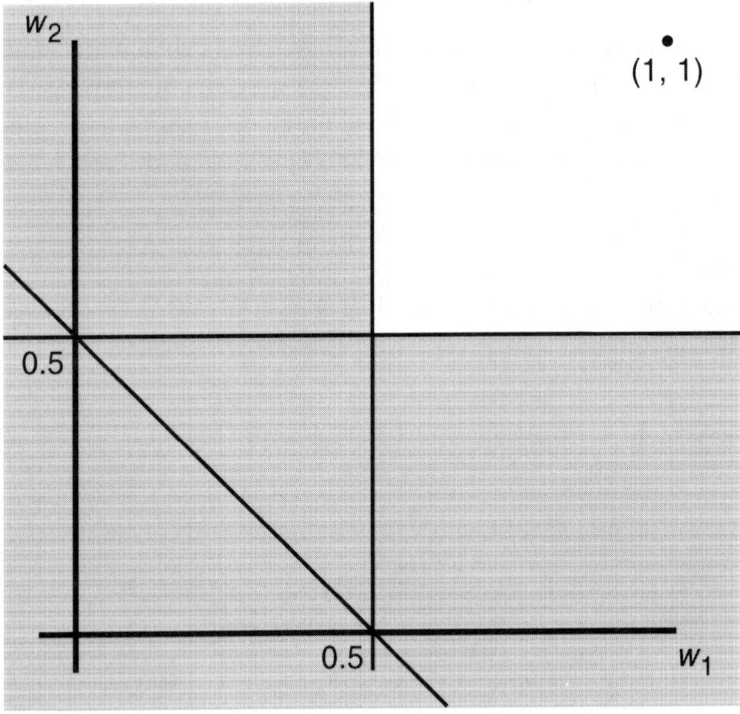

Fig. 2.4

$w_1 + w_2 < 0.5.$

The shading must be moved to the other side of the sloping line in Fig. 2.4. There will then be no region unshaded, and the problem is *infeasible*, as we decided previously.

The dual representation can in fact be extended a little further. Instead of arbitrarily fixing the threshold at 0.5, we could allow it to be a third variable. This variable, say c, could appear as a third axis in our representation: i.e. we would then be working with triples (w_1, w_2, c) which we would display in $\mathbb{R}^3$, with the conditions appearing as bounding planes. Figure 2.4 is simply a slice through this three-dimensional picture corresponding to $c=0.5$.

As we shall see later in this book, the problems of machine learning and optimisation are closely related. It is a characteristic of problems in these fields that they permit a dual representation of this type.

2.3 Linear transformations

In spite of the restrictions inherent in linear systems, a good understanding of them is a vital foundation for studying their non-linear counterparts. The first essential is a precise definition of the concept of linearity itself, since our geometrical intuition is going to be unreliable in systems with more than three variables.

Definition 2.2

Let $\mathbf{w}$ and $\mathbf{x}$ be vectors in $\mathbb{R}^n$. Regarding $\mathbf{w}$ as $1 \times n$ matrix or row vector as above, the quantity

$$\mathbf{w} . \mathbf{x} = \sum_{i=1}^{n} w_i x_i$$

is called the *inner product* of $\mathbf{w}$ and $\mathbf{x}$. This quantity is, of course, a real number (i.e. a scalar).

□

Closely related to the inner product is the concept of length.

Definition 2.3

Let $\mathbf{x}$ be a vector in $\mathbb{R}^n$. The *length* or *norm* of $\mathbf{x}$, denoted $\|\mathbf{x}\|_2$ is given by

$$\|\mathbf{x}\|_2 = \sqrt{(\mathbf{x}.\mathbf{x})} = \sqrt{x_1^2 + x_2^2 + \ldots + x_n^2}.$$

(Application of Pythagorous' Theorem will show that this is the usual concept of length in two- or three-dimensional space. The subscript 2 is for consistency with a more general concept of length to be introduced in later chapters.)

□

Remarks 2.4

(a) You will observe that we have already made considerable use of the inner product in an informal way. Compare for instance equations (2.2) and (2.3).

(b) The definition of the product of a matrix and vector given towards the beginning of the previous section can be re-interpreted in terms of inner products. Comparing equation (2.1), Definition 2.1, and the remarks following this definition, we see that *i*th element of the vector $W\mathbf{x}$, where W is a matrix, is formed by taking the inner product of the ith row of W with $\mathbf{x}$.

(c) The following three properties of the inner product follow easily from Definition 2.2:

(i) $\mathbf{w}.\mathbf{x}=\mathbf{x}.\mathbf{w}$

(ii) $\mathbf{w}.(\mathbf{x}+\mathbf{y})=\mathbf{w}.\mathbf{x}+\mathbf{w}.\mathbf{y}$

(iii) $(\lambda\mathbf{w}).\mathbf{x}=\lambda(\mathbf{w}.\mathbf{x})$ for any real number λ.

(d) We note also these properties of the norm:

(i) $\|\lambda\mathbf{x}\|_2=|\lambda|\,\|\mathbf{x}\|_2$.

(ii) $\|\mathbf{x}+\mathbf{y}\|_2 \le \|\mathbf{x}\|_2 + \|\mathbf{y}\|_2$ (the *triangle inequality*).

The first of these is a simple consequence of Definition 2.3. In $\mathbb{R}^2$ or $\mathbb{R}^3$ the second is geometrically obvious: see Fig. 2.2(c). However it is surprisingly difficult to give a formal proof for $\mathbb{R}^n$, so we will defer this until the more systematic exposition of vector norms in the next chapter. If we define $d(\mathbf{x}, \mathbf{y}) = \|\mathbf{x}-\mathbf{y}\|_2$. the norm makes $\mathbb{R}^2$ into the metric space described in Section 1.9.

In $\mathbb{R}^2$ or $\mathbb{R}^3$ the inner product also has a nice geometrical interpretation which can help to give further insight.

Theorem 2.5

$\mathbf{w}.\mathbf{x}=\|\mathbf{w}\|_2\,\|\mathbf{x}\|_2 \cos\theta$, where θ is the angle between $\mathbf{w}$ and $\mathbf{x}$.

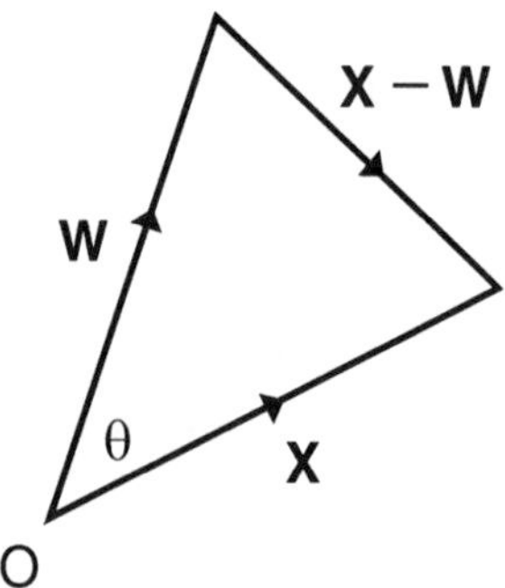

Fig. 2.5

Proof

See Fig. 2.5. From the cosine rule we find

$$2\,\|\mathbf{w}\|_2\,\|\mathbf{x}\|_2 \cos\theta = \|\mathbf{w}\|_2^2 + \|\mathbf{x}\|_2^2 - \|\mathbf{x}-\mathbf{w}\|_2^2$$

$$= 2\mathbf{w}.\mathbf{x}$$

as may be easily verified from Definition 2.4.

□

Theorem 2.5 can in fact be used as a definition of angle in $\mathbb{R}^n$ when $n>3$. Of particular importance is the general concept of vectors being at right angles to each other. So fundamental is this idea to linear algebra that it is given a special name, as expressed in the following definition. Note that in two- or three-dimensional space, the definition simply means that the angle between the two vectors is 90°.

Definition 2.6

Let $\mathbf{w}$ and $\mathbf{x}$ be vectors in $\mathbb{R}^n$. If $\mathbf{w}.\mathbf{x}=0$, then $\mathbf{w}$ and $\mathbf{x}$ are said to be *orthogonal*.

□

Now, working from this basic geometry, we can give a formal definition of linearity. Recall that if $\mathbf{u}$ and $\mathbf{v}$ are column vectors in $\mathbb{R}^n$, then they may be added by adding their corresponding elements, and that for any $\lambda \in \mathbb{R}$ the vector $\lambda\,\mathbf{v}$ is formed by multiplying each element of $\mathbf{v}$ by λ. From Remark 2.4(c), we have

$$\mathbf{w}.(\mathbf{u}+\mathbf{v}) = \mathbf{w}.\mathbf{u} + \mathbf{w}.\mathbf{v} \text{ and } \mathbf{w}.(\lambda\mathbf{u}) = \lambda(\mathbf{w}.\mathbf{v})$$

for any n-vectors $\mathbf{w}$, $\mathbf{u}$, $\mathbf{v}$.

Since here $\mathbf{w}$ could represent any of the rows of an $m \times n$ matrix W, it follows from Remark 2.4(b) that

$$W(\mathbf{u}+\mathbf{v}) = W\mathbf{u} + W\mathbf{v} \text{ and } W(\lambda\mathbf{u}) = \lambda W\mathbf{u}, \tag{2.4}$$

or in terms of the transformation $f\colon \mathbb{R}^n \to \mathbb{R}^m$ defined by

$$f(\mathbf{u}) = W\mathbf{u},$$

we have

$$f(\mathbf{u}+\mathbf{v}) = f\mathbf{u} + f\mathbf{v} \text{ and } f(\lambda\mathbf{u}) = \lambda f(\mathbf{u}). \tag{2.5}$$

Definition 2.7

A transformation f that satisfied the conditions (2.5) is said to be *linear* or *homomorphic*. (We will use only the former term in this book.)

□

To summarise so far, we have seen that the operation of multiplying a vector by a matrix W defines a transformation which is linear in the sense of Definition 2.7, and that these are precisely the transformations realisable by a perceptron with n input units, m output units and weight matrix W. We now proceed to complete the characterization of the perceptrons by showing that in fact *any* linear transformation from $\mathbb{R}^n$ to $\mathbb{R}^m$ can be represented by an $m \times n$ matrix W and hence realised as a perceptron. In order to do this, we need to introduce a little more mathematical machinery.

Definition 2.8

The *standard basis* in $\mathbb{R}^n$ is the set of column vectors $\{\mathbf{e}_1, \mathbf{e}_2, \ldots, \mathbf{e}_n\}$ where $\mathbf{e}_j$ is the vector which has jth element 1 and all other elements 0.

□

For example in $\mathbb{R}^3$ we have

$$\mathbf{e}_1 = \begin{pmatrix} 1 \\ 0 \\ 0 \end{pmatrix}, \mathbf{e}_2 = \begin{pmatrix} 0 \\ 1 \\ 0 \end{pmatrix} \text{and } \mathbf{e}_3 = \begin{pmatrix} 0 \\ 0 \\ 1 \end{pmatrix}.$$

We have for any $\mathbf{x} \in \mathbb{R}^n$, $\mathbf{x} = x_1\mathbf{e}_1 + x_2\mathbf{e}_2 + \ldots + x_n\mathbf{e}_n$. For example

$$\begin{pmatrix} 1 \\ 1 \\ 2 \end{pmatrix} = 1\begin{pmatrix} 1 \\ 0 \\ 0 \end{pmatrix} + 1\begin{pmatrix} 0 \\ 1 \\ 0 \end{pmatrix} + 2\begin{pmatrix} 0 \\ 0 \\ 1 \end{pmatrix}.$$

Now we need two simple lemmas.

Lemma 2.9

For any linear transformation f, we have $f(\mathbf{x}) = x_1 f(\mathbf{e}_1) + \ldots + x_n f(\mathbf{e}_n)$.

Proof

Compare Definition 2.7 and the remark preceding this lemma.

□

Lemma 2.10

For any matrix W, $W\mathbf{e}_j$ is the jth column of W.

Proof

Before giving a formal proof of this, we will illustrate it by a simple example. Consider

$$\begin{pmatrix} 3 & 1 & 2 \\ 4 & 0 & -5 \end{pmatrix}\begin{pmatrix} 0 \\ 1 \\ 0 \end{pmatrix} = \begin{pmatrix} 3\times 0 + 1\times 1 + 2\times 0 \\ 4\times 0 + 0\times 1 - 5\times 0 \end{pmatrix}$$

$$= \begin{pmatrix} 1 \\ 0 \end{pmatrix}.$$

Notice that in this calculation, elements from all columns of the matrix except the second get multiplied by zero elements of $\mathbf{e}_2$, whereas elements from the second column are multiplied by one. We can make this into a formal proof. From Definition 2.2, the inner product of a row vector $\mathbf{w}$ with $\mathbf{e}_j$ will yield w_j. Thus by Remark 2.4(b), the ith element of $W\mathbf{e}_j$ is the ith element of the jth column of W, as required.

□

We draw these ideas together in the following theorem.

Theorem 2.11

(a) Any linear transformation $f: \mathbb{R}^n \to \mathbb{R}^m$ can be represented by an $m\times n$ matrix, and conversely every such matrix yields a linear transformation.

(b) For a given matrix W, the corresponding transformation is given by $f(\mathbf{x}) = W\mathbf{x}$.
(c) For a given transformation f, the corresponding matrix W is formed by taking as its jth column $f(\mathbf{e}_j)$.
(d) A perceptron with n inputs and m outputs defines a linear transformation from $\mathbb{R}^n$ to $\mathbb{R}^m$ with weights defined by the corresponding matrix. Conversely, any linear transformation can be realised as a perceptron.

Proof

Parts (a), (b) and (c) simply summarise the results above. Part (d) is (2.1) and the remarks following.

□

Note that this result is completely constructive: Theorem 2.11(c) actually tells us how to get the matrix. For example, suppose f is a rotation through an angle θ about the origin in $\mathbb{R}^2$. Clearly, rotating a vector will not change its length, so $f(\lambda\mathbf{u})=\lambda f(\mathbf{u})$ for any $\mathbf{u}$. Moreover, a consideration of the effect of rotating Fig. 2.2(b) reveals that $f(\mathbf{u}+\mathbf{v})=f(\mathbf{u})+f(\mathbf{v})$, so f is indeed a linear transformation. To find its matrix, we need only to determine $f(\mathbf{e}_1)$ and $f(\mathbf{e}_2)$,

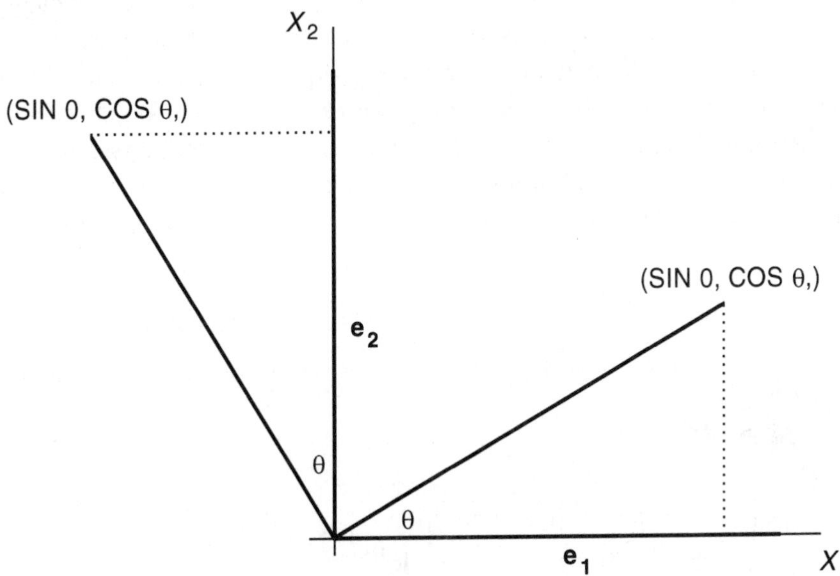

Fig. 2.6

i.e. what vectors do we get by rotating the basis vectors? By elementary trigonometry (see Fig. 2.6) we find that

$$f(\mathbf{e}_1) = \begin{pmatrix} \cos\theta \\ \sin\theta \end{pmatrix} \text{and}\, f(\mathbf{e}_2) = \begin{pmatrix} -\sin\theta \\ \cos\theta \end{pmatrix}.$$

The corresponding matrix W is thus

$$\begin{pmatrix} \cos\theta & -\sin\theta \\ \sin\theta & \cos\theta \end{pmatrix}.$$

The reader might like to calculate $W\mathbf{x}$ for a few vectors $\mathbf{x}$, until convinced that W does indeed give the required rotation!

We see then, that the transformations realised by the perceptrons are precisely the linear transformations. In the next section, we consider the composition of such transformations.

2.4 Matrix algebra

We have seen that perceptrons can only solve a restricted class of classification problems, namely those that are linearly separable. We now consider the question, 'Suppose the output from a perceptron is fed, without thresholding, into another perceptron. Can this system classify a larger range of problems?' The qualification 'without thresholding' is crucial here: we will find later that thresholding at an intermediate layer introduces a non-linearity which considerably increases the representational power of the perceptron, but at the expense of making the mathematics much more complicated! Cascading perceptrons without thresholding amounts to composing the corresponding linear transformations. The following lemma shows that we do not gain any more representational power by doing this.

Lemma 2.12

Let s: $\mathbb{R}^m \to \mathbb{R}^n$ and t: $\mathbb{R}^n \to \mathbb{R}^l$ be linear. Then $t \circ s$ is a linear transformation from $\mathbb{R}^m \to \mathbb{R}^l$.

Proof

$$\begin{aligned} t \circ s\,(\mathbf{x} + \lambda\mathbf{y}) &= t\,[s(\mathbf{x} + \lambda\mathbf{y})] \text{ by definition} \\ &= t\,[s\,(\mathbf{x}) + \lambda s\,(\mathbf{y})] \text{ since } s \text{ is linear} \\ &= t\,[s\,(\mathbf{x})] + \lambda t\,[s\,(\mathbf{y})] \text{ since } t \text{ is linear} \\ &= t + s\,(\mathbf{x}) + \lambda t + s\,(\mathbf{x}) + \lambda t + s\,(\mathbf{y}). \end{aligned}$$

□

Since the composition of linear transformations is linear, we can represent it as a matrix and realise it as a single perceptron using the methods of the previous section. Note that we are *not* claiming that cascading two perceptrons is necessarily useless. In certain circumstances the learning behaviour may be improved, and moreover such a system can be used for data compression. We claim only that there is no gain in representational power. Moreover, these considerations raise a further important question, namely, 'What is the relationship between the matrix representing the composed transformation, and the two matrices representing the individual transformations?' We can answer this question by using the standard basis, in the same way as in the previous section.

Let B represent s, A represent t and C represent $t \circ s$ (See Theorem 2.11). We require an expression for C in terms of A and B. However we know from Theorem 2.11 that the jth column of C is

$$t \circ s(\mathbf{e}j) = t[s(\mathbf{e}j)] = t(\,j\text{th col. of } B) = A(\,j\text{th col. of } B).$$

Thus *the ith element of the jth column of C is obtained as the inner product of the ith row of A with the jth column of B*. We write

$$C = AB$$

where

$$c_{ij} = \sum_{k=1}^{n} a_{ik} b_{kj}. \tag{2.6}$$

The matrix C is, of course, $l \times m$. Remember that it represents the composite transformation $t \circ s$, or the equivalent single perceptron which is result of feeding the output of an unthresholded perceptron with weight matrix B into another one with weight matrix A. C is called the *product* of the matrices A and B.

For example if

$$B = \begin{pmatrix} 3 & 1 & 2 \\ 4 & 0 & -5 \end{pmatrix} A = \begin{pmatrix} 1 & 2 \\ 2 & 1 \end{pmatrix} \mathbf{x} = \begin{pmatrix} 1 \\ 1 \\ 2 \end{pmatrix}$$

Then

$$B\mathbf{x} = \begin{pmatrix} 3 & 1 & 2 \\ 4 & 0 & -5 \end{pmatrix} \begin{pmatrix} 1 \\ 1 \\ 2 \end{pmatrix} = \begin{pmatrix} 8 \\ -6 \end{pmatrix}$$

and

$$A\,(B\mathbf{x}) = \begin{pmatrix} 1 & 2 \\ 2 & 1 \end{pmatrix} \begin{pmatrix} 8 \\ -6 \end{pmatrix} = \begin{pmatrix} -4 \\ 10 \end{pmatrix}.$$

On the other hand,

$$C = AB = \begin{pmatrix} 1 & 2 \\ 2 & 1 \end{pmatrix} \begin{pmatrix} 3 & 1 & 2 \\ 4 & 0 & -5 \end{pmatrix} = \begin{pmatrix} 3+8 & 1+0 & 2-10 \\ 6+4 & 2+0 & 4-5 \end{pmatrix}$$
$$= \begin{pmatrix} 11 & 1 & -8 \\ 10 & 2 & -1 \end{pmatrix}$$

whence

$$Cx = \begin{pmatrix} 11 & 1 & -8 \\ 10 & 2 & -1 \end{pmatrix} \begin{pmatrix} 1 \\ 1 \\ 2 \end{pmatrix} = \begin{pmatrix} 11+1-16 \\ 10+2-2 \end{pmatrix} = \begin{pmatrix} -4 \\ 10 \end{pmatrix}$$
$$= A\,(Bx)$$

as expected.

Remarks 2.13

(a) Obviously the product only makes sense if the number of columns of A is the same as the number of rows of B, in which case A and B are said to be *compatible.*

(b) In general, the matrix product is *not commutative*, i.e. $BA \neq AB$. In terms of perceptrons, this means that we do not get the same result by switching the order. The non-commutativity means that when multiplying matrices, *it is very important to preserve the order*.

(c) On the other hand, the matrix product is associative, i.e. $(AB)C=A(BC)$, since both these mean 'Perform the transformation represented by C followed by that represented by B followed by that represented by A.' We may write ABC without ambiguity.

□

To complete this section we mention briefly some other algebraic aspects of matrices.

As we have seen, it is often convenient to treat a matrix as an ordered set of column vectors. Since for obvious reasons we need to be able to add vectors, it is also convenient to extend the definition of the vector sum to matrices. For vectors, we form the sum by adding corresponding elements. Thus we make the same definition for matrices of the same size, namely

$$(A+B)_{ij} = (A)_{ij} + (B)_{ij}.$$

Since we know that

$$A(\mathbf{x}+\mathbf{y}) = A\mathbf{x} + A\mathbf{y},$$

and in the product AB, B is treated as a set of column vectors, it follows immediately (assuming the matrices are of the appropriate sizes for either side to exist) that

$$A(B+C) = AB + AC.$$

Similarly

$$(A+B)C = AC + BC.$$

These identities are the *left* and *right distributive laws*. Note, however, that these expressions only make sense for matrices of the appropriate sizes, and that the correct order must be preserved in each product.

Obviously we can in a similar fashion also talk of multiplying a matrix by a scalar, simply by multiplying it elementwise.

Another operation that turns out to be useful on occasions is to interchange the rows and columns of a matrix. This operation is called *transposing*. It is denoted by a superscript T. More formally,

$$(A^{\mathrm{T}})_{ij} = (A)_{ji}.$$

For example with

$$B = \begin{pmatrix} 3 & 1 & 2 \\ 4 & 0 & -5 \end{pmatrix} \quad B^{\mathrm{T}} = \begin{pmatrix} 3 & 4 \\ 1 & 0 \\ 2 & -5 \end{pmatrix}.$$

This at first sight useless operation will in fact be employed extensively. An $n \times n$ matrix such that $A^{\mathrm{T}} = A$ is said to be *symmetric* (e.g. the matrix A of the example before Remarks 2.13 is symmetric). Again we will make frequent use of symmetric matrices. We also occasionally meet matrices for which $A^{\mathrm{T}} = -A$. These are said to be *anti-symmetric* or *skew-symmetric*. Note that a matrix A

can only be skew-symmetric if all the elements a_{ii} on its main diagonal are zero.

Algebraically, the most important property of the transpose is the following.

Proposition 2.14
$(AB)^{\mathrm{T}} = B^{\mathrm{T}}A^{\mathrm{T}}$ (or in words, 'When transposing a product we reverse the order.')

Proof
If A has n rows, and B has n columns, we have

$$\begin{aligned}[(AB)^{\mathrm{T}}]_{ji} &= (AB)_{ij} \\ &= \sum_{k=1}^{n} (A)_{ik}(B)_{kj} \\ &= \sum_{k=1}^{n} (B^{\mathrm{T}})_{jk}(A^{\mathrm{T}})_{ki} \\ &= (B^{\mathrm{T}}A^{\mathrm{T}})_{ji}.\end{aligned}$$

□

Up to now we have regarded the matrix product as a kind of extension of the scalar product for vectors. Equally, we can regard the scalar product as a special case of the matrix product. If **x** and **y** are column n-vectors, we simply treat them as $1 \times n$ matrices. Then it is easily seen that $\mathbf{x}^{\mathrm{T}}\mathbf{y}$ is in fact a 1×1 matrix whose single element is **x.y**. But for 1×1 matrices, the sum and product operations reduce to those of the ordinary real numbers applied to the single element. Thus we can identify the 1×1 matrices with the real numbers and $\mathbf{x}^{\mathrm{T}}\mathbf{y}$ can be regarded as the inner product of **x** and **y**. Hence, (for instance) the square of the length of **x** is given by $\mathbf{x}^{\mathrm{T}}\mathbf{x}$ (compare Definition 2.4). We will use this notation for the inner product from now on. For printing purposes it saves space to write row vectors rather than column vectors. For example we can write the column vector from the examples above as $(1, 1, 2)^{\mathrm{T}}$. Thus, from now on, we will often express column vectors in this form.

We have now defined the fundamental operations of matrix algebra. But we will also need some of the elementary computational techniques associated with matrices, and it is also convenient at this stage to discuss the connection with systems of linear equations.

2.5 Subspaces, dimension, rank and the inverse matrix

Look again at Fig. 2.1 showing a simple perceptron with input vector $\mathbf{x} \in \mathbb{R}^n$ and output vector $\mathbf{y} \in \mathbb{R}^m$, related by $m \times n$ weight matrix W so that

$$\mathbf{y} = W\mathbf{x}.$$

Suppose we feed the output of this perceptron directly into another perceptron with $n \times m$ weight matrix V and output vector $\mathbf{z} \in \mathbb{R}^n$. Thus

$$\mathbf{z} = V\mathbf{y} = VW\mathbf{x}. \tag{2.7}$$

This situation is illustrated in Fig. 2.7, with $n=4$ and $m=3$. If $m<n$, such a network (or rather the two layers of it separately) can be used for data compression. The n-vector $\mathbf{x}$ is fed into the first layer and the smaller intermediate vector $\mathbf{y}$ stored. Then we want to reconstruct the original vector $\mathbf{x}$ by means of the second layer of the network. We would like to choose V and W so that

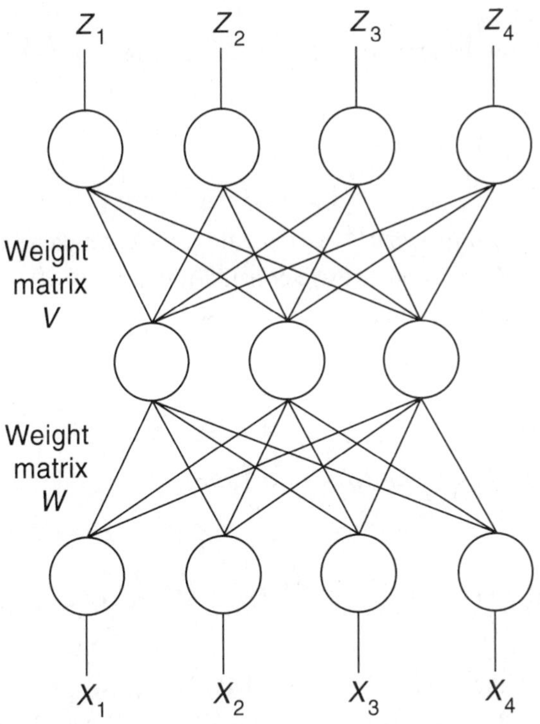

Fig. 2.7

$$\mathbf{z} = \mathbf{x}. \tag{2.8}$$

However it seems intuitively clear that for $m<n$, it will not be possible to choose V and W for this to work for all possible $\mathbf{x}$. In this section we will show that this intuition is correct, and introduce some of the basic concepts needed to understand what is going on. Later we will analyse this problem fully. This will require some of the most powerful tools of linear algebra.

Note, however, that (2.8) will certainly be satisfied if in (2.7) we can choose V such that $VW=I$. In terms of the transformation $f(\mathbf{x})=W\mathbf{x}$, we want W to be a matrix representing the inverse transformation f^{-1} where

$$f^{-1} \circ f(\mathbf{x}) = \mathbf{x}$$

for any $\mathbf{x}$. We recall some general observations about this problem from Section 1.3 in Chapter 1.

(a) A function is said to be *1–1* (read 'one to one') if distinct points have distinct images, i.e. if $f(\mathbf{x}_1)=f(\mathbf{x}_2)$ implies $\mathbf{x}_1=\mathbf{x}_2$. Also f is said to be *onto* if for *each* $\mathbf{y}$ there is an $\mathbf{x}$ with $f(\mathbf{x})=\mathbf{y}$. The inverse exists if and only if the transformation f is 1–1 and onto.

(b) Again from our general knowledge of functions, if f^{-1} exists it is also true that

$$f \circ f^{-1}(\mathbf{y}) = \mathbf{y} \text{ for any } \mathbf{y}$$
[just put $\mathbf{y}=f(\mathbf{x})$].

To these two general properties, we can add a third which applies specifically to the linear transformations we are considering here.

(c) If f^{-1} exists, then it is linear. For suppose

$$\mathbf{y}_1 = f(\mathbf{x}_1) \text{ and } \mathbf{y}_2 = f(\mathbf{x}_2).$$

Since f is linear,

$$\mathbf{y}_1 + \lambda\mathbf{y}_2 = f(\mathbf{x}_1) + \lambda f(\mathbf{x}_2) = f(\mathbf{x}_1 + \lambda\mathbf{x}_2).$$

Thus

$$f^{-1}(\mathbf{y}_1 + \lambda\mathbf{y}_2) = \mathbf{x}_1 + \lambda\mathbf{x}_2 \qquad = f^{-1}(\mathbf{y}_1) + \lambda f^{-1}(\mathbf{y}_2)$$

as required.

The second of these remarks means that if f^{-1} exists and is represented by V, so that VW = I, it will also be true that WV = I. We shall call such a V the *inverse* of W and write $V=W^{-1}$.

We may therefore pose the following crucial questions:

(a) Under what conditions on W is the transformation f defined by $f(\mathbf{x}) = W\mathbf{x}$ 1–1 onto?
(b) If the transformation is 1–1 onto, then W^{-1} will exist, but how do we find it?
(c) If the inverse does *not* exist, how can we understand the structure of the transformations so as to see under what circumstances we *will* be able to solve $VW\mathbf{x} = \mathbf{x}$?

This entire section is really concerned with these three questions. In answering them we shall introduce some of the deeper concepts which are usually considered as part of the study of abstract vector spaces. However since our purpose is to show their relevance to neural networks, it seems more appropriate here to introduce them in this more concrete context. Nevertheless an understanding of abstract vector spaces will be required by the serious student of the theory of neural networks, so they will be introduced later in the chapter. Fortunately the proofs are essentially the same whether working in $\mathbb{R}^n$ or more abstract spaces, so it will not be necessary to repeat them.

As a first step to addressing the three questions above, we note the following.

Lemma 2.15

If a linear transformation $f: \mathbb{R}^m \to \mathbb{R}^n$ is 1–1 onto (and thus has an inverse), then necessarily $m = n$.

Proof

Since f is linear it is represented by a matrix W. Since f^{-1} is linear, there is a matrix W^{-1} representing f^{-1} which satisfies $W^{-1}W = I = WW^{-1}$. However the products on the left and right of this expression only make sense if $m = n$.

□

This result goes some way towards meeting our intuition that (2.8) cannot hold if $m < n$, but it is far from being the full story. What happens if $m > n$? We know from Section 1.3 that f may still have a left inverse allowing (2.8) to hold. Nonetheless we will start with the case $m = n$. (Matrices with the same number of rows and columns are said to be *square*.)

However merely considering square matrices is not enough in itself to guarantee that the transformation is invertible. Consider the following example.

Let a linear transformation f: $\mathbb{R}^3 \to \mathbb{R}^3$ be defined as follows.

$$f(\mathbf{e}_1) = \begin{pmatrix} 2 \\ 1 \\ 3 \end{pmatrix} = \mathbf{a}_1, \text{ say}$$

$$f(\mathbf{e}_2) = \begin{pmatrix} 1 \\ 1 \\ 0 \end{pmatrix} = \mathbf{a}_2$$

$$f(\mathbf{e}_3) = \begin{pmatrix} 4 \\ 3 \\ 3 \end{pmatrix} = \mathbf{a}_3.$$

The matrix W representing f has of course columns $\mathbf{a}_1$, $\mathbf{a}_2$ and $\mathbf{a}_3$, respectively, and we may write concisely in block matrix form

$$W = (\mathbf{a}_1 \mid \mathbf{a}_2 \mid \mathbf{a}_3).$$

If $\mathbf{x}=(x_1, x_2, x_3)^{\mathrm{T}}$ is a general vector in $\mathbb{R}^3$, then

$$\mathbf{x} = x_1\mathbf{e}_1 + x_2\mathbf{e}_2 + x_3\mathbf{e}_3$$

and hence

$$W\mathbf{x} = f(\mathbf{x}) = x_1\mathbf{a}_1 + x_2\mathbf{a}_2 + x_3\mathbf{a}_3. \tag{2.9}$$

But notice that in this particular case,

$$\mathbf{a}_3 = \mathbf{a}_1 + 2\mathbf{a}_2, \tag{2.10}$$

so

$$f(\mathbf{x}) = (x_1+x_3)\mathbf{a}_1 + (x_2+2x_3)\mathbf{a}_2.$$

We can visualise this by thinking of $\mathbf{a}_1$ and $\mathbf{a}_2$ as position vectors starting at the origin. For any $\mathbf{x}$, the image vector $W\mathbf{x}$ lies in the plane defined by $\mathbf{a}_1$ and $\mathbf{a}_2$. See Fig. 2.8. The transformation cannot be 1–1 onto, and W is not invertible. A matrix such as this which has no inverse is called *singular*. Conversely, if a matrix has an inverse, it is said to be *non-singular*, or *invertible*.)

Rewriting (2.10) gives

$$\mathbf{0} = \mathbf{a}_1 + 2\mathbf{a}_2 - \mathbf{a}_3.$$

An expression of the form of the right-hand side of this equation is called a *linear combination* of the vectors $\mathbf{a}_1$, $\mathbf{a}_2$ and $\mathbf{a}_3$. If, as in this case, there is a linear

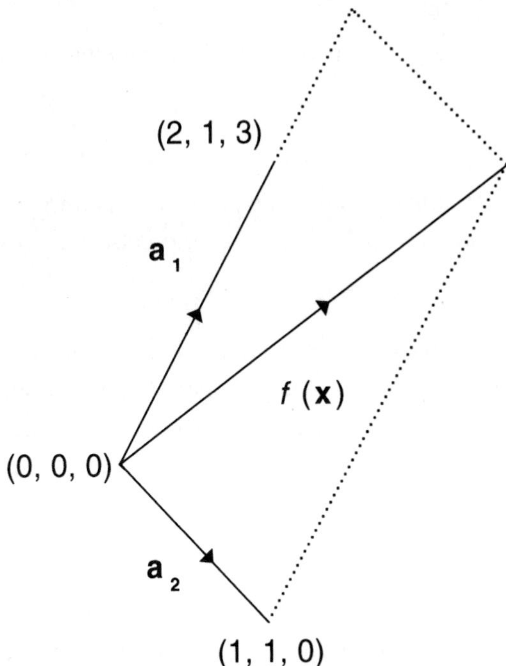

Fig. 2.8

combination of the vectors (with at least one non-zero coefficient) which equals **0**, the vectors are said to be *linearly dependent*. If not, they are said to be *linearly independent*. For instance $\mathbf{a}_1$ and $\mathbf{a}_2$ are independent.

We may also observe some other properties of the set of linear combinations of $\mathbf{a}_1$ and $\mathbf{a}_2$ which form the plane illustrated in Fig. 2.8.

Properties 2.16

(a) If we add any two vectors in this set, the resulting vector remains in the set.
(b) If we multiply a vector in the set by a scalar, the resulting vector remains in the set.
(c) The set contains the zero vector.

□

In fact the plane behaves very much like a space of vectors in its own right and it is useful to think of it as such.

Definition 2.17

A subset of $\mathbb{R}^n$ which satisfies Properties 2.16 is called a *subspace* of $\mathbb{R}^n$.

□

(Note that $\mathbb{R}^n$ is a subspace of itself.)

It is also natural to think of the plane defined by $\mathbf{a}_1$ and $\mathbf{a}_2$ as being in some sense two-dimensional. To make this concept precise requires a little work.

Definition 2.18

(a) Let P be a subspace of $\mathbb{R}^n$. If every vector in S can be expressed as a linear combination of the set $S=\{\mathbf{s}_1, \mathbf{s}_2, \ldots, \mathbf{s}_k\}$ then the set S is said to *span P*.
(b) If the vectors in S are also linearly independent, S is said to be a *basis* for P. (Note that no basis can contain the vector $\mathbf{0}$, since any set containing this vector is linearly dependent).

□

We shall show later (Theorem 2.2(c)) with P taken to be $\mathbb{R}^n$ and R the standard basis) that any subspace of $\mathbb{R}^n$ must have a finite spanning set. For example the set $\{\mathbf{a}_1, \mathbf{a}_2\}$ spans the plane illustrated in Fig. 2.8. However so does the set $\{\mathbf{a}_1, \mathbf{a}_2, \mathbf{a}_3\}$. In order to define the *dimension* of the plane we need to capture the idea that the former set is somehow minimal. We cannot delete any elements without the spanning property breaking down. The key here is that the first set of vectors is a basis whereas the second one is not. It is intuitively clear from Fig. 2.8 that any set of linearly independent vectors which spans the plane can have only two elements and that this is what we mean by the plane being two dimensional. However an appeal to a diagram and to intuition is not a proof: we need to show that any basis for S in Definition 2.18 must have the same number of elements. Although a little technical it is worth coming to grips with this proof as it introduces some further important ideas.

Definition 2.19

Let $f(\mathbf{x})=W\mathbf{x}$ be a linear transformation from $\mathbb{R}^m$ to $\mathbb{R}^n$. The *kernel* of f is the set of vectors $\mathbf{x}$ such that $f(\mathbf{x})=\mathbf{0}$. We denote this set by $\ker(f)$ or $\ker(W)$.

□

Since $W\mathbf{0}=\mathbf{0}$, the kernel of f contains at least the zero vector. Two important properties of the kernel are given in the following theorem.

Theorem 2.20

With f as in Definition 2.19, we have

(a) ker (f) is a subspace of $\mathbb{R}^m$.
(b) The linear transformation f is 1–1 if and only if ker(f) contains *only* the zero vector.

Proof

(a) We know that ker(f) contains at least the zero vector. In general, it may not contain any other vectors, but if it does they form a subspace of $\mathbb{R}^m$. For (compare Properties 2.16) if $W\mathbf{x}_1=\mathbf{0}$ and $W\mathbf{x}_2=\mathbf{0}$, then $W(\mathbf{x}_1+\mathbf{x}_2)=W\mathbf{x}_1+W\mathbf{x}_2=\mathbf{0}+\mathbf{0}=\mathbf{0}$ and similarly for multiplication by a scalar. In fact even if the kernel contains only the single vector $\mathbf{0}$ we can still think of it as a trivial subspace.
(b) We have $f(\mathbf{0})=\mathbf{0}$. If f is 1–1 then by definition there can be no other $\mathbf{x}$ with $f(\mathbf{x})=\mathbf{0}$. We still need to show the converse, namely that if ker$(f)=\{\mathbf{0}\}$, then f is 1–1. This proof is by contradiction: if f is not 1–1, there exist two different vectors $\mathbf{x}_1$ and $\mathbf{x}_2$, and a vector $\mathbf{y}$, such that $f(\mathbf{x}_1)=\mathbf{y}$ and $f(\mathbf{x}_2)=\mathbf{y}$. Since f is linear, $f(\mathbf{x}_1-\mathbf{x}_2)=\mathbf{y}-\mathbf{y}=\mathbf{0}$, so $(\mathbf{x}_1-\mathbf{x}_2)\in$ ker(f), or $(\mathbf{x}_1-\mathbf{x}_2)=\mathbf{0}$. But this is a contradiction since $\mathbf{x}_1\neq\mathbf{x}_2$.

□

The following lemma is a corollary of Theorem 2.20(b).

Lemma 2.21

Let f and W be as in Definition 2.19, and suppose also that $n<m$ and further that f is onto. Then there is a vector $\mathbf{x}\neq\mathbf{0}$ such that $f(\mathbf{x})=\mathbf{0}$, or, equivalently, $W\mathbf{x}=\mathbf{0}$.

Proof

In view of Theorem 2.20(b), it is sufficient to prove that f is not 1–1. Lemma 2.15 tells us that f must fail either to be 1–1 or onto. But we exclude the second case in the hypothesis of the theorem.

□

We are finally ready for the key result, namely that any bases for a given subspace must have the same number of elements.

Theorem 2.22

Let P be a subspace of $\mathbb{R}^n$. Suppose that the sets $\{\mathbf{x}_1 \ldots \mathbf{x}_r\}$ and $\{\mathbf{y}_1 \ldots \mathbf{y}_s\}$ are both bases for P. Then $r=s$.

Proof

The proof is by contradiction. Suppose that $r \neq s$. Then we may assume without loss of generality that $s>r$. For each $i \leq s$ we have (since the $\mathbf{x}_1 \ldots \mathbf{x}_r$ form a basis)

$$\mathbf{y}_i = a_{1i}\mathbf{x}_1 + a_{2i}\mathbf{x}_2 + \ldots + a_{ri}\mathbf{x}_r \tag{2.11}$$

for some numbers a_{ij}. Let X be the $n \times r$ matrix whose columns are the $\mathbf{x}_i$'s and similarly Y the $n \times s$ matrix whose columns are the $\mathbf{y}_i$'s. Then all of the s expressions (2.11) may be written as the single matrix equation

$$Y = XA\,, \tag{2.12}$$

where, of course, A is the $r \times s$ matrix of the a_{ij}. Now consider the mapping $g\colon \mathbb{R}^s \to \mathbb{R}^r$ defined by $g(\mathbf{v}) = A\mathbf{v}$. Suppose first that this mapping is onto. By Lemma 2.21, there exists a $\mathbf{v} \neq \mathbf{0}$ such that $A\mathbf{v}=\mathbf{0}$. Hence $Y\mathbf{v}=XA\mathbf{v}=\mathbf{0}$. But $Y\mathbf{v}$ is a linear combination of the columns of Y, i.e. of the $\mathbf{y}_i$ (compare (2.9) above). Thus, the hypothesis that the $\mathbf{y}_i$ s are linearly independent is contradicted. The only other possibility is that the mapping g is not onto. In this case, by definition, there exists a vector $\mathbf{p}$ such that $\mathbf{p} \neq A\mathbf{v}$ for any $\mathbf{v}$. On the other hand since the $\mathbf{y}_i$'s form a basis, there must be a vector $\mathbf{v}$ such that $Y\mathbf{v}=X\mathbf{p}$. Substituting for Y from (2.12) gives $XA\mathbf{v}=X\mathbf{p}$, or $X(A\mathbf{v}-\mathbf{p})=\mathbf{0}$. Since the vector $A\mathbf{v}-\mathbf{p}$ is not $\mathbf{0}$, we have a linear combination of the $\mathbf{x}_i$'s equal to $\mathbf{0}$, contradicting the hypothesis that they are linearly independent.

□

At last we can give a formal definition of dimension.

Definition 2.23

Let P be a subspace of $\mathbb{R}^n$. Suppose that the set $\{\mathbf{x}_1 \ldots \mathbf{x}_r\}$ is a basis for P. Then r is said to be the *dimension* of P. We write $\dim(P)=r$. (By convention, the trivial subspace $\{\mathbf{0}\}$ is assumed to have dimension 0: compare Definition 2.18(b)).

□

For example, since the vectors $\mathbf{a}_1$ and $\mathbf{a}_2$ form a basis for the planar subspace illustrated in Fig. 2.8, this subspace has dimension 2 as we would expect from our simple geometric intuition. As a further example, note that $\mathbb{R}^3$ (say) is a subspace of itself. The standard basis $\mathbf{e}_1$, $\mathbf{e}_2$, $\mathbf{e}_3$ is a basis for $\mathbb{R}^3$ so $\mathbb{R}^3$ is (of course!) 3-dimensional.

We now have most of the machinery we need to answer the three questions posed towards the beginning of this Section 2.5. However, before doing this, we give for completeness two further theorems about bases.

Theorem 2.24

Let P be a subspace of $\mathbb{R}^n$ and suppose that the set $R=\{\mathbf{x}_1 \ldots \mathbf{x}_r\}$ spans P.

(a) There is a subset of R which is a basis for P.
(b) Suppose that the set $S=\{\mathbf{y}_1 \ldots \mathbf{y}_s\}$ is linearly independent and $\dim(P)\geq s$. Then there is a basis of P of which S is a subset (i.e. any linearly independent set can be extended to a basis by adding extra vectors.) In particular, if $\dim(P)=s$, then S is a basis.
(c) If Q is a subspace of P then Q has a (finite) basis and $\dim(Q)\leq\dim(P)$. If $\dim(Q)=\dim(P)$, then $Q=P$.

Proof

(a) Work through R discarding any vectors which are linear combinations of previous ones. The resulting set still spans P since any linear combinations involving the discarded vectors can be replaced by combinations of the remaining ones. Also the resulting set is linearly independent, so it is a basis.
(b) Let T be any basis of P. Then $T\cup S$ spans V. Applying the argument of (a) with the S vectors listed first establishes the result.
(c) We start by constructing a basis for Q. If Q contains only $\mathbf{0}$, the dimension is 0 and the result is trivial. If not, choose $\mathbf{q}_1\in Q$. If $\{\mathbf{q}_1\}$ spans Q then stop. If not find $\mathbf{q}_2$ not in this span. Note that $\mathbf{q}_1$ and $\mathbf{q}_2$ must be linearly independent. Continue adding independent elements in this way until Q is spanned: note that we can never require more than $\dim(P)$ elements, or we would have a set of independent elements of P larger than the dimension. The final part of (c) is easy: by (b), a basis of Q will span P, and since Q consists of all linear combinations of P, $Q=P$.

□

Again, remember that this theorem also applies to the case that $P=\mathbb{R}^n$. Thus no subspace of $\mathbb{R}^n$ can have dimension greater than n and equality occurs only for $\mathbb{R}^n$ itself. Moreover if we have a basis for any subspace of $\mathbb{R}^n$, we can extend it to a basis for the whole space. The last sentence of Theorem 2.24(b) is particularly useful. It means that if we have a space known to be of dimension s, then any s linearly independent vectors will form a basis.

Now, once again return to the notation of Definition 2.19, with $f(\mathbf{x})=W\mathbf{x}$ a linear transformation from $\mathbb{R}^m$ to $\mathbb{R}^n$. We have seen (Theorem 2.20(a)) that $\ker(f)$ is a subspace of $\mathbb{R}^m$. We have also seen that the image of f, i.e. the set of $\mathbf{y}$ such that $f(\mathbf{x})=\mathbf{y}$ for some $\mathbf{x}$ is a subspace of $\mathbb{R}^n$. This image is, of course, just the plane illustrated in Fig. 2.7 consisting of all linear combinations of the columns of W. We denote the image of f by $\mathrm{im}(f)$ or $\mathrm{im}(W)$.

Definitions 2.25

(a) The *column rank* of the $n\times m$ matrix W is the maximum number of linearly independent columns. (We write it as 'col.rank(W)' for short.) The *rank* of the linear transformation f (rank(f)) defined by W is the dimension of the image. Since $f(\mathbf{x})$ for any $\mathbf{x}$ is a linear combination of the columns of W, rank $(f)=$ col.rank(W).

(b) The *nullity* of f (denoted null(f) or null (W)) is the dimension of $\ker(f)$. □

The next theorem shows that these are related in a very simple way.

Theorem 2.26 (The Dimension Theorem)

With the notation of Definition 2.25, rank $(f)+\mathrm{null}(f)=m$ where m here is the dimension of the space $\mathbb{R}^m$ on which f is defined.

Proof

This apparently mysterious theorem is actually very simple. Let $S_1=\{\mathbf{s}_1 \ldots \mathbf{s}_j\}$ be a basis for $\ker(f)$ so rank$(f)=j$. Extend it (see Theorem 2.24(b)) to a basis $S=\{\mathbf{s}_1 \ldots \mathbf{s}_m\}$ for $\mathbb{R}^m$. Any element of the image of f must be a linear combination of the $f(\mathbf{s}_i)$ $i=1,\ldots,m$. However, only those elements not in S_1 will contribute non-zero vectors to the image, so the set $R=\{f(\mathbf{s}_{j+1})\ldots f(\mathbf{s}_m)\}$ spans im(f). Since rank$(f)=j$, $\dim(\mathbb{R}^m)=m$, and R contains $m-j$ elements, it remains only to show that the set R is linearly independent. Suppose that it is not. Then there exist real numbers $\alpha_{j+1}\ldots\alpha_m$ such that

$\alpha_{j+1} f(\mathbf{s}_{j+1}) + ... + \alpha_m f(\mathbf{s}_m) = \mathbf{0}.$

whence

$f(\alpha_{j+1}\mathbf{s}_{j+1} + ... + \alpha_m\mathbf{s}_m) = \mathbf{0}$ since f is linear .

But this means that $(\alpha_{j+1}\mathbf{s}_{j+1} + \ldots + \alpha_m \mathbf{s}_m) \in \ker(f)$ and is therefore a linear combination of the elements of S_1, contradicting the fact that the set S is linearly independent. This actually completes the proof, but it is worth remarking that of course it is possible that $\ker(f)$ is the trivial space consisting only of the vector $\mathbf{0}$. In this case the set S_1 is empty. This is why this space is considered to have dimension 0. The theorem is still valid in this case.

□

To exemplify all these ideas, we refer again to the example described after Lemma 2.15 and illustrated in Fig. 2.8. We have already seen that the image plane shown in the diagram has dimension 2. Since m is in this case 3, Theorem 2.26 indicates that $\ker(f)$ will have dimension 1. But we do not yet know how to find a basis for $\ker(f)$ explicitly. Obviously, to do this we need to find the general solution of $W\mathbf{x}=\mathbf{0}$. This problem will be addressed in the next section. Before commencing this, let us return to the study of the network of Fig. 2.7 and the three questions which we posed towards the start of this section. Recall that these were

(a) Under what conditions on W is the transformation f defined by $f(\mathbf{x}) = W\mathbf{x}$ 1–1 onto?
(b) If the transformation is 1–1 onto, then W^{-1} will exist, but how do we find it?
(c) If the inverse does *not* exist, how can we understand the structure of the transformations so as to see under what circumstances we *will* be able to solve $VW\mathbf{x}=\mathbf{x}$?

We can now give a fairly complete answer to the first question. For $f: \mathbb{R}^m \to \mathbb{R}^n$ to be 1–1 onto we must first have $m=n$ (Lemma 2.15). In terms of the network of Fig. 2.7, this means that we must have the same number of hidden units as input units (which is also the same as the number of output units). Assume this condition is satisfied. Theorem 2.20(b) and Definition 2.25(b) tells us that f will be 1–1 if and only if $\text{null}(f)=0$. On the other hand, by definition f is onto if its image is the whole of $\mathbb{R}^n$ but then Definition 2.25(a) and Theorem 2.24(c) tell us that this will be the case if rank(f)=n=m. Finally, in the Dimension Theorem 2.26 we can put null(f)=0 or rank(f)=m and conclude that for square matrices, the mapping $f(\mathbf{x})=W\mathbf{x}$ is 1–1 **if and only if** it is onto.

We can also give a partial answer to question (c) (whether or not W is square). Examine again the proof of Theorem 2.26. We chose a basis S_1 for ker(f) and then extended this to a basis S for $\mathbb{R}^m$. Any vector $\mathbf{x}$ can be expressed in terms of this basis. Any component of $\mathbf{x}$ in S_1 is mapped to $\mathbf{0}$ by f, so there is no way it can be reconstructed. On the other hand if $\mathbf{x}$ can be expressed purely as a linear combination of the elements of $S-S_1$, there is hope. Suppose that with j as in the proof,

$$\mathbf{x} = \alpha_{j+1}\mathbf{s}_{j+1} + \ldots + \alpha_m\mathbf{s}_m \tag{2.13}$$

so

$$f(\mathbf{x}) = \alpha_{j+1}f(\mathbf{s}_{j+1}) + \ldots + \alpha_m f(\mathbf{s}_m). \tag{2.14}$$

To reconstruct $\mathbf{x}$ from $f(\mathbf{x})$ we need to find the numbers $\alpha_{j+1} \ldots \alpha_j$. But this is certainly possible in principle since we know that $R=\{f(\mathbf{s}_{j+1}) \ldots f(\mathbf{s}_m)\}$ forms a basis for the image space. (Actually we have not yet shown that the numbers $\alpha_{j+1} \ldots \alpha_m$ are uniquely defined, but this is easy to see. If any vector has two *different* expressions in terms of a given basis, subtracting one of these from the other would give a linear dependence relation for the elements of the basis, contradicting their linear independence.) In order to reconstruct $\mathbf{x}$ (given that we have the basis S), proceed as follows.

R has $k=m-j$ elements and spans im(f). If $k=n$ then im(f)=$\mathbb{R}^n$. If not then we can extend R to a basis R_1 for $\mathbb{R}^n$ by adding additional vectors: say $R_1=\{\mathbf{r}_1 \ldots \mathbf{r}_n\}$ with $\mathbf{r}_1=f(\mathbf{s}_{j+1}) \ldots \mathbf{r}_k=f(\mathbf{s}_m)$. Form the matrix B whose columns are $\mathbf{r}_1 \ldots \mathbf{r}_n$, and let $\mathbf{a}=(\alpha_{j+1} \ldots \alpha_m, 0 \ldots 0)^T$ where, of course, the number of trailing zeros added is $n-k$. Then (2.14) can be written in matrix form as

$$f(\mathbf{x}) = B\mathbf{a}.$$

Now $f(\mathbf{x})=W\mathbf{x}$ by definition, and the matrix B is invertible as it is an $n\times n$ matrix with linearly independent columns. Thus

$$\mathbf{a} = B^{-1}W\mathbf{x}. \tag{2.15}$$

Now form an $m\times n$ matrix A as follows. The first k columns are the vectors $\mathbf{s}_{j+1} \ldots \mathbf{s}_m$. The last $n-k$ columns may be chosen arbitrarily: say just $n-k$ copies of $\mathbf{0}$. In matrix form, (2.13) becomes

$$\mathbf{x} = A\mathbf{a}$$
$$= AB^{-1}W\mathbf{x}.$$

Comparing this equation with the required expression $VW\mathbf{x}=\mathbf{x}$ from question (c), we find that V may be taken as AB^{-1}. Note that the matrices A and B here do not depend on the particular choice of **x**, but only on ker(f) and the basis S that is chosen for it. A matrix V which behaves as a kind of partial inverse to W in this way is often called a *pseudoinverse* or *generalised inverse*: (Ben-Israel and Greville, 1974). However the construction here raises several new questions. How do we choose the basis S? Does it matter which basis we choose? Suppose **x** does not exactly satisfy (2.13), but is close to a vector that does (i.e. if **x** is expressed in terms of the basis S, the coefficients $\alpha_1 \ldots \alpha_j$ are small). How close is $VW\mathbf{x}$ to **x**? Finally, how do we compute B^{-1}? This brings us back to our question (b)! We will begin to answer some of these questions in the next section, although questions of closeness and optimal choice of basis will have to await the spectral theory to be developed in the next chapter.

2.6 Elementary matrices and elementary row operations

The elementary row operations are the key to practical matrix calculations and also to proving many results. It must be admitted that they are *not* generally used in algorithms in neural computation: learning algorithms are used instead. Nevertheless, in view of the importance of these operations both in matrix theory and practical calculation, the reader is strongly advised to study the material in this section.

Elementary operations come in three flavours. Consider first the matrix

$$E = \begin{pmatrix} 1 & 0 & 0 \\ 0 & 1 & s \\ 0 & 0 & 1 \end{pmatrix} \text{where } s \text{ is non zero real number .}$$

Let A denote a general 3×3 matrix

$$\begin{pmatrix} a_{11} & a_{12} & a_{13} \\ a_{21} & a_{22} & a_{23} \\ a_{31} & a_{32} & a_{33} \end{pmatrix}.$$

Then

$$EA = \begin{pmatrix} 1 & 0 & 0 \\ 0 & 1 & s \\ 0 & 0 & 1 \end{pmatrix} \begin{pmatrix} a_{11} & a_{12} & a_{13} \\ a_{21} & a_{22} & a_{23} \\ a_{31} & a_{32} & a_{33} \end{pmatrix}.$$

$$= \begin{pmatrix} a_{11} & a_{12} & a_{13} \\ a_{21} + sa_{31} & a_{22} + sa_{32} & a_{23} + sa_{33} \\ a_{31} & a_{32} & a_{33} \end{pmatrix}.$$

Thus, *premultiplication by E is equivalent to adding s times the third row to the second row*. In practice we do not explicitly perform the premultiplication, but it it important to understand that the operation is equivalent to premultiplying by a certain matrix. We call E an *elementary matrix*, and the operation of adding a multiple of one row to another is one of the *elementary row operations*. The other types have the forms

$$C = \begin{pmatrix} 1 & 0 & 0 \\ 0 & s & 0 \\ 0 & 0 & 1 \end{pmatrix}$$

and

$$P = \begin{pmatrix} 1 & 0 & 0 \\ 0 & 0 & 1 \\ 0 & 1 & 0 \end{pmatrix} \text{(called a \textit{permutation matrix}).}$$

If we work out CA and PA we find that that we have three elementary row operations:

(a) Adding a multiple of one row of a matrix to another row.
(b) Multiplying a row by a non zero scalar.
(c) Interchanging two rows.

A more formal way to define an elementary matrix, is *any matrix obtained by applying an elementary row operation to an identity matrix*.

Applying any of these row operations to a matrix is exactly equivalent to premultiplying it by the corresponding elementary matrix. We emphasise again that in practice we do *not* explicitly perform the premultiplication: we simply perform the row operation. However the fact that these operations can be considered as multiplications by matrices is very important in proofs, as we shall see below.

We now consider application of the elementary row operations to the calculation of matrix inverses. In fact there are many ways known to do this.

The one described here is probably the most generally useful. It is called the *Gauss-Jordan method.* We will first give the general idea of the method and then consider the practical implementation. Given a matrix A whose inverse is required, we first form a so-called *augmented matrix* by writing down an identity matrix next to A thus:

$$(A|I)$$

(The bar in the middle is for convenience of description only. If A is $n \times n$, the augmented matrix is an ordinary $n \times 2n$ matrix.) We then perform elementary row operations on this augmented matrix, to reduce the 'A part' to the identity. This is of course equivalent to premultiplication by a sequence E_1, E_2, . . . , E_k of elementary matrices. Hence we arrive at

$$(E_k \ldots E_2 E_1 A = I \mid E_k \ldots E_2 E_1 I).$$

Notice that the inverse of A is given by the product E_k . . . E_2, E_1. Moreover, this is precisely what is left in the 'I part' of the augmented matrix! In other words, *when we have reduced the 'A part' of the augmented matrix to I, the 'I part' will contain the inverse.*

All we need now is a systematic way of reducing the 'A part' to I. This is achieved by working one column at a time from the left. There are minor differences between the way the method is implemented by hand with simple numbers, and practical calculator/computer implementations. We consider a simple example first.

$$A = \begin{pmatrix} 2 & 4 & 2 \\ 1 & 2 & 2 \\ 2 & 5 & -1 \end{pmatrix}.$$

Form the augmented matrix $(A|I)$.

$$\begin{matrix} 2 & 4 & 2 & 1 & 0 & 0 \\ 1 & 2 & 2 & 0 & 1 & 0 \\ 2 & 5 & -1 & 0 & 0 & 1 \end{matrix}$$

Now by elementary row operations, we systematically reduce the 'A part' to I, working column by column and eliminating using the diagonal elements. Watch out for the row interchange when we get a zero on the diagonal. We will refer to row 2, say, of the current tableau by r2, and use an obvious shorthand notation for the operations. For example, 'r2 × 2' means multiply the second row by 2.

	2	4	2	1	0	0
$r\,2\times2$	2	4	4	0	2	0
	2	5	−1	0	0	1

	2	4	2	1	0	0
$r\,2-r\,1$	0	0	2	−1	2	0
$r\,3-r\,1$	0	1	−3	−1	0	1

	2	4	2	1	0	0
exchange $r\,2, r\,3$	0	1	−3	−1	0	1
	0	0	2	−1	2	0

	2	0	14	5	0	−4
$r\,1-4\times r\,2$	0	1	−3	−1	0	1
	0	0	2	−1	2	0

	2	0	14	5	0	−4
$r\,2\times2$	0	2	−6	−2	0	2
	0	0	2	−1	2	0

	2	0	0	12	−14	−4
$r\,1-7\times r\,3$	0	2	0	−5	6	2
$r\,2+3\times r\,3$	0	0	2	−1	2	0

$r\,1/2$	1	0	0	6	−7	−2
$r\,2/2$	0	1	0	−5/2	3	1
$r\,3/2$	0	0	1	−1/2	1	0

Thus

$$A^{-1}=\begin{pmatrix} 6 & -7 & -2 \\ -5/2 & 3 & 1 \\ -1/2 & 1 & 0 \end{pmatrix}.$$

You should check that $AA^{-1}=A^{-1}A=I$.

For a practicable computer algorithm, this must be modified in two ways, one minor and one very important. Firstly, in the calculation above, we avoided fractions as long as possible. There is no particular advantage in doing this on a computer, so the multiplication of r2 by 2 would not be performed. Instead we would subtract half r1 from r2 in the elimination. Some implementations also get a ‘1’ on the diagonal before eliminating in each column. This requires simply dividing the row in which the diagonal element occurs by the diagonal element.

The second and much more important difference concerns row interchanges. In the example above, we only used a row interchange when it was forced on us by a zero on the diagonal. However it often occurs that in practical calculations, we can get a diagonal element that is not exactly zero but very small. Since we need to divide by these diagonal elements, this is bad news and numerical instability is an almost inevitable consequence. For instance suppose we are working to 4 decimal places and our diagonal element is .0001. This could actually represent anything between .00005 and .00015. Hence if another row had a '1' in this column, when we divide by the diagonal element we would get 10000, but the true value could be anywhere between 6666 and 20000. If at a later stage we were to subtract this from 10000, the answer would be completely meaningless. Thus in a practical general purpose matrix inversion algorithm we must **always** perform row interchanges. More specifically, we look on and below the diagonal (why not above?) to *find the element in the current column which is largest in magnitude* (sign does not really matter here). This element is called the *pivot*. We swap rows so that this element is on the diagonal. This process is known as *partial pivoting*, and is *essential* for a stable algorithm. (Note: the more sophisticated programmer does not explicitly interchange rows in memory as this would waste time: instead the row order is kept in an integer array.) Although this particular algorithm is not usually used in neural computation, the principle illustrated is important. Hardware neural networks often store weights to only 8 or 16 bits. Algorithms which are correct for exact arithmetic might well fail with this relatively small number of significant figures.

We have now answered the question (b) of the previous section: how to calculate the inverse. Another problem we met in that section was how to identify the kernel of a linear transformation, and find a basis for it. If $f(\mathbf{x}) = W\mathbf{x}$, then the kernel is the set of all vectors $\mathbf{x}$ which satisfy $W\mathbf{x} = \mathbf{0}$. Written out in terms of the elements of $\mathbf{x}$, this is a system of linear equations. Rather than deal with this system specifically, we will approach the study of linear equations systematically. As we shall see, there are very close connections between such systems and matrix theory. Consider first the system

$$\begin{aligned} 2x_1 + 4x_2 + 2x_3 &= 1 \\ x_1 + 2x_2 + 2x_3 &= 1. \\ 2x_1 + 5x_2 - x_3 &= 2 \end{aligned}$$

If $\mathbf{x} = (x_1, x_2, x_3)^T$, $\mathbf{b} = (1, 1, 2)^T$ and

$$A = \begin{pmatrix} 2 & 4 & 2 \\ 1 & 2 & 2 \\ 2 & 5 & -1 \end{pmatrix},$$

then it is easily verified that the system of equations may be written in the matrix form

$$A\mathbf{x} = \mathbf{b}. \tag{2.16}$$

We are now familiar with the geometrical interpretation of the columns of A, and the connection with linear transformations. We now see that the *rows* of A are closely connected with linear equations: changing one of the equations changes a row of A. It is this interaction between the row versus column interpretations (geometry versus linear equations) which gives the subject of linear algebra much of its distinctive flavour. Our intuition about one field can be used to understand and prove results about the other.

We want to find the vector $\mathbf{x}$ in (2.16). Since we have already calculated A^{-1} for this particular A, we can easily obtain $\mathbf{x}$ here. We have

$$A^{-1}A\mathbf{x} = A^{-1}\mathbf{b}.$$

Thus

$$\begin{aligned} \mathbf{x} &= A^{-1}\mathbf{b} \\ &= \begin{pmatrix} 6 & -7 & -2 \\ 5/2 & 3 & 1 \\ 1/2 & 1 & 0 \end{pmatrix} \begin{pmatrix} 1 \\ 1 \\ 2 \end{pmatrix} \\ &= \begin{pmatrix} -5 \\ 5/2 \\ 1/2 \end{pmatrix}, \end{aligned}$$

i.e. $x_1 = -5$, $x_2 = 2.5$, $x_3 = 0.5$. You should verify that this is indeed the solution of (2.16) by substituting these values back into the equations.

However this method is really begging the question since of course we would not normally have the inverse available. In fact it is more work to calculate this than to solve the equations directly by eliminating variables. In order to indicate how this is done systematically, we will write out the calculation in the form of an augmented matrix tableau. You should convince yourself that this process can be considered either as the well known process of elimination of variables written out in a formal fashion, or alternatively as performing elementary operations on the matrix $(A \mid \mathbf{b})$. Since these elementary operations are reversible, this interpretation actually proves the validity of the elimination process. The formal elimination process is called *Gaussian elimination*.

We have only one right hand side **b** here so the augmented matrix consists only of A and **b**.

$$\begin{array}{lrrrr} & 2 & 4 & 2 & 1 \\ & 1 & 2 & 2 & 1 \\ & 2 & 5 & -1 & 2 \end{array}$$

$$\begin{array}{lrrrr} & 2 & 4 & 2 & 1 \\ r\,2 - r\,\tfrac{1}{2} & 0 & 0 & 1 & \tfrac{1}{2} \\ r\,3 - r\,1 & 0 & 1 & -3 & 1 \end{array}$$

$$\begin{array}{lrrrr} & 2 & 4 & 2 & 1 \\ \text{exchange} & 0 & 1 & -3 & 1 \\ r\,2 \text{ and } r\,3 & 0 & 0 & 1 & \tfrac{1}{2} \end{array}$$

We have now reduced the tableau to triangular form and *no more elimination is necessary*. Written out in full, the final tableau represents the equations

$$\begin{aligned} 2x_1 + 4x_2 + 2x_3 &= 1 \\ x_2 + 3x_3 &= 1 \\ x_3 &= \tfrac{1}{2} \end{aligned}$$

Thus we have $x_3 = \tfrac{1}{2}$, and *substituting back* into the second and first equations in turn yields

$$x_2 = 1 + 3(\tfrac{1}{2}) = 2\tfrac{1}{2}$$

and

$$2x_1 = 1 - 4(2\tfrac{1}{2}) - 2(\tfrac{1}{2}),$$

whence $x_1 = -5$ as before.

Although many methods for solving linear equations are known, this simple technique is actually the best in a large majority of cases. As far as computer implementation is concerned, similar considerations apply as for finding inverses, although it is not necessary to get '1's on the diagonal. Partial pivoting **must** be applied to retain numerical stability for a general purpose algorithm.

What we have not considered yet is the case when A is not invertible. This is of course the case of main interest when calculating the kernel of the mapping

$f(\mathbf{x}) = W\mathbf{x}$ by solving $W\mathbf{x} = \mathbf{0}$. If W^{-1} exists, we have $\mathbf{x} = W^{-1}\mathbf{0} = \mathbf{0}$, as we could have deduced anyway from Theorem 2.20(b).

Suppose, for instance, that A in (2.16) has rank 2. The set of all possible vectors $A\mathbf{x}$ which is by definition im(A) is thus a plane through the origin as illustrated in Fig. 2.8. Whether (2.16) has a solution therefore obviously depends on whether or not $\mathbf{b} \in$ im(A). In this case the Dimension Theorem 2.26 tells us that ker(A) has dimension 1. Moreover if $\mathbf{x}$ is a solution of (2.16) and $\mathbf{v} \in$ ker(A), then

$$A\,(\mathbf{x} + \mathbf{v}) = A\mathbf{x} + A\mathbf{v} = \mathbf{b} + \mathbf{0} = \mathbf{b}.$$

Thus $\mathbf{x} + \lambda\mathbf{v}$ is also a solution of (2.16). Conversely if $\mathbf{x}_1$ and $\mathbf{x}_2$ are both solutions of (2.16) so that

$$A\mathbf{x}_1 = \mathbf{b} \text{ and } A\mathbf{x}_2 = \mathbf{b}$$

then subtracting the second of these equations from the first gives $A(\mathbf{x}_1 - \mathbf{x}_2) = \mathbf{0}$ so $(\mathbf{x}_1 - \mathbf{x}_2) \in$ ker(A).

To sum up, we have:

Theorem 2.27

The solutions of (2.16) are described as follows. If $\mathbf{b} \notin$ im(A), there is no solution. On the other hand if $\mathbf{b} \in$ im(A), the most general solution of (2.16) takes the form $(\mathbf{x} + \mathbf{v})$ where $\mathbf{x}$ is any particular solution and $\mathbf{v}$ is any vector in ker(A).

□

Recall that the dimension of ker(A) is called null(A). If A is $n \times m$, null(A) = m − col.rank(A). The case of invertible A is of course the special case where $m = n =$ col.rank(A). But we still have not seen how to get $\mathbf{v}$ or indeed $\mathbf{x}$ when A is not invertible. However, the Gaussian elimination process can be modified to deal with this case. Consider the following example.

$$A = \begin{pmatrix} 3 & 2 & 1 \\ 2 & 1 & -2 \\ 1 & 5 & -5 \end{pmatrix} \mathbf{b} = \begin{pmatrix} 5 \\ 4 \\ 15 \end{pmatrix}.$$

In tableau form

$$\begin{matrix} 3 & 2 & 1 & 5 \\ 2 & 1 & -2 & 4 \\ 1 & 0 & -5 & 15 \end{matrix}$$

	3	2	1	5
$r\,2 - \frac{2}{3}\times r\,1$	0	$-\frac{1}{3}$	$-2\frac{2}{3}$	$\frac{2}{3}$
$r\,3 - \frac{1}{3}\times r\,1$	0	$-\frac{2}{3}$	$-5\frac{1}{3}$	$13\frac{1}{3}$

	3	2	1	5
Swap $r\,2$, $r\,3$	0	$-\frac{2}{3}$	$-5\frac{1}{3}$	$13\frac{1}{3}$
	0	$-\frac{1}{3}$	$-2\frac{2}{3}$	$\frac{2}{3}$

	3	2	1	5
	0	$-\frac{2}{3}$	$-5\frac{1}{3}$	$13\frac{1}{3}$
$r\,3 - \frac{1}{2}\times r\,2$	0	0	0	-6

Written out in full, the final triangular system is

$$\begin{aligned} 3x_1 + 2x_2 + \quad x_3 &= 5 \\ \tfrac{2}{3}x_2 - 5\tfrac{1}{3}x_3 &= 13\tfrac{1}{3} \\ 0x_3 &= -6. \end{aligned}$$

Obviously there is no solution. Now suppose we repeat the calculation with the same A, but $\mathbf{b}=(5, 3, 1)^T$. Note that this $\mathbf{b}$ is in the span of the columns of A: add up the first two columns! The final triangular system obtained is now

$$\begin{aligned} 3x_1 + 2x_2 + \quad x_3 &= 5 \\ \tfrac{2}{3}x_2 - 5\tfrac{1}{3}x_3 &= \tfrac{2}{3} \\ 0x_3 &= 0. \end{aligned}$$

The left-hand sides are, of course, the same as before. The third equation is now trivially satisfied. Now we write the first two equations out again but with the x_3 terms transferred to the right-hand side.

$$\begin{aligned} 3x_1 + 2x_2 &= 5 - x_3 \\ \tfrac{2}{3}x_2 &= \tfrac{2}{3} + 5\tfrac{1}{3}x_3 \end{aligned} \qquad (2.17)$$

Note that for *any* choice of x_3 you can solve for x_1 and x_2. Using back substitution we can write down the general solution as a function of $x_3=\lambda$, say. This solution may be written as

$$\begin{pmatrix} x_1 \\ x_2 \\ x_3 \end{pmatrix} = \begin{pmatrix} 1 \\ 1 \\ 0 \end{pmatrix} + \lambda \begin{pmatrix} 5 \\ -8 \\ 1 \end{pmatrix}.$$

This solution is exactly as predicted by Theorem 2.27. The vector $(1, 1, 0)^T$ is a particular solution of the equations corresponding to $\lambda=0$. The vector

$(5, -8, 1)^T$ is a basis for the one-dimensional space ker(A) as is easily verified by setting $\mathbf{b} = (0, 0, 0)^T$.

Gaussian elimination thus provides us with a simple method of determining ker(A): it should be noted, however, that the example above does not in fact capture the most general behaviour possible, as it can happen that we obtain zeros on and below the diagonal *before* reaching the last column. Suppose we wish to determine ker(B) where B is the 4×4 matrix

$$\begin{pmatrix} 1 & 2 & 3 & 4 \\ 2 & 4 & 6 & 4 \\ 3 & 6 & 9 & 8 \\ 1 & 2 & 1 & 2 \end{pmatrix}.$$

The elimination breaks down at the stage

$$\begin{matrix} 3 & 6 & 9 & 8 & 0 \\ 0 & 0 & 0 & -1\tfrac{1}{3} & 0 \\ 0 & 0 & 0 & 1\tfrac{1}{3} & 0 \\ 0 & 0 & -2 & -\tfrac{2}{3} & 0 \end{matrix}$$

since we have zeros on and below the diagonal in the second column. The procedure in this case is simply to skip this column and proceed to the next, but to restart the elimination in the *same* row. For this example we need only interchange the second and fourth rows, and then add the third row to the fourth to complete the elimination with the tableau

$$\begin{matrix} 3 & 6 & 9 & 8 & 0 \\ 0 & 0 & -2 & -\tfrac{2}{3} & 0 \\ 0 & 0 & 0 & 1\tfrac{1}{3} & 0 \\ 0 & 0 & 0 & 0 & 0 \end{matrix}$$

The fourth row is redundant and the third gives $x_4=0$. Substituting into the second gives also $x_3=0$. Finally the first equation gives $3x_1 + 6x_2 = 0$. Setting $x_2=\lambda$ yields $x_1=-2\lambda$. So $\mathbf{x}=\lambda(-2, 1, 0, 0)^T$ and ker(B) is one-dimensional, spanned by $(-2, 1, 0, 0)^T$. The column rank of B is $4-1=3$.

In the two examples we have given the column rank is deficient only by one, and the kernel is one-dimensional. A greater rank deficiency yields only more zero rows at the bottom of the final tableau, enabling two or more of the variables to be set equal to free parameters. While it is not too hard to write down a completely formal description of this process considering all the possible cases, this is rather tedious and not particularly illuminating. Instead, we will use the formal process to prove another closely related result. The reader may have noticed an odd fact about the arguments above. The image and kernel depend on the *columns* of the matrix. But the operations are performed on rows, as is natural for linear equations. More specifically, we fail to get a unique solution to (2.16) if the columns of A are linearly dependent. But we would expect the process to break down if the *rows* of A are dependent since this means that we effectively have two or more equations with the same left-hand side.

Clearly there must be some relationship between linear dependence of rows and columns. To see what this is, define the *row space* of A to be the span of the rows of A, and the *row rank* of A its dimension. The crucial observation is the following lemma.

Lemma 2.28

Let A be an $n \times m$ matrix and E an $n \times n$ elementary matrix. Then

(a) col.rank(EA)=col.rank(A) and
(b) row rank(EA)=row rank(A).

Proof

(a) All the elementary matrices are invertible: to see this note that all the row operations themselves are reversible. Now suppose col.rank$(A)=k$. Let $S=\{\mathbf{s}_1 \ldots \mathbf{s}_k\}$ be a basis for im(A). Then we claim that $R=\{E\mathbf{s}_1 \ldots E\mathbf{s}_k\}$ is a basis for im(EA). For any vector in im(EA) must be the of the form $E\mathbf{x}$ for some $\mathbf{x} \in$ im(A). But $\mathbf{x}$ can be written $\mathbf{x}=\alpha_1\mathbf{s}_1=\ldots \alpha_k\mathbf{s}_k$ for some real numbers $\alpha_1 \ldots \alpha_k$. Then $E\mathbf{x}=\alpha_1 E\mathbf{s}_1+\ldots+\alpha_k E\mathbf{s}_k$, which shows that R spans im(EA). On the other hand if R is not linearly independent then there exist numbers $\beta_1 \ldots \beta_k$, not all zero, with $\beta_1 E\mathbf{s}_1+\ldots+\beta_k E\mathbf{s}_k=\mathbf{0}$. But since E is invertible, this implies $\beta_1\mathbf{s}_1+\ldots+\beta_k\mathbf{s}_k=\mathbf{0}$, contradicting the independence of S. Thus col.rank $(EA)=k$.

(b) If E is an elementary matrix, the rows of EA are linear combinations of those of A and vice versa, so EA has the same row space as A.

□

This lemma tells us that if we perform Gaussian elimination on A we will change neither the row or column ranks. We can now prove:

Theorem 2.29

Let A by any $n \times m$ matrix. The row rank(A)=col.rank(A).

Proof

The idea is to use elimination to reduce A to a form in which both the row and column ranks are obvious. In fact we will see Gauss-Jordan elimination (as we did for finding the inverse), in which we attempt to reduce the columns of A to columns of I. As in the 4×4 example discussed above, we may get stuck with a zero on the diagonal, arriving at the form

$$
\begin{array}{lcccccccc}
 & 1 & 0 & 0 & \cdots & 0 & c_{1,j} & c_{1,j+1} & \cdots \\
 & 0 & 1 & 0 & \cdots & 0 & c_{2,j} & c_{2,j+1} & \cdots \\
 & 0 & 0 & 1 & \cdots & 0 & . & . & \cdots \\
 & . & 0 & 0 & \cdots & . & . & . & \cdots \\
 & . & . & . & \cdots & 1 & . & . & \cdots \\
j\text{th row} \rightarrow & . & . & . & \cdots & . & 0 & c_{j,j+1} & \cdots \\
 & . & . & . & \cdots & . & 0 & . & \cdots \\
 & . & . & . & \cdots & . & . & . & \cdots \\
 & . & . & . & \cdots & . & . & / & \cdots \\
 & 0 & 0 & 0 & \cdots & 0 & 0 & c_{n,j+1} & \cdots
\end{array}
$$

where the c's denote elements in the reduced tableau not known to be either 1 or 0. If this occurs, then we simply proceed to the next column, and eliminate elements off the jth row. Proceeding in this fashion, we eventually reach a matrix in so-called *reduced row echelon form*, in which we have two types of column: Type 1, which are columns of the identity matrix; and type 2, columns with 0 on the row below that on which 1 occurred in the previous type 1 row, and with zeros below that in the column. The jth column above is of this type. (If $m>n$, the latter case may include some complete columns on the right.) Moreover, each row of this matrix starts with at least one more zero than the one above it.

By Lemma 2.28, this matrix has the same row and column rank as A. Notice however that each type 2 column is a linear combination of the type 1 columns to its left. Thus the number of type 1 columns is precisely the column rank of A. On the other hand the 1 in type 1 column is always the first non-zero element in a row, and all rows are of this form except for any zero rows at the bottom. Thus all the non-zero rows are linearly independent, and the number of type 1 columns is also the row rank.

□

Since the column and row ranks of any matrix are always the same, we shall from now on refer only to the rank of the matrix.

2.7 Abstract vector spaces

There are many other mathematical structures which share the basic properties of $\mathbb{R}^n$ that we have discussed in this chapter. Some of these will be of use to us in later chapters, so it is worth making the jump to the abstract mathematical structure known as a *vector* or *linear space*. It will avoid confusion to realise that in mathematics, the term 'space' does not have any particular connotation of physical space: it simply refers to a set with an imposed structure. (Hence we have metric spaces, topological spaces, etc.) We will not have much actual work to do since the proofs in the abstract context are essentially the same as in $\mathbb{R}^n$ and need not be repeated. Our purpose in this section is to understand the nature of the abstraction, and the utility of it. The first generalization to consider is the number set from which the scalars are chosen. For instance we will sometimes need scalars in the complex numbers $\mathbb{C}$ rather than $\mathbb{R}$. The properties that are necessary to form our set of scalars are those of the mathematical structure known as a *field.* (Do not confuse this definition with a field in the sense of an electrical or gravitational field.) All of these properties are, of course, exhibited by $\mathbb{R}$ or $\mathbb{C}$.

Definition 2.30

A *field* $\mathcal{F}$ is a set on which are defined two binary operations + (plus) and $\times$ (times) with the following properties:

(a) $x+y=y+x$ and $x\times y=y\times x$.
(b) If $x, y\in \mathcal{F}$, $x+y$ and $x\times y\in \mathcal{F}$.
(c) If $x, y, z\in \mathcal{F}$, $x\times(y+z)=x\times y+x\times z$.
(d) If $x, y, z\in \mathcal{F}$, $(x\times y)\times z=x\times(y\times z)$.
(e) If $x, y, z\in \mathcal{F}$, $(x+y)+z=x+(y+z)$.
(f) There is an element $0\in \mathcal{F}$ such that $x+0=x$.
(g) There is an element $1\in \mathcal{F}$ such that $1\times x=x$.
(h) If $x\in \mathcal{F}$, there exists an element $-x\in \mathcal{F}$ such that $x+(-x)=0$.
(i) If $x\in \mathcal{F}$, $x\neq 0$, then there is an element $x^{-1}\in \mathcal{F}$ such that $x\times x^{-1}=1$.

□

Other ordinary properties of arithmetic can be obtained from these axioms. Most importantly, we have for any x, $x \times 0 = 0$, for

$$
\begin{aligned}
x^{-1} + 0 &= x^{-1} && \text{:Definition 2.30(i) and (f)} \\
x \times x^{-1} + x \times 0 &= x \times x^{-1} \\
1 + x \times 0 &= 1 && \text{:Definition 2.30(i)} \\
(-1) + 1 + x \times 0 &= (-1) + 1 \\
0 + x \times 0 &= 0 && \text{:Definition 2.30(h)} \\
x \times 0 &= 0 && \text{:Definition 2.30(f)}
\end{aligned}
$$

and also $(-1) \times x = -x$, for

$$
\begin{aligned}
x + -x &= 0 && \text{:Definition 2.30(h)} \\
x + -x + (-1) \times x &= (-1)x \\
(1 + (-1)) \times x &= (-1)x && \text{:Definition 2.30(a) and (c)} \\
0 \times x + -x &= (-1)x && \text{:Definition 2.30(h)} \\
0 + -x &= (-1)x \\
-x &= (-1)x && \text{:Definition 2.30(f)}
\end{aligned}
$$

The rational numbers $\mathbb{Q}$ also form a field. In most cases we use either $\mathbb{R}$ or $\mathbb{C}$. However another useful example is $\mathbb{Z}_p$, where p is a prime number. This consists of the integers $0, 1, \ldots, (p-1)$. Addition and multiplication are defined in the usual way except that if the result is greater than $(p-1)$, the appropriate multiple of p is subtracted to bring it into the right range. For instance in $\mathbb{Z}_7$, $6\times6=36-5\times7=1$. Or, to put it another way, $1/6=6$. (This definition does not require that p be prime, but the condition turns out to be needed to guarantee the existence and uniqueness of the multiplicative inverse.) Vector spaces over $\mathbb{Z}_2$ are used in digital signal processing. Since any field must contain at least 0 and 1, $\mathbb{Z}_2$ is in fact the smallest possible field as it contains only these elements. We will not prove that $\mathbb{Z}_p$ is a field, but the reader may wish to write out the complete multiplication table for $\mathbb{Z}_2$ and $\mathbb{Z}_3$, and verify that every non-zero element does have a multiplicative inverse, i.e. that property (i) holds. $\mathbb{Z}_n$ where n is not prime is an example of the weaker arithmetical structure called a *ring*. It is also possible to discuss linear spaces over rings: these are called *modules*. However we will not consider these further.

In practice, of course we usually omit the 'times' symbol $\times$ when writing expressions, just as in ordinary arithmetic in $\mathbb{R}$.

The formal definition of a vector space over a field $\mathcal{F}$ mirrors the well known behaviour of geometric vectors.

Definition 2.31

A *vector space* V over a field $\mathcal{F}$ is a set on which is defined a binary operation + (plus) and the operation of scalar multiplication of elements of V by $\mathcal{F}$, denoted by writing the element of $\mathcal{F}$ (called the scalar) followed by the element of V with no symbol. These must satisfy the following properties:

(a) If $\mathbf{u}, \mathbf{v}, \mathbf{w}, \in V$, $(\mathbf{u}+\mathbf{v})+\mathbf{w}=\mathbf{u}+(\mathbf{v}+\mathbf{w})$.
(b) If $\mathbf{u}, \mathbf{v} \in V$, $\mathbf{u}+\mathbf{v}=\mathbf{v}+\mathbf{u}$.
(c) There is an element $\mathbf{0} \in V$ such that $\mathbf{0}+\mathbf{u}=\mathbf{u}$ for any $\mathbf{u} \in V$.
(d) For each $\mathbf{u} \in V$, $\mathbf{u}+(-1)\ \mathbf{u}=\mathbf{0}$. (Here -1 is of course the element of $\mathcal{F}$ satisfying $1+(-1)=0$.)
(e) If $t \in \mathcal{F}$ and $\mathbf{u}, \mathbf{v} \in V$, $t(\mathbf{u}+\mathbf{v})=t\mathbf{u}+t\mathbf{v}$.
(f) If $t, s \in \mathcal{F}$ and $\mathbf{u} \in v$, $(t+s)\ \mathbf{u} = t\mathbf{u} + s\mathbf{u}$.
(g) If $t, s \in \mathcal{F}$ and $\mathbf{u} \in V$, $(ts)\mathbf{u} = t(s\mathbf{u})$.
(h) If $\mathbf{u} \in V$, $1\mathbf{u} = \mathbf{u}$ (Here, of course $1 \in \mathcal{F}$.)

□

Convince yourself that all these properties are satisfied when $\mathcal{F}=\mathbb{R}$ and $V=\mathbb{R}^n$.

The following additional properties follow fairly easily from the axioms:

Theorem 2.32

Let $t \in \mathcal{F}$ and $\mathbf{u}, \mathbf{v} \in V$.

(a) $0\ \mathbf{u}=\mathbf{0}$
(b) $t\mathbf{0}=\mathbf{0}$
(c) If $t \neq 0$, and $t\ \mathbf{u}=\mathbf{0}$, then $\mathbf{u}=\mathbf{0}$.
(d) If $\mathbf{u}+\mathbf{v}=\mathbf{0}$, $\mathbf{u}=(-1)\ \mathbf{v}$. (We write $\mathbf{u}=-\mathbf{v}$.)
(e) If $\mathbf{u}+\mathbf{v}=\mathbf{u}$, $\mathbf{v}=\mathbf{0}$.

Proof

(a)

$$\mathbf{u}+(-1)\ \mathbf{u}=\mathbf{0}$$:Definition 2.3(d)

$$(1+(-1))\ \mathbf{u}=\mathbf{0}$$:Definition 2.3(f)

$$0\ \mathbf{u}=\mathbf{0}$$ as required.

Whence

(b)

$$\mathbf{u}+(-1)\ \mathbf{u}=\mathbf{0}$$:Definition 2.3(d)

$$t\mathbf{u}+(-t)\ \boldsymbol{u}=t\ \mathbf{0}$$:Definition 2.3(e) and (h).

$$(t-t)\,\mathbf{u} = t\,\mathbf{0} \qquad \text{:Definition 2.31(e)}$$
$$0\,\mathbf{u} = t\,\mathbf{0} \qquad \text{:Definition 2.30(f)}$$
$$\mathbf{0} = t\,\mathbf{0} \qquad \text{:(a) just proved.}$$

So

$$t\,\boldsymbol{u} = \mathbf{0} \qquad \text{:by hypothesis}$$
$$t^{-1}\,t\,\mathbf{u} = t^{-1}\,\mathbf{0} \qquad \text{:see Definition 2.30(i)}$$
$$1\,\mathbf{u} = \mathbf{0} \qquad \text{:using (b) just proved}$$
$$\mathbf{u} = \mathbf{0} \qquad \text{:Definition 2.31(h)}$$

(d)

$$\mathbf{u} + \mathbf{v} = \mathbf{0} \qquad \text{:by hypothesis}$$
$$\mathbf{u} + \mathbf{v} + (-1)\,\mathbf{v} = \mathbf{0} + (-1)\,\mathbf{v}$$
$$\boldsymbol{u} + \mathbf{0} = (-1)\,\mathbf{v} \qquad \text{:Definition 2.31(d) and (c)}$$
$$\mathbf{u} = (-1)\,\mathbf{v} \qquad \text{:Definition 2.3(c)}$$

(e) Add $-\mathbf{u}$ to each side.

□

These details are rather tedious to check, but worthwhile as in addition to the obvious case of geometric vectors, there are many other examples of vector spaces.

Examples 2.33

(a) Clearly $\mathbb{R}^n$ with the usual elementwise addition and scalar multiplication is a vector space over $\mathbb{R}$.

(b) For any field $\mathcal{F}$, $\mathcal{F}^n$ is a vector space over $\mathcal{F}$, defining the operations in the same way as for the case of $\mathbb{R}$. In particular, bytes of (say) eight bits form a vector space $\mathbb{Z}_2^8$, when addition and scalar multiplication are defined bitwise according to the arithmetic of $\mathbb{Z}_2$. (Of course, this is *not* the same as adding the bytes as binary numbers since no place carry operation is involved!)

(c) For any field $\mathcal{F}$, consider the set of all infinite sequences in $\mathcal{F}$. Such a sequence takes the form $(x_i)=(x_0, x_1, x_2, \ldots)$, where $x_i \in \mathcal{F}$ for all i. If $(y_i)=(y_0, y_1, y_2, \ldots)$ is another such sequence, we define

$$(x_i) + (y_i) = (x_i + y_i) = (x_0 + y_0, x_1 + y_1, x_2 + y_2, \ldots),$$

and for $t \in \mathcal{F}$,

$$t(x_i) = (tx_i) = (tx_0, tx_1, tx_2, \ldots).$$

The zero 'vector' is the sequence with $x_i=0$ for all i. With these operations, the sequences (x_i) form a vector space over $\mathcal{F}$.

(d) Consider the set V of all functions f: $[0, 1]\to\mathbb{R}$.
We define

$$(f+g)(x)=f(x)+g(x)$$

For example, if $f(x)=x^2$, $g(x)=\sin x$, then

$$(f+g)(x)=x^2+\sin x.$$

Define the zero vector to be the function $z(x)=0$ for all x, and multiplication by a real scalar by

$$(tf)(x)=tf(x),$$

so

$$3(\sin x)=3\sin x.$$

Then V is a vector space over $\mathbb{R}$.

□

We shall meet other examples later. Examples 2.33(b) and (c) are fairly straightforward extensions of the space $\mathbb{R}^n$ that we are familiar with. However (d) may seem surprising and take a little getting used to. Treating functions as vectors turns out to be a very powerful idea that will be used extensively in later chapters. As well as example (d) itself, there are many important subspaces. For instance, $C[0, 1]$, the space of all *continuous* functions from $[0, 1]$ to $\mathbb{R}$ is very often used, as are the spaces of polynomials of degree $\leq n$ for some fixed n.

Definition 2.34

A subset P of a vector space V which is itself a vector space under the same operations is called a *subspace* of V. (Note that P must be closed under the vector operations in the sense that if $\mathbf{s}_1$ and $\mathbf{s}_2$ are in P so is $\mathbf{s}_1+t\mathbf{s}_2$.)

□

Example 2.35

The set of polynomial functions of degree ≤ 3 form a subspace of the space in Example 2.33(d).

□

Note that a subset P of a vector space V will automatically inherit most of the vector space properties. To check that P is a subspace, we only need to check Properties 2.16, as in the case of subspaces of $\mathbb{R}^n$.

Definition 2.36 (compare Definition 2.18)

(a) Suppose that in a vector space V, there exists a set S of k vectors, $\mathbf{s}_1, \mathbf{s}_2 \ldots \mathbf{s}_k$ such that any vector $\mathbf{v}$ in V can be expressed as a linear combination of vectors in S, i.e. there exist real numbers $a_1, a_2, \ldots, a_k$ such that

$$\mathbf{v} = a_1\mathbf{x}_1 + a_2\mathbf{x}_2 + \ldots + a_k\mathbf{x}_k.$$

Then V is said to be *finite dimensional*, and S is said to *span* V.

(b) If S spans V, and the vectors of S are linearly independent, then S is said to be a *basis* for V. We write $V=\text{span}(S)$ or $V=\text{span}\{\mathbf{s}_1, \mathbf{s}_2 \ldots \mathbf{s}_k\}$.

□

Note that there is one important difference between Definitions 2.18 and 2.13. In $\mathbb{R}^n$ and its subspaces, there is always a finite spanning set. This may not be the case for a general vector space. Neither Example 2.33(c) nor (d) are finite dimensional. We have already seen the use of bases in $\mathbb{R}^n$. Here is a different example.

Example 2.37

The 'vectors' $1, x, x^2, x^3$ span the space of Example 2.35.

□

As for $\mathbb{R}^n$, we need, in order properly to define the concept of dimension, to show that any basis for V has the same number of elements. The proof is essentially the same as for $\mathbb{R}^n$, but there is a slight complication in that to prove Lemma 2.21 we made use of the equivalence of matrices and linear transformations. We have not yet extended this to the general case. In fact this is best approached in two stages: first the generalization to $\mathcal{F}^n$ and then to an arbitrary finite dimensional space *after* we have defined the dimension.

There is no problem at all in discussing the representation of linear transformations $f: \mathcal{F}^n \rightarrow \mathcal{F}^m$, and we will not even bother to formally restate the Definitions and Lemmas. The definition of a matrix over $\mathcal{F}$ is exactly as Definition 2.1 except that references to the real numbers are replaced by references to $\mathcal{F}$. Linear transformations are defined by Definitions 2.7. The *standard basis* is defined exactly in Definition 2.8, remembering that any field must have elements 0 and 1. Lemmas 2.9 and 2.10 transfer immediately to the general case. Thus we arrive at the following theorem, proved in exactly the same way as Theorem 2.11.

Theorem 2.38

(a) Any linear transformation $f\colon \mathcal{F}^n \to \mathcal{F}^m$ can be represented by an $m \times n$ matrix, and conversely every such matrix yields a linear transformation.
(b) For a given matrix W, the corresponding transformation is given by $f(\mathbf{x}) = W\mathbf{x}$.
(c) For a given transformation f, the corresponding matrix W is formed by taking its jth column as $f(\mathbf{e}_j)$.

□

With this machinery, Lemma 2.15 holds with $\mathbb{R}$ replaced by $\mathcal{F}$.

We can define ker(f) and im(f) as in Definition 2.19, retaining the analogous subspace properties that we found previously: see for instance Theorem 2.20. The definitions of ker(W) and im(W) remain valid but so far only when considering $f\colon \mathcal{F}^n \to \mathcal{F}^m$. Similarly, Lemma 2.21 requires $f\colon \mathcal{F}^n \to \mathcal{F}^m$. We now wish to prove the corresponding result to Theorem 2.22 for *abstract* vector spaces.

Theorem 2.39

Let V be a vector space. Suppose that the sets $\{\mathbf{x}_1 \ldots \mathbf{x}_r\}$ and $\{\mathbf{y}_1 \ldots \mathbf{y}_s\}$ are both bases for V. Then $r=s$.

Proof

The proof is essentially the same as Theorem 2.22, but it does require some care. Since the basis vectors are not vectors in $\mathcal{F}^n$, we cannot form the matrices X and Y used in the previous proof. This makes the argument look somewhat messier, but the basic idea still works.

Suppose that $s \neq r$. Then we may assume without loss of generality that $s > r$. For each $i \leq s$ we have (since the $\mathbf{x}_1 \ldots \mathbf{x}_r$ form a basis)

$$\mathbf{y}_i = a_{1i}\mathbf{x}_1 + a_{2i}\mathbf{x}_2 + \ldots + a_{ri}\mathbf{x}_r$$

for some numbers a_{ij}. We want to show that there are scalars $v_1, v_2, \ldots, v_s$, not all zero, such that

$$v_1\mathbf{y}_1 + v_2\mathbf{y}_2 + \ldots + v_s\mathbf{y}_s = \mathbf{0}$$

since this will contradict the property of a basis that the y_i's are linearly independent. Thus we want

$$v_1(a_{11}\mathbf{x_1} + a_{21}\mathbf{x_2} + ... + a_{r1}\mathbf{x_r}) + ... + v_s(a_{1s}\mathbf{x_1} + a_{2s}\mathbf{x_2} + ... + a_{rs}\mathbf{x_r}) = \mathbf{0}.$$

Rearranging, we see that this will hold if and only if

$$(v_1a_{11} + ... + v_sa_{1s})\mathbf{x_1} + ... + (v_1a_{r1} + ... + v_sa_{rs})\mathbf{x_r} = \mathbf{0}.$$

Since the x_i's are linearly independent, it follows that for each i, $1<i<m$, $v_1a_{i1} + \ldots + v_na_{im}=0$, or, in matrix form, $A\mathbf{v}=\mathbf{0}$. Here $\mathbf{v}$ is a vector in $\mathcal{F}^s$ and A is an $r \times s$ matrix. By Lemma 2.21 either there is a solution $\mathbf{v} \neq \mathbf{0}$, in which case we are done, or there is a vector $\mathbf{p}$ such that $A\mathbf{v}=\mathbf{p}$ has no solution. In this case, we observe that there must, on the other hand, be a vector $\mathbf{v}$ such that

$$v_1\mathbf{y_1} + v_2\mathbf{y_2} + ... + v_s\mathbf{y_s} = p_1\mathbf{x_1} + p_2\mathbf{x_2} + ... + p_r\mathbf{x_r}$$

since the right-hand side is a vector in V and the $\mathbf{y_i}$'s form a basis. Substituting for the $\mathbf{y_i}$'s from (2.18) gives a linear combination of the $\mathbf{x_i}$'s equal to zero and with coefficients the elements of $A\mathbf{v}-\mathbf{p}$. But these cannot all be zero, contradicting the independence of the $\mathbf{x_i}$'s.

□

Now we can give a formal definition of dimension for a general vector space.

Definition 2.40 (compare Definition 2.23)

Let V be a finite dimensional vector space. Suppose that the set $\{\mathbf{x_1} \ldots \mathbf{x_r}\}$ is a basis for V. Then r is said to be the *dimension* of V. We write dim(P)=r. (By convention, the trivial subspace $\{\mathbf{0}\}$ is assumed to have dimension 0).

□

The analogues of Theorems 2.24 and 2.26 present no problems: the proof of the first is identical and the second requires only obvious modifications.

Theorem 2.41

Let P be a subspace of a vector space V and suppose that the set $R=\{\mathbf{x_1} \ldots \mathbf{x_r}\}$ spans P.

(a) There is a subset of R which is a basis for P.

(b) Suppose that the set $S=\{\mathbf{v_1} \ldots \mathbf{y_s}\}$ is linearly independent and dim(P)$\geq s$. Then there is a basis of P of which S is a subset (i.e. any linearly independent

set can be extended to a basis by adding extra vectors.) In particular, if dim(P) $=s$, then S is a basis.
(c) If Q is a subspace of P then Q has a (finite) basis and dim(Q)$\leq$dim(P). If dim(Q)=dim(P), then $Q=P$.

□

Theorem 2.42 (The Dimension Theorem)
Let V and W be finite dimensional vector spaces, and f: $V \rightarrow W$ be a linear transformation. Then rank(f)+null(f)=dim(V).

□

Note that this last result involves linear transformations between *arbitrary* vector spaces, not just $\mathcal{F}^m$ and $\mathcal{F}^n$. While there is no problem in defining these via Definition 2.1 and equation (2.5), we appear to lose the close connection between linear transformations and matrices. But we would like to use the matrix methods of Section 2.6 to find ranks, kernels and so on. Now compare again the proofs of Theorem 2.39 and 2.22. Although identical in concept, the proof of 2.39 looks much messier since we lose the compact matrix representation of the bases. Nevertheless, we were able to use a matrix argument in the proof, which suggest that there should be some way to apply this elegant representation for abstract vector spaces. In fact the proof suggests the way forward: the *coefficients* of linear combinations of vectors in an n-dimensional vector space over $\mathcal{F}$ are elements of the 'concrete' spaces $\mathcal{F}^n$. To do this we need to introduce a new concept, or rather extend one we have already met!

Definition 2.43
Let V and W be finite dimensional vector spaces over a field $\mathcal{F}$ and let f: $V \rightarrow W$ be a linear transformation. If f is 1–1 and onto (i.e. if it has an inverse), then t is said to be an *isomorphism* and the spaces V and W are said to be *isomorphic.*

□

The term 'isomorphic' obviously means 'same form' and we shall see that this is an appropriate description. Since an isomorphism is linear, the vector space properties of V are transferred intact to W. If $\mathbf{v}_1$, $\mathbf{v}_2 \in V$, and $\lambda \in \mathcal{F}$, then $f(\mathbf{v}_1+\lambda\mathbf{v}_2)=f(\mathbf{v}_1)+\lambda f(\mathbf{v}_2)$. Since f is 1–1, any properties that hold in W must hold for the corresponding vectors in V. For example, if $f(\mathbf{v}_1)+\lambda f(\mathbf{v}_2)=\mathbf{0}$, then $f(\mathbf{v}_1+\lambda\mathbf{v}_2)$ $=\mathbf{0}$ and hence $(\mathbf{v}_1+\lambda\mathbf{v}_2)=\mathbf{0}$. Independent vectors in V correspond to independent vectors in W, and conversely dependency relations in V correspond to dependency relations in W. In particular

Theorem 2.44

Let V and W be finite dimensional vector spaces over a field $\mathcal{F}$. Then V and W are isomorphic if and only if $\dim(V)=\dim(W)$.

Proof

'If': Suppose V, W have the same dimension, say n. Let $\{\mathbf{x}_1 \ldots \mathbf{x}_n\}$ be a basis for V and $\{\mathbf{y}_1 \ldots \mathbf{y}_n\}$ be a basis for W.

Define $f(\mathbf{x}_j)=\mathbf{y}_j$, $j=1, 2, \ldots, n$, and extend this linearly to the whole of V, i.e. if

$$\mathbf{v} = \alpha_1\mathbf{x}_1 + \ldots + \alpha_n\mathbf{x}_n,$$

$$f(\mathbf{v}) = \alpha_1\mathbf{y}_1 + \ldots + \alpha_n\mathbf{y}_n.$$

Then f has an inverse defined by $f^{-1}(\mathbf{y}_j) = \mathbf{x}_j = 1, 2, \ldots, n$, (and extended linearly), so it is by definition an isomorphism.

'Only if': Suppose f is an isomorphism from V to W. Since f is 1–1, $\ker(f)$ consists only of the trivial space $\{\mathbf{0}\}$, which has dimension 0. Since f is onto, $W = \mathrm{im}(t)$. Thus by the Dimension Theorem 3.3, $\dim(V)=\dim[\mathrm{im}(t)]=\dim(W)$.

□

This theorem is in a sense 'the same as' Lemma 2.15, but now expressed in the much more powerful and general language of vector spaces.

Theorem 2.44 tells us that all vector spaces over $\mathcal{F}$ of a given dimension are essentially the same, at least as far as their linear structure is concerned, even if their interpretation as concrete spaces is quite different. In particular *every vector space of dimension n over $\mathcal{F}$ is isomorphic to $\mathcal{F}^n$*. If $\{\mathbf{x}_1 \ldots \mathbf{x}_n\}$ is any basis for V,

$$f(\mathbf{x}_j) = \mathbf{e}_j \tag{2.19}$$

defines an isomorphism which we will call the *standard isomorphism*.

Method 2.45

Let V, W be vector spaces of dimension m and n respectively over $\mathcal{F}$, and let g: $V \to W$ a linear transformation. Then g can be represented as an $m \times n$ by a matrix by the following method:

(a) Map V and W to $\mathcal{F}^m$ and $\mathcal{F}^n$ respectively by the standard isomorphisms.
(b) Represent the transformation from $\mathcal{F}^m \to \mathcal{F}^n$ using Theorem 2.38.

□

This might seem complicated, but is actually very simple to do. It is best illustrated by a simple example.

Example 2.46

Let V be the space of polynomials of degree ≤3, and W the space of polynomials of degree ≤2. (Compare Examples 2.35 and 2.37.)

For $p \in V$, define $g(p)$ to be the derivative of p. More specifically if $p(x) = a + bx + cx^2 + dx^3$, then $g(p) = b + 2cx + 3dx^2$. Obviously g is a linear transformation. A basis for V is $\{1, x, x^2, x^3\}$ and for W is $\{1, x, x^2\}$. These correspond to the standard bases in $\mathbb{R}^4$ and $\mathbb{R}^3$. Under the standard isomorphisms, the general element $p(x)$ is represented by $(a, b, c, d)^T$ and its derivative $g(p)$ by $(b, 2c, 3d)^T$. If the matrix representing g is W, the columns of W are the images of the standard basis vectors in $\mathbb{R}^4$. Now $\mathbf{e}_1$ in $\mathbb{R}^4$ corresponds to the polynomial $1 + 0x + 0x^2 + 0x^3$ in V with derivative 0 in W. This corresponds to $\mathbf{0}$ in $\mathbb{R}^3$. The first column of W is therefore $\mathbf{0}$. Similarly $\mathbf{e}_2$ in $\mathbb{R}^4$ corresponds to the polynomial $0 + 1x + 0x^2 + 0x^3$ in V with derivative 1 in W. This corresponds to $\mathbf{e}_1$ in $\mathbb{R}^3$. The second column of W is therefore $\mathbf{e}_1$. Continuing in this way $\mathbf{e}_3$ in $\mathbb{R}^4$ corresponds to the polynomial $0 + 0x + 1x^2 + 0x^3$ in V with derivative $2x$ in W. This corresponds to $2\mathbf{e}_1$ in $\mathbb{R}^3$ giving the third column of W, and the fourth column of W is $3\mathbf{e}_3$. So

$$W = \begin{pmatrix} 0 & 1 & 0 & 0 \\ 0 & 0 & 2 & 0 \\ 0 & 0 & 0 & 3 \end{pmatrix}.$$

To see that this matrix does indeed represent the operation of differentiation, note that

$$\begin{pmatrix} 0 & 1 & 0 & 0 \\ 0 & 0 & 2 & 0 \\ 0 & 0 & 0 & 3 \end{pmatrix} \begin{pmatrix} a \\ b \\ c \\ d \end{pmatrix} = \begin{pmatrix} b \\ 2c \\ 3d \end{pmatrix}.$$

□

As you can see from the example above, the standard isomorphism simply takes a vector $\mathbf{v}$ to its vector of coefficients with respect to the given basis.

Obviously, if we used a different basis for V, we would get a different matrix representing it.

When V is a subspace of $\mathcal{F}^n$, then the standard isomorphism f itself, being linear, can be represented by a matrix. In fact it is easier to write down the matrix of f^{-1}. From (2.19), $f^{-1}(\mathbf{e_j})=\mathbf{x_j}$, where $\mathbf{x_j}$ is the jth basis vector for V. The matrix of f^{-1} is thus the matrix whose columns are the basis vectors. We have already made use of this matrix: see the matrices X and Y in the proof of Theorem 2.22. As in this proof, sometimes it is desirable to use a non-standard basis in $\mathcal{F}^n$. (We shall see a good example when we study eigenvectors in the next chapter.) This can cause confusion if we do not distinguish carefully in our minds between a vector and its coefficients with respect to a given basis: unfortunately the column vector notation obscures this distinction.

Example 2.47

Consider a vector $\mathbf{x}=(x_1, x_2, x_3)^T$ in $\mathbb{R}^3$. Suppose we want to represent $\mathbf{x}$ with respect to the basis

$$\begin{pmatrix}1\\0\\0\end{pmatrix}\begin{pmatrix}1\\1\\0\end{pmatrix}\begin{pmatrix}1\\1\\1\end{pmatrix}.$$

Let $\mathbf{c}$ be the coefficient representation of $\mathbf{x}$ with respect to this basis, i.e.

$$\begin{aligned}\mathbf{x} &= c_1\begin{pmatrix}1\\0\\0\end{pmatrix}+c_2\begin{pmatrix}1\\1\\0\end{pmatrix}+c_3\begin{pmatrix}1\\1\\1\end{pmatrix}\\ &= P\mathbf{c} \qquad (2.20)\end{aligned}$$

where P is the matrix whose columns are the basis, i.e.

$$\begin{pmatrix}1&1&1\\0&1&1\\0&0&1\end{pmatrix}.$$

If we actually want $\mathbf{c}$, we can solve the system (2.20) of linear equations, or, of course, invert P.

□

2.8 The determinant

The final section of this chapter has something of the nature of an appendix. Readers already familiar with determinants can safely omit it. As a computational device, the determinant is now of little importance. However, some use of it is made in theoretical arguments, particularly those relating to eigenvalues which we will need in the next chapter. Thus it is necessary to have some knowledge of determinants. Unfortunately a complete and rigorous exposition of this topic is lengthy and tedious. To avoid this, we will just consider determinants in $\mathbb{R}^2$ and $\mathbb{R}^3$ in detail, finishing with a brief discussion of the general case. In Section 2.5, we found that an $n \times n$ matrix is invertible if it has full rank n. However, the rank is an integer. Either the matrix has rank n or it does not. The rank gives us no idea how close a non-singular matrix might be to being rank deficient. A quantity that gives us some information about this is the determinant. (There are more sophisticated tests for near singularity, but these require more machinery than we have available at present.) Just as linear transformations and matrices are intimately related to the geometrical concept of the scalar product, so the determinant is closely related to another geometrical construct: the vector product. We will in fact use determinants of 2×2 matrices in our study of the vector product, and then use the vector product to get at 3×3 determinants.

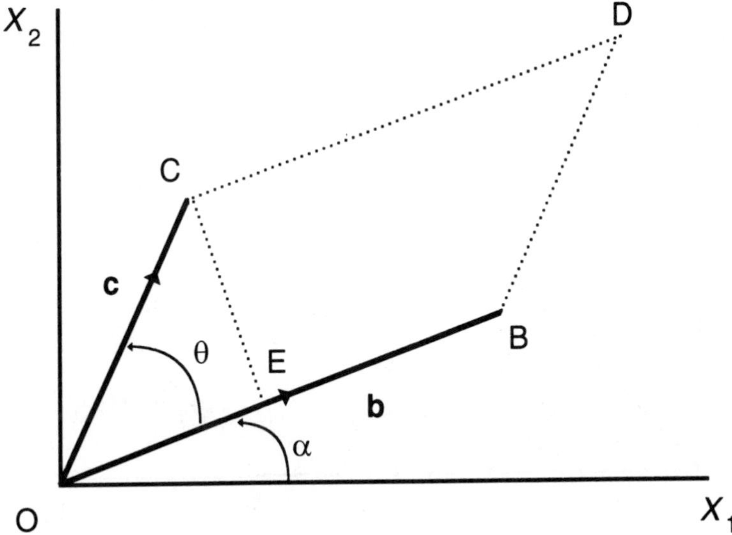

Fig. 2.9

Consider Fig. 2.9. Suppose we form the matrix whose columns are **b** and **c**:

$$\begin{pmatrix} b_1 & c_1 \\ b_2 & c_2 \end{pmatrix}.$$

With $\theta \neq 0$ the matrix will have rank 2. But as θ becomes small, the matrix will become closer and closer to rank deficiency. A natural way to measure this closeness is the area of the parallelogram OCDB. We call this area the *determinant* of the matrix, and we write it as

$$\begin{vmatrix} b_1 & c_1 \\ b_2 & c_2 \end{vmatrix}.$$

Note the use of straight lines instead of brackets. So

$$\begin{aligned} \begin{vmatrix} b_1 & c_1 \\ b_2 & c_2 \end{vmatrix} &= \text{area OCDB} \\ &= \text{OB} \times \text{EC} \end{aligned} \tag{2.21}$$

(i.e. twice the area of triangle OCB).

Formula (2.21) is not very useful however: we want an expression in terms of the elements of **b** and **c**. We could get this by some *ad hoc* geometry, but a more elegant approach is to use our knowledge of linear transformations. Suppose we rotate the parallelogram so that **b** becomes **b′** lying along the x_1

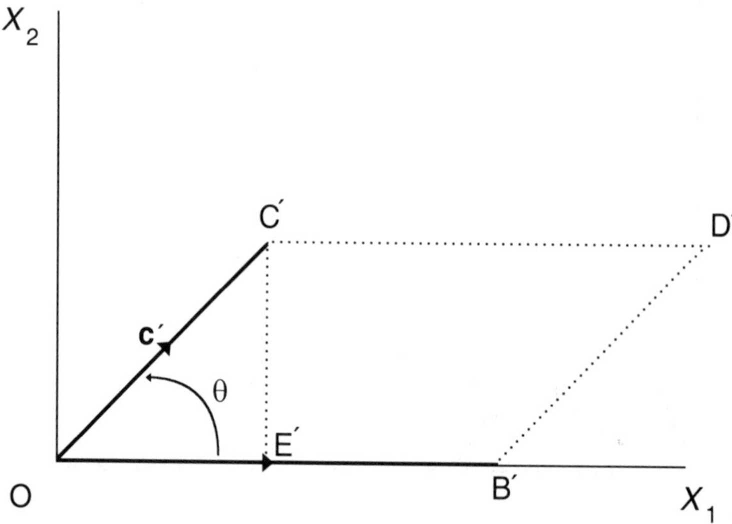

Fig. 2.10

axis (see Fig. 2.10). Obviously a rotation will not change the area or the lengths and angles in the parallelogram. We see immediately that

$$\begin{vmatrix} b_1 & c_1 \\ b_2 & c_2 \end{vmatrix} = \begin{vmatrix} b'_1 & c'_1 \\ b'_2 & c'_2 \end{vmatrix} = c'_2 b'_1. \tag{2.22}$$

Moreover $b'_1 = \|\mathbf{b}\|_2$. But we need to express c'_2 in terms of the original vectors **b** and **c**. We have

$$\mathbf{c}' = R\mathbf{c}$$

where R is the matrix corresponding to a rotation through $-\alpha$. So (compare Fig. 2.6)

$$R = \begin{pmatrix} \cos\alpha & \sin\alpha \\ -\sin\alpha & \cos\alpha \end{pmatrix}$$

$$= \begin{pmatrix} b_1/\|\mathbf{b}\|_2 & b_2/\|\mathbf{b}\|_2 \\ -b_2/\|\mathbf{b}\|_2 & b_1/\|\mathbf{b}\|_2 \end{pmatrix} \text{from Fig. 2.9}$$

$$= \frac{1}{\|\mathbf{b}\|_2} \begin{pmatrix} b_1 & b_2 \\ -b_2 & b_1 \end{pmatrix}.$$

Thus

$$\mathbf{c}' = R\mathbf{c} = \frac{1}{\|\mathbf{b}\|_2} \begin{pmatrix} b_1c_1 + b_2c_2 \\ -b_2c_1 + b_1c_2 \end{pmatrix}.$$

Finally we substitute c_2 and $b_1 = \|\mathbf{b}\|_2$ into (2.22) to get

$$\begin{vmatrix} b_1 & c_1 \\ b_2 & c_2 \end{vmatrix} = c'_2 b'_1 = (b_1c_2 - b_2c_1). \tag{2.23}$$

Note the diagonal pattern: opposite corners are multiplied. In terms of the normal notation for matrices, i.e.

$$A = \begin{pmatrix} a_{11} & a_{12} \\ a_{21} & a_{22} \end{pmatrix} \text{ we get } \begin{vmatrix} a_{11} & a_{12} \\ a_{21} & a_{22} \end{vmatrix} = a_{11}a_{22} - a_{21}a_{12}.$$

This is the standard formula for the determinant of a 2×2 matrix. Although it represents an area, it is clear from (2.23) that the determinant can be negative. If we rotate from **b** to **c** in the usual anticlockwise direction as we showed it in the diagrams, we will get a positive determinant. Reversing the roles of **b** and **c** will give a clockwise angle and a negative determinant. To see this simply observe that interchanging **b** and **c** in (2.23) reverses the sign.

We now need to discuss planes in three dimensional space. We need some way to describe the direction that they face. The convenient way to do this is in terms of a vector perpendicular to the plane. Such a vector is called a *normal* to the plane. (The term is also used as an adjective: we talk about a vector being normal to a plane.) In three dimensions, two vectors **b** and **c** define a plane. We will call the normal to this plane **n**. See Fig. 2.11. To standardise the scale we make **n** a unit vector: a vector satisfying $\|\mathbf{n}\|_2=1$. Unfortunately there are still two choices for **n**, up (as we have drawn it in Fig. 2.11) or down. By convention, we adopt a so-called right-handed system. Consider an ordinary right-hand thread screw at the point 0. Turn a screwdriver in the anticlockwise sense from **b** to **c**, as indicated by the direction of the angle θ marked. We will be unscrewing the screw. We agree to choose **n** in the direction of movement of this screw, which is the direction is is shown in the figure.

Definition 2.48

The vector product $\mathbf{b} \wedge \mathbf{c}$ is defined to be

$$\mathbf{b} \wedge \mathbf{c} = \mathbf{n}\, \|\mathbf{b}\|_2\, \|\mathbf{c}\|_2 \sin\theta. \tag{2.24}$$

(We usually read the '$\wedge$' symbol as 'cross', even though it isn't a cross. Some books actually use the $\times$ symbol, but as we have used this extensively for other purposes, we will stick to the alternative inverted v.)

□

For example, $\mathbf{e}_1 \wedge \mathbf{e}_2 = \mathbf{e}_3$ since the angle between $\mathbf{e}_1$ and $\mathbf{e}_2$ is 90°.

Remark 2.49

Observe the relationship of the vector product to the 2×2 determinant. The length AC in Fig. 2.11 is $\|\mathbf{c}\|_2 \sin\theta$, so $\|\mathbf{b} \wedge \mathbf{c}\|_2 = \|\mathbf{b}\|_2\, \|\mathbf{c}\|_2\, |\sin\theta|$ is the area of the parallelogram formed by **b** and **c**.

□

We need to get an expression for the vector product in terms of the elements of the vectors **b** and **c**. We do this by first proving the distributive law. This is a little technical, and readers wishing to get an overview of the subject, rather than fill in every mathematical detail, might prefer to take Theorem 2.51 as read, and proceed from there.

To get a handle on the distributive law, we split **c** into components parallel and perpendicular to **b**. (This is called resolving **c** in the two directions.) It turns out that the component parallel to **b** does not contribute to the vector product.

Lemma 2.50

(a) $\mathbf{b} \wedge \mathbf{c} = \mathbf{b} \wedge \mathbf{c}'$, where $\mathbf{c}'$ is the projection of **c** onto a plane perpendicular to **b**.

(b) The mapping $\mathbf{c} \to \mathbf{c}'$ is given by $\mathbf{c}' = (I - \mu \mathbf{b}\mathbf{b}^T)\mathbf{c}$ where $\mu = 1 / \|\mathbf{b}\|_2$, and is therefore linear (for fixed **b**).

Proof

(a) Refer again to Fig. 2.11. The vector $\mathbf{c}'$ is the line segment AC. Since **b**, **c** and $\mathbf{c}'$ are coplanar, $\mathbf{b} \wedge \mathbf{c}$ and $\mathbf{b} \wedge \mathbf{c}'$ share the same unit vector **n**. But the area of the parallelogram (equal to $\|\mathbf{b} \wedge \mathbf{c}\|_2$ in view of Remark 2.49) defined by **b** and **c** is precisely $\|\mathbf{b}\|_2 \, \|\mathbf{c}'\|_2$. This is also equal to $\|\mathbf{b} \wedge \mathbf{c}'\|_2$ by Remark 2.49, since $\sin 90° = 1$. Hence $\mathbf{b} \wedge \mathbf{c} = \mathbf{b} \wedge \mathbf{c}'$.

(b) The formula for $\mathbf{c}'$ given here may look complicated, but actually it simply expresses the fact that **c** is the sum of $\mathbf{c}'$ and the vector line segment OA. A unit vector in the direction of **b** is $\mathbf{b} / \|\mathbf{b}\|_2$. The length of OA is $\|\mathbf{c}\|_2 \cos \theta = \mathbf{c}^T\mathbf{b} / \|\mathbf{b}\|_2$ by Theorem 2.5. Hence vector OA is $(\mathbf{c}^T\mathbf{b} / \|\mathbf{b}\|_2) \, \mathbf{b} / \|\mathbf{b}\|_2$ which we may express as $\mathbf{b} \, (\mu \, \mathbf{b}^T\mathbf{c})$. (Note that the term in brackets is a scalar.) Then

$$\mathbf{c} = \mathbf{b} \, (\mu \mathbf{b}^T \mathbf{c}) + \mathbf{c}'$$

so

$$\begin{aligned} \mathbf{c}' &= \mathbf{c} - \mathbf{b} \, (\mu \mathbf{b}^T \mathbf{c}) \\ &= \mathbf{c} - \mu \mathbf{b} \, (\mathbf{b}^T \mathbf{c}) \\ &= (I - \mu \mathbf{b}\mathbf{b}^T)\mathbf{c}. \end{aligned}$$

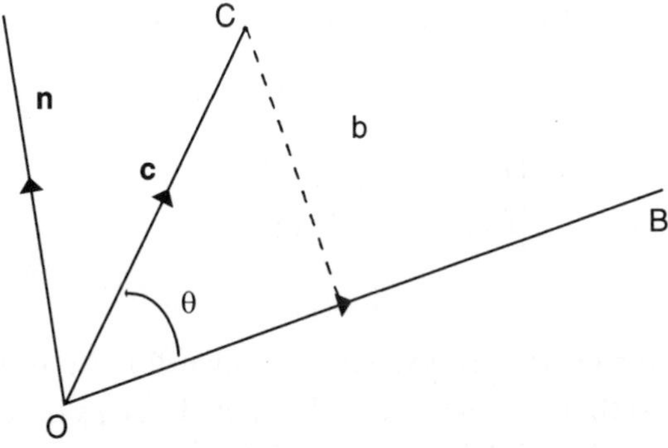

Fig. 2.11

Since the quantity in brackets is a matrix, the mapping is linear.

□

We are now in a position to prove the distributive law (or rather laws, since we have left and right ones).

Theorem 2.51

(a) $\mathbf{b} \wedge \mathbf{c} = -\mathbf{c} \wedge \mathbf{b}$.
(b) $\mathbf{b} \wedge (\mathbf{c}+\mathbf{d}) = \mathbf{b} \wedge \mathbf{c} + \mathbf{b} \wedge \mathbf{d}$ (the Left Distributive Law)
(c) $(\mathbf{c}+\mathbf{d}) \wedge \mathbf{b} = \mathbf{c} \wedge \mathbf{b} + \mathbf{d} \wedge \mathbf{b}$ (the Right Distributive Law)

Proof

(a) This is an immediate consequence of Definition 2.48. If θ is measured in the reverse direction (so the screw is turned the other way) the direction of the unit vector is reversed.
(b) To prove this, it is obviously sufficient to show that the mapping $\mathbf{c} \to \mathbf{b} \wedge \mathbf{c}$ (for fixed $\mathbf{b}$) is linear. With the same notation as Lemma 2.50(b), we already know that the mapping $\mathbf{c} \to \mathbf{c}'$ is linear, and that $\mathbf{b} \wedge \mathbf{c} = \mathbf{b} \wedge \mathbf{c}'$. It remains to show that the map $\mathbf{c}' \to \mathbf{b} \wedge \mathbf{c}'$ is linear. But a study of Fig. 2.11 reveals that this map simply takes $\mathbf{c}'$, rotates it through 90° anticlockwise, and then stretches it by a factor $\|\mathbf{b}\|_2$. Both rotation and stretching are linear. Thus the proof is complete.
(c) follows immediately from (a) and (b).

□

Now we can obtain our formula for the vector product in terms of the elements of $\mathbf{b}$ and $\mathbf{c}$. An obvious but tedious way to do this is to write $\mathbf{b}$ and $\mathbf{c}$ in terms of the standard basis and multiply out. We obtain

Theorem 2.52

$$\mathbf{b} \wedge \mathbf{c} = \mathbf{e}_1 \begin{vmatrix} b_2 & c_2 \\ b_3 & c_3 \end{vmatrix} - \mathbf{e}_2 \begin{vmatrix} b_1 & c_1 \\ b_3 & c_3 \end{vmatrix} + \mathbf{e}_3 \begin{vmatrix} b_1 & c_1 \\ b_2 & c_2 \end{vmatrix}.$$

Proof

Note that $\mathbf{e}_1 \wedge \mathbf{e}_2 = \mathbf{e}_3$ with equivalent formulae for the other pairs of basis vectors. Note also that $\mathbf{e}_1 \wedge \mathbf{e}_1 = 0$, etc. We write $\mathbf{b} \wedge \mathbf{c}$ as $(b_1\,\mathbf{e}_1 + b_2\,\mathbf{e}_2 + b_3\,\mathbf{e}_3) \wedge (c_1\,\mathbf{e}_1 + c_2\,\mathbf{e}_2 + c_3\,\mathbf{e}_3)$. Multiplying out all the terms gives the required result.

□

This formula has many applications in geometry and physics, but they are not particularly relevant here. Our purpose is to obtain a formula for the determinant in three dimensions.

Figure 2.12 shows a parallelopiped formed from three vectors **b**, **c**, and **d**. We wish the determinant det(B) of the matrix

$$B = \begin{pmatrix} d_1 & b_1 & c_1 \\ d_2 & b_2 & c_2 \\ d_3 & b_3 & c_3 \end{pmatrix}$$

to be the volume of this parallelopiped.

We already know that the area of the base formed by **b** and **c** is $\|\mathbf{b} \wedge \mathbf{c}\|_2$. If **n** is the unit vector perpendicular to this base, the height of the parallelopiped is $\mathbf{d}^{\mathrm{T}}\mathbf{n}$. Thus (apart from possibly the sign), the volume is given by the so-called *scalar triple product* $\mathbf{d}^{\mathrm{T}}(\mathbf{b} \wedge \mathbf{c})$. We therefore take this as the definition of the 3×3 determinant:

$$\begin{vmatrix} d_1 & b_1 & c_1 \\ d_2 & b_2 & c_2 \\ d_3 & b_3 & c_3 \end{vmatrix} = d_1 \begin{vmatrix} b_2 & c_2 \\ b_3 & c_3 \end{vmatrix} - d_2 \begin{vmatrix} b_1 & c_1 \\ b_3 & c_3 \end{vmatrix} + d_3 \begin{vmatrix} b_1 & c_1 \\ b_2 & c_2 \end{vmatrix}. \tag{2.25}$$

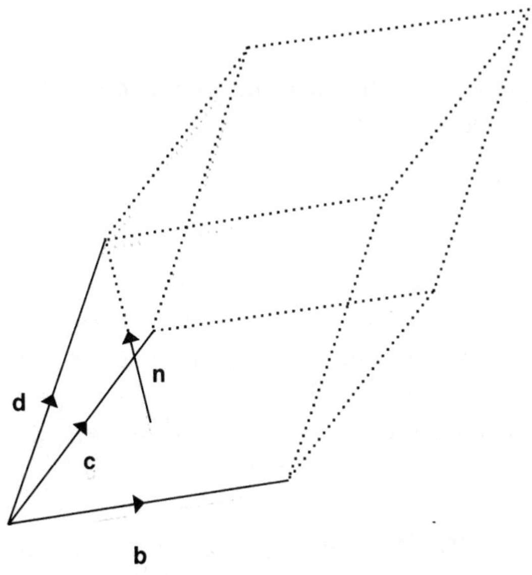

Fig. 2.12

Note the alternation in sign, and the fact that each 2×2 sub-determinant is obtained by deleting the first column, and the row corresponding to the d element, from the 3×3 determinant. This makes the formula easy to remember! Use of the formula (2.25) is called *expanding* the determinant.

The volume of the parallelopiped and hence the *determinant will be zero if and only if the matrix has no inverse* since this means it does not have full rank.

Example

$$\begin{vmatrix} 1 & 2 & -1 \\ 0 & 1 & 3.5 \\ 0 & 2 & 7 \end{vmatrix} = 1\begin{vmatrix} 1 & 3.5 \\ 2 & 7 \end{vmatrix} - 0\begin{vmatrix} 2 & -1 \\ 2 & 7 \end{vmatrix} + 0\begin{vmatrix} 2 & -1 \\ 1 & 3.5 \end{vmatrix}$$

$$= 1\ (7-7) = 0.$$

□

The two key properties of determinants are given by the following theorem.

Theorem 2.53

(a) $\det(A\ B)=\det(A)\ \det(B)$.

(b) $\det(B^{\mathrm{T}})=\det(B)$

Proof

These results depend on the fact that the product $\mathbf{d}^{\mathrm{T}}(\mathbf{b}\wedge\mathbf{c})$ is linear in each of $\mathbf{d}$, $\mathbf{b}$ and $\mathbf{c}$. For example, if $t\in\mathbb{R}$,

$$\mathbf{d}^{\mathrm{T}}(\mathbf{b}\wedge(\mathbf{c}_1+\mathbf{t}\mathbf{c}_2)) = \mathbf{d}^{\mathrm{T}}(\mathbf{b}\wedge\mathbf{c}_1) + t\mathbf{d}^{\mathrm{T}}(\mathbf{b}\wedge\mathbf{c}_2)$$

and similarly for $\mathbf{d}$ and $\mathbf{b}$.

(a) This surprising and beautiful result can be proved in two ways. The first is based on elementary matrices. If A or B is singular, each side of the equation is zero, so we need only consider the case where neither A nor B is singular. We saw in Section 2.6 that B^{-1} can be expressed as a product of elementary matrices. Since each of these is non singular we can write B itself as

$$B = E_1 E_2 \ldots E_k. \tag{2.26}$$

So if we can show that $\det(AE)=\det(A)\ \det(E)$ for any elementary matrix E, then repeated application of this will yield the required result. AE is an elementary column operation on A. (We need to use columns since the determinant (2.25) is defined in terms of columns.) Thus det(AE) can be found by considering the effect of a column operation on the scalar triple product, and det(E) can be found explicitly: E has mostly zero elements. This approach is not too hard to carry out, but it is tedious as there are lots of cases to check, so we will not give the details here.

The following alternative proof is somewhat more demanding, but much shorter. Let B be the matrix with columns **d**, **b** and **c** as above. Let A have columns $\mathbf{a}_1$, $\mathbf{a}_2$ and $\mathbf{a}_3$. We recall that the columns of AB are $A\mathbf{d}$, $A\mathbf{b}$ and $A\mathbf{c}$. Hence

$$\begin{aligned} \det(B) &= \mathbf{d}^{\mathrm{T}}(\mathbf{b} \wedge \mathbf{c}) \\ &= \mathbf{d}^{\mathrm{T}}[(b_1\mathbf{e}_1 + b_2\mathbf{e}_2 + b_3\mathbf{e}_3) \wedge (c_1\mathbf{e}_1 + c_2\mathbf{e}_2 + c_3\mathbf{e}_3)] \end{aligned} \tag{2.27}$$

and

$$\begin{aligned} \det(AB) &= (A\mathbf{d}^{\mathrm{T}})[(A\mathbf{b}) \wedge (A\mathbf{c})] \\ &= \mathbf{d}^{\mathrm{T}}A^{\mathrm{T}}[(b_1\mathbf{a}_1 + b_2\mathbf{a}_2 + b_3\mathbf{a}_3) \wedge (c_1\mathbf{a}_1 + c_2\mathbf{a}_2 + c_3\mathbf{a}_3)] \\ &= \mathbf{d}^{\mathrm{T}}[b_1A^{\mathrm{T}}\mathbf{a}_1 + b_2A^{\mathrm{T}}\mathbf{a}_2 + b_3A^{\mathrm{T}}\mathbf{a}_3) \wedge (c_1\mathbf{a}_1 + c_2\mathbf{a}_2 + c_3\mathbf{a}_3)] \end{aligned} \tag{2.28}$$

The crucial observation is that the coefficient of $\mathbf{e}_i \wedge \mathbf{e}_j$ in the vector product term of (2.27) is the same as the coefficient of $A^{\mathrm{T}}\mathbf{a}_i \wedge \mathbf{a}_j$ in (2.28).

For example, the coefficient of $\mathbf{e}_1 \wedge \mathbf{e}_2$ in (2.27) (not including the coefficient of $\mathbf{e}_2 \wedge \mathbf{e}_1$) is $b_1 c_2$, which is the same as the coefficient of $\mathbf{A}^{\mathrm{T}}\mathbf{a}_1 \wedge \mathbf{a}_2$. (If it is not obvious from the expressions that these coefficients must be the same, consider the special case of (2.28) where $A=I$.) So we need only to show that

$$A^{\mathrm{T}}\mathbf{a}_i \wedge \mathbf{a}_j = \det(A)\mathbf{e}_i \wedge \mathbf{e}_j. \tag{2.29}$$

Now if $i=j$, each side of (2.29) is zero, since the vector product of any vector with itself is zero. For the case $i \neq j$, we observe that the left-hand side of (2.29) is the vector

$$\begin{pmatrix} \mathbf{a}_1^{\mathrm{T}}(\mathbf{a}_i \wedge \mathbf{a}_j) \\ \mathbf{a}_2^{\mathrm{T}}(\mathbf{a}_i \wedge \mathbf{a}_j) \\ \mathbf{a}_3^{\mathrm{T}}(\mathbf{a}_i \wedge \mathbf{a}_j) \end{pmatrix}.$$

Consider for instance the case $i=1, j=2$. Since $\mathbf{a}_1 \wedge \mathbf{a}_2$ is orthogonal to both $\mathbf{a}_1$ and $\mathbf{a}_2$, the first two elements of this vector are zero. The third element is det(A). The vector is thus det(A) $\mathbf{e}_3$=det(A) $\mathbf{e}_1 \wedge \mathbf{e}_2$ as required. The other elements are dealt with similarly.

(b) This result is best proved using elementary matrices. As in (2.26) we write

$$B = E_1 E_2 \ldots E_k.$$

In view of part (a)

$$\det(B) = \det(E_1) \times \det(E_2) \times \ldots \times \det(E_k).$$

But

$$B^{\mathrm{T}} = E_k{}^{\mathrm{T}} \ldots E_1{}^{\mathrm{T}}$$

and

$$\det(B^{\mathrm{T}}) = \det(E_k{}^{\mathrm{T}} \times \ldots \times \det(E_1{}^{\mathrm{T}}).$$

Hence we need only to prove that $\det(E^{\mathrm{T}}) = \det(E)$ for elementary matrices. We consider the three types separately. Multiplication of a row by a scalar s corresponds to a matrix of the form

$$\begin{pmatrix} 1 & 0 & 0 \\ 0 & s & 0 \\ 0 & 0 & 1 \end{pmatrix}. \tag{2.30}$$

This matrix is symmetric, i.e. $E^{\mathrm{T}} = E$. So $\det(E^{\mathrm{T}}) = \det(E)$. Similarly, matrices corresponding to row interchanges are symmetric. Adding a multiple s of a row to another corresponds to a matrix of the form

$$\begin{pmatrix} 1 & 0 & 0 \\ 0 & 1 & s \\ 0 & 0 & 1 \end{pmatrix}. \tag{2.31}$$

From (2.25) we see that wherever the s element appears in the matrix, in the determinant it is multiplied by zero. So $\det(E) = 1$, and E^{T} is another matrix of the same type which therefore also has determinant 1. This completes the proof. □

Theorem 2.53(b) means that we can expand determinants by rows or columns, whichever is easier.

It is also useful to be able to perform elementary operations on rows and columns of matrices. The permissible operations are given in the following theorem.

Theorem 2.54

(a) Multiplying a row or column of a determinant by s multiplies the determinant by s.
(b) Adding a scalar multiple of a row or column to another does not change the determinant.
(c) Interchanging two adjacent rows or columns multiples the determinants by -1.

Proof

In view of Theorem 2.53(b) it is sufficient to prove each of these for rows or columns.

They can each be proved in two ways: either by direct reference to the scalar triple product, or alternatively by considering the determinant of the corresponding elementary matrix. We will use the second method. As an exercise, you might like to try the other approach.

(a) This operation corresponds to multiplying the matrix by an elementary matrix F of the form (2.30). Then $\det(FB)=\det(F)\det(B)$ by Theorem 2.53(a). If we expand the determinant of F, we find that $\det(F)=s$.
(b) We have already seen that an elementary matrix E of the form (2.31) has determinant 1.
(c) Interchanging adjacent rows corresponds to an elementary matrix which is almost the identity matrix, but with one pair of adjacent 1's shifted off the diagonal, e.g.

$$\begin{pmatrix} 1 & 0 & 0 \\ 0 & 0 & 1 \\ 0 & 1 & 0 \end{pmatrix}.$$

Expanding the determinant of this matrix yields -1, as required.

□

For example, using c for column and r for row,

$$\begin{vmatrix} 203 & 200 & 201 \\ 412 & 401 & 403 \\ 520 & 510 & 504 \end{vmatrix}$$

$$\begin{matrix} c2 \text{ from} = \\ c1 \text{ and } c3 \end{matrix} \begin{vmatrix} 3 & 200 & 1 \\ 11 & 401 & 2 \\ 10 & 510 & -6 \end{vmatrix}$$

$$\begin{array}{ll} 2\times r1\text{from } r2 \\ 2\times r1\text{from } r3 \end{array} = \begin{vmatrix} 3 & 200 & 1 \\ 5 & 1 & 0 \\ 4 & 110 & -8 \end{vmatrix}.$$

$$\text{Swap } c2, c3 \quad = - \begin{vmatrix} 3 & 1 & 200 \\ 5 & 0 & 1 \\ 4 & -8 & 110 \end{vmatrix}$$

$$\text{Swap } c1, c2 \quad = + \begin{vmatrix} 1 & 3 & 200 \\ 0 & 5 & 1 \\ -8 & 4 & 110 \end{vmatrix}$$

which expands to 8522.

□

For most of the material in this chapter, the extension from $\mathbb{R}^3$ to $\mathcal{F}\mathbb{R}^n$ is easy, but the determinant, defined as it is as a volume, requires some thought. There are also computational problems associated with large determinants. So we will give a very brief discussion here of determinants in more than three dimensions. It might be thought that the concept of a volume in more than three dimensions is meaningless or at least useless, but this is far from the case. The integral introduced in Chapter 1 works in any number of dimensions. As a concrete application, a particle of mass m moving in $\mathbb{R}^3$ can be described by six coordinates: three spatial ones x_1, x_2 and x_3, and three momentum coordinates mv_1, mv_2 and mv_3, where the v's denote the components of velocity in the coordinate directions. This representation is called the phase space (see Chapter 5). It turns out that if the particle conserves energy, the volume traced out in the six-dimensional phase space remains constant (the system is said to be *Hamiltonian*), whereas if energy is dissipated, the volume tends to zero. The volume here is defined as an integral and expressed as a determinant.

There are various ways to get at n-dimensional determinants. One approach which retains the geometrical flavour is to extend the idea of a vector product. For instance if we take three 4-vectors $\mathbf{b}_1$, $\mathbf{b}_2$, $\mathbf{b}_3$ we can define their vector product by analogy with Theorem 2.52, with the coefficient of $\mathbf{e}_j$ to be $(-1)^j+1$ times the 3×3 determinant obtained by deleting the jth element from each of the $\mathbf{b}$'s. This can be shown to have most of the desirable properties of the vector product. The projection of a four-dimensional volume onto a three-dimensional space is a three-dimensional volume. Extension to higher dimensions works in the same way.

In order to make the theorems work, we need to know that the vector product is linear in each of the **b**'s. Since we know that this is true for the 3 ×3 determinants, this can be proved by induction over the dimension: i.e. we prove that if it is true for dimension n, it must also be true for dimension $n+1$.

The determinant of a matrix A is obtained as above as the scalar product of the first column with the vector product. Thus:

Definition 2.55

Let an $n\times n$ matrix A have first column **a**, and let A_j denote the $(n-1)\times(n-1)$ matrix obtained by deleting the 1st column and jth row of A. Then

$$\det(A) = \sum_{j=1}^{n} (-1)^{j+1}\mathbf{a_j} \det(A_j).$$

□

For example,

$$\begin{vmatrix} 1\,2\,3\,4 \\ 2\,4\,6\,4 \\ 3\,6\,9\,8 \\ 1\,2\,1\,1 \end{vmatrix} = 1\begin{vmatrix} 4\,6\,4 \\ 6\,9\,8 \\ 2\,1\,2 \end{vmatrix} - 2\begin{vmatrix} 2\,3\,4 \\ 6\,9\,8 \\ 2\,1\,2 \end{vmatrix} + 3\begin{vmatrix} 2\,3\,4 \\ 4\,6\,4 \\ 2\,1\,2 \end{vmatrix} - 1\begin{vmatrix} 2\,3\,4 \\ 4\,6\,4 \\ 6\,9\,8 \end{vmatrix}.$$

and the 3×3 determinants expanded as previously.

Theorems 2.53 and 2.54 can be proved for the general case in the same way.

However, it should be emphasised that expanding determinants by rows or columns is not practicable in more than about three dimensions. The example above gives an indication of the amount of work required to expand even a 4×4 determinant. We have four 3×3 determinants to calculate. Even with computers, expansion of determinants soon becomes impossible. Clearly the number of multiplications required for an $n\times n$ determinant is $n!$: we have n terms each involving an $(n-1)\times(n-1)$ determinant. For instance, a 20×20 matrix would be regarded as small by today's standards. Even the smallest microcomputers could invert it using Gauss–Jordan elimination. But 20! is about 10^{18}. Even assuming a million floating point multiplications per second, we would thus require about 10^{12} seconds for the multiplications, to say nothing of the additions and general overheads. This is rather more than 30,000 years! On the other hand systems of equations are now routinely solved in hundreds or even thousands of variables, but not, of course, using determinants. The tendency nowadays is therefore to avoid determinant methods, but occasionally they are useful from a theoretical point of view. If we *do* need to evaluate large determinants, the best way is to use row operations to reduce them to diagonal form, accumulating the determinants of the elementary matrices as we go along.

3 Eigenvectors and normed vector spaces

3.1 Introduction to eigenvectors

Refer again to Fig. 2.7 in the previous chapter. We considered the case of using a perceptron with weight matrix V to invert the output of a perceptron with weight matrix W (equations (2.7) and (2.8)). The question of when this is *exactly* possible was answered in terms of the rank and kernel of the weight matrix W: equations (2.13) to (2.15) and the surrounding discussion. In fact for a given weight matrix W, an input vector $\mathbf{x}$ could be reconstructed if and only if it satisfied equation (2.13). That discussion led naturally to the question of whether an $\mathbf{x}$ which did *not* satisfy (2.13) could be reconstructed approximately. In this chapter we will develop the machinery for discussing questions of this type. This will require the construction of two distinct but closely related tools: eigenvectors and normed vector spaces. Although we will use the problem of Fig. 2.7 to some extent to motivate the discussion, in fact these tools provide the basic language for handling a wide range of problems relating to neural systems, and thus our development will be rather more general than is required just to solve this particular problem. Eigenvectors will be used extensively in Chapters 4 (Optimisation) and 5 (Dynamical Systems), and the whole of Chapter 6 (Approximation Theory) depends crucially on the concept of a normed vector space.

The fundamental idea behind equation (2.13) was the selection of a particular basis S, with respect to which the problem we were trying to solve had a simple structure. Much of this chapter will be based on this idea. In this section, we will show how a particularly useful basis can be constructed for square matrices. While it is possible to develop this theory in the context of abstract vector spaces, there is no real advantage in doing this at least for finite dimensional spaces, since by Method 2.45 using the standard isomorphism, any such space over a field $\mathcal{F}$ can be regarded as $\mathcal{F}^n$. The use of matrix methods permits a concrete representation of our basis as in Example 2.47. This example, and also the proof of Theorem 2.22, indicate the advantage to be gained in forming the matrix P with the basis vectors as columns. Such a matrix is certainly invertible, since its columns are linearly independent. From equation (2.20) we see that the coefficient vector $\mathbf{c}$ of a vector $\mathbf{x}$ with respect to the basis is given by $\mathbf{c}=P^{-1}\mathbf{x}$. Now consider the linear transformation $f(\mathbf{x})=A\mathbf{x}$, where $\mathbf{x}$ is expressed here with respect to the standard basis. What is the matrix representation of the transformation in terms of $\mathbf{c}$? More precisely, what matrix B represents the linear transformation $g(\mathbf{c})=B\mathbf{c}$, with $B\mathbf{c}=P^{-1}A\mathbf{x}$? The pre-multiplication by P^{-1} is to arrange that the image vector is also expressed in terms of the basis whose columns form P. Since $\mathbf{x}=P\mathbf{c}$, it follows that

$$B = P^{-1}AP. \tag{3.1}$$

Definition 3.1

Two matrices A and B are said to be *similar* if there exists a non-singular matrix P such that $B=P^{-1}AP$.

□

Similarity is an equivalence relation on the set of $m\times n$ matrices (see Theorem 1.3). More concretely, two matrices A and B can be thought of as being similar if they represent the same transformation with respect to different bases. Similar matrices must have the same rank, nullity and (by Theorem 2.53(a)) determinant. Such quantities are said to be *invariant* under the similarity transformation (3.1). A fourth invariant is described in the following definition.

Definition 3.2

The *trace* of an $n\times n$ matrix A is the sum of the elements on the main diagonal, i.e.

$$\text{trace}\,(A) = \sum_{j=1}^{n} a_{jj}.$$

□

To see that the trace is invariant under (3.1), we express P as the product of elementary matrices: compare (2.26). This shows that it is sufficient to prove invariance just for the case when P is elementary. It is then simply a matter of verifying the three cases: the details are left to the reader.

For convenience of reference, we collect these results in a theorem.

Theorem 3.3

Let A and B satisfy (3.1). Then

(a) $\text{rank}(B)=\text{rank}(A)$
(b) $\text{null}(B)=\text{null}(A)$
(c) $\det(B)=\det(A)$
(d) $\text{trace}(B)=\text{trace}(A)$.

□

Actually the trace is less useful than the other invariants, but it has the virtue of being very easy to calculate. Thus is can be used to show that matrices are *not* similar, or as a quick check of hand calculations.

Our task now is to try to find a basis $\{\mathbf{p}_1, \ldots, \mathbf{p}_n\}$ such that

$$P^{-1}AP = D, \tag{3.2}$$

where D is a diagonal matrix: D is said to be *diagonal* if $(D)_{ij}=0$ for $i \neq j$. We start with an example.

Example 3.4

Let

$$A = \begin{pmatrix} 5 & -6 & -6 \\ -1 & 4 & 2 \\ 3 & -6 & -4 \end{pmatrix},\ P = \begin{pmatrix} 2 & 2 & 3 \\ 1 & 0 & -1 \\ 2 & 1 & 3 \end{pmatrix} \text{ and } D = \begin{pmatrix} 2 & 0 & 0 \\ 0 & 2 & 0 \\ 0 & 0 & 1 \end{pmatrix}.$$

Then it is easy to verify that $AP=PD$, which is of course equivalent to (3.2) provided P is not singular. The reader may wish calculate P^{-1} by the method of Section 2.6 and verify that (3.2) does indeed hold. Observe also that trace(A)=trace(D)=5. Also rank(D)=3, which must therefore also be the rank of A.

□

In the next section we shall see how P is constructed: it turns out that we can usually, although not always, find such a matrix. As a partial motivation for such a choice we note that all the invariants of Theorem 3.3 are trivially calculated for a diagonal matrix: the rank is the number of non-zero diagonal elements in D, the nullity is the number of zero diagonal elements, the determinant is simply the product of the diagonal elements and of course the trace is the sum of them. Rewrite (3.2) as

$$PD = AP. \tag{3.3}$$

Let the columns of P be ($\mathbf{p}_1, \ldots, \mathbf{p}_n$) and the diagonal elements of D be ($\lambda_1, \ldots, \lambda_n$). Thus (3.3) is

$$\begin{pmatrix} \\ \mathbf{p}_1 : \mathbf{p}_2 : \ldots : \mathbf{p}_n \\ \\ \end{pmatrix} \begin{pmatrix} \lambda_1 & 0 & \ldots & & 0 \\ 0 & \lambda_2 & 0 & \ldots & 0 \\ 0 & 0 & \lambda_3 & & . \\ . & . & . & & \\ . & . & . & & \\ 0 & \ldots & \ldots & & \lambda_n \end{pmatrix} = A \begin{pmatrix} \\ \mathbf{p}_1 : \mathbf{p}_2 : \ldots : \mathbf{p}_n \\ \\ \end{pmatrix},$$

or, considering the jth column

$$\lambda_j \mathbf{p}_j = A\mathbf{p}_j. \tag{3.4}$$

A basis for ker(A) is provided by those $\mathbf{p}_j$ for which λ_j=0. We emphasize again that even for square matrices we cannot always find a basis such that (3.2) holds, but the foregoing should indicate why it is worth searching for one. We shall see that many other problems involving neural networks can be decomposed by this or similar methods. Equation (3.4) motivates the following definition.

Definition 3.5

If $\mathbf{p}$, λ satisfy

$$A\mathbf{p} = \lambda\mathbf{p} \tag{3.5}$$

with $\mathbf{p} \neq \mathbf{0}$, then $\mathbf{p}$ is said to be an *eigenvector* of A corresponding to the *eigenvalue* λ.

□

If f is the linear transformation $f(\mathbf{x}) = A\mathbf{x}$, $\mathbf{p}$ is also said to be an *eigenvector* of f. Geometrically, the condition (3.5) means, of course, that the direction of $\mathbf{p}$ is not changed by the transformation. If a particular vector $\mathbf{p}$ satisfies (3.5), then so will any non-zero scalar multiple of $\mathbf{p}$. We do not regard these as being essentially different eigenvectors. Instead, we consider the eigenvectors to be defined only up to multiplication by a scalar.

Now let us put this idea into a connectionist context.

Example 3.6

Figure 3.1 *a* and *b* show two 4×4 binary images. We code a black pixel as '1' and a white pixel as '0'. We record the pixels in the normal raster scan order, i.e. by reading left to right across the rows from the top. So each image is described by a vector in $\mathbb{R}^{16}$ whose entries are either 0 or 1. Specifically (*a*) is represented by the vector $\mathbf{x}_1 = (1, 0, 0, 0, 1, 0, 0, 0, 1, 0, 0, 0)^T$ and (*b*) by the vector $\mathbf{x}_2 = (0, 0, 1, 0, 0, 0, 1, 0, 0, 0, 1, 0, 0, 0, 1, 0)^T$. Notice that these two 0–1 vectors are orthogonal: in fact any two vectors of this type are orthogonal if and only if they have no 'on' pixel in common. Moreover $\|\mathbf{x}_1\|_2 = \|\mathbf{x}_2\|_2 = (1^2 + 1^2 + 1^2 + 1^2) = 2$. In fact for any such 0–1 vector, the norm is simply the square root of the number of 'on' pixels. The Euclidean norm is thus closely related to the Hamming metric $d_H(\mathbf{u}, \mathbf{v})$ which is the number of pixels for which $\mathbf{u}$ and $\mathbf{v}$ differ. Specifically $d_H(\mathbf{u}, \mathbf{v}) = \|\mathbf{u} - \mathbf{v}\|_2{}^2 = (\mathbf{u} - \mathbf{v})^T(\mathbf{u} - \mathbf{v})$. Conversely $\mathbf{u}^T\mathbf{v} = d_H(\mathbf{u}, -\mathbf{v}) - d_H(\mathbf{u}, \mathbf{v})$. The Hamming metric is a metric on the set of 0–1 vectors in the sense of Section 1.8. This useful connection allows us to use either geometric methods

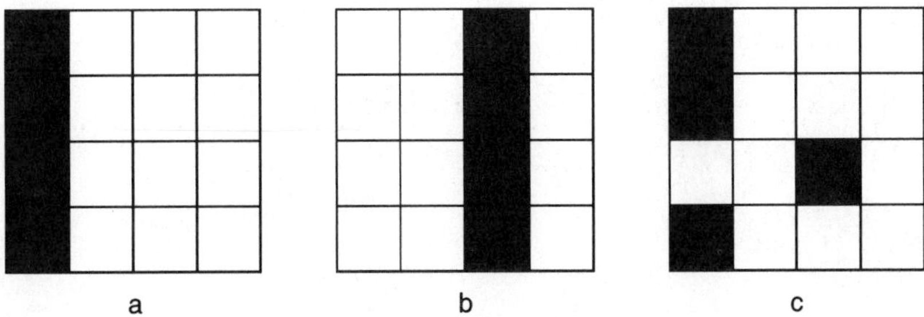

Fig. 3.1

or 'bit counting' methods when discussing 0–1 vectors and matrices, or indeed to mix them.

Figure 3.1 (*c*) shows an image that we might regard as a noisy version of (*a*): two pixels have been flipped. This image corresponds to the vector $\mathbf{y}=(1, 0, 0, 0, 1, 0, 0, 0, 0, 0, 1, 0, 1, 0, 0, 0)^T$. Our aim is to produce a network that will take $\mathbf{y}$ as input and restore it as $\mathbf{x}_1$. Such a network is called an *autoassociative memory*. (The 'auto' part in this title refers to the fact that the network should reconstruct the learned patterns $\mathbf{x}_i$.) We will use a linear network like Fig 2.1. However, here we need the same number of outputs as inputs, and for input $\mathbf{y}$ we want output $\mathbf{x}_1$. So we seek a 16×16 weight matrix W with eigenvectors $\mathbf{x}_1$ and $\mathbf{x}_2$, i.e. scalars λ_1, λ_2 with $W\mathbf{x}_1=\lambda_1\mathbf{x}_1$ and $W\mathbf{x}_2=\lambda_2\mathbf{x}_2$. (As we shall see, it is convenient not to insist that $\lambda_1=\lambda_2=1$.) Moreover we would like $W\mathbf{y}\approx\lambda_1\mathbf{x}_1$. Further, we would like any vector $\mathbf{u}$ which is orthogonal to $\mathbf{x}_1$ and $\mathbf{x}_2$ not to be 'recognised', i.e. $W\mathbf{u}=\mathbf{0}$. Thus we wish $\mathbf{x}_1$ and $\mathbf{x}_2$ to be eigenvectors of W corresponding to eigenvectors λ_1 and λ_2, and any orthogonal vector $\mathbf{u}$ to be an eigenvector corresponding to $\mathbf{0}$. For the simple situation we have here, we can achieve this by means of a simple learning algorithm known as *Hebbian reinforcement*. (See, e.g. Kohonen (1972).) Specifically, start with $W=0$. For each of our t standard patterns $\mathbf{x}_i$, $i=1, 2 \ldots t$, where in this example $t=2$, we add $\mathbf{x}_i\mathbf{x}_i^T$ to W. When we have done this for all the patterns we have

$$W=\sum_{i=1}^{t} \mathbf{x}_i\mathbf{x}_i^{T}. \tag{3.6}$$

The matrix W is too large to write out here, but you may find it illuminating to calculate it for yourself. We can see from (3.11) that W has the required properties. For

$$W\mathbf{x}_j=\sum_{i=1}^{t} \mathbf{x}_i\mathbf{x}_i^{T}\mathbf{x}_j=\|\mathbf{x}_j\|_2^2\mathbf{x}_j$$

since the $\mathbf{x}_i$'s are orthogonal. We have $\lambda_i=\|s\mathbf{x}_j\|_2^2$, $i=1, 2$.

For the input $\mathbf{y}$ we get

$$W\,\mathbf{y}=\sum_{i=1}^{t} \mathbf{x}_i\mathbf{x}_i^{T}\mathbf{y}. \tag{3.7}$$

Now $\mathbf{x}_i^T\mathbf{y}$ is the number of 'on' pixels in which $\mathbf{y}$ agrees with $\mathbf{x}_i$: 3 for $\mathbf{x}_1$ and 1 for $\mathbf{x}_2$. So $W\mathbf{y}=3\mathbf{x}_1+\mathbf{x}_2=(3, 0, 1, 0, 3, 0, 1, 0, 3, 1, 0, 3, 0, 1, 0)^T$. In fact if a threshold of 2 is applied to this vector to make it into a 0–1 vector again, i.e. the elements larger than 2 are set to 1, and elements smaller than 2 to 0, we reconstruct $\mathbf{x}_1$ exactly.

For a general $\mathbf{y}$, suppose $\mathbf{y}$, had d_1 'on' pixels in common with $\mathbf{x}_1$ and d_2 in common with $\mathbf{x}_2$. Suppose $d_1 > d_2$. In (3.7) we will get

$$(W\,\mathbf{y})/d_1 = \mathbf{x}_1 + (d_1/d_2)\mathbf{x}_2.$$

Thus any choice of threshold between 1 and (d_1/d_2) will recover $\mathbf{x}_1$ exactly. Of course in practice we would not know d_1 or d_2, but it is sufficient simply to set all the elements in $W\mathbf{y}$ which are equal to the maximum value, to 1, and all other elements of zero.

□

This example may seem very artificial in that the two learned patterns are orthogonal, which in this context of course means that they have no 1's in common. In general it would not be reasonable to expect this. On the other hand, consider a more realistically sized image: say 256×256. Suppose that this image has had an edge detector applied to it, followed by a threshold operation. The result is likely to be an image made up of lines only one or two pixels wide. Assuming there were not too many objects in the original scene, only a small proportion of the pixels will be 'on'. If we are planning to recognise a set of simple features in the scene, these training features will be made up of edges, and the edges representing different features will intersect at only a very few points. Images are two dimensional whereas edges are made up of line segments which are one-dimensional and thus edge pixels are 'rare'. *Intersections* of edges are points (zero-dimensional) and are thus rare even compared to edge pixels. This means that the features will be *nearly* orthogonal, even if not exactly so.

Definition 3.7

A set of vectors $\{\mathbf{v}_1, \mathbf{v}_2, \ldots, \mathbf{v}_t\}$ are said to be ε-*quasiorthonormal* if $\|\mathbf{v}_j\|_2 = 1$, $j = 1, \ldots, t$, and $|\mathbf{v}_i^T\mathbf{v}_j| < \varepsilon$ for $i \neq j$.

□

While orthogonal feature vectors are unlikely, sets of t feature vectors $\{\mathbf{x}_j\}$ which when normalised are quasi-orthonormal can be regarded as generic in this context. It is not too difficult to generalise the argument of the example to show that a Hebbian network will also work in this case, but this will take us away from eigenvectors, so we will not pursue it here.

Observe that the problem of diagonalizing A (as (3.2)) or equivalently of finding a basis $\mathbf{p}_j$ as in (3.4) amounts to finding n independent eigenvectors of A. So how can we solve (3.5)? Sometimes, as in Example 3.6, eigenvectors arise naturally from the problem under discussion. But in other cases they must be calculated. We will describe a determinant based method for finding eigenvalues: although this is of limited practical use it serves to introduce the key ideas and concepts. For various reasons, it is impracticable to use this method to find eigenvectors of large matrices. However in neural networks eigenvectors are mostly used for theoretical analysis. This is not true in many other branches of mathematics in which the computation of eigenvectors and eigenvalues is an important problem. Practical methods may be found in textbooks of numerical computation (e.g. Isaacson and Keller (1966)).

Observe that (3.5) may be re-written as

$$(A - \lambda I)\mathbf{p} = \mathbf{0}. \tag{3.8}$$

Thus we need to find λ's for which the matrix $A - \lambda I$ is not invertible. One way to do this is to solve the equation

$$\det(A - \lambda I) = 0. \tag{3.9}$$

This is called the *characteristic equation* of A. Note that A and A^{T} have the same characteristic equation and hence the same eigenvalues.

Example 3.8

We will continue with the matrix A from Example 3.4. Recall

$$A = \begin{pmatrix} 5 & -6 & -6 \\ -1 & 4 & 2 \\ 3 & -6 & -4 \end{pmatrix}. \text{ Hence } A - \lambda I = \begin{pmatrix} 5-\lambda & -6 & -6 \\ -1 & 4-\lambda & 2 \\ 3 & -6 & -4-\lambda \end{pmatrix}.$$

Thus

$$\det(A - \lambda \mathrm{I}) = (5-\lambda) \begin{vmatrix} 4-\lambda & 2 \\ -6 & -4-\lambda \end{vmatrix} - (-6) \begin{vmatrix} -1 & 2 \\ 3 & -4-\lambda \end{vmatrix} + (-6) \begin{vmatrix} -1 & 4-\lambda \\ 3 & -6 \end{vmatrix}$$

$$= -\lambda^3 + 5\lambda^2 - 8\lambda + 4$$

after simplification. The characteristic equation (3.9) is thus a cubic:

$$0 = -\lambda^3 + 5\lambda^2 - 8\lambda + 4.$$

We see by inspection that $\lambda = 1$ is a solution of the equation, i.e. $(\lambda - 1)$ is a factor. In fact

$$0=(\lambda-1)(-\lambda^2+4\lambda-4)$$
$$=-(\lambda-1)(\lambda-2)(\lambda-2)$$

whence we obtain the three eigenvalues $\lambda_1=1$, $\lambda_2=2$, $\lambda_3=2$. As we expect these are precisely the elements of the diagonal matrix D of Example 3.4. Now we have the eigenvalues, it is relatively easy to find the eigenvectors which form the columns of P.

First consider the case $\lambda=1$. $A-1I$ is

$$\begin{pmatrix} 5-1 & -6 & -6 \\ -1 & 4-1 & 2 \\ 3 & -6 & -4-1 \end{pmatrix} = \begin{pmatrix} 4 & -6 & -6 \\ -1 & 3 & 2 \\ 3 & -6 & -5 \end{pmatrix}.$$

We now solve (3.8) for $\mathbf{p}$ with $\lambda=1$. The system becomes

$$\begin{aligned} 4p_1-6p_2-6p_3&=0\\ -p_1+3p_2+2p_3&=0\\ 3p_1-6p_2-5p_3&=0. \end{aligned}$$

By construction, the rank of $A-1I$ is less than 3, so one of these equations must be redundant. Nonetheless we can perform Gaussian elimination in the normal way. This yields the pair of equations

$$\begin{aligned} 2p_1-3p_2-3p_3&=0\\ 3p_2+p_3&=0 \end{aligned}$$

with the coefficients in the third equation all 0 as expected. Clearly these two equations are independent, and the solution of (3.8) in this case is thus a one-dimensional subspace. If we set $p_3=1$, we get $p_2=-\frac{1}{3}$ and $p_1=1$. Thus our solution space is spanned by $(1, -\frac{1}{3}, 1)^T$. Any element of this space will do as our eigenvector, and obviously the tidiest choice is $(3, -1, 3)^T$. This is the third column of P in Example 3.4, and corresponds to the eigenvalue 1 which is the third diagonal element of D.

The case of $\lambda=2$ is slightly more complicated since the eigenvalue is repeated. $(A-2I)$ is

$$\begin{pmatrix} 5-2 & -6 & -6 \\ -1 & 4-2 & 2 \\ 3 & -6 & -4-2 \end{pmatrix} = \begin{pmatrix} 3 & -6 & -6 \\ -1 & 2 & 2 \\ 3 & -6 & -6 \end{pmatrix}.$$

Performing elimination for $(A-2I)\mathbf{p}=\mathbf{0}$ reduces the system to the *single* equation

$$p_1 - 2p_2 - 2p_3 = 0.$$

There is a two-dimensional subspace of solutions. If we set $p_2=1$ and $p_2=0$ we get the first column of P, namely $(2, 0, 1)^T$. Conversely, if we set $p_2=0$ and $p_2 = 1$ we get the second column of P, namely $(2, 0, 1)^T$.

□

For an $n \times n$ matrix the characteristic equation will be a polynomial equation of degree n. To summarise then, given an $n \times n$ matrix A, we perform the following steps to find P and diagonal D such that $P^{-1}AP = D$.

(a) Find the eigenvalues, i.e. solve the polynomial equation of degree n given by $\det(A - \lambda I) = 0$. These eigenvalues are the elements of D.
(b) Corresponding to each eigenvalue, find an eigenvector (independent of the previous ones). These form the columns of P.

It might be thought from Example 3.8 that for any $n \times n$ matrix A, it is always possible to find P and D. Unfortunately this is not the case. Firstly, we may observe that if we are working over the real numbers $\mathbb{R}$, some of the eigenvalues may be complex. In this case, P and D will have to be complex matrices. Because of the problem of complex eigenvalues, it is often necessary to work in $\mathbb{C}$ rather than $\mathbb{R}$, even if our actual matrices only have real coefficients. We will make this extension when required. However, this is not sufficient to guarantee that diagonalization is possible. The problem is caused by repeated roots. In Example 3.8, this did not prevent us finding a complete set of independent eigenvalues. But consider the following example.

Example 3.9

$$A = \begin{pmatrix} 3 & 1 & -1 \\ 2 & 2 & -1 \\ 2 & 2 & 0 \end{pmatrix}.$$

The characteristic equation of this matrix is again

$$(1-\lambda)(\lambda-2)^2 = 0.$$

so the eigenvalues are again 1 and 2 (twice). In this case the eigenspace corresponding to 1 is spanned by the eigenvector $(1, 0, 2)^T$. However with $\lambda = 2$, when we eliminate to get the eigenvectors find *two* independent equations have to be satisfied, namely

$$p_1 + p_2 - p_3 = 0$$
$$-2p_2 + p_3 = 0$$

So we only get a *one*-dimensional eigenspace, which is the span of $(1, 1, 2)^T$. In this case we cannot get three independent eigenvectors to form the columns of P, so the matrix A is **not** similar to a diagonal matrix.

□

There are some so-called *normal* forms for matrices to which we can reduce every matrix by a similarity transformation: the most important are the *Jordan* and *rational* normal forms. Reference to these will be found in some advanced texts on linear algebra. In fact a (very indirect!) derivation of the Jordan Normal Form will be given in Chapter 5. See Theorem 5.16 and the remarks following it. So we will not pursue this here: instead we will consider conditions under which a real or complex matrix *can* be diagonalized (over the complex numbers if necessary). Firstly, distinctness of the eigenvalues is sufficient to guarantee the existence of a basis of eigenvectors.

Theorem 3.10

Suppose an $n \times n$ matrix A over $\mathbb{R}$ has a set S of j independent eigenvectors $(\mathbf{p}_1, \ldots, \mathbf{p}_j)$, corresponding to (real or complex) eigenvalues $(\lambda_1, \ldots, \lambda_j)$. Suppose further that λ is another eigenvalue with eigenvector $\mathbf{p}$, and that $\lambda \neq \lambda_k$, $k = 1, 2, \ldots, j$. Then $\mathbf{p}$ is linearly independent of S.

Proof

Suppose we have a dependence relation

$$\alpha_1\mathbf{p}_1 + \alpha_2\mathbf{p}_2 + \ldots + \alpha_j\mathbf{p}_j = \mathbf{p}.$$

Multiplying this equation by A gives

$$\alpha_1 A\mathbf{p}_1 + \alpha_2 A\mathbf{p}_2 + \ldots + \alpha_j A\mathbf{p}_j = A\mathbf{p}$$

whence

$$\alpha_1\lambda_1\mathbf{p}_1 + \alpha_2\lambda_2\mathbf{p}_2 + \ldots + \alpha_j\lambda_j\mathbf{p}_j = \lambda\mathbf{p}.$$

If $\lambda = 0$, we have a dependence relation for S, contrary to hypothesis. If $\lambda \neq 0$, we may divide by it to obtain

$$\alpha_1(\lambda_1/\lambda)\mathbf{p}_1 + \alpha_2(\lambda_2/\lambda)\mathbf{p}_2 + \ldots + \alpha_j(\lambda_j/\lambda)\,\mathbf{p}_j = \mathbf{p}.$$

Subtracting this from (3.1) gives

$$\alpha_1(1-\lambda_1/\lambda)\mathbf{p_1}+\alpha_2(1-\lambda_2/\lambda)\mathbf{p_2}+\ldots+\alpha_j(1-\lambda_j/\lambda)\mathbf{p_j}=\mathbf{0},$$

which again gives a dependence relation for S, since all the quantities in brackets and at least one of the α_j are non-zero.

□

Thus we see that provided an $n \times n$ matrix has n distinct eigenvalues, it has a complete eigenvector basis, and is similar to a diagonal matrix. If the matrix does not have distinct eigenvalues it may or may not be diagonalisable, as shown by the examples above. However, this is the non-typical case corresponding to the non-typical situation of repeated roots in a polynomial equation.

Unfortunately, the condition of Theorem 3.10 can in many cases only be verified *a posteriori*. We cannot tell whether a given matrix A is diagonalizable until we have found the eigenvalues and eigenvectors. Moreover, it is obviously inconvenient when using real matrices to have to work over $\mathbb{C}$. There is one case when everything is much simpler: this is when A is symmetric. Recall, a matrix A is symmetric if $A^T = A$. For simplicity here we will just consider real matrices. (A matrix whose elements are in $\mathbb{R}$ is called a *real* matrix.) At this stage, considering symmetric matrices may seem very artificial. However, we shall find that symmetric matrices arise in a very natural fashion when considering machine learning, particularly in the context of least distance problems and optimisation.

Recall that real vectors $\mathbf{x}$ and $\mathbf{y}$ are said to be *orthogonal* if $\mathbf{x}^T\mathbf{y}=0$ (Definition 2.6). Geometrically in $\mathbb{R}^2$ or $\mathbb{R}^3$ this means that the angle between them is 90°. A set of vectors $\{\mathbf{v_1}, \ldots, \mathbf{v_k}\}$ are said to be *mutually orthogonal* if $\mathbf{v_i}^T\mathbf{v_j}=\mathbf{0}$ for $i \neq j$. If in addition $\|\mathbf{v_i}\|=1$ for each i, the set is said to be mutually *orthonormal*. Note that any set of mutually orthogonal non-zero vectors must be linearly independent, for suppose

$$\alpha_1\mathbf{v_1}+\alpha_2\mathbf{v_2}+\ldots+\alpha_k\mathbf{v_k}=\mathbf{0}.$$

Then for any i, we have

$$\alpha_1\mathbf{v_i}^T\mathbf{v_1}+\alpha_2\mathbf{v_i}^T\mathbf{v_2}+\ldots+\alpha_k\mathbf{v_i}^T\mathbf{v_k}=0$$

so $\alpha_i\mathbf{v_i}^T\mathbf{v_i}=0$, since all the other terms on the left hand side are zero. Thus $\alpha_i\,\|\mathbf{v_i}\|_2^2=0$, and since $\mathbf{v_i} \neq \mathbf{0}$ by hypothesis, we must have $\alpha_i=0$.

Theorem 3.11

Let A be a real symmetric matrix.

(a) All the eigenvalues of A are real.
(b) Let $\mathbf{p}_1$ and $\mathbf{p}_2$ be eigenvectors corresponding to eigenvalues λ_1 and λ_2 with $\lambda_1 \neq \lambda_2$. Then $\mathbf{p}_1^T\mathbf{p}_2=\mathbf{0}$.

Proof

(a) Suppose $A\mathbf{p}=\lambda\mathbf{p}$ with $\mathbf{p}\neq\mathbf{0}$. Then $A^2\mathbf{p}=\lambda A\mathbf{p}=\lambda^2\mathbf{p}$. But since A is symmetric, $A^2\mathbf{p}=A^TA\mathbf{p}$. Thus $A^TA\mathbf{p}=\lambda^2\mathbf{p}$. Premultiply each side of this equation by $\mathbf{p}^T$. This gives $\mathbf{v}^T\mathbf{v}=\lambda^2\mathbf{p}^T\mathbf{p}$ where $\mathbf{v}=A\mathbf{p}$. Hence $\lambda^2=\|\mathbf{v}\|_2^2/\|\mathbf{p}\|_2^2\geq 0$. Since λ^2 is a non-negative real number, λ is real.
(b) We have $A\mathbf{p}_1=\lambda_1\mathbf{p}_1$ so $\lambda_1\mathbf{p}_1^T=\mathbf{p}_1^TA^T=\mathbf{p}_1^TA$ since A is symmetric. Thus $\lambda_1\mathbf{p}_1^T\mathbf{p}_2=\mathbf{p}_1^T\mathrm{A}\mathbf{p}_2=\lambda_2\mathbf{p}_1^T\mathbf{p}_2$. Hence $(\lambda_1-\lambda_2)\mathbf{p}_1^T\mathbf{p}_2=0$. Since $(\lambda_1-\lambda_2)\neq 0$, this is only possible with $\mathbf{p}_1^T\mathbf{p}_2=0$.

□

In particular, if the eigenvalues are distinct, then from Theorem 3.10 the eigenvalues must be real and we get a complete set of real eigenvectors which are also orthogonal. Moreover since eigenvalues are in any case only defined up to multiplication by a scalar, we can choose them to be orthonormal. While Theorem 3.11 is fairly straightforward, it is rather more difficult to prove that we can get a complete set of eigenvectors even if there are repeated eigenvalues. To do this we introduce a matrix called a *Householder matrix* which has the form

$$H=I-2\mathbf{w}\mathbf{w}^T \tag{3.11}$$

with $\mathbf{w}^T\mathbf{w}=1$. Note that the term $\mathbf{w}\mathbf{w}^T$ is not an inner product, in fact it is sometimes called an *outer* or *exterior* product. (Such products occur very frequently in neural computing as they are related to Hebbian reinforcement: compare Example 3.6.) If $\mathbf{w}$ is an n-vector i.e. an $n\times 1$ matrix, $\mathbf{w}^T$ is a $1\times n$ matrix and hence $\mathbf{w}\mathbf{w}^T$ is an $n\times n$ matrix. The jth column of $\mathbf{w}\mathbf{w}^T$ is $w_j\mathbf{w}$, so every column is a scalar multiple of $\mathbf{w}$ and hence rank $(\mathbf{w}\mathbf{w}^T)=1$. The matrix H is easily verified to be symmetric and to satisfy $H^2=I$. In other words H is its own inverse. In fact H is a (very) special case of an important class of matrices.

Definition 3.12

A $n\times n$ real matrix Q is said to be *orthogonal* if $Q^TQ=I$ (or equivalently $Q^T=Q^{-1}$)

□

Orthogonal matrices have very nice properties, and we will be making extensive use of them from now on. The most important properties are given in the following theorems.

Theorem 3.13

An $n \times n$ real matrix Q is orthogonal if and only if *any* of the following properties hold.

(a) the columns of Q are orthonormal.
(b) the rows of Q are orthonormal.
(c) $\mathbf{v}^T\mathbf{w} = \mathbf{v}^T Q^T Q\mathbf{w}$ for *every* $\mathbf{v}, \mathbf{w} \in \mathbb{R}^n$ (i.e. inner products are preserved under multiplication by Q)
(d) $\|Q\mathbf{v}\|_2 = \|\mathbf{v}\|_2$ for *every* $\mathbf{v} \in \mathbb{R}$ (i.e. lengths are preserved under multiplication by Q).

Proof

(a) This is essentially a restatement of the definition. If the columns of Q are $\mathbf{q}_1 \ldots \mathbf{q}_n$ then from the definition of the matrix product, the *i,jth* element of Q^TQ is $\mathbf{q}_i^T\mathbf{q}_j$. So the vectors are orthonormal if and only if $Q^TQ = 1$.
(b) This follows immediately from (a), since obviously Q is orthogonal if and only if Q^T is orthogonal.
(c) If Q is orthogonal, condition (c) holds since $Q^TQ = I$. Conversely if condition (c) holds, then $\mathbf{q}_i^T\mathbf{q}_j = (Q\mathbf{e}_j)^T(Q\mathbf{e}_j) = \mathbf{e}_i^T Q^T Q\mathbf{e}_j = \mathbf{e}_i^T\mathbf{e}_j$ so the columns are orthonormal.
(d) If Q is orthogonal $\|Q\mathbf{v}\|_2^2 = \mathbf{v}^T Q^T Q\mathbf{v} = \mathbf{v}^T\mathbf{v} = \|\mathbf{v}\|_2^2$ so condition (d) holds. The converse follows from the observation that for any two vectors $\mathbf{v}$ and $\mathbf{w}$,

$$2\mathbf{v}^T\mathbf{w} = (\mathbf{v}+\mathbf{w})^T(\mathbf{v}+\mathbf{w}) - (\mathbf{v}-\mathbf{w})^T(\mathbf{v}-\mathbf{w}) = 2\,\|\mathbf{v}+\mathbf{w}\|_2^2 - 2\,\|\mathbf{v}-\mathbf{w}\|_2^2. \qquad (3.13)$$

Now replace $\mathbf{v}$ and $\mathbf{w}$ by $Q\mathbf{v}$ and $Q\mathbf{w}$, and observe that if (d) holds, the right-hand side will be unchanged, so Q is orthogonal by (c).

□

It is the distance preserving property (Theorem 3.13(d)) which makes orthogonal matrices particularly useful when analysing neural systems. Householder matrices (3.11) are orthogonal, as are rotation matrices as illustrated in Fig. 2.6. These two simple types of orthogonal matrix can be used in a similar way to elementary matrices when we want to handle orthogonal matrices. Householder matrices are crucial in the following theorem, which establishes that symmetric matrices can always be diagonalized (even if the eigenvalues are repeated).

Theorem 3.14

Let A be a real symmetric $n \times n$ matrix. Then there exists a set $\{\mathbf{p}_1, \mathbf{p}_2, \ldots, \mathbf{p}_n\}$ of independent eigenvectors of A which are mutually orthonormal.

Proof

The proof is by induction over n. If $n=1$ only $\mathbf{p}_1$ is required and there is nothing to prove. So suppose that the theorem is valid for $(n-1)\times(n-1)$ matrices.

The characteristic equation (3.9) must have at least one solution λ and by Theorem 3.11 this eigenvalue must be real. Hence there is a real eigenvector, say $\mathbf{p}$ and we assume that it is normalised, i.e. $\|\mathbf{p}\|_2=1$. Moreover, by multiplying by -1 if necessary, we may assume its first element satisfies $p_1 \geq 0$. (Do not get confused here between the vector $\mathbf{p}_1$ and the element p_1.) We construct a matrix H of the form (3.11) with the property that $H\mathbf{e}_1=\mathbf{p}$. More specifically, $H\mathbf{e}_1$ is of course the first column of H, so $p_1=1-2w_1^2$ and $p_j=2w_1w_j$ for $j>1$. Rearranging the first equation yields $w_1^2=(1-p_1)/2$ which in view of the normalisation of $\mathbf{p}$ can be solved to get a real solution for w_1. The second equation then gives $w_j, j=2, \ldots, n$. This $\mathbf{w}$ must satisfy $\mathbf{w}^T\mathbf{w}=1$ by Theorem 3.13 (d).

Now $AH\mathbf{e}_1=\mathbf{A}\mathbf{p}=\lambda\mathbf{p}=\lambda H\mathbf{e}_1$. So $HAH\mathbf{e}_1=\lambda\mathbf{e}_1$ (recall $H^{-1}=H$). Let $B=HAH$. We see that $\mathbf{e}_1$ is an eigenvector of B corresponding to λ. But $B\mathbf{e}_1=\lambda\mathbf{e}_1$ is the first column of B Moreover B is symmetric, for $B^T=(HAH)^T=H^TA^TH^T=HAH=B$. Thus the first row of B is $\lambda\mathbf{e}_1^T$. Let C be the $(n-1)\times(n-1)$ submatrix formed by deleting the first row and column of B. Thus

$$B=\begin{pmatrix} \lambda & 0 \;\ldots\; 0 \\ 0 & \\ \cdot & C \\ \cdot & \\ 0 & \end{pmatrix}. \tag{3.14}$$

By the inductive hypothesis, C has $(n-1)$ orthonormal eigenvectors, say $\mathbf{q}_2, \ldots, \mathbf{q}_n$. Then it is easy to see from (3.14) that these form eigenvectors of B if we *preppend* 0 to them, i.e. the eigenvectors have the form

$$\begin{pmatrix} 0 \\ \hline \mathbf{q}_j \end{pmatrix}.$$

Together with $\mathbf{e}_1$ we therefore have a complete set of n orthonormal eigenvectors of B. Multiplying these vectors by H completes the proof.

□

Putting all these ideas together we get the following theorem.

Theorem 3.15

Let A be a real, symmetric $n \times n$ matrix. There exists a real orthogonal matrix P and a real diagonal matrix D such that $D = P^{\mathrm{T}}AP$. The columns of P are eigenvectors of A, and the diagonal elements of D are eigenvalues (in the corresponding order).

Proof

Theorem 3.14 tells us that there is an orthonormal basis of eigenvectors. The result follows from (3.2)

□

3.2 Normed vector spaces

Our next task is to look in more detail at the concept of distance in vector spaces. We have a similar problem to that encountered in the previous chapter: we can develop the ideas needed immediately just with the ordinary Euclidean length $\| \|_2$, but for future use we need to put the material in a more general and abstract context. We cannot always allow ourselves the luxury of going through the theorems twice as we did in Chapter 2. Instead we will develop the abstract theory directly, but illustrate it partly with the simple networks we have considered so far. Other examples will indicate the wider applicability of the ideas.

Refer again to Examples 2.33 and the remarks immediately following. What is the 'length' of a function $f \in C[0, 1]$ when we consider it as a vector? And is the Euclidean length the only meaningful and useful idea of length even in $\mathbb{R}^n$? Moreover we have seen that the inner product is fundamental to the geometry of $\mathbb{R}^n$ and to our understanding of neural networks. Can this concept be extended to other vector spaces? We will find that this last question turns out to be a particularly fruitful one.

Now we could of course think of all kinds of 'length functions' for a vector space, but as always it is best to be guided by two considerations. In order to apply our geometric intuition, we want to generalise properties of the space we understand, i.e. $\mathbb{R}^n$ with $\| \|_2$. Secondly, it is a good idea to think about what we want to use the generalization *for*. Let us take the second consideration first.

Examples 3.16

(a) In Chapter 2 (Section 2.2) we introduced the simple linear perceptron (see Fig. 2.1). The perceptron with weight matrix W and input pattern vector $\mathbf{x}$ produces an output $\mathbf{y} = W\mathbf{x}$. If the *desired* output for this pattern is $\mathbf{b}$, how do we measure the error for this particular pattern and weight matrix? We could (and often do) consider the Euclidean length of the residual $\mathbf{r} = W\mathbf{x} - \mathbf{b}$. But this is not the only sensible choice. One might argue that what we actually want is to minimise the error in each individual element. In other words we want to make max $|r_i|$ small, where the maximum is taken over all the elements. Alternatively we might want to have the *sum* of the errors, $\sum |r_i|$ to be as small as possible. Clearly, neither of these quantities is the same as the Euclidean distance.

(b) Now think about $C[a, b]$ and suppose we have some f in this space. For definiteness, suppose $f(x) = \exp(x)$. We need to compute this function, for instance, to simulate popular activation functions on a digital computer (see Section 1.3). Of course, our high level computer language will have the exponential function built in, but nevertheless it is interesting to consider *how* the machine calculates it. To compute the exponential function exactly requires summation of an infinite series. When we represent it in a digital computer, direct summation of the series to a given error turns out to be too expensive computationally. The usual approach is to employ an approximation. Since digital computers can really only do summation, multiplication and division, this approximation is nearly always either a polynomial, a rational function (the ratio of two polynomials) or a spline (a piecewise polynomial function). Let the approximation be p. The *error* of the approximation is obviously itself a function of x, say $e(x) = f(x) - p(x)$. However we are not really interested in the error at any *particular* x. We want to know that the approximation has an error of (say) 5×10^{-11} (so it is correct to 10 decimal places) for *any* value of x in [0, 1] (or for sin x, more realistically $[0, {}^{\pi}/_{2}]$). Thus we are interested in max $|f(x) - p(x)|$, where here the maximum is over the range of x values.

□

Now in Section 1.8 we met the concept of a *metric space*. This is a general concept of distance used in mathematics, but it does not reflect the special linear properties of vector spaces: for these it is useful to have a slightly more restrictive idea of distance. We define $\mathbb{R}^+$ to be the set of non-negative real numbers, so $\mathbb{R}^+=\{x\in\mathbb{R}\mid x\geq 0\}$. We will use the symbol $\|\ \|$ to denote our general distance and abstract the following properties of $\|\ \|_2$.

Properties 3.17

If V is a vector space over $\mathbb{R}$ or $\mathbb{C}$, a *norm* $\|\ \|$ is a function $\|\ \|: V\to\mathbb{R}^+$ such that for each $\mathbf{v}, \mathbf{w}\in V$ and scalar λ.

(a) $\|\mathbf{v}\|=0$ if and only if $\mathbf{v}=\mathbf{0}$

(b) $\|\mathbf{v}+\mathbf{w}\|\leq\|\mathbf{v}\|+\|\mathbf{w}\|$ (the triangle inequality)

(c) $\|\lambda\mathbf{v}\|=|\lambda|\ \|\mathbf{v}\|$.

V is then said to be a *normed vector space*.

□

Remark and Definition 3.18

Note that this definition is similar to that of a metric, but has the concepts of vector addition and multiplication by a scalar built in. In fact the reader should verify that $d(\mathbf{u}, \mathbf{v})=\|\mathbf{u}-\mathbf{v}\|$ is a metric as defined in Section 1.8. Thus, in a normed vector space we have a concept of convergence. Specifically, we say that a sequence $\mathbf{v_n}$ of elements of V *converges in norm* to $\mathbf{v}$ as $n\to\infty$ if $\|\mathbf{v_n}-\mathbf{v}\|\to 0$. When it is clear from the context that we mean convergence in norm, we just say $\mathbf{v_n}$ converges to $\mathbf{v}$ and write $\mathbf{v_n}\to\mathbf{v}$. The contraction mapping theorem holds **provided V is analytically complete**. It will be necessary to discuss the completeness of various spaces encountered. A complete normed vector space is called a *Banach Space*.

□

This is all very well for a definition, but are their any useful examples?

Examples 3.19

(a) $\mathbb{R}^n$ with $\|\ \|_2$ is a normed vector space. However there is a difficulty in that while the triangle inequality (Properties 3.17(b)) is geometrically obvious for $n=1$ or 2, we have not actually proved this for general n. This is not completely trivial, but neither is it very difficult. Rather than give a proof here, we will deal with the general case of inner product spaces later.

(b) Considering either $\mathbb{R}^n$ or $\mathbb{C}^n$, define

$$\|\mathbf{v}\|_\infty = \max_{1 \le 1 \le n} |v_i| .$$

So for example, $\|(1, 2, -3)^T\|_\infty = 3$. With this norm, $\mathbb{R}^n$ or $\mathbb{C}^n$ is a normed vector space. Actually it is much easier to check that $\| \|_\infty$ is a norm than it is for $\| \|_2$, so the details are left as an exercise.

(c) Considering either $\mathbb{R}^n$ or $\mathbb{C}^n$, define

$$\|\mathbf{v}\|_p = \left(\sum_{i=1}^{n} | v_i |^p \right)^{1/p} .$$

So for example, with $p=1$, $\|(1, 2, -3)^T\|_1 = 1+2+3=6$. With this norm, $\mathbb{R}^n$ or $\mathbb{C}^n$ is a normed vector space. The case $p=2$ is of course the ordinary Euclidean norm we have used all along. Again it is difficult to prove the triangle inequality. We need a result called Minkowski's inequality which requires a bit of effort to prove, so we shall not bother to do the general case. A proof may be found in Kreyszig (1978, p. 14). However it is fairly easy to check the triangle inequality for the case $p=1$ directly (exercise). The main reason for mentioning the general case is to explain the notation of example (b). The larger the value of p, the more emphasis the expression above gives to larger values of v_i compared to the smaller values. We have already seen $\|(1, 2, -3)^T\|_1 = 1+2+3 = 6$. On the other hand when $p=2$, we get $\|(1, 2, -3)^T\|_2 = \sqrt{(1^2+2^2+3^2)} = \sqrt{(1 + 4 + 9)}$. The element -3 has a relatively larger effect on the answer. $\| \|_\infty$ is the limiting case of this as $p \to \infty$.

(d) Now for some more interesting examples. Consider $C[0, 1]$. Define

$$\|f\|_\infty = \max_{0 \le x \le 1} |f(x)| .$$

So for example $\|\exp(x)\|_\infty = e^1 = 2.718281828\ldots$. Similarly $\|\cos x\|_\infty = 1$ and $\|x^2\|_\infty = 1$. Then $C[0, 1]$ is a normed vector space (and a very important one).

(e) Again consider $C[0, 1]$. Define

$$\|f\|_p = \left(\int_0^1 |f(x)|\, p \,dx \right)^{1/p} .$$

With this norm, $C[0, 1]$ is a normed vector space. Again, the most important cases are $p=2$ followed by $p=1$. Note that the symbol for this norm is the same as that for example (c)). In most cases the context makes it clear which is intended.

(f) Consider the space of all real sequences (x_i). and let S be the subspace of absolutely summable sequences, i.e. the sequences such that

$$\sum_{i=1}^{\infty} |x_i|$$

is convergent. Then this sum itself is a norm on S.

□

Much of this book is concerned with the dynamic behaviour of networks. To handle this topic properly requires familiarity with the ideas relating to convergence in vector spaces. In the rest of this section we will discuss the issue of analytic completeness of certain important normed vector spaces. This discussion is quite technical. Readers lacking a very strong mathematical background may prefer to omit the proofs on first reading. However it is important to understand what the theorems mean, as extensive use will be made of the Contraction Mapping Theorem, which requires analytic completeness. For brevity, we will restrict ourselves to discussion of vector spaces over $\mathbb{R}$, although in most cases the extension to spaces over $\mathbb{C}$ requires only straightforward modifications.

Firstly, then, consider finite dimensional spaces. Here we can give a full answer to the question of completeness: all finite dimensional normal vector spaces over $\mathbb{R}$ are complete. This is a consequence of the following theorem, which shows in fact that all finite dimensional normed vector spaces over $\mathbb{R}$ are analytically equivalent with respect to convergence.

Theorem 3.20 (Norm Equivalence)

Let $\|\ \|_\alpha$ and $\|\ \|_\beta$ be any norms on an n dimensional space V over $\mathbb{R}$. Then there exist real, strictly positive constants K_1 and K_2 such that for any $\mathbf{v} \in V$,

$$K_1 \|\mathbf{v}\|_\alpha \leq \|\mathbf{v}\|_\beta \leq K_2 \|\mathbf{v}\|_\alpha$$

(The important thing here, of course, is that K_1 and K_2 are independent of the particular choice of $\mathbf{v}$.)

Proof
It is sufficient to prove the result for a particular choice of $\| \|_\alpha$ since any other norms can then be compared via this one. Let $\mathbf{v}_1, \ldots, \mathbf{v}_n$ be a basis for V. For any $\mathbf{v} \in V$, we may write

$$\mathbf{v} = x_1\mathbf{v}_1 + x_2\mathbf{v}_2 + \ldots + x_n\mathbf{v}_n \qquad (3.15)$$

and moreover it is straightforward to check that

$$\|\mathbf{v}\|_\alpha = \max_{i=1,\ldots n} |x_i|$$

is a norm on V. Then

$$\|\mathbf{v}\|_\beta = \|x_1\mathbf{v}_1 + x_2\mathbf{v}_2 + \ldots + x_n\mathbf{v}_n\|_\beta \leq |x_1|\ \|\mathbf{v}_1\|_\beta + \ldots + |x_n|\ \|\mathbf{v}_1\|_\beta$$

$$\leq \|\mathbf{v}\|_\alpha\ (\ \|\mathbf{v}_1\|_\beta + \ldots + \|\mathbf{v}_1\|_\beta).$$

Thus we may choose K_2 to be $\|\mathbf{v}_1\|_\beta + \ldots + \|\mathbf{v}_1\|_\beta$. (Note that this does not depend on the particular choice of $\mathbf{v}$, although it does of course depend on the choice of basis.)

It is a little more tricky to get the lower bound. The case $\mathbf{v}=0$ will work for any K_1 so we can ignore this.
Let

$$S = \{\mathbf{x} \in \mathbb{R}^{\triangle} \mid |x_i| \leq 1, i = 1,\ldots,n \text{ and } |x_i| = 1 \text{for some } i\}.$$

S is precisely the set of $\mathbf{x}$'s for which $\mathbf{v}$ given by (3.15) has $\|\mathbf{v}\|_\alpha = 1$. Let $f(\mathbf{x})$: $S \to \mathbb{R}$ be defined by $f(\mathbf{x}) = \|x_1\mathbf{v}_1 + x_2\mathbf{v}_2 + \ldots + x_n\mathbf{v}_n\|_\beta$. Now S is the surface of a hypercube in $\mathbb{R}^n$, so clearly the continuous function $f(\mathbf{x})$ must achieve its minimum for some $\mathbf{x}_0$, say, by a multidimensional version of Theorem 1.19. Let $K_1 = f(\mathbf{x}_0)$. Now $K_1 > 0$, for $\| \|_\beta$ is a norm and so the $\mathbf{v}_0$ corresponding to the (non-zero) $\mathbf{x}_0$ is not zero. Thus $\|\mathbf{v}\|_\beta \geq K_1$ provided $\|\mathbf{v}\|_\alpha = 1$. But for *any* non-zero $\mathbf{v}$, $\mathbf{v}/\|\mathbf{v}\|_\alpha$ has α-norm 1. Thus $\|\mathbf{v}\|_\beta \geq K_1\|\mathbf{v}\|_\alpha$ as required.

□

Corollary 3.21
Retaining the notation of Theorem 3.20,

(a) Let $\|\mathbf{v}_n - \mathbf{v}\|_\alpha \to 0$ as $n \to \infty$. Then $\|\mathbf{v}_n - \mathbf{v}\|_\beta \to 0$ also. So for finite dimensional spaces over $\mathbb{R}$, we may write $\mathbf{v}_n \to \mathbf{v}$ unambiguously, without specifying a particular norm.

(b) Every finite dimensional normed vector space V over $\mathbb{R}$ is a Banach space, i.e. is analytically complete.

Proof

(a) This is an immediate consequence of Theorem 3.20.

(b) This is obtained by using the particular choice of $\|\mathbf{v}\|_\alpha$ defined in the proof of Theorem 3.20. Let the norm on V be $\| \|_\beta$. Suppose $(\mathbf{v_n})$ is a Cauchy sequence with respect to this norm. Then it will also be Cauchy with respect to $\| \|_\alpha$, and hence also the elements of each of the coefficient vectors $\mathbf{x}$ of the $\mathbf{v_i}$ will be Cauchy sequences of real numbers. These must have a limit (Theorem 1.9), showing that there exists $\mathbf{v}$ such that $\mathbf{v_n} \to \mathbf{v}$ in $\| \|_\alpha$ and thus also in $\| \|_\beta$.

□

Not surprisingly the situation for infinite dimensional spaces is much more complicated. We can have no general result like Theorem 3.20 as is shown by the following example.

Example 3.22

Consider $C\,[0, 1]$ and let $f_n(x)$ be the function illustrated in Fig. 3.2. Note that $\|f_n\|_1$ is simply the area under the curve, i.e. $1/2n$ (Examples 3.19(e) with $p=1$). So, with respect to the 1-norm, $f_n \to 0$ (more precisely the zero *function*) as $n \to \infty$. On the other hand $\|f_n\|_\infty$ is simply the maximum value of the function: thus 1 for all n. Theorem 3.10 does not hold for this pair of norms, and with respect to the ∞-norm, the sequence does not converge.

□

In general, when dealing with questions of convergence and completeness in infinite dimensional spaces we have no choice but to consider each space and norm separately. On the other hand we can sometimes get relations between norms in particular spaces: for instance it is easy to see that for $f \in C[0, 1]$, we always have $\|f\|_p \leq \|f\|_\infty$.

So what can we say about analytic completeness in the important function spaces? We first deal with $C\,[a, b]$ and consider $\| \|_\infty$. Actually it makes life easier to introduce a bigger space than $C\,[a, b]$, as follows. A function f: $[a, b] \to \mathbb{R}$ is said to be *bounded* if there exists $M \in \mathbb{R}$ such that $|f(x)| \leq M$ for all $x \in [a, b]$. For example take $[a, b]$ to be $[0, 1]$ and consider the function

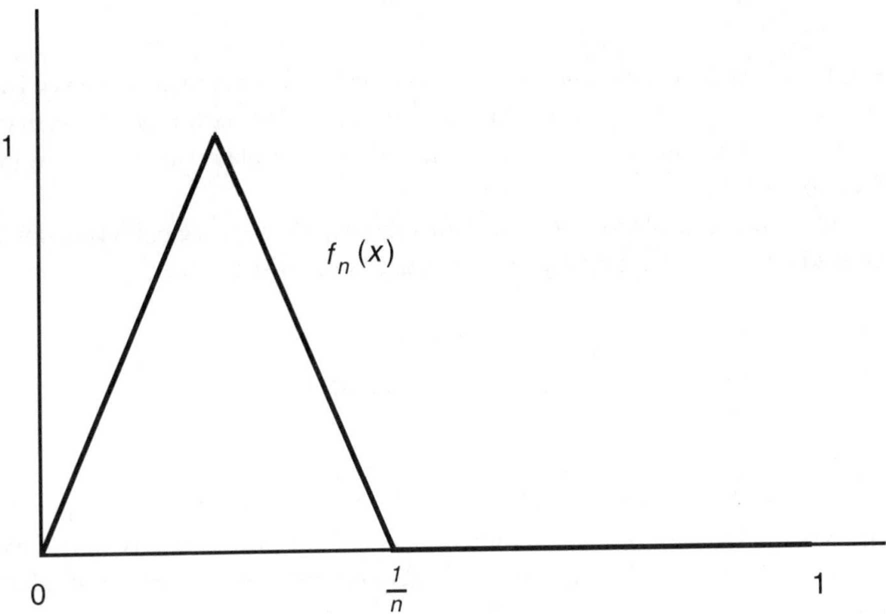

Fig. 3.2

$$h(x) = \begin{cases} x \text{ if } x < 0.5 \\ 0 \text{ if } x \geq 0.5. \end{cases}$$

This function is bounded (take $M = 0.5$) even though it is not continuous. On the other hand if we choose

$$g(x) = \begin{cases} 0 \text{ if } x = 0 \\ 1/x \text{ if } x > 0 \end{cases}$$

this function is not bounded. We denote the set of bounded functions on $[a, b]$ by $B[a, b]$. Note that we do not require all the functions to have the *same* bound: $B[a, b]$ is the set of all functions that have a bound. Clearly $B[a, b]$ is a vector space and moreover we can use $\| \|_\infty$ as a norm on this space, although to be absolutely precise we must replace the maximum in Examples 3.19(d) by the least bound valid for that particular function. This quantity is called the *supremum* (sup for short) of the function values. That the supremum exists is a consequence of Axiom 1.7: see Spivak (1967, Chapter 8) for a detailed discussion of this. Similarly, any bounded set of real numbers has a greatest lower bound, or *infimum* (inf for short). For $f \in B[a, b]$,

$$\|f\|_\infty = \sup_{x\in[a,b]} |f(x)|\ .$$

For the example h above, $\|h\|_\infty=0.5$, but this value is not actually achieved by $h(x)$ for any x. On the other hand if f is continuous, Theorem 1.19 tells us that f achieves its maximum value, so it is acceptable to replace sup by max as in Example 3.19(d).

Indeed $B[a, b]$ is obviously the *largest* subspace of the space of all functions defined on $[a, b]$, such that $\|\ \|_\infty$ makes sense. We first show that:

Theorem 3.23

The space $B[a, b]$ with $\|\ \|_\infty$ is analytically complete.

Proof

We have to show that if $(f_n)\subset B[a, b]$ is a Cauchy sequence, then the sequence converges (in the norm) to a function in $B[a, b]$. Suppose we are given $\varepsilon>0$. By definition if (f_n) is a Cauchy sequence, there is a natural number K such that for $m, n>K$

$$\|f_n - f_m\|_\infty < \varepsilon.$$

But for any particular x in $[a, b]$,

$$|f_n(x) - f_m(x)| \le \|f_n - f_m\|_\infty < \varepsilon. \tag{3.16}$$

This shows that the sequence (of real numbers) $[f_n(x)]$ is Cauchy. So by Theorem 1.9, it has a limit. We may define a function f: $[a, b]\to\mathbb{R}$ by $f(x)=$limit $f_n(x)$ as $n\to\infty$. It remains to show that f is bounded and that $f_n\to f$ in norm.

$$\begin{aligned}|f_n(x)| &= |f_n(x) - f_m(x) + f_m(x)|\\ &\le |f_n(x) - f_m(x)| + f_m(x)|\\ &< \varepsilon + \|f_m(x)\|_\infty \text{ from (3.16).}\end{aligned}$$

If we now fix m and allow $n\to\infty$, we find

$$|f(x)| \le \varepsilon + \|f_m(x)\|_\infty.$$

showing that $f\in B\,[a, b]$. On the other hand, if we let $m\to\infty$ in (3.16) we get

$$|f_{n(x)} - f(x)| < \varepsilon.$$

Since this holds for any x independent of ε, and, with a suitable choice of K, for any $\varepsilon > 0$, it follows that $f_n \to f$ in norm.

□

Corollary 3.24
The space $C[a, b]$ with $\|\ \|_\infty$ is analytically complete.

Proof
In view of Theorem 3.23, we know that a Cauchy sequence (f_n) of functions in $C[a, b]$ will converge in norm to some function f in $B[a, b]$. By definition, the functions f_n must be continuous. We need only show that this implies that f is also continuous. Let x be some point in $[a, b]$. Given $\varepsilon>0$ we may choose n such that $\|f-f_n\|_\infty < \varepsilon/3$, since $f_n \to f$ in norm. Also we may choose δ such that for $|x-y|<\delta$, $|f_n(x)-f_n(y)|<\varepsilon/3$. Then we have for $|x-y|<\delta$

$$\begin{aligned} |f(x) - f(y)| &= |f(x) - f_n(x) + f_n(x) - f_n(y) + f_n(y) - f(y)| \\ &\leq |f(x) - f_n(x)| + |f_n(x) - f_n(y)| + |f_n(y) - f(y)| \\ &< \varepsilon/3 + \varepsilon/3 + \varepsilon/3 = \varepsilon, \end{aligned}$$

confirming that f is continuous.

□

We cannot expect a similar result to hold for $C[a, b]$ with $\|\ \|_p$. Example 3.22 shows a sequence of continuous functions that converges with respect to $\|\ \|_1$, but the limit is not continuous. Instead, we can use the same approach as for $B[a, b]$ and use the *largest* space for which $\|\ \|_p$ makes sense.

The idea then is is to define the space $L_p[a, b]$ as the space of all functions f on $[a, b]$ for which $\|f\|_p$ is finite. However, there is a further subtlety here. Two functions f and g, say, which are equal almost everywhere (see Definition 1.24) will satisfy $\|f-g\|_p=0$, even if $f(x) \neq g(x)$ for *every* **x**. This contradicts Property 3.17i). So if we took this definition for $L_p\ [a, b]$, $\|\ \|_p$ would not be a genuine norm. Instead we define an equivalence relation R by $f\,R\,g$ if and only if $f=g$ almost everywhere. Clearly this preserves the vector space structure: if $f_1=f_2$ a.e. and $g_1=g_2$ a.e., then for any real number λ, $f_1+\lambda g_1=f_2+\lambda g_2$ a.e. In other words, we should only think of functions in L_p being defined up to a set of measure zero. Formally we need this rather clumsy definition:

Definition 3.25

Let R be equivalence relation $f\ R\ g$ if and only if $f=g$ almost everywhere on $[a, b]$. The space $L_p[a, b]$, $1 \leq p < \infty$ is defined to be the set of equivalence classes E of this relation for which there is an $f \in E$ for which $\|f\|_p$ is finite. This definition makes sense since all elements of a given class E have the same norm and, moreover, two functions f and g with $\|f-g\|_p=0$ belong to the same equivalence class. Also the vector space structure is preserved.

□

The universal convention here is to refer to an equivalence class by any of its members, rather than using a special notation. So we refer to a function f belonging to $L_p[a, b]$ when we *really* mean that the *equivalence class* of f belongs to $L_p[a, b]$. We may forget about Definition 3.26 provided we always remember that when talking about $f, g \in L_p[a, b]$, we think of them as being the same function if they are equal almost everywhere.

The completeness proof is somewhat technical and probably only of interest to pure mathematicians. Here an outline is given in sufficient detail to enable a competent analyst to fill in the missing parts! Readers not interested in grasping every detail of the theory may safely ignore these proofs. As in the proof for $B[a, b]$ we start by showing that a particular sequence of functions must have a so called *pointwise* limit, i.e. that the sequence $(g_n(x))$ converges for almost all values of x. We can then use the convergence theorems from Chapter 1 to prove norm convergence.

Lemma 3.26

Let (g_n) be an almost everywhere monotone increasing sequence of functions in $L_p[a, b]$, and suppose that for all n and for some positive real number M, $\|g_n\|_p < M$. Then there is a function g: $[a, b] \rightarrow \mathbb{R}$ such that for almost all x, $g_n(x) \rightarrow g(x)$. Moreover the sequence also converges in norm, i.e. $\|g_n - g\|_p \rightarrow 0$.

Proof

The sequence $(g_n - g_1)$ is in $L_p[a, b]$ and is non-negative. We apply Theorem 1.38 to the sequence $(g_n - g_1)^p$ and obtain a limit, say $h(x)$. Then choose $g(x) = [h(x)]^{1/p} + g_1(x)$.

Convergence in norm follows by applying Theorem 1.39 twice. First apply it to the sequence $(g_n)^p$ to deduce that $\|g\|_p \leq M$. It follows by the triangle inequality that $\|g - g_n\|_p < 2M$. Thus we can apply Theorem 1.39 again, this time that to the sequence $\|g - g_n\|^p$, to obtain the required result.

□

The actual completeness theorem is now fairly straightforward, if somewhat tedious!

Theorem 3.27
The space $L_p[a, b]$, $1 \leq p < \infty$, is analytically complete.

Proof
Let (f_i) be a Cauchy sequence in $L_p[a, b]$. It is not difficult to show that if a subsequence of a Cauchy sequence converges, then the whole sequence must converge. Thus, extracting a subsequence if necessary, we may assume without loss of generality that for $m \geq n$,

$$\| f_i - f_{i+1} \|_p < 2^{-n}.$$

Define $g_{m,i}$ by

$$g_{m,i}(x) = \sum_{j=m+1}^{m+i} | f_{j+1}(x) - f_j(x) | .$$

Since $L_p[a, b]$ is a vector space, and each term of the sum is in $L_p[a, b]$, it follows that $g_{m,i}$ is in $L_p[a, b]$.

Moreover

$$\|g_{m,i}\|_p \leq \sum_{j=m+1}^{\infty} \| f_{j+1} - f_j\|_p \leq \sum_{j=m}^{\infty} 2^{-j} = 2^{-m+1}.$$

Now consider what happens if we fix m and let $i \to \infty$. We see from Lemma 3.26 that the sequence $(g_{m,i})$ will converge almost everywhere and in norm to some limit, say h_m, in $L_p[a, b]$, where

$$h_m = \sum_{j=m+1}^{\infty} | f_{j+1} - f_j|$$

and $\|h_m\|_p \leq 2^{-m+1.}$

Now define $g_m = f_m - h_m$. Then for almost all x we have

$$g_{m+1}(x) - g_m(x) = f_{m+1}(x) - f_m(x) - h_{m+1}(x) + h_m(x) = f_{m+1}(x) - f_m(x) + |f_{m+1}(x) - f_m(x)| \geq 0.$$

In other words the sequence $g_m(x)$ is almost everywhere monotone. So applying Lemma 3.26 again we obtain a limit g, say. Then

$$\|g - f_m\|_p = \|g - g_m + g_m - f_m\|_p = \|g - g_m - h_m\|_p \leq \|g - g_m\|_p = \|h_m\|_p .$$

But both the terms on the right tend to zero as $m \to \infty$, showing that $f_m \to g$ in norm.

□

Remarks 3.28

(a) Referring to the end of the proof, note that the Cauchy sequence (f_m) converges not only in norm to g, but also pointwise almost everywhere. On the other hand it will not necessary converge at *every* point: on the contrary pointwise behaviour may be very complicated.

(b) What is the space $L_\infty[a, b]$? One possibility is to use this notation for the space $B[a, b]$ defined above. A more consistent usage is to define this space as the set of equivalence classes under R such that one element of the class is in $B[a, b]$. L_∞ is thus the space of functions which are bounded except on a set of measure zero: so called *essentially bounded* functions. Every essentially bounded function f is R-equivalent to a function g in $B[a, b]$: simply define $g(x)=0$ for those x belonging to the set of measure zero where f may be unbounded, and $g(x)=f(x)$ otherwise. Thus $L_\infty[a, b] \subset B[a, b]$ (more precisely $L_\infty[a, b]$ can be embedded in $B[a, b]$) and in fact it is a proper subspace since two different elements of $B[a, b]$ may be R-equivalent. The completeness of $L_\infty[a, b]$ is easily deduced from that of $B[a, b]$. However, in practice, $\| \, \|_\infty$ is usually used with $C[a, b]$.

3.3 Matrix iterations, matrix norms and the delta rule

We will now leave the esoteric realms of analysis and return to the study of finite dimensional vector spaces. We require only on more tool (the matrix norm) before we can begin a serious discussion of the behaviour of linear networks. But before introducing this, we will introduce the network learning algorithm that will motivate our discussion throughout this section. Refer again to Fig. 2.1, which shows the simple neural network known as a perceptron. We now address the question of the determination of the weights in this network. These will be determined by a process known as *supervised learning.*

We assume that we have a set of learning vectors for which we *know* the desired output. We will use these to *train* the network to produce the desired response. (This mimics the biological process of learning from examples rather than an established theory.) Of course, to obtain a set of weights that will produce the correct output over all (or even a large range) of possible inputs requires the training vectors to be well chosen. The choice of training vectors is an important (and difficult) problem in itself, but this is not our concern here. We will assume that we have a set of vectors which is representative of the general population of possible inputs. Denote one of the training vectors (generically) by $\mathbf{x}$ ($\mathbf{x} \in \mathbb{R}^n$) and corresponding desired output vector by $\mathbf{y}$. W is the weight matrix. We want to find W such that $\mathbf{y} = W\mathbf{x}$ for all training pairs $(\mathbf{x}, \mathbf{y})$ of patterns and corresponding outputs.

Definition 3.29 The Delta Rule

We assume that we have an initial weight matrix W and we want to update W by means of a new training pattern. The *delta rule* (or *LMS rule*) uses the following learning algorithm: the change in W when the pattern $\mathbf{x}$ is presented is given (Rumelhart and McClelland, 1986, p. 322) by

$$\delta W_{ji} = \eta[\, y_j - (W\mathbf{x})_j]x_i \tag{3.17}$$

where η is a real parameter called the *learning rate*, and $(W\mathbf{x})_j$ denotes the jth element of $W\mathbf{x}$.

□

The initials LMS stand for Least Mean Square: the reason for this will be apparent shortly. This version of the delta rule is the so called *on-line* version. The *off-line* or *epoch* version is considered in Section 3.5.

The new W is then the old $W + \delta W$. Heuristically, this algorithm can be justified as follows. The term $[\, y_j - (W\mathbf{x})_j]$ is the error of the network for the jth element of the output $\mathbf{y}$, when the input $\mathbf{x}$ is applied. The method adds this multiple of $\mathbf{x}$ to the jth row of W. Then

$$\begin{aligned}(W\mathbf{x} + \delta W\mathbf{x})_j &= (W\mathbf{x})_j + \sum \delta W_{ji} x_i \\ &= (W\mathbf{x})_j + \eta y_j \sum (x_i)^2 - \eta\, (W\mathbf{x})_j \sum (x_i)^2 \\ &= (W\mathbf{x})_j + \eta\, y_j \|\mathbf{x}\|_2 - \eta\, (W\mathbf{x})_j \|\mathbf{x}\|_2 \,.\end{aligned}$$

So if η were chosen to be $1/\|\mathbf{x}\|_2$, the new weight matrix would produce precisely the desired output y_j. However this would of course work only for this particular pattern. The idea of the delta rule is to choose a smaller value of η, hopefully improving the response of the system to this pattern, without destroying its behaviour for the other training patterns. But clearly this heuristic justification is not very satisfactory. How do we *know* what the behaviour is for the other patterns? Will the method work at all over a range of training patterns? What is the best choice of η? Actually there are various ways to approach this problem. One method is to consider what happens when η is *very* small. We can then approximate the delta rule by a differential equation. But in practice we do not want to make η too small: we want to make it as close to $1/\|\mathbf{x}\|_2$ as possible, so as to get the best response for a given training pattern. The asymptotic approach gives us no information as to how best to choose η. For a simple network such as this it is both possible and preferable to analyse the system (3.17) directly. It is also arguable that it is actually easier!

We can simplify matters here by observing that *there is no coupling between the rows of W in this formula*: the new jth row of W depends only on the old jth row. This enables us to drop the subscript j, denoting y_j just by y, and the jth row of W by the vector $\mathbf{w}^{\mathrm{T}}$. In other words we can consider, without loss of generality, a perceptron with a *single* output. (Note that this is *not* true for the non-linear version of the delta rule known as back-propagation.) Of course any estimate for η we get will have to apply to all rows, but we shall see later that this is actually not a problem. So we get

$$\delta w_i = \eta\,(y - \mathbf{w}^{\mathrm{T}}\mathbf{x})x_i\,,$$

or

$$\delta \mathbf{w} = \eta\,(y - \mathbf{w}^{\mathrm{T}}\mathbf{x})\mathbf{x}.$$

Thus given a current iterate weight vector $\mathbf{w_k}$,

$$\begin{aligned}
\mathbf{w_{k+1}} &= \mathbf{w_k} + \delta\mathbf{w_k} \\
&= \mathbf{w_k} + \eta(y - \mathbf{w_k}^{\mathrm{T}}\mathbf{x})\mathbf{x} \\
&= (I - \eta\mathbf{x}\mathbf{x}^{\mathrm{T}})\mathbf{w_k} + \eta y\mathbf{x} \qquad (3.18)\\
&= B\mathbf{w_k} + \eta y\mathbf{x}, \qquad (3.19)
\end{aligned}$$

where $B=(I-\eta\mathbf{x}\mathbf{x}^{\mathrm{T}})$. Equation (3.18) is obtained by transposing the (scalar) quantity in brackets. Note the bold subscript k here, denoting the kth iterate, not the kth element.

However, up to now we have only considered a single training pattern $\mathbf{x}$. In practice we actually have a set of these. Suppose there are t pattern vectors $\mathbf{x}_1$, . . . , $\mathbf{x}_t$. (3.18) applies for each of these individually, but how are we going to present the patterns to the system? The most obvious approach is to start with $\mathbf{x}_1$, then $\mathbf{x}_2$ and so on until we get to $\mathbf{x}_t$. We then start again with $\mathbf{x}_1$ and repeat the cycles until the system appears to have settled down. Each presentation of a complete set of training patterns is called an *epoch*. Note that the matrix B in (3.19) depends (only) on η and $\mathbf{x}$. If we regard η as fixed, we will have a matrix B_p corresponding to each input pattern $\mathbf{x}_p$. Suppose that at the start of an epoch of training patterns we have some weight vector $\mathbf{w}_k$. Then from (3.19) we get

$$\mathbf{w}_{k+1} = B_1\mathbf{w}_k + \eta y_1\mathbf{x}_1$$
$$\mathbf{w}_{k+2} = B_2\mathbf{w}_{k+1} + \eta y_2\mathbf{x}_2 = B_2B_1\mathbf{w}_k + \eta B_2 y_1\mathbf{x}_1 + \eta y_2\mathbf{x}_2\,,$$

etc. leading to

$$\mathbf{w}_{k+t} = \Lambda\mathbf{w}_k + \mathbf{h}, \tag{3.20a}$$

where $[\Lambda] = B_tB_{t-1}\ldots B_1$ and

$$\mathbf{h} = \eta[\, y_1(B_tB_{t-1}\ldots B_2)\mathbf{x}_1 + \ldots + y_{t-1}B_t\mathbf{x}_{t-1} + y_t\mathbf{x}_t]. \tag{3.20b}$$

It is important to notice that both Λ and $\mathbf{h}$ are independent of any particular weight vector $\mathbf{w}$: they depend only on the input patterns $\mathbf{x}_p$, the output patterns y_p and the learning rate η. Let us renumber (3.20) by setting $\mathbf{v}_0 = \mathbf{w}_0$, $\mathbf{v}_1 = \mathbf{w}_t$, $\mathbf{v}_2 = \mathbf{w}_{2t}$, etc. If we put $k = 0$ in (3.20) we get

$$\mathbf{v}_1 = \Lambda\mathbf{y}_0 + \mathbf{h}$$

and in general

$$\mathbf{v}_{j+1} = \Lambda\, \mathbf{v}_j + \mathbf{h}. \tag{3.21}$$

A recurrence of this form is called a *matrix iteration*. We wish to know what happens to $\mathbf{v}_j$ as $j \to \infty$. Actually iterations of this kind are extremely common in mathematics and their behaviour is well understood.

As a first attempt at analysing the behaviour of (3.21) let us make two assumptions, neither of which necessarily holds for arbitrary Λ and $\mathbf{h}$ (although we shall show later that at least the first does always hold in our case). However, an understanding of this simplest case is important. First, suppose that there is a fixed point, i.e. there is a vector $\mathbf{v}$ such that

$$\mathbf{v} = \Lambda\, \mathbf{v} + \mathbf{h}. \tag{3.22}$$

(Note that this assumption is equivalent to assuming that the system of equations $(\Lambda - I)\mathbf{v} = -\mathbf{h}$ has a solution: compare Theorem 2.27). The second assumption is that Λ is similar to a diagonal matrix (see Definition 3.1, equation (3.2) and the subsequent discussion.) More specifically, suppose $\Lambda = PDP^{-1}$ where D is diagonal with diagonal elements the eigenvalues of Λ, and P is the matrix formed from a complete set of eigenvectors in the same order as the eigenvalues. If we subtract (3.22) from (3.21) we get

$$(\mathbf{v_{j+1}} - \mathbf{v}) = \Lambda\ (\mathbf{v_{j+1}} - \mathbf{v}).$$

Substituting for Λ gives

$$(\mathbf{v_{j+1}} - \mathbf{v}) = PDP^{-1}(\mathbf{v_{j+1}} - \mathbf{v}).$$

Starting from $\mathbf{v_0}$ gives

$$(\mathbf{v_1} - \mathbf{v}) = PDP^{-1}(\mathbf{v_0} - \mathbf{v})$$
$$(\mathbf{v_2} - \mathbf{v}) = PDP^{-1}(\mathbf{v_1} - \mathbf{v}) = PDP^{-1}PDP^{-1}(\mathbf{v_0} - \mathbf{v}) = PD^2P^{-1}(\mathbf{v_0} - \mathbf{v}).$$

Note the cancellation of the $P^{-1}P$ term in the middle. Similarly we get

$$(\mathbf{v_3} - \mathbf{v}) = PDP^{-1}(\mathbf{v_2} - \mathbf{v}) = PDP^{-1}PD^2P^{-1}(\mathbf{v_0} - \mathbf{v}) = PD^3P^{-1}(\mathbf{v_0} - \mathbf{v})$$

and in general

$$(\mathbf{v_j} - \mathbf{v}) = PD^jP^{-1}(\mathbf{v_0} - \mathbf{v}). \tag{3.23}$$

Now recall that

$$D = \begin{pmatrix} \lambda_1 & 0 & \dots & & 0 \\ 0 & \lambda_2 & 0 & \dots & 0 \\ 0 & 0 & \lambda_3 & & . \\ \vdots & \vdots & \vdots & & \\ 0 & \dots & \dots & & \lambda_n \end{pmatrix}$$

where $\lambda_1 \dots \lambda_n$ are the eigenvalues of Λ. (Remember that the pattern vectors $\mathbf{x_p}$ are in $\mathbb{R}^n$.) It is easy to verify that

$$Dj = \begin{pmatrix} \lambda_1^j & 0 & \dots & & 0 \\ 0 & \lambda_2^j & 0 & \dots & 0 \\ 0 & 0 & \lambda_3^j & & . \\ \vdots & \vdots & \vdots & & \\ 0 & \dots & \dots & & \lambda_n^j \end{pmatrix}. \tag{3.24}$$

Thus $\mathbf{v}_j \to \mathbf{v}$ *if and only if* $|\lambda_k|<1$ *for all k*. This crucial observation is the fundamental property of matrix iterations.

Definition 3.30

The quantity $\rho(\Lambda)=\max |\lambda_k|$, $k=1, \ldots, n$, is called the *spectral radius* of Λ.

□

But recall the two assumptions we have made. In fact these can be removed if we know $\rho(\Lambda)<1$.

Theorem 3.31

Consider the iteration (3.21). Then, if and only if $\rho(\Lambda)<1$, (3.21) has a unique fixed point $\mathbf{v}$ as in (3.22) and $\mathbf{v}_k \to \mathbf{v}$.

□

A complete proof of this result requires either the use of complex matrices: see, e.g. Isaacson and Keller (1966, p. 14), or some relatively sophisticated algebra (Hartley and Hawkes, 1970, Ch. 11) and either way is somewhat technical. A related result for continuous systems will be proved in Chapter 5. We will omit the complete proof of Theorem 3.31 here since instead we are going to use a much more powerful tool to establish the existence of a fixed point, namely the Contraction Mapping Theorem (Theorem 1.51). We remark however that the existence and uniqueness of the fixed point $\mathbf{v}$ is easy to show. Notice that the condition $\rho(\Lambda)<1$ implies that 1 is not an eigenvalue of Λ and thus that $(I-\Lambda)$ is non-singular. The result then follows as in the sentence following (3.22).

Before returning to the special case of the delta rule we make one further observation.

Suppose in (3.24) $|\lambda_1|>|\lambda_k|$, $k=2, \ldots, n$. Then as $j\to\infty$, we see that $\lambda_1^{-j}D^j$ tends to the matrix which has a 1 as entry (1, 1) and 0 everywhere else. Call this matrix Γ. Then from (3.23) we see that

$$\lambda_1^{-j}(\mathbf{v}_j - \mathbf{v}) \to P\,\Gamma P^{-1}(\mathbf{v}_0 - \mathbf{v}).$$

Moreover the vector $\mathbf{c}=\Gamma P^{-1}(\mathbf{v}_0-\mathbf{v})$ *has zero for all its elements except* c_1, since only the first row of Γ is non-zero. Thus we obtain the following important property.

Remark 3.32 (Generic Behaviour of Matrix Iterations)
$\lambda_1^{-j}(\mathbf{v}_j - \mathbf{v}) \to c_1\mathbf{p}_1$ where $\mathbf{p}_1$ is the first column of P, i.e. the eigenvector corresponding to λ_1. So if Λ has a single largest eigenvalue λ_1, we expect in general that, up to multiplication by the scalar λ_1^{-j}, $(\mathbf{v}_j - \mathbf{v})$ *approaches the corresponding eigenvector*. This remark is crucial in understanding the generic behaviour of matrix iterations. Notice that it applies whether or not $\mathbf{v}_j \to \mathbf{v}$. Note also that with exact arithmetic, we would have to include the condition $c_1 \neq 0$ which we would not know in practice. However, in a real system, rounding error (on a digital system) or noise (on an analogue system) will introduce a component of $\mathbf{p}_1$ so the condition can be ignored.

More generally, if there is more than one largest eigenvalue, $(\mathbf{v}_j - \mathbf{v})$ will approach the span of the corresponding eigenvectors.

□

Now let us return to the neural network. Theorem 3.31 applies for any iteration of the form (3.21) but for the case of the delta rule it is very unlikely that we can determine $\rho(\Lambda)$ in general, since Λ is made up of the complicated product in equation (3.20). On the other hand, as we shall see, the B matrices are quite simple. But it is very difficult in general to relate directly the spectral radius of a product to the individual matrices making up the product. We require an alternative tool. Look again equation (3.19). If we were to be guided by the more general Contraction Mapping Theorem (Theorem 1.51) instead of the special properties of matrices, the natural question to ask is whether the mapping defined by B is contractive. Since this mapping is linear, this question is equivalent to asking how big $B\mathbf{w}$ can be for a given size of $\mathbf{w}$. Once again we digress from the particular example in hand to consider this in detail.

How do we measure the 'size' of a real matrix A? Since the set of $m \times n$ matrices over $\mathbb{R}$ form an mn dimensional vector space over $\mathbb{R}$, we could just take any matrix norm over $\mathbb{R}$ and use this as a norm for matrices, just thinking of the matrix as a vector in $\mathbb{R}^{mn}$. For instance we can define $\|A\|_S$ to be $(\sum a_{ij}^2)^{1/2}$, where the sum is over all the elements. If $\mathbf{a}_i$ is the ith column of A, then the i, ith element of A^TA is $\mathbf{a}_i^T\mathbf{a}_i$, so in fact $\|A\|_S = \sqrt{\text{trace}(A^TA)}$. $\|A\|_S$ is called the *Schur norm*. Because of these nice properties this norm is often used. However, the other possible norms on $\mathbb{R}^{mn}$ are not generally used in this way. We really want our definition of matrix norm to reflect the status of matrices as defining linear transformations, and it turns out to be convenient to add an extra condition in addition to those of Properties 3.17.

Properties 3.33

Let S be the set of $m \times n$ matrices over $\mathbb{R}$. A *matrix norm* $\| \ \|$ is a function $\| \ \|: S \to \mathbb{R}^+$ such that for each A, $B \in V$ and $\lambda \in \mathbb{R}$

(a) $\|A\| = 0$ if and only if $A = 0$
(b) $\|A + B\| \leq \|A\| + \|B\|$ (the triangle inequality)
(c) $\|\lambda A\| = |\lambda| \, \|A\|$
(d) $\|AB\| \leq \|A\| \, \|B\|$.

□

Note the additional condition (d). It turns out that $\| \ \|_S$ actually satisfies this condition, but we will not give a proof. Instead we shall develop a much more natural way of defining matrix norms.

Definition 3.34

Let $\| \ \|_\alpha$ and $\| \ \|_\beta$ be vector norms on $\mathbb{R}^n$ and $\mathbb{R}^m$ respectively. We define the *induced norm* (or *operator norm*) on the set of by $m \times n$ matrices over $\mathbb{R}$, by

$$\|A\| = \max_{\|\mathbf{x}\|_\alpha = 1} \|A\mathbf{x}\|_\beta$$

□

Properties 3.33 can be checked as an exercise. It is conventional to use the same symbol for a vector norm and its induced matrix norm when dealing with actual examples. For example if we were using $\| \ \|_2$ on $\mathbb{R}^n$ and $\mathbb{R}^m$, we would write $\|A\|_2$ for the corresponding matrix norm. The point of this definition is that it means that for any vector $\mathbf{x}$, we have

$$\|A\mathbf{x}\| \leq \|A\| \, \|\mathbf{x}\| , \tag{3.25}$$

i.e. it tells us how big $A\mathbf{x}$ can be compared with $\mathbf{x}$. There is always some $\mathbf{x}$ for which equality holds. To see this think of $\mathbf{x}$ moving over the unit sphere $\|\mathbf{x}\| = 1$. $\|A\mathbf{x}\|$ will trace out a closed surface in $\mathbb{R}^n$. At some point it will reach its farthest distance from the origin: this corresponds to the $\mathbf{x}$ required.

If, conversely, we have a matrix norm (perhaps defined by some other method) which satisfies (3.25) for a particular vector norm, the matrix and vector norms are said to be *compatible*.

We will see how to calculate $\|A\|$ for the matrix norms induced by the standard vector norms shortly. First let us look at some properties.

If A is square (i.e. $m=n$), then we can chose $\mathbf{x}$ to be an eigenvector in (3.25), say $\mathbf{v}$ is an eigenvector corresponding to λ. Then substituting in (3.25) gives

$$\|A\mathbf{v}\| \leq \|A\| \, \|\mathbf{v}\|$$

or

$$|\lambda| \, \|\mathbf{v}\| \leq \|A\| \, \|\mathbf{v}\|$$

so

$$|\lambda| \leq \|A\|$$

Since this is true for any eigenvalue λ, we get the important condition

$$\rho\,(A) \leq \|A\| \tag{3.26}$$

for any square matrix A and compatible matrix norm $\|A\|$.

Note that for an induced norm, $I\mathbf{x}=\mathbf{x}$, so $\|I\|=1$. This shows that $\| \, \|_S$ cannot be induced by any vector norm, since $\|I\|_S = \sqrt{n}$ for $n \times n$ matrices.

Another important property follows from Property 3.33(d) and thus holds for any matrix norm. Again if A is square, we get $\|A^k\| \leq \|A\|^k$. Thus $A^k \to 0$ if $\|A\| < 1$ for any norm. On the other hand we already know that $A^k \to 0$ if *and only if* $\rho(A) < 1$ (a simple consequence of Theorem 3.31), so this new condition is weaker, and you may wonder why it is useful. However the point is that $\|A\|$ is usually easier to work with, and calculate or estimate, than $\rho(A)$. Obviously, it is easier to calculate $\|A\|_S$ than solve an eigenvalue problem. Moreover $\|A\|_1$ and $\|A\|_\infty$ are also easy to calculate as is shown by the following theorem, which gives explicit expressions for the norms induced by the usual vector norms.

Theorem 3.35

Let A be an $m \times n$ matrix.

(a) $\|A\|_\infty$ may be calculated as follows. Take the absolute values of all the elements and then add up each row. The largest such row sum is $\|A\|_\infty$. In other words

$$\|A\|_\infty = \max_i \sum_{j=1}^{n} |a_{ij}|$$

(b) $\|A\|_1 = \|A^{\mathrm{T}}\|_\infty$.

(c) $\|A\|_2 = \sqrt{(p\ A^{\mathrm{T}} A)}$

Proof

(a) Let $\mathbf{x}$ satisfy $\|\mathbf{x}\|_\infty=1$. Then the ith element of $A\mathbf{x}$ is $(A\mathbf{x})_i=\sum a_{ij}x_j$, whence $|(A\mathbf{x})_i|\le\sum |a_{ij}|\ |x_j|\le\sum |a_{ij}|$ since $\|\mathbf{x}\|_\infty=1$. Hence $\|A\|_\infty \le \max \sum |a_{ij}|$, where the maximum is taken over i. To show that equality is achieved, define $\mathbf{x}$ by $x_j=\operatorname{sign}(a_{ij})$, where i is the value for which the maximum absolute row sum occurs. (The sign function is defined by sign $a=1$ if a is positive, 0 if a is zero, and -1 if a is negative.) Then assuming $A\neq 0$ (in which case the result is trivial) $|(A\mathbf{x})_i| =\sum |a_{ij}|\ |x_j|=\sum |a_{ij}|$ showing that the bound is achieved.

(b) Let $\mathbf{y}$ be a vector such that $\|\mathbf{y}\|_1=1$ and

$$\|A\|_1 = \|A\mathbf{y}\|_1 = \sum_{j=1}^{m}\sum_{k=1}^{n}|a_{jk}y_k| \le \sum_{j=1}^{m}\sum_{k=1}^{n}|a_{jk}|\ |y_k| = \sum_{k=1}^{n}|y_k|\sum_{j=1}^{m}|a_{jk}|$$

$$\le \sum_{k=1}^{n}|y_k|\left(\max_i \sum_{j=1}^{m}|a_{ji}|\right) \le \|y\|_1 \max_i \sum_{j=1}^{m}|a_{ji}| = \max_i \sum_{j=1}^{m}|a_{ji}| .$$

The bound is attained by considering $\|A\mathbf{e}_M\|_1$ where M is the value of i for which the maximum occurs, since then

$$\|A\mathbf{e}_M\|_1 = \sum_{j=1}^{m}|a_{jM}| .$$

(c) There is a direct proof of this in Isaacson and Keller (1966, p. 10), but a much shorter proof can be given using the singular value decomposition, to be discussed in the next section. Thus we will defer it until then.

□

Computing $\|A\|_2$ exactly is therefore apparently almost as hard as computing $\rho(A)$ although we do have a symmetric matrix to deal with (and hence real eigenvalues). This is unfortunate since many neural net algorithms are based on minimising errors with respect to the ordinary Euclidean vector norm. However we shall see that it is sometimes much easier to estimate $\|A\|_2$ than $\rho(A)$. (We should remark, however, that there are also tools for estimating eigenvalues directly, see Isaacson and Keller, Ch. 4, particularly Theorem 1). If we do not need to use the 2-norm then we can get away with a simpler computation.

Example 3.36

Let

$$A = \begin{pmatrix} 0.4 & 0.3 & -0.2 \\ -0.1 & 0.7 & 0.1 \\ 0.2 & 0.2 & 0.2 \end{pmatrix}.$$

Adding up the absolute values of the elements in each row gives $0.4+0.3+0.2=0.9$, $0.1+0.7+0.1=0.9$ and $0.2+0.2+0.2=0.6$. The largest value is 0.9, so $\|A\|_\infty=0.9$. We can deduce that the iteration $\mathbf{x}_{k+1}=A\mathbf{x}_k$ will converge to zero *without* solving the eigenvalue problem. On the other hand if we compute the column sums (i.e. the rows sums of A^T) we get 0.7, 1.2 and 0.5. Thus $\|A\|_1=1.2$, which is greater than 1 and therefore does not help us. Actually $\rho(A)=0.7049$, so even $\|A\|_\infty$ is not a very sharp estimate of $\rho(A)$.

□

Now let us use this machinery to discuss the delta rule again. (The following result first appeared in this form in Ellacott (1990). It is related to a result of Kaczmarz from 1937, which may be found in Parkes (1993). Compare also Oja (1983, Chapter 5.) We know from Theorem 3.31 that the iteration (3.21) will converge to the fixed point provided $\rho(\Lambda)<1$. However up to now we have had no way of checking this condition in general. The matrix norm provides us with the necessary machinery. For

$$\begin{aligned} \rho(\Lambda) &\le \|\Lambda\|_2 \\ &\le \|B_t B_{t-1} \ldots B_1\|_2 \text{ [see (3.20)]} \\ &\le \|B_t\|_2\,\|B_{t-1}\|_2 \ldots \|B_1\|_2 \text{ (repeated application of Properties 3.33 (d)).} \end{aligned} \tag{3.27}$$

Each matrix B has a very simple structure and its norm is easy to obtain. We have (3.19)

$$B = (I - \eta \mathbf{x}\mathbf{x}^T),$$

where we have dropped the pattern number subscript for notational convenience. It is easy to check that B is symmetric and thus has a complete orthogonal basis of real eigenvectors (whereas on the other hand Λ is not symmetric). Thus

$$\|B\|_2 = \sqrt{\rho(B^T B)} = \sqrt{\rho(B^2)} = \rho(B)$$

since if $\mathbf{y}$ is an eigenvector of B corresponding to the eigenvalue λ, $B^2\mathbf{y} = B(\lambda\mathbf{y}) = \lambda^2\mathbf{y}$, i.e. the eigenvalues of B^2 are the squares of those of B. Actually it is easy to determine the eigenvectors and eigenvalues of B by inspection:

$$\begin{aligned} B\mathbf{x} &= (I - \eta\mathbf{x}\mathbf{x}^{\mathrm{T}})\mathbf{x} \\ &= \mathbf{x} - \eta\mathbf{x}(\mathbf{x}^{\mathrm{T}}\mathbf{x}) \\ &= (1 - \eta\,\|\mathbf{x}\|_2^2)\mathbf{x}. \end{aligned}$$

Thus $\mathbf{x}$ is an eigenvector of B with eigenvalue $(1 - \eta\|\mathbf{x}\|_2^2)$. On the other hand, if $\mathbf{y}$ is any vector orthogonal to $\mathbf{x}$, we get

$$\begin{aligned} B\mathbf{y} &= (I - \eta\mathbf{x}\mathbf{x}^{\mathrm{T}})\mathbf{y} \\ &= \mathbf{y} - \eta\mathbf{x}(\mathbf{x}^{\mathrm{T}}\mathbf{y}) \\ &= \mathbf{y}. \end{aligned}$$

So any such $\mathbf{y}$ is an eigenvector with eigenvalue 1. Thus, provided η is sufficiently small that $|1 - \eta\|\mathbf{x}\|_2^2| < 1$, we find that $\rho(B) = 1$. It follows from (3.27) that $\rho(\Lambda) \le 1$. Unfortunately this is not enough in itself to use Theorem 3.31: we need strict inequality. But we can get this by a more careful analysis. Let $\mathbf{u}$ be a vector such that $\|\mathbf{u}\|_2 = 1$ and

$$\begin{aligned} \|\Lambda\|_2 &= \|\Lambda\mathbf{u}\|_2 \\ &= \|B_t B_{t-1} \ldots B_1\mathbf{u}\|_2 && (3.28) \\ &\le \|B_t B_{t-1} \ldots B_2\|_2\, \|B_1\mathbf{u}\|_2 \\ &\le \|B_1\mathbf{u}\|_2. && (3.29) \end{aligned}$$

By choosing a basis for the space of vectors orthogonal to $\mathbf{x}_1$, we may write

$$\mathbf{u} = \alpha\mathbf{x}_1 + \beta\mathbf{u}' \tag{3.30}$$

where we may assume without loss of generality that $\|\mathbf{u}'\|_2 = 1$. Then recalling that both $\mathbf{x}_1$ and $\mathbf{u}'$ are eigenvectors of B_1, we get

$$B_1\mathbf{u} = \alpha B_1\mathbf{x}_1 + \beta B_1\mathbf{u}' = \alpha(1 - \eta\,\|\mathbf{x}_1\|_2^2)\mathbf{x}_1 + \beta\mathbf{u}'.$$

Thus

$$\begin{aligned} \|B_1\mathbf{u}\|_2^2 &= (B_1\mathbf{u})^{\mathrm{T}}(B_1\mathbf{u}) = \{\alpha(1 - \eta\,\|\mathbf{x}_1\|_2^2)]\mathbf{x}_1 + \beta\mathbf{u}')^{\mathrm{T}}[\alpha(1 - \eta\,\|\mathbf{x}_1\|_2^2)]\mathbf{x}_1 + \beta\mathbf{u}'\} \\ &= [\alpha(1 - \eta\,\|\mathbf{x}_1\|_2^2)]^2\,\|\mathbf{x}_1\|_2^2 + \beta^2. \end{aligned}$$

On the other hand,

$$\|\mathbf{u}\|_2^2 = (\alpha\mathbf{x}_1 + \beta\mathbf{u}')^{\mathrm{T}}(\alpha\mathbf{x}_1 + \beta\mathbf{u}') = \alpha^2\,\|\mathbf{x}_1\|_2^2 + \beta^2$$

If $\mathbf{u}$ is *not* orthogonal to $\mathbf{x}_1$ then (provided of course $|1-\eta\|\mathbf{x}_1\|_2^2| < 1$) we have $\|\mathbf{u}\|_2 < \|B_1\mathbf{u}\|_2$.

Substitution into (3.29) then shows that for this case $\|\Lambda\|_2 < 1$. On the other hand if $\mathbf{u}$ *is* orthogonal to $\mathbf{x}_1$ then $\mathbf{u}$ is an eigenvector of B_1 with eigenvalue 1, so $B_1\mathbf{u}=\mathbf{u}$. Substitution into (3.28) then yields by a similar argument to (3.29) that

$$\|\Lambda\|_2 \leq \|B_2\mathbf{u}\|_2.$$

Repeating the argument above we see that $\|\Lambda\|_2 < 1$ unless $\mathbf{u}$ is orthogonal to *all* the $\mathbf{x}_i$'s. Now recall that the $\mathbf{x}_i$'s are vectors in $\mathbb{R}^n$. If we were to make the assumption that the $\mathbf{x}_i$'s span $\mathbb{R}^n$ then it is obviously impossible for $\mathbf{u}$ to be orthogonal to all of them: if it were we would have $n+1$ independent vectors in $\mathbb{R}^n$. In this case we may conclude

$$\rho(\Lambda) \leq \|\Lambda\|_2 < 1 \tag{3.31}$$

and hence that the delta rule iteration (3.21) converges by Theorem 3.31. However there are two drawbacks with this approach. The first is that we have not actually given a proof of Theorem 3.31. More seriously, the second disadvantage is that Theorem 3.31 cannot cope with the case that the $\mathbf{x}_i$'s do not span. Thus it is more satisfactory to use the Contraction Mapping Theorem 1.51. Let

$$F(\mathbf{v}) = \Lambda v + \mathbf{h} \tag{3.32}$$

(compare (3.21)). We have for any $\mathbf{v}$, $\mathbf{w}$

$$\|F(\mathbf{v}) - F(\mathbf{w})\|_2 = \|(\Lambda\mathbf{v}+\mathbf{h}) - (\Lambda\mathbf{w}+\mathbf{h})\|_2 = \|\Lambda(\mathbf{v}-\mathbf{w})\|_2 \leq \|\Lambda\|_2\,\|\mathbf{v}-\mathbf{w}\|_2.$$

In the case that the $\mathbf{x}_i$'s span it follows immediately from (3.31) that the mapping F is contractive and that the iteration (3.21) converges. The non-spanning case requires only a little more care. Let $S=\text{span}\{\mathbf{x}_1, \mathbf{x}_2, \ldots, \mathbf{x}_p\}$. We shall show shortly (see equation (3.51)) that it is always possible to construct an orthogonal basis for S. If we extend this basis to an orthogonal basis for $\mathbb{R}^n$ and let P be the span of those basis vectors *not* in S, then we have decomposed $\mathbb{R}^n$ into two mutually orthogonal subspaces. Now observe that for any vector $\mathbf{v}$ in S, $B_i\mathbf{v}$ is also in S. To see this we note that in a similar way to (3.30), $\mathbf{v}$ may be written as a linear combination of $\mathbf{x}_i$ and a vector orthogonal to $\mathbf{x}_i$ (but still in S). B_i leaves the latter vector unchanged and maps the $\mathbf{x}_i$ component onto a scalar multiple of $\mathbf{x}_i$, so the resulting vector remains in S. From this we observe (a) that the vector $\mathbf{h}$ appearing in (3.32) is in S (compare its definition in (3.20b)) and (b) that $\Lambda\mathbf{v}$ is in S. Thus F maps S to itself and it follows from our previous discussion that the mapping F is contractive on S. So if we start with a weight vector $\mathbf{w}$ which is in S, then certainly the Contraction Mapping Theorem tells us that we get convergence to a unique fixed point in S. We are nearly done: it remains only to consider the case that $\mathbf{w}$ has a component in P. If so, let us write

$$\mathbf{w} = \mathbf{w}' + \mathbf{w}''$$

where $\mathbf{w}' \in S$ and $\mathbf{w}'' \in P$. Then in (3.32)

$$F(\mathbf{w}) = \Lambda\mathbf{w}' + \Lambda\mathbf{w}'' + \mathbf{h}.$$

But $\Lambda\mathbf{w}''=\mathbf{w}''$ since $\mathbf{w}''$ is an eigenvector of each B_i with eigenvalue 1. Hence

$$F(\mathbf{w}) = F(\mathbf{w}') + \mathbf{w}'',$$

and further iterations will simply have the effect of applying the iterated mapping (3.32) to $\mathbf{w}'$ and leaving the $\mathbf{w}''$ part untouched. Since $\mathbf{w}' \in S$ we have established convergence in the general case. In summary, let us state all this as:

Theorem 3.37

Suppose the delta rule (Definition 3.29) is applied by repeatedly cycling through the given training patterns in the same order. We form a sequence $(\mathbf{v}_j)$ from the weight vectors obtained at the end of the successive epochs of patterns (as in (3.21)). Then provided that the learning rate η is such that for each training pattern $\mathbf{x}_i$, $|1-\eta\|\mathbf{x}_i\|_2| < 1$, this sequence $(\mathbf{v}_j)$ converges.

□

Remarks 3.38

(a) It is now easy to see what happens to the intermediate weight vectors not at the end of the epoch of patterns. Suppose the fixed point obtained from (3.21) is $\mathbf{v}$. If we apply the pattern $\mathbf{x}_1$ starting with $\mathbf{w}_0=\mathbf{v}$ we will get a sequence of weight vectors $\mathbf{w}_1, \mathbf{w}_2 \ldots$ defined by (3.18) with $\mathbf{x}=\mathbf{x}_1, \mathbf{x}_2, \ldots$. But of course we must have $\mathbf{w}_t=\mathbf{v}=\mathbf{w}_0$. Continuing to apply further patterns will just cycle through the weight sequence $\mathbf{w}_1, \mathbf{w}_2 \ldots \mathbf{w}_t$ again. This behaviour is known as a *limit cycle*. It occurs frequently in iterated and differential systems.

(b) We may also consider the case when the successive epochs of patterns are presented in random order. Instead of a single mapping F in (3.32) we will obtain a different one corresponding to each possible rearrangement of the training patterns. However there is only a finite number of such rearrangements so we can choose a contraction parameter uniformly for all possible rearrangements. This situation is known mathematically as an *iterated function scheme*. In general the limit will not be a simple limit cycle: it will be fractal. See Falconer (1990, Chapter 9) for a detailed discussion of iterated function schemes.

□

It is all very well to show that the delta rule will converge to a limit cycle, but of course we do not know whether the resulting network is any use. As it turns out, the resulting weight vectors are closely related to the vector which would be obtained by minimising the sum of squares of the errors over all patterns. Our general aim in the rest of this chapter is to prove this result. However, once again we will not take a direct route to this. Instead we introduce two powerful and important ideas which are fundamental to the analysis of neural networks: the inner product space and the singular value decomposition.

3.4 Inner product and Hilbert spaces

The inner product $\mathbf{x}^T\mathbf{y}$ is fundamental to the geometry of $\mathbb{R}^n$. We wish to extend this useful idea to other vector spaces, and prove some results about them. We will meet with the important idea of an *orthogonal expansion*. Just as for the norm, we abstract the important properties of the inner product on $\mathbb{R}^n$. However, to avoid confusion a different notation is used for inner products. To keep life simple, our exposition will consider only inner products on vector spaces over $\mathbb{R}$. However, later we will need to extend the results to spaces over $\mathbb{C}$. Inner products over $\mathbb{C}$ are called *hermitian products*. Generally speaking, converting the results to this case requires only the judicious use of complex conjugates.

We will also need the following definition and theorem.

Definition 3.39

An $n \times n$ real symmetric matrix A is said to be *positive definite* if for any real n-vector $\mathbf{x} \neq \mathbf{0}$, $\mathbf{x}^T A\mathbf{x} > 0$. If only weak inequality holds, i.e. we may only assert $\mathbf{x}^T A\mathbf{x} \geq 0$, then A is said to be *positive semi-definite*.

□

Theorem 3.40

Since A in Definition 3.39 is symmetric it has n real eigenvalues. We have:

(a) A is positive definite if and only if all its eigenvalues are strictly positive, and

(b) A is positive semi-definite if and only if all its eigenvalues are non-negative.

Proof

According to Theorem 3.15, there is an orthogonal matrix P and a diagonal matrix D such that $A=PDP^{\mathrm{T}}$. Thus $\mathbf{x}^{\mathrm{T}}A\mathbf{x}=\mathbf{x}^{\mathrm{T}}PDP^{\mathrm{T}}\mathbf{x}=\mathbf{v}^{\mathrm{T}}D\mathbf{v}$ say, where $\mathbf{v}=P^{\mathrm{T}}\mathbf{x}$. The diagonal elements of D are the eigenvalues of A, say $\lambda_1, \lambda_2, \ldots, \lambda_n$. So $\mathbf{v}^{\mathrm{T}}D\mathbf{v}=\lambda_1 v^2+\lambda_2 v^2+\ldots \lambda_n v^2$. Both cases of the theorem are now apparent.

□

In fact there are some variations between different authors over the definition of an inner products. The one we shall use is called by some writers a *non-degenerate positive definite* inner product, with a weaker definition for the inner product itself.

Definition 3.41

Let V be a vector space over $\mathbb{R}$. An *inner product* is a mapping $< , >: V\times V\rightarrow \mathbb{R}$ with the following properties.

(a) $<\mathbf{v}, \mathbf{w}>=<\mathbf{v}, \mathbf{w}>$

(b) $<\mathbf{v}, \mathbf{w}+\mathbf{u}>=<\mathbf{v}, \mathbf{w}>+<\mathbf{v}, \mathbf{u}>$

(c) $<\mathbf{v}, \lambda\mathbf{w}>=\lambda <\mathbf{v}, \mathbf{w}>$.

(d) $<\mathbf{v}, \mathbf{v}>\geq 0$ with equality if and only if $\mathbf{v}=\mathbf{0}$.

□

So an inner product is non-negative and is linear in each of its arguments: (b) and (c) show that it is linear in its second argument, and in view of (a) this must hold for the first one also. In addition, if we take the inner product of a non-zero vector $\mathbf{v}$ with itself, this vector must be positive.

Examples 3.42

(a) On $\mathbb{R}^n$, $<\mathbf{x}, \mathbf{y}>=\mathbf{x}^{\mathrm{T}}\mathbf{y}$ is an inner product.

(b) On $\mathbb{R}^n$, $<\mathbf{x}, \mathbf{y}>=\mathbf{x}^{\mathrm{T}}A\mathbf{y}$, where A is a positive definite matrix, is an inner product. Note that A must be positive definite for (d) to hold, and that the symmetry of A is required for (a) to hold since $<\mathbf{y}, \mathbf{x}> = \mathbf{y}^T A\mathbf{x} = (\mathbf{y}^T A\mathbf{x})^T = \mathbf{x}^T A^T \mathbf{y}$ (remembering that $\mathbf{x}^T A\mathbf{y}$ is a scalar and so equal to its transpose). This will only equal $<\mathbf{x}, \mathbf{y}>$ if A is symmetric.

(c) On $C[0, 1]$ or on $L_2[0, 1]$,

$$<p, q> = \int_0^1 p(x)q(x)\,\mathrm{d}x$$

is an inner product.

(d) On the subspace of $L_2[0, 1]$ consisting of functions with almost everywhere bounded derivatives,

$$<p, q> = \int_0^1 p(x)q(x) + p'(x)q'(x)\mathrm{d}x$$

where $'$ denotes differentiation, is an inner product. Products of this type, involving derivatives, are called *Sobolev products* and the appropriate subspace of $L_2[0, 1]$ is called a *Sobolev space*. They are important in the analysis of finite element methods and in some branches of approximation theory.

□

Corresponding to any inner product we have a norm. Specifically, $\|\mathbf{v}\| = \sqrt{<\mathbf{v}, \mathbf{v}>}$. In particular, Example 3.41(a) gives the usual norm $\|\ \|_2$ on $\mathbb{R}^n$. Also Example 3.41(c) gives $\|\ \|_2$ on $L_2[0, 1]$. However we do need to prove that the triangle inequality holds: recall that we have not yet done this even for $\mathbb{R}^n$. The result is a consequence of the following theorem.

Theorem 3.43 (The Cauchy–Schwarz Inequality)

Let $< , >$ be an inner product on a vector space V. Then

$$|<\mathbf{v}, \mathbf{w}>| \le \|\mathbf{v}\|\ \|\mathbf{w}\|,$$

where, of course, the norm here is that corresponding to the inner product. Equality holds if and only if $\mathbf{v} = \lambda\mathbf{w}$ for some scalar λ.

Proof

For any real number t, consider $<t\mathbf{v} + \mathbf{w}, t\mathbf{v} + \mathbf{w}>$. We have

$$\begin{aligned} 0 &\le <t\mathbf{v} + \mathbf{w}, t\mathbf{v} + \mathbf{w}> \text{ (by Definition 3.41(d))} \\ &= t^2 <\mathbf{v}, \mathbf{v}> + 2t <\mathbf{v}, \mathbf{w}> + <\mathbf{w}, \mathbf{w}> \\ &= t^2 \|\mathbf{v}\|^2 + 2t <\mathbf{v}, \mathbf{w}> + \|\mathbf{w}\|^2. \end{aligned}$$

The right-hand side is quadratic in t. Since it is non-negative, its discriminant 'b^2-4ac' must be non-positive (otherwise the quadratic would have two real roots). So

$$4 <\mathbf{v}, \mathbf{w}>^2 \leq 4\,\|\mathbf{v}\|^2\,\|\mathbf{w}\|^2 \text{ as required.}$$

For the last part of the theorem, note that the quadratic can only be exactly zero if $t\mathbf{v}+\mathbf{w}=0$: so if $t=0$ set $\lambda=0$ else set $\lambda=-1/t$.

□

Corollary 3.44

The norm $\|\ \|$ corresponding to $<\,,\,>$ *is* a norm.

Proof

Most of the Properties 3.17 follow directly from those of the inner product. Only the triangle inequality requires comment. But

$$\begin{aligned}\|\mathbf{v}+\mathbf{w}\|^2 &= <\mathbf{v}+\mathbf{w}, \mathbf{v}+\mathbf{w}> \\ &= <\mathbf{v}, \mathbf{v}> + 2<\mathbf{v},\mathbf{w}> + <\mathbf{w}, \mathbf{w}> \\ &\leq \|\mathbf{v}\|^2 + 2\,\|\mathbf{v}\|\,\|\mathbf{w}\| + \|\mathbf{w}\|^2,\end{aligned}$$

by Theorem 3.43. Taking the square root of each side, we get $\|\mathbf{v}+\mathbf{w}\| \leq \|\mathbf{v}\| + \|\mathbf{w}\|$, as required.

□

Definitions 3.45

(a) A vector space V which has an inner product is called an *inner product space*. An inner product space is always a normed vector space, with the norm defined above.

(b) Suppose V is analytically complete with this norm (i.e. V is a Banach space, see Remark and Definition 3.18). Then V is called a *Hilbert space.*

Examples 3.46

(a) $\mathbb{R}^n$ with any inner product is a Hilbert space (Corollary 3.21 (b)).

(b) $L_2[0, 1]$ with the inner product of Example 3.44(c) is a Hilbert space (Theorem 3.27).

□

Other definitions are obvious extensions of those in $\mathbb{R}^n$. For instance two vectors **v**, **w** are said to be *orthogonal* with respect to $< , >$ if $<\mathbf{v}, \mathbf{w}>=0$. Orthonormal sets are defined analogously. We have already seen many examples of orthogonal vectors in $\mathbb{R}^n$. Here is an important set of orthonormal vectors in a function space.

Example 3.47

The set of functions

$$\{½, \sin x, \cos x, \sin 2x, \cos 2x, \ldots, \sin nx, \cos nx\}$$

is orthonormal with respect to the inner product

$$<p,q> = \frac{1}{\pi}\int_{-\pi}^{\pi} p(x)q(x)\,\mathrm{d}x.$$

Obviously there are several different cases to check here. But, for example if $p(x)=\sin kx$ and $q(x)=\cos jx$ with $k\neq j$,

$$\begin{aligned}
<p, q> &= \frac{1}{\pi}\int_{-\pi}^{\pi} \sin kx \cos jx\,\mathrm{d}x \\
&= \frac{1}{2\pi}\int_{-\pi}^{\pi} \sin (k+j)x + \sin (k-j)x\,\mathrm{d}x \\
&= \left[\frac{-\cos(k+j)x}{(k+j)} + \frac{-\cos (k-j)x}{(k-j)}\right]_{-\pi}^{\pi} \\
&= 0,
\end{aligned}$$

whereas if $p(x)=q(x)=\sin kx$, $k\neq 0$,

$$\begin{aligned}
<p, q> &= \frac{1}{\pi}\int_{-\pi}^{\pi} \sin kx \sin kx\,\mathrm{d}x \\
&= \frac{1}{\pi}\int_{-\pi}^{\pi} \sin^2 kx\,\mathrm{d}x \\
&= \frac{1}{2\pi}\int_{-\pi}^{\pi} 1 - \cos 2kx\,\mathrm{d}x \\
&= \frac{1}{2\pi}\left[x - \frac{\sin 2kx}{2k}\right]_{-\pi}^{\pi} \\
&= 1
\end{aligned}$$

You might like to verify some of the other cases as an exercise.

□

3.5 Least squares problems

Hilbert spaces are the natural environment for a discussion of least squares problems and orthogonal expansions, ideas which pervade much of the theory of neural computing. Any neural network can be thought of as in some way approximating an unknown or abstract relationship between its inputs and outputs. There are many ways of constructing such an approximation, but one of the simplest and most popular is the method of least squares. Approximation will be considered in much more detail in Chapter 6, but the study of linear least squares problems is intimately related to the study of spectral properties of matrices. Thus a brief consideration of linear least squares is appropriate here.

Once again we will consider for the purposes of motivation a simple perceptron with a single output. We may ignore any threshold on the output unit: since in a classification problem we want the outputs to be 0 or 1, we can choose weights so that the outputs are approximately 0 or 1 for the different inputs, and then set a threshold of (say) $\frac{1}{2}$. We have a set of input patterns $\{\mathbf{x}_1, \mathbf{x}_2, \ldots, \mathbf{x}_t\}$ and a weight vector $\mathbf{w}$. The actual output for a given pattern $\mathbf{x}_i$, is of course $\mathbf{w}^T\mathbf{x}_i = w_1(\mathbf{x}_i)_1 + w_2(\mathbf{x}_i)_2 \ldots + w_n(\mathbf{x}_i)_n$. Let us form the *pattern matrix* X whose ith column is the pattern vector $\mathbf{x}_i$. Then the actual output for pattern i is the ith element of the vector $X^T\mathbf{w}$. Suppose the desired output is y_i. Let $\mathbf{b} = (y_1, y_2, \ldots, y_t)^T$. In matrix terms we want the weight vector $\mathbf{w}$ to be such that $X^T\mathbf{w}$ is approximately equal to $\mathbf{b}$. So to be specific, one natural approach (and there are also statistical reasons for this) is to try to choose $\mathbf{w}$ so that $\|\mathbf{b} - X^T\mathbf{w}\|_2$ is small. In other words we try to minimise the sum of the squares of the individual errors: hence the term *least squares*.

Now let us consider an abstract version of this problem. We wish to find scalars $w_1 \ldots w_n$ to minimise $\|\mathbf{b} - (w_1\mathbf{a}_1 + \ldots + w_n\mathbf{a}_n)\|$ where $\mathbf{b}$ is some fixed element of an inner space V, and $\mathbf{a}_1 \ldots \mathbf{a}_n$ is a basis for some finite dimensional subspace S of V: for the perceptron of the previous paragraph V is $\mathbb{R}^n$ and $\mathbf{a}_1 \ldots \mathbf{a}_n$ are the columns of X^T, or the *rows* of X. (Note that these are *not* the patterns, which are the *columns* of X.) Moreover we assume that $\mathbf{b} \notin S$. Let us call $\mathbf{p} = w_1\mathbf{a}_1 + \ldots + w_n\mathbf{a}_n$. (So in the matrix case, $\mathbf{p} = X^T\mathbf{w}$, i.e. the actual output vector.)

As a very simple example, consider V to be $\mathbb{R}^2$ with the usual inner product and S the span of a single vector $\mathbf{a}$. Thus S is a line through the origin. If $\mathbf{b}$ is a vector not on this line, the nearest point to $\mathbf{b}$ on the line is the point $\mathbf{p}$ where the error $\mathbf{b} - \mathbf{p}$ is orthogonal to the subspace S. Similarly in three dimensions with S a plane through the origin (the span of two vectors), we would find that the error was normal to the plane describing the subspace. This is the origin of the term *normal equations* which we shall meet shortly. So in the general inner product case, we might expect that the condition for our $\mathbf{p}$ to be optimal is that $<\mathbf{b}-\mathbf{p}, \mathbf{s}>=0$ for each $\mathbf{s}\in S$. Let us prove that this is the case. We do not even need S to be finite dimensional.

Theorem 3.48

(a) Let V be an inner product space and S a (non-empty) subspace. Let $\mathbf{b}\in V$ but $\mathbf{b}\notin S$. Suppose there exists $\mathbf{p}\in S$ such that $<\mathbf{b}-\mathbf{p}, \mathbf{s}>=0$ for each $\mathbf{s}\in S$. Then $\|\mathbf{b}-\mathbf{p}\|<\|\mathbf{b}-\mathbf{y}\|$ for any $\mathbf{y}\in S$, $\mathbf{y}\neq\mathbf{p}$.
(b) Conversely, if there exists $\mathbf{p}\in S$ such that $\|\mathbf{b}-\mathbf{p}\|<\|\mathbf{b}-\mathbf{y}\|$ for any $\mathbf{y}\in S$, $\mathbf{y}\neq\mathbf{p}$, then $<\mathbf{b}-\mathbf{P}, \mathbf{s}>=0$ for each $\mathbf{s}\in S$.
(c) If in addition, S is a Hilbert space (i.e. if it is analytically complete with the inner product norm of V) then the existence of such a $\mathbf{p}$ is guaranteed. (Note that we require S to be complete here: not V. In many practical cases, S is finite dimensional and thus necessarily complete even if V itself is not. See Corollary 3.21.)

Proof

(a) Let $\mathbf{u}=\mathbf{y}-\mathbf{p}$, so $\mathbf{y}=\mathbf{u}+\mathbf{p}$. Then

$$\begin{aligned}\|\mathbf{b}-\mathbf{y}\|^2 &= <\mathbf{b}-\mathbf{y}, \mathbf{b}-\mathbf{y}> \\ &= <\mathbf{b}-\mathbf{p}-\mathbf{u}, \mathbf{b}-\mathbf{p}-\mathbf{u}> \\ &= <\mathbf{b}-\mathbf{p},\mathbf{b}-\mathbf{p}-\mathbf{u}> - <\mathbf{u}, \mathbf{b}-\mathbf{p}-\mathbf{u}> \\ &= <\mathbf{b}-\mathbf{p}, \mathbf{b}-\mathbf{p}> - 2<\mathbf{b}-\mathbf{p}, \mathbf{u}> + <\mathbf{u}, \mathbf{u}> \\ &= \|\mathbf{b}-\mathbf{p}\|^2 + \|\mathbf{u}\|^2\end{aligned}$$

since the second term is zero by hypothesis. But since $\mathbf{y}\neq\mathbf{p}$, $\mathbf{u}\neq\mathbf{0}$, so $\|\mathbf{u}\|>0$, from which the result follows.

(b) Suppose we have an $\mathbf{s}\in S$ with $<\mathbf{b}-\mathbf{p}, \mathbf{s}>=h\neq 0$. We may assume $h<0$: if not replace s by $-\mathbf{s}$. For any $t\in\mathbb{R}$, $t>0$,

$$\begin{aligned}\|\mathbf{b}-\mathbf{p}+ts\|^2 &= <\mathbf{b}-\mathbf{p}+ts, \mathbf{b}-\mathbf{p}+ts> \\ &= <\mathbf{b}-\mathbf{p}, \mathbf{b}-\mathbf{p}> + 2t<s, \mathbf{b}-\mathbf{p}> + t^2<\mathbf{s}, \mathbf{s}> \\ &= \|\mathbf{b}-\mathbf{p}\|^2 + 2th + t^2\|\mathbf{s}\|^2.\end{aligned}$$

Thus for t sufficiently small $\|\mathbf{b}-\mathbf{p}+t\mathbf{s}\|<\|\mathbf{b}-\mathbf{p}\|$.

(c) Let $\delta=\inf\|\mathbf{b}-\mathbf{y}\|$ where the infimum is taken over all $\mathbf{y}\in S$. From the definition of the infimum (see the discussion between Example 3.22 and Theorem 3.23), it follows that there is a sequence of vectors $\mathbf{y}_i$ such that $\delta_i=\|\mathbf{b}-\mathbf{y}_i\| \to \delta$. We show that the sequence $(\mathbf{y}_i)$ is Cauchy. Writing $\mathbf{u}_i=\mathbf{b}-\mathbf{y}_i$, we have

$$\begin{aligned}\|\mathbf{u}_i + \mathbf{u}_j\| &= \|\mathbf{y}_i + \mathbf{y}_j - 2\mathbf{b}\| = 2\|\tfrac{1}{2}(\mathbf{y}_i + \mathbf{y}_i) - \mathbf{b}\| \\ &\geq 2\delta \text{ since } \tfrac{1}{2}(\mathbf{u}_i + \mathbf{y}_j)\in S.\end{aligned}$$

Moreover

$$\begin{aligned}\|\mathbf{y}_i - \mathbf{y}_j\|^2 &= \|\mathbf{u}_i - \mathbf{u}_j\|^2 = <\mathbf{u}_i - \mathbf{u}_j, \mathbf{u}_i - \mathbf{u}_j> \\ &= <\mathbf{u}_i, \mathbf{u}_i> + <\mathbf{u}_j, \mathbf{u}_j> - 2<\mathbf{u}_i, \mathbf{u}_j>.\end{aligned}$$

Similarly

$$\|\mathbf{u}_i + \mathbf{u}_j\|^2 = <\mathbf{u}_i + \mathbf{u}_j, \mathbf{u}_i + \mathbf{u}_j> = <\mathbf{u}_i, \mathbf{u}_i> + <\mathbf{u}_j, \mathbf{u}_j> + 2<\mathbf{u}_i, \mathbf{u}_j>$$

and adding these two equations gives

$$\begin{aligned}\|\mathbf{y}_i - \mathbf{y}_j\|^2 &= - \|\mathbf{u}_i + \mathbf{u}_j\|^2 + 2(\|\mathbf{u}_i\|^2 + \|\mathbf{u}_j\|^2) \\ &\leq - (2\delta)^2 + 2(\delta_i^{\,2} + \delta_j^{\,2}).\end{aligned}$$

Since the expression on the right-hand side can be made arbitrarily small by sufficiently large choices of m and n, we find that the sequence $(\mathbf{y}_n)$ is indeed Cauchy as claimed. Since S is complete there is a vector $\mathbf{p}\in S$ such that $\mathbf{y}_i\to\mathbf{y}$ in norm (i.e. $\|\mathbf{y}_i-\mathbf{p}\|\to 0$) as $i\to\infty$. Finally we note that

$$\|\mathbf{b} - \mathbf{p}\| = \|\mathbf{b} - \mathbf{y}_n + \mathbf{y}_n - \mathbf{p}\| \leq \|\mathbf{b} - \mathbf{y}_n\| + \|\mathbf{y}_n - \mathbf{p}\| = \delta_n + \|\mathbf{y}_n - \mathbf{p}\| \to \delta$$

which from the definition of δ means that **p** indeed satisfies the conditions of (a) and (b).

□

Now let us consider again the finite dimensional case. As above, we let $\{\mathbf{a}_1 \ldots \mathbf{a}_n\}$ be a basis for S and write $\mathbf{p}=w_1\mathbf{a}_1+\ldots+w_n\mathbf{a}_n$. Theorem 3.48 tells us that we are looking for scalars $w_1 \ldots w_n$ such that

$$<\mathbf{b} - (w_1\mathbf{a}_1 +\ldots+ w_n\mathbf{a}_n), \mathbf{a}_j> = 0 \text{ for } j = 1, \ldots, n$$

whence

$$<(w_1\mathbf{a}_1 +\ldots+ w_n\mathbf{a}_n), \mathbf{a}_j> = <\mathbf{b}, \mathbf{a}_j>$$

so

$$\sum_{i=1}^{n} \langle w_i\mathbf{a_i}, \mathbf{a_j}\rangle = \langle\mathbf{b}, \mathbf{a_j}\rangle, j = 1, \ldots, n$$

or

$$\sum_{i=1}^{n} w_i\langle\mathbf{a_i}, \mathbf{a_j}\rangle = \langle\mathbf{b}, \mathbf{a_j}\rangle, j = 1, \ldots, n. \tag{3.33}$$

Define B to be the *autocorrelation matrix* with $b_{ij}=\langle\mathbf{a_i}, \mathbf{a_j}\rangle$, $\mathbf{f}$ to be the vector $(\langle\mathbf{b}, \mathbf{a_1}\rangle, \ldots, \langle\mathbf{b}, \mathbf{a_n}\rangle)^{\mathrm{T}}$ and of course $\mathbf{w}=(w_1, \ldots, w_n)^{\mathrm{T}}$, then we can write this system of equations in matrix form as

$$B\mathbf{w} = \mathbf{f}. \tag{3.34}$$

(3.33) or (3.34) form the *normal equations* for the least squares problem in a finite dimensional inner product space. Note that Theorem 3.48 guarantees the existence and uniqueness of $\mathbf{p}=w_1\mathbf{a_1}+\ldots+w_n\mathbf{a_n}$ and hence that (3.34) must have a solution for $\mathbf{w}$. It does not, however guarantee that $\mathbf{w}$ itself is unique. If the $\mathbf{a_i}$ are not linearly independent, there will be more than one possible choice of $\mathbf{w}$ giving the same $\mathbf{p}$. On the other hand if the $\mathbf{a_i}$ are independent, $\mathbf{w}$ is unique.

Of course if we are working in $\mathbb{R}^n$ the inner products just become the scalar products. For example, $b_{ij}=\langle\mathbf{a_i}, \mathbf{a_j}\rangle=\mathbf{a_i}^{\mathrm{T}}\mathbf{a_j}$. If A is the matrix whose columns are the $\mathbf{a_i}$, then an examination of the structure of the matrix B shows that in fact $B=A^{\mathrm{T}}A$. (It is easiest to see this using block matrix multiplication.) In the case of the perceptron, we have already seen that the $\mathbf{a_i}$ are the rows of the pattern matrix X. Thus $A=X^{\mathrm{T}}$ and $B=XX^{\mathrm{T}}$. Similarly $\mathbf{f}=A^{\mathrm{T}}\mathbf{b}=X\mathbf{b}$. So a choice according to the least squares criterion of weight vector $\mathbf{w}$ for a simple perceptron should satisfy

$$XX^{\mathrm{T}}\mathbf{w} = X\mathbf{b}. \tag{3.35}$$

(Recall that in this context $\mathbf{b}=(y_1, y_2, \ldots, y_t)^{\mathrm{T}}$.) It is possible to construct a version of the delta rule which attempts to compute this $\mathbf{w}$ directly: it is called the *epoch* or *off-line* method. We start with some initial vector $\mathbf{w_0}$ and compute a correction according to (3.17) except that as in (3.18) and the preceding remarks we are only considering a single output perceptron. Thus for the first pattern $\mathbf{x_1}$ with desired output y_1, we calculate

$$\delta\mathbf{w}' = \eta(y_1 - \mathbf{w_0}^{\mathrm{T}}\mathbf{x_1})\mathbf{x_1}.$$

However, instead of updating $\mathbf{w_0}$ at once, we store this $\delta\mathbf{w}$ and proceed to the next pattern, i.e. compute a new

$$\delta\mathbf{w}'' = \eta(y_1 - \mathbf{w_0}^T\mathbf{x_2})\mathbf{x_2}.$$

This correction is added to the correction already in store, and we continue in this way until we have cycled through the entire epoch of patterns $\mathbf{x_1}, \mathbf{x_2}, \ldots,$ $\mathbf{x_t}$. At this point we have a total correction

$$\delta\mathbf{w_0} = \eta \sum_{i=1}^{t} (y_i - \mathbf{w_0}^T\mathbf{x_i})\mathbf{x_i}.$$

Finally add this total correction to $\mathbf{w_0}$ and then repeat the entire process, leading to an iteration

$$\begin{aligned}\mathbf{w_{k+1}} &= \mathbf{w_k} + \eta \sum_{i=1}^{t} (y_i - \mathbf{w_k}^T\mathbf{x_i})\mathbf{x_i} \\ &= \mathbf{w_k} + \eta \sum_{i=1}^{t} y_i\mathbf{x_i} - \eta \sum_{i=1}^{t} (\mathbf{x_i}\mathbf{x_i}^T)\mathbf{w_k} \quad \text{by a similar argument to (3.18)} \\ &= (I - \eta XX^T)\mathbf{w_k} + \eta X\mathbf{b} \qquad (3.36)\end{aligned}$$

with the same notation as (3.35). Observe the use of the important identity

$$XX^T = \sum_{i=1}^{t} (\mathbf{x_i}\mathbf{x_i}^T) \qquad (3.37)$$

which may be verified by writing X in terms of its columns (the $\mathbf{x_i}$) and applying block multiplication.

If the iteration (3.36) converges to some fixed point $\mathbf{w}$, then it will satisfy

$$\mathbf{w} = (I - \eta XX^T)\mathbf{w} + \eta X\mathbf{b} \qquad (3.38)$$

which when rearranged gives (3.35). So *if* it converges, the iteration (3.36) will give that $\mathbf{w}$ which is optimal in the least squares sense.

The convergence of (3.36) can be tackled using the methods of Section 3.3, since (3.36) is of the general form of (3.22) with $\Lambda=(I-\eta\ XX^T)$ and $\mathbf{h}=\eta\ X\mathbf{b}$. In this case we know that there is a fixed point: Theorem 3.48 implies that (3.35) must have a solution. Moreover $(I-\eta XX^T)$ is symmetric so it is similar to a diagonal matrix. Hence the restricted version of the proof of Theorem

3.31 that we have given is valid in this case: as in many practical situations we do not actually need the full version even for complete rigour.

Since we have used Λ generically, let us define $\Omega=(I-\eta\, XX^{\mathrm{T}})$ (3.36). (Note that it depends on η.) We wish to know under what conditions $\rho(\Omega)<1$.

Clearly $L=XX^{\mathrm{T}}$ is symmetric. Moreover for any $\mathbf{v}\in\mathbb{R}^n$, $\mathbf{v}^{\mathrm{T}}L\mathbf{v}=(X\mathbf{v})^{\mathrm{T}}(X\mathbf{v})\geq 0$, i.e. L is positive semi-definite. Thus it has real non-negative eigenvalues. In fact we have $\mathbf{v}^{\mathrm{T}}L\mathbf{v}=(X\mathbf{v})^{\mathrm{T}}(X\mathbf{v})=0$ if and only if $\mathbf{v}\in\ker(X)$. Now the columns of X are the input patterns $\mathbf{x_p}$, $p=1, \ldots, t$. So X is an $n\times t$ matrix. If the t patterns $\{\mathbf{x_p}\}$ span $\mathbb{R}^n$ (for which it is necessary but not sufficient that $t\geq n$) we have rank $(X)=n$. In this case it follows from the Dimension Theorem 2.26 that null$(X)=0$ and we must have $\mathbf{v}=\mathbf{0}$. So if the patterns span, L is strictly positive definite and has strictly positive eigenvalues. As we did for the ordinary delta rule, let us assume for simplicity that this holds. The case of rank deficient X is best handled using the singular value decomposition with which this chapter concludes.

Suppose $L=XX^{\mathrm{T}}$ has eigenvalues λ_j, $j=1 \ldots n$, with $0<\lambda_n\leq\lambda_{n-1}\leq\ldots\leq\lambda_1$. If $\mathbf{u_j}$ is the eigenvector corresponding to λ_j, note that $\Omega\mathbf{u_j}=(I-\eta\, L)\,\mathbf{u_j}=\mathbf{u_j}-\eta\,\lambda_j\mathbf{u_j}=(1-\eta\,\lambda_j)\,\mathbf{u_j}$. Thus the eigenvalues of Ω are $1-\eta$ (the corresponding eigenvalues of L) and $\rho(\Omega)$ is the larger of $|1-\eta\lambda_n|$ or $|1-\eta\lambda_1|$. Since all the λ_j, are positive, both these will be less than one for sufficiently small η. We conclude that the iteration (3.36) will converge, provided the patterns span and η is sufficiently small. *But how small does η have to be*? (Recall that for the usual delta rule we need only the simple normalisation condition $|1-\eta\|\mathbf{x_i}\|_2|<1$ of Theorem 3.37.) To answer this question we need more precise estimates for the spectrum of L and the norm of Ω. From these we will be able to see why the epoch algorithm does not always work well in practice.

The eigenvalues of Ω are $(1-\eta\lambda_1)\leq(1-\eta\lambda_2)\leq\ldots\leq(1-\eta\lambda_n)$, and $\rho(\Omega)=\max(|1-\eta\lambda_1|, |1-\eta\lambda_n|\}$. (Observe that Ω is positive definite for small η, but ceases to be so when η becomes large.) Since $L=XX^{\mathrm{T}}$ is symmetric, we find from Theorem 3.35 (c)) that

$$\begin{aligned}\lambda_1 &= \|X^{\mathrm{T}}\|_2^2=\max_{\|\mathbf{v}\|_2=1}\|X^{\mathrm{T}}\mathbf{v}\|_2^2=\max_{\|\mathbf{v}\|_2=1}\mathbf{v}^{\mathrm{T}}XX^{\mathrm{T}}\mathbf{v}.\\ &=\sum_{p=1}^{t}(\mathbf{v}^{\mathrm{T}}\mathbf{x_p})^2 \quad \text{for the maximal } \mathbf{v}\text{, using (3.37)}\\ &\leq\sum_{p=1}^{t}\|\mathbf{x_p}\|_2^2.\end{aligned}$$

On the other hand, we can get a lower bound by substituting a particular **v** into the expression on the right-hand side of of the expression for λ_1. For instance, we have for any k, $k=1, \ldots, t$,

$$\lambda_1 \geq \frac{1}{\|\mathbf{x_k}\|}\left(\sum_{p=1}^{t} (\mathbf{x_k}^T\mathbf{x_p})^2\right) \geq \|\mathbf{x_k}\|. \tag{3.39}$$

Now consider a particular case. Suppose the $\mathbf{x_p}$ cluster around two vectors **u** and **v** which are mutually ortho*normal*. If these represent two classes which are to be separated, we are in an ideal situation for machine learning: the pattern classes are in two widely separated sets. However, even in this case the behaviour of the epoch method is not good (Ellacott, 1990). If the clusters are of equal size, we have from the first inequality in (3.39)

$$\lim_{\varepsilon \to o} \lambda_1 \geq t/2 \text{ and since the rank of } L = XX^T \text{collapses to } 2, \lim_{\varepsilon \to 0} \lambda_n = 0.$$

Thus, unlike the ordinary delta rule for which the convergence condition depends only on the norm of the individual patterns, for the epoch method (which is a form of steepest descent: see Chapter 4) we may require an arbitrary small η *to get convergence. But the rate of convergence depends on* λ_1 *which does not become small.* The on-line delta rule is in this sense much more stable.

This analysis illustrates the importance of the ratio of λ_1 to λ_n.

Definition 3.49

Let an $n \times n$ matrix A be non-singular. The *condition number* $\mu_2(A)$ is defined as

$$\mu_2(A) = \|A\|_2\|A^{-1}\|_2.$$

□

Remarks 3.50

(a) We can of course define a condition number for any matrix norm, but the 2-norm is by far the most commonly used.

(b) From Theorem 3.37 it follows that $\mu_2(A)=\{\rho(A^TA)\rho[(A^TA)^{-1}]\}^{1/2}$.

(c) If λ is an eigenvalue of a square matrix B (necessarily non-zero if B is not singular), then $1/\lambda$ is an eigenvalue of B^{-1}, since if $B\mathbf{u}=\lambda\mathbf{u}$, $B^{-1}\mathbf{u}=\lambda^{-1}\mathbf{u}$. Setting $B=A^TA$, in (b) we find that $\{\mu_2(A)\}^2$ is precisely the ratio of the largest eigenvalue of A^TA to its smallest.

□

Now returning to the pattern matrix X, we conclude $\mu_2(X)=\lambda_1/\lambda_n$. For a more practical discussion of the significance of the condition number of this matrix, see Brown and Harris (1994, Chapters 4 and 5). Here we derive some theoretical results.

It appears that we are getting 'something for nothing' by using the on-line version of the delta rule rather than the off-line version. Unfortunately this is only partly so. It is true that we can avoid divergence of the iteration with a larger value of η. On the other hand we have not yet considered what the limit cycle generated by the on-line delta rule actually is. Let us do this now.

First we require a well-known standard result on the continuous behaviour of solutions of linear equations.

Theorem 3.51

Consider the system of linear equations $A\mathbf{v}=\mathbf{b}$ and a perturbed form $(A+\delta A)(\mathbf{v}+\delta\mathbf{v})=(\mathbf{b}+\delta\mathbf{b})$. How does the change $\delta\mathbf{v}$ of the solution $\mathbf{v}$ change as a function of δA and $\delta\mathbf{b}$? The following bound provides the answer.

Suppose $\|\delta A\|_2<1/\|A^{-1}\|_2$, Then

$$\frac{\|\delta\mathbf{v}\|_2}{\|\mathbf{v}\|_2}\leq\frac{\mu_2(A)}{1-\|A^{-1}\|_2\|\delta A\|_2}\left(\frac{\|\delta\mathbf{b}\|_2}{\|\mathbf{b}\|_2}+\frac{\|\delta A\|_2}{\|A\|_2}\right).$$

Proof

Note that $\|A^{-1}\delta A\|_2\leq\|A^{-1}\|_2\|\delta A\|_2<1$ by the hypothesis of the theorem. So all the eigenvalues of $A^{-1}\delta A$ are smaller than 1 in modulus. It follows that 0 cannot be an eigenvalue of $I+A^{-1}\delta A$ and hence that this matrix is not singular. Now we have

$$I=(I+A^{-1}\delta A)\,(I+A^{-1}\delta A)^{-1}$$

whence

$$(I+A^{-1}\delta A)^{-1}=I-A^{-1}\delta A\,(I+A^{-1}\delta A)^{-1}.$$

Taking the norm of each side we obtain

$$\begin{aligned}\|(I+A^{-1}\delta A)^{-1}\|_2&=\|I-A^{-1}\delta A(I+A^{-1}\delta A)^{-1}\|_2\\&\leq 1+\|A^{-1}\delta A\|_2\|(I+A^{-1}\delta A)^{-1}\|_2.\end{aligned}$$

Since $\|A^{-1}\delta A\|_2<1$, this may be rearranged to

$$\|(I+A^{-1}\delta A)^{-1}\|_2 \leq \frac{1}{1-\|A^{-1}\delta A\|_2} \leq \frac{1}{1-\|A^{-1}\|_2\|\delta A\|_2}. \tag{3.40}$$

Moreover we also have $(A+\delta A)(\mathbf{v}+\delta\mathbf{v})=(\mathbf{b}+\delta\mathbf{b})$ which rearranges to

$$\delta\mathbf{v} = (I+A^{-1}\delta A)^{-1}A^{-1}(\delta\mathbf{b}-\delta A\mathbf{v})$$

when we recall that also $A\mathbf{v}=\mathbf{b}$. So

$$\|\delta\mathbf{v}\|_2 \leq \|(I+A^{-1}\delta A)^{-1}\|_2\|A^{-1}\|_2\|\delta\mathbf{b}-\delta A\mathbf{v}\|_2.$$

Now apply (3.40) and divide $\|\mathbf{v}\|_2$ to get

$$\frac{\|\delta\mathbf{v}\|_2}{\|\mathbf{v}\|_2} \leq \frac{\|A^{-1}\|_2}{1-\|A^{-1}\|_2\|\delta A\|_2}\left(\frac{\|\delta\mathbf{b}\|_2}{\|\mathbf{v}\|_2}+\|\delta A\|_2\right)$$

But since $A\mathbf{v}=\mathbf{b}$, we have $\|\mathbf{v}\|_2 \geq \|\mathbf{b}\|_2/\|A\|_2$, from which the desired result easily follows.

□

With this theorem we can determine what the delta rule (3.17)–(3.20) actually computes. Let $\mathbf{w}$ be the fixed point of (3.20), which is unique provided the patterns $\{\mathbf{x}_1, \ldots, \mathbf{x}_t\}$ span. (Compare Theorem 3.37 and Remark 3.38 (a).) So $\mathbf{w}=\mathbf{w}(\eta)$ is that element of the limit cycle which is obtained when the complete epoch of patterns has been presented. As in (3.22) (with $\mathbf{v}$ now renamed $\mathbf{w}$) we have

$$\mathbf{w}(\eta) = \Lambda(\eta)\mathbf{w}(\eta) + \mathbf{h}(\eta),$$

where we have indicated that each of the terms depends on η: see (3.20). So

$$[I-\Lambda(\eta)]\mathbf{w}(\eta) = \mathbf{h}(\eta). \tag{3.41}$$

Again from (3.20) we note that

$$\begin{aligned}
\Lambda &= B_tB_{t-1}\ldots B_1 \\
&= (I-\eta\mathbf{x}_t\mathbf{x}_t^{\mathrm{T}})(I-\eta\mathbf{x}_{t-1}\mathbf{x}_{t-1}^{\mathrm{T}})\ldots(I-\eta\mathbf{x}_1\mathbf{x}_1^{\mathrm{T}}) \\
&= I-\eta\sum_{i=1}^{t}\mathbf{x}_i\mathbf{x}_i^{\mathrm{T}} + O(\eta^2) \\
&= I-\eta XX^{\mathrm{T}} + O(\eta^2).
\end{aligned} \tag{3.42}$$

Similarly

$$\begin{aligned}\mathbf{h} &= \eta[y_1(B_tB_{t-1}\ldots B_2)\mathbf{x_1} + \ldots + y_{t-1}B_t\mathbf{x_{t-1}} + y_t\mathbf{x_t}]\\ &= \eta(y_1\mathbf{x_1} + \ldots + y_{t-1}\mathbf{x_{t-1}} + y_t\mathbf{x_t}) + O(\eta^2).\\ &= \eta X\mathbf{b} + O(\eta^2) \text{ where, as in (3.35), } \mathbf{b} = (y_1, y_2, \ldots, y_t)^{\mathrm{T}}.\end{aligned} \tag{3.43}$$

Substituting these into (3.41), and dividing by η yields

$$[XX^{\mathrm{T}} + O(\eta)]\mathbf{w}(\eta) = X\mathbf{b} + O(\eta). \tag{3.44}$$

Corollary 3.52

Let the patterns $\{\mathbf{x_1}, \ldots, \mathbf{x_t}\}$ span $\mathbb{R}^n$, and let $\mathbf{w}(\eta)$ be that element of the weight limit cycle of the delta rule which obtains at the end the complete cycle of patterns. Then as $\eta \to 0$, $\mathbf{w}(\eta)$ approaches the weight obtained as the best least squares approximation to the outputs, i.e. the solution of (3.35).

Proof

Compare (3.44) with (3.35) (and (3.38)) in the light of Theorem 3.53.

□

Remarks 3.53

(a) Note that the rate of convergence in this result depends on the condition number of XX^{T}, as we might well have expected. A closer examination of the $O(\eta^2)$ in (3.42) and (3.43), (i.e. examining the η^2 terms in the products) reveals that these too depend on correlations between the patterns.

(b) If $\varepsilon(\eta)$ is the root mean square error corresponding to $\mathbf{w}(\eta)$, and ε^* is the corresponding error for the least squares optimal $\mathbf{w}$, then $\varepsilon(\eta) - \varepsilon^* = O(\eta^2)$. Although convergence of weights is linear with η, convergence of the error is quadratic (proportional to η^2). This is a consequence of the fact that at the least squares optimum point, the error is orthogonal to the approximating subspace. Thus an $O(\eta)$ perturbation in this subspace causes only an $O(\eta^2)$ change in error.

□

A very important question is '*Even if we get the least squares optimal solution, does this guarantee that the resulting weight will separate linearly separable patterns?*' The answer to this is 'No' for a linear network! In order to understand why, let us consider the pattern classification problem in more detail. Suppose we have two sets of patterns $R = \{\mathbf{x_1}, \ldots, \mathbf{x_j}\}$ and $S = \{\mathbf{x_{j+1}}, \ldots, \mathbf{x_t}\}$. We wish to find a weight $\mathbf{w}$ and threshold c such that $\mathbf{w}^{\mathrm{T}}\mathbf{x} < c$ for $\mathbf{x} \in R$ and $\mathbf{w}^{\mathrm{T}}\mathbf{x} > c$ for

$\mathbf{x} \in S$. For example, if $n=2$ and we are trying to create a network to solve the OR problem, we have $R=\{(0, 0)^T\}$ and $S=\{(0, 1)^T, (1, 0)^T, (1, 1)^T\}$. Thus $j=1$ and $t=4$. Our aim is to construct a network which will output 1 if $\mathbf{x} \in S$ and 0 if $\mathbf{x} \in R$. We emphasize again that linear separation is not always possible. For the XOR problem we have $R=\{(0, 0)^T, (1, 1)^T\}$ and $S=\{(0, 1)^T, (1, 0)^T\}$. These sets cannot be separated by a straight line.

For these logical examples the output is naturally coded as 1 or 0, but we can use this as a clue to attack the general classification problem. In general our sets may not suggest a numerical output, but we will always be classifying with respect to some binary quantity (on/off, full/empty, male/female, etc.). For instance we might be trying to develop a system for automatic sex typing of chromosomes from microscopic images. Then the male/female classification is what is required. We can code this as output 0 or 1. Actually it is mathematically more convenient to change the activation function of the threshold unit slightly, and to make the output -1 or $+1$. Thus we specify that the output unit will produce -1 if $\mathbf{w}^T\mathbf{x} < c$ and $+1$ if $\mathbf{w}^T\mathbf{x} > c$. In summary then, we want to choose $\mathbf{w}$ and c such that the network outputs -1 if $\mathbf{x} \in R$, and $+1$ if $\mathbf{x} \in S$. Clearly if we can find $\mathbf{w}$ such that

$$\mathbf{w}^T\mathbf{x} = -1 \text{ for } \mathbf{x}\ R \text{ and } \mathbf{w}^T\mathbf{x} = 1 \text{ for } \mathbf{x} \in S \tag{3.45}$$

we may simply choose $c=0$. But we have n weights and t patterns. Hence (3.45) gives t linear equations for the n unknown weights w_i. Let us identify the different cases. The simplest case is $t=n$, with the patterns linearly independent. Then the patterns span $\mathbb{R}^n$ and the equations (3.45) will have a unique solution. Note that in this case the patterns are *always* separable: for example in three dimensions with any three non-colinear points, any division of the points into two sets is separable. If $t<n$, $t>n$ or if the patterns are not independent, the situation is more complicated.

In order to deal with these cases we introduce homogeneous co-ordinates. More specifically,

$$\begin{aligned} &\text{for } \mathbf{x} \in S, \text{ let } \mathbf{u}^T = (\mathbf{x} : -1)^T, \\ &\text{and for } \mathbf{x} \in R, \text{ let } \mathbf{u}^T = (-\mathbf{x} : 1)^T. \end{aligned} \tag{3.46}$$

(Note the minus signs here.) Also define $\mathbf{v}^T = (\mathbf{w} : c)^T$. Then we have for $\mathbf{x} \in S$,

$$\mathbf{v}^T\mathbf{u} = \mathbf{w}^T\mathbf{x} - c$$

so

$$\mathbf{w}^T\mathbf{x} > c \text{ if and only if } \mathbf{v}^T\mathbf{u} > 0.$$

Similarly for $\mathbf{x} \in R$,

$$\mathbf{v}^T\mathbf{u} = -\mathbf{w}^T\mathbf{x} + c$$

so

$$\mathbf{w}^T\mathbf{x} < c \text{ if and only if } \mathbf{v}^T\mathbf{u} > 0.$$

We have reduced the problem to the following standard form:

For a given set of t vectors $\{\mathbf{u}_1, \ldots, \mathbf{u}_t\}$ in $\mathbb{R}^{n+1}$, find a vector $\mathbf{v}$ such that $\mathbf{v}^T\mathbf{u}_i > 0$, $i=1, \ldots, t$.

Let us try to solve this problem by satisfying $\mathbf{v}^T\mathbf{u}_i=1$, $i=1, \ldots, t$. (In view of the homogeneity, any positive constant will do on the right-hand side. In our original problem, it makes no difference if we multiply the threshold and all the weights by a positive constant.) If we can satisfy these equations, then certainly we have a separator. But obviously this is only possible if all the points $\mathbf{u}_i$ are colinear. In terms of the original variables, we want

$$\mathbf{w}^T(-\mathbf{x}_i) = 1 - c, \text{ for } i = 1,\ldots,j,$$
$$\mathbf{w}^T\mathbf{x}_i = 1 + c, \text{ for } i = j+1,\ldots,t.$$

Let A be the $t\times(n+1)$ matrix whose rows are $(-\mathbf{x}_i\!: 1)^T$ for $i=1, \ldots, j$, and $(\mathbf{x}_i\!: -1)^T$ for $i=j+1, \ldots, t$. Also, let $\mathbf{e}$ be the vector all of whose elements are 1. The equations can then be written in matrix form as

$$A\mathbf{v} = \mathbf{e}. \tag{3.47}$$

An exact solution of this system of equations with $|c| < 1$ gives a separator. We can now get a complete description of the various cases.

Firstly, if $t=n$ and the $\mathbf{x}_i$'s are linearly independent, we can set $c=0$ and solve for $\mathbf{w}$: separation is always possible if we have as many dimensions as patterns.

The second case is when the $\mathbf{x}_i$'s are linearly independant span a space of dimension r, where $r<n$. Let A' be the matrix obtained be deleting the last column of A (the one with either 1 or -1 in each entry). Note that rank(A') $=r$. Pick r independent columns of A' and set the w_i's corresponding to the *other* columns to be zero. Then set $c=0$ and solve for the remaining w_i's. Again separation of the sets is guaranteed. (If the **xi**'s are not independant separation is not possible: just consider three points in a line and try to seperate the middle one from the other two.)

The third case is when the $\mathbf{x}_i$'s span a space of dimension r, where $r>n$. We attempt to solve (3.47) in the least squares sense. (Note that this formulation is almost the same as that given in the paragraphs preceding Theorem 3.48: the only differences are that the sign of some of the rows has been changed, and, rather than fix the threshold at $\frac{1}{2}$, we have introduced it as an extra variable c.) For any given (extended) weight $\mathbf{v}$ and (extended) pattern $\mathbf{u}_i$, the error for that particular pattern is $(\mathbf{v}^T\mathbf{u}_i - 1)$. So the total least squares error measures the divergence from non-colinearity of the patterns. Now consider a situation such as that illustrated in Fig. 3.3. A large cluster of nearly colinear points to the right of the y-axis causes the separating line to adopt a steep gradient, with the result that the isolated point to the left of the y-axis is *misclassified*, even though a separating line *is* possible. (Note that the row of (3.47) corresponding to this point will have a very large error compared with the others. It is possible overcome the misclassification in an iterative way by adding a large term with the appropriate sign to just the appropriate row of the right-hand side of (3.47). This increases the term in the error corresponding to the isolated point, causing the line to be 'dragged' in the appropriate direction. However we are then no longer using a simple learning system: an iterative algorithm is involved. See Tou and Gonzales (1978) for more details of this method: we will not pursue it here as it is taking us rather far from the subject of neural nets.)

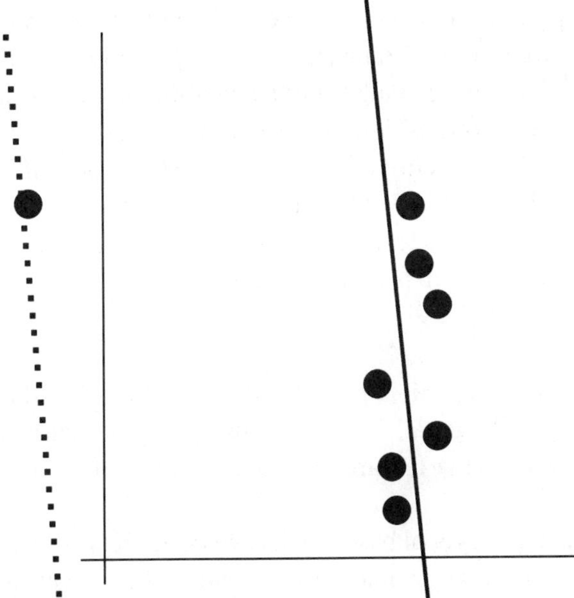

Fig. 3.3

3.6 Orthogonal expansions

In this section we temporarily put aside our study of the perceptron to consider a topic which is of vital importance in understanding filtering and preprocessing of data. A common requirement of such preprocessing is to reduce the dimension of the data. Obviously if the input vectors to our network can be mapped onto a space of smaller dimension, a smaller network will be required and redundancy eliminated. A natural way to do this is to make use of least squares approximation. For example, if our input data is in an inner product space V (e.g. $V=\mathbb{R}^n$), we could choose a suitable (finite dimensional) subspace S of V and approximate each item of data by its least squares approximation from S. Then, instead of feeding our original data into the network, we can use the coefficients of this approximation with respect to a suitable basis of S. In order for this to be feasible, we need to choose both a suitable subspace S and a suitable basis for S. The choice of S itself is of course highly dependent on the nature of our data: we will meet examples below. However it is possible to construct a general theory about the choice of basis: specifically we seek a basis with respect to which the least squares approximation may be easily found.

Thus our starting point is the normal equations (3.33) and (3.34). It is rarely advisable to tackle (3.34) by ordinary Gaussian Elimination methods. It has been found in practice that B is often very ill-conditioned, so it is impossible to determine $\mathbf{x}$ accurately. (Compare Theorem 3.51.) For the matrix case we obtain B as $A^{\mathrm{T}}A$ and we can alleviate the conditioning problem by applying the singular value decomposition to A to get the pseudoinverse: this approach is discussed in the next section. However in (3.33) we do not have a natural factorization of B. Also, it would take a lot of work to evaluate the inner products to get the matrix form. Instead, we exploit the special structure of (3.33). The key observation is that if $<\mathbf{a_i}, \mathbf{a_j}>=0$ for $i \neq j$, we get simply

$$w_j = <\mathbf{b}, \mathbf{a_j}>/<\mathbf{a_j}, \mathbf{a_j}>. \tag{3.48}$$

But the condition $<\mathbf{a_i}, \mathbf{a_j}>=0$ is precisely the condition that the basis vectors $\{\mathbf{a_j}\}$ be mutually orthogonal! If we have an orthogonal basis, each required least squares coefficient w_j requires only evaluation of the two inner products of (3.48).

How do we get orthogonal bases? In fact we have already seen one way. The eigenvectors of any real symmetric $n \times n$ matrix form such a basis for $\mathbb{R}^n$ (Theorem 3.11). There are many other ways: we shall see later that we can construct an orthogonal basis from any basis at all. However, let us first consider the important explicit Example 3.47: we saw that the set of functions

$$\{½, \sin x, \cos x, \sin 2x, \cos 2x, \ldots, \sin nx, \cos nx\}$$

is orthonormal with respect to the inner product

$$<p, q> = \frac{1}{\pi}\int_{-\pi}^{\pi} p(x)q(x)\,\mathrm{d}x.$$

Now let us consider approximation of an actual function with this basis.

Example 3.54

Let f be the function

$$f(x) = \begin{cases} 1, & x \geq 0 \\ -1, & x < 0 \end{cases}.$$

Thus is the restriction of a square wave to the interval $[-\pi, \pi]$. We wish to approximate f by the orthonormal basis of Example 3.47. Approximating waveforms by sinusoidal components is a common problem in acoustics and signal processing. Note that since the basis is 2π-periodic, if we approximate on $[-\pi, \pi]$, we will in fact get an approximation for any value of x. We write

$$f(x) \approx ½\, a_0 + a_1 \cos x + b_1 \sin x + a_2 \cos 2x + b_2 \sin 2x + \ldots$$
$$+ a_n \cos nx + b_n \sin nx.$$

(The use of a_j and b_j for these coefficients is traditional in this context.) Recalling that the basis of Example 3.47 is actually orthonormal with respect to the given inner product so the denominator inner product is 1, we find from (3.48) that

$$a_j = \frac{1}{\pi}\int_{-\pi}^{\pi} f(x) \cos jx\,\mathrm{d}x \tag{3.49a}$$

and

$$b_j = \frac{1}{\pi}\int_{-\pi}^{\pi} f(x) \sin jx\,\mathrm{d}x \tag{3.49b}$$

For our particular example, f is defined in two parts, from $-\pi$ to 0 and from 0 to π. We can deal with this simply by splitting the region of integration into these two parts. So

$$
\begin{aligned}
b_j &= \frac{1}{\pi}\int_{-\pi}^{0} f(x)\sin jx\,\mathrm{d}x + \frac{1}{\pi}\int_{0}^{\pi} f(x)\sin jx\,\mathrm{d}x \\
&= \frac{1}{\pi}\int_{-\pi}^{0} -\sin jx\,\mathrm{d}x + \frac{1}{\pi}\int_{0}^{\pi} \sin jx\,\mathrm{d}x \\
&= \frac{1}{j\pi}\left[\cos jx\right]_{-\pi}^{0} + \frac{1}{j\pi}\left[-\cos jx\right]_{0}^{\pi} \\
&= 2\left(\frac{1-(-1)^i}{j\pi}\right),
\end{aligned}
$$

making use of the useful identity $\cos j\pi=(-1)^j$. Thus if j is odd, we get $b_j = 4/(j\pi)$, and if j is even, $b_j=0$. A similar calculations shows

$a_j = 0$ for all j,

(Actually we could see that a_j must be zero in view of the symmetry about the origin.) Taking, for example, $n=3$, we find that the best least squares approximation to f(x) is $(4/\pi)\sin x + (4/3\pi)\sin 3x$.

□

Remarks 3.55

There are several important points to notice about Example 3.54.

(a) $f(x)$ is not continuous, i.e. it is not in $C[-\pi, \pi]$. We are actually working in $L_2[-\pi, \pi]$.

(b) Another very important observation is that (3.48) and hence the expressions (3.49) for a_j and b_j in the example do not explicitly involve the dimension n. If we wish to increase the dimension of the approximating space S we can add more elements of the orthonormal set *without* re-calculating the coefficients. In fact we can go on adding more functions *ad infinitum*. This yields the *Fourier series* of f:

$$
\tfrac{1}{2}a_0 + \sum_{j=1}^{\infty} (a_j \cos jx + b_j \sin jx) \tag{3.50}
$$

where the a_js and b_js are given by (3.49). Each truncation of this series is the best least squares approximation to f of the appropriate dimension but note that is does *not* follow that the series converges to f for any particular value of x. However, it can be shown that (for this particular basis) the series converges in the sense of the norm for any $f \in L_2[-\pi, \pi]$. A useful subspace of $L_2[-\pi, \pi]$ is the space of functions that are piecewise continuous and differentiable, with only simple jump discontinuities. For this subspace it can be shown (again using some careful and detailed analysis) that the series converges to $f(x)$ at points x where f is continuous, and at the jumps (including the points $-\pi$ and π) it converges to the average of the left- and right-hand values. At the end points this of course means the average of $f(-\pi)$ and $f(\pi)$.

□

Having examined at some length the very important special case of the Fourier series, we return to the case of approximation of **b** by an element of a general finite dimensional subspace S. If we have an orthogonal basis for S, then obviously using (3.48) we can get least squares approximations in the same way. If the basis can be extended (and the dimension of S increased) indefinitely, we get an expansion of **b** which is equivalent of (3.50). Such an expansion is called an *orthogonal expansion* or *generalised Fourier series.* A further important extension of these ideas is the *wavelet*, in which an orthogonal basis is chosen which incorporates local behaviour and different spatial scalings. Wavelets are an extensive topic, so we will content ourselves here with a reference: Chui (1992).

We have reduced the problem of finding least squares approximations to that of constructing an orthogonal basis for S. Our final topic in this section is to describe how such a basis is constructed from any given basis. We will introduce a method applicable to any subspace.

The idea of the construction is very simple. Suppose we have a basis $\{\mathbf{c}_1 \ldots \mathbf{c}_n\}$ for S which is not orthogonal. We construct an orthogonal basis $\{\mathbf{a}_1 \ldots \mathbf{a}_n\}$ inductively as follows. Start with $\mathbf{a}_1=\mathbf{c}_1$. For, the inductive step suppose that we have got $\mathbf{a}_1 \ldots \mathbf{a}_k$ as an orthogonal basis for span$(\mathbf{c}_1 \ldots \mathbf{c}_k)$. We construct a new basis vector $\mathbf{a}_{k+1}$ as $\mathbf{c}_{k+1}-\mathbf{d}_k$ where $\mathbf{d}_k$ is the best least squares approximation to $\mathbf{c}_{k+1}$ from span$(\mathbf{c}_1 \ldots \mathbf{c}_k)=$span$(\mathbf{a}_1 \ldots \mathbf{a}_k)$. Then since $\mathbf{a}_{k+1}=$ $\mathbf{c}_k-$an element of span$(\mathbf{c}_1 \ldots \mathbf{c}_k)$, we will certainly have span$(\mathbf{a}_1 \ldots \mathbf{a}_{k+1})=$ span$(\mathbf{c}_1 \ldots \mathbf{c}_{k+1})$. But also in view of Theorem 3.48 (b), $\mathbf{a}_{k+1}$ will be orthogonal to span$(\mathbf{c}_1 \ldots \mathbf{c}_k)$ as required. Note also that $\mathbf{d}_k$ certainly exists as we have already an orthogonal basis for span$(\mathbf{c}_1 \ldots \mathbf{c}_k)$ and so $\mathbf{d}_k$ is given explicitly by (3.48). Specifically we get for $k=0, 1, \ldots, n-1$

$$\mathbf{a}_{k+1} = \mathbf{c}_{k+1} - \mathbf{d}_k \tag{3.51a}$$

where $\mathbf{d}_0=\mathbf{0}$ and for $k>0$

$$\mathbf{d}_k = w_1\mathbf{a}_1 + \ldots + w_k\mathbf{a}_k \tag{3.51b}$$

with the w_j given by (3.48) with **b** replaced by $\mathbf{c}_{k+1}$ (so they depend on k, of course). This construction is known as the *Gram–Schmidt process.*

Examples 3.56

(a) Consider $\mathbb{R}^3$ with the standard inner product and let $\mathbf{c}_1=(1, 1, 1)^T$, $\mathbf{c}_2=(1, 1, 0)^T$, $\mathbf{c}_3=(1, 0, 0)^T$,

We set $\mathbf{a}_1 = \mathbf{c}_1 = (1, 1, 1)^T$,

Now $\mathbf{d}_1 = w_1\mathbf{a}_1$ where $w_1 = (\mathbf{c}_2{}^T\mathbf{a}_1)/(\mathbf{a}_1{}^T\mathbf{a}_1) = 2/3$. Thus

$$\mathbf{a}_2 = \mathbf{c}_2 - 2/3\mathbf{a}_1 + (1, 1, 0)^T - (2/3, 2/3, 2/3)^T$$
$$= (1/3, 1/3, -2/3)^T.$$

Note that

$$\mathbf{a}_1{}^T\mathbf{a}_2 = 1/3 + 1/3 - 2/3 + 0, \text{ as required .}$$

Now

$$\mathbf{a}_3 = \mathbf{c}_3 - \mathbf{d}_2 \text{ and } \mathbf{d}_2 = w_1\mathbf{a}_1 + w_2\mathbf{a}_2.$$

Remember that this is not the same w_1 and w_2 as before. In fact

$$w_1 = (\mathbf{c}_3{}^T\mathbf{a}_1)/(\mathbf{a}_1{}^T\mathbf{a}_1) = 1/3$$

and

$$w_2 = (\mathbf{c}_3{}^T\mathbf{a}_2)/(\mathbf{a}_2{}^T\mathbf{a}_2) = (1/3)/(2/3) = 1/2.$$

So

$$\mathbf{d}_2 = (1/3, 1/3, 1/3)^T + (1/6, 1/6, -1/3)^T$$

$$\mathbf{a}_3 = (1/2, -1/2, 0)^T.$$

Thus

$$\mathbf{a}_3 = (1/2, -1/2, 0)^T.$$

Note

$$\mathbf{a}_3{}^T\mathbf{a}_1 = 1/2 - 1/2 = 0$$

and

$$\mathbf{a}_3{}^T\mathbf{a}_2 = 1/6 - 1/6 = 0 \text{ as expected .}$$

(b) Consider the space spanned by $\{1, \exp(x), \exp(2x)\}$ where $\exp(x) = e^x$.

Fitting exponentials to data is quite a common problem, so it is useful to find an orthogonal basis for the space with respect to some suitable inner product. For definiteness we use the inner product

$$<p, q> = \int_0^1 p(x)q(x)\,\mathrm{d}x.$$

Let the orthogonal basis be $\{f_0(x), f_1(x), f_2(x)\}$. It is natural to number from zero here, as we did for the Fourier basis, since 1 can be thought of as exp(0). Set $f_0 = 1$. Then

$$f_1(x) = \exp(x) - w_1 f_0$$

where

$$w_1 = <\exp(x), 1>/<1, 1> .$$

But

$$<\exp(x), 1> = \int_0^1 \exp(x)\,\mathrm{d}x = \mathrm{e} - 1$$

and

$$<1, 1> = \int_0^1 1\,\mathrm{d}x = 1.$$

Thus

$$f_1(x) = \exp(x) + 1 - \mathrm{e} .$$

The determination of f_2 is left as an exercise!

□

While it is important to know about the Gram–Schmidt process, this is not of course a connectionist technique, and neither is it very stable numerically. However, an important special case of the Gram–Schmidt process can in some circumstances much simplify the construction orthogonal bases. Here we will look at orthogonal polynomials. The conjugate gradient method described in Chapter 4 also avails itself of the following beautiful result of Forsyth.

The natural starting basis for polynomial spaces is of course the power functions $1, x, x^2, x^3 \ldots$. The important thing about this basis is the simple and obvious fact that we get each element by multiplying the previous one by x. If we define $q_i = x^i$, and a (linear) operator $L(f) = xf$, then we have

$$q_{i+1} = L(q_i). \tag{3.52}$$

Now for most real inner products that we use in practice, it is true for this L that

$$<L(p), q> = <p, L(q)>. \tag{3.53}$$

This probably looks horribly abstract but is actually a triviality. For example if

$$<p, q> = \int_0^1 p(x)q(x)\, dx$$

then

$$\begin{aligned} <L(p),q> &= \int_0^1 [xp(x)]q(x)\, dx \\ &= \int_0^1 p(x)[xq(x)]\, dx \\ &= <p, L(q)>. \end{aligned}$$

A linear operator that satisfies (3.53) is said to be *self-adjoint* with respect to the inner product. In function spaces, self-adjoint operators play a similar role to symmetric matrices in matrix theory. In fact a symmetric matrix A is self-adjoint with respect to the standard inner product: $(A\mathbf{x})^{\mathrm{T}}\mathbf{y} = \mathbf{x}^{\mathrm{T}}(A^{\mathrm{T}}\mathbf{y}) = \mathbf{x}^{\mathrm{T}}(A\mathbf{y})$ if A is symmetric. Forsyth's theorem is a result about self-adjoint operators, and we might as well give the general form as it is no harder to prove and we will need it in Chapter 4. But remember that here we are just interested in the simple operator 'multiply by x', and that this operator is self-adjoint with respect to the usual real inner products. (It is *not* self-adjoint with respect to hermitian products due to the need to take a complex conjugate. Although Forsyth's theorem itself works for hermitian products, unfortunately it does not apply to orthogonal polynomials. This is one of the few cases where results in the real case fail to go over to the complex plane.)

Now the point of Forsyth's theorem is that if our subspace S has a basis generated like (3.52) by a self-adjoint linear operator, the Gram–Schmidt process takes a particularly simple form. Before proceeding to the theorem, we need to make one more observation. Since in (3.51), $\mathrm{span}\{\mathbf{c}_1 \ldots \mathbf{c}_j\} = \mathrm{span}\{\mathbf{a}_1 \ldots \mathbf{a}_j\}$ and $\mathbf{a}_{j+1}$ is orthogonal to each $\mathbf{a}_i$, $i = 1, \ldots, j$, it follows that in fact $\mathbf{a}_{j+1}$ is orthogonal to *any* vector in span $\{\mathbf{c}_1 \ldots \mathbf{c}_j\}$.

Theorem 3.57 (Forsyth's Theorem)
Let V be an inner product space, and let S be a finite dimensional subspace with a basis $\{\mathbf{c}_1, \ldots, \mathbf{c}_n\}$ satisfying $\mathbf{c}_{i+1} = L(\mathbf{c}_i)$ where L is a self-adjoint linear operator. Then the associated orthogonal basis $\{\mathbf{a}_j\}$ generated by the Gram–Schmidt process satisfies the three term recurrence

$$\mathbf{a}_{j+1} = L(\mathbf{a}_j) + A_j\mathbf{a}_j + B_j\mathbf{a}_{j-1}$$

where

$$A_j = -<\mathbf{a}_j, L(\mathbf{a}_j)>/<\mathbf{a}_j, \mathbf{a}_j>$$

and

$$B_j = -<\mathbf{a}_j, \mathbf{a}_j>/<\mathbf{a}_{j-1}, \mathbf{a}_{j-1}> .$$

Proof
From equation (3.51) we have $\mathbf{c}_j = \mathbf{a}_j - \mathbf{d}_{j-1}$. Thus $\mathbf{c}_{j+1} = L(\mathbf{c}_j) = L(\mathbf{a}_j) - L(\mathbf{d}_{j-1})$ since L is linear. Hence

$$\begin{aligned} \mathbf{a}_{j+1} &= \mathbf{c}_{j+1} - \mathbf{d}_j \text{ from } (3.51a) \\ &= L(\mathbf{a}_j) - L(\mathbf{d}_{j-1}) - \mathbf{d}_j . \end{aligned}$$

So

$$\mathbf{a}_{j+1} - L(\mathbf{a}_j) = -L(\mathbf{d}_{j-1}) - \mathbf{d}_j .$$

Now $\mathbf{d}_{j-1} \in \text{span}\{\mathbf{c}_1 \ldots \mathbf{c}_{j-1}\}$ so $L(\mathbf{d}_{j-1}) \in \text{span}\{\mathbf{c}_1 \ldots \mathbf{c}_j\} = \text{span}\{\mathbf{a}_1 \ldots \mathbf{a}_j\}$, as does $\mathbf{d}_j$. Thus there exist numbers $y_1 \ldots y_j$ such that

$$\mathbf{a}_{j+1} - L(\mathbf{a}_j) = y_j\mathbf{a}_j + y_{j-1}\mathbf{a}_{j-1} + \ldots + y_1\mathbf{a}_1.$$

If we take the inner product of this equation with $\mathbf{a}_i$, remembering that the $\mathbf{a}_j$s are orthogonal, we find that

$$y_i <\mathbf{a}_i, \mathbf{a}_i> = <\mathbf{a}_{j+1} - L(\mathbf{a}_j), \mathbf{a}_i> = <\mathbf{a}_{j+1}, \mathbf{a}_i> - <L(\mathbf{a}_j), \mathbf{a}_i> .$$

The first of these terms is zero, again because of the orthogonality, so we can use the self-adjointness of L to write

$$y_i <\mathbf{a}_i, \mathbf{a}_i> = -<\mathbf{a}_j, L(\mathbf{a}_i)> .$$

Now comes the magic bit! $L(\mathbf{a}_i) \in \text{span}\{\mathbf{a}_1, \ldots, \mathbf{a}_{i+1}\}$ by a similar argument as we used for $\mathbf{d}_{j-1}$ above. It follows from the remark preceding the statement of the theorem that $y_i = 0$ for $i = 1, \ldots, j-2$. Only y_j and y_{j-1} are non-zero. We are nearly finished. To complete the proof we set $A_j = y_j$ and $B_j = y_j - 1$, and then note that $<\mathbf{a}_j, L(\mathbf{a}_{j-1})> = <\mathbf{a}_j, \mathbf{a}_j>$ since $\mathbf{a}_j - L(\mathbf{a}_{j-1}) \in \text{span}\{\mathbf{a}_1, \ldots, \mathbf{a}_{i-1}\}$ and is therefore orthogonal to $\mathbf{a}_j$.

□

For the case of a set of orthogonal polynomials $p_k(x)$ where $L(p) = xp(x)$ we get

$$p_{j+1}(x) = (x + A_j)p_j(x) + B_j\, p_{j-1}(x) \tag{3.54}$$

where

$$A_j = -<p_j(x), xp_j(x)>/ <p_j(x), p_j(x)>$$

and

$$B_j = -<p_j(x), p_j(x)>/<p_{j-1}(x), p_{j-1}(x)> .$$

Example 3.58

Orthogonal polynomials are usually constructed on [−1, 1] in order to exploit even/odd symmetry. Other intervals can be obtained by a linear change of variable. So consider

$$<p, q> = \int_{-1}^{1} p(x)q(x)\, \mathrm{d}x.$$

The polynomials orthogonal with respect to this inner product are called *Legendre polynomials*. $P_n(x)$. (Actually a different normalisation for $P_n(x)$ is used in many books, but this need not concern us here.) We start with $P_0(x) = 1$. We could find $P_1(x)$ from (3.51), but since

$$0 = \int_{-1}^{1} 1x\, \mathrm{d}x.$$

it is easy to spot that $P_1(x) = x$. Further polynomials are obtained from (3.54). So

$$P_2(x) = (x + A_1)P_1(x) + B_1 P_0(x) = (x + A_1)x + B_1.$$

Now

$$A_1 = -< P_1(x), xP_1(x) >/<P_1(x), P_1(x)> .$$

$$< P_1(x), xP_1(x) > = \int_{-1}^{1} P_1(x), xP_1(x)\,\mathrm{d}x.$$

$$= \int_{-1}^{1} x^3\,\mathrm{d}x = 0.$$

Thus $A_1 = 0$, as in fact we might have deduced by even/odd symmetry. Also

$$B_1 = -< P_1(x), P_1(x) >/< P_0(x), P_0(x) > .$$

$$< P_0(x), P_0(x) > = \int_{-1}^{1} P_0(x)P_0(x)\,\mathrm{d}x.$$

$$= \int_{-1}^{1} \mathrm{d}x = 2.$$

And

$$< P_1(x), P_1(x) > = \int_{-1}^{1} P_1(x)P_1(x)\,\mathrm{d}x.$$

$$= \int_{-1}^{1} x^2\,\mathrm{d}x = 2/3.$$

So $B_1 = -\frac{1}{3}$ and we get

$$P_2(x) = (x + A_1)x + B_1 = x^2 - 1/3.$$

To check this, note that

$$< P_2(x), P_0(x) > = \int_{-1}^{1} x^2 - 1/3\,\mathrm{d}x = 2/3 - 2/3 = 0.$$

$$< P_2(x), P_1(x) > = \int_{-1}^{1} x^3 - 1/3x\,\mathrm{d}x = 0.$$

This computation is quite economical. Each polynomial is defined in terms of the previous two, and requires only three inner products. Moreover even one of these is used twice, for the denominator of A_j is the denominator of B_{j+1}. Further savings can be made by remembering that P_j is orthogonal to all polynomials of degree $j-1$ or less. Thus when evaluating the inner products, only the leading terms of (say) the second argument need be considered. There is in fact an explicit expression for the coefficients in the three term recurrence for the Legendre polynomials: see, e.g. Abramowitz and Stegun (1964, Chapter 22).

□

Where possible, in practice it is normally best to avoid direct techniques of orthogonalization and employ alternative methods. A technique which is both important numerically and also intimately related to neural computation is the singular value decomposition.

3.7 The singular value decomposition

The singular value decomposition (SVD) is closely related to the concept of principal components and the stochastic analysis of neural systems. However the decomposition as such belongs to the field of linear algebra, and, indeed, many of the results which are often clothed in statistical language are actually algebraic. It is therefore appropriate to consider the SVD here. It is in fact a natural extension of the ideas discussed in Theorems 3.10, 3.11 and 3.15. As previously remarked, the problem with Theorem 3.10 is that a general square matrix may not have a distinct set of real eigenvalues and thus not be diagonalizable. Symmetric matrices by contrast *are* always diagonalizable (Theorem 3.15). The SVD enables us to extend these spectral methods to general real (or complex) matrices. Again, our exposition will only consider the real case. The matrices do not even need to be square!

Theorem 3.59 (The Singular Value Decomposition or SVD)
Let A be an $m\times n$ real matrix. Then

(a) A may be factorised in the form

$$A = PSQ^{\mathrm{T}}$$

where P and Q are orthogonal matrices ($m\times m$ and $n\times n$ respectively), and S is an $m\times n$ matrix which (although not necessarily square) is diagonal in the sense that $s_{ij}=0$ if $i\neq j$. The diagonal elements $\sigma_i=s_{ii}$ are non negative, and may be assumed ordered so that $\sigma_1\geq\sigma_2 \ldots \geq\sigma_{\min(m,n)} \geq 0$. These σ's are called the *singular values* of A. (Some authors define the singular values to be the non-zero σ's.)

(b) The columns of Q are eigenvectors of $A^{\mathrm{T}}A$, the columns of P are eigenvectors of AA^{T}, and the non-zero singular values are the positive square roots of the non-zero eigenvalues of $A^{\mathrm{T}}A$ or equivalently of AA^{T}.

Proof

In fact, (b) is used to prove (a). We consider first the case $n \geq m$.

The matrix A^TA is $n \times n$ and symmetric. It is also and positive semi-definite: to see this note that for any real $\mathbf{x}$, $\mathbf{x}^TA^TA\mathbf{x} = (A\mathbf{x})^T(A\mathbf{x}) \geq 0$.

Let Q be as defined in (b), Since A^TA has non-negative eigenvalues we can write them as σ_i^2 arranged in non-increasing order in the diagonal matrix D. Then we have

$$Q^TA^TAQ = D. \tag{3.55}$$

If A is of rank r, so is A^TA, since the subset of vectors $\mathbf{x}$ for which $\mathbf{x}^TA^TA\mathbf{x} = 0$ is precisely ker(A). Thus the last $n-r$ of the σ_i are zero. Let $\mathbf{q_i}$ denote the ith column of Q, and

$$\mathbf{p_i} = A\mathbf{q_i}/\sigma_i, \; i = 1,\ldots,r.$$

It follows from (3.55) that the $\mathbf{p_i}$ form an orthonormal set. If $r < n$, extend this set to an orthonormal basis for $\mathbb{R}^n$, by adding additional vectors $\mathbf{p_{r+1}}, \ldots, \mathbf{p}_n$. Then for $i = 1, \ldots, n$, we have

$$(i\text{th column of } AQ) = A\mathbf{q_i} = \sigma_i\mathbf{p_i}.$$

Thus if P is the orthogonal matrix formed from the columns $\mathbf{p_i}$, and S is as defined in (a),

$$AQ = SP \text{ or } A = PSQ^T.$$

This completes the proof of (a) for $n \geq m$. The final part of (b), namely that the $\mathbf{p_i}$ are eigenvectors of AA^T, follows from the observation that

$$AA^T = PSQ^TQS^TP^T = PSS^TP^T.$$

The case $n < m$ may be deduced by transposing A.

□

Notice that a nice property of the SVD is that we always get real singular values, and there is no problem with 'missing' eigenvectors, when A is not symmetric. Generally speaking, it is not a good idea to use Theorem 3.59(b) as a method of actually calculating the SVD, since the squaring of the eigenvalues involved tends to cause underflow and consequent problems of numerical stability. As with eigenvalues, consideration of numerical computation of the SVD is outside the scope of this book: one standard algorithm is given in Golub and Reinsch (1970).

Using this immensely powerful tool we can tie up several loose ends in this chapter and address many further issues relating to neural computation.

To begin with, we can easily prove Theorem 3.35 (c). Note that in fact the result may now be restated as $\|A\|_2=\sigma_1$, where σ_1 is the largest singular value of A.

Proof of Theorem 3.35 (c)

Let $A=PSQ^T$ be the SVD of A. Since Q is an orthogonal matrix, $\|Q^T\mathbf{v}\|_2=\|\mathbf{v}\|_2$ for any $\mathbf{v}$, and since P is orthogonal, $\|PAQ^T\mathbf{v}\|_2=\|AQ^T\mathbf{v}\|_2$. It follows that $\|A\|_2=\max\|S\mathbf{v}\|_2$, where as usual the maximum is taken over $\mathbf{v}$ such that $\|\mathbf{v}\|_2=1$. But $\|S\mathbf{v}\|_2=\sigma_1 v_1^2+\ldots+\sigma_n v_n^2$. Since we must have $v_1^2+\ldots+v_n^2=1$, $\sigma_1 v_1^2+\ldots+\sigma_n v_n^2$ is clearly maximised when $v_1=1$ and all the other v_i are zero.

□

Remark 3.60

Observe that the method of proof of this theorem shows that $\|PA\|_2=\|A\|_2$ for any orthogonal matrix P. Also the theorem shows that $\|A\|_2=\|A^T\|_2$.

□

We can also use the SVD to obtain a direct solution to matrix least squares problems. (Compare (3.33), (3.34) and (3.35).)

Example 3.61

Again we consider the problem of finding $\mathbf{w}$ to minimise $\|B\mathbf{w}-\mathbf{f}\|_2$. This time we will tackle it directly. Recall once again that for an orthogonal matrix P, $\|Q\mathbf{v}\|_2=\|\mathbf{v}\|_2$. Applying the SVD to B gives

$$\begin{aligned}\|B\mathbf{w}-\mathbf{f}\|_2 &= \|PSQ^T\mathbf{w}-\mathbf{f}\|_2\\ &= \|P(SQ^T\mathbf{w}-P^T\mathbf{f})\|_2\\ &= \|SQ^T\mathbf{w}-P^T\mathbf{f}\|_2\end{aligned}$$

Now write $\mathbf{v}=Q^T\mathbf{w}$ and $\mathbf{c}=P^T\mathbf{f}$. Then

$$\begin{aligned}\|B\mathbf{w}-\mathbf{f}\|_2^2 &= \|S\mathbf{v}-\mathbf{c}\|_2^2\\ &= \sum_{i=1}^{n}(\sigma_i v_i - c_i)^2.\end{aligned}$$

Suppose that the first r singular values are non-zero (i.e. rank$(B)=r$). Obviously the minimum occurs when $v_i=c_i/\sigma_i$ for $i=1,\ldots,r$. The residual square error is $\sum c_i^2$ where the sum is taken over the zero singular values, thus from $r+1$ to n.

We can write this solution in matrix form by defining $S^{\#}$ to be the matrix with

$s_{ij}^{\#} = 0$ if $i \neq j$,
$s_{ii}^{\#} = 1/\sigma_i$ for $i = 1,\ldots,r$,
$s_{ii}^{\#} = 0$ if $i > r$. Then

$$\mathbf{v} = S^{\#}\mathbf{c}$$

or

$$Q^{\mathrm{T}}\mathbf{w} = S^{\#}P^{\mathrm{T}}\mathbf{f}$$

$$\mathbf{w} = QS^{\#}P^{\mathrm{T}}\mathbf{f} \tag{3.56}$$

□

With the notation of this example, let us define $B^{\#} = QS^{\#}P^{\mathrm{T}}$. Note that if the matrix B is square and non singular, then the system of equations $B\mathbf{w} = \mathbf{f}$ would, of course, have the solution $\mathbf{w} = B^{-1}\mathbf{f}$. Comparing this with (3.56), we see that $B^{\#}$ behaves as a *generalized inverse* of B.

Definition 3.62

The matrix $B^{\#} = QS^{\#}P^{\mathrm{T}}$, with the notation of Example 3.61, is called the *Moore–Penrose Pseudoinverse* of B.

□

This is not actually the simplest definition of the Moore–Penrose Pseudoinverse, or indeed the fastest way to calculate it. However it is one of the most natural definitions, and provided a good algorithm is used for the SVD, it is numerically very stable. For a full discussion of generalized inverses, see Ben-Israel and Greville (1974).

An extension of this idea can be employed to approximate one matrix by another (of smaller size or rank). This process can be given a very natural connectionist context, where it provides a method of data compression. We will look in at an example based on Baldi and Hornik (1989) but we modify it somewhat. Consider a multilayer perceptron with n inputs and n outputs. We have one hidden layer with m units. For this network the activation of the hidden units (as well as the input and output units) is simply the identity function $\sigma(x)=x$. Thus if W is the matrix of weights in the first layer, and V is the matrix of weights in the second layer, the output for input vector $\mathbf{x}$ is simply $\mathbf{g}(\mathbf{x})=VW\mathbf{x}$. Now for any given $\mathbf{x}$ we specify our target output $\mathbf{y}$ as $\mathbf{y}=\mathbf{x}$. Obviously if we have $m \geq n$, then any V and W with $VW=I$ would achieve this exactly. But what happens for $m<n$? More specifically, let our input patterns $\mathbf{x_j}$, $j=1, \ldots, t$, to be the columns of an $n \times t$ matrix X. We train the network, perhaps by backpropagation (see Chapter 4), to minimise $\sum \|\mathbf{x_j}-\mathbf{g}(\mathbf{x_j})\|_2^2$, where the sum is over j. Our minimisation problem can therefore be restated as follows: find V and W so that $\|X-VWX\|_s$ is minimised (note the use of the Schur norm here: see the paragraph before Properties 3.33. As we have seen, training with a finite learning rate η will not in fact solve the least squares problem exactly, but let us suppose that η is sufficiently small that for practical purposes we have the true minimum. (Since this is actually an overdetermined linear problem there are no local minima.) To understand what the matrix W does here, we write X in terms of its singular value decomposition $X=PSQ^{\mathrm{T}}$ where P and Q are orthogonal and S is diagonal (but not necessarily square). The diagonal elements of S are the singular values $\sigma_1 \geq \sigma_2 \geq \ldots \geq \sigma_n$, Suppose rank $(X)=r$ so that in fact $\sigma_{r+1} \ldots \sigma_n=0$. The crucial stage is to find a matrix H satisfying rank $(H) \leq m$ and which minimises $\|X-PHP^{\mathrm{T}}X\|_s$. Once we have H it is not difficult to factorize PHP^{T} to get W and V. The Schur norm of a matrix is unchanged if we multiply by an orthogonal matrix, since the 2-norm of each column is unchanged (or observe that the eigenvalues and hence the trace are unchanged). So for any H,

$$\begin{aligned}\|X-PHP^{\mathrm{T}}X\|_s^2 &= \|(I-PHP^{\mathrm{T}})X\|_s^2 = \|(I-PHP^{\mathrm{T}})PSQ^{\mathrm{T}}\|_s^2 \\ &= \|(P-PH)S\|_s^2 = \|(I-H)S\|_s^2 \\ &= \sum_{i=1}^{r} \sigma_i^2\Big\{(1-h_{ii})^2 + \sum_{j \neq i} h_{ji}^2\Big\}.\end{aligned}$$

Obviously, at the minimum H is diagonal. But we require rank $(H) \leq m$. Thus the minimising H is obtained by setting $h_{ii}=1$, $i=1, \ldots, \min(r, m)$ and all the other elements to zero. If $r \geq m$, there is no loss of information in this process, and the patterns $\mathbf{x_p}$ are reconstructed exactly. If $r>m$, then the total error over all patterns is given by the square root of

$$\sum_{i=m+1}^{r} \sigma_i^{\,2}. \tag{3.57}$$

It remains to perform the factorization $VW=PHP^T$. While the choice of H is unique, this is not so for the factorization. However, since PHP^T is symmetric, it makes sense to set $V=W^T$. In fact we have for the minimising H,

$$HH^T = H$$

whence

$$PHP^T = PHH^TP^T = PH(PH)^T.$$

PH has (at most) m non-zero columns: we may take these as V and make $W=V^T=$the first m rows of H^TP^T. Then $VW=PHP^T$ as required. The rows of W are those eigenvectors of XX^T corresponding to the largest singular values. The effect of W is to project the input patterns $\mathbf{x_p}$ onto the span of these vectors. If $r\leq m$ (which is certainly the case, for instance, if the number of patterns $t\leq m$) then the t n-vectors $\mathbf{x_p}$ are compressed by W onto m-vectors $\mathbf{y_p}$ with no loss of information, since we can recover X as W^TY. Here, of course, the columns of Y are the $\mathbf{y_p}$s. More usefully, even if $r>m$ there will be little loss in this compression provided the quantity (3.57) is small.

Moreover, VWX is the closest rank m matrix to X in terms of the Schur norm, and can be constructed using the trained network by feeding the columns of X thought the network one at a time to get the columns of VWX. It is well known and not hard to show that this matrix is also closest with respect to the matrix 2-norm: the proof is left for the reader!

As well as helping us to understand the representation of data in neural networks, the SVD can help us to understand the convergence behaviour of learning algorithms. Firstly, we can provide a simple explanation for the well known phenomenon of *overgeneralization* reported in many practical studies with neural networks. This is the observation that better results may well be obtained if the iteration is *not* continued to convergence. These problems are closely related to the issue of non-spanning patterns which we have already encountered. In many network applications such as vision, we may have a very large number of free weights. For example, even a low resolution 64×64 image will have 4096 pixels. If we feed this into the network without any compression we will have at least this many weights. If we are training the network to recognise (say) a certain object in a set of images, it is most unlikely that we will have enough data to prevent the problem being severely under-determined. But in fact, the delta rule (even in epoch form) can cope with this if the number of iterations is restricted: it includes a kind of built in compression. Recall (3.38):

$$\mathbf{w_{k+1}} = \Omega \mathbf{w_k} - \eta X\mathbf{b},$$

where $\Omega = (I - \eta\ XX^{\mathrm{T}})$ and $\mathbf{b}$ is the vector of required outputs. We decompose X in singular value form. Specifically we write

$$X = PSQ^{\mathrm{T}}$$

where P and Q are orthogonal and S is diagonal (but not necessarily square). We find

$$\begin{aligned}\mathbf{w_{k+1}} &= (I - \eta PSS^{\mathrm{T}}P^{\mathrm{T}})\mathbf{w_k} - \eta X\mathbf{b}\\ &= P(I - \eta SS^{\mathrm{T}})P^{\mathrm{T}}\mathbf{w_k} - \eta PSQ^{\mathrm{T}}\mathbf{b}\end{aligned}$$

or with $\mathbf{z}_k = P^{\mathrm{T}}\mathbf{w_k}$ and $\mathbf{u} = Q^{\mathrm{T}}\mathbf{b}$.

$$\mathbf{z_{k+1}} = (I - \eta SS^{\mathrm{T}})\mathbf{z_k} - \eta S\mathbf{u}. \tag{3.58}$$

Note that SS^{T} is diagonal. At this point the notation becomes a little messy: let us denote by $(\mathbf{z_k})_i$ the ith element of $\mathbf{z_k}$. These elements are decoupled by the singular value decomposition. More specifically, suppose X has r non-zero singular values (the diagonal elements of S) $\sigma_1 \geq \sigma_2 \geq \ldots \geq \sigma_n$, Then (3.58) when written elementwise gives

$$(\mathbf{z_{k+1}})_i = (1 - \eta\sigma_i{}^2)(\mathbf{z_k})_i - \eta\sigma_i u_i, \text{ for } i = 1,\ldots,r$$

and

$$(\mathbf{z_{k+1}})_i = (\mathbf{z_k})_i \text{ for } i = r + 1,\ldots,n.$$

Assuming that η is sufficiently small to guarantee convergence (i.e. all terms $(1 - \eta\ v_i^2) < 1$), it is easy to see that convergence will be very much faster for the $(\mathbf{z_k})_i$ corresponding to the larger singular values. This is exactly what we would like. Since P and Q are orthogonal matrices their rows and columns have norm 1. Thus we see from (3.58) that the large singular values correspond to the actual information in the pattern data X. (This approach is called *principal component analysis*.) The delta rule (in the epoch form at least) has the nice property of converging on the principal components of the data *first*. Unfortunately it is very hard to tell from the iteration when this has occurred since small singular values can make a large contribution to the least squares error. This explains the phenomenon of *overtraining*. Initially the iteration picks out significant features in the variability of the data. Continued iteration makes it try to separate insignificant features or noise.

In view of the problems of slow convergence and underdetermination, many authors have commented on the advisability of performing some preprocessing of the input patterns before feeding them to the network. Often (not always, of course) the preprocessing suggested is linear. At first sight this seems to be a pointless exercise, for if the raw input data vector is $\mathbf{x}$, with dimension n', say; the preprocessing operation is represented by the $n \times n'$ matrix T, W is the input matrix of the net and we denote by the vector $\mathbf{h}$ the input to the next layer of the net, then

$$\mathbf{h} = WT\mathbf{x}. \tag{3.59}$$

Obviously, *the theoretical representational power of the network is the same as one with unprocessed input and input matrix* WT. However, this does *not* mean that these preprocessing operations are useless. We can identify at least the following three uses of preprocessing.

(a) To reduce work by reducing dimension and possibly using fast algorithms e.g. the Fast Fourier Transform, Brigham (1974). (So we do not want this information to increase the contraction parameter in the delta rule iteration.)
(b) To improve the search geometry by removing principal components of the data and corresponding singular values that are irrelevant to the classification problem.
(c) To improve the stability of the iteration by removing near zero singular values (which correspond to noise) and clustering the other singular values near to 1: in the language of numerical analysis to *precondition* the iteration.

We will not address all these three points explicitly here. Instead we will derive some theoretical principles with the aid of which the issues may be attacked (Ellacott, 1993, 1994a, 1994b). The first point to consider is the effect of the filter on the stability of the learning process. For simplicity, we again consider only the linear epoch algorithm here.

We hope, of course, that a suitable choice of filter will make the learning properties better, but the results here show that whatever choice we make, the dynamics will not be made much worse unless the filter has very bad singular values. In particular, we show that if the filter is an orthogonal projection, then the gradient descent mapping with filtering will be at least as contractive as the unfiltered case.

We see from (3.36) that the crucial issue is the relationship between the unfiltered update matrix

$$\Omega = (I - \eta XX^{\mathrm{T}}) \tag{3.60}$$

and its filtered equivalent

$$(I - \eta TXX^{\mathrm{T}}T^{\mathrm{T}}) + \Omega'$$

say.

Note that these operators may be defined on spaces of different dimension: indeed for a sensible filtering process we would expect the filter T to involve a significant dimension reduction. Recall that Ω in (3.60) is $n \times n$ and let us take Ω' to be $n' \times n'$ with $n' < n$. Note also that for purposes of comparison we have assumed the learning rates η are the same.

A natural question is to try to relate the norms of these two operators, and hence the rate of convergence of the corresponding iterations. As before, we suppose $L = XX^{\mathrm{T}}$ has eigenvalues λ_j, $j = 1, \ldots, n$, with

$$0 < \lambda_n \leq \lambda_{n-1} \leq \ldots \leq \lambda_1 = \rho(XX^{\mathrm{T}}) = \|XX^{\mathrm{T}}\|_2 = \|X^{\mathrm{T}}\|_2^2.$$

(Note here we assume the **x**'s span so $\lambda_n \neq 0$. In terms of the singular values σ_i of X, $\sigma_i^2 = \lambda_i$.)

We need to relate the eigenvalues of XX^{T} with those of $TXX^{\mathrm{T}}T^{\mathrm{T}} = L'$, say. Let L' have eigenvalues $\mu_1 \geq \mu_2 \geq \ldots \geq \mu_n > 0$ and T have singular values $\nu_1 \geq \nu_2 \geq \ldots \geq \nu_n > 0$. Note that we are assuming T has full rank n' and so has no non-zero singular values. This is a reasonable assumption since there is no point in using a filter which has a non-trivial kernel. We should reduce the dimension of the operator's image space instead.

Proposition 3.63

With the notation above, $\mu_1 \leq \nu_1^2 \lambda_1$ and $\mu_{n'} \geq \nu_{n'}^{2} \lambda n$.

Proof

The first inequality is straightforward. Since L and L' are symmetric

$$\mu_1 = \|TXX^{\mathrm{T}}T^{\mathrm{T}}\|_2 \leq \|T\|_2 \|XX^{\mathrm{T}}\|_2 \, \|T^{\mathrm{T}}\|_2 = \nu_1^2 \lambda_1.$$

The second inequality is slightly more difficult. Let $\mathbf{u}_{n'}$ be the normalised eigenvector of L' corresponding to $\mu_{n'}$. Also let X have SVD PSQ^{T} as above (remembering the singular values satisfy $\sigma_i^2 = \lambda_i$.), and T have SVD UNV^{T} where the ν_i are the non-zero entries in N. Then

$$\mu_n = \mathbf{u}_{n'}^{\mathrm{T}} \mu_n \mathbf{u}_n' = \mathbf{u}_n'^{\mathrm{T}} TXX^{\mathrm{T}}T^{\mathrm{T}} \mathbf{u}_n' = \|X^{\mathrm{T}}T^{\mathrm{T}}\mathbf{u}_n'\|_2^2.$$

But $\|X^T T^T \mathbf{u_n}\|_2 = \|QS^T P^T T^T \mathbf{u_n}\|_2 = \|S^T P^T T^T \mathbf{u_n}\|_2 \geq \lambda_n^{1/2} \|P^T T^T \mathbf{u_n}\|_2 = \lambda_n^{1/2}$ $\|N^T U^T \mathbf{u_n}\|_2 \geq \lambda_n^{1/2} \nu_n'$ since $\|U^T \mathbf{u}_n\|_2 = 1$.

□

This result means that $\|\Omega'\|_2$ cannot be much larger than $\|\Omega\|_2$ if T has singular values close to 1.

Most linear filters T applied in practical applications are examples of a particular type of linear operation known as a *projection.*

Definition 3.64

Let V be a finite dimensional vector space and W a subspace. A linear mapping P from V onto W is called a *projection* if it satisfies $P^2(\mathbf{v}) = P[P(\mathbf{v})] = P(\mathbf{v})$ for each $\mathbf{v} \in V$.

□

Note that the mapping must be onto: i.e. W is the image of V under P. This definition may look odd at first, but the idea is actually very simple. Think of P as producing an approximation $\mathbf{w} = P(\mathbf{v})$ to $\mathbf{v}$ from the subspace W. The condition of the definition merely requires that if we apply P to $\mathbf{w}$ (which we may certainly do since W is a subspace of V) then we get $\mathbf{w}$ back: $P(\mathbf{w}) = \mathbf{w}$. If we approximate an element of W we get the same element.

The requirement that V be finite dimensional is not crucial. (See, e.g. Kreyszig (1978, p. 480).) For any normed vector space, we can define the norm of an operator in a similar manner to Definition 3.34 (except that the maximum needs to be replaced by the supremum). However in infinite dimensional spaces it is possible to have linear mappings for which the quantity of Definition 3.34 is not finite, i.e. the mapping does not have a finite norm. If the norm *is* finite, the mapping is said to be *bounded.* When defining projections in infinite dimensional spaces, it is usual to require the condition that V be a normed vector space and P be bounded (although actually Kreyszig does not follow this convention). In the finite dimensional spaces which are generally used in neural computation, all operators are bounded.

The usual way to define projections is to select a basis for our approximating space W, or conversely choose W as the span of our set of approximating functions. (For example, if we wish to approximate by cubic polynomials in one variable, we might choose the basis $1, x, x^2, x^3$.) Extend this basis to all of V. So suppose $W = \text{span}\{\mathbf{v}_1, \mathbf{v}_2, \ldots, \mathbf{v}_k\}$ and $V = \text{span}\{\mathbf{v}_1, \mathbf{v}_2, \ldots, \mathbf{v}_k, \mathbf{v}_{k+1}, \ldots, \mathbf{v}_n\}$. Any element $\mathbf{v}$ of V can be expressed uniquely as

$$\mathbf{v} = \alpha_1\mathbf{v_1} + \alpha_2\mathbf{v_2} + \ldots + \alpha_k\mathbf{v_k} + \alpha_{k+1}\mathbf{v_{k+1}} + \ldots + \alpha_n\mathbf{v_n}.$$

To get a projection onto W choose simply $\mathbf{w} = P(\mathbf{v})$, where

$$\mathbf{w} = \alpha_1\mathbf{v_1} + \alpha_2\mathbf{v_2} + \ldots + \alpha_k\mathbf{v_k}.$$

Since this expression for $\mathbf{w}$ is unique in terms of the basis, we certainly have $\mathbf{w} = P(\mathbf{w})$. Note that

$$\mathbf{v} - P(\mathbf{v}) = \alpha_{k+1}\mathbf{v_{k+1}} + \ldots + \alpha_n\mathbf{v_n}.$$

The effect of a projection is to decompose V into two subspaces $W = \text{im}(P)$ and $\ker(P)$. The intersection of these subspaces is only the zero vector. (V is said to be the *direct sum* of these two subspaces. Any element of V is uniquely expressible as the sum of an element of W and an element of $\ker(P)$.)

Now if V is an inner product space and the basis $\{\mathbf{v_1}, \mathbf{v_2}, \ldots \mathbf{v_k}, \mathbf{v_{k+1}}, \ldots, \mathbf{v_n}\}$ is orthogonal, we have in addition $<\mathbf{v} - P(\mathbf{v}), \mathbf{u}> = 0$ for any $\mathbf{u} \in W$. In this case P is said to be an *orthogonal projection*. It follows from Theorem 3.48 that $\mathbf{w} = P(\mathbf{v})$ is the best least squares approximation to $\mathbf{v}$ from $\mathbf{W}$. Conversely, since the orthogonal expansions of Section 3.6 merely express the least squares approximation in terms of an orthogonal basis, we see that taking a least squares approximation (or equivalently truncating an orthogonal expansion) defines an orthogonal projection. To relate these ideas to Proposition 3.63, we identify the singular values of an orthogonal projection. This is easy with the aid of the following lemma.

Lemma 3.65

Let A be the $k \times r$ matrix representation of a linear transformation with respect to the standard basis in $\mathbb{R}^r$ and $\mathbb{R}^k$, and A' be the matrix representation with respect to alternative orthonormal bases in $\mathbb{R}^r$ and $\mathbb{R}^k$. Then A and A' have the same singular values. (Hence we can talk about the singular values of the transformation, provided we allow only orthonormal bases.)

Proof

Let the alternative orthonormal bases be $\mathbf{v_1}, \mathbf{v_2}, \ldots, \mathbf{v_r}$ for $\mathbb{R}^r$ and $\mathbf{u_1}, \mathbf{u_2}, \ldots, \mathbf{u_k}$ for $\mathbb{R}^k$. Construct matrices V and U respectively, with the basis vectors as columns. Since the columns are orthonormal, U and V are orthogonal matrices (Theorem 3.13). Then $A' = U^T A V$ (compare Method 2.45 and Example 2.47).

If A has SVD PSQ^T, we have $A' = (U^T P)S(Q^T V)$ which provides an SVD for A'. But the singular values of A' are unique, being the eigenvalues of AA^T, which establishes that A and A' have the same singular values.

□

Now we can easily show:

Theorem 3.66

Let W be a subspace of $\mathbb{R}^r$, and P an orthogonal projection of $\mathbb{R}^r$ onto W. Then all the singular values of P (or any matrix representing P with respect to an orthonormal basis) are equal to 1.

Proof

Choose an orthonormal basis $\mathbf{u}_1, \mathbf{u}_2, \ldots, \mathbf{u}_k$ for W, and extend it to a basis for $\mathbb{R}^r$. We have $P(\mathbf{u}_j) = \mathbf{u}_j$ for $j = 1, \ldots, k$ and $P(\mathbf{u}_j) = \mathbf{0}$ for $j = k+1, \ldots, r$. Thus, with respect to this basis, the matrix representation of P is simply the first k rows of the $r \times r$ identity matrix.

□

Corollary 3.67

Let a filter matrix T be the matrix of an truncated orthogonal projection. Then with filtering applied the epoch method will converge at least as fast (as expressed by its contraction parameter) as the unfiltered version.

Proof

Compare Proposition 3.63 with Theorem 3.66

□

Now let us look at two important examples of this. One is from signal processing and the other machine vision: both have immediate relevance to neural computation.

Example 3.68

It is a very common operation in signal processing to approximate a signal by a truncated Fourier series. This has the effect of removing high frequency noise while retaining the main low frequency structure of the signal. Such processing is often applied to data before feeding it to a neural net. Examples 3.56 and

3.57 and Remarks 3.55 describe the basic idea. In this case (Example 3.53) we apparently have an inner product on $L^2[-\pi, \pi]$ rather than $\mathbb{R}^n$. We could approximate the integrals by sums (e.g. using the Trapezium rule) and thus obtain a discrete finite dimensional inner product. The basis of Example (3.56) might be only approximately orthogonal with respect to this inner product, but we might expect Corollary 3.67 to hold at least approximately. It so happens, however, that we can do better than this. At this point it becomes much more convenient to deal with complex valued functions. If $\mathbf{y}$ and $\mathbf{z} \in \mathbb{C}^n$, consider the hermitian product

$$<\mathbf{y}, \mathbf{z}> = \sum_{j=1}^{n} y_j \bar{z}_j, \tag{3.61}$$

where $-$ denotes complex conjugation. The use of the complex conjugate is required here to ensure that Property (d) of Definition 3.41 holds: a conjugation is then also required in (a) and (c). The point of introducing this is the following observation. Let the complex n-vector $\mathbf{z_k}$ be defined by

$$(\mathbf{z_k})_j = \exp\left(\frac{2\pi i(k-1)(j-1)}{n}\right) \text{for } k, j = 1,\ldots,n. \tag{3.62}$$

Here i denotes the square root of -1. The vectors $\mathbf{z_k}$ are orthogonal with respect to the hermitian product (3.61). To see this, observe that

$$<\mathbf{z_k}, \mathbf{z_h}> = \sum_{j=1}^{n} \exp\left(\frac{2\pi i(k-h)(j-1)}{n}\right).$$

If $k=h$ the right-hand side of this expression is obviously equal to n. For $k \neq h$, we observe that the right-hand side is actually a geometric series with common ratio $\exp(2\pi i\,(k-h)/n)$. Using the formula (1.8) for summation of a geometric series, we find that the sum is zero as required. This result means that we can express vectors in terms of the basis (3.62) obtaining a discrete Fourier series and truncate this. The complex terms of course cancel for real data and we can apply Corollary 3.67. Moreover, there exists a very fast and stable numerical algorithm for carrying out the computations, known as the Fast Fourier Transform (Brigham, 1974) making the application of this filter a very attractive option.

□

The second example is less obvious, and is not based on an orthogonal expansion.

Example 3.69

Consider an $n \times n$ bit mapped grey scale image, and suppose that n is even. Each pixel is an intensity level (usually in the range 0 to 255). An obvious way to reduce the amount of data is to average the intensity of a block of four pixels. Thus we have a mapping from $\mathbb{R}^{n^2}$ to $\mathbb{R}^{n^2/4}$. This mapping is actually an orthogonal projection. To see this, think of $\mathbb{R}^{n^2/4}$ being embedded in $\mathbb{R}^{n^2}$ by setting each of the four averaged pixels in the latter space to the same average value. Specifically, let us call our image vector $\mathbf{x}$ and consider four pixels numbered 1, 2, 3 and 4 with intensities x_1, x_2, x_3 and x_4. We replace each of these values by $(x_1+x_2+x_3+x_4)/4$ in our new vector: let us call the latter $\mathbf{y}$. So $y_1=y_2=y_3=y_4=(x_1+x_2+x_3+x_4)/4$. The error for pixel i is thus $x_i-(x_1+x_2+x_3+x_4)/4$ $i=1, 2, 3, 4$. Now any vector $\mathbf{u}$ in the subspace must have all these pixels with the same value: say u. Finally consider $(\mathbf{x}-\mathbf{y})^T\mathbf{u}$. The contribution of the four pixels under consideration is

$$\sum_{i=1}^{4} u\{x_i - (x_1 + x_2 + x_3 + x_4)/4\} = 0.$$

This applies equally to each block of pixels averaged. Hence $(\mathbf{x}-\mathbf{y})^T\mathbf{u}=0$. But $\mathbf{u}$ was an arbitrary vector in the approximating subspace, whence we find from Theorem 3.48 that $\mathbf{y}$ is the best least squares approximation to $\mathbf{x}$, i.e. that the mapping $\mathbf{x}\to\mathbf{y}$ is an orthogonal projection.

It is interesting that when using this averaging process with a multilayer perceptron and backpropagation, Hand, Evans and Ellacott (1992) did find variation of the convergence behaviour at different resolutions. This must either be because the scaling between levels was not correct, or, more likely, because of the non-linear effects introduced by backpropagation.

□

The result above gives us some insight into the uses of filters for data compression, although its extension to the non-linear case is not obvious: filters are applied to the input of a multilayer perceptron, whereas to employ this result directly we would need to apply them to the tangent space: see the next chapter. Let us turn now to the issue of preconditioning. An ideal choice of filter to act as a preconditioner would not require knowledge of the particular data set under consideration, but this would seem to be an almost impossible requirement since the matrix Ω is defined in terms of this data. The best one might hope for is something that would work for large classes of data sets in a particular context such as vision or speech recognition. In other words we might try to derive information from the problem domain, and use this to construct the filter. As an illustration of the difficulties, we show that the theoretically optimal preconditioner for the delta rule in epoch form is both easily described and completely useless! Suppose, as above, X has singular value decomposition PSQ^{T}. We set the filter matrix T to be the Moore–Penrose pseudoinverse of X (see Definition 3.62) which we denote by $X^{\#}$. So

$$T = X^{\#} = QS^{\#}P^{\mathrm{T}}.$$

Then

$$TX = QS^{\#}P^{\mathrm{T}}PSQ^{\mathrm{T}} = QS^{\#}SQ^{\mathrm{T}}.$$

Thus (with the same notation as above)

$$L' = TXX^{\mathrm{T}}T^{\mathrm{T}} = QS^{\#}SS^{\mathrm{T}}S^{\#\mathrm{T}}Q^{\mathrm{T}},$$

and $S^{\#}SS^{\mathrm{T}}S^{\#\mathrm{T}}$ is a diagonal matrix with diagonal elements either 0 or 1. Thus all the eigenvalues of L' are either 0 or 1, and indeed, if the $\mathbf{x}$'s span so that XX^{T} has no zero eigenvalues, then all the eigenvalues of L' are 1. With $\eta = 1$, the iteration will converge in a single iteration. This is not surprising, since once we know $X^{\#}$, the least squares solution for $\mathbf{w}$ may be given explicitly! (For the non-linear case we would need to compute the local pseudoinverses for the relevant tangent vectors.)

A modification of the approach which might be slightly more practicable is just to remove the large eigenvalues of XX^{T} based on computation of the dominant singular values, and corresponding singular vectors, of X. An algorithm for removing the principal components one at a time was presented in Ellacott (1993): see also Ellacott and Easdown (1996). (Oja (1992) also has some relevance to this problem, as does the method of Almeida and Silva (1992) discussed next.)

As always, we consider a matrix X whose columns are our patterns. If the patterns were orthonormal, the matrix $X^{\mathrm{T}}X$ would obviously be the identity. An important operation in statistics is the construction of a transformation of the set of data vectors such that XX^{T} is diagonal: let us say that for definiteness that all its diagonal elements are either 0 or 1 since given a diagonal

XX^T, the latter condition only requires rescaling of the transformation. This process is called *decorrelation.* Orthogonalization and decorrelation are not the same thing, but Theorem 3.59(b) shows that, unexpectedly perhaps, they are closely related, since X^TX and XX^T have the same non zero eigenvalues. Either orthonormalizing or decorrelating the pattern vectors has a profound effect on the behaviour of learning algorithms as either process will pre-condition the learning algorithm.

Almeida and Silva (1992) propose using a separate perceptron to decorrelate the data. The weight matrix of this perceptron is T so that for a given input pattern $\mathbf{x}$ the output is simply $T\mathbf{x}$. Given a set of patterns $\{\mathbf{x}_1, \ldots, \mathbf{x}_t\}$ and denoting, as always, by X the matrix whose columns are the $\mathbf{x}_i$, we can write this condition in matrix form as $TXX^TT^T=I$. Starting with $T=I$, they update T according to the rule

$$T_{n+1} = (1+\alpha)T_n - \alpha(T_nLT_n^T)T_n, \tag{3.63}$$

where, as before, $L=XX^T$. Now if L has full rank, certainly there exits a non-singular T^* such that

$$T^*LT^{*T} = I. \tag{3.64}$$

To see this write $L=PDP^T$, where P is orthogonal, and let $T^*=D^{-1/2}P^T$. To see that it is a fixed point, simply set T^* satisfying (3.64) as T_n in (3.63). Almeida and Silva give as a sufficient condition for convergence $\alpha<\min\{\frac{1}{2}, (3\rho(L)-1)^{-1}\}$. However, it is perhaps worth pointing out that convergence is sublinear, for let

$$F(T) = (1+\alpha)T - \alpha(TLT^T)T \tag{3.65}$$

and suppose T^* satisfies (3.64). Direct calculation yields for $h\in\mathbb{R}$ and any $n\times n$ matrix S

$$\begin{aligned}F(T^*+hS) &= T^* + (1+\alpha)hS - \alpha T^*LT^{*T}hS - \alpha(hSLT^{*T}T^* + hT^*LS^TT^*) \\ &\quad + O(h^2) \\ &= T^* + (1+\alpha)hS - \alpha hS - \alpha(hS + hT^*LS^TT^*) + O(h^2)\end{aligned}$$

since T^* satisfies (3.64) and this condition also implies $LT^{*T}T^*=I$. Thus

$$\begin{aligned}F(T^*+hS) &= T^* + (1-\alpha)hS - \alpha h(T^{*T})^{-1}S^TT^* + O(h^2). \\ &= [I + (1-\alpha)hS(T^*)^{-1} - \alpha h(T^{*T})^{-1}S^T]T^* + O(h^2).\end{aligned}$$

Now if we choose S so that $(T^*)^{-1}S$ is antisymmetric we obtain

$$F(T^* + hS) = [I + hS(T^*)^{-1}]T^* + O(h^2)$$
$$= T^* + hS + O(h^2).$$

Thus the improvement can be at best $O(h^2)$ near the fixed point. This is not a true on-line learning network anyway since all the patterns are required at once. Hence use of an optimisation routine might be preferable. Or simply compute the SVD instead! Almeida and Silva do give a version which uses the patterns one at a time, but this requires a sequence of α's tending to zero. Thus it seems that a better update rule than (3.63) would be worth seeking, but the particular interest of this method is that Almeida and Silva have performed numerical experiments with networks interleaving ordinary backpropagation layers with layers trained by (3.63). Improved convergence of the backpropagation was found on two test problems.

We remark finally that another way to satisfy (4.3) is actually to compute the principle components of X. Oja, Ogawa and Wangviwattana (1992) describe a network to do this.

In closing this section, we should point out that these remarks are far from exhausting the applications of the SVD to neural computation. But to proceed further, we need to introduce statistical ideas which are outside the scope of this book.

3.7 Learning vector quantization

In most of this chapter we have considered supervised learning: the patterns $\{\mathbf{x}_1 \ldots \mathbf{x}_t\}$ have known associated outputs $\{y_1 \ldots y_t\}$. Often the y_p take values 0 or 1, and the network then functions as a classifier. However we do not know the desired classes *a priori*. We may wish to divide $\{\mathbf{x}_1 \ldots \mathbf{x}_t\}$ up into classes according to some internal structure. This process is akin to the clustering algorithms of classical statistical theory. In other contexts it is known as *data mining*, or *feature detection*. It can be regarded as a form of data preprocessing similar to that described in the previous sections, but as we shall see it is generally non-linear.

We will look briefly at the simplest neural network for this purpose, the *learning vector quantizer* (LVQ). Figure 3.4 shows the architecture: each output neuron corresponds to a possible class so in Fig. 3.4 only three classes are permitted and the input vectors are in $\mathbb{R}^4$. The classification property used for LVQ is simply geometrical closeness: we wish to partition $\{\mathbf{x}_1 \ldots \mathbf{x}_2\}$ into sets of nearby vectors. Basic LVQ uses a *winner take all* strategy. This means that

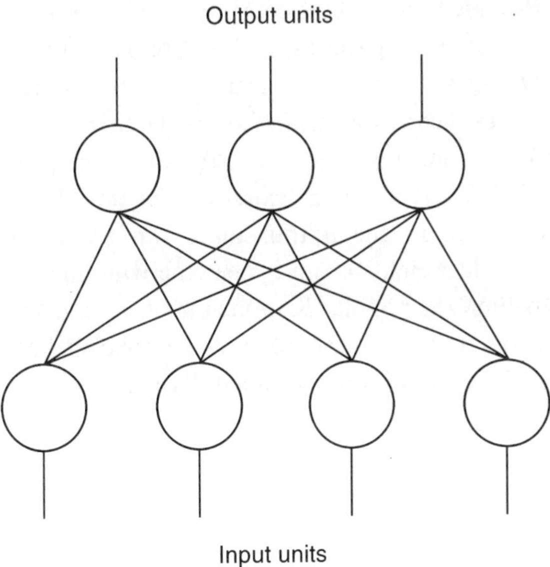

Fig. 3.4

the synaptic weights are modified only for one output unit. More specifically let $\mathbf{w_j}^T$ denote the (row) vector joining the inputs to the jth output unit for $j=1, \ldots, m$ where m is the number of output units. All the weights are initially randomised with some suitable scaling, e.g. $\|\mathbf{w_j}\|=1$ for some suitable vector norm. Often $\| \|=\| \|_2$, the Euclidean distance, but this is not essential so we will use a general norm symbol. It is also convenient to normalise input patterns in the same way: $\|\mathbf{x_p}\|=1$, $p=1, \ldots, t$.

The learning proceeds as follows.

For $i=i, 2, \ldots$
  For each input pattern $\mathbf{x_p}$ $p=1, 2, \ldots, t$.
    Step 1: Find the nearest $\mathbf{w_j}$ to $\mathbf{x}$, i.e. find j such that $\|\mathbf{x_p}-\mathbf{w_j}\| \leq \|\mathbf{x}-\mathbf{w_k}\|$ for $k=1, \ldots, m$. If there is more than one such j, just the first.
    Step 2: modify $\mathbf{w_j}$ (only) according to the learning rule $\Delta\mathbf{w_j}=\eta_i(\mathbf{x_p}-\mathbf{w_j})$.
  Next p
Next i.

Note that the learning rate η_i depends on i. The usual approach is to choose a sequence such that $\eta_i \to 0$ as $i \to \infty$. For example, $\eta_i=1/i$ is a possible choice. The effect of Step 2 is of course simply to move $\mathbf{w_j}$ closer to $\mathbf{x_p}$. If $S_j \subset \{\mathbf{x_1} \ldots \mathbf{x_2}\}$ is the subset of pattern vectors 'grabbed' by $\mathbf{w_j}$, the same multiple of each $\mathbf{x_p} \in S_j$

is added to $\mathbf{w_j}$. Provided the process converges, eventually, therefore, $\mathbf{w_j}$ will approach the average of the patterns in S_j and $\mathbb{R}^n$ is partitioned into regions centered around these $\mathbf{w_j}$ vectors. Any particular pattern vector $\mathbf{x_p}$ can only be nearest to one of these centres so $\{\mathbf{x_1} \ldots \mathbf{x_2}\}$ is classified.

The iteration is non-linear and we will not give a convergence analysis here: see Kohonen (1986). There are many extensions of this basic idea. Instead of just updating one weight, the output units can be arranged in a two-dimensional array and weights of units near the winning unit also updated. This is the idea behind the popular Kohonen net (see, e.g. Wasserman (1989, p. 63). Also 'soft competition', rather than winner take all, has been proposed. See Bezdek and Nikhil (1995) for a detailed discussion of this.

4 Optimisation

4.1 Multivariate calculus

In this chapter, we move away from linear theory and work towards a systematic exposition of non-linear methods. The first topic to be considered is multivariate calculus and its applications to classical optimisation. This theory forms the basis of all optimisation methods, including the stochastic and genetic ones not explicitly considered here. This is because it is connected with the geometry of the error surfaces with which any learning algorithm must cope. In the previous chapter, we saw that the delta rule can be regarded as a method to minimise the least squares error of the output over a set of patterns. For non-linear networks, the geometry of these error is more complex.

In this first section we consider the basic theory of smooth surfaces. The fundamental tool is the partial derivative. Suppose S is a subset of $\mathbb{R}^n$ and f: $S \to \mathbb{R}$, so we may write

$$z = f(\mathbf{x}) = f(x_1, x_2, \ldots, x_n) \text{ for } z \in \mathbb{R} \tag{4.1}$$

At a given point $\mathbf{x}$, the *partial derivative* of f with respect to x_j (provided it exists) is simply the derivative of f considered as a function of x_j with the other variables held constant. (Geometrically, this is simply the slope of f along the x_j co-ordinate direction.) We write any of

$$\frac{\partial f}{\partial x_j}, \frac{\partial z}{\partial x_j} \text{ or } f_j(\mathbf{x}) \text{ for this derivative.}$$

In other words

$$f_j(\mathbf{x}) = \lim_{h\to 0} \frac{f(x_1, x_2, \ldots, x_j + h, \ldots, x_n) - f(x_1, x_2, \ldots, x_n)}{h}.$$

The argument $\mathbf{x}$ is omitted from the notation when the meaning is clear. The *gradient* of f is the vector $(f_1, f_2, \ldots, f_n)^{\mathrm{T}}$. This is written ∇f. (Note that ∇f *is* a vector, although conventionally it is not written in bold type). If all the partial derivatives exist at $\mathbf{x}$, f is said to be *differentiable* there. If they are continuous functions of $\mathbf{x}$ on S, f is said to be *differentiable* on S.

Now consider a smooth path $\mathbf{x}=\mathbf{x}(t)$ in the $\mathbf{x}$ space. The equation defines a point $\mathbf{x}$ as a function of a parameter t, which is often thought of as being time. For example, in two dimensions we might have $\mathbf{x}=(\cos t, \sin t)^{\mathrm{T}}$. $x_1=\cos t$ and $x_2=\sin t$ are called the *co-ordinate functions*. As t increases from zero, the point moves round a circle of radius 1. 'Smooth' here indicates that the co-ordinate functions are differentiable. The derivative of $\mathbf{x}$ is a vector:

$$\frac{\mathrm{d}\mathbf{x}}{\mathrm{d}t} = \left(\frac{\mathrm{d}x_1}{\mathrm{d}t}, \frac{\mathrm{d}x_2}{\mathrm{d}t}, \ldots, \frac{\mathrm{d}x_n}{\mathrm{d}t}\right)^{\mathrm{T}}.$$

So $f[\mathbf{x}(t)]$ is a function of t, which we might expect to be differentiable. What is the derivative of f? This basic theorem of multivariate calculus provides the answer.

Theorem 4.1 (The Chain Rule or Total Increment Theorem)
With the notation of the previous paragraphs, f is differentiable as a function of t, and

$$\frac{\mathrm{d}f}{\mathrm{d}t} = f_1 \frac{\mathrm{d}x_1}{\mathrm{d}t} + f_2 \frac{\mathrm{d}x_2}{\mathrm{d}t} + \ldots + f_n \frac{\mathrm{d}x_n}{\mathrm{d}t} = (\nabla f)^{\mathrm{T}} \frac{\mathrm{d}\mathbf{x}}{\mathrm{d}t}. \qquad (4.2)$$

Proof

For clarity we will just consider the case of two dimensions. The general case is simply a repeated application of the same argument. So (provided the right-hand side exists)

$$\frac{\mathrm{d}f}{\mathrm{d}t} = \lim_{\delta t\to 0} \frac{f[x_1(t+\delta t), x_2(t+\delta t)] - f[x_1(t), x_2(t)]}{\delta t}$$

$$= \lim_{\delta t\to 0} \frac{f[x_1(t+\delta t),x_2(t+\delta t)] - f[x_1(t),x_2(t+\delta t)] + f[x_1(t),x_2(t+\delta t)] - f[x_1(t),x_2(t)]}{\delta t}$$

The result now follows merely by evaluating the right-hand side limit (using the single variable 'function of a function' rule, which also establishes its existence.

□

Example 4.2

By way of a simple illustration of these ideas, consider again $\mathbf{x}=(\cos t, \sin t)^T$ and suppose $f(x_1, x_2)=x_1^2+x_2^2$. Then according to (4.2),

$$\begin{aligned}\frac{df}{dt} &= f_1\frac{dx_1}{dt}+f_2\frac{dx_2}{dt}\\ &= 2x_1(-\sin t)+2x_2(\cos t)\\ &= (2\cos t)(-\sin t)+2(\sin t)(\cos t)\\ &= 0.\end{aligned}$$

This is as we would expect, since $f(x_1, x_2)=x_1^2+x_2^2$ is in fact constant on the circle traced out by $\mathbf{x}$. Note that we obtain exactly the same result by actually substituting for x_1 and x_2 since

$$f(x_1, x_2)=x_1^2+x_2^2=\cos^2 t+\sin^2 t=1.$$

□

Now in many applications, the actual path $\mathbf{x}=\mathbf{x}(t)$ is irrelevant. We only want to know about the change δf in f for a given change $\delta\mathbf{x}$ in $\mathbf{x}$. From (4.2) we get, using the order notation (Section 1.10)

$$\delta f=\delta x_1 f_1+\delta x_2 f_2+\ldots+\delta x_1 f_1+o(t).$$

By assumption $\mathbf{x}=\mathbf{x}(t)$ is smooth, so $o(t)=o(\|\delta\mathbf{x}\|_2)$. Hence, for small $\delta\mathbf{x}$,

$$\delta f=(\delta\mathbf{x})^T\nabla f+o(\|\delta\mathbf{x}\|_2)$$

or equivalently

$$f(\mathbf{x}+\delta\mathbf{x})=f(\mathbf{x})+(\delta\mathbf{x})^T\nabla f+o(\|\delta\mathbf{x}\|_2). \qquad (4.3)$$

To a first order approximation, the change in f when we move a small distance $\delta\mathbf{x}$ is simply the inner product of $\delta\mathbf{x}$ with ∇f!

Now consider a very small sphere of radius ε about the point $\mathbf{x}$. Since we will be considering minimisation of the function f, the following question is of obvious importance. Which direction $\delta\mathbf{x}$, with $\|\delta\mathbf{x}\|_2=\varepsilon$, will give the largest decrease in f? We call this direction the *direction of steepest descent*. In view of the Cauchy–Schwarz inequality (Theorem 3.43) we have $|(\nabla\mathbf{x})^T\nabla f| \leq \varepsilon\|\nabla f\|_2$ with equality only if $\delta\mathbf{x}=\lambda\,\nabla f$ for some $\lambda\in\mathbb{R}$. Suppose for the moment that $\nabla f\neq 0$. Examination of (4.3) shows that to get a descent direction at all we must have $(\delta\mathbf{x})^T\nabla f<0$, so we need $\lambda<0$ and the direction of steepest descent is given by $-\nabla f$.

These ideas are sufficiently important to be collected into a theorem.

Theorem 4.3

Suppose S is a subset of $\mathbb{R}^n$ and f: $S\rightarrow\mathbb{R}$ is differentiable on S. Let $\mathbf{x}$ be an interior point of S, and $\mathbf{h}\in\mathbb{R}^n$. Suppose moreover that $\nabla f\neq\mathbf{0}$.

(a) If $\mathbf{h}^T\nabla f<0$, then for t sufficiently small $f(\mathbf{x}+t\mathbf{h})<f(\mathbf{x})$.
(b) The direction of steepest descent is given by $\mathbf{h}=-\nabla f$.

□

As in the previous chapter (see the second paragraph of Section 3.5), we will consider the least squares criterion for a simple perceptron. This will also enable us to introduce some practical methods of vector differentiation.

We have a set of input patterns $\mathbf{x}_1, \mathbf{x}_2, \ldots, \mathbf{x}_t$, and a weight vector $\mathbf{w}$. The actual output for a given pattern $\mathbf{x}_i$ is $\mathbf{w}^T\mathbf{x}_i=w_1(\mathbf{x}_i)_1+w_2(\mathbf{x}_i)_2+\ldots+w_n(\mathbf{x}_i)_n$. The pattern matrix X has ith column as the pattern vector $\mathbf{x}_i$. Thus the output for pattern i is the ith element of the vector $X^T\mathbf{w}$. Suppose the desired output is y_i. Let $\mathbf{b}=(y_1,y_2,\ldots,y_t)^T$. We try to choose $\mathbf{w}$ so that $f(\mathbf{w})=\|\mathbf{b}-X^T\mathbf{w}\|_2^2$ is small. (Note that we have squared the error term here. Minimising the square of the error term will also minimise the two norm error itself.)

Now

$$\begin{aligned} f(\mathbf{w}) &= \|\mathbf{b}-X^T\mathbf{w}\|_2^2 \\ &= (\mathbf{b}-X^T\mathbf{w})^T(\mathbf{b}-X^T\mathbf{w}) \\ &= \mathbf{b}^T\mathbf{b}-2\mathbf{b}^TX^T\mathbf{w}+\mathbf{w}^TXX^T\mathbf{w}. \end{aligned} \tag{4.4}$$

We need to calculate ∇f. (Differentiating with respect to the elements of $\mathbf{w}$, of course.) The first term on the right-hand side is constant, and will vanish on differentiation. The second term has the general form $\mathbf{c}^T\mathbf{w}$ with in this case $\mathbf{c}=-2X\mathbf{b}$. But $\mathbf{c}^T\mathbf{w}=c_1w_1+c_2w_2+\ldots+c_nw_n$, so differentiation with respect to w_i just gives c_i. Thus $\nabla(\mathbf{c}^T\mathbf{w})=\mathbf{c}=-2X\,\mathbf{b}$. The third term is conveniently written $\mathbf{v}^T\mathbf{v}$ where $\mathbf{v}=X^T\mathbf{w}$. Then $\mathbf{v}^T\mathbf{v}=v_1{}^2+v_2{}^2+\ldots+v_n{}^2$, and differentiation with respect to $\mathbf{w}_i$ gives $\sum 2v_j\times\partial v_j/\partial w_i$ with the summation over j. Write this as $2A_\mathbf{v}$ where A

is the matrix with $a_{ij}=\partial v_j/\partial w_i$. Furthermore v_j is $\mathbf{x_j}^T\mathbf{w}$. The derivative with respect to w_i is therefore the ith element of $\mathbf{x_j}$. Thus in fact $A=X$ and $\nabla(\mathbf{w}^T XX^T\mathbf{w})=2XX^T$. Putting all this together we obtain

$$\nabla f=-2X\,\mathbf{b}+2XX^T\mathbf{w}. \tag{4.5}$$

The steepest descent for f is thus to choose $\delta\mathbf{w}$ as a small multiple of $X\,\mathbf{b}-XX^T\mathbf{w}$. Observe that this is precisely the step chosen by the delta rule in its epoch or off-line formulation (3.36).

Remark 4.4

(a) The reader might like to show that for any $n\times n$ matrix A, $\nabla(\mathbf{w}^T A\mathbf{w})=(A+A^T)\mathbf{w}$, and hence that if A is symmetric, $\nabla(\mathbf{w}^T A\mathbf{w})=2A\mathbf{w}$. This was shown above for the case $A=XX^T$. Probably the easiest way to proceed is to write $\mathbf{w}^T A\mathbf{w}$ as $\mathbf{w}^T(A\mathbf{w})$ and differentiate this with respect to w_i by the product rule. Observe that in general in such differentiations we get what we might expect if we regard the inner product as a square. This can be an aid to getting the right answer, but of course in any particular application we need to check that it makes sense.

(b) An expression of the form $f(\mathbf{w})=\mathbf{w}^T A\mathbf{w}+\mathbf{b}^T\mathbf{w}+c$ for fixed matrix A and vector $\mathbf{b}$ and scalar c is known as a *quadratic form* (compare (4.4)). Any quadratic form can be written with A symmetric: if not just replace A by $\frac{1}{2}(A+A^T)$. Provided we have done this, we have $\nabla f=2A\mathbf{w}+\mathbf{b}$ and it is also often useful to 'complete the square' and write $f(\mathbf{w})=(\mathbf{w}-\mathbf{w_0})^T A(\mathbf{w}-\mathbf{w_0})+c'$ where a simple calculation reveals $\mathbf{w_0}=-\frac{1}{2}A^{-1}\mathbf{b}$, and $c'=c-\mathbf{w_0}^T A\mathbf{w_0}$. This does obviously require A to be non-singular: this will certainly be true if A is positive definite since it cannot then have a zero eigen value.

□

Theorem 4.3 obviously implies that if $\nabla f(\mathbf{x})\neq\mathbf{0}$, then there are points near $\mathbf{x}$ at which f is less than $f(\mathbf{x})$, and also where f is greater than $f(\mathbf{x})$. So at a maximum or minimum point, we must have $\nabla f(\mathbf{x})=\mathbf{0}$. A point $\mathbf{x}$ at which $\nabla f(\mathbf{x})=\mathbf{0}$ is said to be *stationary*. We will examine the structure of stationary points in more detail in the next section. For the moment, just observe that setting $\nabla f=\mathbf{0}$ in (4.5) gives

$$X\,\mathbf{b}=XX^T\mathbf{w},$$

which is precisely the condition for the least square minimum we obtained in Chapter 3, equation (3.35).

Before studying the structure of stationary points in more detail, let us look a little more at the geometrical properties of the gradient operator. Instead of the explicit form of a hypersurface (4.1), it is convenient here to consider implicit equations. Suppose U is a subset of $\mathbb{R}^{n+1}$ and $\varphi: U \to \mathbb{R}$. An equation of the form

$$\varphi(\mathbf{u}) = c, \text{ where } c \in \mathrm{IR} \text{ is a constant} \tag{4.6}$$

typically defines an 'n-dimensional' surface in $\mathbb{R}^{n+1}$. (We will make this concept of dimension more precise shortly.) For example, the equation $\varphi(x_1, x_2, x_3) = x_1^2 + x_2^2 + x_3^2 = 1$ defines a sphere of radius 1 in three dimensional space. Surfaces defined by explicit equations (4.1) can be written in the form of (4.6) simply by setting $\mathbf{u}^T = (\mathbf{x}^T : z)^T$ and $\varphi(\mathbf{u}) = f(\mathbf{x}) - z$, with $c = 0$. Then $(\nabla\varphi)^T = (\nabla f : -1)^T$.

According to (4.3), we have

$$\varphi(\mathbf{u} + \delta\mathbf{u}) = \varphi(\mathbf{u}) + (\delta\mathbf{u})^T \nabla\varphi + o(\|\delta\mathbf{u}\|_2).$$

Now if $\delta\mathbf{u}$ is such that $\mathbf{u} + \delta\mathbf{u}$ remains in the surface (4.6), then by definition we have $\varphi(\mathbf{u} + \delta\mathbf{u}) = c$. So to a first order approximation we have $(\delta\mathbf{u})^T \nabla\varphi = 0$. This tells us that $\nabla\varphi$ is orthogonal to small changes lying in the surface (4.6). In other words $\nabla\varphi$ is perpendicular or *normal* to the surface.

Example 4.5

Consider the sphere $\varphi(x_1, x_2, x_3) = x_1^2 + x_2^2 + x_3^2 = 1$. $\nabla\varphi = (2x_1, 2x_2, 2x_3)^T$. At any point on the surface of the sphere, $\nabla\varphi$ is twice the position vector of the point, which is obviously normal to the surface.

□

At any point $\mathbf{u}$ on the surface (4.6), the set V of vectors $\mathbf{v} \in \mathbb{R}^{n+1}$, satisfying $\mathbf{v}^T \nabla\varphi = 0$, are all tangent to the surface. The expression $l(\mathbf{v}) = \mathbf{v}^T \nabla\varphi$ constitutes a linear functional on $\mathbb{R}^{n+1}$ (see p. 304). Provided $\nabla\varphi \neq 0$, this linear functional has an image space of dimension 1. The kernel is by definition the set V which forms a vector space of dimension n (Theorem 2.26). V is said to be the *tangent space* to the surface. The set of all tangent spaces as $\mathbf{u}$ moves in the surface is called the *tangent bundle*. Since V is n-dimensional, it makes sense to think of the surface as n-dimensional, at least at points at which $\nabla\varphi \neq 0$. The pathological points (if any) at which $\nabla\varphi = 0$ are points at which the surface does not have a clearly defined normal and may not have a natural n-dimensional structure. This concept of the dimension of a surface will be further developed in the next chapter.

We can now visualise stationary points of (4.1) as points at which $(\nabla\varphi)^{\mathrm{T}} = (\nabla f: -1)^{\mathrm{T}} = (\mathbf{0}: -1)^{\mathrm{T}}$. $\nabla\varphi$ is 'vertical' and the tangent space is 'horizontal'.

4.2 Taylor's theorem and stationary points in *n*-dimensions

The structure of n-dimensional stationary points is a little more complicated than the one-dimensional case. To understand them properly, we need to make use of Taylor's Theorem. Equation (4.3) may be thought of as the first step in the Taylor expansion of f. Can we go further? Actually, it is not necessary to start again from scratch. We can get an n-dimensional version of Taylor's Theorem by application of the one dimensional version (Theorems 1.36 and 1.37). Suppose that f is twice (partially) continuously differentiable in each of its arguments. Then for small $t \in \mathbb{R}$, and fixed $\mathbf{x}, \mathbf{h} \in \mathbb{R}^n$ with $\|\mathbf{h}\|_2 = 1$,

$$f(\mathbf{x} + t\mathbf{h}) = f(\mathbf{x}) + tf'(\mathbf{x}) + \tfrac{1}{2}tf''(\mathbf{x}) + o(t^2), \tag{4.7}$$

where $'$ denotes differentiation with respect to t. (If f has continuous third derivatives, the $o(t^2)$ term may be replaced by $O(t^3)$.) Now according to Theorem 4.1,

$$f'(\mathbf{x}) = [(\mathbf{x} + t\mathbf{h})']^{\mathrm{T}}\nabla f = \mathbf{h}^{\mathrm{T}}\nabla ft \text{ since } \mathbf{x} \text{ and } \mathbf{h} \text{ are constant . (Compare (4.2).)} \tag{4.8}$$

Also

$$f''(\mathbf{x}) = [f'(\mathbf{x})]' = (\mathbf{h}^{\mathrm{T}}\nabla f)' = \mathbf{h}^{\mathrm{T}}(\nabla f)',$$

where by $(\nabla f)'$ we mean differentiate each element ∇f of with respect to t. The ith element of ∇f is by definition f_i. Applying (4.8) with f replaced by f_i (and transposing) gives $(\nabla f_i)^{\mathrm{T}}\mathbf{h}$ for the ith element of $(\nabla f)'$. Hence we may write $f''(\mathbf{x}) = \mathbf{h}^{\mathrm{T}}H(\mathbf{x})\mathbf{h}$ where H is the matrix with $h_{ij}(\mathbf{x}) = f_{ij}(\mathbf{x})$, called the *Hessian*. Here of course, f_{ij} denotes differentiation of f first by the ith component, then the jth.

Substituting this into (4.7) we get

$$f(\mathbf{x} + t\mathbf{h}) = f(\mathbf{x}) + (t\mathbf{h})^{\mathrm{T}}\nabla f(\mathbf{x}) + \tfrac{1}{2}(t\mathbf{h})^{\mathrm{T}}H(\mathbf{x})(t\mathbf{h}) + o(t^2). \tag{4.9}$$

We now want to set $\delta\mathbf{x} = t\mathbf{h}$ to get our generalization of (4.3). However, there is a complication here that we have glossed over. The order term will only be valid for arbitrary $\delta\mathbf{x}$ if $o(t^2)$ holds uniformly over *all* directions $\mathbf{h}$. To avoid unnecessary complication, let us assume that f has continuous third partial derivatives. The error term in the expansion will then have the form $t^3/6$ times $f'''(\mathbf{x}+\theta\mathbf{h})$, where $\theta \in (0, 1)$. The derivative term can be evaluated in terms of the partial derivatives of f in a similar manner to above. Since by hypothesis these are all continuous, $f'''(\mathbf{x}+\theta\mathbf{h}) \to f'''(\mathbf{x})$ as $t \to 0$, so we obtain the following result.

Theorem 4.6

Suppose S is a subset of $\mathbb{R}^n$ and $f\colon S \to \mathbb{R}$ has continuous derivatives up to and including order three on S. Let $\mathbf{x}$ be an interior point of S, and $\delta\mathbf{x} \in \mathbb{R}^n$. Then as $\|\delta\mathbf{x}\|_2 \to 0$ we have

$$f(\mathbf{x}+\delta\mathbf{x}) = f(\mathbf{x}) + (\delta\mathbf{x})^{\mathrm{T}}\nabla f(\mathbf{x}) + \tfrac{1}{2}(\delta\mathbf{x})^{\mathrm{T}}H(\mathbf{x})(\delta\mathbf{x}) + O(\|\delta\mathbf{x}\|_2^3). \tag{4.10}$$

□

Of course we could develop the expansion further to higher order terms. But observe that differentiation of f once gives rise to the vector ∇f, and twice to a matrix H. Higher order terms require tensor notation to express them properly. Fortunately, Theorem 4.6 is adequate for most applications in optimisation.

Observe that ignoring the order term, the right-hand side of (4.10) is a quadratic form. Locally, we can investigate the behaviour of general smooth surfaces by considering quadratic forms. We emphasise, however, that this only works for local analysis: globally the structure of general non-linear surfaces may be very complicated. The next result is also useful.

Theorem 4.7

Under the same conditions as Theorem 4.6, the matrix $H(\mathbf{x})$ is symmetric.

Proof

Since only two variables are involved in any given term in H, it is sufficient to consider the case $n=2$. We require to show that $f_{1,2}=f_{2,1}$. But for $h, k \in \mathbb{R}$

$$f_1(x_1, x_2) = \lim_{h\to 0}\frac{f(x_1+h, x_2) - f(x_1, x_2)}{h}$$

whence

$$f_{1,2}(x_1, x_2) = \lim_{k\to 0}\lim_{h\to 0}\frac{[f(x_1+h, x_2+k) - f(x_1, x_2+k)] - [f(x_1+h, x_2) - f(x_1, x_2)]}{kh}$$

$$= \lim_{k\to 0} \lim_{h\to 0} \frac{[f(x_1+h, x_2+k) - f(x_1+h, x_2)] - [f(x_1, x_2+k) - f(x_1, x_2)]}{hk}$$

$f_{2,1}, (x_1, x_2)$ is the same as this last expression, but with the order of the limits reversed. Reversing the order of the limits is a valid operation provided the operand is continuous in both its variables. This will be the case, since by hypothesis, f has continuous second derivatives.

□

For example, if $f(x_1, x_2)=x_1^p x_2^q$ for some natural numbers p and q, $f_1= px_1^{p-1} x_2^q$, $f_2=qx_1^p x_2^{q-1}$, and $f_{1,2}=f_{2,1}=pqx_1^{p-1} x_2^{q-1}$.

Let us proceed to consider the structure of the stationary points of f. By definition, at a stationary point $\mathbf{x}$, $\nabla f(\mathbf{x})=0$. So from (4.10)

$$f(\mathbf{x}+\delta\mathbf{x}) = f(\mathbf{x}) + ½(\delta\mathbf{x})^T H(\mathbf{x})(\delta\mathbf{x}) + O(\|\delta\mathbf{x}\|_2^3).$$

We see at once that if $H(\mathbf{x})$ is strictly positive definite, $\mathbf{x}$ must be a local minimum of f, and conversely if $H(\mathbf{x})$ is strictly negative definite, it is a local maximum. Actually, we can say a little more than this. Since H is symmetric, we may write $H=PDP^T$, where P is orthogonal and D is the diagonal matrix whose entries are the eigenvalues $\lambda_1, \lambda_2, \ldots, \lambda_n$ of H. Make a change of variable $\mathbf{u}=P^T\delta\mathbf{x}$. Then

$$\begin{aligned} f(\mathbf{x}+\delta\mathbf{x}) - f(\mathbf{x}) &= ½\mathbf{u}^T D\mathbf{u} + O(\|\mathbf{u}\|_2^3) \\ &= ½\mathbf{u}^T D\mathbf{u} + O(\|\mathbf{u}\|_2^3) \\ &= ½(\lambda_1 u_1^2 + \lambda_2 u_2^2 + \ldots + \lambda_n u_n^2) + O(\|\mathbf{u}\|_2^3). \end{aligned}$$

If H has some positive and some negative eigenvalues, f will have a minimum in some of the u_i coordinate directions and a maximum in others. Such a stationary point is called a *saddle point*, since the surface takes the shape of a horse's saddle. Saddle points occur only in two or more dimensions, and constitute a third type of simple stationary point, besides maxima and minima. Of course, as in one dimensional calculus, one can also get points of inflexion and other more complicated behaviour if H has any zero eigenvalues.

4.3 Gradient descent, the generalised delta rule and back propagation

As will be already apparent from the previous section, a simple solution to the problem of minimising a function f such as (4.1) is repeatedly to take a small step in the direction of steepest descent. Provided we are not at a stationary point, (4.4) will guarantee that if each step is small enough, f will be reduced. Of course we do not necessarily have to use the direction of steepest descent: any step $\delta\mathbf{x}$ such that $(\delta\mathbf{x})^T\nabla f(\mathbf{x}) < 0$ will suffice. Algorithms of this type are known as *gradient descent* methods. You should note that the fact that a method reduces the value of f is not sufficient in itself to guarantee convergence to a stationary point. Consider for example the one-dimensional function $f(x) = x^2$ and restrict attention to the region $x \geq 0$. Start at $x=1$ and set

$$x_{k+1} = \tfrac{1}{2}\{f(x_k)^{\frac{1}{2}} + \tfrac{1}{2}\} = \tfrac{1}{2}\{x_k + \tfrac{1}{2}\}.$$

With $x_0=1$, this generates the sequence $1, \frac{3}{4}, \frac{5}{8}, \frac{9}{16}, \ldots$. Each step is in the direction of steepest descent, but the limit is $\frac{1}{2}$ which is not a stationary point. In this case, the limit *is* a fixed point of the iteration, but even this is not always the case. If we allow negative x's in the example, and set

$$x_{k+1} = \tfrac{1}{2}(-1)^{k+1}\{f(x_k)^{\frac{1}{2}} + \tfrac{1}{2}\}$$

we will get $1, -\frac{3}{4}, \frac{5}{8}, -\frac{9}{16}, \ldots$. Each step is still a descent for f, yet the iteration has no fixed points and does not converge. We need extra conditions to ensure that a gradient descent algorithm will get to a stationary point. In any case we may not care too much that the sequence $(\mathbf{x}_k)$ itself converges. What we really want to know is whether the sequence $[f(\mathbf{x}_k)]$ approaches an at least local minimum value of f. We can say a little more about this in general terms. If f has a global minimum, then obviously f is bounded below. Moreover if our method generates a sequence of descent steps, then by definition $f(\mathbf{x}_{k+1}) < f(\mathbf{x}_k)$. So the sequence $[f(\mathbf{x}_k)]$ is monotone decreasing and bounded below. Hence it must converge to something. The most common approach is to design an algorithm so that this 'something' must be a stationary point. This issue will be addressed more systematically in Chapter 5: for the moment we will adopt an *ad hoc* approach.

For various reasons, strict gradient descent methods are not always the best choice. Unlike the quadratic function (4.5), a general f may have many local minima. Clearly a gradient descent method can at best hope only to get to the bottom of whatever 'bowl' we happen to start in. Moreover, as we have seen in the previous chapter, steepest descent may require very small steps to ensure convergence. And it does of course require full knowledge of the function f itself: for on-line learning we may not have this information. However, it is in the nature of learning to be a local process, and the vast majority of optimisation algorithms used for neural computation employ some variant of gradient descent, perhaps modified to improve the convergence in some way.

Now our immediate purpose is to consider the method of training non-linear networks which is an extension of the delta rule considered in the previous chapter. An early application of this was to multilayer perceptrons, where, for reasons which will become apparent later, it was given the name *backpropagation*. This name has stuck, and is often used to describe the more general form of the method when applied to other networks: indeed sometimes the term is used in such a way as to include classical steepest descent, as if this was invented for the express purpose of training neural networks! This nomenclature is rather unsatisfactory. Instead, we will use the alternative term *generalised delta rule* to describe the extension of the delta rule to non-linear systems. The application of this to multilayer perceptrons and similar feedforward networks will be called *backpropagation.* In this context, the term actually has some meaning.

Most elementary textbooks on neural computation get to the method by considering multilayer perceptrons directly, and immediately get involved with differentiation of the least squares error term with respect to the weights. But this approach needs a fresh start for each new network architecture. Moreover it hides much of the general structure of such methods, and certainly clouds the relationship with the linear delta rule. Instead, we will approach the algorithm from the top down. We will state a fairly general model of a non-linear delta rule. For simplicity we do not consider time dependent problem explicitly: these are in any case usually handled by treating time delayed quantities as extra data. We will give a general local convergence result and then derive backpropagation as a special case. We will also restrict attention to networks with a fixed number of inputs, outputs and weights.

With these restrictions, a neural network can in very general terms be thought of as a machine to transform an input vector into an output vector, the machine being determined by its fundamental architecture and a set of parameters called the weights. For the linear network the dimension of the input space and the number of weights are the same: n in our previous notation. Now we will let M denote the *total number* of weights and n the input dimension.

So the input patterns $\mathbf{x}$ to our network are in $\mathbb{R}^n$, and we have a vector $\mathbf{w}$ of parameters in $\mathbb{R}^M$ describing the particular instance of our network: i.e. the vector of synaptic weights. For a single layer perceptron with m outputs, the 'vector' $\mathbf{w}$ is the $m \times n$ weight matrix, and thus $M = mn$. For a general system with m outputs, the network computes a function $\mathbf{g}$: $\mathbb{R}^M \times \mathbb{R}^n \to \mathbb{R}^m$. Say

$$\mathbf{v} = \mathbf{g}(\mathbf{w}, \mathbf{x}) \tag{4.11}$$

where $\mathbf{v} \in \mathbb{R}^m$. We equip $\mathbb{R}^M$, $\mathbb{R}^m$ and $\mathbb{R}^n$ with suitable norms (usually the 2-norm in each case).

Now $\mathbf{g}$ here is a vector valued quantity which we are going to differentiate with respect to the weights. Up to now we have only considered differentiation of scalar valued functions f as in (4.1). So before we can proceed to a discussion of (4.11) we need to think about the differentiation of such objects. Actually this does not require anything fundamentally new: after all each co-ordinate function of $\mathbf{g}$ (i.e. each individual output of the network) is a scalar function. But some notation will lead to a much more elegant language for discussing this. To avoid formulating our definitions with the two arguments $\mathbf{w}$ and $\mathbf{x}$, let us first discuss differentiation of a vector valued function $\mathbf{F}$: $\mathbb{R}^n \to \mathbb{R}^m$. So $\mathbf{F}(\mathbf{x}) = [F_1(\mathbf{x}), F_2(\mathbf{x}), \ldots, F_m(\mathbf{x})]^T$. Each co-ordinate function F_j is a scalar valued function of $\mathbf{x}$: do not confuse the notation here with that for partial derivatives. For a small change $\delta\mathbf{x}$, the change in F_j is given, according to (4.3), by $(\nabla F_j)^T(\delta\mathbf{x})$. (The reason for transposing this will soon be apparent). The total change $\delta\mathbf{F}$ is therefore given by the expression

$$\delta\mathbf{F} = J\delta\mathbf{x},$$

where J is the matrix whose jth row is $(\nabla F_j)^T$. We shall call J is called the *Jacobian* of $\mathbf{F}$. (Some authors use the term for the determinant of J, which is important in multivariate integration.)

We shall need a generalization of Theorem 4.1 in order to combine derivatives. It is possible to extend the theorem in simple minded terms, but the whole issue is made a lot clearer if we step back and take a broader view. We have seen that the derivative of a scalar function f is a vector ∇f, and the derivative of a vector function $\mathbf{F}$ is the matrix J. However in (4.3), ∇f is actually used as a linear functional applied to the change $\delta\mathbf{x}$, in order to get the change in f. In the same way, J behaves as a linear transformation to $\delta\mathbf{x}$ to give the change in $\mathbf{F}$. This is what the derivative is 'really for': to see how a small change in the argument of a function changes its value. So why not use this as a definition?

Definition 4.8

Let V and W be normed vector spaces. Suppose further that $S \subset V$, and $\mathbf{F}: S \rightarrow W$. $\mathbf{F}$ is said to be *Fréchet differentiable* at a point $\mathbf{v} \in S$, if there is a bounded linear mapping $H: V \rightarrow W$ such that $\delta\mathbf{F} = \mathbf{F}(\mathbf{v} + \delta\mathbf{v}) - \mathbf{F}(\mathbf{v})$ satisfies

$$\|\delta\mathbf{F} - H(\delta\mathbf{v})\| = o(\|\delta\mathbf{v}\|)$$

as $\delta\mathbf{v} \rightarrow \mathbf{0}$. H is called the *Fréchet derivative* of $\mathbf{F}$.

□

(Note Fréchet is pronounced French style: 'Fresh-Eh'.) With this definition, we can even talk about derivatives in infinite dimensional spaces. Recall that a linear map is said to be *bounded* if it has a finite operator norm. (We need this condition to ensure that $H(\delta\mathbf{v})$ cannot be arbitrarily large. In finite dimensions, of course, all linear transformations are bounded.) In (4.12), J is simply the matrix representation of the Fréchet derivative. (For an explicit calculation of such a matrix, see Example 5.18 in the next chapter.)

However our purpose here is not generalisation for its own sake. We want to clarify how derivatives can be combined. Consider a third normed space V. Suppose $\mathbf{F}: S \rightarrow W$ and $\mathbf{G}: W \rightarrow U$, with Fréchet derivatives H and K respectively. To a first order approximation we have $\delta\mathbf{F} = H(\delta\mathbf{v})$ and $\delta\mathbf{G} = K(\delta\mathbf{F})$. So the change in $\mathbf{G}$ as a function of $\mathbf{v}$ is simply $K[H(\delta\mathbf{v})]$. For future reference, let us state this as a proposition.

Proposition 4.9 (Multivariate Function of a Function Rule)

The Fréchet derivative of the composition of $\mathbf{G}$ and $\mathbf{F}$ is the composition of the Fréchet derivatives. In finite dimensional spaces, composition of derivatives is merely multiplication of the Jacobian matrices in the corresponding order.

□

When employing this result, remember that for a scalar valued function f, the Jacobian is $(\nabla f)^{\mathrm{T}}$. The Hessian matrix of Theorem 4.7 is the Jacobian of ∇f.

Now we return to our study of (4.11). For pattern $\mathbf{x}_\mathbf{p}$, denote the corresponding output by $\mathbf{v}_\mathbf{p}$, i.e.

$$\mathbf{v}_\mathbf{p} = \mathbf{g}(\mathbf{w}, \mathbf{x}_\mathbf{p}).$$

We assume that $\mathbf{g}$ is Fréchet differentiable with respect to $\mathbf{w}$, and denote by $D = D(\mathbf{w}, \mathbf{x})$ the $m \times M$ matrix representation of the derivative with respect to the standard basis. Thus, for a small change $\delta\mathbf{w}$ and fixed $\mathbf{x}$, we have (by the definition of the derivative)

$$\mathbf{g}(\mathbf{w} + \delta\mathbf{w}, \mathbf{x}) = \mathbf{g}(\mathbf{w}, \mathbf{x}) + D(\mathbf{w}, \mathbf{x})\delta\mathbf{w} + o(\|\delta\mathbf{w}\|_2). \tag{4.12}$$

On the other hand for given $\mathbf{w}$, corresponding to a particular pattern $\mathbf{x_p}$, we have a desired output $\mathbf{y_p}$ and thus an error ε_p given by

$$\varepsilon_p^2 = (\mathbf{y_p} - \mathbf{v_p})^{\mathrm{T}}(\mathbf{y_p} - \mathbf{v_p}) = \mathbf{q_p}^{\mathrm{T}}\mathbf{q_p}, \text{ say.} \tag{4.13}$$

The total error is obtained by summing the $\varepsilon_p{}^2$s over the t available patterns, thus

$$\varepsilon^2 = \sum_{p=1}^{t} \varepsilon_p^2.$$

An ordinary descent algorithm will seek to minimise ε^2. However the class of methods we are considering generate, not a descent direction for ε^2, but rather successive steepest descent direction for $\varepsilon_p{}^2$. Now for a change $\delta\mathbf{q_p}$ in $\mathbf{q_p}$ we have from (4.13)

$$\begin{aligned}\delta\varepsilon_p^2 &= (\mathbf{q_p} + \delta\mathbf{q_p})^{\mathrm{T}}(\mathbf{q_p} + \delta\mathbf{q_p}) - \mathbf{q_p}^{\mathrm{T}}\mathbf{q_p}\\ &= 2\delta\mathbf{q_p}^{\mathrm{T}}\mathbf{q_p} + \delta\mathbf{q_p}^{\mathrm{T}}\delta\mathbf{q_p}.\end{aligned}$$

Since $\mathbf{y_p}$ is fixed,

$$\delta\mathbf{q_p} = -\delta\mathbf{v_p} = -D(\mathbf{w}, \mathbf{x_p})\delta\mathbf{w} + o(\|\delta\mathbf{w}\|_2) \text{ by (4.12).}$$

Thus

$$\begin{aligned}\delta\varepsilon_p^2 &= -2[D(\mathbf{w},\mathbf{x_p})\delta\mathbf{w}]^{\mathrm{T}}[\mathbf{y_p} - \mathbf{g}(\mathbf{w}, \mathbf{x_p})] + o(\|\delta\mathbf{w}\|_2)\\ &= -2\delta\mathbf{w}^{\mathrm{T}}[D(\mathbf{w}, \mathbf{x_p})]^{\mathrm{T}}[\mathbf{y_p} - \mathbf{g}(\mathbf{w}, \mathbf{x_p})] + o(\|\delta\mathbf{w}\|_2).\end{aligned}$$

Hence, ignoring the $o(\|\delta\mathbf{w}\|_2)$ term, and for a fixed size of small change $\delta\mathbf{w}$, the largest decrease in $\varepsilon_p{}^2$ is obtained by setting

$$\delta\mathbf{w} = \eta[D(\mathbf{w}, \mathbf{x_p})]^{\mathrm{T}}[\mathbf{y_p} - \mathbf{g}(\mathbf{w}, \mathbf{x_p})].$$

This is the *generalised delta rule*. Compare this with the single output linear perceptron, for which the second term in this expression is scalar with

$$\mathbf{g}(\mathbf{w}, \mathbf{x_p}) = \mathbf{w}^{\mathrm{T}}\mathbf{x_p},$$

and the derivative is the gradient vector (considered as a row vector) obtained by differentiating this with respect to $\mathbf{w}$, i.e. $\mathbf{x_p}^T$. Thus we indeed have a generalization of the delta rule. Given a kth weight vector $\mathbf{w_k}$, we have

$$\begin{aligned}\mathbf{w_{k+1}} &= \mathbf{w_k} + \delta\mathbf{w_k}\\ &= \mathbf{w_k} + \eta[D(\mathbf{w_k}, \mathbf{x_p})]^T[\mathbf{y_p} - \mathbf{g}(\mathbf{w_k}, \mathbf{x_p})].\end{aligned} \tag{4.13}$$

To proceed further, we need to make evident the connection between (4.13) and the analysis of Sections 3.3 to 3.5. However, there is a problem in that, guided by the linear case considered above, we actually expect a limit cycle rather than convergence to a minimum. Nevertheless it is necessary to fix attention to some neighbourhood of a local minimum, say $\mathbf{w}^*$, of the least square error ε: clearly we cannot expect any global contractivity result as in general ε may have many local minima, as is well known in the backpropagation case. Now assume that D is continuous and uniformly bounded in a neighbourhood of $\mathbf{w}^*$. By *uniformly bounded* we mean there is a bound on $\|D\|_2$ that is valid for every $\mathbf{w}$ in the neighbourhood and for each $\mathbf{x_p}$. By Theorem 3.35(c) this will be the case unless the singular values of D are very badly behaved. From (4.12) and (4.13) we obtain

$$\begin{aligned}w_{k+1} &= \mathbf{w_k} + \eta[D(\mathbf{w_k}, \mathbf{x_p})]^T[\mathbf{y_p} - \mathbf{g}(\mathbf{x}^*, \mathbf{x_p}) - D(\mathbf{w}^*, \mathbf{x_p})(\mathbf{w_k} - \mathbf{w}^*)] + o(\|\mathbf{w_k} - \mathbf{w}^*\|_2)\\ &= [I - \eta\ D(\mathbf{w_k}, \mathbf{x_p})^T D(\mathbf{w}^*, \mathbf{x_p})]\mathbf{w_k}\\ &\quad + \eta[D(\mathbf{w_k}, \mathbf{x_p})]^T[\mathbf{y_p} - \mathbf{g}(\mathbf{w}^*, \mathbf{x_p}) + D(\mathbf{w}^*, \mathbf{x_p})\mathbf{w}^*] + o)\|\mathbf{w_k} - \mathbf{w}^*\|_2).\end{aligned} \tag{4.14}$$

The connection between (4.13) and (3.18) is now clear. The iteration matrix $[I - \eta D(\mathbf{w_k}, \mathbf{x_p})^T D(\mathbf{w}^*, \mathbf{x_p})]$ is not exactly symmetric in this case, although it will be nearly so if $\mathbf{w_k}$ is close to $\mathbf{w}^*$. More precisely, let us assume that $D(\mathbf{w}, \mathbf{x})$ is Lipschitz continuous (see Definition 1.49) at $\mathbf{w}^*$, uniformly over the space of pattern vectors $\mathbf{x}$. Then we have

$$\begin{aligned}\mathbf{w_{k+1}} &= [I - \eta D(\mathbf{w}^*, \mathbf{x_p})^T D(\mathbf{w}^*, \mathbf{x_p})]\mathbf{w_k}\\ &\quad + \eta[D(\mathbf{w}^*, \mathbf{x_p})]^T[\mathbf{y_p} - \mathbf{g}(\mathbf{w}^*, \mathbf{x_p}) + D(\mathbf{w}^*, \mathbf{x_p})\mathbf{w}^*] + O(\|\mathbf{w_k} - \mathbf{w}^*\|_2).\end{aligned} \tag{4.15}$$

Suppose we apply the patterns $\mathbf{x_1}, \ldots, \mathbf{x_t}$ cyclically, as for the linear case. If we can prove that the linearized part (i.e. what we would get if we applied (4.15) without the O term) of the mapping $\mathbf{w_k} \to \mathbf{w_{k+t}}$ is contractive, it will follow by continuity that there is a neighbourhood of $\mathbf{w}^*$ within which the whole mapping is contractive. This is because, by hypothesis, we have only a finite number of patterns. To establish contractivity of the linear part, we may proceed as follows.

First observe that $D(\mathbf{w}^*, \mathbf{x_p})^T D(\mathbf{w}^*, \mathbf{x_p})$ is positive semi definite. Thus for η sufficiently small,

$$\|I - \eta D(\mathbf{w}^*, \mathbf{x_p})^T D(\mathbf{w}^*, \mathbf{x_p})\|_2 \leq 1.$$

We may decompose the space of weight vectors into the span of the eigenvectors corresponding to zero and non-zero eigenvalues respectively. These spaces are orthogonal complements of each other, as the matrix is symmetric. On the former space, the iteration matrix does nothing. On the latter space it is contractive provided

$$\eta < 1/\rho[D(\mathbf{w}^*, \mathbf{x_p})^T D(\mathbf{w}^*, \mathbf{x_p})].$$

We may then proceed in a similar manner to equations (3.27)–(3.31), provided the contractive subspaces for each pattern between them span the whole weight space. (If this condition fails then a difficulty arises, since the linearized product mapping will have norm 1, so the non-linear map could actually be expansive on some subspace. We will not pursue this detail here.) For the single output case, $D(\mathbf{w}^*, \mathbf{x_p})$ is just a row vector, and we can identify the eigenvectors explicitly as in Lemma 3.1.

The *backpropagation rule* (Rumelhart and McClelland, 1986, pp. 322–328) used in many neural net applications is a special case of this. To see how this works, consider (4.13). Dropping the subscripts, we have

$$\delta\mathbf{w} = \eta[D(\mathbf{w}, \mathbf{x})]^T[\mathbf{y} - \mathbf{g}(\mathbf{w}, \mathbf{x})].$$

For simplicity we consider just a single output. (The general case only requires application of the same argument for each output.) The quantities $\mathbf{y}$ and $\mathbf{g}$ are therefore actually scalars, and the matrix D is $(\nabla g)^T$, where it is important to remember that the gradient operator is applied with respect to $\mathbf{w}$, $\mathbf{x}$ being regarded as fixed. Thus

$$\delta\mathbf{w} = \eta[y - g(\mathbf{w}, \mathbf{x})]\nabla g(\mathbf{w}, \mathbf{x}). \qquad (4.16)$$

To evaluate $\delta\mathbf{w}$ we need to know ∇g. A multilayer perceptron is made up of simple perceptrons in cascade. Figure 4.1 shows the architecture with an input layer, one or more 'hidden layers' (two in the diagram) and an output layer, which in the diagram consists of a single output. We are going to need Proposition 4.9. There is no problem with this in principle, since all the required quantities are available. However the differentiation needs a little care. Firstly, of course, the gradient is taken with respect to $\mathbf{w}$. Secondly, we are not in the

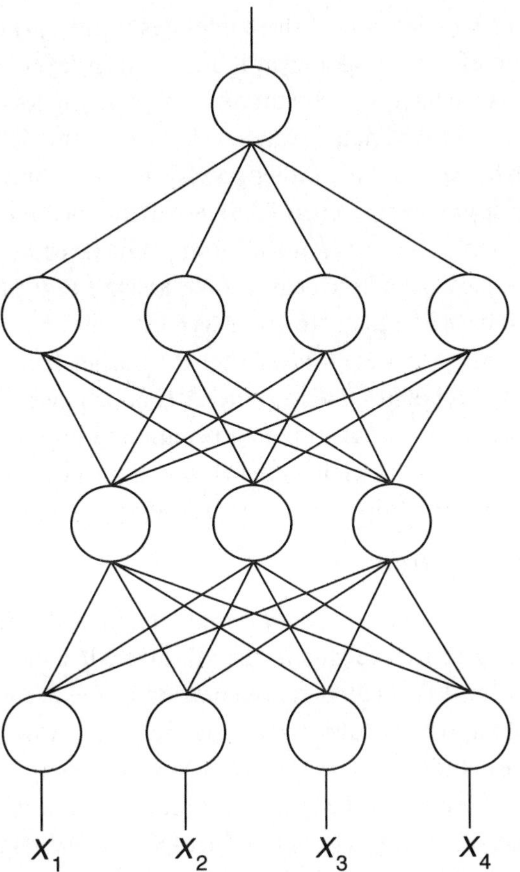

Fig. 4.1

simple situation of the Proposition, where the differentiation is only with respect to the input vector. The different layers depend on the different parts of **w**. Nevertheless, the at first sight daunting process is actually not difficult once the following principle has been grasped: a change of weights in any given layer will cause a (linear) change in the *input* vector to the successive hidden weights and layers. Thus the required gradient is obtained by (a) differentiating with respect to the weights in the layer and (b) multiplying this by the matrix representation of the Fréchet derivative in the succeeding layers. The first step is easy since the weights occur linearly, and the second is an immediate application of Proposition 4.9. The most difficult part is a reasonable notation: it is desirable to suppress as many subscripts as practicable.

Let the kth weight layer, $k=1, 2, \ldots, K$, say, have weight matrix W_k. (In the notation of (4.16) each row of these matrices forms part of the parameter vector $\mathbf{w}$.) On top of each weight layer is a non-linear layer. At each of the m (say) hidden units we have an activation function, say h_j for the jth unit. The function $\mathbf{h}$ whose jth co-ordinate function is h_j is a mapping $\mathbb{R}^m \to \mathbb{R}^m$. However for a multilayer perceptron it is rather special in that h_j only depends on the jth element of its argument: in terms of derivatives this means that the Jacobian, H say, of $\mathbf{h}$ is diagonal. Let the H and $\mathbf{h}$ for the units layer sitting on top of the kth weight layer also be subscripted k. (We assume that input units to the bottom layer just have identity activation, as is conventional.) Finally suppose that the input to the kth weight layer (i.e. the output from the units of the previous layer) are denoted $\mathbf{v_k}$, with $\mathbf{v_1}=\mathbf{x}$. A small change of δW_k in the kth weight matrix causes the input to the corresponding unit layer to change by $\delta W_k \mathbf{v}_k$. The derivative of a weight layer $W_r \mathbf{v_r}$ with respect to its input $\mathbf{v_r}$ is of course just W_r. Thus by Proposition 4.9, the output is changed by

$$H_K W_K H_{K-1} W_{K-1} \ldots H_k \delta W_k \mathbf{v_k}. \tag{4.17}$$

Since this expression is linear in δW_k it is that section of the Fréchet derivative of g corresponding to the weights in the kth layer. It is not yet quite in the correct form: we need the matrix representation of the derivative. In fact we might as well split up W_k by rows and consider a change $(\delta \mathbf{w_{i,k}})^T$ in the ith row (only). This corresponds to $\delta W_k = \mathbf{e_i}(\delta \mathbf{w_{i,k}})$, so $\delta W_k \mathbf{v_k} = \mathbf{e_i}(\delta \mathbf{w_{i,k}})\mathbf{v_k} = \mathbf{e_i}\mathbf{v_k}^T(\delta \mathbf{w_{i,k}})^T = V_{i,k}(\delta \mathbf{w_{i,k}})^T$, say, where $V_{i,k}$ is the matrix with ith row $\mathbf{v_k}$, and zeros elsewhere. Thus, that section of ∇g in (4.16) which corresponds to changes in the ith row of the kth weight matrix is $H_K W_K H_{K-1} W_{K-1} \ldots H_k V_{i,k}$ and the delta rule update for these weights is this quantity multiplied by $\eta[y - g(\mathbf{w}, \mathbf{x})]$. The name backpropagation derives from the fact that the output error is reflected back by this expression onto the kth layer. The necessary terms in can be calculated recursively back from the top layer. Note that normally the activation functions whose derivatives occur in the H_k are all the same. However this does not mean that the matrices are scalar multiples of I since the derivatives are evaluated at different points.

The process is made much simpler to understand by the following example, which was worked out in detail by A. Easdown (private communication). Figure 4.2 shows the architecture. The shaded neurons represent bias neurons with activation functions the identity, and the input to the one in the input layer is fixed at 1. The smaller dashed connections have weights fixed at 1, and the larger dashed ones have weights fixed at 0. (This approach to bias has been adopted to keep the matrix dimensions consistent.) All other neurons have the

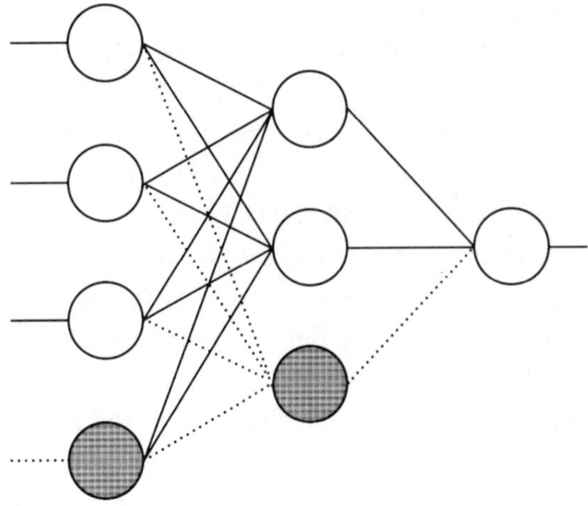

Fig. 4.2

standard activation function $a = 1/(1+e^{-x})$. Other than the bias input, the data are a 'toy' problem taken from Ellacott (1994, p. 113). There are four patterns in $\mathbb{R}^3$: $\mathbf{x}_1=(1, 0, 0)^T$, $\mathbf{x}_2=(1, 1, 0)^T$, $\mathbf{x}_3=(1, 1, 1)^T$ and $\mathbf{x}_4=(1, 0, 1)^T$. The corresponding outputs are $y_1=0$, $y_2=y_3=y_4=1$. Let the initial weights be

0.01	0.03	0.05	0
0.02	0.04	0.06	0
0	0	0	1

between the input and hidden layers numbering from the top in Fig. 4.2. Thus no bias is applied (but weights in rows 1 and 2 in the last column are trainable), and the bottom row of weights is fixed. Weights are

0.01	0.02	0.03

between hidden and output layer, so a bias of 0.03 is applied to the output neuron and this is trainable. With input $\mathbf{x}_1=(1, 0, 0, 0)^T$ and $y_1=1$, we find that (working to 4 dp) the output from the non-bias hidden units are 0.5025 and 0.5050. The bias output is of course 1. The output from the output unit is 0.5113. Using the fact that the derivative of the standard activation function is $a(1-a)$, the diagonal elements of the 3×3 matrix H_1 are 0.2500, 0.2500 and 1 from the bias unit. The off diagonal elements are, of course, 0. H_2 is a 1×1 matrix (i.e. a scalar) with value 0.2499. Ignoring terms corresponding to fixed weights we have 11 trainable weights: 8 below the hidden layer and 3 above. ∇g is a thus an 11-vector with the first three elements (say) corresponding to the hidden-to-output weights. (This is the convenient ordering for back-propagation, as the output gradient terms must be computed first.) So the first three elements of ∇g are given by $H_2 V_{1,2}=0.2499\, V_{1,2}=0.2499\mathbf{v}_2^{\mathrm{T}}$ (since $\mathbf{e}_1$ is here a 1-vector with element 1)$=(0.1256, 0.1262, 0.2499)$. Proceeding to the sub-hidden layer weights, the first four elements are given by $H_2 W_2 H_1 V_{1,1}$. The product $H_2 W_2 H_1$ evaluates to $(0.0006, 0.0012, 0.0075)$. $V_{1,1}=\mathbf{e}_1\mathbf{v}_1^{\mathrm{T}}$, which has $(1, 0, 0, 1)$ as first row and zeros elsewhere. Hence elements 4 to 7 of ∇g are $(0.0006, 0, 0, 0.0006)$. Similarly elements 8 to 11 of ∇g are $(0.0012, 0, 0, 0.0012)$. We remark that for on line learning, one might update the weights in the upper layers *before* computing the products. (Most books are not clear on this point!) With this approach, the matrix W_2 is changed by the delta rule update and $H_2 W_2 H_1$ becomes $(0.0002, 0.0009, 0.0043)$.

We should make it clear, however, that backpropagation is rarely used in this ‘pure’ form. Rumelhart and McClelland (1986) themselves advocate the use of a ‘momentum term’ which is somewhat analogous to the Levenberg–Marquardt method used in classical optimisation (Moré 1978; Gill, Murray and Wright, 1981, p. 136). See also equation (4.38) below. Moreover, the literature abounds with acceleration techniques. Fombellida and Destiné (1992) discuss two of the most popular: the *delta-bar-delta* and *quickprop* methods. They do some numerical comparisons and actually suggest a hybrid of the two methods as the most effective. However, none of the methods appear to have been subjected to any serious numerical analysis! An novel approach to accelerating backpropagation has been suggested by (Almeida and Silva, 1992).

4.4 Conjugate gradients

Of all the methods of classical optimisation, the one most closely linked to neural computation is that of conjugate gradients. This method is easily applied to neural networks, it is effective on large problems and moreover in some ways seems a natural extension of the ideas of the delta rule and backpropagation. We should emphasise, however, that it is not a true on-line learning method, and so does not replace these entirely. We will examine conjugate gradients in some detail: other classical optimisation methods will be considered more briefly in Section 4.5. Conjugate gradients have been used by many authors for neural computation, but for a further discussion of the connections between backpropagation and conjugate gradients, see van der Smagt (1994). For further reading on classical techniques of optimisation see for example Greig (1980) or Gill, Murray and Wright (1981).

By way of introduction, let us take another look at steepest descent. We have already seen that the delta rule in its epoch form is actually a version of steepest descent (4.5). The length of the step along the descent direction is determined by the learning rate. But in fact this is *not* the original version of steepest descent. A natural way to proceed is to search along the the descent direction to find the minimum value of f in this direction: this is called a *line search*. Specifically, we wish to find the least value of $f(\mathbf{x}_0 + t\mathbf{h})$, where $\mathbf{x}_0$ is our current position, $\mathbf{h}$ is a search direction and $t \in \mathbb{R}$. By elementary calculus, this minimum will occur when the derivative of f with respect to t is zero. We can use Theorem 4.1, with $\mathbf{x}(t) = \mathbf{x}_0 + t\mathbf{h}$. Thus $\mathrm{d}x_i/\mathrm{d}t = h_i$, and (4.2) yields the condition

$$\mathbf{h}^{\mathrm{T}} \nabla f(\mathbf{x}_0 + t_0\mathbf{h}) = 0 \tag{4.18}$$

for the point $t = t_0$ where the minimum occurs. In practice we may be able to use this condition to solve for t_0, but more usually the line search is carried out by some systematic trial and error process. However we are not interested here in the practical details. Instead, look what happens when $\mathbf{h}$ is chosen to be the steepest descent direction: $\mathbf{h} = -\nabla f(\mathbf{x}_0)$. We find that $[\nabla f(\mathbf{x}_0)]^{\mathrm{T}} \nabla f(\mathbf{x}_0 + t_0\mathbf{h}) = 0$. Of course, $-\nabla f(\mathbf{x}_0 + t_0\mathbf{h})$ is simply the new steepest descent direction at the point $\mathbf{x}_1 = \mathbf{x}_0 + t_0\mathbf{h}$. So steepest descent with line searches yields a sequence of *orthogonal* search directions. This property is not particularly useful in itself, but does have interesting implications in certain circumstances. A contour map of the surface can be illuminating: a contour is a line of constant f and therefore ∇f is always orthogonal to the contours. (Compare (4.6) and Example 4.5.) Figure 4.3 illustrates various possibilities for a quadratic form. Note that the contours are elliptical. Figure 4.3(a) shows the application of steepest descent with a small fixed step length. This is analogous to walking downhill in a fog: if we always take a short step in the downhill direction we will eventually land up at the bottom by a reasonably sensible route, but with a lot of steps. Figure 4.3(b) and (c) shows what happens when we employ steepest descent with line searches. If we start on one of the axes of the ellipse, the minimum is attained in a single step. But if we start slightly off the longer axis, the algorithm oscillates about this axis and takes a long time to converge. The problem is caused by the eccentricity of the contours: if they were circular we would get convergence in one step from any starting point. In this case, even if our first search direction is not the steepest descent, an orthogonal direction with line searches will get to minimum in 2 steps (n in n-dimensions). However, to make the contours circular requires us to find the eigenvalues of the matrix of the

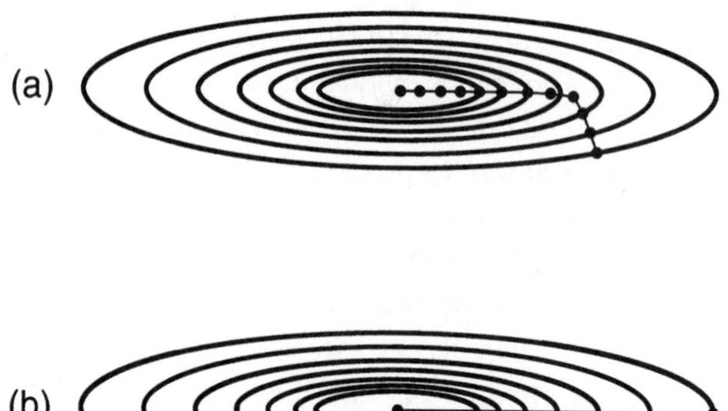

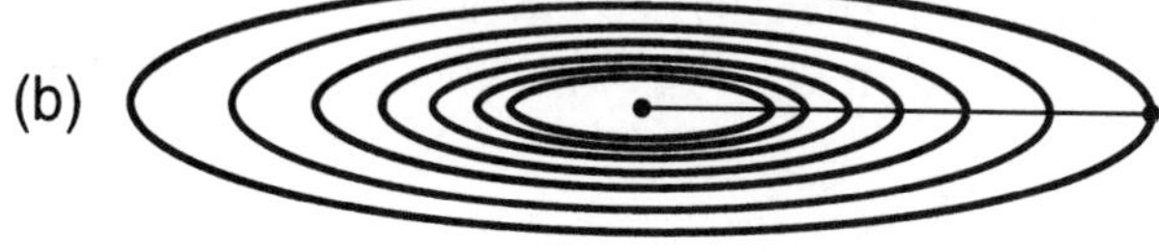

Fig. 4.3

quadratic form and rescale them: actually the eccentricity of the ellipses is the ratio of the two eigenvalues as may be determined by diagonalization of the matrix. If we have found the eigenvalues and eigenvectors of the quadratic form we can write down the solution explicitly in any case (compare Section 3.7), so this is of no value directly.

But consider a quadratic form $f(\mathbf{x})=\frac{1}{2}\mathbf{x}^{\mathrm{T}}A\mathbf{x}+\mathbf{b}^{\mathrm{T}}\mathbf{x}+c$ (Remark 4.4(b)) with A symmetric and positive definite. Thus $\nabla f(\mathbf{x})=A\mathbf{x}+\mathbf{b}$. We will make use of the inner product

$$<\mathbf{x}, \mathbf{y}> = \mathbf{x}^{\mathrm{T}}A\mathbf{y}. \tag{4.19}$$

Vectors $\mathbf{x}$, $\mathbf{y}$ which are orthogonal with respect to this inner product are said in this context to be *conjugate*, to avoid confusion with ordinary orthogonality with respect to the standard inner product. In the usual fashion we may write, for P orthogonal and D diagonal with strictly positive diagonal elements,

$$A = PDP^{\mathrm{T}} = PD^{½}D^{½}P^{\mathrm{T}}.$$

Here $D^{½}$ is simply the diagonal matrix whose entries are the square roots of those of D. Now for conjugate **x**, **y** we have $<\mathbf{x}, \mathbf{y}>=0$. Let $\mathbf{u}=D^{½}P^{\mathrm{T}}\mathbf{x}$, $\mathbf{v}=D^{½}P^{\mathrm{T}}\mathbf{y}$. Then **u** and **v** orthogonal with the standard inner product. Also $\mathbf{x}^{\mathrm{T}}A\mathbf{x}=\mathbf{u}^{\mathrm{T}}\mathbf{u}$: *hence f has circular contours in* **u** *space.* So searching conjugate directions in the original **x** space means searching orthogonal directions with circular contours in **u** space! In fact, let us suppose that the minimum of f occurs at the point $\mathbf{x}^*$. Start at some point $\mathbf{x}_1$, and let $\mathbf{d}_1, \mathbf{d}_2, \ldots, \mathbf{d}_n$ be a set of mutually conjugate directions. Since these are orthogonal with respect to the conjugation inner product, they must be linearly independent and therefore span $\mathbb{R}^n$. So we may write

$$\mathbf{x}^* - \mathbf{x}_1 = \sum_{i=1}^{n} \alpha_i \mathbf{d}_i,$$

where from (3.48)

$$\begin{aligned}\alpha_i &= \mathbf{d}_i^{\mathrm{T}} A(\mathbf{x}^* - \mathbf{x}_1)/\mathbf{d}_i^{\mathrm{T}} A\mathbf{d}_i.\\ &= [\mathbf{d}_i^{\mathrm{T}}\nabla f(\mathbf{x}^*) - \mathbf{d}_i^{\mathrm{T}}\nabla f(\mathbf{x}_1)]/\mathbf{d}_i^{\mathrm{T}} A\mathbf{d}_i \\ &= -\,\mathbf{d}_i^{\mathrm{T}}\nabla f(\mathbf{x}_1)/\mathbf{d}_i^{\mathrm{T}} A\mathbf{d}_i\end{aligned} \tag{4.20}$$

since $\mathbf{x}^*$ is a stationary point. So $\mathbf{x}^*$ can be reached in (at most) n steps from $\mathbf{x}_1$, where the kth step is

$$\mathbf{x}_{k+1} = \mathbf{x}_k + \alpha_k \mathbf{d}_k.$$

Hence

$$\mathbf{x}_{k+1} - \mathbf{x}_1 = \sum_{i=1}^{k} \alpha_i \mathbf{d}_i.$$

and

$$A\mathbf{x}_{k+1} = A\mathbf{x}_1 + \sum_{i=1}^{k} \alpha_i A\mathbf{d}_i$$

or

$$\nabla f(\mathbf{x}_{k+1}) = \nabla f(\mathbf{x}_1) + \sum_{i=1}^{k} \alpha_i A\mathbf{d}_i,$$

whence for $1 \leq r \leq k$,

$$\begin{aligned} \mathbf{d_r}^T \nabla f(\mathbf{x_{k+1}}) &= \mathbf{d_r}^T \nabla f(\mathbf{x_1}) + \alpha_r \mathbf{d_r}^T A \mathbf{d_r} \\ &= 0 \text{ by (4.20).} \end{aligned} \tag{4.21}$$

Thus setting $r=k$, (4.18) *tells us that* $\mathbf{x_{k+1}}$ *is precisely the point we would reach by doing a line search for the minimum of f from* $\mathbf{x_k}$ *in the direction* $\mathbf{d_k}$! Or to put it the other way round, if we start at $\mathbf{x_1}$ and minimise f along a set of mutually conjugate directions, we will reach the minimum of f in at most n steps. But (4.21) is a much stronger condition than (4.18): it shows us that with conjugate directions the gradient at $\mathbf{x_{k+1}}$ is orthogonal to *all* the previous search directions. Note that we do not actually need to calculate P and D: the searches are carried out in $\mathbf{x}$ space.

To employ the method we need to generate the conjugate directions. This can be done with the Gram–Schmidt process. The algorithm described so far is called the *method of conjugate directions.* But it has disadvantages. Firstly we need to store all previous directions, and secondly the Gram–Schmidt process is not very stable numerically: rounding error can quickly result in loss of conjugacy for the search directions. Remarkably, Forsyth's Theorem (Theorem 3.57) comes to our aid. Consider the linear transformation $L(\mathbf{x})=A\mathbf{x}$. Since A is symmetric, this is self-adjoint with respect to the conjugation inner product (4.19). *Thus there exists a three term recurrence for our conjugate search directions.* The coefficients are given by the usual inner products of Forsyth's Theorem. We therefore define the *conjugate gradient method* for minimising the quadratic form f as follows:

1. Choose an initial search point $\mathbf{x_1}$. Choose also an initial search direction $\mathbf{d_1}$, generally the steepest descent direction $\mathbf{d_1}=-\nabla f(\mathbf{x_1})$.
2. At each point $\mathbf{x_i}$, generate a new conjugate search direction $\mathbf{d_i}$, using the previous search directions and Theorem 3.57. Set $\mathbf{x_{i+1}}=\mathbf{x_i}+\alpha_i\mathbf{d_i}$, where α_i is chosen to minimise $f(\mathbf{x_i}+\alpha\mathbf{d_i})$ for $\alpha \in \mathbb{R}$.

This method will, at least in theory, find the minimum of any n-dimensional quadratic form in at most n steps. Certain changes are made in practice. Since we need to store the current search point $\mathbf{x_i}$ anyway, we can avoid storing the two previous $\mathbf{d}$'s. Instead use $\mathbf{x_i}=\mathbf{x_{i-1}}+\alpha_{i-1}\mathbf{d_{i-1}}$ to eliminate $\mathbf{d_{i-1}}$ from the recurrence. Also some care is needed in implementing the method, in order to minimise the number of matrix multiplications and inner products that are required. Most importantly, conjugacy will eventually be lost due to rounding error. Thus it is best to reinitialise the method from time to time by using step 1 instead of 2, but starting from the current point.

Non-quadratic optimisation problems are tackled using the approximation (4.10) with the error term ignored. At each step 2, a new matrix is used, so the directions are not really conjugate but will be so asymptotically near the minimum. Ideally, a good starting point is required, but the method is reasonably robust if a preconditioner is applied: see below. Of course, it will not converge (even in principle) in a finite number of steps, but (4.10) guarantees fast convergence near the minimum.

The conjugate gradient method is generally applied with a preconditioner. Although in principle the method avoids the problem of elongated contours by mapping A in (4.19) onto a space where the contours are circular, in practice it can be unstable if the contours are too eccentric: i.e. if the condition number of A is very large. Hence, as in the paragraphs following Example 3.71, our aim here is to produce a matrix with reduced condition number. The basic idea works like this.

We would like to find a matrix M such that $\mu(M^{-1}A) \ll \mu(A)$. (The symbol $\ll$ means 'very much less than'.) Think of M as being a matrix that is an approximation to A, but much easier to invert. Since A is symmetric and positive definite, it is sensible to insist that M is also symmetric and positive definite. However, $M^{-1}A$ may be neither. But we can find a matrix T such that $EE^{\mathrm{T}} = M$: to see this consider the diagonalization of M. (This matrix E^{T} will perform a similar role to that of the filtering matrix T in Section 3.7: see equation (3.59) and Proposition 3.63.) The matrix $E^{-1}A(E^{-1})^{\mathrm{T}}$ is symmetric and positive definite. Moreover it has the same eigenvalues, and hence the same condition number, as $M^{-1}A$, because if $\mathbf{v}$ is a eigenvector of $M^{-1}A$ with eigenvalue λ,

$$[E^{-1}A(E^{-1})^{\mathrm{T}}](E^{\mathrm{T}}\mathbf{v}) = [E^{\mathrm{T}}(E^{-1})^{\mathrm{T}}]E^{-1}A\mathbf{v} = E^{\mathrm{T}}M^{-1}A\mathbf{v} = \lambda E^{\mathrm{T}}\mathbf{v} \tag{4.22}$$

i.e. $E^{\mathrm{T}}\mathbf{v}$ is an eigenvector of $E^{-1}A(E^{-1})^{\mathrm{T}}$ with the same eigenvalue. To make use of this, we substitute $\mathbf{x}' = E^{\mathrm{T}}\mathbf{x}$ into the quadratic form $f(\mathbf{x}) = \mathbf{x}^{\mathrm{T}}A\mathbf{x} + \mathbf{b}^{\mathrm{T}}\mathbf{x} + c$. Only the quadratic term is really important here: thus $\mathbf{x}^{\mathrm{T}}A\mathbf{x} = \mathbf{x}'^{\mathrm{T}}E^{-1}A(E^{-1})^{\mathrm{T}}\mathbf{x}'$. In view of (4.22), the quadratic form will indeed be much better conditioned if $\mu(M^{-1}A) \ll \mu(A)$. It might be inconvenient in practice to compute E: if so the conjugate gradient recurrence can be written in terms of M^{-1} instead. In applying preconditioning to the non-linear case in which the matrix A (i.e. H in (4.10)) changes at each iteration, it is obviously not worthwhile to expend much effort on finding a very sophisticated M. The simplest choice is to choose M to be the diagonal matrix formed from the diagonal elements of A. M^{-1} (and indeed E) are then trivially calculated. This choice of M is called the *Jacobi preconditioner*. But it is not always very effective in practice. For large non-linear problems, there is a trade off between the work involved in obtaining a preconditioner and its usefulness (see, e.g. Gill, Murray and Wright, 1981, Section 4.8, for a more detailed discussion).

4.5 Other methods of optimisation

Minimising the quadratic form $f(\mathbf{x})=\mathbf{x}^T A\mathbf{x}+\mathbf{b}^T\mathbf{x}+c$ is of course equivalent to solving the equations $A\mathbf{x}=-\mathbf{b}$, or in terms of a least squares problem to solving the normal equations (3.34). In the last section we saw the advantage to be gained by computing an approximate inverse to A. Of course if we know A^{-1} exactly there is nothing to do: $\mathbf{x}=-A^{-1}\mathbf{b}$. A class of methods for non-linear problems is based on this idea. Ignoring the order term, (4.10) gives (using '≈' to denote 'approximately equal')

$$f(\mathbf{x}+\delta\mathbf{x}) \approx f(\mathbf{x}) + (\delta\mathbf{x})^T\nabla f(\mathbf{x}) + \tfrac{1}{2}(\delta\mathbf{x})^T H(\mathbf{x})(\delta\mathbf{x}).$$

For fixed $\mathbf{x}$, the right-hand side, as we have already observed, is a quadratic form in $\delta\mathbf{x}$. Suppose we are at some point $\mathbf{x}=\mathbf{x}_k$, and we select a new point $\mathbf{x}_{k+1}=\mathbf{x}_k+\delta\mathbf{x}$ where $\delta\mathbf{x}$ is chosen to minimise the quadratic form. So $\delta\mathbf{x}=-H^{-1}\nabla f$ where both items are evaluated at $\mathbf{x}_k$. (Compare this with the steepest descent direction $-\nabla f$.) Provided all the required quantities can be evaluated, this gives an iteration

$$\mathbf{x}_{k+1} = \mathbf{x}_k - H(\mathbf{x}_k)^{-1}\nabla f(\mathbf{x}_k) \tag{4.23}$$

to find the minimum of f. This method is known as *Newton's method*. Alternatively, we can think of Newton's method as being steepest descent for the conjugate norm arising from the inner product (4.19). If the Newton step does not actually reduce f, a line search can be applied. In practice Newton's method is of limited usefulness, since it is often hard work to get even H, let alone H^{-1}. We can make life a little easier by writing (4.23) as

$$\delta\mathbf{x}_k = \mathbf{x}_{k+1} - \mathbf{x}_k$$

with

$$H(\mathbf{x}_k)\delta\mathbf{x}_k = -\nabla f(\mathbf{x}_k) \tag{4.24}$$

and solving for $\delta\mathbf{x}_k$. But this is of only marginal assistance. However it does form the basis for a class of methods which attempt to obtain estimates of H^{-1} near the minimum. These are called *quasi-Newton methods*. These take the form

$$\mathbf{x_{k+1}} = \delta\mathbf{x_k} + \mathbf{x_k}$$

with

$$\delta\mathbf{x_k} = -\alpha_k B_k \nabla f(\mathbf{x_k}), \tag{4.25}$$

where B_k is an estimate of H^{-1} and $\alpha_k \in \mathbb{R}$ is a line search parameter. α_k is chosen to minimise f along the search direction: thus from (4.18)

$$(\delta\mathbf{x_k})^T \nabla f(\mathbf{x_{k+1}}) = 0. \tag{4.26}$$

Normally B_0 is I, so that the first step is steepest descent. If we expand the gradient in the direction of $\delta\mathbf{x_k}$ we get

$$\delta\nabla f(\mathbf{x_k}) = \nabla f(\mathbf{x_{k+1}}) - \nabla f(\mathbf{x_k}) \approx H(\mathbf{x_k})\delta\mathbf{x_k}.$$

We want B_{k+1} to make use of this information while retaining the previously computed information in B_k. Specifically we insist that

$$B_{k+1}\delta\nabla f(\mathbf{x_k}) = \delta\mathbf{x_k}. \tag{4.27}$$

So write

$$B_{k+1} = B_k + \delta B_k \tag{4.28}$$

with δB_k to be determined. We would like all the B_k to be symmetric, so we require δB_k symmetric. We would also like each B_k to be positive definite, since then (if $\mathbf{x_k}$ is not a stationary point) $(\delta\mathbf{x_k})^T\nabla f(\mathbf{x_k}) = -\alpha_k[\nabla f(\mathbf{x_k})]^T B_k \nabla f(\mathbf{x_k}) < 0$ with $\alpha_k > 0$. In other words a step with positive α_k will have a component in the descent direction and f will therefore be reduced by the step. One choice that satisfies all these conditions is the well known *Davidon–Fletcher–Powell method* (usually abbreviated to DFP), where

$$\delta B_k = \frac{\delta\mathbf{x_k}(\delta\mathbf{x_k})^T}{(\delta\mathbf{x_k})^T\delta\nabla f(\mathbf{x_k})} - \frac{[B_k\delta\nabla f(\mathbf{x_k})][B_k\delta\nabla f(\mathbf{x_k})]^T}{\delta\nabla f(\mathbf{x_k})^T B_k \delta\nabla f(\mathbf{x_k})}. \tag{4.29}$$

Clearly δB_k and hence B_{k+1} are symmetric provided B_k is symmetric. To see that B_{k+1} is positive definite, let $\mathbf{z}$ be any vector. Then from (4.28)

$$\begin{aligned}\mathbf{z}^T B_{k+1}\mathbf{z} &= \mathbf{z}^T B_k \mathbf{z} + \mathbf{z}^T \delta B_k \mathbf{z} \\ &= \frac{(\mathbf{z}^T\delta\mathbf{x_k})^2}{(\delta\mathbf{x_k})^T\delta\nabla f(\mathbf{x_k})} + \frac{[\mathbf{z}^T B_k \mathbf{z})\,(\delta\nabla f(\mathbf{x_k})^T B_k \delta\nabla f(\mathbf{x_k})] - (\mathbf{z}^T B_k \delta\nabla f(\mathbf{x_k})]^2}{[\delta\nabla f(\mathbf{x_k})]^T B_k \delta\nabla f(\mathbf{x_k})}\end{aligned}$$

Note that $(\delta \mathbf{x_k})^T \delta \nabla f(\mathbf{x_k}) = -(\delta \mathbf{x_k})^T \nabla f(\mathbf{x_k})$ in view of (4.26), and we have already seen that this quantity is strictly positive if B_k is positive definite. To understand the structure of the second term, consider the inner product $<\mathbf{x}, \mathbf{y}>_k = \mathbf{x_k}^T B_k \mathbf{y}$ and let its corresponding norm be $\| \ \|$. The denominator of the second term is simply $\|\delta \nabla f(\mathbf{x_k})\|^2$ and is thus positive: it cannot be zero as we always take a non-zero step at a non-stationary point. The numerator is $\|\mathbf{z}\| \ \|\delta \nabla f(\mathbf{x_k})\| - <\mathbf{z}, \delta \nabla f(\mathbf{x_k})>_k$ which is non-negative by the Cauchy–Schwarz inequality, Theorem 3.43. Thus $\mathbf{z}^T B_{k+1} \mathbf{z} > 0$, as required.

It remains to show that (4.27) is valid.

$$
\begin{aligned}
&B_{k+1}\delta\nabla f(\mathbf{x_k}) \\
&\quad = B_k \delta \nabla f(\mathbf{x_k}) + \delta B_k \delta \nabla f(\mathbf{x_k}) \\
&\quad = B_k \delta \nabla f(\mathbf{x_k}) + \delta B_k \delta \nabla f(\mathbf{x_k}) \\
&\quad = B_k \delta \nabla f(\mathbf{x_k}) + \frac{\delta \mathbf{x_k} (\delta \mathbf{x_k})^T \delta \nabla f(\mathbf{x_k})}{(\delta \mathbf{x_k})^T \delta \nabla f(\mathbf{x_k})} - \frac{[B_k \delta \nabla f(\mathbf{x_k})][B_k \delta \nabla f(\mathbf{x_k})]^T \delta \nabla f(\mathbf{x_k})}{\delta \nabla f(\mathbf{x_k})^T B_k \delta \nabla f(\mathbf{x_k})} \\
&\quad = B_k \delta \nabla f(\mathbf{x_k}) + \delta \mathbf{x_k} - B_k \delta \nabla f(\mathbf{x_k}) \\
&\quad = \delta \mathbf{x_k}.
\end{aligned}
$$

These arguments should explain some of the reasoning behind the update formula (4.29) and they also prove that DFP generates a sequence of descent steps for f. However they do not really reveal that the method gives Newton-like behaviour near the minimum. When we are near the minimum, f may, on the basis of (4.10), be assumed to be quadratic. To understand the asymptotic behaviour, we need to consider what happens when H is constant. We shall show that in this case

$$B_{k+1}\delta\nabla f(\mathbf{x_r}) = \delta \mathbf{x_r} \text{ for } 1 \le r \le k, \tag{4.30}$$

holds for each k (compare (4.27)) and moreover that the search directions $(\delta \mathbf{x_r})$, $r = 1, \ldots, k+1$ are H-conjugate. This is achieved by induction. Suppose that at some k we have reached a neighbourhood of the minimum where the quadratic approximation is valid. For simplicity, we renumber the steps from $k=1$. First consider the case $k=1$ itself. We have already observed that (4.27) holds, and (4.30) reduces to (4.27) for $k=1$. Moreover

$$
\begin{aligned}
\delta\nabla f(\mathbf{x_1}) &= \nabla f(\mathbf{x_2}) - \nabla f(\mathbf{x_1}) \\
&= H\mathbf{x_2} - H\mathbf{x_1} \text{ (Remark 4.4}(b)) \\
&= H\delta\mathbf{x_1},
\end{aligned}
$$

whence

$$B_2 H\delta\mathbf{x_1} = \delta\mathbf{x_1} \text{ by (4.30).} \tag{4.31}$$

Thus

$$\begin{aligned}(\delta\mathbf{x_2})^{\mathrm{T}} H\delta\mathbf{x_1} &= [-\alpha_2 B_2 \nabla f(\mathbf{x_2})]^{\mathrm{T}} \delta\mathbf{x_1} \text{ by (4.25)} \\ &= -\alpha_2 [\nabla f(\mathbf{x_2})]^{\mathrm{T}} B_2{}^{\mathrm{T}} \delta\mathbf{x_1} \\ &= -\alpha_2 [\nabla f(\mathbf{x_2})]^{\mathrm{T}} \delta\mathbf{x_1} \\ &= 0 \text{ by (4.26).}\end{aligned}$$

This completes the first step of the induction. So let us assume as an inductive hypothesis that $\delta\mathbf{x_1}, \delta\mathbf{x_2}, \ldots, \delta\mathbf{x_k}$ are mutually H-conjugate and that (4.30) holds up to $k-1$. We need to show that $\delta\mathbf{x_{k+1}}$ is conjugate and that (4.30) holds for k. The case $r=k$ in (4.30) is just (4.27) again. Moreover

$$(\delta\mathbf{x_k})^{\mathrm{T}} H\delta\mathbf{x_{k-1}} = 0$$

by the same argument as above for $k=1$. The tricky bit is $r<k$. We have

$$B_{k+1}\delta\nabla f(\mathbf{x_r}) = B_k \delta\nabla f(\mathbf{x_r}) + \delta B_k \delta\nabla f(\mathbf{x_r}). \tag{4.32}$$

The first term on the right-hand side is $\delta\mathbf{x_r}$ by the (4.30) part of the inductive hypothesis. Also recalling that (similarly to above) $\delta\nabla f(\mathbf{x_r}) = H\delta\mathbf{x_r}$, we find

$$(\delta\mathbf{x_k})^{\mathrm{T}} \delta\nabla f(\mathbf{x_r}) = (\delta\mathbf{x_k})^{\mathrm{T}} H\delta\mathbf{x_r} = 0$$

by the conjugacy part of the inductive hypothesis. Moreover

$$B_k \delta\nabla f(\mathbf{x_r}) = \delta\mathbf{x_r} \text{ (the (4.30) part again !).}$$

It follows from (4.31) that the second term on the right of (4.22) is zero, so (4.30) is established. Finally,

$$\begin{aligned}(\delta\mathbf{x_{k+1}})^{\mathrm{T}} H\delta\mathbf{x_r} &= -\alpha_{k+1}[B_{k+1}\nabla f(\mathbf{x_{k+1}})]^{\mathrm{T}} \delta\mathbf{x_r} \text{ by (4.25)} \\ &= -\alpha_{k+1}[\nabla f(\mathbf{x_{k+1}})]^{\mathrm{T}} B_{k+1}{}^{\mathrm{T}} \delta\mathbf{x_r} \\ &= -\alpha_{k+1}[\nabla f(\mathbf{x_{k+1}})]^{\mathrm{T}} \delta\mathbf{x_r} \\ &= 0 \text{ by (4.21).}\end{aligned}$$

The induction is complete.

Before leaving the proof we observe that from (4.30)

$$\begin{aligned}B_{k+1} H\delta\mathbf{x_r} &= B_{k+1}\delta\nabla f(\mathbf{x_r}) \\ &= \delta\mathbf{x_r} \text{ for } 1 \le r \le k.\end{aligned}$$

Thus in this case where H is constant we indeed have $B_n = H^{-1}$, since the complete set of conjugate directions spans $\mathbb{R}^n$. The effect of DFP is to start off as steepest descent and gradually work towards a Newton step (4.23).

The theory of DFP may seem a little hair-raising, but it is important to realise that application is fairly straight forward. Just use (4.25), (4.28) and (4.29). Other quasi-Newton methods may be found in the literature. It has been shown that most of them are actually equivalent in the sense that, using exact arithmetic, they will generate the same sequence of points. (They may differ in terms of the numerical stability and amount of work involved.) An outline of the proof is given in Greig (1980, p. 63). Unlike conjugate gradients. DFP has not been used extensively in neural computing. One reason for this, of course, is the need to store the approximate inverse Hessian. However, storing such a matrix only requires the construction of an associated simple perceptron to hold it: such a network could be thought of as learning the geometric structure of the data space. This approach could well repay further study in future.

The methods considered so far have been applicable to general minimisation problems. However as we have seen, neural learning is often formulated as a least squares problem. There are methods which attempt to exploit the special structure of such problems. In particular they make use of the fact that the Hessian matrix is factorizable. Look again at equations (3.34) and (3.35), and the remarks between them. Consider also the exposition of the backpropagation method in the previous section. In both cases the problems under consideration make use of the fact that we are minimising a quantity which takes the general form

$$f(\mathbf{x}) = \tfrac{1}{2}(\mathbf{g}(\mathbf{x}))^{\mathrm{T}}\mathbf{g}(\mathbf{x}) \text{ with } \mathbf{g}(\mathbf{x}) \in \mathbb{R}^{\mathrm{m}}. \tag{4.33}$$

Let D be the Jacobian matrix of $\mathbf{g}$. Then proceeding in much the same way as we did for the generalised delta rule (equations (4.11) and (4.12)),

$$\mathbf{g}(\mathbf{x}+\delta\mathbf{x}) = \mathbf{g}(\mathbf{x}) + D(\mathbf{x})\delta\mathbf{x} + [\tfrac{1}{2}(\delta\mathbf{x})^{\mathrm{T}}G_i(\mathbf{x})\delta\mathbf{x}] + O(\|\delta\mathbf{x}\|_2^3)$$

where $G_i(\mathbf{x})$ is the Hessian of the ith co-ordinate function $g_i(\mathbf{x})$ and $[\frac{1}{2}(\delta x)^{\mathrm{T}}G_i(\mathbf{x})\delta\mathbf{x}]$ denotes the vector whose ith term is that shown in the square brackets, and hence

$$\begin{aligned} f(\mathbf{x}+\delta\mathbf{x}) &= \tfrac{1}{2}[\mathbf{g}(\mathbf{x}+\delta\mathbf{x})]^{\mathrm{T}}\mathbf{g}(\mathbf{x}+\delta\mathbf{x}) \\ &= \tfrac{1}{2}\{\mathbf{g}(\mathbf{x}) + D(\mathbf{x})\delta\mathbf{x} + [\tfrac{1}{2}(\delta\mathbf{x})^{\mathrm{T}}G_i(\mathbf{x})\delta\mathbf{x}] + O(\|\delta\mathbf{x}\|_2^3\}^{\mathrm{T}} \\ &\qquad \mathbf{g}(\mathbf{x}) + D(\mathbf{x})\delta\mathbf{x} + [\tfrac{1}{2}(\delta\mathbf{x})^{\mathrm{T}}G_i(\mathbf{x})\delta\mathbf{x}] + O(\|\delta\mathbf{x}\|_2^3) \end{aligned}$$

$$= f(\mathbf{x}) + [\mathbf{g}(\mathbf{x})]^{\mathrm{T}} D(\mathbf{x})\delta\mathbf{x} + \tfrac{1}{2}[D(\mathbf{x})\delta\mathbf{x}]^{\mathrm{T}}[D(\mathbf{x})\delta\mathbf{x}] + [\tfrac{1}{2}(\delta\mathbf{x})^{\mathrm{T}} G_i(\mathbf{x})\delta\mathbf{x}]^{\mathrm{T}}\mathbf{g}(\mathbf{x}) + O(\|\delta\mathbf{x}\|_2^3).$$

(When deriving this line, we make use of the fact that this is a scalar equation so all the terms may be transposed at will.) Thus

$$\nabla f(\mathbf{x}) = [D(\mathbf{x})]^{\mathrm{T}}\mathbf{g}(\mathbf{x}) \tag{4.34}$$

and

$$[\tfrac{1}{2}(\delta\mathbf{x})^{\mathrm{T}} G_i(\mathbf{x})\delta\mathbf{x}]^{\mathrm{T}}\mathbf{g}(\mathbf{x}) = \tfrac{1}{2}\sum g_i(\mathbf{x})(\delta\mathbf{x})^{\mathrm{T}} G_i(\mathbf{x})\delta\mathbf{x} = \tfrac{1}{2}(\delta\mathbf{x})^{\mathrm{T}} \left[\sum g_{ii}(\mathbf{x}) G_i(\mathbf{x})\right]\delta\mathbf{x}$$

(where the summations are over i) so if $H(\mathbf{x})$ is the Hessian of f, we have

$$H(\mathbf{x}) = \sum_{i=1}^{m} g_i(\mathbf{x}) G_i(\mathbf{x}) + [D(\mathbf{x})]^{\mathrm{T}} D(\mathbf{x}). \tag{4.35}$$

Special least squares methods are based on the assumption that (at least near the minimum) $f(\mathbf{x})$ and hence the quantities $g_i(\mathbf{x})$ will be very small. In the context of neural networks, this means that the errors between the required outputs and the actual outputs are small, i.e. that the model is a good fit (compare equation (4.13)). Of course, this assumption may not be valid, but if it is, then it seems sensible to ignore the first term of (4.35), giving

$$H(\mathbf{x}) \approx [D(\mathbf{x})]^{\mathrm{T}} D(\mathbf{x}). \tag{4.36}$$

The great advantage of this approximation is that it involves only first derivative information about $\mathbf{g}$. Applying this information to Newton's method (4.23) yields the update

$$D_k^{\mathrm{T}} D_k(\mathbf{x_{k+1}} - \mathbf{x_k}) = -D_k^{\mathrm{T}}\mathbf{g}(\mathbf{x_k}) \tag{4.37}$$

where $D_k = D(\mathbf{x_k})$, or, if we wish to use linear searches,

$$D_k^{\mathrm{T}} D_k \mathbf{d_k} = -D_k^{\mathrm{T}}\mathbf{g}(\mathbf{x_k})$$

for the search direction $\mathbf{d_k}$ with $\mathbf{x_{k+1}} = \mathbf{x_k} + \alpha_k\mathbf{d_k}$. This approach is called the *Gauss–Newton method*. If you compare (4.37) with (3.35), you will observe that Gauss–Newton actually amounts to approximating the non-linear least squares problem by a linear one. Parallels with the generalised delta rule should be obvious.

In practice, the Gauss–Newton method suffers from several disadvantages. As might be expected, the matrix $D_k^T D_k$ is likely to be ill-conditioned and inversion impracticable. This can to some extent be alleviated by applying the singular value decomposition to D_k instead, but clearly for a large neural system this method will involve a lot of computation. It is possible to use techniques like those employed for Quasi Newton methods to estimate the Hessian or its inverse: see, e.g. Gill, Murray and Wright (1981, p. 137).

A variant of Gauss–Newton is the *Levenberg–Marquardt method* (Moré, 1978). Although not actually very popular among the optimisation fraternity at present, we mention it in view of its similarities with the backpropagation technique of adding a 'momentum term'. The Levenberg–Marquardt method replaces (4.37) with

$$(D_k^T D_k + \lambda_k I)(\mathbf{x_{k+1}} - \mathbf{x_k}) = -D_k^T \mathbf{g}(\mathbf{x_k}), \tag{4.38}$$

where λ_k is a parameter which must be chosen at each stage in order to ensure that $(D_k^T D_k + \lambda_k I)$ is sufficiently well conditioned.

Up to now we have assumed that the values that our independent variable $\mathbf{x}$ may take are unconstrained. We have concentrated on this case since this is generally true for the optimisation problems occurring in neural computation. However the reader should be aware that there is also an extensive theory concerned with optimisation problems in which $\mathbf{x}$ is constrained to lie within some set S. Implicit here is the assumption that S is a fairly simple set: perhaps a hypersphere or a simplex (a region bounded by hyperplanes). At least it is generally assumed that S has a reasonable boundary: if the boundary is fractal there is of course little hope of success. Constrained optimisation problems have the property that the optimum may occur at either a stationary point or a boundary point. For example the one-dimensional function $f(x) = x^2$, $-1 \le x \le 1$, achieves its minimum at the stationary point 0, but has two maxima (at ± 1) neither of which is stationary. In n-dimensions the optimum may occur at some point of the boundary which is not a vertex, in which case the component of ∇f along the boundary will be zero, but the normal component may not be. The exact conditions for an optimum point are summed up in the well-known *Kuhn–Tucker conditions* (Greig, 1980, p. 13), but it would take us too far afield to consider these here.

5 Differential equations and dynamical systems

5.1 Introduction

We have up to now considered only artificial neural systems that operate in discrete time. Systems that operate in continuous time and employ feedback during recall need to be able rapidly to map all inputs to equilibria. These equilibria are states where information can be deliberately stored. Globally stable neural networks are dynamical systems (typically non-linear) that are capable of such a mapping of inputs to equilibria. This topic presents some difficulties of exposition, since most of the neural applications are actually somewhat technical, and therefore less than ideal for illustrative purposes. Thus the examples presented in this chapter are mostly not explicit neural networks. However, many papers applying dynamical systems theory to neural nets exist: Leen (1991) is a typical example which the reader might like to consult for motivational purposes! In addition, virtually all applications of neural methods to control depend on these ideas to a greater or lesser extent. At the end of the chapter we will give a proof of the Cohen–Grossberg Theorem used in proving the stability of certain artificial neural systems.

In this chapter we will extend our discrete results and introduce fundamental notions and theorems concerning the stability of continuous time non-linear systems. Just as the study of discrete time non-linear systems is founded on that of linear systems, the starting point for understanding continuous time non-linear systems is the analysis of *linear* systems of differential equations. We shall meet the notions of flow, equilibrium, hyperbolic equilibrium and stability of both linear and non-linear systems, and state various fundamental theorems concerned with these concepts. The material here focuses on the classical theory of simple attractors, since this is what is usually employed in practical neural models. However the non-linear models are sufficiently rich in principle to exhibit chaotic behaviour. The theory of chaotic systems depends on the classical theory in any case, so a study of this chapter will provide a firm foundation for the study of so-called *strange attractors* (basically asymptotic behaviour that has a fractal or other complex structure). Readers requiring explicit discussion of chaotic systems are directed to Baker and Gollub (1990), for a painless introduction, or to Falconer (1990) for a more formal and rigorous approach. For further reading on the classical theory, see Perko (1991).

5.2 Linear differential systems

A differential equation relates a function and its derivatives. If this equation is linear and only the first derivative of the function is present in the equation then we have a *linear first order ordinary differential equation*. For example

$$\frac{\mathrm{d}x}{\mathrm{d}t} + 3x = 0$$

or

$$\frac{\mathrm{d}y}{\mathrm{d}x} + 2y = x^2.$$

In the first example, x is (implicitly) a function of t and in the second y is a function of x. In the first of these examples, the right-hand side is zero. Such an equation is said to be *homogeneous.*

Here we will be mostly concerned with systems of differential equations. For instance

$$\frac{dx}{dt} + 3x = 0$$

$$\frac{dy}{dt} - 2y = 0,$$

or

$$\frac{dx}{dt} + x + 3y = 0$$

$$\frac{dy}{dt} - 2y = 0,$$

The first system is *uncoupled* in that neither of the equations involves both unknown functions. When two or more functions and/or their derivatives are connected in the equations, as in the first equation of the second pair, the system is said to be *coupled.*

We shall first of all study uncoupled systems and then build on that to solve coupled systems. Look first at a very simple equation.

$$\frac{dx}{dt} = ax, \tag{5.1}$$

where $a \in \mathbb{R}$ is a (given) constant. Now consider the function

$$x(t) = ce^{at}, \tag{5.2}$$

where $c \in \mathbb{R}$ is an arbitrary constant. We have

$$\frac{dx}{dt} = cae^{at} = cx(t),$$

so (5.2) is indeed a solution of the differential equation (5.1). It can be shown (see Section 5.2) that in fact (5.2) is the most general solution.

From now it will be convenient to use the notation $\dot{x}$ to denote differentiation of x with respect to t. Consider the uncoupled system

$$\begin{aligned} \dot{x}_1 &= -x_1 \\ \dot{x}_2 &= 2x_2. \end{aligned} \tag{5.3}$$

This system has the general solution

$$x_1 = c_1e^{-t}, \; x_2 = c_2e^{2t}. \tag{5.4}$$

We can write (5.3) and (5.4) in matrix form: (5.3) becomes

$$\dot{\mathbf{x}} = A\mathbf{x} \tag{5.5}$$

where

$$\mathbf{x} = \begin{pmatrix} x_1(t) \\ x_1(t) \end{pmatrix} \text{and } A = \begin{pmatrix} -1 & 0 \\ 0 & 2 \end{pmatrix}, \tag{5.6}$$

and (5.4) becomes

$$\mathbf{x}(t) = \begin{pmatrix} \mathrm{e}^{-t} & 0 \\ 0 & \mathrm{e}^{2t} \end{pmatrix} \mathbf{c} \tag{5.7}$$

where $\mathbf{c}=(c_1, c_2)^{\mathrm{T}}=\mathbf{x}(0)$. We shall show that this solution can in fact be written $\mathrm{e}^{At}\mathbf{c}$, echoing the form of (5.2). Specifically,

Theorem 5.1

Let A be an $n \times n$ real matrix and $t_0>0$. The series

$$\sum_{k=0}^{\infty} (A^k t^k)/n! \tag{5.8}$$

is absolutely convergent and uniformly continuous for all $t \in \mathbb{C}$ with $|t| < t_0$. The sum is a matrix which we call e^{At}. If t is real, then e^{At} is also real.

Proof

For simplicity we will assume A is similar to a diagonal matrix: $A=PDP^{-1}$. See Definition 3.1, equation (3.2) and the subsequent discussion. Compare also equations (3.22)–(3.24) and Theorem 3.31. We may actually need to use complex matrices here since in many practical applications the A will have complex eigenvalues. Even then of course we may have repeated eigenvalues. Actually we shall see how to deal with this a bit later (Method 5.6), so for the moment just look at the simple case. Now if

$$A = PDP^{-1},$$
$$A^k = (PDP^{-1})^k = PD^kP^{-1} \text{ (Compare (3.23)).}$$

Then (5.8) can be written

$$P\left(\sum_{k=0}^{\infty} (D^k t^k)/n!\right)P^{-1}$$

and the term in brackets is simply a diagonal matrix whose diagonal element corresponding to the eigenvalue λ is $e^{\lambda t}$. Although this argument involves complex matrices, the sum for real t must be real as each partial sum of the series is real.

□

(Note that we could equally apply the argument to an abstract linear operator from $\mathbb{R}^n \to \mathbb{R}^n$.)

Example 5.2
Consider

$$A = \begin{pmatrix} -2 & -1 \\ 1 & -2 \end{pmatrix}.$$

The characteristic equation is

$$(-2-\lambda)^2 + 1^2 = 0,$$

whence $\lambda = -2 \pm i$. We could of course calculate the matrix P as in the proof, but this matrix will be complex and we will have to invert it. As an alternative, for this matrix there is a neat trick which depends on the fact that the eigenvalues are a complex conjugate pair. Choose $\lambda = -2 + i$. A simple induction shows that in fact

$$A^k = \begin{pmatrix} \mathrm{Re}(\lambda^k) & -\mathrm{Im}(\lambda^k) \\ \mathrm{Im}(\lambda^k) & \mathrm{Re}(\lambda^k) \end{pmatrix}.$$

Hence

$$e^{At} = \begin{pmatrix} \mathrm{Re}(e^{\lambda}t) & -\mathrm{Im}(e^{\lambda}t) \\ \mathrm{Im}(e^{\lambda}t) & \mathrm{Re}(e^{\lambda}t) \end{pmatrix}.$$

$$= e^{-2t} \begin{pmatrix} \cos t & -\sin t \\ \sin t & \cos t \end{pmatrix}.$$

□

Before looking more systematically at computation of e^{At}, let us return to our application to linear systems. In (5.6) the matrix is already diagonal and obviously

$$e^{At} = \begin{pmatrix} e^{-t} & 0 \\ 0 & e^{2t} \end{pmatrix}.$$

So (5.7) is $\mathbf{x}(t)=e^{At}\mathbf{c}$. where $\mathbf{c}=\mathbf{x}(0)$, as advertised. Our task now is to show that this result holds not just for diagonal systems, but for coupled ones also.

Lemma 5.3

Let A be a real square matrix. Then

$$\frac{d(e^{At})}{dt} = Ae^{At}.$$

Proof

For real x, y, we have $e^{x+y}=e^x e^y$. Thus the product of the two series for the right-hand side must give the series for the left-hand side. But to multiply power series, we need only the distributive and commutative laws or arithmetic. Since A commutes with itself, it follows that the multiplication identity will also hold for the power series (5.8). For for $t, h \in \mathbb{R}$, $e^{A\,(t+h)}=e^{At}e^{Ah}$. Thus

$$\begin{aligned}\frac{d(e^{At})}{dt} &= \lim_{h\to 0} \frac{e^{A(t+h)} - e^{At}}{h}, \\ &= \lim_{h\to 0} \frac{e^{At}(e^{Ah} - I)}{h} \\ &= e^{At} \lim_{h\to 0} \left(A + \frac{A^2 h}{2!} + \frac{A^3 h^2}{3!} + \ldots\right) \\ &= e^{At}A.\end{aligned}$$

The termwise evaluation of the limit is justified here, since the series is absolutely convergent.

□

Now we can prove our basic result.

Theorem 5.4

Let A be an $n\times n$ real matrix. Then for a given $\mathbf{x}_0 \in \mathbb{R}^n$, the initial value problem

$$\begin{aligned}\dot{\mathbf{x}} &= A\mathbf{x} \\ \mathbf{x}(0) &= \mathbf{x}_0\end{aligned} \tag{5.9}$$

has a unique solution $\mathbf{x}(t)=e^{At}\mathbf{x}(0)$.

Proof
That $e^{At}\mathbf{x}(0)$ is a solution of (5.9) is an immediate consequence of Lemma 5.3. To see it is unique, let $\mathbf{x}^*(t)$ be any solution of (5.9). Define $\mathbf{y}(t)=e^{At}\mathbf{x}^*(t)$. Then by an obvious extension of the product rule to matrix differentiation (consider it elementwise) we get

$$\begin{aligned}\dot{\mathbf{y}} &= -Ae^{-At}\mathbf{x}^*(t) + e^{-At}\dot{\mathbf{x}}^*(t)\\ &= -Ae^{-At}\mathbf{x}^*(t) + e^{-At}A\dot{\mathbf{x}}(t)\\ &= 0.\end{aligned}$$

Thus $\mathbf{y}(t)$ is a constant vector, but $\mathbf{y}(0)=\mathbf{x}(0)$ so $\mathbf{y}(t)=\mathbf{x}(0)$. The definition of $\mathbf{y}(t)$ now implies that

$$e^{At}\mathbf{y}(t) = e^{At}e^{-At}\mathbf{x}^*(t) = \mathbf{x}^*(t).$$

□

Example 5.5
Consider again the equations (5.3), and suppose $x_1(0)=x_2(0)=1$. In matrix form the system is

$$\dot{\mathbf{x}} = \begin{pmatrix} -1 & 0 \\ 0 & 2 \end{pmatrix}\mathbf{x}(t),$$

and for this A we have shown previously that

$$e^{At} = \begin{pmatrix} e^{-t} & 0 \\ 0 & e^{2t} \end{pmatrix}.$$

Thus

$$\mathbf{x}(t) = \begin{pmatrix} e^{-t} & 0 \\ 0 & e^{2t} \end{pmatrix}\begin{pmatrix} 1 \\ 1 \end{pmatrix}$$

is the unique solution (i.e. $x_1(t)=e^{-t}$, $x_2(t)=e^{2t}$).

□

Of course, the main difficulty in using Theorem 5.4 is the calculation of e^{At} for a given A. As we have seen, closed form solutions can sometimes be found, but in general this is very complicated. What can be done, however, is to find n linearly independent $\mathbf{x}_0$ such that $e^{At}\mathbf{x}_0$ can be summed exactly. This way, n linearly independent solutions of (5.9) can be generated, and the required solution for a given $\mathbf{x}_0$ is a linear combination of these.

So how do we find these independent solutions? Our starting point is the observation that $e^{At}\mathbf{v}=e^{(A-\lambda I)t}e^{\lambda It}\mathbf{v}$ for any constant λ, since $(A-\lambda I)$ and λI commute. Moreover it follows from the power series (5.8) that $e^{\lambda It}\mathbf{v}=e^{\lambda t}\mathbf{v}$. Hence $e^{At}\mathbf{v}=e^{(A-\lambda I)t}e^{\lambda t}\mathbf{v}=e^{\lambda t}e^{(A-\lambda I)t}\mathbf{v}$ since $e^{\lambda t}$ is a scalar. We now make the crucial observation that if $(A-\lambda I)^m\mathbf{v}=\mathbf{0}$, then the infinite series $e^{(A-\lambda I)t}\mathbf{v}$ actually terminates after m terms. This is because for any positive integer k,

$$(A-\lambda I)^{m+k}\mathbf{v}=(A-\lambda I)^k(A-\lambda I)^m\mathbf{v}=\mathbf{0}.$$

The vector $\mathbf{v}$ is called a *generalised eigenvector*: of course if $m=1$ we just get an ordinary eigenvector. This leads to the following algorithm for finding n linearly independent solutions:

Method 5.6

(a) Find all the eigenvalues and eigenvectors of A. Suppose we have k linearly independent eigenvectors $\mathbf{v}_1, \mathbf{v}_2, \ldots, \mathbf{v}_k$ with corresponding eigenvalues $\lambda_1, \lambda_2, \ldots, \lambda_k$. By the observation above, there is only one term in the expansion of $e^{(A-\lambda_j I)t}\mathbf{v}_j$, namely $\mathbf{v}_j$. In other words, $\mathbf{v}_j$ is also an eigenvector of e^{At}, with eigenvalue $e^{\lambda_j t}$. Therefore $e^{\lambda_j t}\mathbf{v}_j$ for $j=1, \ldots, k$, provide k independent solutions. If $k=n$ we are done, but if not we need some more solutions. So:

(b) If $k<n$, pick an eigenvalue λ of A and find all vectors $\mathbf{v}$ for which $(A-\lambda I)^2\mathbf{v}=\mathbf{0}$, but $(A-\lambda I)\mathbf{v}\neq\mathbf{0}$. For each vector $\mathbf{v}$, $e^{At}\mathbf{v}=e^{\lambda}te^{(A-\lambda I)t}\mathbf{v}=e^{\lambda t}\{\mathbf{v}+t(A-\lambda I)\mathbf{v}\}$ is an additional solution. Do this for all the eigenvalues of A. If we still need more solutions:

(c) Find all vectors $\mathbf{v}$ for which $(A-\lambda I)^3\mathbf{v}=\mathbf{0}$, but $(A-\lambda I)^2\mathbf{v}\neq\mathbf{0}$. For each $\mathbf{v}$, $e^{\lambda t}\{\mathbf{v}+t(A-\lambda I)\mathbf{v}+\frac{1}{2!}t^2(A-\lambda I)^2\mathbf{v}\}$ is a further solution.

(d) Proceed in this manner until n linearly independent solutions are obtained.

□

Before proving that this algorithm always works, we will give a simple example.

Example 5.7

$$\dot{\mathbf{x}}=\begin{pmatrix}1 & 1 & 0\\ 0 & 1 & 0\\ 0 & 0 & 2\end{pmatrix}\mathbf{x},$$

The characteristic polynomial for this matrix is $(1-\lambda)^2(2-\lambda)=0$. The eigenvector corresponding to $\lambda=2$ is $(0, 0, 1)^T$, so $\mathbf{x}_1(t)=e^{2t}(0, 0, 1)^T$ is a solution.

Similarly $(1, 0, 0)^T$ is the eigenvector corresponding to $\lambda=1$, yielding the solution $\mathbf{x}_2(t)=e^t(1, 0, 0)^T$. To get a third independent solution, we seek $\mathbf{v}$ such $(A-I)^2\mathbf{v}=\mathbf{0}$, but $(A-I)\mathbf{v}\neq\mathbf{0}$.

$$(A-I)^2=\begin{pmatrix}0&0&0\\0&0&0\\0&0&1\end{pmatrix},$$

so it is easy to see that $\mathbf{v}=(0, 1, 0)^T$ satisfies these conditions. Thus, the third solution is $\mathbf{x}_2(t)=e^t\{I+t(A-I)\}\ \mathbf{v}=e^t(t, 1, 0)^T$.

The general solution is given by $\mathbf{x}(t)=c_1\mathbf{x}_1(t)+c_2\mathbf{x}_2(t)+c_3\mathbf{x}_3(t)=(c_2e^t+c_3te^t,\ c_3e^t,\ c_1e^{2t})^T$.

□

Notice that in this example, the multiplier of e^t in $\mathbf{x}_2$ is $(t, 1, 0)^T=t(1, 0, 0)^T+(0, 1, 0)^T$; *a linear combination of the generalised eigenvectors corresponding to the eigenvalue 1*. Why is this? Look again at Method 5.6(b). The first term of $\{\mathbf{v}+t(A-\lambda I)\mathbf{v}\}$ is $\mathbf{v}$ itself: the second term is an element of the image (i.e. the column span) of $(A-\lambda I)$. By definition, any non-zero element of this span is an eigenvector of A corresponding to the eigenvalue λ. Similar arguments will apply to the higher order terms in Method 5.6(c). *We reach the important conclusion that for any eigenvalue λ and for any t, the solution*

$$e^{\lambda t}\left\{\mathbf{v}+t(A-\lambda I)\mathbf{v}+\frac{1}{2!}t(A-\lambda I)^2\mathbf{v}\right\}$$

is a linear combination of the generalised eigenvectors corresponding to λ. This remark will prove fundamental in our study.

But before proceeding further, we need to justify the Method 5.6. We first note that the process certainly does generate solutions of (5.10) since each function generated is of the form $e^{At}\mathbf{v}(0)$. We need to prove two results: firstly that steps (b) and (c) are actually possible, and secondly that all the solutions generated are independent.

We will look first at step (b) in detail. (Step (c) is merely an extension of the same argument and we will omit the detail.) So we have an eigenvalue λ of A, and a corresponding eigenvector $\mathbf{v}_1$. Assume that λ has multiplicity at least 2. (The multiplicity is the number of times the eigenvalue is repeated in the characteristic equation.) If null $(A-\lambda I)\geq 2$, we can find another eigenvector, so step (b) is not required. (Recall that for any matrix Λ, null (Λ) is the dimension of the kernel of Λ.) Thus we assume null $(A-\lambda I)=1$, and hence $\ker(A-\lambda I)=\text{span}\ \{\mathbf{v}_1\}$. Now extend $\{\mathbf{v}_1\}$ to a basis of $\mathbb{C}^n$ ($\mathbf{v}_1$ might be complex), and form the vectors into a matrix P (s0 the first column of P is $\mathbf{v}_1$). Let $B = P^{-1}AP$: then B has the same characteristic polynomial as A. Since $\mathbf{v}_1$ is an eigenvector corresponding to λ, the first column of B is $\lambda\mathbf{e}_1$ (i.e. $b_{11}=\lambda$ and $b_{i1}=0$ for $i>1$.) Let C be the $(n-1)\times(n-1)$ matrix obtained by deleting the first row and column of B. Expanding the determinant by the first column shows that $\det(B-\mu I_n)=(\lambda-\mu)\det(C-\mu I_{n-1})$ where I_n is the identity matrix in n dimensions. Since λ is an eigenvalue of A (and thus B) of multiplicity at least 2, we must have $\det(C-\lambda I_{n-1})=0$, so λ is an eigenvalue of C. Let $\mathbf{u}'$ be a corresponding eigenvector of C, and set $\mathbf{u}=(0 \mid \mathbf{u}'^{T})^{T}$. Then we have

$$B\mathbf{u} = \lambda\mathbf{u} + \alpha\mathbf{e}_1$$

for some $\alpha \in \mathbb{C}$ (actually α is – the inner product of $\mathbf{u}'$ with the first row of B ignoring the first element). Now set $\mathbf{v}_2 = P\mathbf{u}$. We have

$$A\mathbf{v}_2 = PBP^{-1}\mathbf{v}_2 = PB\mathbf{u} = P(\lambda\mathbf{u} + \alpha\mathbf{e}_1) = \lambda\mathbf{v}_2 + \alpha\mathbf{v}_1,$$

since the first column of P is $\mathbf{v}_1$. Hence

$$(A - \lambda I)\mathbf{v}_2 = \alpha\mathbf{v}_1,$$

whence

$$(A - \lambda I)^2\mathbf{v}_2 = \mathbf{0},$$

since $\mathbf{v}_1 \in \ker(A-\lambda I)$. Note that $\mathbf{v}_2$ cannot be a multiple of $\mathbf{v}_1$, since $\mathbf{u}=P^{-1}\mathbf{v}_2$ has 0 for its first element, whereas $P^{-1}\mathbf{v}_1=\mathbf{e}_1$. Observe also that the equation $(A)-\lambda I)\mathbf{v}_2=\mathbf{v}_1$ can be used to find $\mathbf{v}_2$: the value of α does not matter since we are not interested in the normalization. If we need further generalised eigenvectors (step (c) of the method), then define a matrix whose first columns are $\mathbf{v}_1$ and $\mathbf{v}_2$ and proceed in the same manner.

Since the sum of the multiplicities of the eigenvectors is n, we have now shown that the Method 5.6 can always be carried out to generate n solutions. It remains finally to be shown that these are independent. We already know that eigenvectors corresponding to distinct eigenvalues are independent (Theorem 3.10). And we have just shown that generalised eigenvectors corresponding to the same eigenvalue are independent of each other. But is it possible that they could be dependent on generalised eigenvectors corresponding to other eigenvalues? To show that this is impossible is unfortunately not quite as easy as Theorem 3.10, but one way to do it is to modify the argument of the previous paragraphs. When we have exhausted all the generalised eigenvectors corresponding to λ, sponding to λ, we can pick a different eigenvalue and continue the process. The construction and independency part of the argument does not depend on the eigenvalues being the same, and in fact can be used to prove that any matrix is similar to a triangular matrix (Isaacson and Keller, 1966, p. 2).

5.3 Qualitative theory of linear differential systems

In this section we consider some questions relating to the generic behaviour of solutions of differential systems, for the case of $\dot{\mathbf{x}}=A\mathbf{x}$. These questions are:

(a) Do there exist equilibrium values? In other words, is there a constant vector $\mathbf{c}$ such that $\mathbf{x}(t)=\mathbf{c}$ is a solution of the system?
(b) What happens to a solution $\mathbf{x}(t)$ as t approaches infinity? Do all solutions approach equilibrium values? If not, are they periodic?
(c) Suppose we have two solutions $\mathbf{x}(t)$ and $\mathbf{y}(t)$ such that $\mathbf{x}(0)$ is 'very close to' $\mathbf{y}(0)$. Will $\mathbf{x}(t)$ remain 'very close to' $\mathbf{y}(t)$ for all t? This is a fundamental question in the qualitative theory of differential systems. It is referred to as the problem of stability.

For the simple system $\dot{\mathbf{x}}=A\mathbf{x}$, question (a) can be answered very simply. If $\mathbf{x}(t)=\mathbf{c}$, $\dot{\mathbf{x}}=\mathbf{0}$, so $\mathbf{x}(t)$ will solve the system if and only if $A\mathbf{c}=0$, i.e. if $\mathbf{c}\in \ker(A)$. Thus $\mathbf{c}=\mathbf{0}$ is always an equilibrium solution. Non-trivial solutions occur if and only if A is singular.

As we shall see later, an answer to (c) will largely answer (b), so we shall now concentrate on stating (c) more precisely, and then proving a theorem that answers it. Since we are working on $\mathbb{R}^n$, we can use any vector norm such as the ordinary Euclidean norm $\|\ \|_2$ to measure closeness. We now give a formal definition of stability.

Definition 5.8

The solution $\mathbf{x}(t)$ of

$$\dot{\mathbf{x}} = A\mathbf{x} \tag{5.10}$$

is *stable* if for every $\varepsilon>0$, there exists δ (which may depend on ε) such that for every solution $\mathbf{y}(t)$ of (5.10) with $\|\mathbf{x}(0)-\mathbf{y}(0)\|_2<\delta, \|\mathbf{x}(t)-\mathbf{y}(t)\|_2<\varepsilon$ for all t.

□

Conversely a solution $\mathbf{x}(t)$ is *unstable* if there is at least one solution $\mathbf{y}(t)$ which starts off near $\mathbf{x}(t)$ but does not remain near it in the sense of the definition, i.e. if for all $\delta>0$, there is a solution $\mathbf{y}(t)$ and an $\varepsilon>0$ such that $\|\mathbf{x}(0)-\mathbf{y}(0)\|_2<\delta$, but $\|\mathbf{x}(t)-\mathbf{y}(t)\|_2>\varepsilon$, for at least one $t>0$. The stability question for (5.10) can be resolved completely, since we know the solution. (Compare the following result with Theorem 3.31).

Theorem 5.9

(a) Every solution of (5.10) is stable if all the eigenvalues of A have negative real part.
(b) Every solution of (5.10) is unstable if at least one eigenvalue of A has positive real part.
(c) If the eigenvalues of A are non-positive, but one or more has zero real part (i.e. is purely imaginary), the situation is more complicated. Suppose that $\lambda_1=i\sigma_1$, $\lambda_2=i\sigma_2$ . . . $\lambda_l=i\sigma_l$ are the purely imaginary eigenvalues and let λ_k have multiplicity m_k. If A has m_k linearly independent eigenvectors for every λ_k, then every solution is stable. Otherwise every solution is unstable.

Proof

Since (5.10) is linear, the difference of two solutions is also a solution. Thus it follows from Definition 5.7 that every solution is stable if and only if the solution $\mathbf{x}(t)=\mathbf{0}$ is stable.

(a) Every solution $\mathbf{x}(t)$ of (5.10) is of the form $e^{At}\mathbf{x}(0)$. Now Method 5.6 shows that the kth element of e^{At} is in fact a linear combination of functions of the form $q_k(t)e^{\lambda t}$, where q_k is a polynomial in t and λ is an eigenvalue of A. Let $M_k = \max q_k(t)e^{-\alpha}t$, for $0 \leq t<\infty$, where α is that real part of an eigenvalue of A which is algebraically largest. M_k is finite since by hypothesis $\alpha<0$. Now let $M = \sum M_k$. Then $\|e^{A}t\|_\infty \leq M\, e^{-\alpha t}$. It follows from the equivalence (Theorem 3.20) of all finite dimensional norms that there exists a constant K such that $\|e^{At}\|_2 \leq K\, e^{-\alpha t}$, So $\|\mathbf{x}(t)\|_2\leq K\, e^{-\alpha t}\,\|\mathbf{x}(0)\|_2$. Then, given $\varepsilon>0$, choose $\delta=\varepsilon/\,(K\,\|\mathbf{x}(0)\|_2)$. Thus $\|\mathbf{x}(t)-\mathbf{0}\|_2<\varepsilon$, if $\|\mathbf{x}(0)-\mathbf{0}\|_2<\delta$ i.e. the zero solution, and hence any other solution, is stable.
(b) Let λ be an eigenvalue of A with positive real part, and let $\mathbf{v}$ be the corresponding eigenvector. Then from Method 5.6(a), $c\, e^{\lambda t}\mathbf{v}$ is a solution of (5.10) for any $c\in\mathbb{R}$. Obviously this solution tends to infinity with t: however one may object that this solution could be complex. We are really interested only in real

solutions. If $\lambda = \alpha + i\beta$ is complex, then so is the eigenvector $\mathbf{v}$. Say $\mathbf{v} = i\mathbf{v}^2$. In this case,

$$\begin{aligned}\mathbf{y}(t) &= ce^{\lambda t}\mathbf{v} \\ &= ce^{(\alpha+i\beta)t}(\mathbf{v}^1 + i\mathbf{v}^2) \\ &+ ce^{\alpha t}\{(\mathbf{v}^1 \cos \beta t - \mathbf{v}^2 \sin \beta t) + i(\mathbf{v}^1 \sin \beta t + \mathbf{v}^2 \cos \beta t)].\end{aligned}$$

But for any complex solution of (5.10) it follows just by taking the real part of each side that the real part of the solution also solves (5.10). So $ce^{\alpha t}$ $(\mathbf{v}^1 \cos \beta t - \mathbf{v}^2 \sin \beta t)$ is also a solution. For any value of t for which βt is an integer multiple of 2π, this expression takes the value of $ce^{\alpha}t$. No matter how small c, these values become arbitrarily large, establishing that the zero solution is unstable.
(c) As in part (a), we note that every element of e^{At} is in fact a linear combination of functions of the form $q(t)e^{\lambda}t$, where q is a polynomial in t and λ is an eigenvalue of A. Now in the case that each purely imaginary eigenvalue has m_k independent eigenvectors, the $q(t)$ will be constant for these eigenvalues hence $\|e^{At}\|_2 \leq K$ for some K, whence the stability follows by a similar argument to part (a). Conversely, if A has fewer than m_k eigenvectors corresponding to λ_k, there is a solution $ce^{i\sigma_k t}$ $[I + t(A - i\sigma_k)]\mathbf{v}$. In a similar way to (b), we find that the real part of this is unbounded for arbitrarily small $c \neq 0$, establishing that the zero solution is unstable.

□

Note that the roof of part (a) actually establishes rather more than is required. It shows that in fact every solution $\mathbf{x}(t)$ approaches the equilibrium solution $\mathbf{0}$ as $t \to \infty$. This very strong behaviour is known as *asymptotic stability*. More precisely, a solution $\mathbf{y}(t)$ is *asymptotically stable* if there exists $\delta > 0$ such that every solution $\mathbf{x}(t)$ with $\|\mathbf{x}(0) - \mathbf{y}(0)\|_2 < \delta$ satisfies $\|\mathbf{x}(t) - \mathbf{y}(0)\|_2 \to 0$ as $t \to \infty$.

Examples 5.10

(a) We discuss the stability of solutions of

$$\dot{\mathbf{x}} = \begin{pmatrix} 2 & -1 & 0 \\ 1 & -2 & 0 \\ 0 & 0 & 0 \end{pmatrix} \mathbf{x}.$$

The eigenvalues of this matrix are $\lambda = 3, -2 \pm i$. Since the first of these has positive real part, every solution is unstable.
(b) We discuss the stability of solutions of

$$\dot{\mathbf{x}} = \begin{pmatrix} 0 & -3 \\ 2 & 0 \end{pmatrix} \mathbf{x}.$$

The eigenvalues are $\lambda = \pm i\sqrt{6}$. Every solution is stable, by part (c) of the theorem. The general solution is in fact $\mathbf{x}(t) = c_1 \, (-\sqrt{6} \sin \sqrt{6}\,t, \, 2 \cos \sqrt{6}\,t)^{\mathrm{T}} + c_2(\sqrt{6} \cos \sqrt{6}\,t, \, 2 \sin \sqrt{6}\,t)^{\mathrm{T}}$. The solutions are periodic: they do not approach the equilibrium solution $\mathbf{0}$ as $t \to \infty$, and thus are not asymptotically stable.

□

You may wonder why we have spent so much time discussing the simple linear system (5.10). However, it turns out that an understanding of this simple case is an essential step in coming to grips with more complicated systems. We are now ready to take the next step by introducing the concept of a phase plane, which enables us to illustrate stability graphically.

5.4 Phase portraits and stability

We shall again start by looking at the very simple uncoupled system

$$\dot{\mathbf{x}} = \begin{pmatrix} -1 & 0 \\ 0 & 2 \end{pmatrix} \mathbf{x}(t). \tag{5.11}$$

Solutions of this system take the form $x_1(t) = c_1 e^{-t}$, $x_2(t) = c_2 e^{2t}$ (see (5.4)), where $\mathbf{x}(0) = (c_1, c_2)^{\mathrm{T}}$. We can think of the solution as defining a 'motion' in the sense that each such point $(c_1, c_2)^{\mathrm{T}}$ moves to the point $(c_1 e^{-t}, c_2 e^{2t})^{\mathrm{T}}$ after time t. This motion can be described geometrically by drawing the curve traced out by $(c_1 e^{-t}, c_2 e^{2t})^{\mathrm{T}}$ as t goes from zero to infinity. In this particular case the equations of the curves are easy to determine: since $e^{2t} = 1/(e^{-t})^2$, we have $x_2 = c_1^2 c_2 / x_1^2$. A set of these curves for each point $(c_1, c_2)^{\mathrm{T}}$ is called the *phase portrait* of the system. Of course in practice we cannot plot all of them since there are infinitely many. However we can plot representative examples to illustrate the phase portrait. Arrows are drawn on these curves to indicate the direction of motion. Figure 5.1 shows the phase portrait of (5.11). Note the following types of behaviour:

(a) The equilibrium solution is given by $(c_1, c_2)^{\mathrm{T}} = \mathbf{0}$. The solution does not move from the origin.
(b) The solution given by $(c_1, c_2)^{\mathrm{T}} = (1, 0)^{\mathrm{T}}$ is $x_1(t) = e^{-t}$, $x_2(t) = 0$. It converges to $\mathbf{0}$ as $t \to \infty$. We have asymptotic stability in the subspace of solutions starting on the x_1-axis. This axis is called the *stable subspace* of (5.11), written E^S.

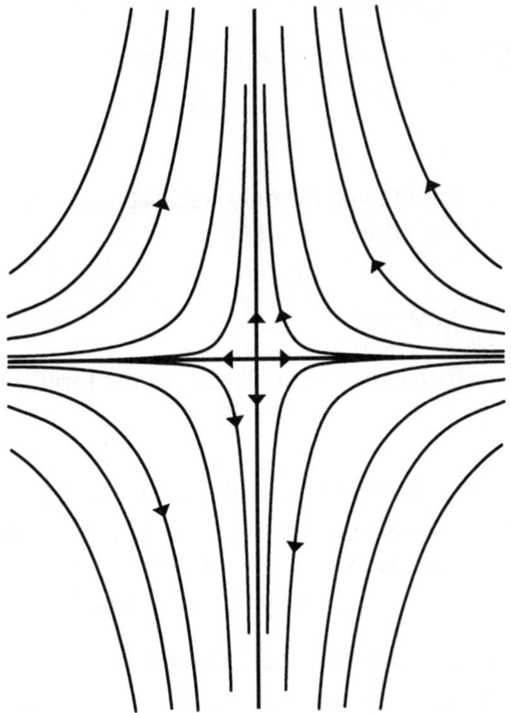

Fig. 5.1

(c) Solutions starting at any point off the x_1 axis tend to infinity asymptotically to the x_2 axis. In particular, paths on the axis travel to infinity along it. The x_2 axis is called the *unstable subspace* of (5.11), written E^U.

Now the eigenvalues of A in (5.11) are $\lambda = -1$ and $\lambda = 2$ corresponding to eigenvectors $(1, 0)^T$ and $(0, 1)^T$ respectively. For this example at least, E^S is the subspace spanned by $(1, 0)^T$ and E^U is the subspace spanned by $(0, 1)^T$. We shall now develop this approach to characterise the stability properties of the system (5.10). We have already seen (Theorem 5.9) how the eigenvalues of A determine the stability or otherwise of the solutions. Parts (a) and (b) of the theorem allow us to define the stable and unstable subspaces. Part (c) will lead to the notion of a *centre subspace* E^C. However we need to be able to cope with complex eigenvalues, and also the case of A failing to have a complete set of eigenvectors. We can do this as in Method 5.6. The vectors $\mathbf{v}$ introduced in parts (b) and (c) of the method will be referred to as *generalised eigenvectors*. As already indicated we can always find a basis of eigenvectors and generalised eigenvectors.

Example 5.11

As a very simple illustration of this idea, consider

$$A = \begin{pmatrix} 0 & 0 \\ 1 & 0 \end{pmatrix}$$

The only eigenvalue is $\lambda=0$, and the only eigenvector (up to scalar multiplication, of course) is $(0, 1)^{\mathrm{T}}$. But

$$A^2 = \begin{pmatrix} 0 & 0 \\ 0 & 0 \end{pmatrix}$$

so $(1, 0)^{\mathrm{T}}$ is a generalised eigenvector. These vectors form a basis for $\mathbb{R}^2$.

□

Now let $\mathbf{w_j}=\mathbf{u_j}+\mathrm{i}\mathbf{v_j}$ denote a generalised eigenvector of the (real) $n\times n$ matrix A corresponding to the eigenvalue $\lambda_j=a_j+\mathrm{i}b_j$. Suppose further that in fact $\lambda_1 \ldots \lambda_k$ are real, so in fact $\mathbf{v_1}=\mathbf{v_2}=\ldots=\mathbf{v_k}=\mathbf{0}$. The other eigenvectors occur in complex conjugate pairs, so we retain only one of each pair. Let

$$B=\{\mathbf{u_1}, \mathbf{u_2},\ldots,\mathbf{u_k}, \mathbf{u_{k+1}}, \mathbf{v_{k+1}}, \mathbf{u_{k+2}}, \mathbf{v_{k+2}},\ldots,\mathbf{u_m}, \mathbf{v_m}\}.$$

Then we claim that B is a basis for $\mathbb{R}^n$. We already know that the generalised eigenvectors are independent as complex vectors, but we need to show that the real and imaginary parts are independent as real vectors. To see this we use the fact that the complex generalised eigenvectors also occur in conjugate pairs. We can write $a\mathbf{u_j}+b\mathbf{v_j}$ as $\alpha\,(\mathbf{u_j}+\mathrm{i}\mathbf{v_j})+\beta\,(\mathbf{u_j}-\mathrm{i}\mathbf{v_j})$ with $\alpha=\frac{1}{2}(a-\mathrm{i}\,b)$ and $\beta=\frac{1}{2}(a+\mathrm{i}\,b)$. Hence any dependence relation among the real and imaginary parts would yield a corresponding dependence relation on the complex generalised eigenvectors, contradicting their independence. This establishes the independence of the elements of B.

Definition 5.12

The stable, unstable and centre subspaces E^S, E^U and E^C of the linear system (5.10) are defined as

$$E^s=\mathrm{span}\{\mathbf{u_j}, \mathbf{v_j}, 1\le j\le n \mid a_j<0\}$$
$$E^u=\mathrm{span}\{\mathbf{u_j}, \mathbf{v_j}, 1\le j\le n \mid a_j>0\}$$
$$E^c=\mathrm{span}\{\mathbf{u_j}, \mathbf{v_j}, 1\le j\le n \mid a_j=0\}$$

□

Example 5.13

(a) Consider again the Example 5.10 (a). We have already seen that the eigenvalues are $\lambda=3$, $-2\pm i$, Further, the eigenvector $(0, 0, 1)^T$ corresponds to eigenvalue 3, and $(0, 1, 0)^T + i(1, 0, 0)^T$ corresponds to $-2+i$. Thus $\mathbf{u_1}=(0, 0, 1)^T$, $\mathbf{u_2}=(0, 1, 0)^T$, $\mathbf{v_2}=(1, 0, 0)^T$, and $B=\{\mathbf{u_1}, \mathbf{u_2}, \mathbf{v_2}\}$ spans $\mathbb{R}^3$. Further

$$E^s = \text{span}\{\mathbf{u_2}, \mathbf{v_2}\} = \text{the } x_1x_2 \text{ plane}$$
$$E^u = \text{span}\{\mathbf{u_1}\} = \text{the } x_3 \text{ axis.}$$

E^C is empty.

(b) Consider the matrix in Example 5.11. The only eigenvector is $\mathbf{u_1}=(0, 1)^T$; $\mathbf{u_2}=(1, 0)^T$ is a generalised eigenvector. These span $\mathbb{R}^2$. E^S and E^U are empty. $E^C=\mathbb{R}^2$. The solution of the system is $x_1(t)=c_1$, $x_2(t)=c_1t+c_2$. Solutions with $c_1=0$ are bounded, others are not!

□

We now proceed to explore further the structure of solutions starting in E^S, E^U and E^C. Any solution to (5.10) starting at $\mathbf{x_0}$ has moved to the point $\mathbf{x}(t)=e^{At}\mathbf{x_0}$ at time t. In other words, the mapping e^{At}: $\mathbb{R}^n \to \mathbb{R}^n$ may be regarded as describing the motion of points along the trajectories which are the solutions of (5.10). The mapping is called the *flow* of the system. We have seen that the simplest case is when A has no eigenvalues with zero real part (i.e. when E^C is empty). The following definition captures this information.

Definition 5.14

If all the eigenvalues of the matrix A in the system (5.10) have non-zero real part, the flow e^{At}: $\mathbb{R}^n \to \mathbb{R}^n$ is called a *hyperbolic flow* and the system (5.10) itself is called a *hyperbolic linear system.*

□

Now we have also seen that solutions that start in one of the subspaces E^S, E^U and E^C actually remain in the same subspace for all time, *because for all time they are linear combinations of the appropriate generalised eigenvalues*. (If this is not clear, look at the actual solutions as they are given in the previous section.) This very important property is encapsulated in the following two definitions and a theorem.

Definition 5.15

If a vector space U can be decomposed into two subspaces V and W such that any vector $\mathbf{u} \in U$ can be uniquely expressed as $\mathbf{u}=\mathbf{v}+\mathbf{w}$, where $\mathbf{v} \in V$ and $\mathbf{w} \in W$, we say that U is the direct sum of V and W, and write $U=V \oplus W$.

□

There is nothing deep or mysterious about this definition: it is just a notational convenience. If $[\mathbf{u}_1, \mathbf{u}_2, \ldots, \mathbf{u}_n]$ is a basis for U, then partitioning the basis $[\mathbf{u}_1, \mathbf{u}_2, \ldots, \mathbf{u}_k]$ and $[\mathbf{u}_{k+1}, \mathbf{u}_2, \ldots, \mathbf{u}_n]$ automatically decomposes U as the direct sum of span $[\mathbf{u}_1, \mathbf{u}_2, \ldots, \mathbf{u}_k]$ and span $[\mathbf{u}_{k+1}, \mathbf{u}_2, \ldots, \mathbf{u}_n]$. This is indeed the usual way of constructing direct sums. The only point to notice is that the fact that $\mathbf{u}$ must be expressed *uniquely* as $\mathbf{u}=\mathbf{v}+\mathbf{w}$ means that $V \cap W=\{\mathbf{0}\}$, otherwise we could add an element of the intersection to $\mathbf{v}$ and subtract it from $\mathbf{w}$, contradicting the uniqueness.

Definition 5.16

A subspace $E \subset \mathbb{R}^n$ is said to be *invariant* with respect to the flow e^{At}, if $\mathbf{x} \in E$ implies that $e^{At}\mathbf{x} \in E$ for all t (or for short we write $e^{At}E \subset E$).

□

Finally we put all our previous analysis together to get the following theorem. No further proof is required for the first part. The second part gives a concrete matrix representation of the ideas which we will require later.

Theorem 5.16

(a) Consider the linear system (5.10) with A real and $n \times n$. We have

$$\mathbb{R}^n = E^s \oplus E^c \oplus E^u$$

where E^S, E^C and E^U are respectively the stable, centre and unstable subspaces of the system. Furthermore E^S, E^C and E^U are each invariant with respect to the flow e^{At} of (5.10).

(b) There is a matrix B and a nonsingular matrix V such that $B=V^{-1}AV$ (so B has the same eigenvalues as A) and B takes the block form

$$B=\begin{pmatrix} P & 0 & 0 \\ 0 & Q & 0 \\ 0 & 0 & R \end{pmatrix}$$

where P, Q, and R are matrices such that P has the eigenvalues with negative real part, Q has the purely imaginary (or zero) eigenvalues, and R has the eigenvalues with positive real part. (Of course in any given case one or two of P, Q or R may be absent depending on the absence of appropriate eigenvalues of A.)

Proof

Part (a) follows from the arguments of the previous paragraphs and definitions. The proof of part (b) is an easy consequence. Choose a basis for E^S. Extend this to a basis for $E^S \oplus E^C$ and then finally to $\mathbb{R}^n = E^S \oplus E^C \oplus E^U$. Let V be the matrix whose columns are this basis and $B = V^{-1}AV$. With respect to this basis a vector $\mathbf{v}$, say in (for example) E^C, will have components only involving those columns of V corresponding to the basis of E^C. This implies that B has the structure given.

□

This theorem is all that is needed to prove the Stable Manifold Theorem, and readers wishing to hurry on to the non-linear theory may omit the rest of this section. But for those still reading, it is illuminating to explore the structure of Theorem 5.16 in more detail. In the proof we saw that (a) implies (b). The first observation is that, equally, (b) implies (a). To see this, let V be as constructed in the proof of (b). Such a choice automatically decomposes $\mathbb{R}^n$ as the direct sum of the individual spaces. Note that any vector $\mathbf{v}$, can be expressed uniquely in terms of the columns of V. The corresponding solution is $e^{Bt}\mathbf{v}$, and

$$e^{Bt} = \begin{pmatrix} e^{Pt} & 0 & 0 \\ 0 & e^{Qt} & 0 \\ 0 & 0 & e^{Rt} \end{pmatrix}.$$

If $\mathbf{v}$ is in, say, E^S, it has non-zero components only in the first entries which get multiplied by the e^{Pt}, thus establishing the invariance of the subspaces. So parts (a) and (b) are equivalent: (b) is merely a matrix representation of (a).

However as stated, we do not really get any feeling for the properties of the basis and the matrix V. We will give here an explicit construction of V in terms of the generalised eigenvectors of A, which will lead to the matrices P, Q and R having a particularly simple structure. This construction is thus a concrete proof of part (b) and hence of (a) also.

Alternative Proof of Theorem 5.16(b)

We first show that e^{At} can be decomposed in the block form similar to B, and then deduce the decomposition of A by a limit argument.

Let $\mathbf{v_1}, \ldots, \mathbf{v_n}$ be the generalised eigenvectors of A, ordered so that $\mathbf{v_1}, \ldots, \mathbf{v_j}$ correspond to eigenvalues with negative real part and $\mathbf{v_{j+1}}, \ldots, \mathbf{v_k}$ correspond to eigenvalues with zero real part. We also assume that the generalised eigenvectors corresponding to an eigenvalue are listed in increasing order of the power of $(A-\lambda I)$ following the true eigenvector from which they are generated. (We here regard two eigenvalues as 'different' if they have different true eigenvectors, even if they are numerically equal.) Let V be the matrix whose ith column is $\mathbf{v_i}$. We have then

$$e^{At}\mathbf{v_i} = e^{\lambda t}\{\mathbf{v_i} + t(A-\lambda)\mathbf{v_i} + t^2(A-\lambda)^2\mathbf{v_i} + \ldots + t^{\nu}(A-\lambda)^{\nu}\mathbf{v_i}\}$$

for some non-negative integer ν, with λ the eigenvalue corresponding to $\mathbf{v_i}$. However, as we have already observed (see the paragraph following Example 5.7), the expression in brackets is actually a linear combination of generalised eigenvectors corresponding to the same eigenvalue. So we can write

$$e^{At}\mathbf{v_i} = e^{\lambda t}\mathbf{g_i}(t)^{\mathrm{T}}V$$

where $\mathbf{g_i}: \mathbb{R} \to \mathbb{C}^n$. However only those elements of $\mathbf{g_i}$ corresponding to the same eigenvalue as $\mathbf{v_i}$ are non-zero. More specifically if $g_{i,k}(t)$ is the kth element of $\mathbf{g_i}(t)$, we have $g_{i,i}(t)=1$ for all t. Moreover, $g_{i,k}(t)=0$ for all t unless $\mathbf{v_i}$ and $\mathbf{v_k}$ correspond to the same eigenvalue. Even in this latter case, we have $g_{i,k}(0)=0$ for $k \neq i$. The functions $g_{i,k}(t)$ are actually polynomials in t. Hence, considering each column of V separately, we may write

$$e^{At}V = VH(t),$$

where H is the matrix whose ith column is $e^{\lambda}t\mathbf{g_i}(t)$. Thus $H(t)$ has the structure

$$H(t) = \begin{pmatrix} H_1(t) & 0 & 0 \\ 0 & H_2(t) & 0 \\ 0 & 0 & H_3(t) \end{pmatrix},$$

and $H(t) = V^{-1}e^{At}V$. Now we observe that $(e^{At} - I)/t \to A$ as $t \to 0$. Hence we may set $B = V^{-1}AV$, so

$$B = \begin{pmatrix} P & 0 & 0 \\ 0 & Q & 0 \\ 0 & 0 & R \end{pmatrix}$$

where $P = \lim(H_1(t) - \mathrm{I})/t$ as $t \to 0$, and similarly for Q and R. Of course, we need to verify that these limits exist. The off diagonal limits certainly exist since

$g_{i,k}(0)=0$ and $g_{i,k}$ is a polynomial. For the diagonal elements we note that $g_{i,i}(0)=1$ and hence $(e^{\lambda_i t}-1)\,g_{i,i}(t)\to\lambda_i$ as $t\to 0$.

□

This completes the concrete proof of part (b), but it is perhaps worth making a short digression to observe that we can actually deduce a lot more about P, Q and R. Firstly, the proof shows that the diagonal elements of these submatrices are the eigenvalues. Furthermore if $\mathbf{v}_i$ is not a true eigenvector, as $t\to 0$,

$$[e^{\lambda t}\{\mathbf{v}_i + t(A-\lambda)\mathbf{v}_i + t^2(A-\lambda)^2\mathbf{v}_i + \ldots + t^{\nu}(A-\lambda)^{\nu}\mathbf{v}_j\} - \mathbf{v}_i]/t$$

converges to $\lambda\mathbf{v}_i+(A-\lambda)\mathbf{v}_i=A\mathbf{v}_i=\lambda\mathbf{v}_i+\alpha\mathbf{v}_{i-1}$ (see the justification of Method 5.6). With a suitable choice of normalisation, we can make $\alpha=1$. It follows that the submatrices P, Q and R are made up of square blocks on the diagonal, each of which has λ for each diagonal element, 1 on the superdiagonal and 0 everywhere else. (Some blocks are only 1×1 with just λ on the diagonal.) Obviously there is nothing special here about A occurring in a system of differential equations. Any square matrix A is similar to a matrix with this structure, which is called the *Jordan Normal Form*.

To summarise this section, solutions have the following behaviour. If they start in E^S, they remain there for all time and approach $\mathbf{0}$ exponentially fast as $t\to\infty$. If they start in the unstable subspace they remain there for all time and they go to infinity with t. If the system is not hyperbolic, there is also a centre subspace E^C. Solutions that start in E^C stay there for all time. They may be bounded or unbounded depending on the properties of A (Theorem 5.9(c)). Finally 'most' solutions, of course, do not start in any of the subspaces. However the initial point $\mathbf{x}_0$ can be decomposed as in Definition 5.15 and the consequent motion understood as a combination of these three types.

5.5 Non-homogeneous systems

We now wish to extend these ideas to non-linear systems. However, before we are ready to do this we must briefly consider non-homogeneous linear systems. These take the form

$$\dot{\mathbf{x}} = A\mathbf{x} + \mathbf{f}(t). \tag{5.12}$$

Readers who have studied differential equations before will be aware that there are various approaches to solving (5.12). However, our interest here is the method of *variation of parameters*. Method 5.6 provides us with n-independent solutions $\mathbf{v}_1(t), \ldots, \mathbf{v}_n(t)$ for the solution $\mathbf{x}(t)$ of the system (5.10). We seek solutions to (5.12) of the form

$$\begin{aligned}\mathbf{x}(t) &= u_1(t)\mathbf{v}_1(t) + u_2(t)\mathbf{v}_2(t) + \ldots + u_n(t)\mathbf{v}_n(t)\\ &= V(t)\mathbf{u}(t),\end{aligned}$$

where $V(t)$ is the matrix whose columns are the $\mathbf{v}_i(t)$ and $\mathbf{u}(t) = [u_1(t), u_2(t), \ldots, u_n(t)]^T$. V is called a *fundamental matrix solution* of (5.10). Clearly $e^{At} = V(t)V^{-1}(0)$ and $\dot{V}(t) = AV(t)$. We can now derive a formula for solving (5.12) as follows. We search for a solution to (5.12) of the form

$$\mathbf{x}(t) = V(t)\mathbf{u}(t) \tag{5.13}$$

so

$$\begin{aligned}A\mathbf{x} + \mathbf{f}(t) &= \dot{\mathbf{x}}\\ &= \dot{V}(t)\mathbf{u}(t) + V(t)\dot{\mathbf{u}}(t)\\ &= AV(t)\mathbf{u}(t) + V(t)\dot{\mathbf{u}}(t)\\ &= A\mathbf{x}(t) + V(t)\dot{\mathbf{u}}(t) \text{ from (5.13).}\end{aligned}$$

Thus

$$\mathbf{f}(t) = V(t)\dot{\mathbf{u}}(t)$$

or

$$\dot{\mathbf{u}}(t) = V^{-1}(t)\mathbf{f}(t).$$

Integrating between 0 and t gives

$$\mathbf{u}(t) = \mathbf{u}(0) + \int_0^t V^{-1}(s)\mathbf{f}(s)\mathrm{d}s.$$

with $\mathbf{u}(0) = V^{-1}(0)\mathbf{x}(0)$. Since both the quantities in the integrand are known, this expression can, at least in principle, be used to find $\mathbf{u}(t)$ and thus $\mathbf{x}(t)$ from (5.13). Specifically, (5.13) gives

$$\mathbf{x}(t) = V(t)V^{-1}(0)\mathbf{x}(0) + V(t)\int_0^t V^{-1}(s)\mathbf{f}(s)\mathrm{d}s$$

or

$$\mathbf{x}(t) = e^{At}\mathbf{x}(0) + V(t)\int_0^t V^{-1}(s)\mathbf{f}(\mathbf{s})\mathrm{d}s. \tag{5.14}$$

Note that the first term is the solution of the homogeneous equation. What we have done so far works for any set of solutions of (5.10). Suppose, however we choose the n-independent solutions $\mathbf{v}_1(t), \mathbf{v}_2(t), \ldots, \mathbf{v}_n(t)$ to satisfy $\mathbf{v}_j(0)=\mathbf{e}_j$. In this case $V(0)=I$, $V(t)=\mathrm{e}^{At}$, and (5.14) can be reduced to the simpler form

$$\mathbf{x}(t) = \mathrm{e}^{At}\mathbf{x}(0) + \int_0^t \mathrm{e}^{A(t-s)}\mathbf{f}(s)\mathrm{d}s, \tag{5.15}$$

since $V^{-1}(s)=\mathrm{e}^{-As}$. Note that (5.15) does not actually involve the matrix V: this integral is an explicit solution of (5.12).

Example 5.17

Consider the forced harmonic oscillator $\ddot{x} + x = g(t)$. By setting $x_1=x$, $x_2=\dot{x}$, This can be written as

$$\begin{aligned}\dot{x}_1 &= -x_2\\ \dot{x}_2 &= x_1 + g(t),\end{aligned}$$

i.e. in the form of (5.12) with

$$A = \begin{pmatrix} 0 & -1 \\ 1 & 0 \end{pmatrix} \text{ and } \mathbf{f}(t) = \begin{pmatrix} 0 \\ g(t) \end{pmatrix}$$

In this case

$$\mathrm{e}^{At} = \begin{pmatrix} \cos t & -\sin t \\ \sin t & \cos t \end{pmatrix}$$

and hence

$$\mathrm{e}^{-At} = \begin{pmatrix} \cos t & \sin t \\ -\sin t & \cos t \end{pmatrix}$$

Using (5.15)

$$\begin{aligned}\mathbf{x}(t) &= \mathrm{e}^{At}\mathbf{x}(0) + \begin{pmatrix} \cos t & -\sin t \\ \sin t & \cos t \end{pmatrix} \int_0^t \begin{pmatrix} \cos s & \sin s \\ -\sin s & \cos s \end{pmatrix} \begin{pmatrix} 0 \\ g(s) \end{pmatrix} \mathrm{d}s \\ &= \mathrm{e}^{At}\mathbf{x}(0) + \begin{pmatrix} \cos t & -\sin t \\ \sin t & \cos t \end{pmatrix} \int_0^t \begin{pmatrix} \sin s \times g(s) \\ \cos s \times g(s) \end{pmatrix} \mathrm{d}s.\end{aligned}$$

Hence

$$x(t) = x_1(t) = x(0)\cos t + \dot{x}(0)\sin t + \int_0^t g(s)\sin(s-t)\mathrm{d}s.$$

□

Solutions like (5.14) and (5.15) will be used later when discussing stability properties of equilibrium solutions of non-linear systems of equations.

5.6 Non-linear systems

In this section we shall indicate some of the main notions and important theorems concerning the local existence of solutions of non-linear systems of differential equations and the local behaviour of the system near an equilibrium point. Since the proofs can be very technical we shall concentrate more on understanding the ideas and meaning of the theorems rather than the details of proof. For full technical details one may consult Perko (1991).

We consider *autonomous systems* of ordinary differential equations

$$\dot{\mathbf{x}} = \mathbf{f}(\mathbf{x}) \tag{5.16}$$

as opposed to the most general case $\dot{\mathbf{x}}=\mathbf{f}(\mathbf{x}, t)$. This is actually without loss of generality: the system $\dot{\mathbf{x}}=\mathbf{f}(\mathbf{x}, t)$ can be written in autonomous form by introducing an extra variable: set $u=t$ and $\dot{u}=1$. Then with $\mathbf{y}=(\mathbf{x}^{\mathrm{T}}: u)^{\mathrm{T}}$ and $\mathbf{g}(\mathbf{y})=[\mathbf{f}^{\mathrm{T}}(\mathbf{x}, u): 1]^{\mathrm{T}}$ we have $\dot{\mathbf{y}}=\mathbf{g}(\mathbf{y})$. Many neural models are in any case naturally autonomous.

In general, (5.16) will have a solution provided $\mathbf{f}$ is continuous (Perko, 1991, p. 6), but continuity is not sufficient to guarantee uniqueness (compare Theorem 5.4). Moreover unlike linear systems, it is possible (even for continuous $\mathbf{f}$) that the solution may become unbounded in finite time. In other words the solution may only exist on some time interval $(\alpha, \beta)\subset\mathbb{R}$. We need theorems to cover all these possibilities.

The fundamental existence and uniqueness theorem requires the Fréchet derivative. The reader should consult the definition of this (Definition 4.8) and the explanatory remarks following. To indicate the function being differentiated here we will write $D\mathbf{f}$ for the derivative of $\mathbf{f}$ and recall that in these finite dimensional spaces $D\mathbf{f}$ is given by the $n\times n$ Jacobian matrix, i.e.

$$D\mathbf{f} = \left(\frac{\partial f_i}{\partial x_j}\right).$$

Example 5.18

Let $\mathbf{f}(\mathbf{x})=[f_1(x, y), f_2(x, y)]^{\mathrm{T}}=(2x-3y^2, -y+6xy)^{\mathrm{T}}$ where $\mathbf{f}$: $\mathbb{R}^2\rightarrow\mathbb{R}^2$. Then

$$\mathbf{Df}(x,y)=\begin{pmatrix}\dfrac{\partial f_1}{\partial x} & \dfrac{\partial f_1}{\partial y}\\ \dfrac{\partial f_2}{\partial x} & \dfrac{\partial f_2}{\partial y}\end{pmatrix}$$

$$=\begin{pmatrix}2 & -6y\\ 6y & -1+6x\end{pmatrix}.$$

So in particular at $x=1$, $y=-1$, for instance,

$$\mathbf{Df}(1,-1)=\begin{pmatrix}2 & 6\\ -6 & 5\end{pmatrix}$$

□

From now on we will assume that $\mathbf{f}\colon \mathbb{R}^n \to \mathbb{R}^n$ is *continuously differentiable.* (i.e. that $\mathbf{Df}(x)$ is a continuous function of $\mathbf{x}$ in some open set $E\subset\mathbb{R}^n$. More precisely, we use the notation $L(\mathbb{R}^n)$ (do not confuse this with L_p spaces) for the vector space of all linear operators from $\mathbb{R}^n\to\mathbb{R}^n$, which in fact we can identify with the n^2 dimensional space of $n\times n$ matrices, since each linear operator is uniquely represented (with respect to the standard basis) by a matrix. Note that in fact for a fixed function $\mathbf{f}$ and with $D\mathbf{f}$ considered as a function of $\mathbf{x}$, $D\mathbf{f}\colon \mathbb{R}^n\to L(\mathbb{R}^n)$. If $\mathbb{R}^n$ has the usual Euclidean norm, $L(\mathbb{R}^n)$ is a normed vector space equipped with the corresponding matrix norm. Continuity then means that for each $\mathbf{x}\in\mathbb{R}^n$, and for each $\varepsilon>0$, there exists δ such that

$$\|\mathbf{x}-\mathbf{y}\|_2<\delta \Rightarrow \|D\mathbf{f}(\mathbf{x})-D\mathbf{f}(\mathbf{y})\|_2<\varepsilon.$$

Definition 5.19

Let $E\subset\mathbb{R}^n$ and suppose that $\mathbf{f}\colon \mathbb{R}^n\to\mathbb{R}^n$ is differentiable on E. We say that $\mathbf{f}\in C^1(E)$ if $D\mathbf{f}\colon \mathbb{R}^n\to L(\mathbb{R}^n)$ is continuous on E.

□

$C^1(E)$ is itself a vector space (a subspace of the space of all continuous functions on E), since if $\mathbf{f}$ and $\mathbf{g}$ are continuously differentiable so is $\mathbf{f}+t\mathbf{g}$ for any $t\in\mathbb{R}$: indeed the derivative is just $D\mathbf{f}+tD\mathbf{g}$. Now let us state the fundamental existence theorem.

Theorem 5.20

Let $E\subset\mathbb{R}^n$ be open, and $\mathbf{x}_0\in E$. Suppose further that $\mathbf{f}\in C^1(E)$. Then there exists $a>0$ such that the initial value problem

$$\dot{\mathbf{x}} = \mathbf{f}(\mathbf{x}) \tag{5.17a}$$

with

$$x\,(0) = x_0 \tag{5.17b}$$

has a unique solution $\mathbf{x}(t)$ for t on the interval $[-a, a]$.

Proof

We need to prove that $\mathbf{x}(t)$ is differentiable on the interval $[-a, a]$; that $\mathbf{x}(t) \in E$, and that it satisfies (5.17). The proof depends on the Contraction Mapping Theorem (Theorem 1.51). However a complication arises in that the space of differentiable vectors $\mathbf{x}(t)$ is not analytically complete. This space is of course just $(C^1[-\mathbf{a}, \mathbf{a}])^n$, the Cartesian product of n copies of $C^1[-a, a]$. We need instead to work in $(C\,[-a, a])^n$, i.e. n copies of the space of functions continuous on $[-a, a]$ equipped with the uniform norm $\|\mathbf{x}\|_\infty$ defined as the maximum over i of $\|x_i\|_\infty$ where x_i is the ith element function of the vector function $\mathbf{x}$. This space is complete, by Corollary 3.24. (Deal with each co-ordinate function separately.) But (5.17) is not defined on $(C\,[-a, a])^n$: the equation requires $\mathbf{x}(t)$ to be differentiable. So how do we proceed? Our strategy will be as follows: (a) We rewrite (5.17) as an integral equation. The definition of this can be extended to $(\mathrm{C}\{-a, a\})^n$. (b) We then use the Contraction Mapping Theorem to show that there is a solution to the integral equation in $C(E)$. Such a solution is called a *weak solution* of (5.17). (c) Finally we show that this solution is actually differentiable and therefore solves (5.17).

(a) If we integrate (5.17) with respect to t, we get for $t \in [-a, a]$ where $a \in \mathbb{R}$,

$$\mathbf{x}(t) = \mathbf{x}_0 + \int_0^t \mathbf{f}[\mathbf{x}(s)]\mathrm{d}s. \tag{5.18}$$

Observe that this $\mathbf{x}(t)$ has the correct initial value. However the operator on the right-hand side is in fact defined for any $\mathbf{x} \in (C\,[-a, a])^n$ provided $\mathbf{x}(s) \in E$. To ensure this holds, let $G \subset E$ be closed and contain a neighbourhood of $\mathbf{x}_0$. Then clearly the set $\mathcal{F}$ of vector functions $\mathbf{x}(t)$ such that $\mathbf{x}(t) \in G$ for $t \in [-a, a]$ is a closed subset of $(C\,[-a, a])^n$. Moreover if a is chosen sufficiently small and

$$\mathbf{y}(t) = \mathbf{x}_0 + \int_0^t \mathbf{f}[\mathbf{x}(s)]\mathrm{d}s. \tag{5.19}$$

then $\mathbf{y}(t) \in G$ for any $\mathbf{x}(t) \in G$ since **f** is continuous and thus bounded. In other words the operator (5.19) maps $\mathcal{F}$ to itself.

(b) In order to apply the Contraction Mapping Theorem, we need to show that (5.19) defines a contractive mapping. Let

$$\mathbf{y}(t) = \mathbf{x}_0 + \int_0^t \mathbf{f}[\mathbf{x}(s)]\mathrm{d}s$$

and

$$\mathbf{v}(t) = \mathbf{x}_0 + \int_0^t \mathbf{f}[\mathbf{u}(s)]\mathrm{d}s.$$

Then

$$\begin{aligned} \|\mathbf{y} - \mathbf{v}\|_\infty &\le a\|\mathbf{f}[\mathbf{x}(\cdot)] - \mathbf{f}[\mathbf{u}(\cdot)]\|_\infty \\ &\le aK\|\mathbf{x}(\cdot) - \mathbf{u}(\cdot)\|_\infty \text{ for some real } K \text{ (depending on } \mathbf{f}\text{)}. \end{aligned}$$

(The second inequality here is because $\mathbf{f} \in C^1(G)$ and hence $\|D\mathbf{f}\|_\infty$ is bounded on G. The definition of the Fréchet derivative then establishes the existence of K.) It follows that provided a is sufficiently small, (5.19) does indeed define a contractive mapping from $\mathcal{F}$ to itself. So the Contraction Mapping Theorem tells us that there is a fixed point in G, i.e. there exists a vector function **x** such that $\mathbf{x}(t) \in G$ for $t \in [-a, a]$ and which satisfies (5.18).

(c) Finally we observe need to show that $\mathbf{x}(t)$ satisfying (5.18) is differentiable. To do this we simply calculate $[\mathbf{x}(t+\delta t)-\mathbf{x}(t)]/\delta t$ from (5.18). In fact this is just the integrand of the right-hand side integrated from t to $t+\delta t$ and then the result divided by δt. The Intermediate Value Theorem (Theorem 1.30) shows that the limit as $\delta t \to 0$ exists, and indeed is equal to $\mathbf{f}[x(t)]$ as required by (5.17). This completes the proof.

□

Actually Theorem 5.20 is not quite strong enough for us. It only shows that there is some interval $[-a, a]$ on which there is a unique solution. However since equation (5.16) is autonomous, we can look again for a solution starting at $t=a$ and $\mathbf{x}_1=\mathbf{x}(a)$. Theorem 5.20 does not really depend on starting at $t=0$. In (5.18) and (5.19), just replace $\mathbf{x}_0$ by $\mathbf{x}_1$ and the lower limit on the integral by a. Then we can extend the solution forwards in time by a further distance b. This solution must coincide with the initial one on the intersection of $[-a, a]$ and $[a-b, a+b]$ in view of the uniqueness of any solution starting in this interval. Equally, we can extend our original solution backward in time. Of course this does not necessarily mean we that can extend the solution to the whole of $\mathbb{R}$: the intervals on which we get a solution may decrease in size. However it does imply the following.

Corollary 5.21

Under the conditions of Theorem 5.20, there is a maximal open interval of existence (α, β) say, with possibly $\alpha=\infty$ and/or $\beta=\infty$, of the solution of (5.17). Moreover the solution is unique in the sense that there cannot be two distinct solutions of (5.16) which take the same value $\mathbf{x}(t_0)$ at any $t_0 \in (\alpha, \beta)$.

□

Example 5.22

The equation $\dot{x}=x^2$ with $x_0=1$ has the solution $x(t)=(1-t)^{-1}$ on the maximal interval $(-\infty, 1)$.

□

This property permits us to define the flow of non-linear systems. We will then later be able to connect the stability of solutions of (5.16) with that of a corresponding linear system. Previously we defined the matrix function e^{At} to be the flow of the linear system (5.10). If $\Phi_t(\mathbf{x})=e^{At}\mathbf{x}$, we note the following properties for all $s, t \in \mathbb{R}$.

Properties 5.23

(a) $\Phi_0(\mathbf{x})=\mathbf{x}$,
(b) $\Phi_s[\Phi_t(\mathbf{x})]=\Phi_{s+t}(\mathbf{x})$
(c) In particular, $\Phi_{-t}[\Phi t(\mathbf{x})] = \Phi t[\Phi_{-t}(\mathbf{x})] = \mathbf{x}$.

□

The following definition extends these properties to solutions of (5.16), except that (b) will only hold for s, t, $-t$ and $(s+t)$ in the maximal interval of Corollary 5.21.

Definition 5.24

Under the conditions of Theorem 5.20, let $\Phi(t, \mathbf{x}_0)$ be the solution of (5.17), defined on its maximal interval of existence, $I(\mathbf{x}_0)$ say. Then for any $t \in I(\mathbf{x}_0)$, the mapping Φ_t: $E \rightarrow E$ defined by $\Phi_t(\mathbf{x})=\Phi(t, \mathbf{x})$ is called the *flow* of the differential equation (5.16). It is also sometimes referred to as the flow of the vector field $\mathbf{f}(\mathbf{x})$.

□

Property 5.24 (a) is immediate: $\Phi_t(\mathbf{x})=\Phi(t, \mathbf{x})$ and $\Phi(0, \mathbf{x})=\mathbf{x}$ from the definition of $\Phi(t, \mathbf{x})$ as the solution starting at $\mathbf{x}$. Property 5.24(b) is just the uniqueness part of the argument of the paragraph before Corollary 5.21. It says that if we follow the solution starting at $t=0$ to arrive at $\mathbf{x}(t)$, and then start again from this point, we just get the same thing as if we continued on with the original solution. The third property is of course an immediate consequence of the first two.

We need to get a geometrical feel for the notion of a flow and the related idea of a trajectory. If we think of $\mathbf{x}_0$ as varying throughout some set $K\subset E$, then the flow Φ_t: $K\rightarrow E$ can be thought of as the motion of all points in the set K. For example if the differential equation (5.16) actually described the motion of a fluid, then the flow describes the motion of the entire fluid. Focussing now on a single point $\mathbf{x}_0$, the flow defines a single curve or *trajectory* through $\mathbf{x}_0$: in terms of a fluid it describes the actual motion of an individual particle.

Now in the previous section we found that the stable, unstable and centre subspaces of the linear system (5.10) are invariant under the flow $\Phi_t=e^{At}$. We seek now to establish the corresponding result for non-linear systems. Our approach will in fact be to linearize the system and apply our previous result. This process is very similar to the linearization of the generalised delta rule in the previous chapter: we approximate the non-linear function $\mathbf{f}$ by means of its Fréchet derivative.

Definition 5.25

A point $\mathbf{x}_0\in \mathbb{R}^n$ is said to be an *equilibrium point* or *critical point* of (5.16) if and only if $\mathbf{f}(\mathbf{x}_0)=\mathbf{0}$.

□

An equilibrium point is therefore a solution of (5.16) which is time independent. The trajectory through $\mathbf{x}_0$ is simply the constant $\mathbf{x}_0$. In other words $\Phi_t(\mathbf{x}_0)=\mathbf{x}_0$, i.e. $\mathbf{x}_0$ is a fixed point of the flow. It is also called a *zero*, *critical point* or *singular point* of the vector field $\mathbf{f}$.

The *linearization* of (5.16) at an equilibrium point $\mathbf{x}_0$ is the linear system

$$\dot{\mathbf{x}} = D\mathbf{f}(\mathbf{x}_0)\mathbf{x}. \tag{5.20}$$

Definition 5.26

The equilibrium point $\mathbf{x}_0$ is said to be *hyperbolic* if the system (5.20) is hyperbolic, i.e. if none of the eigenvalues of $D\mathbf{f}(\mathbf{x}_0)$ have zero real part. (Compare Definition 5.14.)

□

As in the linear case the study of non-hyperbolic equilibria is much more complicated, and will be deferred for the present. The hyperbolic equilibria are further classified as follows.

Definition 5.27

The hyperbolic equilibrium point $\mathbf{x}_0$ is said to be a *sink* if all the eigenvalues of $D\mathbf{f}(\mathbf{x}_0)$ have negative real part, a *source* if they all have positive real part, and a *saddle* if some eigenvalues have negative real part and others positive real part.

□

These terms are suggestive of the behaviour of the trajectories near the hyperbolic equilibria: that they are accurate descriptions is the substance of the Stable Manifold Theorem. This theorem will make precise the connection between the behaviour of the non-linear system (5.16) at a hyperbolic equilibrium, and that of the stable and unstable subspaces of the linearization (5.20). We will illustrate first by an example. Note that from now on we will assume that the maximal interval (α, β) of Corollary 5.21 is in fact $(-\infty, \infty)$. In actual fact, any system (5.16) can be converted to this interval by a suitable (non-linear) transformation of t: for brevity we omit the details. This assumption means that we can focus on the behaviour of trajectories as $t \to \infty$ and $t \to -\infty$, rather than having to worry about asymptotic behaviour of trajectories for finite t.

Now suppose there is a set S such that for all $\mathbf{c} \in S$, $t(\mathbf{c}) \to \mathbf{x}_0$ as $t \to \infty$. Then this set S will correspond to the stable subspace E^S of a linear system. Similarly the unstable subspace E^U will correspond to a set U such that for all $\mathbf{c} \in U$, $\Phi_t(\mathbf{c}) \to \mathbf{x}_0$ as $t \to -\infty$. We will illustrate this first with an example (Perko, 1990).

Example 5.28

Consider the system

$$\dot{x}_1 = -x_1$$
$$\dot{x}_2 = -x_2 + x_1^2$$
$$\dot{x}_3 = x_3 + x_1^2.$$

The only equilibrium point is $\mathbf{x}_0=\mathbf{0}$.

$$D\mathbf{f}(\mathbf{0}) = \begin{pmatrix} -1 & 0 & 0 \\ 0 & -1 & 0 \\ 0 & 0 & 1 \end{pmatrix}.$$

Thus for the linearized system (5.20) we see that E^S is the x_1, x_2-plane and E^U is the x_3 axis. However in this case the non-linear system can be easily solved. From the first equation we get $x_1(t)=c_1e^{-t}$, and this can be substituted into the other two equations, which then yield $x_2(t)=c_2e^{-t}+c_1^2\,(e^{-t}-e^{-2t})$ and $x_3(t)=c_3e^t + \frac{1}{3}c_1^2\,(e^t-e^{-2t})$, where $\mathbf{x}(0)=\mathbf{c}=(c_1, c_2, c_3)^T$. Thus $\Phi_t(\mathbf{c})\to\mathbf{x}_0=\mathbf{0}$ as $t\to\infty$ if and only if $c_3+\frac{1}{3}c_1^2=0$. Let S be the set of all vectors $\mathbf{c}$ which satisfy this condition. S is a surface in $\mathbb{R}^3$, and the vector $\nabla\varphi$, where $\varphi(\mathbf{c})=c_3+\frac{1}{3}c_1^2$, is normal to the surface. (Compare (4.6) and Example 4.5.) $\nabla\varphi(\mathbf{c})=(\frac{2}{3}c_1, 0, 1)^T$, whence $\nabla\varphi(\mathbf{0})=(0, 0, 1)^T$. Moreover S contains the point $\mathbf{0}$. It follows that the surface S is tangential to E^S (the x_1, x_2-plane) at $\mathbf{0}$. On the other hand $\Phi_t(\mathbf{c})\to\mathbf{x}_0=\mathbf{0}$ as $t\to-\infty$ if and only if $c_1=c_2=0$. The set U of all vectors $\mathbf{c}$ which satisfy these conditions is in fact precisely the x_3 axis, i.e. E^U.

□

In the previous chapter we described surfaces like S in this example, and suggested that they had in a sense a dimension, in this case 2. But we need to be rather more precise here. The term 'surface' is actually too closely linked to our idea of two-dimensionality. In the example, U is not a surface, it is a line. Or to look at it another way, a two-dimensional surface in $\mathbb{R}^3$ is defined by one equation: a line requires two. To avoid confusing our terminology, we introduce a different nomenclature to cover 'surfaces' of varying dimensions. However the basic approach remains the same. We said that in $\mathbb{R}^3$, a surface in the terms of the previous chapter was two dimensional because it locally 'looked like' its tangent space which was isomorphic to $\mathbb{R}^2$. Using this isomorphism, the tangent space induces a local co-ordinate system onto the surface. Now we give a simple formula for such a co-ordinate system. Let us take S from the example as an illustration. S is the set of points satisfying $0=c_3+\frac{1}{3}c_1^2$ where $\mathbf{c}\in\mathbb{R}^3$. Any point on the surface can be represented with position vector $(c_1, c_2, -\frac{1}{3}c_1^2)^T$. Since this vector depends only on c_1 and c_2, it defines a mapping

$\mathbf{h}$: $\mathbb{R}^2 \to \mathbb{R}^3$, namely $\mathbf{h}(c_1, c_2)^T = (c_1, c_2, -\frac{1}{3}c_1^2)^T$ Conversely, suppose $(c_1, c_2, c_3)^T$ is a point on S, then c_3 must satisfy the defining condition, so the point can be mapped uniquely onto $\mathbb{R}^2$ by $\mathbf{h}^{-1}(c_1, c_2, c_3)^T = (c_1, c_2)^T$. Both $\mathbf{h}$ and its inverse are differentiable functions.

Definition 5.29

If P and Q are open sets in $\mathbb{R}^n$, a differentiable function $\mathbf{h}{:}P \to Q$ with a differentiable inverse $\mathbf{h}^{-1}$: $Q \to P$ is called a *diffeomorphism*. If a diffeomorphism exist between P and Q, they are said to be *diffeomorphic*.

□

We have just shown that S is diffeomorphic to $\mathbb{R}^2$. Now what is the local co-ordinate system induced on S by h? Firstly consider the origin in $\mathbb{R}^2$, and make a small movement $\delta\mathbf{c}$ away from it. The corresponding change in the surface S is given by $D\mathbf{h}(\mathbf{0})\delta\mathbf{c}$. In particular, we can consider changes in the two co-ordinate vectors in $\mathbb{R}^2$, say $\delta t\ \mathbf{e}_1$ and $\delta t\ \mathbf{e}_2$ for some small real number δt. These two vectors will be mapped to $\delta t\ D\mathbf{h}(\mathbf{0})\mathbf{e}_1$ and $\delta t\ D\mathbf{h}(\mathbf{0})\mathbf{e}_2$ respectively. *The image vectors will be independent provided* $D\mathbf{h}(\mathbf{0})$ *has rank 2*. Assuming this is the case, a point very close to $\mathbf{h}(\mathbf{0})$ (actually $\mathbf{0}$ itself for this S) in the surface can be expressed in terms of the two vectors $D\mathbf{h}(\mathbf{0})\mathbf{e}_1$ and $D\mathbf{h}(\mathbf{0})\mathbf{e}_2$, say $\delta t_1\ D\mathbf{h}(\mathbf{0})\mathbf{e}_1 + \delta t_2\ D\mathbf{h}(\mathbf{0})\mathbf{e}_2$ and the inverse image of this point is to a first-order approximation $\delta t_1\mathbf{e}_1 + \delta t_2\mathbf{e}_2$. In fact

$$D\mathbf{h}(\mathbf{c}) = \begin{pmatrix} 1 & 0 \\ 0 & 1 \\ -2/3 c_1 & 0 \end{pmatrix}, \tag{5.21}$$

which is of rank 2 at every point $\mathbf{c}$. Since $Dh(\mathbf{0})$ is 3×2 it does not actually have an inverse, but the Moore–Penrose pseudoinverse (or equivalently the singular value decomposition) can be used to give an explicit expression for the inverse mapping, which of course is the Fréchet derivative of h^{-1}. It should be clear from this argument that the fact that $Dh(\mathbf{0})$ has full rank actually guarantees that the inverse mapping is locally differentiable and that the defining mapping h is therefore at least locally a diffeomorphism. That this is actually the case in general is a result known as the Implicit Function Theorem. We will omit a formal proof since for our purposes the rank condition will be sufficient.

Next observe that actually there is nothing special about the origin in the argument of the previous paragraph: it was used only to simplify the notation. At any point $\mathbf{c} \in \mathbb{R}^2$, we can consider small changes in the directions of the standard basis vectors, and hence define a local co-ordinate system on S based at the point $\mathbf{h}(\mathbf{c})$, provided only that $D\mathbf{h}(\mathbf{c})$ has full rank 2.

The great advantage of this way of looking at dimension is that it works for sets of any dimension $k \leq n$ in $\mathbb{R}^n$. For instance the set U of Example 5.28 is defined by the mapping $\mathbf{h}(c)=(0, 0, c)^{\mathrm{T}}$. Therefore

$$D\mathbf{h}(c) = \begin{pmatrix} 0 \\ 0 \\ 1 \end{pmatrix}.$$

This obviously has rank 1, indicating that U is one-dimensional.

In other words we can, roughly speaking, think of the local dimension as the rank of $D\mathbf{h}(\mathbf{c})$. However to avoid technical complications we insist that in fact the co-ordinate function $\mathbf{h}$ is set up as a mapping from $\mathbb{R}^k$ and that $D\mathbf{h}(\mathbf{c})$ has full rank k. This simply avoids redundancy. We could have defined U as the image of $\mathbb{R}^2$ with the mapping $\mathbf{h}(c_1, c_2)=(0, 0, c)^{\mathrm{T}}$ but this would not be a very sensible choice and is best excluded in our definitions.

Now we need to move from a purely local definition of dimension to something that makes sense on the macroscopic scale. To do this we need to look at an open set in $\mathbb{R}^k$.

Definition 5.30

Suppose there is a 1–1 mapping $\mathbf{h}$: $W \rightarrow V$, where W is an open subset of $\mathbb{R}^k$ and V is an open subset of $\mathbb{R}^n$. Suppose further that $D\mathbf{h}$ has rank k at every point of W. We will call $\mathbf{h}(W)$, i.e. the image of W, a *k-dimensional patch* or *chart*.

□

Usually we take V to be $\mathbb{R}^n$ itself, but the introduction of V gives us a bit more flexibility in the definition of $\mathbf{h}$. Although the rank condition will guarantee that $\mathbf{h}$ is 1–1 locally, we want to avoid the situation where points far apart in W are mapped to the same point in V, so we insist that h is 1–1 throughout W. The term 'patch' in this context is actually derived from computational geometry, which is the application of differential geometry to computer graphics and computer aided design. Writers on 'pure' differential geometry mostly use the term chart, indicating a local map!

In the example we have been looking at, S and U were definable as a single patch. But this is not always possible. For example we cannot define a suitable $\mathbf{h}$ over the whole of the sphere $x_1^2+x_2^2+x_3^2=1$. A little thought should convince you that no simple minded attempt to do this will work. The fact that it is actually impossible is a theorem from differential topology known as the Hairy Ball Theorem: we will not prove it. You should note however that the openness of W is important. We can define a co-ordinate system for the sphere (e.g. latitude and longitude) but this system necessarily has at least one singularity (one of the poles). The fact that W must be open outlaws nasty joins. We may now state the key definition.

Definition 5.31

Suppose a set $M \subset \mathbb{R}^n$ can be expressed as the (possibly infinite but countable) union of k-dimensional charts. Then M is said to be a *k-dimensional differentiable* (or *smooth*) *manifold.* Where the meaning is clear from the context, we shorten the terminology and say simply that M is a k-manifold. The set of all charts for the manifold is called its *atlas.*

□

As indicated above, the nomenclature 'manifold' is to be preferred to 'surface', but geometrical surfaces are of course manifolds. The sphere is a two manifold which can be constructed using two patches: the details are left for the reader! This definition is actually all we need, but it does require a little thought to convince ourselves that manifolds are well defined. Two objections present themselves. (a) Is the dimension of a patch actually dependent on the choice of $\mathbf{h}$? (b) Could something nasty happen in passing from one patch to an overlapping one? The first question may be disposed of as follows. Suppose $\mathbf{h}$ and $\mathbf{k}$ map subsets of $\mathbb{R}^h$ and $\mathbb{R}^k$ respectively onto intersecting patches of the same manifold M. At any point $\mathbf{x}$ in the subset of $\mathbb{R}^h$, let $\mathbf{y}=\mathbf{h}(\mathbf{x})$. Then $[D\mathbf{k}]^{\#}(\mathbf{y})D\mathbf{h}(\mathbf{x})$, where # denotes the pseudoinverse, defines an isomorphism of $\mathbb{R}^h$ and $\mathbb{R}^k$. Thus $h=k$. A similar approach works for the second question. This time consider $\mathbf{h}$ and $\mathbf{k}$ mapping subsets of $\mathbb{R}^k$ respectively onto intersecting patches of M. Then where the patches intersect, $[D\mathbf{k}]^{\#}(\mathbf{y})D\mathbf{h}(\mathbf{x})$ is the derivative of $\mathbf{h} \circ \mathbf{k}^{-1}$ establishing that this composite function is differentiable. So there is a smooth mapping from one co-ordinate system to an adjacent one where they overlap. Manifolds and their dimensions are well defined.

We note that any k-dimensional subspace W of $\mathbb{R}^n$ is *a fortiori* a k-manifold. To see this, let $\{\mathbf{w}_1, \mathbf{w}_2, \ldots, \mathbf{w}_k\}$ span W and set $\mathbf{h}(\mathbf{x})=x_1\mathbf{w}_1+x_2\mathbf{w}_2+\ldots+x_k\mathbf{w}_k$ for $\mathbf{x} \in \mathbb{R}^k$. $D\mathbf{h}(\mathbf{x})$ is then the constant matrix whose jth column is $\mathbf{w}_j$. Thus $D\mathbf{h}(\mathbf{x})$ has rank k.

Definition 5.32

Let M and N be smooth manifolds. We say that M and N are *tangent* at a point $\mathbf{x}$ if $\mathbf{x} \in M$ and $\mathbf{x} \in N$ (i.e. they meet at $\mathbf{x}$) and $D\mathbf{h}(\mathbf{u})$ spans the same subspace as $D\mathbf{k}(\mathbf{v})$ where $\mathbf{h}$ and $\mathbf{k}$ are co-ordinate functions for M and N respectively, with $\mathbf{h}(\mathbf{u})=\mathbf{k}(\mathbf{v})=\mathbf{x}$. The columns of $D\mathbf{h}(\mathbf{u})$ and $D\mathbf{k}(\mathbf{v})$ each provide a basis for the *tangent space* at $\mathbf{x}$. This tangent space is therefore a k-dimensional subspace of $\mathbb{R}^n$.

□

Note that tangent manifolds must have the same dimension. From (5.21) we see that for the manifold S of Example 5.28, S is tangent to the x_1, x_2-plane at $\mathbf{0}$, agreeing with our informal geometrical explanation in the example. As in this example, by choosing $\mathbf{h}$ and $\mathbf{k}$ suitably in the definition, we can of course make $D\mathbf{h}(\mathbf{u})=D\mathbf{k}(\mathbf{v})$, so that the manifolds share geometrically the same tangent space. Note that we insist that $D\mathbf{h}(\mathbf{u})$ spans the *same* subspace of $\mathbb{R}^n$ as $D\mathbf{k}(\mathbf{v})$, not just an isomorphic one. The latter condition would say no more than that they have the same dimension!

At last we are in a position to state the key theorem about the behaviour of non-linear systems near hyperbolic equilibria (a brief discussion of the non-hyperbolic case will be given at the end of this section). As in the discussion of manifolds that we have just completed, it is convenient to assume that the point of interest is the origin. If not a linear change of variable in $\mathbf{x}$ will move it there. The proof is somewhat long and technical. Readers not interested in a completely rigorous development may wish to skip it, and to keep the level of detail within reasonable bounds we will assume that those who do wish to struggle through it have some facility in real analysis.

Theorem 5.33 (Stable Manifold Theorem)

Let E be an open subset of $\mathbb{R}^n$ containing the origin, let $\mathbf{f} \in C^1(E)$ and let Φ_t be the flow of the system (5.16). Suppose further that $\mathbf{f}(\mathbf{0})=\mathbf{0}$, and that $D\mathbf{f}(\mathbf{0})$ has k eigenvalues with negative real part and $n-k$ eigenvalues with positive real part. Then there exists a k-dimensional differentiable manifold S tangent to E^S at $\mathbf{0}$, such that for all $t \geq 0$, $\Phi_t(S) \subset S$, and for all $\mathbf{x_0} \in S$, $\Phi_t(\mathbf{x_0}) \rightarrow \mathbf{0}$ as $t \rightarrow \infty$. Furthermore there exists an $n-k$-dimensional differentiable manifold U tangent to E^U at $\mathbf{0}$, such that for all $t \leq 0$, $\Phi_t(U) \subset U$, and for all $\mathbf{x_0} \in U$, $\Phi_t(\mathbf{x_0}) \rightarrow \mathbf{0}$ as $t \rightarrow -\infty$.

Proof

We prove here the existence of the stable manifold. The unstable manifold is obtained in exactly the same way, but reversing the sign of t. The proof of this theorem is actually a little delicate and involves several stages. These are as follows: (a) express the problem in a 'natural' basis so as to decouple the stable and unstable subspaces of the linearized system; (b) write the problem as an integral equation similar to that of the non-homogeneous systems in Section 5.5; (c) obtain a local solution to this integral equation using the Contraction Mapping Theorem as in Theorem 5.20; (d) use the solution to define a chart for the stable manifold. Let us now work through these stages in order.

(a) Let $A = D\mathbf{f}(\mathbf{0})$. Since A is hyperbolic, there is no centre subspace. By Theorem 5.16(b) We can chose a basis whose columns form a matrix V such that $V^{-1}AV$ has the structure

$$\begin{pmatrix} P & 0 \\ 0 & R \end{pmatrix}. \tag{5.22}$$

Here P is $k \times k$ and has the k eigenvalues of A with negative real part, and R has those $n-k$ with positive real part. Since this choice of basis is simply an invertible matrix transformation (i.e. a linear diffeomorphism of $\mathbb{R}^n$ onto itself) it will not effect the analytical properties of the system (5.16). Thus we may assume without loss of generality that $A = D\mathbf{f}(\mathbf{0})$ has the decomposed structure (5.22).

Let

$$U(t) = \begin{pmatrix} e^{Pt} & 0 \\ & 0 \; 0 \end{pmatrix}$$

and

$$V(t) = \begin{pmatrix} 0 & 0 \\ 0 & e^{Rt} \end{pmatrix}.$$

Note that $e^{At} = U(t) + V(t)$. Also the terms of $U(t)$ decay at worst at a rate proportional $p(t)e^{\mu t}$, where p is a polynomial and $0 > \mu > \mathrm{Re}(\lambda)$, for each eigenvalue λ of P, as $t \to \infty$. A similar observation holds for $V(t)$ as $t \to -\infty$. Thus we can find positive real numbers K, α and σ such that $\mu < -\alpha < -\sigma < 0$, $\|U(t)\|_\infty \leq K\,e^{-(\alpha+\sigma)t}$ for all $t \geq 0$, and $\|V(t)\|_\infty \leq K\,e^{-\sigma t}$ for all $t \leq 0$.

(b) To get our solution to (5.16) we use the method of variation of parameters as in Section 5.5. Specifically, we write (5.16) as

$$\dot{\mathbf{x}} = A\mathbf{x} + \mathbf{g}(\mathbf{x}), \tag{5.23}$$

where $\mathbf{g} \in C^1(E)$, $\mathbf{g}(\mathbf{0}) = \mathbf{0}$ and $D\mathbf{g}(\mathbf{0}) = \mathbf{0}$. The difference between this equation and (5.12) is that $\mathbf{g}$ here is a function of $\mathbf{x}$ rather than t. This means that we cannot get an explicit solution like (5.14) or (5.15): instead we get an integral equation. A further complication is that we have to deal with the unstable components as well, so we cannot just integrate backwards from infinity. But in the same way as in Section 5.5 we got (5.15), we can derive the integral equation

$$\mathbf{x}(t) = U(t)\mathbf{a} + \int_0^t U(t-s)\mathbf{g}[\mathbf{x}(s)]\mathrm{d}s - \int_t^\infty V(t-s)\mathbf{g}[\mathbf{x}(s)]\mathrm{d}s. \tag{5.24}$$

Note the two integral terms which serve as the indefinite integrals of the stable and unstable terms respectively. The vector $\mathbf{a}$ is a convenient parameter for the system: a suitable choice of $\mathbf{a}$ will give a particular required solution $\mathbf{x}(0) = \mathbf{x}_0$.

(c) Any continuous solution $\mathbf{x}(t)$ of the integral equation (5.24) will give a solution of (5.23) and hence of (5.16). To establish the existence of a solution, we define a mapping F by

$$[F(\mathbf{x})](t) = U(t)\mathbf{a} + \int_0^t U(t-s)\mathbf{g}[\mathbf{x}(s)]\mathrm{d}s - \int_t^\infty V(t-s)\mathbf{g}[\mathbf{x}(s)]\mathrm{d}s.$$

Since $\mathbf{g}$ is Fréchet differentiable and $D\mathbf{g}(\mathbf{0}) = \mathbf{0}$, there exists for any $\varepsilon > 0$, a real number $\delta > 0$ such that for any vectors $\mathbf{x}$, $\mathbf{y}$ with $\|\mathbf{x}\|_\infty, \|\mathbf{y}\|_\infty \le \delta$, $\|\mathbf{g}(\mathbf{x}) - \mathbf{g}(\mathbf{y})\|_\infty \le \varepsilon\|\mathbf{x} - \mathbf{y}\|_\infty$. Now for each ε, let us define M_ε to be the set of continuous vector valued functions $\mathbf{x}(t)$ which satisfy $\|\mathbf{x}(t)\|_\infty \le \delta\, \mathrm{e}^{-\alpha t}$ for all t. For such a function we have, because of the bounds on $U(t)$ and $V(t)$ from part (a) of the proof,

$$\|[F(\mathbf{x})](t)\|_\infty \le \|\mathbf{a}\|_\infty\, \mathrm{e}^{-(\sigma+\alpha)t} + \int_0^t K\, \mathrm{e}^{-(\sigma+\alpha)(t-s)}\varepsilon\delta\, \mathrm{e}^{-\alpha s}\mathrm{d}s + \int_t^\infty K\mathrm{e}^{-\sigma(t-s)}\varepsilon\delta\mathrm{e}^{-\alpha s}\mathrm{d}s. \tag{5.25}$$

Evaluating the integrals and recalling $\alpha > \sigma > 0$, we obtain the bound

$$\|[F(\mathbf{x})](t)\|_\infty \le \delta\, \mathrm{e}^{-\alpha t}\left(\frac{\|\mathbf{a}\|_\infty}{\delta} + \frac{\varepsilon K}{\sigma} + \frac{\varepsilon K}{(\alpha - \sigma)}\right).$$

This needs to be interpreted with care, since, of course, δ depends on ε. Nevertheless, we see that by choosing first ε and then $\mathbf{a}$ sufficiently small, we can ensure that F maps M_ε into itself. We now define the following metric on M_ε:

$$d(\mathbf{x}, \mathbf{y}) = \sup_{0 \le t < \infty} \|\mathbf{x}(t) - \mathbf{y}(t)\|_\infty e^{-\alpha t}$$

Convergence in this metric is uniform convergence on any finite interval $[a, b]$ with $a \ge 0$. Since $C[a, b]$ with $\| \|_\infty$ is complete, it follows that (M_ε, d) is a complete metric space. We now show that the mapping (5.25) is contractive in this metric space. Specifically, let $d = d(\mathbf{x}, \mathbf{y})$ for some particular $\mathbf{x}, \mathbf{y}$. Then

$$F(\mathbf{x})(t) - F(\mathbf{y})(t) = \int_0^t U(t-s)\{\mathbf{g}[\mathbf{x}(s)] - \mathbf{g}[\mathbf{y}(s)]\}\mathrm{d}s$$

$$-\int_t^\infty V(t-s)\{\mathbf{g}[\mathbf{x}(s)] - \mathbf{g}[\mathbf{y}(s)]\}\mathrm{d}s$$

whence

$$\|F(\mathbf{x})(\mathbf{t}) - F(\mathbf{y})(t)\|_\infty \le \int_0^t \|U(t-s)\|_\infty \|\mathbf{g}[\mathbf{x}(s)] - \mathbf{g}[\mathbf{y}(s)]\|_\infty \mathrm{d}s$$

$$-\int_t^\infty \|V(t-s)\|_\infty \|\mathbf{g}[\mathbf{x}(s)] - \mathbf{g}[\mathbf{y}(s)]\|_\infty \mathrm{d}s$$

$$\le \varepsilon \int_0^t K e^{-(\sigma+\alpha)(t-s)} \|\mathbf{x}(s) - \mathbf{y}(s)\|_\infty \mathrm{d}s - \varepsilon \int_t^\infty K e^{-\sigma(t-s)} \|\mathbf{x}(s) - \mathbf{y}(s)\|_\infty \mathrm{d}s.$$

$$\le \varepsilon \int_0^t K e^{-(\sigma+\alpha(t-s)} d e^{-\alpha s} \mathrm{d}s - \varepsilon \int_t^\infty K e^{-\sigma(t-s)} d e^{-\alpha s} \mathrm{d}s$$

$\le M d e^{-\alpha t}$ where the positive constant $M < 1$, for ε sufficiently small.

Thus F is contractive and (5.24) has a continuous solution by Theorem 1.51. But the integral equation (5.24) also shows that any continuous solution must be differentiable and hence a solution of (5.23).

(d) Having shown that the integral equation has a solution for each sufficiently small $\mathbf{a}$, it remains to demonstrate that these solutions form the desired manifold. Let us suppose that we have a solution for $\|\mathbf{a}\|_\infty < H$.

At $t = 0$, we have

$$\mathbf{x}(0) = U(0)\mathbf{a} - \int_0^\infty V(-s)\mathbf{g}[\mathbf{x}(s)]\mathrm{d}s. \tag{5.26}$$

Now, U has non-zero elements only in the first k rows and columns, so in fact only the first k elements of $\mathbf{a}$ affect the solution: the remaining $n-k$ elements can be chosen to be zero. Similarly the matrix V in the integral only has non-zero elements in the last $n-k$ rows and columns, so in fact only contributes to the last $n-k$ elements of $\mathbf{x}(0)$.

Indeed for $j=1, \ldots, n$, and for $\max(a_1, a_2, \ldots, a_k)<H$ we may define the functions

$$\psi_j(a_1, a_2, \ldots, a_k) = x_j(0) \tag{5.27}$$

where $\mathbf{x}(t)$ is the solution corresponding to $\mathbf{a}$. For $j=1, \ldots, k$, we have, therefore,

$$\psi_j(a_1, a_2, \ldots, a_k) = a_j \tag{5.28}$$

and for $j=k+1, \ldots, n$, $\psi_j(a_1, a_2, \ldots, a_k)$ is the jth element of $\mathbf{x}(0)$ minus the value of the integral on the right-hand side of (5.26). Hence (5.27) defines a mapping from the open set $\max(a_1, a_2, \ldots, a_k)<H$ to $\mathbb{R}^n$. This mapping will be the chart for the local stable manifold. We need to show that (i) it is differentiable, (ii) the derivative has rank k and (iii) that the manifold is tangent to E^S (which in this case is just $\mathbb{R}^k$) at $a_1=a_2=\ldots=a_k=0$.

To establish (i), we define $\mathbf{x_0}(t)=U(t)\,\mathbf{a}$ (i.e. a stable solution of the linearized system). Then obviously $\mathbf{x_0}$ depends differentiably on $\mathbf{a}$. Use $\mathbf{x_0}$ to start an iteration with (5.25) as in the Contraction Mapping Theorem. Since $\mathbf{g}$ is differentiable, it follows that the iterates $\mathbf{x_m}$ are differentiable with respect to $\mathbf{a}$ for each m. But the Contraction Mapping Theorem tells us that $\mathbf{x_m} \to \mathbf{x_a}$, the solution of (5.23) corresponding to $\mathbf{a}$, *uniformly* over all $\mathbf{x_a}$ in a suitable closed subset of M_ε. Indeed examination of the proof of the Contraction Mapping Theorem shows that $\mathbf{x_a}$ is the sum of a uniformly and absolutely convergent series of differentiable terms $\mathbf{x_m}-\mathbf{x_{m-1}}$. Thus $\mathbf{x_a}$ is differentiable with respect to $\mathbf{a}$.

Part (ii) is easy. From (5.28), for $j=1, \ldots, k$,

$$\frac{\partial \psi_j}{\partial a_i} = 1 \text{ if } i=j \text{ and } 0 \text{ otherwise.}$$

In other words the first k columns of the derivative matrix will just be the identity matrix, and thus the derivative matrix $(D_a(\mathbf{x_a}))$ will have rank k. We have established the existence of a manifold S of solutions all of which remain in S (because a solution starting from $\mathbf{x}(t)$ is in M_ϵ if $\mathbf{x}(0)$ is) and tend to zero as $t \to \infty$.

To prove (iii) we need to show that the partial derivatives for $j=k+1, \ldots, n$ vanish when $a_1=a_2=\ldots=a_k=0$, i.e. for the equilibrium solution $\mathbf{x}(t)=\mathbf{0}$ for all t. Let $\mathbf{v_j}^{\mathrm{T}}(t)$ be the jth row of $V(t)$, and $\mathbf{x_a}(t)$ the solution corresponding to $\mathbf{a}$. Then for $j=k+1, \ldots, n$,

$$\psi_j(a_1, a_2, \ldots, a_k) = -\int_0^\infty \mathbf{v}_j^{\mathrm{T}}(-s)\mathbf{g}[\mathbf{x}_\mathbf{a}(s)]\mathrm{d}s.$$

The integral is uniformly convergent and all the terms of the integrand are differentiable with respect to the a_i, so the result follows by differentiating with respect to a_i under the integral sign and recalling that $D\mathbf{g}(\mathbf{0})=\mathbf{0}$.

The existence of the unstable manifold U is established in a similar way.

Clearly any particular solution not in either S or U will near $\mathbf{0}$ have components tangent to the stable and unstable subspaces of the linearized system, so the solution will flow out along the unstable manifold U. Thus any solution not completely in S will be unstable: for brevity we will omit the details of this argument.

□

Corollary 5.34

Let E be an open subset of $\mathbb{R}^n$ containing the origin, let $\mathbf{f} \in C^1(E)$ and let Φ_t be the flow of the system (5.16). Suppose further that $\mathbf{f}(\mathbf{0})=\mathbf{0}$.

(a) If all the eigenvalues of $D\mathbf{f}(\mathbf{0})$ have negative real part the equilibrium solution $\mathbf{x}(t)=\mathbf{0}$ is asymptotically stable.
(b) If at least one eigenvalue of $D\mathbf{f}(\mathbf{0})$ has positive real part the equilibrium solution $\mathbf{x}(t)=\mathbf{0}$ is unstable.

Proof

(a) In this case, the stable manifold is a neighbourhood of the origin in $\mathbb{R}^n$. Thus any solution near $\mathbf{0}$ decays exponentially.
(b) Simply choose a solution in the unstable manifold.

□

Note that, unlike the linear case, we cannot conclude from part (b) that the solutions tend to infinity: only that they move away from the origin. All we have said so far is local to the origin: the manifolds S and U are called the *local* stable and unstable manifolds. By construction as in the proof of Theorem 5.33 they are disjoint. We can define global manifolds by letting S flow backward and U flow forward in time.

Definition 5.35

Let Φ_t be the flow of the system (5.16). The *global stable* and *unstable manifolds* are defined respectively as

$$W^s(\mathbf{0}) = \bigcup_{\tau \le 0} \Phi_t(S)$$

and

$$W^u(\mathbf{0}) = \bigcup_{\tau \ge 0} \Phi_t(U).$$

□

It is not necessarily true that $W^s(\mathbf{0})$ and $W^U(\mathbf{0})$ are disjoint. A trajectory starting out near zero in U may flow away from **0** and then curve back and approach **0** again along the local stable manifold S. On the other hand it might head in to another equilibrium solution, or go off to infinity or behave in a variety of more complicated ways. The branch of mathematics known as *chaos theory* is dedicated to the study of trajectories. The asymptotic behaviour can be incredibly intricate, resulting in aptly named strange attractors (Baker and Gollub, 1990; Falconer, 1990).

The Stable Manifold Theorem only characterises the local behaviour of hyperbolic equilibria. It is possible to define a centre manifold, but it is not very useful. Perko (1991) gives the following two examples, which show that the stability of the equilibrium cannot be determined from the linearized equation.

Examples 5.36

(a) $\dot{x}_1 = x_2 - x_1(x_1^2 + x_2^2)$

$\dot{x}_2 = -x_1 - x_2(x_1^2 + x_2^2)$

Then

$$D\mathbf{f}(\mathbf{0}) = \begin{pmatrix} 0 & 1 \\ -1 & 0 \end{pmatrix}.$$

The eigenvalues are $\pm$i. Trajectories of the linear system are circles: thus they are stable, but not asymptotically so. On the other hand a calculation shows that the solutions of the non-linear system satisfy $x_1^2 + x_2^2 = c/(1 + 2ct)$ where $c = x_1^2(0) + \mathbf{x}\ x_2^2(0)$. These tend to **0**: they are asymptotically stable.

(b) $\dot{x}_1 = x_2 + x_1(x_1^2 + x_2^2)$

$\dot{x}_2 = -\ x_1 - x_2(x_1^2 + x_2^2).$

Again

$$D\mathbf{f}(\mathbf{0}) = \begin{pmatrix} 0 & 1 \\ -1 & 0 \end{pmatrix}.$$

but for this system $x_1^2 + x_2^2 = c/(1-2ct)$. Every solution with $c \neq 0$ approaches infinity in finite time. Thus the fixed point $\mathbf{0}$ is unstable.

□

This method of local linearization is often called *Lyapunov's first method.* It has the advantage of giving a simple explanation of the behaviour of a non-linear system near hyperbolic equilibria. But, as we have seen, it cannot cope with non-hyperbolic equilibria, and moreover does not give global results. In order to overcome these restrictions, we now proceed to a different approach known as *Liapunov's second method.* We will then apply the method to a class of continuous time neural models.

5.7 Lyapunov functions

The theory of the previous section showed that a hyperbolic equilibrium point $\mathbf{x_0}$ of (5.16) is either asymptotically stable or unstable. In other words, (5.16) can only have an equilibrium which is stable but not asymptotically so if $D\mathbf{f}(\mathbf{x_0})$ has a zero or purely imaginary eigenvalue. The analysis of non-hyperbolic equilibria is often very delicate.

Let E be an open set in $\mathbb{R}^n$ and let $\mathbf{x_0}$ be the only equilibrium point of (5.16) in E. Suppose $\mathbf{f} \in C^1(E)$. Moreover let V: $E \rightarrow \mathbb{R}$, $V \in C^1(E)$, be any differentiable function. Consider a solution $\mathbf{x}(t) \subset E$. Then by the Chain Rule (Theorem 4.1)

$$\frac{\mathrm{d}V[\mathbf{x}(t)]}{\mathrm{d}t} = \nabla V(\mathbf{x})^{\mathrm{T}} \frac{\mathrm{d}\mathbf{x}}{\mathrm{d}t} = [\nabla V(\mathbf{x})]^{\mathrm{T}} \mathbf{f}(\mathbf{x}) \tag{5.29}$$

from (5.16). If this quantity is less than zero everywhere in E, then $V(\mathbf{x})$ decreases along the solution $\mathbf{x}(t)$. If, in addition there is a real constant V_0 such that $V(\mathbf{x_0}) = V_0$, and $V(\mathbf{x}) > V_0$, for $\mathbf{x} \neq \mathbf{x_0}$, then V is said to be a *Liapunov function* for the system (5.16). (We could of course assert that $V_0 = 0$ without loss of generality: just subtract it from V. However in complicated examples we may only be able to show that $\mathbf{x_0}$ is a minimum of V. It is not necessary to evaluate V_0 explicitly.)

Useful Liapunov functions are often rather hard to find, but if we *can* get one, it can solve the stability problem. Observe that if $\dot{V} \leq 0$ in E then $\mathbf{x_0}$ is a stable equilibrium, since the trajectory of the solution cannot escape from the contour defined by $V(\mathbf{x})=V[\mathbf{x}(0)]$ and this contour can be made arbitrarily close to $\mathbf{x}_0$ by choosing $\mathbf{x}(0)$ close to $\mathbf{x}_0$. Furthermore, suppose that in fact $\dot{V}<0$ in E for $\mathbf{x}\neq\mathbf{x}_0$. (We must of course have $\dot{V}=0$ at $\mathbf{x}_0$ since it is an equilibrium point which means by definition that $\mathbf{f}(\mathbf{x}_0)=\mathbf{0}$.) Choose $\mathbf{x}_1\neq\mathbf{x}_0$ such that $V(\mathbf{x}_1)<V[\mathbf{x}(0)]$. The points between the contours $V(\mathbf{x})=V[\mathbf{x}(0)]$ and $V(\mathbf{x})=V(\mathbf{x}_1)$, together with the contours themselves, form a closed bounded set in $\mathbb{R}^n$. Thus there exists δ such that $\dot{V}=\nabla V(\mathbf{x})^{\mathrm{T}}\,\mathbf{f}(x)<\delta$ on this set. It follows that in finite time $V(\mathbf{x})<V(\mathbf{x}_1)$, i.e. the solution moves inside the contour $V(\mathbf{x})=V(\mathbf{x}_1)$. Since this applies for any $\mathbf{x}_1\neq\mathbf{x}_0$ (i.e. for contours arbitrarily close $\mathbf{x}_0$), the only possibility is that $\mathbf{x}_0$ is an asymptotically stable equilibrium.

Conversely if $\dot{V}>0$ in E, then a similar argument shows that a solution will move outside any contour near $\mathbf{x}_0$ and thus away from $\mathbf{x}_0$. The equilibrium is in this case unstable.

If we do not know the existence of an equilibrium point $\mathbf{x}_0$, the function V might still be useful to show that the solutions are bounded. But note that $\dot{V}\leq 0$ in E is not in itself sufficient to guarantee the existence of an equilibrium point, even if we also know that V is bounded below. This is because a stationary point of V or just a point at which ∇V is orthogonal to f will also make $\dot{V}=0$, as is clear from (5.29). A more careful analysis, using basically the same ideas, can deal with limit cycles and other types of invariant set.

Before going on to apply this to a neural model, we give some simple examples.

Examples 5.37

(a) $\dot{x}_1=-x_2{}^3$

$\dot{x}_2=x_1{}^3$

Then $\mathbf{0}$ is a non-hyperbolic equilibrium point. Let $V(\mathbf{x})=x_1{}^4+x_2{}^4$. Note that $V(\mathbf{0})=0$ and $V(\mathbf{x})>0$ otherwise. So V may serve as a Liapunov function. Now using (5.29)

$$\begin{aligned}\dot{V}&=4x_1^3(-x_2^3)+4x_2^3(x_1^3)\\&=0.\end{aligned}$$

Thus $\mathbf{0}$ is a stable equilibrium point. Note that since in fact $\dot{V}=0$, V is constant along each trajectory, or in other words the trajectories are just the contours of V. Thus the equilibrium point is not asymptotically stable.

$$\dot{x}_1 = -x_1$$
$$\dot{x}_2 = -x_2 + x_1^2$$
$$\dot{x}_3 = x_3 + x_1^2.$$

Thus **0** is an equilibrium point.

$$D\mathbf{f}(\mathbf{0}) = \begin{pmatrix} 0 & -2 & 0 \\ 1 & 0 & 0 \\ 0 & 0 & 0 \end{pmatrix}.$$

The eigenvalues are $0, \pm 2i$. Therefore **0** is a non-hyperbolic equilibrium solution. To construct a suitable Liapunov function consider $V(\mathbf{x}) = c_1 x_1^2 + c_2 x_2^2 + c_3 x_3^2$. Using (5.29) we get

$$\dot{V} = 2(c_1 - c_2 + c_3)x_1 x_2 x_3 + (-4c_1 + 2c_2)x_1 x_2.$$

Hence if $c_2 = 2c_1$, and $c_3 = c_1 > 0$, we have $V(\mathbf{x}) > 0$ for $\mathbf{x} \neq \mathbf{0}$ and $\dot{V} = 0$. Again we conclude that the equilibrium point is stable but not asymptotically stable.
(c) Consider the second order equation $\ddot{x} + f(x) = 0$ where $xf(x) > 0$ for $x \neq 0$. The equation describes the motion of a particle under a restoring force of $-f(x)$ which always has direction opposite to x. This system can be rewritten as

$$\dot{x}_1 = x_2$$
$$\dot{x}_2 = f(x_1),$$

where $x_1 = x$. The total energy of the system can be written

$$V(\mathbf{x}) = \tfrac{1}{2}x_2^2 + \int_0^{x_1} f(s)\mathrm{d}s.$$

The first term is the kinetic energy, and the second the potential energy.

$$\dot{V} = f(x_1)x_2 + x_2[-f(x_1)]$$
$$= 0.$$

Once again we conclude that the equilibrium point **0** is stable but not asymptotically stable. Physically, this is because the energy remains constant. Where appropriate, the use of an energy functional is a very natural and common way to construct Liapunov functions. Sometimes general Lyapunov functions are described as an 'energy', although this can be confusing if it has no physical interpretation.

□

In the next section, we look at a stability theorem for a class of neural networks.

5.8 The Cohen–Grossberg theorem

Many neural networks are best thought of as non-linear dynamical systems. General stability theorems have been developed describing the dynamics of classes of autoassociative and heteroassociative continuous feedback networks. An important example is the Cohen–Grossberg Theorem which is used for proving stability of non-adaptive autoassociators (Cohen and Grossberg, 1983). This reference also contains a discussion of the biological significance of such networks in pattern formation including a consideration of the plausibility of the conditions set out below.

Non-adaptive autoassociators are networks that operate in continuous time with feedback. No learning or adaptation is permitted: the connection weights are assumed constant. The important questions are (a) whether the network has asymptotically stable equilibria, and (b) if so, which (if any) will it go to? The following differential system of equations describes a continuous time generalised Hopfield net.

$$\dot{x}_i = \alpha_i(x_i)\left\{\beta_i(x_i) - \sum_{j=1}^{n} m_{ij}s_j(x_j)\right\}. \tag{5.30}$$

Here x_i describes the *activation* of the *i*th neuron. (This activation is stored in the unit. Unlike a perceptron neuron, a Hopfield unit is time dependent and has storage capacity.) The function s_i is the output activation function for the neuron, i.e. the output is $s_i(x_i)$. The matrix $M=(m_{ij})$ defines inhibitory links from the output of the *j*th neuron to the input of the *i*th. For a network of Hopfield type, the links are bi-directional, and often $m_{ij}=m_{ji}$, i.e. M is symmetric. The activation of the neuron after a small time interval is a function of the current activation and the input: in (5.30) a semilinear form is assumed which is the term in braces. Note that the function β_i can include a constant term indicating a fixed input to the unit. The rate of change of the activation is given in the general case by a weight function α_i (which in general though rarely in practice can depend on x_i) times the former quantity, leading to the differential equation (5.30) for the activation of the *i*th neuron. (The function α_i is in strict mathematical terms redundant as it could be incorporated into the β_i and s_i, but it is included since often we want to make particular choices for β_i and s_i and α_i allows us to include a separate weighting term.)

As for our perceptron models, it is convenient to write the system in matrix form. Let $\mathbf{x}=(x_1, x_2, \ldots, x_n)^T$ be the state vector and $\mathbf{s}(\mathbf{x})$ and $\mathbf{b}(\mathbf{x})$ be the vectors $[s_1(x_1), \ldots, s_n(x_n)]^T$ and $[\beta_1(x_1), \ldots, \beta_n(x_n)]^T$ respectively. It is convenient to encode the α_i as the diagonal matrix $A(\mathbf{x})$ where $a_{ii}=\alpha_i(x_i)$ and $a_{ij}=0$ if $i \neq j$. We shall assume that the $s_i(x_i)$ are differentiable. Then we can write (5.30) as

$$\dot{\mathbf{x}} = A(\mathbf{x})[\mathbf{b}(\mathbf{x}) - M\mathbf{s}(\mathbf{x})]. \tag{5.31}$$

Making the sensible assumption that the weighting terms α_i satisfy $\alpha_i(x_i) > 0$ for all x_i, we observe that any equilibrium point of (5.31) must satisfy

$$M\mathbf{s}(\mathbf{x}) - \mathbf{b}(\mathbf{x}) = \mathbf{0}. \tag{5.32}$$

In general, there is no reason to suppose that such a system of equations has a solution for $\mathbf{x}$: some analysis might be required to show this. But for the moment, let us assume that there are equilibrium points, and try and write down a suitable candidate for a Liapunov function. To do this, we integrate the ith row of (5.32) with respect to s_i, and sum over the rows, yielding the candidate function

$$V(\mathbf{x}) = \tfrac{1}{2}\mathbf{s}^T(\mathbf{x})M\mathbf{s}(\mathbf{x}) - \sum_{i=1}^{n}\int_0^{x_i} s_i'(y_i)\beta_i(y_i)\mathrm{d}y_i. \tag{5.33}$$

Here $'$ denotes differentiation. Let $S(\mathbf{x})=D\mathbf{s}(\mathbf{x})$ and note that S is diagonal: in fact $S(\mathbf{x})=\mathrm{diag}\,[s_i'(y_i)]$. Thus

$$\nabla V(\mathbf{x}) = S(\mathbf{x})[M\mathbf{s}(\mathbf{x}) - \mathbf{b}(\mathbf{x})]. \tag{5.34}$$

Any equilibrium point of (5.31) is a stationary point of (5.33), and provided the $s_i'(y_i)$ are never zero the converse is also true. Moreover (5.29) shows that

$$\dot{V} = -[\mathbf{b}(\mathbf{x}) - M\mathbf{s}(\mathbf{x})]^T S^T(\mathbf{x})A(\mathbf{x})[\mathbf{b}(\mathbf{x}) - M\mathbf{s}(\mathbf{x})]. \tag{5.35}$$

Recall $\mathbf{A}(\mathbf{x})$ is diagonal and positive definite. Provided the functions $s_i(x_i)$ are non-decreasing, we see that the diagonal elements of S, namely $s_i'(x_i)$, are non-negative and we may deduce that $\dot{V} \leq 0$. Thus any equilibrium points are stable. Indeed if $s_i'(x_i) > 0$, we have $\dot{V} < 0$ except at an equilibrium point, so any such points are asymptotically stable.

This argument is the essential feature of the Cohen–Grossberg theorem. We have not shown that there *are* any equilibrium points. Moreover, if we want a *global* convergence result, we need to show that the activation vector **x** cannot wander off to infinity. Let us state the desired result formally.

Theorem 5.38 (The Cohen–Grossberg Theorem)

Consider the dynamical system (5.30), (5.31) and suppose that it has at least one equilibrium point. Suppose further that the following conditions are satisfied

(i) M is symmetric, and $m_{ij} \geq 0$ for all i, j.
(ii) For each i, $\alpha_i(x)$ is continuous for $x \geq 0$, and $\beta_i(x)$ is continuous for $x > 0$.
(iii) For each i, $\alpha_i(x) > 0$ for $x > 0$, and $s_i(x) \geq 0$ for $x \in (-\infty, \infty)$.
(iv) For each i, $s_i(x)$ is differentiable, and $s_i'(x) \geq 0$ for $x \geq 0$.
(v) For each i, $\beta_i(x) - m_{ii}s_i(x) < 0$ for x sufficiently large.
(vi) For each i, one of the following two conditions holds: either

$$\lim_{x \downarrow 0} \beta_i(x) = \infty \text{ (By } x \downarrow 0 \text{ we mean } x \to 0 \text{ only through positive values)} \tag{5.36}$$

or

$$\lim_{x \downarrow 0} \beta_i(x) < \infty \text{ and } \int_0^y \frac{dx}{\alpha_i(x)} = \infty \text{ for all } y > 0. \tag{5.37}$$

Then there exists at least one equilibrium point of (5.30), (5.35) is a Lyapunov function for the system (5.31) and the system is globally stable.

Proof

It remains to show that whatever the initial data (provided of course $x_i(0) > 0$ for each i), the system (5.31) generates positive bounded trajectories. Note that

$$\beta_i(x_i) - \sum_{j=1}^{n} m_{ij}s_j(x_j) \leq \beta_i(x_i) - m_{ii}s_i(x_i) < 0 \text{ in view of (a) and (c).}$$

Since also $\alpha_i(x) > 0$, it follows from (5.30) x_i is large and positive. It follows that x_i cannot go to ∞, so it must be bounded above. Thus there exist $l_i \in \mathbb{R}$ such that $x_i < l_i$ for all t.

Similarly, since the x_i are bounded above, condition (5.36) implies that $\dot{x}_i < 0$ when $x_i \downarrow 0$, since the right-hand side of (5.30) is negative for small positive x_i.

Alternatively if (5.37) holds, let us suppose there exists T such that $x_i(T)=0$. Then

$$-\infty = \int_{x_i(0)}^{0} \frac{dx}{\alpha_i(x)}$$

$$= \int_0^T \beta_i(x_i) - \sum_{j=1}^{n} m_{ij}s_j(x_j)\, dt.$$

But this is impossible, since the integrand is bounded.

□

The original statement of the theorem had the integral in (5.37) infinite for *some* $y>0$. Note that if this holds, (b) and (c) together imply our version so the two are equivalent. We have changed it since in our opinion at least, (5.37) is more natural. It is the behaviour of α_i at zero which is really under discussion here! In the paper, the authors also discuss the question of the existence and nature of equilibrium points and other invariant sets. Kosko (1988) extends the result to the case in which the interconnection weights m_{ij} are allowed to vary and also considers other generalizations of the basic result.

6 Non-linear separation and approximation theory

6.1 Non-linear separation by neural networks

In Chapter 2 (see Section 2.2 and Fig. 2.3) we saw that a linear perceptron can separate some sets of points in $\mathbb{R}^n$, but not others. For example, in two dimensions, we can construct a perceptron that will correctly compute the logical AND and OR functions, but there is no perceptron that will compute the XOR function. A natural question arising from this is to consider what functions a given non-linear network can classify. In this chapter, we are going to discuss this question for the multilayer perceptron, and much more briefly for radial basis networks.

Actually a simple argument shows that a multilayer perceptron with two hidden layers, as shown in Fig. 4.1, and with threshold activation, can separate any finite sets of points in $\mathbb{R}^n$. Let A and B be two finite sets in $\mathbb{R}^n$. In Fig. 6.1,

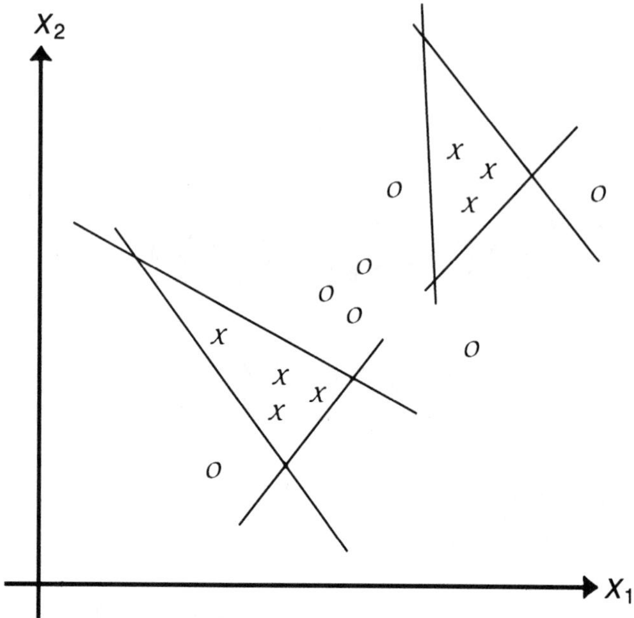

Fig. 6.1

A might consist of the points labelled X and B the points labelled O. Suppose we wish the network to produce output 1 for points in A and 0 for points in B. Clearly it is possible to construct a finite set of polyhedra $P_1 \dots P_k$ such that

$$A \subset Q = \cup P_j \text{ and } B \cap P_j = \varphi \text{ for } j = 1,\dots,k. \tag{6.1}$$

Each P_j consists of a finite intersection of half spaces. The first layer of our network computes these halfspaces. P_j can thus be obtained by a network computing the logical AND function (which is linearly separable). This network constitutes the second layer. The union to include A can then be obtained by a network computing the OR function (also linearly separable) forming the third layer of the network.

This approach is natural, geometrical and simple. The number of units in the second hidden layer is the number of polyhedra required, and the total number of units in the first layer is the number of edges. The network does not have to be completely connected. Consider a unit in the second hidden layer corresponding to a particular polyhedron. Only the units in the first hidden layer which correspond to the edges of that polyhedron need to be connected to the former unit. The construction is local in the sense that nearby points with the same classification can be included in the same polygon as in Fig. 6.1.

However, if we are prepared to abandon this local structure, we shall find later that it is actually possible to make do with only one hidden layer. Moreover the method we have just described applies only to discrete logical functions. We would like our networks to be able to cope with continuous problems such as the control problems involved in balancing a rocket or catching a ball. A different viewpoint proves more fruitful.

As before, we regard our inputs as vectors in $\mathbb{R}^n$. The output $\mathbf{y}$ of the network is a vector in $\mathbb{R}^m$ where usually $m << n$. In many cases $m=1$. In fact to avoid the complication of vector valued function spaces it is usual to make this assumption. The case of $m>1$ can be dealt with by considering each co-ordinate function separately. So we consider a network computing a function g: $\mathbb{R}^n \rightarrow \mathbb{R}$ which we regard as an *approximation* to some other function f: $\mathbb{R}^n \rightarrow \mathbb{R}$. The point classification problem discussed above can be put into this context by choosing $m=1$ and f to be the characteristic function of the set Q in (6.1) (i.e. $f(\mathbf{x})=1$ if $\mathbf{x} \in Q$ and 0 otherwise). This viewpoint means that neural networks can be discussed using methods derived from approximation theory. The point sets A and B are conveniently regarded as interpolation or sample points for approximation of the function f. (Sometimes networks are actually constructed this way: radial basis function networks are of this type (Broomhead and Lowe, 1988; Mason and Parks, 1992). As constructed here the function f is not continuous: however since the point sets A and B are finite, it is clearly possible to overcome this with some smoothing process, creating a continuous function f which takes the value 1 on A and 0 on B.

The question of what a neural net can compute may thus be restated in approximation theoretic terms. The following definition is convenient.

Definition 6.1

Let V be a normed vector space with norm $\| \ \|$, and W a subset. Suppose that for every $\mathbf{v} \in V$ and for every $\varepsilon > 0$, there exists $\mathbf{w} \in W$ such that $\|\mathbf{v}-\mathbf{w}\| < \varepsilon$. Then W is said to be *dense* in V.

□

At first sight this definition may look a little opaque, but it is actually a very simple idea. It merely requires that for each $\mathbf{v} \in V$ we can find $\mathbf{w} \in W$ which approximates it with arbitrarily small error. (Note that we do not require that W be a subspace.)

Armed with this definition, we can rephrase our key question as follows. Specifically we wish to know if our set W of possible functions g, corresponding to our particular class of network, is dense in some suitable function space V which includes our target function f. The set W is defined by the architecture of the network (including the activation functions). It is precisely the set of functions g which the network can compute exactly. Normally in this chapter V will be $C(S)$, the space of continuous functions defined on some suitable subset of $S \subset \mathbb{R}^n$. $C(S)$ is equipped with the uniform norm $\| \, \|_\infty$. For simplicity of exposition, we will assume that S is closed and bounded. Then any continuous function on S must achieve its maximum value, and we may therefore define

$$\| f \|_\infty = \max_{\mathbf{x} \in S} | f(\mathbf{x}) | \, .$$

(If we do not assume S is closed and bounded, we would be forced to replace the maximum in this definition by the supremum, leading to various analytic complications.) Note that we are now working in function spaces, so we cannot employ the discrete forms of the norms which have sufficed up to now.

Although, as we have already seen, the use of the two norm is most convenient for practical calculation, it is natural to use the infinity norm here. It tells us what the maximum error of our approximation will be. Note that if μ is the Lebesgue measure on $\mathbb{R}^n$ (see Definitions 1.22 and 1.29(b)) then

$$\| f \|_2 = \left(\int f(\mathbf{x})^2 \, \mathrm{d}\mathbf{x} \right)^{1/2} \leq \| f \|_\infty [\mu(S)]^{1/2}.$$

(It is perhaps worth remarking here that the notation ‘d**x**’ for the Lebesgue integral is actually a little confusing. We might expect d**x** to mean $\mathrm{d}x_1\mathbf{e}_1 + \mathrm{d}x_2\mathbf{e}_2 + \ldots + \mathrm{d}x_n\mathbf{e}_n$, but as is indicated by Definitions 1.22 and 1.23 it is actually a generalised *volume* element. Loosely, we may think of d**x** as meaning $\mathrm{d}x_1 \times \mathrm{d}x_2 \times \ldots \mathrm{d}x_n$.)

So if W is dense in $C(S)$ with respect to the uniform norm it will also be dense with respect to the two norm. Similarly, in the case of the classification problem (6.1), the discrete sum of squares of the error on the sets A and B can be made arbitrarily small.

In view of the difficulty of dealing with non-differentiable and discontinuous functions, it is usual to use a smooth activation function, instead of a threshold, for the units. (Recall that the activation function is the function that relates the sum of the inputs to a given unit to the output.) Note that the activation function $\sigma: \mathbb{R} \to \mathbb{R}$. Various restrictions need to be put on σ to make a practical network, but we will introduce these as required.

The results to be discussed in the main part of this chapter refer to the case of an multilayer perceptron with a *single* hidden layer of k units. The form of the network is shown in Fig. 6.2. The weight vector relating the inputs to the jth hidden neuron is denoted $\mathbf{w_j}$. Thus for a given input $\mathbf{x}$, the input to this unit is $\mathbf{w_j}^T\mathbf{x}$. We assume that each of the hidden units has identical activation function σ, but that a 'threshold like' shift of the argument by a real scalar c_j is permitted. So the output from the jth hidden unit is $\sigma(\mathbf{w_j}^T\mathbf{x}+c_j)$. Functions of this form are called *ridge functions*. The name derives from the fact that they are obviously constant on the hyperplane $\mathbf{w_j}^T\mathbf{x}=$constant. In two dimensions, this means that the contours of the function form straight ridges. An immediate consequence of this observation is the fact that no non-trivial continuous ridge function can be in $L_1(\mathbb{R}^n)$ if $n>1$. To see this, choose $\mathbf{x_0}$ for which $\sigma(\mathbf{w_j}^T\mathbf{x_0}+c_j)\neq 0$. Then integrate $|\sigma|$ over the infinite strip $|\mathbf{w_j}^T\mathbf{x}-\mathbf{w_j}^T\mathbf{x_0}|<\delta$, where δ is chosen sufficiently small that σ does not vanish in the region.

Now we denote the weight connecting the jth hidden unit to the output by a_j. The output function g of the network is therefore

$$g(\mathbf{x}) = \sum_{j}^{k} a_j\sigma(\mathbf{w_j}^T\mathbf{x} + c_j). \tag{6.2}$$

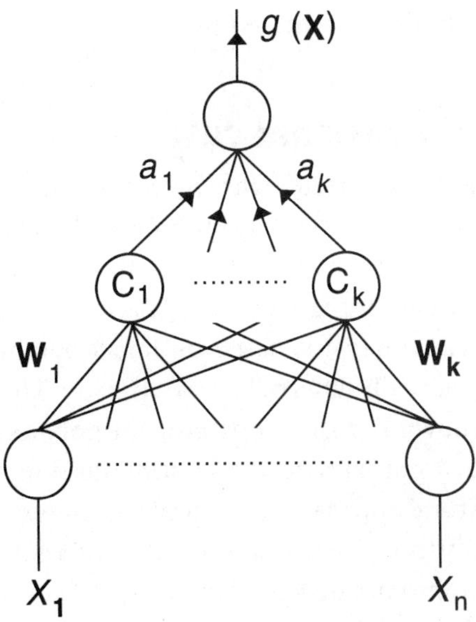

Fig. 6.2

Thus W is the set of all functions of the form (6.2) where the a_j and $c_j \in \mathbb{R}$ and the $\mathbf{w_j} \in \mathbb{R}^n$.

Activation functions σ used in practice have the property of being monotonic increasing, bounded and *sigmoidal*, which means simply that $\sigma(x) \to 1$ as $x \to \infty$, and $\sigma(x) \to 0$ as $x \to -\infty$. Except for the threshold function, they are also generally chosen to be continuous and smooth. The most popular choice is

$$\sigma(x) = 1/[1 + \exp(-x)]. \tag{6.3}$$

However the density proofs do not use all these conditions. For the basic results as we shall give them, only continuity or uniform continuity is required, plus in some cases the condition that σ be sigmoidal. Even these assumptions can be weakened (Leshno *et al*, 1993).

We are interested, then, in approximation by linear combinations of ridge functions. The first papers to establish that one hidden layer is sufficient, i.e. that functions of the form (6.2) are dense in $C(S)$, were by Cybenko (1989), Hornik, Stinchcombe and White (1989) and Funahashi (1989). However, simpler and sharper proofs have since superseded this work. A variety of versions of the basic result now exist, as do various approaches to the proof. Some current proofs are in themselves quite simple, but they do tend to depend on fairly powerful ideas and theorems. Rather than concentrate on a single method, we will introduce and prove some of these theorems and show how they can be used to obtain the required result.

6.2 The one-dimensional case

Several proofs of the density result start by considering the one-dimensional case and we will also adopt this strategy initially. A direct constructive approximation operator has been devised for this case by Chen, Chen and Liu. (Their result is most easily found in Light (1992).) It is of the type known as a *quasi interpolant* which means that it is based on linear combinations of function values. (It does not actually interpolate of course.) The operator is in fact similar to the well-known Bernstein operator for polynomial approximation. The basic idea is to approximate the continuous function f by piecewise constants: a fairly natural approach in a neural net context where the activation functions are generally thought of as smoothed thresholds. For y in the interval $(x, x+\delta)$, f can be approximated by the constant $h(y)=f(x)$; the horizontal dashed line in Fig. 6.3. In this interval, therefore, the error in the approximation of $f(y)$ by $h(y)$ is $|f(y)-f(x)|$. Next consider a closed interval $[a, b]$. Split this

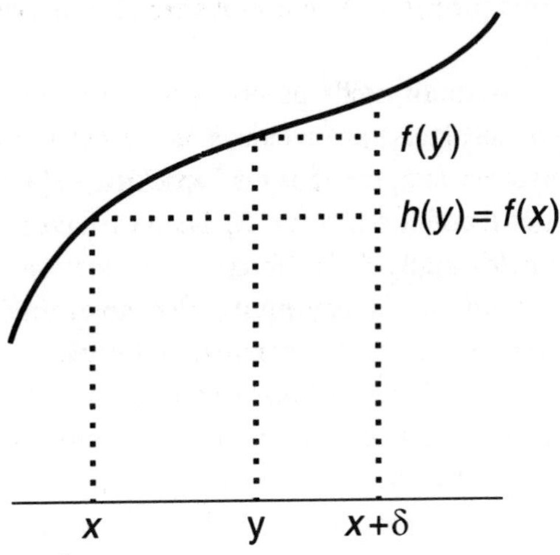

Fig. 6.3

up into subintervals of length δ and approximate on each subinterval as before. For any fixed δ the largest error over the whole interval $[a, b]$ will be finite, and moreover this quantity will clearly decrease monotonically with δ. We now introduce a basic measure of continuity.

Definition 6.2

For $f \in C[a, b]$, the *modulus of continuity* of f is defined as

$$\omega(f; \delta) = \sup_{\substack{x,y \in [a,b] \\ |x-y|<\delta}} |f(x) - f(y)| .$$

□

Observe that ω is finite and decreases monotonically as $\delta \to 0$. In fact it must decrease monotonically *to zero* (i.e. $\omega(f; 0)=0$) for if the limit as $\delta \to 0$ were greater than zero, the continuity of f would be contradicted. Also note that $\omega(f; \delta_1 + \delta_2) \le \omega(f; \delta_1) + \omega(f; \delta_2)$. This is because $|u-v| < \delta_1 + \delta_2$ implies that the δ_1 neighbourhood of u and the δ_2 neighbourhood of v intersect. Thus there exists $t \in [a, b]$ such that $|u-t| < \delta_1$ and $|v-t| < \delta_2$. Hence for any u, v such that $|u-v| < \delta_1 + \delta_2$ we have

$$|f(u) - f(v)| = |f(u) - f(t) + f(t) - f(v)| \le |f(u) - f(t)| + |f(t) - f(v)| .$$
$$\le \omega(f; \delta_1) + \omega(f; \delta_2) \text{ since } |u-t| < \delta_1 \text{ and} |v-t| < \delta_2.$$

Taking the supremum of the left-hand side over all u, v with $|u-v| < \delta_1 + \delta_2$

establishes the desired property. As a useful special case, note that for any $k \in \mathbb{N}$, $w(f; k\delta) \le k\omega(f; \delta)$.

The modulus of continuity tells us how rapidly f can vary with a given variation of x. It encapsulates various ideas of smoothness of f that might be introduced. For example, suppose that f is Lipschitz, so $|f(x)-f(y)|<L\,|x-y|$ for some real number L and for all $x, y \in K$. Then we have immediately $\omega(f{:}\ \delta) \le L\ \delta$. Similar estimates apply for differentiable functions. And as we have already noted, the modulus of continuity also gives an immediate simple estimate of how well f can be approximated by piecewise constants. To complete the density proof for one-dimensional sigmoidal ridge functions, we now approximate these constants by sigmoids. For simplicity (but without loss of generality as we can always rescale) we choose the interval [0, 1], and let $n \in \mathbb{N}$. We consider the step function $h_n(x)$ which takes the value $f(\nu/n)$ in the subinterval $\nu/n \le x < (\nu+1)/n$. Thus $\|f-h_n\|_\infty \le \omega(f;\ 1/n)$. (Actually we could reduce the constant from 1 to $\frac{1}{2}$ by evaluating at mid-points but this choice simplifies the notation.) It is convenient to write

$$h_n(x) = f(0) + \sum_{\nu=1}^{m} \{ f(\nu/n) - f([\nu - 1]/n) \}, \tag{6.4}$$

where m is the largest integer which does not exceed nx.

Now consider a continuous sigmoidal function such as (6.3) (Neither smoothness nor monotonicity are required here.) If we replace x by ax for some $a>1$, we steepen σ in the transitional region around $x=0$. In fact as $a \to \infty$, $\sigma(ax) \to 0$ or 1, according to whether $x<0$ or $x>0$. In other words σ converges pointwise to a simple threshold function with the value $\sigma(0)$ at 0. Thus $\sigma(ax) - \sigma[a(x-1)]$ will approach the unit step function which takes the value 1 on (0, 1) and 0 outside [0, 1]. In view of the discontinuities at 0 and 1, this convergence cannot be uniform. But Chen, Chen and Liu noticed that if one combines the constructions of this and the previous paragraph to approximate f, one *does* get uniform approximation, since the size of the discontinuity approaches 0 as $n \to \infty$. More specifically, suppose σ is continuous (on $\mathbb{R}$) and sigmoidal. They define A_n to be the smallest positive integer such that

$$|\sigma(x)| \le n^{-1} \text{ for } x \le -A_n \text{ and } (1 - n^{-1}) \le \sigma(x) \le (1 + n^{-1}) \text{ for } x \ge A_n.$$

Then they define the quasi-interpolant g_n as

$$g_n(x) = f(0) + \sum_{\nu=1}^{n} \{f(\nu/n) - f([\nu-1]/n)\}\ \sigma(A_n[nx-\nu]) \tag{6.5}$$

for $x \in [0, 1]$. Note that this function is essentially of the form (6.2): the initial constant term $f(0)$ can be approximated arbitrarily closely by $f(0)\,\sigma(t+x)$ with t very large. Observe also that this is precisely the approximation obtained by the construction described above: for those values of ν in the summation with $x < n\nu$, $\sigma(A_n[nx-\nu])$ is approximately zero. A careful estimate yields the following theorem.

Theorem 6.3
There exists a constant c such that for $f \in C[0, 1]$,

$$\|f - g_n\|_\infty \le c\omega(f; 1/n).$$

(Here the uniform norm is of course taken on the interval [0, 1].) Note that c is independent of f and in fact we may choose $c = 4 + 2S$ where $S = \sup |\sigma(x)|$ for $x \in \mathbb{R}$, i.e. the norm of σ taken on the whole of $\mathbb{R}$.

Proof
We have $\|f - g_n\|_\infty = \|f - h_n + h_n + g_n\|_\infty \le \|f - h_n\|_\infty + \|h_n - g_n\|_\infty$. We already know $\|f - h_n\|_\infty \le \omega(f{:}\ 1/n)$ so only the second term need be considered. Now for any $x \in [0, 1]$ with m defined as in (6.4) we have

$$h_n(x) - g_n(x) = f(0) + \sum_{\nu=1}^{m} \{f(\nu/n) - f([\nu-1]/n)\}\{1 - \sigma(A_n[nx-\nu])\} +$$

$$\sum_{\nu=\mu+1}^{n} \{f(\nu/n) - f([\nu-1]/n)\}\sigma(A_n[nx-\nu]).$$

Now $\nu \le m-1$ implies $nx - \nu \ge 1$ so $|1 - \sigma(A_n[nx-\nu])| \le 1/n$ by the definition of A_n. Similarly $\nu \ge m+2$ implies $|\sigma(A_n[nx-\nu])| \le 1/n$. Thus

$$|h_n(x) - g_n(x)| \le \omega(f, 1/n) + |\{f(\mu/n) - f([\mu-1]/n)\}\{1 - \sigma(A_n[nx-\mu])\}$$
$$+ \{f[(\mu+1)/n] - f(\mu/n)\}\sigma(A_n[nx-\mu-1])|\ .$$

The second term on the right-hand side is bounded by $2(1+S)\,\omega(f; 1/n)$, which completes the proof.

□

We remark in passing that if σ is monotone then $S = 1$ and c in Theorem 6.3 may be chosen as 6.

An alternative to this rather brute force construction is provided by dual space methods. Readers who merely wish to see a straightforward proof of density may skip the remainder of this section and pass to the multidimensional case in Section 6.3. However the dual space approach is at least of historical interest, since Cybenko's original proof was of this type (Cybenko, 1989). Moreover it is of considerable importance in approximation theory generally. In fact the final density proof for one-dimensional sigmoidal ridge functions using this approach turns out to be very short indeed, but of course this is due to the powerful machinery used, which must first be derived.

Consider a normed vector space V over $\mathbb{R}$. The (bounded) *dual space* of V, denoted by V', is the space of all bounded linear functionals on V. (A linear functional is a linear mapping from V to $\mathbb{R}$.) V' has a natural norm defined by

$$\|\mathbf{l}\| = \sup_{\substack{\mathbf{v} \in V \\ \|\mathbf{v}\| = 1}} |\mathbf{l}(\mathbf{v})| \,. \tag{6.6}$$

(This norm employs the same idea as the familiar matrix norm, of course. For any $\mathbf{v} \in V$, we have $|l(\mathbf{v})| \leq \|l\| \, \|\mathbf{v}\|$.) V' is always a Banach space, even if X is not. (Readers not familiar with this construction at all are advised to consult a suitable textbook such as Kreyszig (1978, pp. 119–125)).

Now let W be a subspace of V. (A mere subset will not do here, although it is possible to extend some of the following results to cover convex subsets.) We wish to know whether W is dense in V. The relevance of the dual space is shown by the following results. Note that any linear functional may be made into a functional with norm 1 simply by dividing by its norm. Thus there is no loss of generality in these results in considering functionals of norm 1.

Theorem 6.4

Let V be a normed vector space and W be a subspace. Suppose that $l \in V'$, with $\|l\|=1$, and moreover that l satisfies $l(\mathbf{w})=0$ for all $\mathbf{w} \in W$. Then

(a) for any $\mathbf{v} \in V$ we have

$$\|\mathbf{v} - \mathbf{w}\| \geq |\mathbf{l}(\mathbf{v})| \text{ for all } \mathbf{w} \in W, \text{ and}$$

(b) for any $\varepsilon > 0$, there exists $\mathbf{v} \in V$ with $\|\mathbf{v}\|=1$ and

$$\|\mathbf{v} - \mathbf{w}\| > 1 - \varepsilon \text{ for all } \mathbf{w} \in W.$$

Proof

(a) $|l(\mathbf{v})|=|l(\mathbf{v})-l(\mathbf{w})|=|l(\mathbf{v}-\mathbf{w})|\le\|l\|\,\|\mathbf{v}-\mathbf{w}\|$ but $\|l\|=1$.

(b) From (6.6) we can chose $\mathbf{v}\in V$ with $\|\mathbf{v}\|=1$ and $|l(\mathbf{v})|>1-\varepsilon$.

□

This theorem can help us to show that V is *not* dense, and indeed to obtain lower bounds as to how well any given function can be approximated, if we can construct a linear functional which vanishes on W but not on V. Brown and Harris use essentially this argument in a Hilbert space context to discuss the approximation capabilities of the CMAC neural net: see Brown and Harris (1994), Chapter 7, particularly Sections 7.4 and 7.5. A kind of converse to Theorem 6.4 which does establish density will be proved later.

We need some more theory of linear functionals (in particular the Hahn–Banach Theorem 6.10) first. In order for these results to be useful, we need some concrete way of constructing linear functionals. Of course, if V is n-dimensional, a linear functional can be represented by a $1\times n$ matrix: in other words linear functionals are just inner products with (row) vectors. In infinite dimensional spaces the situation is more complex, but it turns out that in most practical function spaces which have been studied the linear functionals are 'inner product like'. Theorems which provide a concrete representation of the dual space of a given function space V are called Riesz Representation Theorems. The simplest and most elegant such theorem refers to Hilbert spaces. If H is a real Hilbert space with inner product $<,>$, then it can be shown (Kreyszig, 1978, p. 188) that every linear functional $l: H\to\mathbb{R}$ can be written as $l(h)=<h, k>$ for some $k\in H$. Moreover $\|l\|=\|k\|$.We will not give a proof here, as we are interested in $C[a, b]$ which is *not* a Hilbert space. Unfortunately, the situation for $C[a, b]$ is rather more complicated. We would like to write linear functionals as Lebesgue–Stieltjes integrals (see Definition 1.29, but here we do not insist that $g(x)\ge 0$, as we are not defining a measure). So we want to write

$$l(f)=\int_a^b f(x)g(x)\mathrm{d}x \tag{6.7}$$

for integrable g in some suitable function space to be identified. However, although such an integral defines a linear functional, there are linear functionals not of this form. For example let $x_0\in[a, b]$ and consider the *point evaluation* functional $l(f)=f(x_0)$. This is easily checked to be a linear functional. In order to try to write it in the form of (6.7) consider $g_\varepsilon(x)=1/(2\varepsilon)$ for $x\in[x_0-\varepsilon, x_0-\varepsilon]$ and 0 outside this interval. Then let

$$
\begin{aligned}
l_\varepsilon(f) &= \int_a^b f(x) g_\varepsilon(x) \mathrm{d}x \\
&= \frac{1}{2\varepsilon} \int_{x_0-\varepsilon}^{x_0+\varepsilon} f(x) \mathrm{d}x \\
&= f(\zeta) \text{ for some } \zeta \in [x_0 - \varepsilon, x_0 + \varepsilon],
\end{aligned}
$$

by the Integral Mean Value Theorem (Theorem 1.30). To recover the point evaluation, we need to let $\varepsilon \to 0$. However, this does not result in a well defined g. (Note that the problem does not occur in the Hilbert space $L_2[a, b]$: elements of this space are equivalence classes of functions which agree almost everywhere, so point evaluation does not make sense.) We need g to have infinite height, zero width and area 1. Such an object is misleadingly called the Dirac δ-function. Of course it is not a true function: see Section 6.5. Instead, we extend the idea of the Lebesgue–Stieltjes integral (6.7) to cover this case. In view of Definition 1.31 and Theorem 1.32 it is natural to define

$$
G(x) = \int_a^x g(t) \mathrm{d}t \tag{6.8}
$$

to be the indefinite integral of g in (6.7), even when g is not continuous. Furthermore in view of Theorem 1.34 it is natural to write

$$
\int_a^b f(x) g(x) \mathrm{d}x = \int_a^b f(x) \mathrm{d}G(x). \tag{6.9}
$$

For g_ε as defined above, it follows immediately from (6.8) that the corresponding G_ε is given by

$$
G_\varepsilon(x) = \begin{cases} 0 & \text{for } x < x_0 - \varepsilon \\ (2/\varepsilon)(x - x_0 + \varepsilon) & \text{for } x_0 - \varepsilon \le x \le x_0 + \varepsilon \, . \\ 1 & \text{for } x > x_0 + \varepsilon \end{cases} \tag{6.10}
$$

Note that G_ε is continuous. However as $\varepsilon \to 0$, G_ε tends almost everywhere to the step function

$$
H(x) = \begin{cases} 0 & \text{for } x < x_0 \\ 0 & \text{for } x = x_0 \, . \\ 1 & \text{for } x > x_0 \end{cases} \tag{6.11}
$$

(The value we choose for $H(x_0)$ is not very important, but in (6.8) we have $G(a) = 0$, and it seems sensible to preserve this property.) In view of (6.7) and (6.9) we would like to write the point evaluation functional at x_0 as

$$l(f)=\int_a^b f(x)\mathrm{d}H(x).$$

But how can we make this argument mathematically respectable? There are two issues to consider. Firstly we need to construct a suitable normed vector space for our indefinite integrals G, and secondly we need to show that for each element G of this space we can give a sensible meaning to

$$\int_a^b f(x)\mathrm{d}G(x).$$

By 'sensible' we mean that it reduces to (6.9) when applicable, and preserves our normal properties of integral and measure.

Now consider (6.7) again. We have

$$\begin{aligned} |l(f)| &\leq \int_a^b |f(x)|\,|g(x)|\mathrm{d}x \\ &\leq \|f\|_\infty \int_a^b |g(x)|\mathrm{d}x \\ &= \|f\|_\infty \|g\|_1 \end{aligned} \tag{6.12}$$

Thus according to (6.6) $\|l\|\leq\|g\|_1$. In fact if g is a non-negative function, equality occurs in (6.12) when f is the function $f(x)=1$ for all x. Thus $\|l\|=\|g\|_1$. If g is not non-negative we need to set $f(x)=\mathrm{sign}[g(x)]$ to get equality, and unfortunately this function is not necessarily continuous. Nevertheless it is plausible $\|l\|=\|g\|_1$ still holds: this turns out to be the case but we will omit the proof here in the interests of brevity, since in fact it follows from the arguments below. So what property of G as defined in (6.8) corresponds to $\|g\|_1$? Consider first the case when g is a step function like g_ε above. Obviously $\|g_\varepsilon\|_1=1$. Examining (6.8) and (6.10) we see that this quantity is given by $G(x_2)-G(x_1)$ for any x_1, x_2 with $x_2>x_0-\varepsilon$ and $x_1<x_0-\varepsilon$, simply because $G(x)$ in (6.10) measures the cumulative contribution to the integral as x increases. (It is of course just this property of the indefinite integral that is employed in the Fundamental Theorem of Calculus.) Now suppose g is a linear combination of two such simple g_ε functions with different ε and x_0. This situation is a little more complicated. The corresponding G will be made up of piecewise linear segments, each segment having gradient equal to the corresponding value of $g(x)$. If g is non-negative, then again we can simply write $\|g\|_1=G(b)-G(a)$. But if g changes sign at some point x_3, then we get $\|g\|_1=|G(x_3)-G(a)|+|G(b)-G(x_3)|$. (Only one sign change is possible!) For three g_ε's we will get an expression of the form

$$\|g\|_1 = |G(x_3) - G(a)| + |G(x_4) - G(x_3)| + |G(b) - G(x_4)| \tag{6.13}$$

and so on. A general g can be expressed as the limit of such step functions (Section 1.7). However we will not in general know where the jumps will occur. To get round this we need to look at (6.13) more closely. Suppose we introduce an extra point x' say, between x_3 and x_4 but *not* corresponding to a sign change. Then $G(x_4)-G(x')$ and $G(x')-G(x_3)$ will have the same sign, so $|G(x_4)-G(x')| + |G(x')-G(x_3)|$. Introducing an additional point in (6.13) does no harm: the important consideration is than one of the subinterval boundaries hits the sign change. Hence we may write for a general *step function g*

$$\|g\|_1 = \sum_{i=0}^{N-1} |G(x_{i+1}) - G(x_i)|\,, \tag{6.14}$$

where the $N+1$ points x_i are chosen so that each sign change occurs at the end of some subinterval $[x_{i+1}, x_i]$. Additional points do not matter. For a step function there can only be a finite number of sign changes, so (6.14) is always possible, but we do need to know where the sign changes occur. Suppose some particular x_i is a sign change. If we move x_i *we will reduce the value of the sum on the right-hand side of* (6.14) since both $|G(x_{i+1})-G(x_i)|$ and $|G(x_i)-G(x_{i-1})|$ will be reduced. Hence (6.14) yields

$$\|g\|_1 = \sup \sum_{i=0}^{N-1} |G(x_{i+1}) - G(x_i)|\,, \tag{6.15}$$

where the supremum is taken over all possible $N+1$ point subdivisions of $[a, b]$, and over all $N>2$. We call the right-hand side of (6.15) the *total variation* of G (often just the variation for short) and write it as $\mathrm{Var}(G)$. Actually when g is a step function there is an obvious choice of points x_i: simply choose them to be the points at which the value of g changes. Sign changes must be such points, so this subdivision will achieve the supremum in (6.15).

Finally we address the case of general $g \in L_1[a, b]$. Again, let G be its indefinite integral. Choose a sequence of subdivisions which approach $\mathrm{Var}(G)$ (or infinity if the supremum is unbounded), and sequence of step functions (φ_n) approaching g almost everywhere, and satisfying $|\varphi_n(x)| \leq |g(x)|$ almost everywhere. We may assume without loss of generality that φ_n has jumps at the points of the nth subdivision: if not simply introduce these as extra jumps. Conversely we may assume that each jump of φ_n is in the nth subdivision since introducing extra points into a subdivision can only make the sum under the supremum in (6.15) larger. Then we note that

(a) $|\varphi_n(x)| \to |g(x)|$ almost everywhere
(b) $\|\varphi_n\|_1 = \mathrm{Var}(\Phi_n)$ where Φ_n is the indefinite integral of φ_n since φ_n is a step function, and
(c) $\mathrm{Var}(\Phi_n) \to \mathrm{Var}(G)$ by construction.

Thus by Theorem 1.39, $\mathrm{Var}(G) = \lim \|\varphi_n\|_1 = \|g\|_1$ as $n \to \infty$, establishing that (6.15) also holds for $g \in L_1[a, b]$. If g is in L_1, its indefinite integral is of bounded variation. But there are functions of bounded variation which do *not* correspond to a g in L_1. Indeed the function H defined by (6.11) is a step function and has variation 1. We shall see that we can we make sense of an integral like the right-hand side of (6.9) for *any* function G of bounded variation. However, before tackling this problem, we need to make an important observation about functions of bounded variation. For any real valued function f, the *left-hand limit* at some point x is defined (if it exists) to be the limit as $y \to x$ from below, i.e. through values with $y < x$. More formally, we say that

$$L = \lim_{y \uparrow x} f(x)$$

if given $\varepsilon > 0$, there exists δ such that for $y < x$ and $x - y < \delta$, $|L - f(x)| < \varepsilon$. (Note the use of the up arrow $\uparrow$ to distinguish the left limit. An alternative nomenclature is to call L the limit as y *tends up to* x.)

If L exists at x and moreover $L = f(x)$, then f is said to be *left* continuous at x. For example, in (6.11), the left-hand limit of H at x_0 is 0, so H is left continuous at x_0. We may similarly define right-hand limits and right continuity. The right-hand limit of H at x_0 is 1, so H is not right continuous. (Obviously if a function is left and right continuous at a given point x, it is continuous there.)

Lemma 6.5

Let G: $[a, b] \to \mathbb{R}$ be of bounded variation. Then at any point $x \in [a, b]$, G has a left-hand limit.

Proof

If G is of bounded variation, then it is bounded: consider $|G(x) - G(0)|$. Suppose G does not have a left-hand limit at some point x. Then we can construct a sequence (x_i) such that $x_i \to x$, but $G(x_i)$ does not converge. Since the sequence $[G(x_i)]$ is bounded, it must have at least two convergent subsequences with different limits. Indeed, deleting points and renumbering as necessary, we can clearly choose the x_i without loss of generality so that $G(x_i) \to G_1$ for i even and $G(x_i) \to G_2$ for i odd. Assuming without loss of generality that $G_1 > G_2$, let $D = G_1 - G_2$. We find that, except for possibly finitely many values of i, which may be deleted, $G(x_i) > G_1 - D/4$ for i even and $G(x_i) < G_2 + D/4$ for i odd. Now consider, for $n \in \mathbb{R}$,

$$S_N = \sum_{i=0}^{N} |G(x_{i+1}) - G(x_i)| \, .$$

We have $S_N > (N+1)\, D/2$. Thus S_N can ne made arbitrarily large by choosing N sufficiently large, contradicting that assumption that G is of bounded variation.

□

Equally, of course, G has a right limit at any point in (a, b). Now if G is the indefinite integral of an L_1 function, it follows from (6.8) that G is actually continuous at each point of $[a, b]$. To see this, note that

$$\begin{aligned} G(x) - G(y) &= \int_y^x g(t)\mathrm{d}t \\ &= \int_a^b \varphi_{y,x}(t) g(t)\mathrm{d}t \, , \end{aligned}$$

where $\varphi_{y,x}(t)$ is the characteristic function of the interval $[y, x]$, i.e. the step function which is 1 in $[y, x]$ and 0 outside it. This function tends to zero as $y \to x$, so by Theorem 1.38, $G(y) \to G(x)$. (Clearly $G(y) \to G(x)$ if and only if $G(y_i) \to G(x)$ for every sequence (y_i) such that $y_i \to x$.) We want to construct a space that includes *discontinuous* functions of bounded variation like H in (6.11). However, the actual value of H at x_0 is not important: it is the value of the jump, i.e. the difference between the left- and right-hand limits, that matters. So we do no harm by insisting that at a point x_0 of discontinuity, $H(x_0)$ is equal to its left-hand limit there. This is consistent with the choice $H(a) = 0$ (but we do not insist $H(x) \to 0$ as $y \downarrow a$). Hence we lose nothing by insisting that our functions be left continuous. We may now make the following definition.

Definition 6.6

Let $BV_0[a, b]$ be the normed vector space of functions G: $[a, b]\to\mathbb{R}$ such that G is of bounded variation, is left continuous at each point $x\in(a, b]$, and satisfies $G(a)=0$, with $\|G\|=\mathrm{Var}(G)$.

□

It is easy to verify that BV_0 is indeed a vector space and that the variation is a norm. The mapping $g\to G$ defined by (6.8) is an *isometric isomorphism* of $L_1[a, b]$ into the subspace of $BV_0[a, b]$ consisting of continuous functions of bounded variation. The term 'isometric' here refers to the fact that $\|g\|_1=\|G\|$. (It is worth noting that there exist continuous functions which are *not* of bounded variation, e.g. $f(x)=x \sin(1/x)$, $f(0)=0$, on $[0, 1]$.) A restriction of this mapping covers the case where g is continuous: then G is differentiable (Theorem 1.32).

Now we proceed to define the generalised integral. In the case that G is monotone increasing, this is not very hard. Simply define the *Lebesgue–Stieltjes measure* of the interval $I=[a, b]$ to be $\mu_G(I)=G(b)-G(a)$ (compare Definition 1.22). The Lebesgue measure is simply the special case $G(x)=x$. If φ is a step function, we define its *Lebesgue–Stieljes integral* by

$$\int_{\mathbb{R}n} \varphi(\mathbf{x})d\mathbf{x}=\sum_{i=1}^{N} \varphi_i\mu_g(I_i) \tag{6.16}$$

as a straightforward extension of Definitions 1.21 and 1.24. The development of the integral proceeds as in Chapter 1, and the argument of the proceeding paragraphs relates the Lebesgue and Lebesgue–Stieljes integrals when G is an indefinite integral (i.e. our new definition is consistent with Definition 1.29). However monotone G is not good enough for our purposes: for example we could not write $l(f)=-f(x_0)$ (for fixed x_0) in the desired form. Clearly we need to express a general G of bounded variation as the difference of two monotone functions and then define the integral as the corresponding difference of the two integrals. But it is not immediately obvious that this is possible. The following theorem provides the necessary machinery.

Theorem 6.7

Any $G\in BV_0[a, b]$ can be expressed as the sum of a monotone non-decreasing function and a monotone non-increasing function in the space: in other words

$$G = G^{\gtrless} + G^{\lessgtr}$$

where $G^{\gtrless}, G^{\lessgtr} \in BV_0[a, b], G^{\gtrless}(x) \geq G^{\gtrless}(y), G^{\lessgtr}(x) \leq G^{\lessgtr}(y)$ if $y \leq x$.

Proof

Consider any particular choice of a partition set $P = \{x_i\}$. For any partition we assume that the x_i are numbered in increasing order with i. By definition

$$S_P = \sum_P |G(x_{i+1}) - G(x_i)| \leq \mathrm{Var}(G). \tag{6.17}$$

Now let P_n be any sequence of such partitions such that $S_{P_n} \to \mathrm{Var}(G)$ as $n \to \infty$. To simplify the notation we will denote S_{P_n} by S_n, but bear in mind that it does depend on P_n. By adding extra points to a partition, we can only increase the sum in the middle member of (6.17). So we can assume without loss of generality that $P_n \subset P_{n+1}$: if not just add the missing points. Furthermore by construction the total number of points in $\cup P_n$ for all n is countable. It follows that we can in fact construct the sequence of partitions P_n in such a way that P_{n+1} contains precisely one more (distinct) point than P_n. Finally, we impose two other conditions on the sequence P_n: namely (a) that the maximum of $|x_{i+1} - x_i| \to 0$ as $n \to \infty$ and (b) that $x_1 = a$ for all n. Again this just requires the addition of extra points if necessary. Now in each partition, and for each i, either $G(x_{i+1}) \geq G(x_i)$ or $G(x_{i+1}) < Gx_i)$. Call the former interval *up intervals*, and the latter *down intervals*. Define

$$G_n^{\gtrless}(x) = \sum G(x_{i+1}) - G(x_i) = \sum |G(x_{i+1}) - G(x_i)|\,,$$

where the summation is over the all the up intervals in P_n that satisfy $x_{i+1} < x$. Suppose that the largest such subscript (if it exists) is I: so $x_{i+1} < x$ but $x_{I+2} \geq x$. Of course, I depends on n. Clearly $G_n^{\lessgtr}(x)$ is monotone non-decreasing as a function of x. If $x = a$, I does not exist: simply set $G_n^{\gtrless}(a) = 0$ for all n.

$G_n^{\lessgtr}(x)$ is defined similarly with the down intervals:

$$G_n^{\lessgtr}(x) = \sum \{G(x_{i+1}) - G(x_i)\} = -\sum |G(x_{i+1}) - G(x_i)|\,.$$

Observe that $G_n^{\gtrless}(x) + G_n^{\lessgtr}(x) = G(x_I) \to G(x)$ as $n \to \infty$, in view of the left continuity of G and the fact that the size of the intervals tends to zero so $x_I \to x$. We need to show that $G_n^{\gtrless}$ and $G_n^{\lessgtr}$ converge to suitable functions $G^{\gtrless}$ and $G^{\lessgtr}$.

In proceeding from P_n to P_{n+1}, we add one additional point: say x'. There are three cases to consider. Possibly $x' \geq x$. In this case $G_n^{\gtrless}(x) = G_{n+1}^{\gtrless}(x)$ and

$G_n^{\lessgtr}(x) = G_{n+1}^{\leq}(x)$. The second possibility is that $x_{I+1} < x' < x$. If $[x_{I+1}, x']$ becomes a new up interval, $G_{n+1}(x) \geq G_n^{\gtrless}(x)$ and $G_{n+1}^{\leq}(x) = G_n^{\lessgtr}(x)$. Conversely if $[x_I^+{}_1, x']$ becomes a new down interval, $G_{n+1}^{\geq}(x) = G_n^{\gtrless}(x)$ and $G_{n+1}^{\leq}(x) \leq G_n^{\lessgtr}(x)$. The third possibility is that $x' < x_I$. Suppose that $x' \in (x_{j+1}, x_j)$ with $j \leq I$, and consider the case that $[x_{j+1}, x_j]$ is an up interval. If $G(x_j) \leq G(x') \leq G(x_{j+1})$ then $[x_j+_1, x_j]$ is split into two up intervals, and $G_{n+1}^{\geq}(x) = G_n^{\gtrless}(x)$. The sum for $G_n^{\lessgtr}(x)$ is unaffected, so also $G_n^{\lessgtr}(x) = G_{n+1}^{\leq}(x)$. On the other hand if $G(x')$ is *not* between $G(x_j)$ and $G(x_{j+1})$, a new down interval and an up interval with a *larger change* in G are created. Then $G_{n+1}^{\geq}(x) \geq G_n^{\gtrless}(x)$ and $G_{n+1}^{\leq}(x) \leq G_n^{\lessgtr}(x)$. Similar considerations apply if $[x_{j+1}, x_j]$ is a down interval. This exhausts all the possible cases, and we see that in every case $G_{n+1}^{\geq}(x) \geq G_n^{\gtrless}(x)$ and $G_{n+1}^{\leq}(x) \leq G_n^{\lessgtr}(x)$. Obviously $G_n^{\gtrless}(x) \leq \mathrm{Var}G$ and $G_n^{\lessgtr}(x) \geq -\mathrm{Var}(G)$. So for any x, we conclude that the sequences $[G_n^{\gtrless}(x)]$ and $[G_n^{\lessgtr}(x)]$ are convergent as $n \to \infty$. Define $G^{\gtrless}(\xi) = \lim G_n^{\gtrless}(x)$ and $G^{\lessgtr}(x) = \lim G_n^{\lessgtr}(x)$.

Now by construction $G{\geq}(x) + G{\leq}(x) = \lim \{G_n{\geq}(x) + G_n{\leq}(x)\} = G(x)$ as required. Also $G^{\gtrless}(a) = G^{\lessgtr}(a) = 0$. The functions satisfy the required monotonicity properties, since these are preserved in passing to the limit (as may be easily shown by contradiction). Monotone functions are necessarily of bounded variation: in fact $\mathrm{Var}(G^{\gtrless}) = G^{\gtrless}(b) - G^{\gtrless}(a)$ and $\mathrm{Var}(G^{\lessgtr}) = G^{\lessgtr}(a) - G^{\lessgtr}(b)$. As constructed, it is possible that $G^{\gtrless}$ is not left continuous. However if this is the case at some point x_0, redefine $G^{\gtrless}$ by replacing $G^{\gtrless}(x_0)$ by its left-hand limit there, and change $G^{\lessgtr}(x_0)$ so that $G^{\gtrless}(x_0) + G^{\lessgtr}(x_0) = G^{\lessgtr}(x_0)$. Since $G^{\gtrless}$ and G are now left continuous at x_0, $G^{\lessgtr}$ will be also. Hence $G^{\gtrless}$ and $G^{\lessgtr} \in BV_0[a, b]$.

□

We will now give a formal definition of the Lebesgue–Stieljes integral.

Definition 6.8

Let $G \in BV_0[a, b]$, and let f: $[a, b] \to \mathbb{R}$, with $f(x) \geq 0$ for all $x \in [a, b]$. Suppose we have a sequence of step functions $\varphi_n(x)$ which is monotone non-decreasing and converges almost everywhere to f.

(a) If G is monotone non-decreasing, define

$$\int_a^b f(x)\mathrm{d}G(x) = \lim_{n \to \infty} \int_a^b \varphi_n(x)\mathrm{d}G(x)$$

(providing it exists) where the integral on the right-hand side is defined by (6.16).

(b) If G is not monotone non-decreasing, define

$$\int_a^b f(x)\mathrm{d}G(x) = \int_a^b f(x)\mathrm{d}G^{\geq}(x) - \int_a^b f(x)\mathrm{d}[-G^{\leq}(x)]$$

with $G^{\geq}$ and $G^{\leq}$ as in Theorem 6.7.

□

Remarks 6.9

(a) If f is not non-negative, write it as the difference of two non-negative functions and define the integral of f as the difference of the integrals of these functions, exactly as in Chapter 1.

(b) The decomposition of G as two monotone functions is not unique. Indeed adding any monotone non-decreasing function (from BV_0) to $G^{\geq}$ and subtracting it from $G^{\leq}$ will yield a different decomposition. However an examination of (6.16) shows that in fact the integral of a step function is independent of the decomposition, for if $I=[c, d]$

$$\begin{aligned} \mu_{G^{\geq}}(I) - \mu_{-G^{\leq}}(I) &= G^{\geq}(d) - G^{\geq}(c) + G^{\leq}(d) - G^{\leq}(c) \\ &= G(d) - G(c). \end{aligned} \tag{6.18}$$

This property will be preserved in passing to the limit f, so the integral is well defined.

(c) In view of remark (b), one may wonder why we bother with Theorem 6.7. However much of the construction of the integral in Chapter 1 depends on monotonicity properties. For example, the Integral Mean Value Theorem (Theorem 1.30) clearly will not work if G is not monotone, and thus there are also problems with extending the Fundamental Theorem of Calculus. And what about convergence theorems such as Theorem 1.38? It is much safer to think of the general integral as being made up of the difference of two measures. In view of Theorem 6.7, this rarely causes any difficulty (except where it ought to!), and can avoid much confusion. Some authors do refer to integrals such as Definition 6.8(b) as defining a measure, but it does not have the normal properties of length which we would expect $\mu_G(\mathcal{I})$ to have. Thus we will avoid this usage.

□

Now recall that our purpose in all this is to obtain an expression for a general linear functional on $C[a, b]$. In view of (6.7) and (6.9), we would like to write a functional as

$$l(f) = \int_a^b f(x)\mathrm{d}G(x) \tag{6.19}$$

for some $G \in BV_0[a, b]$. We have certainly made progress, since choosing G to be H as in (6.11) will give the point evaluation at x_0. To see this, note that the Integral Mean Value Theorem (easily extended to Lebesgue–Stieltjes integrals with monotone G) shows that for any $\varepsilon > 0$,

$$\int_a^b f(x)\mathrm{d}H(x) = \int_{x_0-\varepsilon}^{x_0+\varepsilon} f(x)\mathrm{d}H(x) \text{ (since the H-measure of any interval excluding } x_0 \text{ is zero)}$$

$$= f(\zeta)\int_{x_0-\varepsilon}^{x_0+\varepsilon} \mathrm{d}H(x) \text{ with } \zeta \in [x_0+\varepsilon, x_0-\varepsilon] \text{ (by the integral Mean Value Theorem)}$$

$$= f(\zeta) \text{ (since } H(x_0+\varepsilon) - H(x_0-\varepsilon) = 1).$$

But this holds for any $\varepsilon > 0$, so the only possibility is

$$\begin{aligned} l(f) &= \int_a^b f(x)\mathrm{d}H(x) \\ &= f(x_0) \end{aligned}$$

as required. But of course it is a big jump from this to the conclusion that *every* linear functional on $C[a, b]$ is of the form (6.19). Nevertheless, this turns out to be true. The proof requires the Hahn–Banach Theorem, which in turn requires the use of Zorn's Lemma (which is really an axiom!). For a discussion of Zorn's Lemma, see, e.g. Kreyszig (1978, Chapter 4): in the interests of brevity we will not include it here. This version of the Hahn–Banach Theorem is not the most general form, but covers the common applications in approximation theory.

Theorem 6.10 (Hahn–Banach Theorem)

Let V be a real normed vector space and W a subspace. Further, let l be a linear functional on W with norm $\| l \|_W$. (We introduce the subscript W here to indicate that (6.6) is applied on W only.) Then l can be extended to a linear functional on V; i.e. there is a linear function on V, which we also call l, and which agrees with the definition of l on W. Moreover the extension can be chosen such that $\| l \|_V = \| l \|_W$.

Proof

First of all, note that we might as well assume $\| l \|_w = 1$. For if $\| l \|_w = 0$, just choose l to be the zero functional on V and there is nothing to prove. Otherwise consider the functional $l(v)/\| l \|_w$, extend this to a functional of norm 1, and then multiply this by $\| l \|_w$. So we assume $\| l \|_w = 1$, and seek an extension of l to V that satisfies

$$|l(\mathbf{v})| \leq \|\mathbf{v}\| \tag{6.20}$$

for all $\mathbf{v} \in V$.

The proof is in two distinct parts. (a) The first is elementary, and shows that an extension by dimension 1 is always possible. We will give this in full. (b) The deeper (although fairly short) second part is to show that extension is possible even if the difference between V and W is of uncountable dimension, and we can only give the proof of this in brief form.

(a) Suppose first that the difference between V and W is one-dimensional. This does not imply that V or W are themselves finite dimensional, only that any element of V can be written as

$$\mathbf{v} = \alpha \mathbf{x} + \mathbf{w},$$

where where $\mathbf{x}$ is a **fixed** element of V, $\mathbf{x} \notin W$, $\alpha \in \mathbb{R}$ and $\mathbf{w} \in W$. With $\mathbf{x}$ fixed, it is easy to check that such a representation for any given $\mathbf{v}$ is unique. For if $\mathbf{v} = \alpha_1 \mathbf{x} + \mathbf{w}_1 = \alpha_2 \mathbf{x} + \mathbf{w}_2$, we see that $(\alpha_1 - \alpha_2)\, \mathbf{x} \in W$. But since $\mathbf{x} \notin W$, $\alpha_1 = \alpha_2$ and hence $\mathbf{w}_1 = \mathbf{w}_2$. If $\alpha = 0$, $\mathbf{v} \in W$, and there is nothing to prove. Otherwise we might as well replace $\mathbf{v}$ by $\mathbf{v}/\alpha$. Since $\mathbf{w}$ was just a representative element of W it is sufficient to prove (6.20) for $\mathbf{v}$ satisfying

$$\mathbf{v} = \mathbf{x} + \mathbf{w}. \tag{6.21}$$

We wish to extend l from W to V. From (6.20), any such extension l must satisfy

$$l(\mathbf{v}) = l(\mathbf{x}) + l(\mathbf{w}).$$

To define the extension, the only choice we have is in $c = l(\mathbf{x})$. We have to choose c so that (6.20) holds. Now consider any two vectors $\mathbf{w}_1$ and $\mathbf{w}_2 \in W$ and let $\mathbf{v}_1$ and $\mathbf{v}_2$ be the corresponding $\mathbf{v}$'s as in (6.21). We have

$$l(\mathbf{w}_1) - l(\mathbf{w}_2) = l(\mathbf{w}_1 - \mathbf{w}_2) \leq \|\mathbf{w}_1 - \mathbf{w}_2\| = \|\mathbf{v}_1 - \mathbf{v}_2\| \leq \|\mathbf{v}_1\| + \|\mathbf{v}_2\|.$$

Hence

$$-\|\mathbf{v}_2\| - l(\mathbf{w}_2) \leq \|\mathbf{v}_1\| - l(\mathbf{w}_1).$$

Now the right-hand side depends only on $\mathbf{w}_1$ (since $\mathbf{x}$ is fixed), whereas the left-hand side depends only on $\mathbf{w}_2$. It follows that as $\mathbf{w}_1$ and $\mathbf{w}_2$ range over W, the supremum of the left-hand side must be less than or equal to the infimum of the right-hand side. Thus we can choose c such that

$$-\|\mathbf{v}_2\| - l(\mathbf{w}_2) \leq c \leq \|\mathbf{v}_1\| - l(\mathbf{w}_1),$$

for all $\mathbf{w}_1$ and $\mathbf{w}_2 \in W$. Now given any particular $\mathbf{v}$ of the form of (6.21), set $\mathbf{w}_1 = \mathbf{w}_2 = \mathbf{w}$. Then

$$-\|\mathbf{v}\| - l(\mathbf{w}) \leq c \leq \|\mathbf{v}\| - l(\mathbf{w}),$$

or

$$-\|\mathbf{v}\| \leq l(\mathbf{w}) + c \leq \|\mathbf{v}\|,$$

whence, since we are choosing $l(\mathbf{x}) = c$ in (6.21),

$$-\|\mathbf{v}\| \leq l(\mathbf{v}) \leq \|\mathbf{v}\|,$$

which establishes (6.20).

(b) We now need to proceed from a dimension 1 extension to an arbitrary extension. Note that if V is finite dimensional, this is almost trivial. Select a basis for W, extend it to a basis for V, and apply part (a) inductively for those basis elements not in W. Even if V has a countable basis, with respect to which any vector can be expanded in an infinite series and convergence of infinite series is in terms of norm, simple induction will still work. The problem is that this is not possible in an arbitrary real normed vector space. To cope with the general case, we need some kind of 'non-countable induction': this is where Zorn's Lemma comes in. We will give enough details for those readers already familiar with partial orderings and the Lemma itself. Others should skip the next part, or consult Kreyszig as suggested above.

Denote by l_i an extension of l to the space D_i where where $W \subset D_i \subset V$. We define a partial ordering on the set E of all such extensions. Specifically, we say that $l_i \leq l_j$ if $D_i \subset D_j$ and l_j is an extension of l_i (i.e. the restriction of l_j to D_i is l_i). Now let L be any totally ordered set of such extensions. Thus L consists of a sequence $l_1 \leq l_2 \leq l_3 \ldots$. In order to apply Zorn's lemma, we need to show that L has an upper bound. Actually, this is easy. Let $D = \cup D_i$, $i = 1,2,3, \ldots$ and note that D is a subspace of V. If $\mathbf{v} \in D$, we must have $\mathbf{v} \in D_i$, for some i. Define $l'(\mathbf{v}) = l_i(\mathbf{v})$. Whenever two D_i's intersect, the l_i's give the same answer because of the partial ordering, so $l'(\mathbf{v})$ is uniquely defined. We see that l' is an extension of l, and moreover $l_i \leq l'$ for all $l_i \in L$. Thus (by definition) l' is an upper bound for L. Since this holds for any totally ordered set $L \subset E$, the conditions of Zorn's Lemma are fulfilled and we conclude from the lemma that E has a maximal element. Call this maximal extension l^* and its domain D^*. If $D^* = V$ we are done, so suppose not, i.e. that D^* is a proper subspace of V. Thus there exists $\mathbf{x} \in V$ with $\mathbf{x} \notin D^*$. Then by part (a), l^* can be extended to span$\{\mathbf{x}, D^*\}$, a space strictly larger than D^*. This contradicts the maximality of l', so we must have $D^* = V$, completing the proof.

□

Taking a deep breath, we now at last can give an explicit representation of the linear functionals on $C[a, b]$.

Theorem 6.11 (The Riesz Representation Theorem for $C[a, b]$)
Every linear functional l on $C[a, b]$ can be expressed in the form (6.19), where $G \in BV_0[a, b]$. Moreover $\|l\| = \mathrm{Var}(G)$.

Proof
By Theorem 6.10, l can be extended to $B[a, b]$, the space of bounded, Lebesgue integrable functions on $[a, b]$ with $\| \|_\infty$. We observe first that for $G \in BV_0[a, b]$, the right-hand side of (6.19) certainly defines a linear functional on $C[a, b]$. To avoid confusing the notation, let us call this functional l'. Then

$$|l'(f)| \leq \|f\|_\infty \int_a^b \mathrm{d}G(x) = \|f\|_\infty \mathrm{Var}(G), \tag{6.22}$$

whence $\|l'\| \leq \mathrm{Var}(G)$ so l' is bounded. Again, l' can be extended without increased norm to $B[a, b]$. We now need to show that there is a choice of G which makes l' agree with l. Let $f \in C[a, b]$, and suppose that we have a sequence of functions (f_n) in $B[a, b]$ which converges uniformly to f. Set $h = l - l'$. and note that h is itself a bounded linear functional. Then

$$|h(f) - h(f_n)| \leq \|h\| \, \|f - f_n\|_\infty,$$

whence $h(f) = \lim h(f_n)$ as $n \to \infty$. We shall in fact construct G (independently of f) and a sequence (f_n) such that $l(f_n) = l'(f_n)$ for all n, whence $h(f) = 0$, i.e. $l(f) = l'(f)$. Since the definition of G does not depend on f, this will establish that $l = l'$. To construct the sequence (f_n) we simply note that the properties of the modulus of continuity (Definition 6.2) imply the existence of a sequence of step functions which converge uniformly to f: choose such a sequence as

(f_n). Now define $\chi_t: [a, b] \to \mathbb{R}$ by $\chi_t(x)=1$ if $x \in [a, t),]$ $\chi_t(x)=0$ otherwise. (Thus χ_t is the characteristic function of $[a, t)$. Observe that $\chi_a(x)=0$ for all x.) Obviously every step function on $[a, b]$ is a linear combination (almost everywhere) of these characteristic functions with various choices of t, and l and l' are linear functionals. *So it is sufficient to choose G such that $l(\chi_t)=l'(\chi_t)$ for all t!* But for any G in $BV_0[a, b]$ we have

$$\begin{aligned} l'(\chi_t) &= \int_a^b \chi_t(x)\mathrm{d}G(x) \\ &= \int_a^t \mathrm{d}G(x) \\ &= G(t) - G(a) \text{ by (6.16) and (6.18)} \\ &= G(t) \text{ for } G \in BV_0[a, b]. \end{aligned}$$

Thus the only possible definition of G is

$$G(t) = l(\chi_t). \tag{6.23}$$

But does this lead to a G in $BV_0[a, b]$? To see that it does we note first that $G(0) = l(\chi_a)=l(0)=0$. Moreover let $P=\{t_0, t_i, \ldots, t_n\}$ be any partition of the interval $[a, b]$, where it does no harm to assume $t_0=a$. To avoid proliferation of subscripts, write (by a slight abuse of notation) $\chi_i=\chi_t$ when $t=t_i$. Also set $\sigma_i=\operatorname{sign}(\chi_i-\chi_{i-1})$. Then (with the summation over P)

$$\begin{aligned} \sum |l(\chi_i) - l(\chi_{i-1})| = \sum \sigma_i [l(\chi_i) - l(\chi_{i-1})] &= \sum l(\sigma_i [\chi_i - \chi_{i-1})] \\ &\leq \|l\| \, \|\sigma_i (\chi_i - \chi_{i-1})\|_\infty. \end{aligned}$$

But $(\chi_i-\chi_{i-1})(x)=\chi_i(x)-\chi_{i-1}(x)$. For any particular value of x, only one such term can be non-zero (the one with $t_{i-1}\leq x<t_i$) and this term is equal to 1. Moreover $|\sigma_i|=1$. Thus $\|\sigma_i(\chi_i-\chi_{i-1})\|_\infty=1$, whence $\sum l(\chi_i)-l(\chi_i-1)\,|\leq\|l\,\|$, independently of the partition P. This shows that indeed (6.23) yields G in $BV_0[a, b]$, and hence this choice of G yields $l'=l$.

Furthermore the argument of the previous paragraph also shows that $\operatorname{Var}(G)\leq\|l\,\|$. But we have already noted that (6.22) implies $\operatorname{Var}(G)\geq\|l\,\|$. Hence $\operatorname{Var}(G)=\|l\,\|$ as required.

□

Now in view of Theorem 6.4, and with the notation of that theorem, a necessary condition for W to be dense in V is that every linear functional that vanishes identically on W also vanishes identically on V, i.e. it is the trivial zero functional. The next result shows that this condition is also sufficient. (Recall the notation V' for the dual space of V.)

Theorem 6.12

Let V be a normed vector space and W a subspace. W is dense in V if and only if the only linear functional $l \in V'$ for which $l(\mathbf{w})=0$ for all $\mathbf{w} \in W$ is the trivial one $l(\mathbf{v}) \equiv 0$.

Proof

The 'only if' part is an immediate corollary of Theorem 6.4.

Now suppose that W is *not* dense in V. Then there is a $\mathbf{v} \in V$ and a number $\delta > 0$ such that $\|\mathbf{v}-\mathbf{w}\| > \delta$ for all $\mathbf{w}$ in W. Let X be the space spanned by $\mathbf{v}$ and the space W, i.e. the set of all linear combinations $\alpha\mathbf{v}+\mathbf{w}$, where $\alpha \in \mathbb{R}$ and $\mathbf{w} \in W$. Note that the number α here is unique, for if $\alpha_1 v + \mathbf{w}_1 = \alpha_2 \mathbf{v} + \mathbf{w}_2$ we have $(\alpha_1 - \alpha_2)\,\mathbf{v} = \mathbf{w}_2 - \mathbf{w}_2$, whence we must have $\alpha_1 = \alpha_2$ since $\mathbf{v} \notin W$. Thus we can define the following linear functional on X: $l\,(\alpha\mathbf{v}+\mathbf{w}) = \alpha$. Note that $l(\mathbf{v})=1$ and $l(\mathbf{w})=0$ for all $\mathbf{w} \in W$. Now if $\mathbf{x} = \alpha\mathbf{v}+\mathbf{w}$ with $\alpha \neq 0$,

$$\|\alpha\mathbf{v} + \mathbf{w}\| = |\alpha|\ \|\mathbf{v} + \alpha^{-1}\mathbf{w}\| \geq |l(\mathbf{x})|\delta$$

so

$$|l(\mathbf{x})| \leq \|\mathbf{x}\|/\delta.$$

On the other hand if $\alpha=0$, $|l(w)|=0$ so the inequality above holds trivially. This shows that l is a non-trivial bounded linear functional on W. By the Hahn–Banach Theorem 6.10, l may be extended to a bounded linear functional on the whole of V. This completes the proof.

□

With the aid of all this heavy machinery, the proof of the density of functions of the form (6.2) when σ is sigmoidal becomes almost trivial. Even so, we do not get the explicit estimate of Theorem 6.3. Nevertheless this method does have the advantage of the lower bounds in Theorem 6.4, and moreover provides a general method of establishing density for other choices of σ in (6.2). Since it is part of the aim of this book to set the study of neural nets in the context of established mathematics, this lengthy digression is hopefully justified!

To establish the density of one-dimensional sigmoidal functions we need only show that if the integral (6.19) vanishes whenever f is a sigmoidal function, then necessarily G is constant. This is fairly straightforward. We have for any sigmoidal function σ

$$0 = \int_a^b \sigma(kx + 1)\mathrm{d}G(x)$$

for all $k, l \in \mathbb{Z}$. Once again we adopt the basic idea of making k large enough so that the integrand looks like a step function. For any $p, q \in \mathbb{Z}$ with $p/q \in [a, b]$, define

$$r(x) = \begin{cases} 0 & a \le x < p/q \\ \sigma(l) & x = p/q \\ 1 & p/q < x \le b \end{cases}$$

Now consider the expression $\sigma(nq[t - p/q])$. As $n \to \infty$, this expression converges pointwise to r on $[a, b]$. By the Lebesgue Dominated Convergence Theorem (Theorem 1.39) we conclude that

$$\begin{aligned} 0 &= \int_a^b r(x)\mathrm{d}G(x) \\ &= \int_{(p/q)^+}^b \mathrm{d}G(x) + \sigma(l)[G(p/q^+) - G(p/q^-)]. \end{aligned}$$

The second term denotes the jump in w at the point p/q. Notice that the integral term does not depend on l so we first let $l \to -\infty$. By the definition of a sigmoidal function, $\sigma(l) \to 0$. We conclude that the integral term is zero. By subtraction we may deduce that

$$0 = \int_t^s \mathrm{d}G(x) \tag{6.24}$$

whenever s, t are rational and (by the Lebesgue Dominated Convergence Theorem using sequences of rational numbers to converge monotonically to the required end points) we deduce that in fact (2.9) holds for any $t, s \in [a, b]$. But this integral is precisely $G(s) - G(t)$, showing that G is in fact constant as required.

6.3 Using the Stone–Weierstrass theorem to establish density in *n*-dimensions

Now we need to pass to the n-dimensional case. There are two well-known methods of passing from one dimensional to higher dimensional approximations: the blending operator and the tensor product. The former method has not to these authors' knowledge been applied to neural nets at all: the 'infinite interpolation' properties of blending operators seem likely to cause severe problems. However the tensor product approach offers more hope.

To illustrate both the idea and the problems we will consider briefly the two-dimensional case. Suppose we have two sets of basis functions $\{\varphi_1, \ldots, \varphi_\mu\}$ and $\{\psi_1, \ldots, \psi_\nu\}$ where $\varphi_i, \psi_j\colon \mathbb{R} \to \mathbb{R}$. The *tensor product basis* is the set of $\mu \times \nu$ functions

$$\zeta_{ij}(x, y) = \varphi_i(x)\psi_j(y).$$

Sometimes one can construct a two-dimensional approximation using the tensor product basis by applying a one-dimensional approximation operator in each dimension: for example two-dimensional orthogonal expansions can be constructed in this way. In practice the two sets are usually the same kind of function (e.g. both polynomials or both trigonometric functions) although μ and ν may of course by different. Now let us consider what happens if we apply this construction to ridge functions (6.2). For simplicity we assume that the same function σ is to be used for x and y. So typical one-dimensional ridge functions will be $\sigma(a_i x + c_i)$ and $\sigma(b_j y + d_j)$. The tensor product basis thus consists of functions of the form $\sigma(a_i x + c_i)\, \sigma(b_j y + d_j)$. In general this does *not* give a two-dimensional ridge function so we will not land up with a neural net approximation of the form (6.2). However there is one particular choice of σ for which the construction *does* work, namely $\sigma(x) = \exp(x)$. For then we get

$$\begin{aligned}\sigma(a_i x + c_i)\sigma(b_j y + d_j) &= \exp(a_i x + c_i)\exp(b_j y + d_j)\\ &= \exp(a_i x + b_j y + c_j + d_j)\\ &= \sigma(a_i x + b_j y + c_j + d_j) >\end{aligned}$$

This observation has been used by several authors to produce n dimensional ridge function approximations. The basic idea is to prove the density of the ridge functions for the special case of $\sigma(x) = \exp(x)$ and then to use a one-dimensional result such as Theorem 6.1 to approximate the exponential function by linear combinations of the desired σ.

If we are not interested in constructive methods then a simple application of the Stone–Weierstrass Theorem will do for the first stage (see Cheney, 1966, p. 190; Diaconis and Shashahani, 1984; Hornik, Stinchcombe and White, 1989). Our next task is to prove this theorem. To avoid writing down explicit linear combinations of the form (6.2) all the time, we introduce the following definition.

Definition 6.13

Let V be a normed vector space and S a subset. S is said to be *fundamental* in V if span $\{S\}$ is dense V.

□

Note that S can be infinite here. We wish to show that the set of all sigmoidal functions (or other choice of σ's) is fundamental in $C[a, b]$.

In the previous century, Weierstrass showed that the set of all polynomials (in one variable) is fundamental in $C[a, b]$. Many proofs of this result are now known. The result was extended by Stone to cover other sets of functions which share similar algebraic properties to the polynomials. The Stone–Weierstrass Theorem is the classic density theorem. But the proof requires that a lemma states that the function $|x|$ on $[-1, 1]$ can be approximated by a polynomial. While it is possible to give direct proofs of this lemma, we shall instead give a proof of the Weierstrass result which introduces ideas and methods that we will require later.

Definition 6.14

Consider the function $U_n(x)$: $[-1, 1] \to \mathbb{R}$ defined by

$$U_n(x) = \frac{\sin (n+1)\theta}{\sin \theta} \text{ where } x = \cos \theta \text{ and } n \in \mathbb{N}.$$

$U_n(x)$ is called the nth *Chebyshev polynomial of the second kind.*

□

Proposition 6.15

(a) $U_0(x) = 1$, $U_1(x) = 2x$.
(b) $U_{n+1}(x) = xU_n(x) - U_{n-1}(\mathrm{x})$
(c) $U_n(x)$ is a polynomial of degree n.

Proof

(a) $U_0(x) = \sin \Theta / \sin \Theta = 1$. $U_2(x) = \sin 2\Theta / \sin \Theta = (2 \sin \Theta \cos \Theta)/\sin \Theta = 2x$.
(b) $\sin \Theta\, [U_{n+1}(x) + U_{n-1}(x)] = \sin (n+2)\Theta + \sin n\Theta = 2 \sin (n+1)\Theta \cos \Theta$ from which the result follows.
(c) Is a simple consequence of (a) and (b) by induction.

□

As might be suspected from Proposition 6.15(b) (compare Forsyth's Theorem

3.59) the Chebyshev polynomials of the second kind are orthogonal polynomials on [–1, 1] with inner product

$$<p, q> = \int_{-1}^{1} \sqrt{(1-x^2)}\, p(x)q(x)\mathrm{d}x.$$

Actually of more general importance in approximation theory are the *Chebyshev polynomial of the first kind* defined by $T_n(x) = \cos\theta$. These also satisfy the recurrence of Proposition 6.15(b) and are orthogonal with respect to the inner product

$$<p, q> = \int_{-1}^{1} \{\sqrt{(1-x^2)}\}^{-1} p(x)q(x)\mathrm{d}x.$$

However it is the second kind we need here. Or more precisely we need the properties of a related function.

Lemma 6.16

(a) $$U_n\left(\left\{\frac{y+1}{2}\right\}^{\frac{1}{2}}\right) = \frac{\sin \frac{1}{2}(n+1)\alpha}{\sin \frac{1}{2}\alpha} \quad \text{where } y = \cos\alpha. \tag{6.25}$$

(b) $$\left(\frac{\sin \frac{1}{2}n\alpha}{\sin \frac{1}{2}\alpha}\right)^{2k},$$

where $y = \cos\alpha$, and $k \in \mathbb{N}$, is a polynomial of degree $k(n-1)$ in y.

(c) Let $$\beta_{n,k} = \int_0^{\pi} \left(\frac{\sin \frac{1}{2}n\alpha}{n \sin \frac{1}{2}\alpha}\right)^{2k} \mathrm{d}\alpha \tag{6.26}$$

(note the n in the denominator) and

$$\rho_k = \int_0^{\pi/2} \left(\frac{\sin\mu}{\mu}\right)^{2k} \mathrm{d}\mu.$$

Then $\beta_{n,k} > 2\rho_k/n$.

Proof

(a) Setting $\theta = \frac{1}{2}\alpha$ we have $y = \cos\alpha = 2\cos^2 \frac{1}{2}\theta - 1$. With x as in Definition 6.14 we get the required identity with $y = 2x^2 - 1$.

(b) It is easy to see from Proposition 6.15 that $U_n(x)$ with n even/odd contains only even/odd powers of x. Thus if n is even, the left-hand side of (6.25) is a polynomial of degree $n/2$ in y. If n is odd, $U_n(x)$ can be written as $x \times$(an even polynomial). This even polynomial is a polynomial of degree $(n-1)/2$ in y.

(c) The integrand of (6.26) is an even function of α (i.e. it has the same value if α is replaced by $-\alpha$) so

$$\begin{aligned}\beta_{n,k} &= \int_0^{\pi} \left(\frac{\sin \frac{1}{2} n\alpha}{n \sin \frac{1}{2}\alpha} \right)^{2k} d\alpha \\ &= 2 \int_0^{\pi/2} \left(\frac{\sin n\theta}{n \sin \theta} \right)^{2k} d\theta \text{ where } \theta = \tfrac{1}{2}\alpha \\ &\geq 2 \int_0^{\pi/2} \left(\frac{\sin n\theta}{n\theta} \right)^{2k} d\theta \text{ since } \sin\theta \leq \theta \text{ for } 0 \leq \theta \leq \pi/2. \\ &= \frac{2}{\pi} \int_0^{n\pi/2} \left(\frac{\sin \mu}{\mu} \right)^{2k} d\mu \text{ with } \mu = n\theta \\ &> 2\rho_k/n.\end{aligned}$$

□

The following result strengthens that of Weierstrass, since it actually estimates the error of polynomial approximation in terms of the degree of continuity ω of f (see Definition 6.2).

Theorem 6.17 (Jackson's Theorem)
Let $f \in C[a, b]$. For each $m \in \mathbb{N}$, there exist a polynomial p_m of degree $\leq m$ such that $\| f - p_m \|_\infty \leq M\, \omega\,(f;\, [b-a]\,/m)$. Here M is a certain absolute constant.

Proof
It is convenient to standardise on the interval $[-1, 1]$: other intervals require only a linear change of variable. First observe that for any real number λ

$$\begin{aligned}\beta_{n,2} &= \tfrac{1}{2} \int_{-\pi}^{\pi} \left(\frac{\sin \frac{1}{2} n\alpha}{n \sin \frac{1}{2}\alpha} \right)^{4} d\alpha \\ &= \tfrac{1}{2} \int_{-\pi}^{\pi} \left(\frac{\sin \frac{1}{2} n(\alpha+\lambda)}{n \sin \frac{1}{2}(\alpha+\lambda)} \right)^{4} d\alpha:\end{aligned}$$

just replace α by $\alpha+\lambda$ and observe that the integration is over one period of the integrand. Hence

$$2\beta_{n,2} = \int_0^\pi \left(\frac{\sin \frac{1}{2}n(\alpha+\lambda)}{n \sin \frac{1}{2}(\alpha+\lambda)} \right)^4 d\alpha + \int_{-\pi}^0 \left(\frac{\sin \frac{1}{2}n(\alpha+\lambda)}{n \sin \frac{1}{2}(\alpha+\lambda)} \right)^4 d\alpha$$

$$= \int_0^\pi \left(\frac{\sin \frac{1}{2}n(\alpha+\lambda)}{n \sin \frac{1}{2}(\alpha+\lambda)} \right)^4 d\alpha + \int_0^\pi \left(\frac{\sin \frac{1}{2}n(\alpha-\lambda)}{n \sin \frac{1}{2}(\alpha-\lambda)} \right)^4 d\alpha$$

$$= \int_0^\pi \left(\frac{\sin \frac{1}{2}n(\alpha+\lambda)}{n \sin \frac{1}{2}(\alpha+\lambda)} \right)^4 + \left(\frac{\sin \frac{1}{2}n(\alpha-\lambda)}{n \sin \frac{1}{2}(\alpha-\lambda)} \right)^4 d\alpha,$$

whence, with $x = \cos \lambda$,

$$f(x) = \frac{1}{2\beta_{n,2}} \int_0^\pi f(\cos \lambda) \left\{ \left(\frac{\sin \frac{1}{2}n(\alpha+\lambda)}{n \sin \frac{1}{2}(\alpha+\lambda)} \right)^4 + \left(\frac{\sin \frac{1}{2}n(\alpha-\lambda)}{n \sin \frac{1}{2}(\alpha-\lambda)} \right)^4 \right\} d\alpha.$$

$$= \frac{1}{4\beta_{n,2}} \int_{-\pi}^\pi f(\cos \lambda) \left\{ \left(\frac{\sin \frac{1}{2}n(\alpha+\lambda)}{n \sin \frac{1}{2}(\alpha+\lambda)} \right)^4 + \left(\frac{\sin \frac{1}{2}n(\alpha-\lambda)}{n \sin \frac{1}{2}(\alpha-\lambda)} \right)^4 \right\} d\alpha.$$

since the integrand is even. But from Lemma 6.16(b),

$$\left(\frac{\sin \frac{1}{2}n(\alpha+\lambda)}{\sin \frac{1}{2}(\alpha+\lambda)} \right)^4$$

is a polynomial of degree $2n-2$ in $y = \cos(\alpha+\lambda) = \cos \alpha \cos \lambda - \sin \alpha \sin \lambda$. Replacing λ by $-\lambda$ changes the sign of the last term. Thus in the expression

$$\left\{ \left(\frac{\sin \frac{1}{2}n(\alpha+\lambda)}{n \sin \frac{1}{2}(\alpha+\lambda)} \right)^4 + \left(\frac{\sin \frac{1}{2}n(\alpha-\lambda)}{n \sin \frac{1}{2}(\alpha-\lambda)} \right)^4 \right\}$$

any terms involving odd powers of $\sin \lambda$ will cancel out. Even powers of $\sin \lambda$ can be written in terms of $\cos \lambda$ using the identity $\sin^2 \lambda + \cos^2 \lambda = 1$. So the expression is polynomial of degree $\leq 2n-2$ in $x = \cos \lambda$. (This would, of course remain true if we used the power two rather than four, but the power four is required later.) Hence

$$q(x) = \frac{1}{4\beta_{n,2}} \int_{-\pi}^\pi f(\cos \alpha) \left\{ \left(\frac{\sin \frac{1}{2}n(\alpha+\lambda)}{n \sin \frac{1}{2}(\alpha+\lambda)} \right)^4 + \left(\frac{\sin \frac{1}{2}n(\alpha-\lambda)}{n \sin \frac{1}{2}(\alpha-\lambda)} \right)^4 \right\} d\alpha.$$

is also a polynomial of degree $\leq 2n-2$ in x. It follows that

$$|f(x) - q(x)| \leq \frac{1}{4\beta_{n,2}} \int_{-\pi}^\pi |f(\cos \lambda) - f(\cos \alpha)| \left(\frac{\sin \frac{1}{2}n(\alpha+\lambda)}{n \sin \frac{1}{2}(\alpha+\lambda)} \right)^4 d\alpha$$

$$+\frac{1}{4\beta_{n,2}}\int_{-\pi}^{\pi}|f(\cos\lambda)-f(\cos\alpha)|\left(\frac{\sin\frac{1}{2}n(\alpha-\lambda)}{n\sin\frac{1}{2}(\alpha-\lambda)}\right)^4 d\alpha. \tag{6.27}$$

Now in view of Definition 6.2 and the remarks in the paragraph following it, we get

$$\int_{-\pi}^{\pi}|f(\cos\lambda)-f(\cos\alpha)|\left(\frac{\sin\frac{1}{2}n(\alpha+\lambda)}{n\sin\frac{1}{2}(\alpha+\lambda)}\right)^4 d\alpha$$

$$\leq\int_{-\pi}^{\pi}\omega(f;|\cos\lambda-\cos\alpha|)\left(\frac{\sin\frac{1}{2}n(\alpha+\lambda}{n\sin\frac{1}{2}(\alpha+\lambda)}\right)^4 d\alpha$$

$$=\int_{-\pi}^{\pi}\omega(f;2|\sin\tfrac{1}{2}(\alpha+\lambda)\sin\tfrac{1}{2}(\alpha-\lambda)|)\left(\frac{\sin\frac{1}{2}n(\alpha+\lambda)}{n\sin\frac{1}{2}(\alpha+\lambda)}\right)^4 d\alpha$$

$$=2\int_{\lambda-\pi/2}^{\lambda+\pi/2}\omega(f;2|\sin\mu\sin(\mu-\lambda)|)\left(\frac{\sin n\mu}{n\sin\mu}\right)^4 d\mu$$

$$\leq 4\int_{-\pi/2}^{\pi/2}\omega(f;|\sin\mu|)\left(\frac{\sin n\mu}{n\sin\mu}\right)^4 d\mu \quad \text{(the integrand has period } \pi)$$

$$=8\int_{0}^{\pi/2}\omega(f;|\sin\mu|)\left(\frac{\sin n\mu}{n\sin\mu}\right)^4 d\mu \quad \text{(the integrand is even)}$$

$$\leq\frac{\pi^4}{2}\int_{0}^{\pi/2}\omega(f;\mu)\left(\frac{\sin n\mu}{n\mu}\right)^4 d\mu \quad \text{(since } \sin\mu\geq 2\mu/\pi \text{ on the interval of integration)}$$

$$\leq\frac{\pi^4}{2n}\int_{0}^{n\pi/2}\omega(f;t/n)\left(\frac{\sin t}{t}\right)^4 dt \quad (t=n\mu)$$

$$=\frac{\pi^4}{2n}\sum_{j=o}^{n-1}\int_{j\pi/2}^{(j+1)\pi/2}\omega(f;t/n)\left(\frac{\sin t}{t}\right)^4 dt$$

$$\leq\frac{\pi^4}{2n}\sum_{j=o}^{n-1}\int_{j\pi/2}^{(j+1)\pi/2}\omega\left(f;\frac{(j+1)\pi}{2n}\right)\left(\frac{\sin t}{t}\right)^4 dt$$

$$\leq\frac{\pi^4}{2n}\omega\left(f;\frac{\pi}{2n}\right)\sum_{j=o}^{n-1}\int_{j\pi/2}^{(j+1)\pi/2}(j+1)\left(\frac{\sin t}{t}\right)^4 dt$$

$$\leq\frac{\pi^4}{2n}\omega\left(f;\frac{4}{2n}\right)\sum_{j=0}^{n-1}\int_{j\pi/2}^{(j+1)\pi/2}(t+1)\left(\frac{\sin t}{t}\right)^4 dt$$

$$\leq \frac{\pi^4}{n}\,\omega\left(f:\frac{2}{m}\right)\int_0^\infty (t+1)\left(\frac{\sin t}{t}\right)^4 \mathrm{d}t,$$

where $m=2n$. Since this bound is actually independent of λ, it applies also to the second integral in (6.27). Thus

$$\begin{aligned}|f(x)-q(x)| &\leq \frac{\pi^4}{2n\beta_{n,2}}\,\omega\left(f;\frac{2}{m}\right)\int_0^\infty (t+1)\left(\frac{\sin t}{t}\right)^4 \mathrm{d}t \\ &\leq \frac{\pi^4}{4\rho_2}\,\omega\left(f;\frac{2}{m}\right)\int_0^\infty (t+1)\left(\frac{\sin t}{t}\right)^4 \mathrm{d}t, \qquad (6.28)\end{aligned}$$

where ρ_2 is given in Lemma 6.16(c). This completes the proof with

$$M=\frac{\pi^4}{4\rho_2}\int_0^\infty (t+1)\left(\frac{\sin t}{t}\right)^4 \mathrm{d}t: \qquad (6.29)$$

since q is actually of degree $\leq m-2$ we note that it is *a fortiori* of degrees $\leq m-1$ and m, so the result holds for odd degrees as well.

□

We note that the constant M here is not particularly large. In fact this is not the best possible value of M (see Cheney, 1966, pp. 139–148) but is sufficient for our purposes. Although the proof here is constructive, this is not really a practical method of approximation. However, orthogonal expansion in terms of Chebyshev polynomials of the first kind is a popular method of polynomial approximation (Cheney, 1966, Chapters 3 and 4).

We now proceed to a proof of the Stone–Weierstrass Theorem. The key concept is that of an *algebra*. We will consider real vector spaces, although the results can be generalised with the usual modifications to complex spaces.

Definition 6.18

Let V be a vector space over $\mathbb{R}$, and suppose that there is defined a multiplication operator $\times$ such that the following properties hold for all $\mathbf{u}, \mathbf{v}, \mathbf{w}, \in V$.

(a) $\mathbf{u}\times(\mathbf{v}+\mathbf{w})=\mathbf{u}\times\mathbf{v}+\mathbf{u}\times\mathbf{w}$ (Left distributive law)
(b) $(\mathbf{v}+\mathbf{w})\times\mathbf{u}=\mathbf{v}\times\mathbf{u}+\mathbf{w}\times\mathbf{u}$ (Right distributive law)
(c) $\mathbf{u}\times(\mathbf{v}\times\mathbf{w})=(\mathbf{u}\times\mathbf{v})\times\mathbf{w}$ (Associative law)
(d) $\alpha(\mathbf{u}\times\mathbf{v})=(\alpha\mathbf{u})\times\mathbf{v}=\mathbf{u}\times(\alpha\mathbf{v})$ for all $\alpha\in\mathbb{R}$.

Then V with $\times$ is said to be an *algebra*.

□

Examples 6.19

(a) $C[a, b]$ is an algebra with the product defined pointwise: $(f\times g)(x)=f(x)g(x)$. Similarly the other standard spaces of real functions can be made into algebras this way. More generally, the space $C(X)$ consisting of continuous functions defined on any metric space X form an algebra.

(b) The set of all polynomial functions is a subalgebra of $C[a, b]$ since the product of two polynomials is a polynomial.

(c) Similarly, other spaces of functions which are closed under pointwise product are algebras: linear combinations of exponential or trigonometric functions for example.

(d) The space of all $n\times n$ real matrices with the usual product is an algebra.

□

One technical lemma is required. This requires the notion of a *cover*. Let P be a subset of $\mathbb{R}$. A cover of P is a collection C of sets O_α (not necessarily countable) such that each $O_\alpha\subset\mathbb{R}$, and $P\subset\cup O_\alpha$. If each O_α is open, then C is called an *open cover*. Now let X be a closed, bounded set in $\mathbb{R}^n$.

Lemma 6.20

Every open cover of X contains a finite subcover.

Proof

For simplicity, we will give the proof for $n=1$ and a closed interval $[a, b]$. Essentially the same ideas will handle the general case.

Let $S(x, \varepsilon)$ denote the open interval $(x-\varepsilon, x+\varepsilon)$. We first note that $[a, b]$ can be covered by a finite number of open intervals $S(x, \varepsilon)$ with fixed ε. This is obvious since they are of finitely large length! Now let $C=\{O_\alpha\}$ be an open cover of $[a, b]$. We prove that for ε sufficiently small, every $S(x, \varepsilon)$ (for each x in $[a, b]$) lies in some O_α. For if not, we can construct a sequence $S(x_n, 1/n)$ each of which lies in no O_α. Since the points x_n are confined to the closed interval $[a, b]$, we may assume (by selecting a subsequence if necessary) that they converge, i.e. that $x_n\to x^*$ for some $x^*\in[a, b]$. But the O_α cover the interval, so $x^*\in$ some O_α. Since this O_α is open, $S(x^*, \delta)\subset O_\alpha$ for some $\delta>0$. But since $x_n\to x^*$, $S(x_n, 1/n)\subset S(x^*, \delta)\subset O_\alpha$ for n sufficiently large: a contradiction.

Thus $[a, b]$ is contained in a finite number of $S(x, \varepsilon)$'s, and each such $S(x, \varepsilon)$ is contained in a O_α. This establishes the result.

□

Any set in a metric space which has this property that every open cover contains a finite subcover is said to be *compact*. The Stone–Weierstrass Theorem works for any compact set, but subsets of $\mathbb{R}^n$ will be sufficient for our purposes.

Now for the main result.

Theorem 6.21 (the Stone-Weierstrass Theorem)

Let X be a closed, bounded set in $\mathbb{R}^n$ and A a subalgebra of $C(X)$, and suppose the following properties hold.

(a) A contains 1. More precisely the function $f\in A$ where $f\colon X\to\mathbb{R}, f(x)=1$ for all x.

(b) For each pair of distinct points $x, y\in X$, there exists $g\in A$ such that $g(x) \neq g(y)$.

Then A is dense in $C\,[a, b]$.

Proof

Let B be the closure of A, i.e. set of all f which are limits of uniformly convergent sequences in A. We wish to establish that $B=C(X)$. It is easy to check that B is itself a subalgebra of $C(x)$. To prove the theorem we require three preliminary steps.

Firstly, let $f\in B$. By Theorem 6.17 there exists a sequence p_n of polynomials which converges uniformly to $|x|$ in the interval $[-\|f\|_\infty, \|f\|_\infty]$. Then $|f|=\lim p_n(f)$ as $n\to\infty$, so each $p_n(f)$ is itself the limit of functions in A. It follows that if $f\in B$, then $|f|\in B$.

Secondly, for any $f, g\in B$, we see that

$$\max\{f, g\} = \tfrac{1}{2}(f+g+|f-g|)$$

and

$$\min\{f, g\} = \tfrac{1}{2}(f+g-|f-g|)$$

are also in B, since algebras are closed under addition.

Thirdly, given any two points, $p, q\in X$ and real numbers λ, μ, there exists a function $h_{p,q}\in A$ with $h_{p,q}(p)=\lambda$ and $h_{p,q}(q)=\mu$. Since we know there exists f with $f(p)\neq f(q)$, a suitable linear combination of f and l will establish this result. Specifically,

$$h_{p,q} = mf + cl \text{ where } m = (\lambda-\mu)/[f(p)-f(q)] \text{ and}$$
$$c = [\mu f(p) - \lambda f(q)]/[f(p)-f(q)].$$

We now proceed to the main part of the proof. Suppose $B \neq C(X)$. Then there exists $F \in C(X)$ and $\varepsilon > 0$ such that for every $g \in B$ $\|F-g\|_\infty > \varepsilon$. For each pair of points p, q, set $\lambda = F(p)$, $\mu = F(q)$ and define an open set

$$O_{p,q} = \{x \in X \mid h_{p,q}(x) < F(x) + \varepsilon\}.$$

Now fix q and observe that $p \in O_{p,q}$ since $h_{p,q} = F(p)$. Thus the sets $O_{p,q}$ for fixed q cover X. Lemma 6.20 tells us that we can choose finitely many p's, say $p_1 \ldots p_k$ such that X is still covered. Let

$$h_q = \min\{h_{p_1,q}, \ldots h_{p_k,q}\}.$$

For any $x \in X$, there is an index i with $x \in O_{pi,q}$ whence $h_q(x) < F(x) + \varepsilon$. Now setting

$$O_q = \{x \in X \mid h_q(x) > F(x) - \varepsilon\},$$

a similar argument enables us to select $h \in B$ as the maximum of finitely many h_q's such that for any $x \in X$, $F(x) - \varepsilon < h(x) < F(x) + \varepsilon$.

This contradicts the assumption $\|F-g\|_\infty > \varepsilon$ for all $g \in B$.

□

As a simple example, we note that the polynomials fulfil the conditions of this theorem, and thus are dense in $C(X)$. From the density of polynomials of one variable in $C[a, b]$, we have deduced density of polynomials in multidimensional spaces.

Now to return to our investigation of the density of the ridge functions (6.2). As we indicated at the start of this section, we base our results on the case where σ is the exponential function.

Theorem 6.22

The set E of functions of the form $\mu(\mathbf{x}) = \exp(\mathbf{a}^{\mathrm{T}}\mathbf{x})$, where $\mathbf{a} \in \mathbb{R}^n$, is fundamental in $C[a, b]$.

Proof

By the Stone–Weierstrass Theorem we need only show that the set forms an algebra and separates points. Suppose $\mathbf{x} \in [a, b]$. We have firstly

$$\exp(\mathbf{a}^{\mathrm{T}}\mathbf{x})\exp(\mathbf{b}^{\mathrm{T}}\mathbf{x}) = \exp(\mathbf{a}^{\mathrm{T}}\mathbf{x} + \mathbf{b}^{\mathrm{T}}\mathbf{x}) = \exp([\mathbf{a}^{\mathrm{T}} + \mathbf{b}^{\mathrm{T}}]\mathbf{x}).$$

This establishes that E is an algebra. Also the set contains the function '1': simply choose $\mathbf{a} = \mathbf{0}$. It remains to show that E separates the points of $[a, b]$. Let

$\mathbf{x}, \mathbf{y} \in [a,b]$ with $\mathbf{x} \neq \mathbf{y}$. Set $\mathbf{a}=(\mathbf{x}-\mathbf{y})$. Then $\mathbf{a}^T(\mathbf{x}-\mathbf{y}) \neq 0$ so $\mathbf{a}^T\mathbf{x} \neq \mathbf{a}^T\mathbf{y}$. Thus $\exp(\mathbf{a}^T\mathbf{x}) \neq \exp(\mathbf{a}^T\mathbf{y})$. The proof is complete.

□

Before considering more constructive versions of this result let us complete the density proof.

Theorem 6.23

Let X be a compact set in $\mathbb{R}^n$. Then the set F of functions of the form $g(\mathbf{x})$, defined by (6.2) with σ a continuous sigmoidal function, is dense in $C(X)$.

Proof

Let $f \in C(X)$. For any $\varepsilon>0$, there exists (by Theorem 6.19) a finite number m of vectors $\mathbf{a}_i$ such that

$$\|f - \sum_{i=1}^{m} \exp(\mathbf{a}_i{}^T\mathbf{x})\|_\infty < \varepsilon/2.$$

Since there are only m scalars $\mathbf{a}_i{}^T\mathbf{x}$, we may find a finite interval including all of them. Thus there exists a number ψ such that $\exp(\mathbf{a}_i{}^T\mathbf{x})=\exp(\psi y)$ where $y=(\mathbf{a}_i{}^T\mathbf{x}/\psi) \in [0, 1]$. Then Theorem 6.1 tells us that the function $\exp(\psi y)$ can be approximated by linear combinations functions of the form $\sigma(\mathbf{w}_j{}^T\mathbf{x}+c_j)$ with a uniform error less than $\varepsilon/(2m)$, from which the desired result easily follows.

□

Sun and Cheney (see, e.g. Light, 1992, p. 4) have a more sophisticated version of this argument which shows that the elements of the vectors $\mathbf{w}_j$ and the constants c_j may be chosen to be rational numbers (i.e. there is a countable fundamental set). We will not give the details of their result as it complicates the proof significantly and in any case the existence of such a countable set will be established constructively later.

Neither is there anything particularly special about sigmoidal functions. Hornik (1991) showed that it is sufficient that σ be continuous, bounded and non-constant. Leshno, Lin, Pinkus and Schoken (1993) consider the class M of functions that are locally bonded (i.e. bounded on compact sets), and such that the closure of the set of points of discontinuity of any function in M is of zero Lebesgue measure. In particular, therefore, all continuous functions are in M. They show that density is obtained if σ is any function in M *except* a polynomial. That σ cannot be chosen a polynomial is a triviality: if σ is a polynomial of degree m, so is g defined by (6.2). Clearly the polynomials of degree m are not dense. It is therefore really quite remarkable that any other choice of $\sigma \in M$ will do. The proof is not all that complex, but requires more functional analysis that we introduce here. (In particular, it requires Baire's Category Theorem: for which, see, e.g. Kreyszig, 1978, p. 247.) However important steps in the proof consider approximation by smooth σ's, and the use of Fourier convolutions. Both these issues will be considered below. A reader who has completed this chapter and has looked up Baire's theorem should be in a position to tackle the proof!

6.4 Degree of approximation

Our nest task is to consider how good neural networks are at approximating functions. At the time of writing, there are still many open questions in this area, but some interesting results do exist. Most of these work by comparing the networks with functions such as polynomials or trigonometric functions for which results are already known. Others are based on transforms such as the Fourier Transform. We shall consider both approaches. As a starting point, let us consider approximation of smooth functions by polynomials. The following result, also due to Jackson, is typical. Suppose that f is differentiable in $[-1, 1]$. Then $|f(x)-f(y)| \leq \|f'\|_\infty |x-y|$. It follows from Theorem 6.17 and the definition of the modulus of continuity that for each m there exists a polynomial of degree at most m with

$$\|f-p_m\|_\infty \leq \frac{2M\|f'\|_\infty}{m}$$

Now let q_{m-1} be a polynomial of degree at most $m-1$ $(m \geq 1)$ which satisfies

$$\|f'-q_{m-1}\|_\infty \leq M\omega[f; 2/(m-1)]:$$

the existence of q_{m-1} follows from Theorem 6.17 with f replaced by f'. Further, let Q_m be any indefinite integral of q_{m-1}: thus Q_m is a polynomial of degree at most m. Since $f-Q_m$ is differentiable, we can find a polynomial P_m of degree at most m with

$$\|f-Q_m-P_m\|_\infty \leq \frac{2M\|f'-q_{m-1}\|_\infty}{m}.$$

$$\leq \frac{2M^2\,\omega[f; 2/(m-1)]}{m}.$$

$$\leq \frac{(2M)^2\|f''\|_\infty}{m(m-1)}$$

if f' is itself differentiable, i.e. if $f \in C^2[-1, 1]$. Since $m/(m-1) \to 1$ as $m \to \infty$, it follows that there is a constant K_2 (independent of f) and a polynomial $h_m = Q_m - P_m$ of degree at most m which satisfies, for $m \geq 2$,

$$\|f - h_m\|_\infty \leq \frac{K_2\|f''\|_\infty}{m^2}.$$

Indeed, let us further suppose that $f \in C^k[-1, 1]$, i.e. has k continuous derivatives on the interval. Then we may apply the argument above inductively to conclude that for $m \geq k$, there is a constant K_k (independent of f and m) and a polynomial r_k of degree at most m which satisfies

$$\|f - r_m\|_\infty \leq \frac{K_k\|f^{[k]}\|_\infty}{m^k}. \tag{6.30}$$

In other words, the smoother f is, the more rapidly it may be approximated by a polynomial of degree m as $m \to \infty$. A basic task when presented with any set of approximating functions is to determine whether a corresponding estimate holds for that space. We now proceed to address that question for the class of perceptions with one hidden layer. However, we first need to extend the polynomial result to the multidimensional case. Several complications will present themselves!

Firstly, what set in $\mathbb{R}^n$ are we going to approximate on? In one dimension, it is rarely sensible to choose anything other than a (possibly infinite) interval. But in two or more dimensions there is a wide choice of plausible sets: we might for example work on the unit sphere or an ellipsoid. These sets tend to complicate the arguments somewhat, without adding much essentially new. Thus for simplicity we will restrict attention to rectangular regions, and further by a suitable linear change of variable this case can be reduced to that of approximation on the unit hypercube $[-1, 1]^n = [-1, 1] \times [-1, 1] \times \ldots \times [-1, 1]$. Can we extend Theorem 6.17 to cover polynomial approximation on this set? In (say) two dimensions a polynomial is a function of two variables. Consider for example $3x^2 + xy + xy^3$. What is the degree of this polynomial? For fixed y, it is a polynomial of degree 2 in x. We say that the *degree* in x is 2. Similarly the degree in y is 3. However the *total degree* is what we would get if we replaced each variable by the same one. Replacing both x and y by z we get $3z^2+z^2+z^4$, so the total degree is 4. Another way to look at this is to examine each monomial term in the expression and add up the degrees of each variable. The first term $3x^2$ gives $2+0=2$; the second term xy yields $1+1=2$ and from the last term xy^3 we get $1+3=4$. The largest of these monomial degrees is the total degree 4. Obviously the total degree is an upper bound for the degree in each variable. Indeed in $\mathbb{R}^n$, if the degree in the x_i variable is m_i, and the total degree is d, we have $m \leq d \leq \sum m_i \leq nm$, where m is the largest m_i. The simplest way to generalise Theorem 6.17 is to consider each degree separately. Again, consider two dimensions initially. A continuous function $f(x_1, x_2)$ is certainly continuous in each variable separately. Say we fix x_2 temporarily. Then $f(x_1, x_2)$ will have a modulus of continuity (see Definition 6.2) considered as a function of x_1. If we take now the supremum over *all* values of x_2, we will have a modulus that is valid for all values of x_2 when f is considered as a function of x_1. Specifically, let

$$\omega_1(f; u) = \sup_{x_2} \sup_{|x_1-y_1|<u} |f(x_1, x_2) - f(y_1, x_2)| .$$

We will call this the *partial modulus of continuity* of f with respect to x_1, and of course we make make a similar definition for x_2. We will also need the total modulus of continuity, defined by analogy with Definition 6.2 to be

$$\omega(f; u, v) = \sup_{\substack{|x_1-y_1|<u \\ |x_2-y_2|<v}} |f(\mathbf{x}) - f(\mathbf{y})| .$$

Observe that $\omega_1(f; u) = \omega(f; u, 0)$ and $\omega_2(f; v) = \omega(f; 0, v)$, and that the properties following Definition 6.2 generalise to these moduli. More formally in n dimensions we make the following definition.

Definition 6.25

Let $f \in C[-1, 1]^n$. Define the *modulus of continuity* of f to be

$$\omega(f; \mathbf{u}) = \sup_{|x_i-y_i|<u_i} |f(\mathbf{x}) - f(\mathbf{y})| .$$

By an abuse of notation we will write $\omega(f; \delta)$ as shorthand for $\omega(f; \mathbf{u})$ where $\|\mathbf{u}\|_\infty = \delta$.

Further, for each i, define the *partial modulus of continuity*

$$\omega_i(f;u) = \sup_{\text{All } x_j\, j\neq i} \sup_{|x_i-y_i|<u} |f(x_1,x_2)-f(y_1,x_2)| .$$

□

In addition to the properties of the one-dimensional modules, we have some relationships between the partial and total moduli.

Lemma 6.26
Let $f \in C[-1,1]^n$,

(a) $\omega_i(f;u) \leq \omega(f;\mathbf{u})$ for each i.

(b) $\omega(f;\mathbf{u}) \leq \sum_{i=1}^{n} \omega_i(f;u)$.

Proof
(a) Since $\omega(f;\mathbf{u})$ is a monotone decreasing function of each u_j, we will not increase its value by letting $u_j \to 0$ for each $j \neq i$. But the resulting limit is $\omega_i(f;u)$. (In other words, $\omega_i(f;u) = \omega(f;u\mathbf{e}_i)$, as observed in the two-dimensional case above.)

(b) For clarity we give the proof for two dimensions. (The extension to n dimensions is trivial, but messy notationally.)

$$\omega(f;u,v) = \sup_{\substack{|x_1-y_1|<u \\ |x_2-y_2|<v}} |f(x_1,x_2)-f(y_1,y_2)|$$

$$= \sup_{\substack{|x_1-y_1|<u \\ |x_2-y_2|<v}} |f(x_1,x_2)+f(y_1,x_2)-f(y_1,x_2)-f(y_1,y_2)|$$

$$\leq \sup_{\substack{|x_1-y_1|<u \\ |x_2-y_2|<v}} |f(x_1,x_2)+f(y_1,x_2)| + \sup_{\substack{|x_1-y_1|<u \\ |x_2-y_2|<v}} |f(y_1,x_2)-f(y_1,y_2)|$$

$$\leq \sup_{x_2\in[-1,1]} \sup_{|x_1-y_1|<u} |f(x_1,x_2)+f(t,x_2)| +$$

$$\sup_{y_1\in[-1,1]} \sup_{|x_2-y_2|<v} |f(y_1,x_2)-f(y_1,y_2)|$$

$$= \omega_1(f;u) + \omega_2(f;v).$$

□

Now for the n-dimensional Jackson Theorem.

Theorem 6.27

Let $f \in C[-1, 1]^n$. For each set of degrees $\mathbf{m}=(m_1, m_2 \ldots m_n)$, $m_i \in \mathbb{N}$, there exists a polynomial $p_{\mathbf{m}}$ of degree $\le m_i$ in variable x_i such that

$$\|f - p_{\mathbf{m}}\|_\infty \le M \sum_{i=1}^{n} \omega_i(f; 2/m_i).$$

Here M is the same constant as in Theorem 6.17.

Proof

As in the previous lemma, we avoid notational horrors by giving the proof for two dimensions. The idea is simple. To approximate $f(x_1, x_2)$ we fix x_2 and approximate this by a polynomial in x_1. The coefficients of this polynomial in x_1 will depend on x_2, and are then approximated by a polynomial in x_2. However the problem is that if the first approximating polynomial is chosen to satisfy Theorem 6.17 but otherwise arbitrary, we do not know whether its coefficients depend continuously on x_2. Instead we have to make explicit use of the polynomial approximation process used in the proof. So let us consider $f(x,y)$ and for the moment fix y. With β_{n2} as in Lemma 6.16 and the proof of Theorem 6.17 we construct with $x=\cos\lambda$, and $l_1 \in \mathbb{N}$

$$q(x, y) = \frac{1}{4\beta_{n,2}} \int_{-\pi}^{\pi} f(\cos\alpha\ y) \left\{ \left(\frac{\sin \frac{1}{2} l_1(\alpha+\lambda)}{l_1 \sin \frac{1}{2}(\alpha+\lambda)} \right)^4 + \left(\frac{\sin \frac{1}{2} l_1(\alpha-\lambda)}{l_1 \sin \frac{1}{2}(\alpha-\lambda)} \right)^4 \right\} d\alpha.$$

This is a polynomial of degree $\le 2l_1 - 2$ in x: l_1 is used here to avoid confusion with the dimension n. It follows from (6.27), (6.28) and (6.29) that

$$|f(x, y) - q(x, y) \le M\omega_1 \left(f; \frac{2}{m_1} \right) \text{for each } y, \text{ with } m_1 = 2l_1.$$

(The case of odd m_1 is dealt with as in the proof of Theorem 6.17.) But $q(x, y)$ is not a polynomial in y. However considered as a function of the second variable, we note that

$$|q(x, u) - q(x, v)|$$

$$\le \frac{\omega_2(f; u - v)}{4\beta_{n,2}} \int_{-\pi}^{\pi} \left\{ \left(\frac{\sin \frac{1}{2} l_1(\alpha+\lambda)}{l_1 \sin \frac{1}{2}(\alpha+\lambda)} \right)^4 + \left(\frac{\sin \frac{1}{2} 2l_1(\alpha-\lambda)}{l_1 \sin \frac{1}{2}(\alpha-\lambda)} \right)^4 \right\} d\alpha$$

$= \omega_2(f; u-v)$ from the definition of $\beta_{n,2}$ (compare the first part of the proof of Theorem 6.17).

Since this holds for any u and v, we conclude that $\omega_2(q; u-v) \leq \omega_2(f; u-v)$. Now let

$$r(x, y) = \frac{1}{4\beta_{n,2}} \int_{-\pi}^{\pi} q(x, \cos\alpha) \left\{ \left(\frac{\sin \frac{1}{2} l_2(\alpha+\nu)}{l_2 \sin \frac{1}{2}(\alpha+\nu)} \right)^4 + \left(\frac{\sin \frac{1}{2} l_2(\alpha-\nu)}{l_2 \sin \frac{1}{2}(\alpha-\nu)} \right)^4 \right\} d\alpha,$$

with $y = \cos \nu$. It follows again that

$$|q(x, y) - p(x, y)| \leq M\omega_2\left(q; \frac{2}{m_2}\right) \text{for each } x, \text{ with } m_2 = 2l_2.$$

Moreover r is a polynomial in x (because q is) and y because of the now familiar argument about the integrand. Finally we observe that

$$\begin{aligned} |f(x, y) - p(x, y)| &= |f(x, y) - q(x, y) + q(x, y) - p(x, y)| \\ &\leq |f(x, y) - q(x, y)| + |q(x, y) - p(x, y)| \\ &\leq M\omega_1\left(f; \frac{2}{m_1}\right) + M\omega_2\left(q; \frac{2}{m_2}\right) \\ &\leq M\left\{\omega_1\left(f; \frac{2}{m_1}\right) + \omega_2\left(f; \frac{2}{m_2}\right)\right\} \end{aligned}$$

as required. Since this argument can obviously be extended inductively to any number of dimensions, the proof is complete.

□

This results seems satisfactory, but it hides an important problem. Let us suppose, for example, that $m_1 = m_2 = \ldots = m_n = m$, say. In view of Lemma 6.26(a), we have $\|f - p_m\|_\infty \leq 2\ nM\ \omega(f; m^{-1})$. The total number of coefficients in the polynomial p_m is $\mu = m^n + 1$ (we only need one constant term!). So as $\mu \to \infty$, $\|f - p_m\|_\infty \to 0$ only at a rate proportional to $\omega(f; \mu^{-1/n})$ instead of μ^{-1} as we might perhaps have hoped. This property is known as the *curse of dimensionality*, and it is unavoidable when approximating simple spaces of functions. We will return to this issue later, but let us accept the problem for the moment.

The extension of (6.30) to the multidimensional case requires a little care. By $C^k[-1, 1]^n$ we mean the space of functions which can be differentiated k times with respect to the each variable, and such that the resulting derivatives are all continuous. (We could of course consider different numbers of derivatives with respect to different variables, but this turns out to be considerably more complicated while offering little more in the way of insight.) Now if $f \in C^1[-1, 1]^n$ we see that for $i =, \ldots, n$

$$\omega_i(f;\delta) \le \left\| \frac{\partial f}{\partial x_i} \right\|_\infty \delta.$$

Hence for such an f, we conclude from Theorem 6.27 that there is a polynomial $p_{\mathbf{m}}$ of degree m_i in the ith variable such that

$$\|f - p_m\|_\infty \le 2M \sum_{i=1}^{n} \frac{1}{m_i} \left\| \frac{\partial f}{\partial x_i} \right\|_\infty . \tag{6.31}$$

Now consider $f \in C^2[-1, 1]^2$. (As previously, the initial restriction to two dimensions here is made to simplify the notation and exposition.) From (6.31) we may choose a polynomial q of degree $m_1 - 1$ in x_1 and $m_2 - 1$ in x_2, where $m_1, m_2 \ge 1$, and such that

$$\left\| \frac{\partial^2 f}{\partial x_1 \partial x_2} - q \right\|_\infty \le \frac{2M}{m_1 - 1} \left\| \frac{\partial^3 f}{\partial^2 x_1 \partial x_2} \right\|_\infty + \frac{2M}{m_2 - 1} \left\| \frac{\partial^3 f}{\partial x_1 \partial^2 x_2} \right\|_\infty . \tag{6.32}$$

Note that the definition of $C^2[-1, 1]^2$ implies that the derivatives on the right-hand side exist and are continuous, even though they appear to be 'third' derivatives. Specifically, let

$$q = \sum_{i=0}^{m_1-1} \sum_{j=0}^{m_2-1} a_{ij} x_1^i x_2^j .$$

Now let Q be obtained by integrating q once with respect to *each* variable. The general form of Q is

$$Q = \sum_{i=0}^{m_1-1} \sum_{j=0}^{m_2-1} \frac{a_{ij} x_1^{i+1} x_2^{j+1}}{(i+1)(j+1)} + h(x_1) + g(x_2) ,$$

where h and g are arbitrary differentiable functions. Since we require Q to be a polynomial, we shall insist that in fact h is a polynomial of degree m_1 and g is a polynomial of degree m_2. Moreover

$$\frac{\partial f}{\partial x_1} - \frac{\partial Q}{\partial x_1} = \int_0^{x_2} \frac{\partial^2 f}{\partial x_1 \partial x_2}(x_1, t) - q(x_1, t) \mathrm{d}t + \frac{\partial f}{\partial x_1}(x_1, 0) - h'(x_1) , \tag{6.33}$$

whence

$$\left\| \frac{\partial f}{\partial x_1} - \frac{\partial Q}{\partial x_1} \right\|_\infty \le \left\| \frac{\partial^2 f}{\partial x_1 \partial x_2} - q \right\|_\infty + \left\| \frac{\partial f}{\partial x_1}(x_1, 0) - h' \right\|_\infty .$$

Since the second term on the right is a function of x_1 only, we may choose h so that

$$\left\| \frac{\partial f}{\partial x_1}(x_1, 0) - h' \right\|_\infty \leq \frac{2M}{m_1 - 1} \left\| \frac{\partial^2 f}{\partial x_1^2} \right\|_\infty .$$

Thus from (6.32)

$$\left\| \frac{\partial f}{\partial x_1} - \frac{\partial Q}{\partial x_1} \right\|_\infty \leq \frac{2M}{m_1 - 1} \left\{ \left\| \frac{\partial^3 f}{\partial^2 x_1 \partial x_2} \right\|_\infty + \left\| \frac{\partial^2 f}{\partial x_1^2} \right\|_\infty \right\} + \frac{2M}{m_2 - 1} \left\| \frac{\partial^3 f}{\partial x_1 \partial^2 x_2} \right\|_\infty$$

and for a suitable choice of g we get a similar estimate for the derivatives with respect to x_2.

Now we may chose P of degree m_1 in x_1 and m_2 in x_2 such that

$$\|f - Q - P\|_\infty \leq \frac{2M}{m_1} \left\| \frac{\partial f}{\partial x_1} - \frac{\partial Q}{\partial x_1} \right\|_\infty + \frac{2M}{m_2} \left\| \frac{\partial f}{\partial x_2} - \frac{\partial Q}{\partial x_2} \right\|_\infty$$

which together with (6.34) and (for a suitable choice of g) a similar estimate for the derivatives with respect to x_2, yields a constant K (depending on f but not m_1 or m_2) such that

$$\|f - Q - \_ R\|_\infty \leq K \left\{ \frac{1}{m_1^2} + \frac{1}{m_2^2} \right\} .$$

To extend this result to more than two dimensions requires an induction over the dimension since the second term in the equivalent of (6.33) will involve all the variables except one. Nonetheless we may conclude that if $f \in C^2[-1, 1]^n$, there exists a number $K_{2,n}(f)$ (depending on f and n but not the m_i) such that for each choice of $\mathbf{m}$ there is a polynomial $p_\mathbf{m}$ of degree at most m_i in x_i such that

$$\|f - p_m\|_\infty \leq K_{2,n}(f) \sum_{i=1}^{n} (1/m_i^2) .$$

Further, by induction over the number of derivatives applying the estimate above instead of (6.32), we obtain:

Theorem 6.28

Let $f \in C^r[-1, 1]^n$. For each set of degrees $\mathbf{m} = (m_1, m_2 \ldots m_n)$, $m_i \in \mathbb{N}$, there exists a polynomial $p_\mathbf{m}$ of degree $\leq m_i$ in variable x_i such that

$$\|f - p_m\|_\infty \leq K_{r,n}(f) \sum_{i=1}^{n} (1/m_i^r) .$$

Here $K_{r,n}(f)$ depends on r, n and f but not on the m_i

□

We now seek to relate this result to approximation by ridge functions. The idea is to look at functions called *ridge polynomials* of the form $(\mathbf{w}^T\mathbf{x})^m$ where $\mathbf{w}$ is a vector of coefficients and $m \in \mathbb{N}$. We then realise these by the ridge functions like (6.2). Observe that if $(\mathbf{w}^T\mathbf{x})^m$ is expanded as a polynomial, every non-zero monomial term is of total degree exactly m. For example, with $n=2$ and $m=2$,

$$(\mathbf{w}^T\mathbf{x})^2 = (w_1x_1 + w_2x_2)^2 = w_1^2x_1^2 + 2w_1w_2x_1x_2 + w_2^2x_2^2.$$

(Moreover there are zero terms if and only if one or more of the w_i are zero.) Polynomials in which every term has exactly the same degree are said to be *homogeneous*. Chui and Li showed that any polynomial can be realised as the sum of ridge functions $(\mathbf{w}^T\mathbf{x})^m$ (Chui and Li, 1992). Several authors have used this fact to discuss density issues (see, e.g. Leshno, Lin, Pinkus and Shocken, 1993; Wray and Green, 1995). Our analysis here uses ideas from Chui and Li, and Scarselli and Tsoi (1995). We first show that any homogeneous polynomial of degree m can be expressed in terms of ridge polynomials. We need a simple combinatorial lemma.

Lemma 6.29

$$\sum_{j=0}^{m} \frac{(j+n-1)!}{j}! = \frac{(m+n)!}{nm!} .$$

Proof

If $m=0$, the sum has only the one term $(n-1)! = n!/n$ as required. So we proceed by induction over m. Suppose that the result holds for $m-1$. We have

$$\sum_{j=0}^{m} \frac{(j+n-1)!}{j}! = \sum_{j=0}^{m-1} \frac{(j+n-1)!}{j}! + \frac{(m+n-1)!}{m!}$$

$$= \frac{(m+n-1)!}{n(m-1)!} + \frac{(m+n-1)!}{m!} \quad \text{by the inductive hypothesis}$$
$$= \frac{(m+n-1)!(m+n)}{nm!}$$

which completes the induction.

□

We now prove

Proposition 6.30

Let $H_m{}^n$ denote the set of homogeneous polynomials of degree m in n variables, together with the zero polynomial. Then

$$H_m \text{ is a vector space of dimension } N_m^n = \frac{(m+n-1)!}{(n-1)!m!}.$$

Proof

H_m^n consists of all linear combination of monomials $x_1{}^{m_1}x_2{}^{m_2} \dots x_n{}^{m_n}$ with $m_1 + \dots + m_n = m$. So it is certainly a vector space. The dimension of H_m^n is the number of different monomials, i.e. the number of different choices of the m_i with $0 \le m_i$ for each i and $m_1 + m_2 + \dots + m_n = m$. Let us denote this number of choices by H_m^n. If m_n is chosen arbitrarily to be j, then the other m_i's must be chosen to sum to $m-j$.

Thus

$$N_m^n = \sum_{j=0}^{m} N_{m-j}^{n-1}.$$

We proceed by induction over n. For $n=1$, obviously $N_m^1 = 1 = m!/(0!m!)$ for any m, as we have only one term x^m. So assume that the result is valid for $n-1$ (and all m). Then

$$N_m^n = \sum_{j=0}^{m} \frac{(m-j+n-2)!}{(n-2)!(m-j)!}$$

$$= \sum_{i=0}^{m} \frac{(i+n-2)!}{(n-2)!i\,!} \quad \text{setting } i = m-j$$

$$= \frac{(m+n-1)!}{(n-2)!(n-1)m!} \quad \text{by Lemma 6.29}$$

$$= \frac{(m+n-1)!}{(n-1)!m!} \quad \text{as required.}$$

Note that the dimension may also be written as the binomial coefficient ${}^{(m+n-1)}C_{(n-1)}$.

Our next target is to show that there is a basis for H_m^n consisting of ridge polynomials. Furthermore we shall do it in a way that is constructive and parsimonious in the sense that the same $\mathbf{w_i}$ are used for different degrees. We establish the result by means of several lemmas.

Lemma 6.31

If $(\mathbf{w_i}^T\mathbf{x})^{m-1}$, $i=1, \ldots, N$ are linearly independent, so are $(\mathbf{w_i}^T\mathbf{x})^m$.

Proof

First note that we may assume without loss of generality that for each j there is at least one i such that $(\mathbf{w_i})_j$ (the jth element of $\mathbf{w_i}$) is non-zero. For if not, then the variable x_j does not appear in any $(\mathbf{w_i}^T\mathbf{x})^{m-1}$ and may be removed from consideration.

Now suppose that the Lemma is false, i.e. there exist N numbers β_i (not all zero) with

$$0 = \beta_1(\mathbf{w_1}^T\mathbf{x})^m + \beta_2(\mathbf{w_2}^T\mathbf{x})^m + \ldots + \beta_N(\mathbf{w_N}^T\mathbf{x})^m.$$

For any i, choose j such that $(\mathbf{w_i})_j \neq 0$, differentiate the expression with respect to x_j, and divide by m. We get

$$0 = (\mathbf{w_1})_j\beta_1(\mathbf{w_1}^T\mathbf{x})^{m-1} + (\mathbf{w_2})_j\beta_2(\mathbf{w_2}^T\mathbf{x})^{m-1} + \ldots + (\mathbf{w_N})_j\beta_N(\mathbf{w_N}^T\mathbf{x})^{m-1}.$$

Since this is a dependence relation for the $(\mathbf{w_i}^T\mathbf{x})^{m-1}$ we must have $(\mathbf{w_i})_j\beta_i=0$, and hence $\beta_i=0$. Since this holds for any i, we have a contradiction.

□

Lemma 6.32

Let $s = x_1^{m_1}x_2^{m_2} \ldots x_n^{m_n}$ with $m_1+m_2+\ldots+m_n=m$ be a monomial in H_m^n. Moreover let $\{(\mathbf{w_i}^T\mathbf{x})^{m-1}\}$, $i=1, 2 \ldots N_{m-1}{}^n$ be a basis for $H_{m-1}{}^n$ with $(\mathbf{w_i})_1 \neq 0$ for all i. Then we may write

$$s = \sum \gamma_i (\mathbf{w_i}^{\mathrm{T}}\mathbf{x})^m + h(x_2, x_3,\ldots,x_n) \tag{6.34}$$

where $h \in H_m{}^n$. The γ_i are real numbers.

Proof

The derivative of s with respect to x_1 is in $H_{m-1}{}^n$ and hence s' may be expressed in the form

$$s' = \sum \beta_i (\mathbf{w_i}^{\mathrm{T}}\mathbf{x})^{m-1}.$$

If we integrate this with respect to x_1 we obtain the desired expression with $\gamma_j = \beta_j/(\mathbf{w_i})_1$. (That $h \in H_m^n$ follows from the fact that the other terms in the equation are in this vector space.)

□

This lemma means that given a suitable basis for $H_{m-1}{}^n$ we can obtain a set of functions in H_m^n which allows us to eliminate terms involving x_1 from a polynomial in H_m^n. *Moreover the functions* $\mathbf{w_i}^{\mathrm{T}}\mathbf{x}$ *are preserved in the transition.* We now need to extend our set of independent functions to a basis for H_m^n by the addition of new $\mathbf{w_i}$'s. There are various possible ways to do this, but the following is particularly elegant, arising from a simple construction.

For each $\mathbf{w_i}$ let $\mathbf{w_i}'$ be obtained from $\mathbf{w_i}$ by switching the first two elements. Thus $(\mathbf{w_i}')_2 = (\mathbf{w_i})_1$ and *vice versa*, with the other elements being identical. Since in (6.34) $h \in H_m^n$, it is a linear combination of monomials and so we may write, according to Lemma 6.32,

$$h(x_2, x_3,\ldots,x_n) = \sum \tau_i (\mathbf{w_i}'^{\mathrm{T}}\mathbf{x})^m + g(x_1, x_3,\ldots,x_n)$$

for some real numbers τ_i. Here h is in terms of the original variables, but x_1 is replaced by x_2 in the application of the Lemma. Now the left hand side is independent of x_1, so the equation still holds if x_1 is replaced by zero. Thus

$$h(x_2, x_3,\ldots,x_n) = \sum \tau_i (\mathbf{w_i}''^{\mathrm{T}}\mathbf{x})^m + g(0, x_3,\ldots,x_n),$$

where $\mathbf{w_i}''$ is obtained from $\mathbf{w_i}'$ by replacing the first element by zero. We have shown that any monomials can be written as a linear combination of terms of the form $(\mathbf{w_i}^{\mathrm{T}}\mathbf{x})^{\mathrm{m}}$, $(\mathbf{w_i}''^{\mathrm{T}}\mathbf{x})^m$ and a function involving only $x_3, \ldots, x_n$. The $\mathbf{w_i}''$ were obtained from the $\mathbf{w_i}$ simply by switching the first two elements and then replacing the new first element by zero. Take all these $\mathbf{w}$'s and renumber them as $\mathbf{w_{j}}=\mathbf{w_i}$, $i=1, \ldots, N_{m-1}{}^n$ and $\mathbf{w_j}=\mathbf{w_i}''$ where $j=i+N_{m-1}{}^n$, $i=1, \ldots, N_{m-1}{}^n$. Now repeat the construction, but this time switching the second and third elements, and setting the first two elements in the new $\mathbf{w_j}$'s to zero. In this way we can express any monomial as a linear combination of $(\mathbf{w_j}^T\mathbf{x})^m$ terms and a function involving only variables $x_4, \ldots, x_n$. Proceeding in this fashion we eventually obtain a set of $\mathbf{w_j}$'s such that the $(\mathbf{w_j}^T\mathbf{x})^m$ span H_j^n. Now we prune this spanning set to a basis by removing redundant elements, but retain all the original $\mathbf{w_i}$'s, $i=1, \ldots, N_{m-1}{}^n$ (which we can certainly do since they are independent by Lemma 6.31).

We have now extended these original $\mathbf{w_i}$'s to a basis for H_m^n. However we are not yet quite ready to go on to higher degrees, since the basis does not satisfy the conditions of Lemma 6.32 that $(\mathbf{w_i})_1 \neq 0$ for all i. Indeed we have explicitly set many of the $(\mathbf{w_i})_1$'s to zero. In order to increase the degree, we need the following Lemma. (Recall $\mathbf{e_j}$ denotes the standard basis vector with jth element 1 and all other elements 0.)

Lemma 6.33

Let $\{(\mathbf{w_j}^T\mathbf{x})^m | j=1, 2, \ldots, N=H_m^n\}$ be a basis for H_m^n, but with $(\mathbf{w_i})_1=0$ for some i. Then we may replace $\mathbf{w_i}$ in the basis by $\mathbf{v_i}=\mathbf{w_i}+\beta\mathbf{e_i}$, $\beta \in \mathbb{R}$, except for at most N values of β. In particular, we many choose β positive and sufficiently small.

Proof

$$\begin{aligned}(\mathbf{v_i}^T\mathbf{x})^m &= (\mathbf{w_i}^T\mathbf{x} + \beta x_1)^m \\ &= \beta^m x_1^m + m\beta^{m-1}x_1^{m-1}(\mathbf{w_i}^T\mathbf{x}) + \ldots + (\mathbf{w_i}^T\mathbf{x})^m.\end{aligned}$$

Each term in this binomial expansion is a homogeneous polynomial of degree m (i.e. it is in H_m^n) and is thus a linear combination of elements of the basis $\{(\mathbf{w_i}^T\mathbf{x})^m\}$. It follows that

$$(\mathbf{v_i}^T\mathbf{x})^m = \sum_{j=1}^{N} \lambda_j(\beta)(\mathbf{w_j}^T\mathbf{x})^m, \tag{6.35}$$

where each $\lambda_j(\beta)$ is a polynomial of degree at most N in β. In order to be able to replace $(\mathbf{w_i}^T\mathbf{x})^m$ by $(\mathbf{v_i}^T\mathbf{x})^m$ it is sufficient to ensure that $(\mathbf{v_i}^T\mathbf{x})^m$ is not in the span of $\{(\mathbf{w_i}^T\mathbf{x})^m | j \neq i\}$. But this holds if and only if $\lambda_i(\beta) \neq 0$. Now the polynomial $\lambda_i(\beta)$ cannot vanish identically, for if it did, the case $\beta=0$ in (6.35) would contradict the independence of the basis. For the same reason, it cannot vanish at zero. Thus there are at most N real values of β, not including zero, which will not suffice.

□

Using this lemma we can modify our basis of H_m^n to satisfy the conditions of Lemma 6.32. Thus we can start with homogeneous polynomials of degree $m=1$, and successively construct bases for higher degrees of homogeneous polynomials.

Example 6.34

We explicitly construct a basis for $n=3$ and $m=1$ and 2. (Since we are working in three dimensions, let us call the variables x, y and z rather than x_1, x_2 and x_3.)

For $m=1$, we may choose the basis x, $x+y$ and $x+y+z$. In other words, $\mathbf{w}_1 = (1, 0, 0)^T$, $\mathbf{w}_2 = (1, 1, 0)^T$ and $\mathbf{w}_3 = (1, 1, 1)^T$. We proceed to $m=2$ as follows.

Step 1

Increase the powers to 2, giving x^2, $(x+y)^2$ and $(x+y+z)^2$.

Step 2.1

In each of the above, swap the roles of x and y, then replace the x coefficient by zero. Thus

$x^2 \to y^2 \to y^2$, $(x+y)^2 \to (x+y)^2 \to y^2$ (again), and $(x+y+z)^2 \to (x+y+z)^2 \to (y+z)^2$.

Or in terms of of the $\mathbf{w}_i$, this is written

$$\mathbf{w}_i = (1, 0, 0)^T \to (0, 1, 0)^T \to (0, 1, 0)^T,$$
$$\mathbf{w}_2 = (1, 1, 0)^T \to (1, 1, 0)^T \to (0, 1, 0)^T$$

and

$$\mathbf{w}_3 = (1, 1, 1)^T \to (1, 1, 1)^T \to (0, 1, 1)^T$$

In total we now have the five functions x^2, $(x+y)^2$, $(x+y+z)^2$, y^2, $(y+z)^2$.

Step 2.2

In each of the above, swap the roles of y and z, then replace the x and y coefficients by zero. This in fact yields only one more distinct function, namely z^2.

Step 3

Prune the spanning set to a basis. In fact, no further pruning is required as we have six distinct functions and H_2^3 has dimension $N_2^3=4!/(2!\times 2!)=6$. (Note that the $\mathbf{w}_i$ are *not* all independent: they cannot be since they are in $\mathbb{R}^3$ and we have six of them.)

Step 4

Use Lemma 6.33 to obtain a basis each member of which involves x. This gives a basis

$$\{x^2, (x+y)^2, (x+y+z)^2, (\beta_1 x+y)^2, (\beta_2 x+y+z)^2, (\beta_3 x+z)^2\}$$

where β_1, β_2, and β_3 are to chosen to guarantee independence.

□

Remark 6.35

In practice, of course, it is unlikely to be worth checking which choices of β do not yield independent solutions. Moreover the construction does not yield bases which are symmetrical in the variables. In fact Scarselli and Tsoi suggest fixing the highest value of m required, and produce a basis $(\mathbf{w}_i^T\mathbf{x})^m$, $i=1, \ldots, N_m^n$ for H_m^n. Unless we are very unlucky, choosing $\mathbf{w}_i$'s uniformly distributed on the unit sphere in $\mathbb{R}^n$ will do. They then observe that $(\mathbf{w}_i^T\mathbf{x})^{m-1}$, $i=, \ldots, N_m^n$ spans H_{m-1}^n. To see this, suppose s is any monomial in H_{m-1}^n, so that $s= x_1^{m_1}x_2^{m_2}\ldots x_n^{m_n}$ with $m_1+m_2+\ldots+m_n=m-1$. Thus $x_1^{m_1+1}x_2^{m_2}\ldots x_n^{m_n}\in H_m^n$ and may be expressed as a linear combination of the $(\mathbf{w}_i^T\mathbf{x})^m$. Differentiating this linear combination with respect to x_1 yields the required expression for s in terms of the $(\mathbf{w}_i^T\mathbf{x})^{m-1}$.

□

Putting all this together, we obtain

Theorem 6.36

Let p_m by any polynomial of total degree m in the n variables $x_1, x_2, \ldots, x_n$. Then there exist $N=N_m^n$ (see Proposition 6.30) n-vectors $\mathbf{w}_i$ and single variable polynomials q_i (each of degree not more than m) for $i=1, 2, \ldots, N$, such that $p_m=q_1(\mathbf{w}_1^T\mathbf{x})+q_2(\mathbf{w}_2^T\mathbf{x})+q_N(\mathbf{w}_N^T\mathbf{x})$, where $\mathbf{x}=(x_1, x_2, \ldots, x_n)^T$.

Proof

The polynomial p_m can obviously be expressed as the sum of a constant plus homogeneous polynomials of degree 1, 2, . . . , m. This theorem is thus an immediate consequence of the preceding development.

□

To emphasise this remarkable result, we have shown that a polynomial of degree m in n variables can be expressed as the sum of N_m^n polynomial ridge functions. Clearly the result is best possible in that we cannot in general do this with $N<N_m^n$.

But how does this relate to approximation by sigmoidal ridge functions? At the beginning of this chapter we saw that by squashing them up sufficiently, sigmoidal functions are 'as good as' (discontinuous) step functions for approximating uniformly. We shall now prove that by stretching them out enough, smooth sigmoidal functions are also 'as good as' (very smooth) polynomials! It is perhaps this versatility which makes them so useful as approximators. Once again we follow the method of Scarselli and Tsoi who have one of the simplest expositions of the desired result.

The idea is straightforward. Consider a smooth activation function σ. For simplicity, we will assume that σ is actually *analytic*, i.e. that it is equal to its Taylor expansion in the neighbourhood of some point $\lambda \in [-1, 1]$. This is true of the common activation functions such as $\sigma(x)=1/(1+e^{-x})$. Then we expand σ about λ:

$$\sigma(\lambda + h) = \sigma(\lambda) + h\sigma'(\lambda) + \tfrac{1}{2}h^2\sigma''(\lambda)\dots .$$

So we can approximate a constant to order h. Taking the expansion for some different distance, say $\frac{1}{2}h$ for example, we get

$$\sigma(\lambda + \tfrac{1}{2}h) = \sigma(\lambda) + \tfrac{1}{2}h\sigma'(\lambda) + \tfrac{1}{8}h^{2''}(\lambda)\dots .$$

and subtracting the equations gives

$$h = 2\,[\sigma(\lambda + h) - \sigma(\lambda + \tfrac{1}{2}h)]/\sigma'(\lambda) + O(h^2)$$

provided $\sigma'(\lambda) \neq 0$. So we can approximate the linear term h. Further differences give higher powers of h. Of course these are only approximations, but we are interested in terms of the form $\sigma(\mathbf{w}^T\mathbf{x}+\lambda)$ (compare (6.2)), so by choosing $\mathbf{w}$ small enough we can approximate these powers to any desired accuracy with a *fixed* number of terms. The process can be achieved either with differences, or as a limiting case with derivatives. Scarselli and Tsio, following (Lesho, Lin, Pinkus and Shocken, 1993) and (Kreniovich, 1991) give this explicit construction, which shows that to approximate a polynomial of degree M we only need m copies of σ.

Theorem 6.37

Let σ be analytic in a neighbourhood of λ and suppose that $\sigma^{[i]}(\lambda) \Rightarrow 0$ for any $i \geq 0$. Further, consider the polynomial $q(x) = c_0 + c_1 x + \ldots + c_m x^m$. Let

$$g_\alpha(x) = \sum_{j=0}^{m} \gamma_j(\alpha)\sigma(j\alpha x + \lambda)$$

where

$$\gamma_i(\alpha) = \sum_{k=j}^{m} \frac{(-1)^{k+j} c_k^k C_j}{\alpha_k \, \sigma^{[k]}(\lambda)} \text{ and } {}^kC_j \text{ is the binomial coefficient } \frac{k!}{j!(k-j)!}$$

Then $g_\alpha \to q$ uniformly in x on any bounded interval as $\alpha \to 0$.

Proof

Substituting for γ_j and interchanging the order of summation, we may rewrite $g_\alpha(x)$ as

$$g_\alpha(x) = \sum_{k=0}^{m} \frac{(-1)^k c_k}{\alpha^k \sigma^{[k]}(\lambda)} \sum_{j=0}^{k} (-1)^{j\,k}\} C_j \sigma(j\alpha x + \lambda)\,. \qquad (6.36)$$

Now consider the expression

$$\sum_{j=0}^{k} (-1)^{j\,k} C_j \sigma(j\alpha x + \lambda) = \sum_{j=0}^{k} (-1)^{j\,k} C_j \sum_{i=0}^{\infty} \sigma^{[i]}(\lambda)(j\alpha x)^i / i!$$

$$= \sum_{i=0}^{\infty} \beta_{i,k} \sigma^{[i]}(\lambda)(a\alpha x)^i \qquad (6.37)$$

where

$$\beta_{i,k} = \sum_{j=0}^{k} (-1)^{j\,k} C_j \, j^i / i!\,.$$

We now evaluate these quantities (which are related to Stirling numbers of the second kind (Abramovitz and Stegun, 1968) for $i \leq k$. To perform the evaluation we note that differentiating x^j i times gives

$$\begin{aligned}(x^j)^{[i]} &= j(j-1)(j-2)(j-i+1)x^{j-i} \\ &= (j^i + \text{a linear combination of lower powers of } j)\, x^{j-i}.\end{aligned}$$

(Note that the expression is zero for $i<j$: no negative powers are generated). But

$$(1-x)^k = \sum_{j=0}^{k} (-1)^j\, {}^kC_j x_i.$$

So if we differentiate this i times and then substitute $x=1$ we find that for $i<k$

$$0 = \beta_{i,k} + \text{linear combination of } \beta_{\nu,k} \text{ for } \nu < i.$$

In particular $\beta_{0,k}=(1-1)^k=0$, so it follows by a trivial induction that $\beta_{i,k}=0$ for $i<k$. Furthermore, differentiating $(1-x)^k$ k times and setting $x=1$ we get

$$(-1)^k\, k! = k!\, \beta_{k,k} + \text{linear combination of } \beta_{\nu,k} \text{ for } \nu < k,$$

whence $\beta_{k,\,k}=(-1)^k$. Putting this back into (6.37) we find

$$\sum_{j=0}^{k} (-1)^j\, {}^kC_j \sigma(j\alpha x + \lambda) = (-1)^k \sigma^{[k]}(\lambda)\, (\alpha x)^k + O(\alpha^{k+1}),$$

whence from (6.36)

$$\begin{aligned}g_\alpha(x) &= \sum_{k=0}^{m} \frac{c_k}{\alpha^k \sigma^{[k]}(\lambda)} [\sigma^{[i]}(\lambda)(\alpha x)^k + O(\alpha^{k+1})] \\ &= \sum_{k=0}^{m} c_k x^k + O(\alpha)\end{aligned}$$

as required.

□

Combining this result with Theorem 6.36 gives

Corollary 6.38

Let P_m be any polynomial of total degree m in the n variables x_1 $x_2, \ldots, x_n$, and let σ satisfy the conditions of Theorem 6.37. Further, let g be given by (6.2) but with $k=m\ N_m^n$ (see Proposition 6.30). Then for any $\varepsilon>0$, there exist choices of the k n-vectors $\mathbf{w}_i$, the k thresholds c_j and the k coefficients a_j such that

$$\|p_m - g\|_\infty < \varepsilon.$$

(The norm here may be taken over any compact set in $\mathbb{R}^n$).

□

Remark 6.39

It is important to note here that $\sigma(x)=1/(1-e^{-x})$ does not satisfy the conditions of the theorem if λ is taken to be zero. Indeed the even numbered derivatives are odd functions and hence vanish at zero. However, we note that a non-zero analytic function can have only a finite number of zeros in any closed, bounded interval inside the region of analyticity. Otherwise the set of zeros would have a limit in this closed set, and the expansion about this limit would need to have all coefficients zero and hence the function itself would vanish. It follows that if σ is analytic as $1/(1-e^{-x})$ is, then the set of zeros of its derivatives is countable. Thus in any open interval there exist infinitely many choices λ for which the conditions of the theorem are satisfied. In fact it seems clear that any non-zero λ will do for $1/(1-e^{-x})$, although it is not easy to give a simple proof of this.

If we are prepared to allow a *different* choice of λ for each threshold C_j in (6.2), then Leshno *et al.* show that it is only necessary that σ be infinitely differentiable and non-polynomial to get density. They use the difference idea introduced before Theorem 6.37. Provided we can find a point at which the appropriate difference does not vanish, then we can approximate the relevant power of h. If σ is not a polynomial, its derivatives do not vanish identically, so we can find a suitable threshold. However this method makes it difficult to count the number of units required. Scarselli and Tsoi give a version of Theorem 56.37 based in differences rather than derivatives, but again it is hard to prove that any specified step length for the difference will work.

□

Now, recall that the space of polynomials of total degree m contains the space of polynomials of degree m/n in each variable. We can obtain an estimate of the degree of approximation to a smooth function. Since this is best written in terms of the number of hidden units, i.e. the number of copies of σ required, let us first consider the number of nodes required in Corollary 6.38. Here we will *fix* the number of variables n and consider what happens as $m \to \infty$. If k hidden units are used in Corollary 6.38, we have

$$\begin{aligned} k &= mN_n^m \\ &= \frac{m\,(m+n-1)!}{(n-1)!m!} \\ &= \frac{(m+n-1)!}{(n-1)!\; m-1)!} \\ &= \frac{(m+n-1)\,(m+n-2)\ldots m}{(n-1)!} \end{aligned}$$

Since $m = m + n - n$, there are n terms in the numerator and k grows like m^n. In other words with k hidden units, we can approximate a polynomial of total degree $O(k^{1/n})$. Thus we find

Theorem 6.40

Let $f \in C^r[-1, 1]^n$, and consider approximation by functions of the form

$$g_k(\mathbf{x}) + \sum_j^k a_{k,j}\sigma(\alpha_k \mathbf{w_j}^T \mathbf{x} + \lambda)$$

(where σ and λ satisfy the conditions of Theorem 5.37) representing a single hidden layer perception with activation σ. Then there exists a sequence of vectors $\mathbf{w_j}$, $j = 1 \ldots \infty$, which may be chosen *independently* of f, and for each k a constant K, which depends on r, n and f but not on k, such that for suitable α_k and a_{kj}'s,

$$\|f - g_k\|_\infty \leq Kk^{-r/n.}$$

Proof

First approximate f by a polynomial of total degree less than h. According to Theorem 6.28 there is a polynomial P_h of degree h in each variable and a constant C such that

$$\|f - p_h\|_\infty < Ch^{-r}.$$

This polynomial is of total degree at most nh. Thus according to Corollary 6.38 it may be approximated to arbitrary accuracy by g_k with $k = (nh)N_{nh}{}^n$. Thus

$$\|f - g_k\|_\infty \leq Ch^{-r}.$$

For fixed n, k grows as $O(h^n)$ as $h \to \infty$. So there is a constant B such that $h > B k^{1/n}$. Hence

$$\|f - g_k\|_\infty \leq Ch^{-r} \leq CB^{-r}k^{-r/n}$$

as required.

□

Remarks 6.41

(a) Note that this bound suffers from the curse of dimensionality: if n is large the asymptotic rate of convergence may be very small. On the other hand, if n is large we see from Corollary 6.38 that the value of k required to realise a polynomial of moderate m is actually quite small: there is an $(n-1)!$ in the denominator of N_m^n.

(b) A case of interest in control theory is when n is relatively small and the function to be approximated is smooth. In this case the asymptotic bound is useful, as Scarselli and Tsoi point out.

(c) The direction vectors $\mathbf{w_j}$ are chosen independently of f. Thus the only non-linearly occurring parameter that has to be chosen is α_k. And in fact the requirement is only that it be sufficiently small. So we can approximate smooth f in practice by fixing α_k to some small value, and choosing the $a_{j,k}$'s by a linear approximation algorithm (e.g. linear least squares if we do not insist on uniform approximation). Or if this is not sufficiently precise, vary α_k and solve a sequence of linear problems, choosing α_k to get the smallest error. This is of course much simpler than solving a fully non-linear optimisation problem (see Chapter 4). Alternatively, first approximate f by a polynomial and then use Theorem 6.37 and Corollary 6.38 explicitly.

(d) The result suggests that when approximating smooth functions, the norm of the vector $\alpha_k\mathbf{w_j}$ is small. To compensate for this, we might expect that the $a_{j,k}$'s will get large. Is this a disadvantage of the approach? (Mhaskar, 1996) in fact shows that unless f is infinitely differentiable, *any* sequence of g_k's that satisfy $\|f - g_k\|_\infty \leq Ck^{-\nu}$ for $\nu > 0$ *must* result in some of the $a_{j,k}$'s becoming arbitrarily large as $k \to \infty$. So the difficulty is not an artifact of the method: it is unavoidable.

□

Results such as Theorem 6.40 raise the question of whether it is possible to find bounds that avoid the curse of dimensionality, particularly if we allow the direction vectors $\mathbf{w_j}$ to depend on f. Can we get k^{-r} bounds instead of $k^{-r/n}$

bounds? The answer to this question turns out to be a qualified yes. Such results do exist, but for more complicated classes of functions than $C_r[-1, 1]^n$: compare De Vore, Howard and Micchelli (1989). The first such result was due to Barron (1993), but a much simpler argument has been produced by Mhaskar and Micchelli (1994) so we will give this version. We will then close this chapter and book with a brief discussion of the Fourier methods used by Barron and others, followed by a survey of a few other interesting methods and results.

The result of Mhaskar and Micchelli, like that of Barron, uses a special convexity property of Hilbert spaces and therefore refers to least squares approximation. Moreover the Mhaskar Micchelli result is primarily about periodic functions and activations, although as they point out, it is possible to get round this for the standard sigmoidal activations. However, our purpose is only to show that dimension independent rates of convergence are possible in principle, so the restricted case does not really matter. (Many authors, including indeed Mhaskar and Micchelli themselves, talk of dimension independent *bounds*. However the *constants* in these bounds always do depend on dimension, so the term dimension independent *rate* is more accurate.)

We consider first the space of functions $L_2[-\pi, \pi]^n$. Our activation function σ is considered to be in $L_2[-\pi, \pi]$ and extended in periodic fashion to $(-\infty, \infty)$. This will mean that we have to choose weights which are an integral multiple of 2π, but we have already seen that the choice of a countable set of directions generally makes little difference and the restriction will not matter.

In Section 3.6 we met the idea of an orthogonal expansion. In particular, in Examples 3.55 and 3.56, and in Remark 3.57, we considered the classical Fourier expansion in terms of trigonometric functions. The argument here is more easily expressed in terms of complex Fourier series. Using the identity

$$e^{i\theta} = \cos\theta + i \sin\theta$$

where $i^2 = -1$, which is easily proved from the power series, we can write

$$\cos n\theta = \tfrac{1}{2}\,(e^{in\theta} + e^{-in\theta})$$

with a similar expression for $\sin n\theta$. Thus the Fourier series can be written in the form $\sum A_k e^{ik\theta}$ but in this summation n runs from $-\infty$ to ∞. A_n can be written in terms of the original coefficients a_k and b_k by a simple algebraic manipulation, or alternatively we can regard $\sum A_k e^{ik\theta}$ as an orthogonal expansion in terms of a hermitian product (see below).

We also need to extend the expansion to the multi-dimensional case: indeed this is very easy. We extend the inner product simply by integrating over each dimension, thus

$$<p, q> = \frac{1}{(2\pi)^n}\int_{-\pi}^{\pi}\dots\int_{-\pi}^{\pi} p(\mathbf{x})\overline{q(\mathbf{x})}\mathrm{d}\mathbf{x}.$$

is our required hermitian product. Here $\overline{}$ denotes complex conjugation. Basis functions of the form

$$\mathrm{e}^{\mathrm{i}\mathbf{m}^{\mathrm{T}}\mathbf{x}} = \mathrm{e}^{\mathrm{i}m_1x_1} \times \mathrm{e}^{\mathrm{i}m_2x_2} \times \dots \times \mathrm{e}^{\mathrm{i}m_nx_n}$$

where $\mathbf{m}=(m_1, m_2, \dots, m_n)^{\mathrm{T}}$, will form an orthonormal basis, since orthogonality in one of the dimensions will result in a zero inner product unless all of the indices are the same. So any f in $L_2[-\pi, \pi]^n$ can be expanded as a Fourier series in terms of this basis. The coefficients of this expansion are given by the inner product in the usual way (see (3.48)). Let us label these coefficient $A_{\mathbf{m}}$ where $\mathbf{m}=(m_1, m_2, \dots, m_n)$. Now our requisite class of functions is defined to be

$$SF_n = \{F \in L_2[-\pi, \pi]^n \mid \sum |A_{\mathbf{m}}| \leq 1 \},$$

where the summation is of course over all possible indices $\mathbf{m}$. The approach is firstly to show that functions in SF_n can be approximated at a dimension independent rate by trigonometric functions, and then secondly approximate these by σ. The first part is surprisingly easy, but does require one theorem on orthogonal expansions that we have not yet addressed.

Theorem 6.42 (Parseval's Formula)

Let H be any Hilbert space over $\mathbb{C}$ (not necessarily finite dimensional) with a fundamental set of orthonormal functions $\varphi_1, \varphi_2, \dots,$ and norm $\| \; \|$. Moreover let $f \in H$, and denote by A_i the ith Fourier coefficient in the expansion of f in terms of the φ_i. Let p_m be the orthogonal projection onto span $\{\varphi_1, \dots, \varphi_m\}$ so that

$$p_m = \sum_{i=1}^{m} A_i\varphi_i.$$

Then $\|f-p_m\|^2 = \sum_{i=m+1}^{\infty} |A_i|^2$. (The sum terminates if H is finite dimensional.)

Proof

First consider the case that H is finite dimensional: say it has dimension M. We may write

$$f = \sum_{i=1}^{M} A_i \varphi_i.$$

Hence

$$f - p_m = \sum_{i=m+1}^{M} A_i \varphi_i.$$

Thus

$$\begin{aligned} \|f - p_m\|^2 &= <f - p_m, f - p_m> \\ &= <\sum_{i=m+1}^{M} A_i \varphi_i, \sum_{i=m+1}^{M} A_i \varphi_i> \\ &= \sum_{i=m+1}^{M} |A_i|^2 \text{ since the } \varphi_i \text{ are orthonormal.} \end{aligned}$$

This completes the proof for finite dimensional spaces. For infinite dimensional spaces we use the fact that the φ_i are fundamental, which guarantees that

$$f = \sum_{i=1}^{\infty} A_i \varphi_i.$$

at least in the sense of convergence of the partial sums in norm, and employ a simple limiting argument.

□

Now consider $f \in SF_n$. As above, f has Fourier coefficients $A_{\mathbf{m}}$, and $\sum |A_{\mathbf{m}}| \leq 1$. However the latter condition means that the Fourier series for f is absolutely convergent (see Section 1.5) for all $\mathbf{x}$. This implies that all functions in SF_n must be continuous, since f is the limit of continuous functions. More importantly for our purposes it means that we can reorder the terms of the series in any way we like without changing the sum. Let us suppose the basis functions and hence the coefficients are reordered to use a *single* index m and such that the new coefficients, say B_i, satisfy $|B_{i+1}| \leq |B_i|$. Of course, we still have $\sum |B_m| \leq 1$.

Let us suppose that the relabelled basis functions are called $\varphi_0, \varphi_1, \ldots$, but keep in mind that they are simply multivariate trigonometric functions. Here φ_0 denotes the constant function. We may now express

$$f = \sum_{k=0}^{\infty} B_k \varphi_k.$$

This is an expansion in a single indexed series, and it is this which enables us to get a dimension independent rate of convergence. Specifically, with

$$p_m = \sum_{k=0}^{m} B_k \varphi_k.$$

we have by Parseval's formula

$$\begin{aligned} \|f - p_m\|_2^2 &= \sum_{k=m+1}^{\infty} |B_k|^2 \\ &\leq |B_{m+1}| \sum_{k=m+1}^{\infty} |B_k| \\ &\leq |B_{m+1}| \,. \end{aligned} \tag{6.38}$$

But since the $|B_k|$ form a decreasing sequence,

$$m|B_{m+1}| \leq 2 \sum_{m/2 \leq k \leq m+1} |B_k|$$

and the right-hand side tends to zero as $m \to \infty$, since the sum of all the $|B_k|$ converges by hypothesis. It follows that there is a sequence of real numbers δ_m such that $\delta_m > 0$, $\delta_m \to 0$ as $m \to \infty$, and such that $|B_{m+1}| \leq \delta_m{}^2/m$. Thus by (6.38)

$$\|f - p_m\|_2 \leq \delta_m m^{-\frac{1}{2}}. \tag{6.39}$$

The rate of convergence in terms of the number m of basis functions does not depend on n. However we are not finished yet. The basis functions φ_i are trigonometric functions of arbitrary high frequency. How can we approximate them by σ? Actually, it is not really the frequency that causes difficulty. If we approximate a product of cos and sin terms to a given accuracy by a linear combination of periodic σ's, simply replacing x_i by kx_i will produce an approximation of a suitable frequency in the variable x_i. The real problem is that unlike the polynomial case we cannot approximate the terms to arbitrary accuracy without increasing the number of nodes required. On the other hand if we used the argument above to produce an expansion in orthogonal polynomials, the higher degrees would require more nodes. To get around this, a convexity property is used.

Definition 6.43

Let V be a real vector space. *A* set $S \subset V$ is said to be *convex* if for any $\mathbf{u}, \mathbf{v} \in S$, $t\mathbf{u} + (1-t)\,\mathbf{v} \in S$ for $0 \leq t \leq 1$.

□

This is a very simple idea. Given any two points in the set S, we 'draw a straight line' joining the points. If we can do this without leaving the set, it is convex. So a filled-in square, rectangle or triangle is always convex, as is a filled-in disc or ellipse. But a C shape, or a figure with a hole such as a donut, is not convex. Here are some associated ideas.

Definition 6.44

(a) An expression of the form $t_1\mathbf{u}_1 + t_2\mathbf{u}_2 + \ldots + t_k\mathbf{u}_k$ where $0 \leq t_i \leq 1$ for each i, and $\sum t_i = 1$, is called a *convex combination* of the $\mathbf{u}_i$.
(b) Let V be a real vector space and $S \subset V$ a subset. The set of all convex combinations of the elements of S is called the *convex hull* of S and is written $\mathcal{H}(S)$. Equivalently it is the smallest convex set containing S.
(c) A set of $E \subset S$ such that $\mathcal{H}(E) = \mathcal{H}(S)$, but $\mathcal{H}(D) \neq \mathcal{H}(S)$ for any proper subset D of E, is said to be an *extreme set* of S.

□

For example suppose S is the hollow square in $\mathbb{R}^2$. The convex hull is the filled-in square, and the only extreme set consists of the four corners of the square. As another example, if S is the hollow circle, the convex hull is the filled-in disc, and the only extreme set is S itself.

Clearly if $V = \mathbb{R}^n$ and S is closed, so is $\mathcal{H}(S)$. The key result on convex sets in finite dimensional spaces is the following.

Theorem 6.45 (Carathéodory's Theorem)

Let V be a real vector space of dimension n and $S \subset V$ a subset. Suppose that E is an extreme set of S. Then every point in $\mathcal{H}(S)$ is expressible as a convex combination of at most $n+1$ points of E.

Proof

Let $\mathbf{u} \in S$. By definition of the convex hull, we have $\mathbf{u}$=for some $\mathbf{u}_1, \mathbf{u}_2 + \ldots + \mathbf{u}_k$ and t_i's with $0 \le t_i \le 1$ and $\sum t_i = 1$. Let us suppose that k is the least integer for which such an expression exists. Thus we may assume $0 < t_i$ for each i. We require to show that $k \le n+1$. Now let $\mathbf{v}_i = \mathbf{u} - \mathbf{u}_i$, $i = 1, 2, \ldots, k$, and note that $t_1\mathbf{v}_1 + t_2\mathbf{v}_2 + \ldots + t_k\mathbf{y}_k = \mathbf{0}$. If $k > n+1$, we must have $\alpha_2\mathbf{v}_2 + \alpha_3\mathbf{v}_3 + \ldots + \alpha_k\mathbf{y}_k = \mathbf{0}$, for some α_i's, not all zero, since $\mathbf{v}_2 \ldots \mathbf{v}_k$ constitute $n+1$ or more vectors in an n-dimensional space. Define $\alpha_1 = 0$. Then for any $\lambda \in \mathbb{R}$, we have $(t_1 + \lambda\alpha_1)\mathbf{v}_1 + (t_2 + \lambda\alpha_2)\mathbf{v}_2 + \ldots + (t_k + \lambda\alpha_k)\mathbf{v}_k = \mathbf{0}$. Now choose λ such that $|\lambda|$ is as small as possible under the condition that one of the coefficients $(t_i + \lambda\alpha_i)$ vanish. The remaining coefficients are non-negative and do not all vanish because $(t_1 + \lambda\alpha_1) = t_1 > 0$. But replacing each $\mathbf{v}_i$ by $\mathbf{u} - \mathbf{u}_i$ and dividing by $\sum(t_i + \lambda\alpha_i)$ now gives an expression for $\mathbf{u}$ as a convex combination of fewer than k of the $\mathbf{u}_i$, contradicting the minimality of k.

□

Since $\mathcal{H}(E) = \mathcal{H}(S)$ by definition, the substance of this theorem is the observation that at most $n+1$ points are required. (Note that it does not claim that every point of $\mathcal{H}(S)$ is expressible in terms of the *same* $n+1$ points, only that a choice exists for each point of $\mathcal{H}(S)$.) For example, any point of the unit square in $\mathbb{R}^2$ can be expressed as a convex combination of at most three of the corners. The set of convex combinations of three points is of course the filled triangle with the points at the vertices. A convex combination of $n+1$ points in $\mathbb{R}^n$ is called an *n-simplex*. The (non-degenerate) 2-simplices are triangles, 3-simplices are tetrahedrons and so on. Another way of stating Carathéodory's Theorem is that any convex body in $\mathbb{R}^n$ is the union of n-simplices. Of course we do not necessarily get a finite number of them: we cannot express the unit disc in $\mathbb{R}^2$ as a finite union of triangles.

The application of these ideas to our approximation problem proceeds as follows.

Lemma 6.46

Let $g_1 \ldots g_m$ be continuous complex valued functions on $[-\pi, \pi]^n$. Then there exist $2m+1$ vectors $\mathbf{u}_1, \mathbf{u}_2 + \ldots + \mathbf{u}_{2m+1} \in [-\pi, \pi]^n$ and $2m+1$ non-negative real numbers $t_1 \ldots t_{2m+1}$, *which may be chosen independently of* k, such that

$$\frac{1}{(2\pi)^n} \int g_k(\mathbf{u})d\mathbf{u} = \sum_{j=1}^{m+1} t_k g_k(\mathbf{u}_j),\ k = 1 \ldots m.$$

Proof

First consider the case when the g_k are real. Let $G \subset \mathbb{R}^m$ be the set $\{g_1(\mathbf{u}) \ldots g_m(\mathbf{u}), |\mathbf{u} \in [-\pi, \pi]^n\}$. Since $\mathcal{H}(G)$ is closed, the definition of the integral implies that the point

$$\left(\frac{1}{(2\pi)^n}\int g_1(\mathbf{u})\mathrm{d}\mathbf{u}, \frac{1}{(2\pi)^n}\int g_2(\mathbf{u})\mathrm{d}\mathbf{u}, \ldots, \frac{1}{(2\pi)^n}\int g_m(\mathbf{u})\mathrm{d}\mathbf{u}\right)^{\mathrm{T}}$$

is in $\mathcal{H}(G)$. (To see this partition $[-\pi, \pi]^n$ the same for each integral. The step functions then yield convex combinations.) The Lemma follows from Theorem 6.45. The complex version is obtained by considering the real and imaginary parts of the g_k as separate functions.

□

Before giving the main result, we also need another simple formula.

Lemma 6.47

Let $f \in L_2[-\pi, \pi]$ have Fourier expansion $\sum A_j \mathrm{e}^{ij\theta}$. and suppose $A_1 \neq 0$. Then

$$\mathrm{e}^{\mathrm{i}\theta} = \frac{1}{2\pi A_1}\int_{-\pi}^{\pi} \mathrm{e}^{\mathrm{i}u} f(\theta - u)\mathrm{d}u.$$

Proof

This apparently mysterious result is actually a triviality! First consider the case $f = \mathrm{e}^{\mathrm{i}k\theta}$. The integrand then becomes $\mathrm{e}^{\mathrm{i}u} \times \mathrm{e}^{ik(\theta - u)} = \mathrm{e}^{\mathrm{i}\theta} \times \mathrm{e}^{\mathrm{i}u(1-k)}$ Thus the integrand vanishes by the orthogonality relations unless $k=1$, in which case the integral becomes $2\pi\ \mathrm{e}^{\mathrm{i}\theta}$. The full result follows by substituting the Fourier series for f.

□

Now suppose we expand σ in a (one-dimensional) Fourier series: say

$$\sigma(\theta) = \sum_{k=-\infty}^{\infty} C_k \mathrm{e}^{\mathrm{i}k\theta},$$

and we will make the assumption that $C_1 \neq 0$. Let us denote by σ_N the truncated Fourier series, i.e.

$$\sigma_N(\theta) = \sum_{k=-N}^{N} C_k \mathrm{e}^{\mathrm{i}k\theta},$$

The clever part of the argument is that only this one approximation to σ is used, as follows. Define p_m as in (6.39) and recall that the B_j are the re-ordered Fourier coefficients of f. We have with $\mathbf{m_k}$ the index vector for φ_k, i.e. $\varphi_k(\mathbf{x})= e^{i\mathbf{m_k}^T\mathbf{x}}$,

$$p_m = B_0 + \sum_{k=1}^{m} B_k e^{i\mathbf{m_k}^T\mathbf{x}}$$

$$= B_0 + \frac{1}{2\pi C_1}\sum_{k=1}^{m} B_k \int_{-\pi}^{\pi} e^{iu}\sigma_N(\mathbf{m_k}^T\mathbf{x} - u)du.$$

Now comes the magic bit. We write

$$\frac{1}{2\pi}\int_{-\pi}^{\pi} e^{iu}\sigma_N(\mathbf{m_k}^T\mathbf{x} - u)du$$

$$= \sum_{j=-N}^{N} \frac{C_j}{2\pi}\int_{-\pi}^{\pi} e^{iu}e^{ij(\mathbf{m_k}^T\mathbf{x} - u)}du$$

$$= \sum_{j=-N}^{N}\sum_{l=1}^{4N+3} C_j t_i e^{iu_j} e^{ij(\mathbf{m_k}^T\mathbf{x} - u_1)} \text{ where } \sum t_j = 1, \text{ by Lemma 6.46.}$$

$$= \sum_{l=1}^{4N+3} t_1 e^{iu_j} \sum_{j=-N}^{N} C_j e^{ij(\mathbf{m_k}^T\mathbf{x} - u1)}$$

$$= \sum_{l=1}^{4N+3} t_1 e^{iu_j}\sigma_N(\mathbf{m_k}^T\mathbf{x} - u_1).$$

Thus

$$p_m = B_0 + \frac{1}{C_1}\sum_{k=1}^{m}\sum_{l=1}^{4N+3} t_1 B_k e^{iu_j}\sigma_N(\mathbf{m_k}^T\mathbf{x} - u_1).$$

Now let

$$g(\mathbf{x}) = B_0 + \frac{1}{C_1}\sum_{k=1}^{m}\sum_{l=1}^{4N+3} t_1 B_k e^{iu_j}\sigma(\mathbf{m_k}^T\mathbf{x} - u_l). \tag{6.40}$$

We note that

$$\sigma(\mathbf{m_k}^T\mathbf{x} - u_l) - \sigma_N(\mathbf{m_k}^T\mathbf{x} - u_l) = \sum_{|k|>N} C_k e^{ik(\mathbf{m_k}^T\mathbf{x} - u_l)}.$$

whence

$$\|\sigma(\mathbf{m_k}^T\mathbf{x} - u_l) - \sigma_N(\mathbf{m_k}^T\mathbf{x} - u_l)\|_2 \le \varepsilon_N \text{ where } \varepsilon_N^2 = \sum_{|k|>N} C_k^2.$$

(Note that the norm here is taken in $L_2[-\pi, \pi]^n$.) It follows that

$$\|p_m - g(\mathbf{x})\|_2 \le \varepsilon_N \frac{1}{|C_1|} \sum_{k=1}^{m} \sum_{l=1}^{4N+3} t_l B_k |e^{iu_j}| .$$

$$\le \varepsilon_N \frac{1}{|C_1|} \sum_{k=1}^{m} |B_k|$$

$$\le \varepsilon_N \frac{1}{|C_1|} \text{since } f \in SF_n.$$

Thus for $f \in SF_n$, we have

$$\|f - g(\mathbf{x})\|_2 \le \frac{\delta_m}{m^{\frac{1}{2}}} + \frac{\varepsilon_N}{|C_1|} .$$

Examination of (6.40) shows that g is a single hidden layer perceptron net with m $(4N+3)$ hidden nodes. If we suppose, for instance, that $\sum |C_j| = 1$ then a similar argument to the one we used for f will give

$$\varepsilon_N^2 = \sum_{|k|>N} C_k^2$$

$$\varepsilon_N / |C_1| \le \nu_N N^{-\frac{1}{2}}$$

where if necessary the C_k's are re-ordered in the argument above, and $\nu_N \to 0$ as $N \to \infty$. Then with $N = M$ we will get

$$\|f - g(\mathbf{x})\|_2 \le (\delta_m + \nu_m) m^{-\frac{1}{2}},$$

or since g actually has m $(4m+3)$ hidden nodes, let us put $M = m^2$ and conclude that

$$\|f - g(\mathbf{x})\|_2 = o(M^{-\frac{1}{4}}).$$

We have indeed obtained a rate of approximation of f which is independent of n.

An extension of the Fourier series methods discussed here is to employ Fourier transforms. Many authors have used this approach, including the papers of Barron and of Leshno *et al.* that we have already mentioned. Space will not permit a complete discussion of these methods, but an introduction which will enable the reader to address these papers forms the next section.

6.5 Fourier transform methods

The literature surrounding Fourier transforms is enormous, but fortunately only a relatively small part is relevant to approximation. The transform is defined as follows.

Definition 6.48
Let $f \in L_1(\mathbb{R}^n)$. The *Fourier Transform* $F(s)$ of f is defined to be

$$F(s) = \int_{\mathbb{R}^n} \mathrm{e}^{-\mathrm{i}\mathbf{s}^{\mathrm{T}}\mathbf{x}} f(\mathbf{x})\mathrm{d}\mathbf{x} \tag{6.41}$$

where as above $\mathrm{i}^2 = -1$.

□

The element $\mathrm{d}\mathbf{x}$ here is of course a 'volume' element $\mathrm{d}x_1, \mathrm{d}x_2 \ldots \mathrm{d}x_n$. Note that since $\mathbf{s}^{\mathrm{T}}\mathbf{x}$ can be written $s_1x_1 + s_2x_2 + \ldots + s_nx_n$, it is legitimate to think of (6.41) as simply a repeated application of the one-dimensional transform

$$F(s) = \int_{-\infty}^{\infty} \mathrm{e}^{-\mathrm{i}sx} f(x)\mathrm{d}x \tag{6.42}$$

We give two examples that are important in approximation.

Examples 6.49
(a) For real numbers p and q, let $f \in L_1(\mathbb{R})$ be

$$f(x) = \begin{cases} p \text{ for } |x| < q \\ 0 \text{ for } |x| > q \end{cases}.$$

(Since we are working in L_1, we do not have to specify the value at the discontinuities.) So f takes just the constant value p between $-q$ and q, and is zero outside this range. We have

$$F(s) = \int_{-q}^{q} p\,\mathrm{e}^{-\mathrm{i}sx}\mathrm{d}x$$

$$= \left[\frac{p\,\mathrm{e}^{-\mathrm{i}sx}}{-\mathrm{i}s}\right]_{-q}^{q}$$

$$= \frac{p(\mathrm{e}^{-\mathrm{i}sq} - \mathrm{e}^{\mathrm{i}sq})}{-\mathrm{i}s}$$

$$= \frac{-2p\mathrm{i}\,\sin(sq)}{-\mathrm{i}s}$$

$$= \frac{2pq\,\sin(sq)}{sq}.$$

The function $\sin y/y$ occurs so often in Fourier methods that it is given the special name sinc y (pronounced 'sink y'). We have

$$F(s) = 2pq\,\mathrm{sinc}\,(sq).$$

A special case is when $p = 1/(2q)$ so that the area under f is one. Then

$$F(s) = \mathrm{sinc}\,(sq).$$

If $q \to 0$, $F(s) \to 1$ for any s. This corresponds to a kind of limiting f which is a 'spike' of infinite height and zero width, but with area one, called the *dirac delta function* $\delta(t)$. Of course, δ is not an L_1 function. but it is possible to make its definition rigorous using measure theory. However we need not pursue this here.

(b) The second important case we consider is the Gaussian function

$$f(x) = \mathrm{e}^{-\nu x^2} \tag{6.43}$$

where again $\nu > 0$ is a real parameter. Then

$$F(s) = \int_{-\infty}^{\infty} \mathrm{e}^{-\mathrm{i}sx}\mathrm{e}^{-\nu x^2}\mathrm{d}x. \tag{6.44}$$

There are various ways to evaluate this. The following method introduces another interesting property of the Fourier transform. If we integrate (6.42) by parts we obtain

$$F(s) = \left[\frac{\mathrm{e}^{-\mathrm{i}sx}f(x)}{-\mathrm{i}s}\right]_{-\infty}^{\infty} + \frac{1}{\mathrm{i}s}\int_{-\infty}^{\infty} \mathrm{e}^{-\mathrm{i}sx}f'(x)\mathrm{d}x \tag{6.45}$$

provided the first term exists. In particular if $f(x)\to 0$ as $x\to\pm\infty$, we get

$$\mathrm{i}sF(s)=\int_{-\infty}^{\infty}\mathrm{e}^{-\mathrm{i}sx}f'(x)\mathrm{d}x$$

and the term on the right is the Fourier transform of $f'(t)$. In other words, for f satisfying $f(x)\to 0, x\to\pm\infty$, the Fourier transform of f' is simply $\mathrm{i}\times s\times$ the Fourier transform of f. If f does not satisfy the condition $f(x)\to 0, x\to\pm\infty$, an extra term is required according to (6.45). However for the f given by (6.43), the condition is indeed satisfied. Hence in this case

$$\begin{aligned}\mathrm{i}sF(s)&=\int_{-\infty}^{\infty}\mathrm{e}^{-\mathrm{i}sx}(-2\nu x)\mathrm{e}^{-\nu x^2}\mathrm{d}x\\&=-2\nu[\mathrm{i}F'(s)]\end{aligned}$$

as may be seen by differentiating (6.44) with respect to s. Thus

$$\frac{F'(s)}{F(s)}=\frac{s}{-2\nu}$$

or

$$\begin{aligned}\frac{d[\ln F(s)]}{\mathrm{d}s}&=\frac{s}{-2\nu}\\ \ln F(s)&=\frac{-s^2}{4\nu}+c \text{ for some constant } c\text{, whence}\\ F(s)&=A\mathrm{e}^{-s^2/(4\nu)} \text{ for some constant } A.\end{aligned}$$

The Fourier transform of a Gaussian is a Gaussian, a property which turns out to be important in several branches of mathematics. The constant A can be obtained by putting $s=0$ in (6.44) to obtain

$$A=\int_{-\infty}^{\infty}\mathrm{e}^{-\nu x^2}\mathrm{d}x.$$

This integral is well known to have the value $\sqrt{\pi/\nu}$: see, e.g. Abramowitz and Stegun (1964, p. 931) or the value can be deduced from the inverse Fourier formulae given below (see Example 6.53). This result is easily extended to n dimensions by repeated integration.

□

There are essentially two ways that Fourier transforms are used in approximation: we may either use a convolution or the inverse formula. In fact these ideas are closely related anyway, as we shall now see.

Definition 6.50

Let f, $g \in L_1(\mathbb{R}^n)$. The *Fourier convolution* $f*g$ is defined to be

$$f*g(\mathbf{x}) = \int_{\mathbb{R}^n} f(\mathbf{x} - \mathbf{t})g(\mathbf{t})d\mathbf{t}$$

□

Remarks 6.51

(a) It is easily verified that $f*g=g*f$: just make the substitution $\mathbf{u}=\mathbf{x}-\mathbf{t}$.
(b) An important property of the convolution that is used extensively in signal processing is that if F and G are the Fourier transforms of f and g respectively, then the Fourier transform of $f*g$ is $F(s)\times G(s)$. We omit the proof here as we shall not actually require the result.

□

The convolution may be used to construct sequences of functions that converge in some required fashion to a given function f, and hence to construct approximations. There are various versions of the result based on the same idea, and depending on exactly what conditions are imposed on the functions involved. We give here versions concerned with uniform and pointwise approximation: the second may appear a little contrived, but actually turns out to be precisely what we need for the Fourier Inverse Theorem. A function defined on $\mathbb{R}^n$ is said to be *uniformly continuous* if $\omega(f;\mathbf{u})$ exists and tends to zero as $\|\mathbf{u}\|_\infty \to 0$ (see Definition 6.25). For example, the function $f(x)=x^2$ is *not* uniformly continuous on $\mathbb{R}$, since we would require

$$\omega(f;\delta) = \sup_{\substack{x,y \in \mathbb{R} \\ |x-y|<\delta}} |f(x) - f(y)| .$$

But $|x^2 - y^2| = (x+y)(x-y) \to \infty$ as $x \to \infty$ even if $|x-y| < \delta$. So the modulus of continuity does not exist. Of course, on finite closed intervals, continuous functions are always uniformly continuous.

Theorem 6.52

(a) Let f be bounded and uniformly continuous on $\mathbb{R}^n$ and let $h \in L_1(\mathbb{R}^n)$ with

$$\int_{\mathbb{R}^n} h(\mathbf{x})d\mathbf{x} = 1. \tag{6.46}$$

Define $h_m(\mathbf{x}) = m^n h(m\mathbf{x})$. Then $f * h_m$ exists and converges uniformly to f as to $m \to \infty$.

(b) Suppose on the other hand that $f \in L_1(\mathbb{R}^n)$, is essentially bounded and is continuous at some point $\mathbf{x}$. Suppose moreover that h is merely integrable, rather than absolutely integrable [i.e. perhaps $h \notin L_1(\mathbb{R}^n)$] but that (6.46) holds and also $|h(\mathbf{x})|$ is measurable. Then $f * h_m(\mathbf{x})$ exists and converges pointwise to $f(\mathbf{x})$ as $m \to \infty$.

(Note that in either version of the theorem, we do not insist that m is an integer. We may let $m \to \infty$ through integer or real values, as appropriate for our application.)

Proof

First observe that

$$\begin{aligned}\int_{\mathbb{R}^n} h_m(\mathbf{x})d\mathbf{x} &= \int_{\mathbb{R}^n} m^n h(m\mathbf{x})d\mathbf{x}\\ &= \int_{\mathbb{R}^n} h(m\mathbf{x})d(m\mathbf{x})\\ &= 1 \text{ (setting } \mathbf{y} = m\mathbf{x}).\end{aligned}$$

Now the conditions on f and h_m guarantee that $f(\mathbf{x}-\mathbf{t})h_m(\mathbf{t}) \in L_1(\mathbb{R}^n)$ so the convolution exists. Hence

$$(f * h_m)(\mathbf{x}) - f(\mathbf{x}) = \int_{\mathbb{R}^n} [f(\mathbf{x}-\mathbf{t}) - f(\mathbf{x})]h_m(\mathbf{t})d\mathbf{t}$$

so

$$\begin{aligned}|(f * h_m)(\mathbf{x}) - f(\mathbf{x})| &\le \int_{\mathbb{R}^n} |f(\mathbf{x}-\mathbf{t}) - f(\mathbf{x})|\,|h_m(\mathbf{t})|\,d\mathbf{t}\\ &= \int_{\mathbb{R}^n} |f(\mathbf{x}-\mathbf{t}) - f(\mathbf{x})|\,|h(m\mathbf{t})|m^n d\mathbf{t}\\ &= \int_{\mathbb{R}^n} |f(\mathbf{x}-\mathbf{s}/m) - f(\mathbf{x})|\,|h(\mathbf{s})|\,d\mathbf{s} \text{ where } \mathbf{s} = m\mathbf{t}\\ &\le \int_{\mathbb{R}^n} \omega(f; \mathbf{s}/m)\,|h(\mathbf{s})|\,d\mathbf{s}.\end{aligned}$$

From the definition of ω and properties of the integral, we see that $\omega(f; \mathbf{s/m})$ is an integrable function of $\mathbf{s}$ and converges monotonically pointwise to zero as $m \to \infty$. Hence the integral on the right goes to zero by the Monotone Convergence Theorem (Theorem 1.38). This establishes (a).

To get (b), we note that the conditions are again sufficient to guarantee that $f(\mathbf{x}-\mathbf{t})h_m(\mathbf{t}) \in L_1(\mathbb{R}^n)$ so the convolution exists. We have

$$\begin{aligned}(f * h_m)(\mathbf{x}) &= \int_{\mathbb{R}^n} f(\mathbf{x}-\mathbf{t})h_m(\mathbf{t})d\mathbf{t} \\ &= \int_{\mathbb{R}^n} f(\mathbf{x}-\mathbf{s}/m)h(\mathbf{s})d\mathbf{s} \text{ where } \mathbf{s} = m\mathbf{t}.\end{aligned}$$

Also, since h is integrable at least improperly, we must have

$$\int_{\|\mathbf{x}\|_2 \geq \mathbb{R}} h(\mathbf{x})d\mathbf{x} \to 0$$

as $R \to \infty$. Since f is essentially bounded, it follows that given $\varepsilon > 0$, we can find R such that

$$\left| \int_{\mathbb{R}^n} f(\mathbf{x}-\mathbf{s}/m)h(\mathbf{s})d\mathbf{s} - \int_{\|\mathbf{s}\|_2 \leq \mathbb{R}} f(\mathbf{x}-\mathbf{s}/m)h(\mathbf{s})d\mathbf{s} \right| < \varepsilon/3,$$

independently of m, and also, recalling (6.46), such that

$$\left| f(\mathbf{x}) - f(\mathbf{x}) \int_{\|\mathbf{s}\|_2 \leq \mathbb{R}} h(\mathbf{s})d\mathbf{s} \right| < \varepsilon/3.$$

But $|f(\mathbf{x}-\mathbf{s/m})\, h(\mathbf{s})| \leq \|f\|_\infty\, |h(\mathbf{s})|$ and $f(\mathbf{x}-\mathbf{s}/m) \to f(\mathbf{x})$ pointwise as $m \to \infty$. Thus

$$\int_{\|\mathbf{s}\|_2 \leq \mathbb{R}} f(\mathbf{x}-\mathbf{s}/m)h(\mathbf{s})d\mathbf{s} \to f(\mathbf{x}) \int_{\|\mathbf{s}\|_2 \leq \mathbb{R}} h(\mathbf{s})d\mathbf{s}$$

by the Lebesgue Dominated Convergence Theorem (Theorem 1.39). Consequently, for m sufficiently large, we have

$$\begin{aligned}&\left| f(\mathbf{x}) - \int_{\mathbb{R}^n} f(\mathbf{x}-\mathbf{s}/m)h(\mathbf{s})d\mathbf{s} \right| \\ &\quad < \left| f(\mathbf{x}) - f(\mathbf{x}) \int_{\|\mathbf{s}\|_2 \leq \mathbb{R}} h(\mathbf{s})d\mathbf{s} \right| + \\ &\qquad \left| \int_{\|\mathbf{s}\|_2 \leq \mathbb{R}} f(\mathbf{x}-\mathbf{s}/m)h(\mathbf{s})d\mathbf{s} - f(j\mathbf{x}) \int_{\|\mathbf{s}\|_2 \leq \mathbb{R}} h(\mathbf{s})d\mathbf{s} \right| \\ &\quad + \left| \int_{\mathbb{R}^n} f(\mathbf{x}-\mathbf{s}/m)h(\mathbf{s})d\mathbf{s} - \int_{\|\mathbf{s}\|_2 \leq \mathbb{R}} f(\mathbf{x}-\mathbf{s}/m)h(\mathbf{s})d\mathbf{s} \right| \\ &< \varepsilon.\end{aligned}$$

Since this holds for any $\varepsilon > 0$, the result is established.

□

Before using this result to construct approximations, let us employ it to complete the basic theory of the Fourier transform by proving the inverse formula. This is not the most general possible form, but it is sufficient for our purposes.

Theorem 6.53

Let $f \in L_1(\mathbb{R}^n)$ be essentially bounded and continuous at $\mathbf{x}$. Denote its Fourier transform by $F(s)$. The function

$$g_w(\mathbf{x}) = \frac{1}{(2\pi)^n} \int_{\|\mathbf{s}\| \le W} e^{i\mathbf{s}^T\mathbf{x}} F(\mathbf{s}) d\mathbf{s}$$

exists for all real $W > 0$, and $g_w(\mathbf{x}) \to f(\mathbf{x})$ (pointwise) as $W \to \infty$. In particular if $F \in L_1(\mathbb{R}^n)$, or alternatively, if we interpret the integral as a Cauchy principle value (i.e. as the limit of g_w as $W \to \infty$), we may write

$$f(x) = \frac{1}{(2\pi)^n} \int_{\mathbb{R}^n} e^{i\mathbf{s}^T\mathbf{x}} F(\mathbf{s}) d\mathbf{s}$$

Proof

For simplicity we will give the proof for the case $n = 1$. The multivariate case is obtained by repeated application for each variable. Thus

$$\begin{aligned} g_w(x) &= \frac{1}{2\pi} \int_{-W}^{W} e^{isx} F(s) ds \\ &= \frac{1}{2\pi} \int_{-W}^{W} e^{isx} \int_{-\infty}^{\infty} e^{-ist} f(t) dt\, ds \\ &= \frac{1}{2\pi} \int_{-\infty}^{\infty} f(t) \int_{-W}^{W} e^{is(x-t)} ds\, dt \\ &= \frac{W}{\pi} \int_{-\infty}^{\infty} f(t) \operatorname{sinc} W(x-t) dt \text{ on evaluating the inner integral} \\ &= \frac{W}{\pi} f(x) * \operatorname{sinc}(Wx). \end{aligned} \tag{6.47}$$

Now the function sinc y is *not* in $L_1(\mathbb{R})$. To see this consider each 'loop' of the function between $k\pi$ and $(k+1)\pi$. We find $|\sin y/y| > |\sin y|/((k+1)\pi)$. Hence

$$\int_{k\pi}^{(k+1)\pi} |\sin y/y| \, dy > 2/[(k+1)\pi].$$

Thus

$$\int_{0}^{(k+1)\pi} |\sin y/y| \, dy \to \infty \text{ as } k \to \infty$$

by comparison with the harmonic series $(2/\pi)(k+1)^{-1}$.

On the other hand we also have

$$\int_{k\pi}^{(k+1)\pi} |\sin y/y| \, dy < 2/(k\pi)$$

and clearly the area of the kth loop decreases as k increases. Thus

$$I = \int_{-\infty}^{\infty} \operatorname{sinc} y \, dy$$

does exist improperly (i.e. as a limit when the range becomes infinite) by the Alternating Series Test (Theorem 1.14). Furthermore each negative loop is smaller than the previous positive loop, so certainly $I \neq 0$. It follows from (6.47) and Theorem 6.52(b) that as $W \to \infty$, $g_w(x) \to (I/\pi) f(x)$. To complete the proof we need to evaluate I. Since I does not depend on f, we can evaluate it by choosing a particular f for which we can actually evaluate the integrals explicitly. One suitable choice is $f(x) = e^{-|x|}$. Substitution of this function in (6.42) and evaluating the integral yields $F(s) = 2/(1+s^2)$. Now f is in $L_1(\mathbb{R})$, is bounded by 1 and is continuous at 0 where it takes the value 1. Since $g_w(x) \to (I/\pi) f(x)$, we get

$$\frac{I}{\pi} = \frac{1}{2\pi} \int_{-\infty}^{\infty} \frac{2e^{-is0}}{1+s^2} \, ds$$

whence

$$\begin{aligned} I &= 2[\arctan s]_0^{\infty} \\ &= \pi \text{ as required}. \end{aligned}$$

□

Example 6.54

In Example 6.49(b) we quoted the value of the integral

$$A=\int_{-\infty}^{\infty} e^{-vx^2} dx.$$

when evaluating the Fourier transform of a Gaussian function. In fact we can use the inverse formula to evaluate the integral, We found that with $f(x)=e^{-vx^2}$ $F(s)=Ae^{-s^2/(4v)}$ Setting $x=0$ in the inverse formula gives

$$1=\frac{1}{2\pi}\int_{-\infty}^{\infty} Ae^{-s^2/(4v)} ds.$$

The substitution $s=2vt$ gives

$$1=\frac{Av}{\pi}\int_{-\infty}^{\infty} e^{-vt^2} dt$$
$$=\frac{A^2 v}{\pi},$$

whence $A=\sqrt{(v/\pi)}$ as quoted previously.

□

Let us illustrate the use of the Fourier approach to approximation by proving a simple density result for *radial basis networks* (see, e.g. Park and Sandberg (1991) Instead of (6.2), these networks construct a function (Broomhead and Lowe, 1988; Mason and Parks, 1992); see also Powell, (1992).

$$g(\mathbf{x})=\sum_{j}^{k} a_j\sigma(c_j\,\|\mathbf{w_j}-\mathbf{x}\|),\ c_j>0. \tag{6.48}$$

Here $\|\ \|$ denotes the ordinary Euclidean distance in $\mathbb{R}^n$ so we have dropped the 2 subscript to avoid confusion with the function space norm. Instead of projection of $\mathbf{x}$ on to the weight $\mathbf{w}$, activation is a function of the distance of $\mathbf{x}$ from $\mathbf{w}$. The activation function σ is often a Gaussian, $\sigma(x)=e^{-x^2}$. With this choice, it is easy to verify that $\sigma(c_j\,\|\mathbf{w_j}-\mathbf{x}\|)$ is a multivariate Gaussian, although it is not clear that this is actually the best choice (see, e.g. Anderson (1996)). In any case, let us assume that $\sigma(x)\to 0$ as $x\to\infty$ sufficiently quickly that $\sigma(c_j\,\|\mathbf{w_j}-\mathbf{x}\|)\in L_1(\mathbb{R}^n)$: this is certainly the case for Gaussian σ. We also assume σ is continuous and that it is normalised so that the integral of $\sigma(\|\mathbf{x}\|)$ is 1. (In particular we assume that the integral does not vanish. Again this holds for the Gaussian, which is everywhere positive.)

Let $h(\mathbf{x})=\sigma(\|\mathbf{x}\|)$ and h_m be constructed as in Theorem 6.52. Now suppose f is continuous on the unit sphere $D\subset\mathbb{R}^n$, $D_1=\{\,\mathbf{x}\,|\,\|\mathbf{x}\|\le 1\}$. It possible to extend

f to a function which has compact support $D_2=\{\mathbf{x} \mid \|\mathbf{x}\| \le 2\}$. and which is uniformly continuous on D_2. For example, define a function $p(\mathbf{x})$ which takes the value one on D_1 and which then decreases linearly to zero as $\|\mathbf{x}\|$ increases to 2. For $\mathbf{x} \in D_2 - D_1$, we can extend the definition of f to have the value $f(x/\|x\|) \times p(x)$.

According to Theorem 6.52(a), $f*h_m(\mathbf{x})$ converges uniformly to f as $m \to \infty$. Given $\epsilon > 0$, choose m so that $\|f - f*h_m\|_\infty < \epsilon/2$. Now

$$f*h_m(\mathbf{x}) = \int_{D_2} f(\mathbf{t}) h_m(\mathbf{x}-\mathbf{t}) d\mathbf{t},$$

Since the integral is over a finite region, we may approximate it to arbitrary accuracy by a finite sum: i.e. we may chose a constant a and points $\mathbf{t}_1 \ldots \mathbf{t}_M$ such that $\|f*h_m - S\|_\infty < \epsilon/2$, where

$$S(\mathbf{x}) = a \sum_{j=1}^{M} f(\mathbf{t}_j) h_m(\mathbf{x}-\mathbf{t}_j).$$

The only difficulty here is to show that we can do this uniformly for $\mathbf{x}$. Consider the function $q_\mathbf{x}(\mathbf{t}) = h_m(\mathbf{x}-\mathbf{t})$. Since h_m is continuous.

$$\sup_{\mathbf{x} \in D_2} \omega(q_\mathbf{x}; \mathbf{u})$$

will tend to zero with $\|\mathbf{u}\|$ as may be shown by a contradiction argument. Dividing D_2 into regions for which this quantity is sufficiently small shows the existence of S. Now observe that $S(\mathbf{x})$ is actually a function of the form (6.48) with $\|f - S\|_\infty < \varepsilon$. We have proved:

Theorem 6.55

Let σ satisfy the conditions (a) $\sigma(\|x\|) \in L_1(\mathbb{R}^n)$, (b) the integral of $\sigma(\|\mathbf{x}\|)$ over $\mathbb{R}^n$ does not vanish and (c) σ is continuous. Then the set of radial basis networks with this σ (i.e. the set of functions of the form (6.48)) is dense in $C(D_2)$.

□

Again this is not the strongest possible density result, but it does cover many cases of practical interest. It is also probably the simplest example of the Fourier approach to density. An alternative method is to use the inverse formula. Using Theorem 6.53, we approximate $f(\mathbf{x})$ by a sum of values of $F(s) \times e^{is^T x}$ and then use a one-dimensional approximation result to approximate the exponentials by activation functions.

Both these methods have been used to prove results about one hidden layer perceptrons (6.2): Xu, Light and Cheney (see Light (1992)) used a variant of the first approach to prove density, and Baron's dimension independent rate uses the second method. The general density result of Leshno *et al.* also uses a Fourier convolution. However we will not give details of these as they are all complicated by the already noted awkward property of ridge functions like (6.2), namely that $\sigma(\mathbf{w}^T\mathbf{x}+c) \notin L_1(\mathbb{R}^n)$ and the Fourier transform of $\sigma(\mathbf{w}^T\mathbf{x}+c)$ will in general not exist. Xu *et al.* get around it by averaging the activation functions over the n-dimensional hypersphere to obtain an L_1 function. Baron uses a more general definition of the Fourier transform: under much weaker conditions on f it can be shown that there exists a Lebesgue–Stieljes measure $\mu(\mathbf{s})$ such that

$$f(x) = \int_{\mathbb{R}^n} e^{i\mathbf{s}^T\mathbf{x}} \mu(\mathbf{s}).$$

The ordinary Fourier transform corresponds to the case that $\mu(\mathbf{s})$ can be written as $[1/(2\pi)]\, F(\mathbf{s})\, d\mathbf{s}$. Apart from the problems of actually setting up the measure $\mu(\mathbf{s})$, more delicacy is required in handling the estimates, making Barron's dimension independent rate rather harder to obtain that of Mhaskar and Micchelli described above. Nonetheless, the basic idea is the fairly simple one described above, and virtually all the mathematics required to understand the results has been covered in this and previous chapters. Consult the papers themselves for the messy analytical details!

6.6 Some other aspects of approximation by neural nets

We will make very brief mention of two other interesting lines of development.

First, an examination of Fig. 6.1 might suggest that it would be better to use networks with more than one hidden layer. The problem of approximation by such networks is harder, since we cannot use the 'nearly linear' properties of (6.2) that we have employed in this chapter. However some results have appeared. The approach used is to divide $[-1, 1]^n$ up into subcubes and approximate f on each subcube by a single layer network. Further layers may then be used to combine the subnetworks. See Mhaskar (1993) and Chui, Li and Mhaskar (1995) for details of the methods. At the time of writing, it has not be shown unequivocally that multilayer networks are better, but the latter paper has some results pointing in that direction.

Second, an altogether more abstract approach to neural network approximation is provided by a result known as the Komolgorov Superposition Theorem. In a form due to Sprecher, this states that for any continuous function f: $\mathbb{R}^n \rightarrow \mathbb{R}$, there is a predetermined function ψ, independent of n, functions φ_j (which do depend on f of course) and a constant c_n such that

$$f(\mathbf{x}) = \sum_{j=0}^{2n} \varphi_j \left(\sum_{k=1}^{n} \lambda_k \psi(x_k + jc_n) \right).$$

Algorithms are available for constructing these functions iteratively, thus providing a network whose activation functions depend on f. See Katsuura and Sprecher (1994) for recent work on this approach.

Approximation by neural networks is a lively topic, which has hopefully been demonstrated in this chapter!

References

Abramowitz, M. and Stegun, L.A. (1964) *Handbook of Mathematical Functions.* Dover Publications, New York. ISBN 486-61272-4.

Aleksander, I. and Morton, H. (1990) *An Introduction to Neural Computing.* Chapman and Hall, London.

Almeida, L.B. and Silva, F.M. (1992) Adaptive decorrelation, in *Artificial Neural Networks 2* (eds. I. Aleksander and J. Taylor), Vol. 2, pp. 149–156. North-Holland.

Amari, S.-i. (1989) Mathematical foundations of neurocomputing. *Proc. IEEE* **78**(a), 1143–1463.

Anderson, I.J. (1996) Local modifications to radial basis networks. To appear in *Mathematics of Neural Networks* (eds. J.C. Mason and S.W. Ellacott), comprising the *Proceedings of the 1995 Conference on Mathematics of Neural Networks and Applications at Lady Margaret Hall, Oxford, UK.*

Anthony, M. (1994) *Probabilistic Studies of Learning in Artificial Neural Networks: The PAC Model and its Variants.* Technical report available from the author at: Dept. of Mathematics, The London School of Economics and Political Science, Houghton Street, London WC2A 2AE, UK.

Baker, G.L. and Gollub, J.P. (1990) *Chaotic Dynamics, an Introduction.* Cambridge University Press. ISBN 0-521-38258-0 (hardcover, 0-521-38897-X (paperback).

Baldi, P. and Hornik, K. (1989) Neural networks and principal component analysis: learning from examples without local minima. *Neural Networks,* Vol. 2, No. 1. Pergamon Press.

Barron, A. (1993) Universal approximation bounds for superposition of a sigmoidal function. *IEEE Trans. on Information Theory*, **3**(3), 930–945.

Bartle, R.G. (1966) *The Elements of Integration*. John Wiley and Sons. ISBN 0-471-05457-7.

Ben-Israel, A. and Greville, T.N.E. (1974) *Generalized Inverses: Theory and Applications*. John Wiley and Sons.

Bezdek, J.C. and Nikhil, R.P. (1995) Two soft relatives of learning vector quantization. *Neural Networks*, **8**(5), 729–743.

Bishop, C.M. (1995) *Neural Networks for Pattern Recognition*. Oxford University Press.

Brigham, E.O. (1974) *The Fast Fourier Transform*. Prentice Hall, USA.

Broomhead, D.S. and Lowe, D. (1988) Multivariable function interpolation and adaptive networks. *Complex Systems*, **2**, 321–355.

Brown, M. and Harris, C. (1994) *Neurofuzzy Adaptive Modelling and Control*. Prentice Hall series in systems and control engineering, Prentice Hall. ISBN 0-13-134453-6.

Carling, A. (1992) *Introducing Neural Networks*. Sigma Press, Wilmslow, UK. ISBN 1-85058-174-6

Chui, C.K. (ed.) (1992) *Wavelets: a Tutorial in Theory and Applications*. Academic Press, ISBN 0-12-174590-2.

Chui, C.K., Li, X. and Mhaskar, H.N. (1995) *Limitations of the Approximation Capabilities of Neural Networks with One Hidden Layer*. Preprint available from the third author at Dept. of Math., California State University, Los Angeles, California, 90032, USA.

Cohen, M. and Grossberg, S. (1983) Absolute stability of global pattern formation and parallel memory storage by competitive neural networks. *IEEE Transactions on Systems, Man, and Cybernetics*, **SMC13**(5), 815–825.

Cybenko, G. (1989) Approximation by superpositions of a sigmoidal function. *Math. Control-Signals Systems*, **2**, 303–314.

De Vore, R.A., Howard, R. and Micchelli, C. (1989) Optimal nonlinear approximation. *Manuscripta Math.* **63**, 469–478.

Ellacott, S.W. (1990) An analysis of the delta rule. *Proceedings of the International Neural Net Conference, Paris*, pp. 956–959. Kluwer Academic Publishers.

Ellacott, S.W. (1993) The numerical analysis approach, pp. 103–138 in *Mathematical Studies of Neural Networks*, (ed. J. Taylor). North-Holland, The Netherlands. ISBN 0-444-81692-5.

Ellacott, S.W. (1994a) Techniques for the mathematical analysis of neural networks. *J. Computational and Applied Mathematics*, **50**, 283–297.

Ellacott, S.W. (1994b) Aspects of the numerical analysis of neural networks. *Acta Numerica 1994*, pp. 145–202. (Ed. A. Iserles). Cambridge University Press.

Ellacott, S.W. and Easdown, A. (1996) Numerical aspects of machine learning in artificial neural networks, to appear in *Mathematics of Neural Networks* (eds. J.C. Mason and S.W. Ellacott), comprising the *Proceedings of the 1995 Conference on Mathematics of Neural Networks and Applications at Lady Margaret Hall, Oxford, UK.*

Falconer, K. (1990) *Fractal Geometry: Mathematical Foundations and Applications.* John Wiley and Sons. ISBN 0-471-92287-0.

Finkbeiner, D.T. (1966). Introduction to Matrices and Linear Transformations (2nd edn.) W.H. Freeman and Co. USA.

Fombellida, M. and Destiné, J. (1992) The extended quickprop, in *Artificial Neural Networks 2* (eds. I. Aleksander and J. Taylor), Vol. 2, pp. 973–977. North-Holland.

Funahashi, K.-I. (1989) On the approximate realization of continuous mappings by neural networks. *Neural Networks* **2**, 183–192.

Gerber, H. (1990) *Elementary Linear Algebra.* Brookes/Cole Publishing, USA. ISBN 0-534-11574-8.

Gill, P.E., Murray, W. and Wright, M.H. (1981) *Practical Optimization.* Academic Press.

Golub, G.H. and Reinsch, C. (1970) Singular value decomposition and least squares solutions. *Numerische Mathematik* **14**, 403–420.

Greig, D.M. (1980) *Optimisation.* Longman Mathematical Texts, London.

Hand, C., Evans, M. and Ellacott, S.W. (1992) A neural network feature detector using a multi-resolution pyramid, in *Neural Networks for Images, Speech and Natural Language* (eds. B. Linggard and C. Nightingale). Chapman and Hall.

Hartley, B. and Hawkes, T.O. (1970) *Rings Modules and Linear Algebra.* Chapman and Hall.

Hewitt, E. and Stromberg, L. (1965) Real and abstract analysis. *Springer Graduate texts in Mathematics No. 25*. Springer Verlag, Berlin. ISBN 3-540-90138-8.

Hornik, K. (1991) Approximation capabilities of multilayer feedforward networks. *Neural Networks* **4**, 251–257. Pergamon Press.

Hornik, K., Stinchcombe, M. and White, H. (1989) Multilayer feedforward networks are universal approximators. *Neural Networks* 2, 359–366. Pergamon Press.

Isaacson, E. and Keller, H.B. (1966) *Analysis of Numerical Methods.* John Wiley.

Katsuura, H. and Sprecher, D.A. (1994) Computational aspects of Komolgorov's superposition theorem. Neural Networks **7**(3) 455–461. Pergamon Press.

Kohonen, T. (1972) Correlation matrix memories. *IEEE Transactions on Computers*, **C-21**.

Kohonen, T. (1986) *Learning Vector Quantization for Pattern Recognition.* Helsinki University of Technology, Dept. Tech Physics, Technical Report TKK-F-A601.

Komolgorov, A.N. and Fomin, S.V. (1961) *Functional Analysis*, Vol. 2, *Measure, the Lebesgue Integral, Hilbert Space.* Graylock Press, Albany, New York. (Translated from the Russian by H. Kamel and H. Komm.)

Kosko, B. (1988) Feedback stability and unsupervised learning, *Proc. IEEE Int. Conf. on Neural Networks* **1**, 141–152.

Kreinovich, V. (1991) Arbitrary nonlinearity is sufficient to represent all functions by neural networks: a theorem. *Neural Networks*, **4**, 381–383. Pergamon Press.

Kreyszig, E. (1978) *Introductory Functional Analysis with Applications.* John Wiley and Sons. ISBN 0-471-50731-8.

Leen, T.K. (1991) Dynamics of learning in linear feature discovery networks, *Network* **2**, 85–105.

Leshno, M., Lin, V. Ya, Pinkus, A. and Schocken, S. (1993) Multilayer feedforward networks with a nonpolynomial activation function can approximate any function, *Neural Networks* **6**, 861–867. Pergamon Press.

Light, W. (1992) Ridge functions, sigmoidal functions and neural networks In *Approximation Theory VII (eds. E.W. Cheney, C.K. Chui and L.L. Schumaker), pp. 1–44. Academic Press, Boston. ISBN 0-12-174589-9.*

Mason, J.C. and Parks, P.C. (1992) Selection of neural network structures—some approximation theory guidelines. Chapter 8 (pp. 151–180) in *Neural Networks for Control and Systems* (eds. K. Warwick, G.W. Irwin and K.J. Hunt). IEE Control Engineering Series No. 46, Peter Peregrinus.

Mhaskar, H.N. (1993) Neural networks for localised approximation of smooth and analytic functions, pp. 190–196 in *Neural Networks for Signal Processing, III* (eds. Kamm, Huhn, Chellappa and Kung). IEEE.

Mhaskar, H.N. (1996) On smooth activation functions. To appear in *Mathematics of Neural Networks* (eds. J.C. Mason and S.W. Ellacott), and comprising the *Proceedings of the 1995 Conference on Mathematics of Neural Networks and Applications at Lady Margaret Hall*, Oxford, UK.

Mhaskar, H.N. and Micchelli, C.A. (1994) Dimension-independent bounds on the degree of approximation by neural networks. *IBM J. Research and Development* **38**(3), 277–283.

Minsky, M. and Pappert, S. (1969) *Perceptrons.* MIT Press, Cambridge MA, USA.

Moré, J.J. (1978) The Levenberg-Marquardt algorithm, implementation and theory, pp. 105–116 in the *Proceedings of the Dundee Biennial Conference on Numerical Analysis 1977* (ed. G.A. Watson). Springer Lecture Notes in Mathematics No. 630.

Oja, E. (1983) *Subspace Methods of Pattern Recognition.* John Wiley and Sons. ISBN 0-471-903116.

Oja, E. (1992) Principal components, minor components and linear neural networks. *Neural Networks* **5**, 927–935.

Oja, E., Ogawa, H. and Wangviwattana, J. (1992) PCA in fully parallel neural networks, in *Artificial Neural networks 2* (eds. I. Aleksander and J. Taylor), Vol. 2, pp. 199–202. North-Holland.

Park, J. and Sandberg, J. (1991) Universal approximation by radial-basis-functions networks. *Neural Computation* **5**, 305–316.

Parkes, P. (1993) A translation of a paper by Kaczmarz with a forward by the translator, *Int. J. Control* **57**(6), 1269–1271 with a foreword on 1263–1267.

Perko, L. (1991) Differential equations and dynamical systems. *Texts in Applied Mathematics* **7**. Springer Verlag.

Powell, M.J.D. (1992) The theory of radial basis functions approximation in 1990, pp. 105–210 in *Advances in Numerical Analysis* (ed. W. Light), Vol. II. Oxford University Press.

Rumelhart, D.E. and McClelland, J.L. (1986) *Parallel and Distributed Processing: Explorations in the Microstructure of Cognition*, Vol. 2. MIT Press.

Scarselli, F. and Tsoi, A.C. (1995) *Universal Approximation Using Feedforward Neural Networks: A Survey of Some Existing Methods, and Some New Results.* Report available from the authors: F. Scarselli, Dipartimento di Ingegneria dei Sistemi e Informatica, Université di Firenze, v. S. Marta, n.3, 50139 Firenze, Italy. A.C. Tsoi, Dept. Elec. and Comp. Eng., University of Queensland, St. Lucia, Queensland, 4072, Australia.

Simpson, P.K. (1990) *Artificial Neural Systems: Foundations, Paradigms, Applications and Implementations*. Pergamon Press, New York.

Spivak, M. (1967) *Calculus*. W.A. Benjamin, New York.

Tou, J.T. and Gonzales, R.C. (1978) *Principles of Pattern Recognition*. Addisson Wesley.

van der Smagt, P.P. (1994) Minimisation methods for training feedforward neural networks. *Neural Networks* **7**(1), 1–11.

Wasserman, P.D. (1989) *Neural Computing: Theory and Practice*. Van Nostrand Reinhold, New York. ISBN 0-442-20743-3.

Weir, A.J. (1973) *Lebesgue Integration and Measure*. Cambridge University Press, UK.

Wray, J. and Green, G.G.R. (1995) Neural Networks, approximation theory and finite precision computation. *Neural Networks* **8**(1), 31–37.

Index